REFERENCE

The
New York
Public Library
Business Desk Reference

The
New York
Public Library
Business Desk
Reference

A STONESONG PRESS BOOK

John Wiley & Sons, Inc.
New York • Chichester • Weinheim
Brisbane • Singapore • Toronto

This publication is designed to provide accurate and authoritative information in regard to the subject matter covered. It is sold with the understanding that the publisher is not engaged in rendering professional services. If legal, accounting, medical, psychological, or any other expert assistance is required, the services of a competent professional person should be sought.

Library of Congress Cataloging-in-Publication Data

The New York Public Library Business desk reference.
    p. cm.
    "A Stonesong Press book."
    Includes index.
    ISBN 0-471-14442-8 (cloth : acid-free paper)
    1. Office practice—United States—Hardbooks, manuals, etc.
I. New York Public Library.
HF5547.5.N5 1997
651—dc21   97-7408

Printed in the United States of America

10 9 8 7 6 5 4 3 2 1

The New York Public Library
Project Sponsors

Paul LeClerc, *President*

Michael J. Zavelle, *Senior Vice President for Administration, Finance, and Business Affairs*

William D. Walker, *Senior Vice President and the Andrew W. Mellon Director of The Research Libraries*

Norman Holman, *Senior Vice President and Director of The Branch Libraries*

Karen Van Westering, *Manager of Publications*

Editorial Directors
Paul Fargis
Sheree Bykofsky

Managing Editor
Karen Brunson Kneipp

Associate Editor
Kerry Acker

Contributing Editors
Julia Banks-Rubel
Anne Basye
Donna Coe
Wilbur Cross
Liza Featherstone
Peter M. Gerard
Karen B. Kneipp
Roni Sarig
Erica Sorohan
Suzanne Stone
Laurie Viera

A Note from the Editors

Every attempt has been made to ensure that this publication is as accurate as possible and as comprehensive as space would allow. We are grateful to the many businesspeople, computer experts, friends, librarians, reference editors, researchers, teachers, and state and U.S. government employees who contributed facts, figures, time, energy, ideas, and opinions. Our choice of what to include was aided by their advice and their voices of experience. The contents, however, remain subjective to some extent, because we could not possibly cover everything that office managers and workers need to know. If errors or omissions are discovered, we would appreciate hearing from you, the user, as we prepare future editions. Please address suggestions and comments to The Stonesong Press at 11 East 47th Street, New York, NY, 10017.

We hope you find our work useful.

Contents

Introduction

In an increasingly complex world, even the smallest office generates correspondence and maintains financial, legal, marketing, and personnel records. This book is designed to help office employees and managers organize, retrieve, and communicate needed information efficiently. Business writing and speaking, office design and equipment, accounting practices and budgeting, employee benefits, incorporation, taxation, marketing research, and business travel are included. Personnel administration and safety, time management and recordkeeping, and company image and public relations are also addressed. Many topics are presented from two perspectives (the employee's as well as management's), with the goal of creating a useful reference for every office worker.

The computerization of business has affected every area of office work, so each major subject area includes information about computer technology to make the job easier. Increasing hard drive capacities, CD-ROM technology, and Internet access are continuously changing information storage and retrieval options, yet many office workers still have basic questions about computers. Due to the rapid changes in available software and hardware, an effort has been made to address general issues of computer use in data organization, storage, and presentation, in addition to offering specific suggestions on currently available programs and equipment.

Extensive cross-referencing and a comprehensive index have been included to help you find related topics easily. A section entitled "Sources of Further Information" concludes each chapter, listing organizations, books and literature, and Internet websites for additional research on major topics. The final chapter includes recommendations on researching business issues, including useful reference materials to purchase for office use, a directory of business associations, a list of pertinent government agencies and information sources, and a glossary of business terms.

Large or small, libraries all over the country are constantly dealing with questions about the world of business. At the new Science, Industry and Business Library (SIBL) of The New York Public Library, where a vast number of books, electronic resources, online information, and every recorded U.S. patent and trademark are housed, the librarians answer questions about everything from how far an airport might be from a certain city to the best resources for marketing information. With this book, we have tried to provide frequently needed information based on the experience of librarians with user questions and input from business editors, researchers and statistics from popular on-line sites. The intention has been to present the essentials of commonly needed business information, particularly as it applies to necessities in the office. Admittedly, we have had to make subjective decisions and condense large amounts of information. Still, every effort has been made to ensure that the text presented is accurate, timely, and useful. The editorial staff of The Stonesong Press who prepared the material and the New York Public Library hope that you will find the book browsable, practical, and informative. If errors or omissions are discovered or you would like to make suggestions for future editions, please address your comments to The Stonesong Press at 11 East 47th Street, New York, NY 10017.

The Editors

1

Getting It There

Using the U.S. Postal Service

Mailing and shipping represent significant costs for businesses of all sizes. Most firms can save money by using bulk mailing rates and special discounts to cut expenses in these areas. Understanding the services and rates offered by the United States Postal Service (USPS) and its major competitors is a prerequisite to getting your mail where it is going in the most cost-efficient manner.

It is hard to imagine any business operating without the U.S. Postal Service, whose mail carriers visit almost every home and office in the United States daily. Its employees also provide helpful information and assistance (as they have since the postal department's creation in 1775) at postal counters and by telephone. In addition, the USPS operates about 85 Postal Business Centers nationwide to help small- and medium-sized businesses with their mailing operations. (Companies spending more than $250,000 annually have USPS customer service representatives assigned to their accounts.) Postal Business Center employees can open a corporate account for Express Mail, help to design promotional mailing pieces, and teach you to prepare mail that qualifies for discount rates. They also offer free or low-cost seminars on topics such as bar coding and bulk mailing. (A bar code is made up of a series of tall and short bars printed on a mailing label or directly on an envelope. It can represent a zip code, a zip+4 code, or an 11-digit delivery-point code. A delivery-point bar code combines the zip+4 code with two more digits derived from the street address number so that the mail can be sorted into the order in which carriers will deliver it.)

In 1996 the USPS received approval from the Postal Rate Commission to reform its domestic first-, second-, and third-class mail classification system. Reforms do not affect special services, Express Mail, or nonprofit, international, and fourth-class mail at present, but changes in these areas are pending. Domestic mail includes all classes of mail in the United States, including Alaska, Hawaii, and U.S. territories and possessions. Mail sent to and from Army/Air Force (APO) and Navy (FPO) post offices is considered domestic mail, too. Major changes instituted by classification reform primarily affect the preparation and handling of bulk mailings, affording businesses the opportunity to reduce mailing expenses significantly by using approved addressing, bar coding, and presorting techniques.

The purpose of the reforms is to award greater discounts on mail that can be processed through new USPS automation systems, with higher charges for mail that requires hand sorting. The new automated systems are much faster than older letter-sorting machinery. Properly addressed and/or bar coded mail can be processed by optical character recognition (OCR) technology and bar code sorters, enabling the USPS to cut labor costs, increase efficiency, and enhance its competitive standing. Mail that can be automated meets certain standards of dimension and thickness and is addressed correctly.

Most businesses can save money by following USPS guidelines for addressing, bar coding, and presorting mail. The following standards now apply to domestic mail, and similar standards may soon be in effect for international mail as well.

USPS Domestic Mail: First-Class, Standard, and Periodicals Classifications

All correspondence, including single first-class letters and cards, will be processed and delivered much faster if delivery-point bar codes are used. Even if bar codes are not present, a discount rate may be allowed for bulk mail that is classified *upgradable* by the Postal Service. This includes only letter-size, automation-compatible envelopes, with machine-printed (nonscript) addresses, an OCR read area, a bar code clear zone, and paper that can accept bar coding ink.

1. *First-class mail* continues to offer fast delivery (most first-class mail is delivered within one to three days), as well as maximum privacy of content (first-class mail is not subject to postal inspection). There are now two presorted mail subclassifications for first-class letters (letters, checks, statements, and invoices) and postcards: the Automation and Retail subclasses. The use of Presort Accuracy Verification (PAVE)-certified software is recommended for the preparation of all envelopes and cards to be mailed in bulk (at least 500 pieces for first-class presort rates). Delivery-point bar codes are required. Many of the newer versions of word-processing software include automatic bar code addressing for envelopes and labels. But business postal customers should call the USPS National Customer Support Center at 800-238-3150 to ensure that their software provides accurate delivery-point bar codes, as some programs are not PAVE-certified.

   First-class letter mail must conform to certain physical dimensions of vertical height (3½ inches minimum, 6⅛ inches maximum), horizontal width (5 inches minimum, 11½ inches maximum), thickness (.007 inch minimum, ¼ inch maximum), and weight (less than 11 ounces). To qualify for first-class handling, postcards must be no more than 4¼ inches high and no more than 6 inches in horizontal width. "First-Class Mail" should be imprinted or stamped on items that are not letter-size.

   Priority Mail is first-class mail weighing 11 ounces to 2 pounds. Priority usually moves as quickly as first-class mail but costs less than a first-class rate calculated by weight and destination. Free Priority Mail envelopes, packaging materials, labels, and stickers are available at the post office, but plain envelopes or packages may be used by attaching the labels and stickers. The USPS will pick up Priority Mail from your office for an additional fee; to schedule pickups or get rates and delivery information, call 800-222-1811.

2. *Standard mail* is the new classification for mail previously called third-class and fourth-class mail. The minimum volume for bulk mailings is 200 pieces, and delivery-point bar coding is required. There are no longer any discount rates for the use of zip+4 codes, as OCR technology has replaced the older sorting machines. Nonprofit mail reforms are not yet in place, but they are forthcoming. Contact your local post office or the National Customer Support Center for details on bulk-mailing permits, which are still required for some types of mail.

   Standard mail generally includes mail previously classified as fourth class (parcel post), but with no restructuring of that classification. Fourth-class mail still includes packages, merchandise, or printed materials that weigh 1 to 70 pounds and measure up to 108 inches in size. Packages heavier or larger than these specifications cannot be delivered by the USPS. (Measure the longest side of a package to get its length; measure all the way around the package's height and depth to get its girth; then add length and girth to obtain total package size.) Delivery is usually within two to seven days, depending on distance. Postage is determined by package destination and weight. Nonpersonal communications such as invoices or instructions may be included inside packages at no extra charge, but first-class postage should be added for enclosed or attached correspondence meeting first-class requirements. (When a letter is enclosed rather than attached to the package, you must write "Letter Enclosed" on the box and pay first-class postage for the letter only.)

Package mailings within certain size and weight requirements may qualify for standard mail bulk rates, and a permit imprint may be used if it is filed with the postal location processing the packages. Special rates may still apply to books, printed music, testing materials, recordings, and manuscripts, with additional discounts for presorting. There is also a library rate for certain items, such as books and manuscripts, sent between educational institutions, museums, public libraries, and some nonprofit organizations. Publishers can send materials to these institutions at the library rate, too.

3. *Periodicals mail* is the new name (it was formerly second-class mail) for mailed publications. A new rate structure is now in effect, based on address standards. The purpose of this category is still to promote the free flow of information and ideas. Publishers of subscription periodicals (whether commercial or nonprofit) can qualify for periodicals mailing status by meeting certain USPS requirements for publication frequency, ratio of editorial to advertising content, and circulation. Regular and nonprofit subclasses still apply, and there is a new publications service subclass that provides low-cost rates for printed matter that does not qualify for regular or nonprofit rates.

PREPARING PACKAGES FOR SHIPMENT

- Package items the way they would normally sit or stand, with the destination address on the up side.
- Use sturdy containers. Grocery store cartons work well for most items. Other appropriate containers include mailing tubes, paperboard boxes, metal cans, and wooden boxes.
- Use filament tape to seal the package.
- Avoid using brown paper to wrap packages, as it can tear during transport.
- Imprint or type the destination address and return address clearly, following USPS quality standards for size and type of print and order of information, using all capitals and no punctuation. Use an imprinted address label rather than a handwritten address whenever possible. Use ink that will not smear. Include accurate delivery-point bar codes, if possible, to help speed delivery.

- Put a list of the contents and the names/addresses of the sender and recipient inside the package.
- Use at least 2 inches of padding around each breakable item. Wrap or pack fragile items with Styrofoam peanuts, bubble wrap, shredded newspaper, or other cushioning material.
- Pack very fragile items in double boxes.
- Mark packages as appropriate (for example, "Fragile," "Perishable," or "Do Not Bend").

USPS International Mail Services

The USPS sends letters and packages to almost every country in the world. Its major classifications for international mail follow:

1. *LC Mail.* LC stands for "lettres et cartes" ("letters and cards"). This category includes letters, packages of letters, aerograms, postcards, and postal cards (cards sold by the USPS). The USPS defines letters as "personal handwritten or type-written communications having the character of current correspondence." Type or imprint the word "Letter" or "Lettre" on letters or letter packages. Postcards and postal cards are single cards sent without envelopes or other wrappers. Folded cards must be mailed in envelopes at the letter rate. Aerograms are thin, sealable sheets of stationery.

   The weight limit for LC Mail is 4 pounds. You may send other items, such as merchandise, at the letter rate if this is allowed by the destination country. The items must meet weight and size requirements for LC Mail.

2. *AO Mail.* AO stands for "autre objets" ("other objects"). This category is for printed matter, books, sheet music, small packets, materials for the blind, and periodicals that would be mailed in the periodicals classification, domestically. Audiotapes, videotapes, automated data-processing cards, and magnetic tapes also fall into this class. Weight limits vary for AO Mail. Ask your local post office personnel for specific weights and rates based on the item to be sent and its destination.

   Handwritten and typewritten materials are not classified as printed matter. To mail at least 11 pounds of printed matter to one addressee, the material may be packaged in a sack called an *M-bag* or *direct sack.* The sack and its contents may not weigh more than 66 pounds combined.

   Type or imprint one of the following identifiers on envelopes or packages containing printed matter: "Printed Matter," "Printed Matter—Catalogs," or "Printed Matter Directories" when the item weighs more than 4 pounds, "Printed Matter—Books," "Printed Matter—Sheet Music," "Printed Matter—Periodicals" (for publications that qualify). Post office personnel can help you identify items that qualify as materials for the blind, which can be sent free of charge by surface mail.

   Small packets classified as AO Mail include gifts, merchandise, commercial samples, and documents that are not "personal and current correspondence."

You may not mail small packets to Cambodia, Cuba, or the Democratic People's Republic of Korea (North Korea). Use the identifier "Small Packet" on the envelope or wrapper in English and in the language of the destination country.

3. *CP International Mail.* CP stands for "colis postaux" ("parcel post"). This category is similar to the domestic parcel post classification and is used for merchandise and other nonletter mail. Weight limits vary from country to country, but usually the limit is 22 pounds or 44 pounds.

4. *Express Mail International Service (EMS).* EMS is available to many countries. You may insure items sent by EMS and open an Express Mail corporate account. The USPS does not guarantee EMS service as it does domestic Express Mail. Ask USPS personnel for weight limits, rates, and availability to specific countries.

5. *International Priority Airmail (IPA).* This service is intended to provide business mailers with fast international service. IPA must meet certain volume and sorting requirements. All classes of LC and AO Mail may be sent IPA to any foreign country except Canada. Ask the post office for information about rates and how to prepare IPA, or request a copy of Publication 507, *International Priority Airmail.*

6. *International Surface Air Lift (ISAL).* This service offers a way to send all types of printed matter more quickly than by surface mail, at lower costs than airmail. Customers take their ISAL shipments to sites designated by the USPS. The shipments are flown to destination countries, where they enter surface mail systems for delivery. Rates vary by country. Consult the USPS or request Publication 31, *International Surface Air Lift.*

7. *Worldpost Priority Letter (WPL).* Worldpost Priority Letters are delivered internationally in an average of four days. USPS markets the WPL classification as faster than airmail but less expensive than private air express services. WPL is available for two flat-rate sizes: 9 inches by 11½ inches and 5 inches by 9 inches.

In addition, bulk letter mailing rates are available for service to Canada for letters weighing up to 3 ounces. Advertising materials, books, catalogs, directories, and merchandise may be sent via the USPS Valuepost classification. Use of either service requires the preparation of mail according to the Canadian postal code. Other international services include insurance, recorded delivery, registered mail, return receipt, restricted delivery, special delivery, special handling, C.O.D., and certified mail. The availability of a particular service depends on the destination country.

Customs laws require declaration of the content and value of international mail. Either a Customs Douane C-1 (Form 2976—green label) or a Customs Declaration C-2 (Form 2976-A—white form) must be attached to any small packet, any parcel containing dutiable (taxable) printed matter, or any letter package containing dutiable items. Form 2976-A is used when the value of a package exceeds $400. Either Form 2966-A (Parcel Post Customs Declaration) or Form 2966-B (Parcel Post Customs Declaration and Dispatch Note) must be attached to parcel post items. Form 2976 or Form 2966-A should be included on Express Mail International

Service. Check with the USPS about other requirements that may be applicable when mailing to certain countries.

When addressing international mail, type or imprint addresses in English, following USPS address quality standards. The last line of a foreign address should include only the name of the destination country, in all uppercase letters. Do not use abbreviations. Foreign postal codes, if available, should be included on the line above the country name, next to the city and state or province name. Include the country of origin as the bottom line of the return address, in all capitals.

USPS Address Quality Standards

For fastest delivery, addresses must include complete, up-to-date information and should be prepared according to the following USPS guidelines. Review these carefully—some may surprise you:

- Always include a return address.
- Include the street suffix (identifying the street as a lane, road, street, avenue, boulevard, place, court, or other) and the secondary-unit indicator (such as "Suite" or "Room") if available.
- Include directional indicators (for example, "North" or "Southwest") if these are part of the address.
- When using window envelopes, be sure that the complete delivery address will be visible even if the contents of the envelope shift.
- Locate all delivery address information within these boundaries of an envelope: at least ½ inch from the right edge and the left edge; at least ⅝ inch from the bottom edge, and no more than 2¾ inches from the bottom edge.
- Leave the lower right-hand corner of the envelope clear for USPS bar code application if you do not pre-imprint a bar code. The clear area must measure at least ⅝ inch deep and 4½ inches wide. In addition, the envelope must be made of paper that meets USPS *reflectance* standards—that is, paper that will accept sprayed-on bar code ink without smearing.
- Type or machine-print addresses in all capital letters, and use at least 10-point type but no more than 14-point type, preferably in a *sans serif* font. (*Sans serif* means "without serifs"—the short lines stemming from the ends of letters in many font styles. A sans serif font is one that is plain and easy to read. Fonts that emulate handwriting, called script fonts, are specifically prohibited by USPS standards.)

At present, what the USPS refers to as *uniform address element placement* is not a requirement to qualify for discount rates under the reformed classifications. However, the Postal Service urges all customers to begin following its uniform address element placement guidelines as part of their basic routine for addressing mail. These steps follow the guidelines:

- Put the recipient's name or an attention line on the top (first line) of the address.
- Type the recipient's business title, if included, on the second line of the address.

- Place the company name on the second line of the address unless a business title (such as "Vice President") is used; if so, place the company name on the third line of the address.
- Type the delivery address (street address, post office box number, rural route, or highway contract route/box number) on the next-to-last line of the address. If the delivery address is too long to fit on one line, continue the overflow information on the line above the delivery address line, not on the line below it, as automated sorters read from the bottom up.
- Place the city, state, and zip or zip+4 code on the bottom (last) line of a U.S. address. If the complete city, state, and zip will not fit on the bottom line, the zip or zip+4 code may be placed on the line immediately below the city and state names, aligned with the left edge of the address block. Nothing else should be on or below the last line except the bar code or the required space for bar coding. (For foreign addresses, the city, state or province, and foreign postal code should be on the next-to-last line, with the name of the country—in English—on the last line of the address.)
- Leave one letter space between each word or part of the address except between the state and zip code. Two letter spaces are left here.
- Use no punctuation within an address except the required hyphen in a zip+4 code. (This no-punctuation rule may require some mental adjustment, as it violates the time-honored traditions taught in grammar and typing classes.)
- Use USPS-approved abbreviations for states, street suffixes, directionals, and secondary-unit indicators.

The following examples of addresses meeting USPS standards were included in the USPS publication *Classification Reform,* dated October 1995:

```
MS MILDRED DOE                    MR M MURPHY
MARKETING SPECIALIST             PO BOX 1001
BRAKE CONTROL COMPANY            1201 BROAD ST E
12 E BUSINESS LN STE 209         FALLS CHURCH VA    22942-2101
KRYTON TN    38188-0002

H E BROWN                        ABC COMPANY
RR 3 BOX 9                        PO BOX 7530
CANTON OH    44730-9521          KRYTON TN    38188-7530
```

Another USPS publication (*Max It!,* printed in May, 1996) adds these examples:

```
MR DAVID H ADAMS                    MR & MRS JOHN A SAMPLE
325 W CAPITOL ST E APT 12          5505 W SUNSET BLVD APT 230
ARLINGTON VA    22203-7495         HOLLYWOOD CA    90028-8521
```

Note that in the Arlington address, the *W* is called a *predirectional* and the *E* is a *postdirectional.* The USPS literature emphasizes the importance of including accurate directionals and placing them in the appropriate places to ensure that mail is delivered correctly.

U.S. Postal Service Abbreviations

The United States, its territories and possessions

Alabama	AL	Missouri	MO
Alaska	AK	Montana	MT
Arizona	AZ	Nebraska	NE
Arkansas	AR	Nevada	NV
American Samoa	AS	New Hampshire	NH
California	CA	New Jersey	NJ
Colorado	CO	New Mexico	NM
Connecticut	CT	New York	NY
Delaware	DE	North Carolina	NC
District of Columbia	DC	North Dakota	ND
Federated States of		Northern Mariana Islands	MP
Micronesia	FM	Ohio	OH
Florida	FL	Oklahoma	OK
Georgia	GA	Oregon	OR
Guam	GU	Palau	PW
Hawaii	HI	Pennsylvania	PA
Idaho	ID	Puerto Rico	PR
Illinois	IL	Rhode Island	RI
Indiana	IN	South Carolina	SC
Iowa	IA	South Dakota	SD
Kansas	KS	Tennessee	TN
Kentucky	KY	Texas	TX
Louisiana	LA	Utah	UT
Maine	ME	Vermont	VT
Marshall Islands	MH	Virginia	VA
Maryland	MD	Virgin Islands	VI
Massachusetts	MA	Washington	WA
Michigan	MI	West Virginia	WV
Minnesota	MN	Wisconsin	WI
Mississippi	MS	Wyoming	WY

Directional abbreviations

North	N
East	E
South	S
West	W
Northeast	NE
Southeast	SE
Southwest	SW
Northwest	NW

Secondary address unit indicators

Apartment	APT
Building	BLDG
Floor	FL
Suite	STE
Room	RM
Department	DEPT

Delivery indicators

Post Office Box	PO BOX
Rural Route	RR

U.S. Postal Service Abbreviations (continued)

Common street suffixes

Avenue	AVE	Plaza	PLZ
Boulevard	BLVD	Point	PT
Canyon	CYN	Road	RD
Center	CTR	Square	SQ
Circle	CIR	Station	STA
Court	CT	Street	ST
Drive	DR	Terrace	TER
Freeway	FWY	Trace	TRCE
Highway	HWY	Trail	TRL
Lane	LN	Turnpike	TPKE
Manor	MNR	View	VW
Parkway	PKY	Way	WAY
Place	PL		

Special USPS Services

A number of special services are offered by the U.S. Postal Service for the convenience, security, privacy, and safety of customers and their mail. These include the following:

Post Office Boxes. Most post offices rent boxes of various sizes. The annual or semiannual fee for this service varies with the size of the box. Having your business mail delivered to a post office box provides extra security and privacy, and you can pick up your mail sooner than a postal employee would deliver it to your home or office. It is best to check a post office box at least once each day, and more often if you receive a large volume of business mail.

Certificates of Mailing. A certificate provides proof that you mailed an item. It does not prove that an item was delivered, and insurance coverage is not included. Certificates may be obtained for items sent first class, standard, or fourth class.

Certified Mail. This service for first-class mail provides a record of delivery at the recipient's post office.

C.O.D. (collect on delivery) Mail. Packages sent C.O.D. are not delivered unless the mail carrier receives a specified payment for the merchandise, which is then forwarded to the sender.

Insurance. For a small fee, packages can be insured for the value of the items they contain, up to $600 for standard and fourth class, and up to $25,000 for first-class registered mail. The USPS automatically insures Express Mail for up to $500.

Money Orders. You can buy money orders in amounts up to $700 at all post offices. If you have your receipt, the USPS will replace lost or stolen money orders. You can get copies of paid money orders for a small fee, up to two years after the payment date.

Registered Mail. This service provides extra security for first-class and Priority Mail. You can combine registered mail with insurance, return receipt, and restricted delivery services.

Restricted Delivery. The post office delivers restricted mail only to the addressee or a person authorized in writing to accept mail for the addressee. Restricted delivery is available for registered, certified, and C.O.D. mail, and any item insured for more than $50.

Return Receipts. If you want to know when a particular piece of mail was delivered and who received it, request a receipt. This service is available for Express Mail, mail sent C.O.D., mail insured for more than $50, and registered or certified mail.

Postage Stamps. The USPS sells many different types of stamps in various denominations. For customer convenience, they can be purchased at post offices or ordered by mail or telephone. To order by mail, pick up a preaddressed Stamps by Mail form (Form 3227) from the post office, or ask your mail carrier for one. Complete the form and mail it with a check or money order. You may also order stamps via electronic mail if you subscribe to the Prodigy on-line network. Use Prodigy's U.S. STAMPS file and the "FIND" command to locate the file. To order by phone, call 800-782-6724 and use your Visa, MasterCard, or Discover account number. The phone ordering service is available 24 hours a day, seven days a week. There is no fee for mail orders, but USPS does charge a fee for telephone and Prodigy orders. All three types of orders are filled and mailed within five business days of receipt of the order.

USPS Postal Business Centers. As noted previously, these centers were established to help smaller businesses manage their mail efficiently. The services of the centers have become even more valuable since classification reform has increased the possibilities for reducing mail expenses through use of proper mail preparation and handling procedures. To learn more about USPS Postal Business Center services and how to reach the one nearest you, contact your local post office or call the USPS National Customer Support Center at 800-238-3150.

(*See also* USPS Express Mail, page 19).

Postage Meters

Postage meters have been in use for more than 75 years. In the United States and Canada, you may rent, not purchase, a postage meter, as both the U.S. and Canadian postal services closely regulate their use. In the United States, a license from the USPS is required for meter use. Postage meter dealers will help you fill out the necessary paperwork, teach you how to operate the machine, and serve as your liaison to the post office.

The USPS currently authorizes only four companies to manufacture and rent postage meters (check the yellow pages for authorized dealers in your area):

1. Friden Neopost, 30955 Huntwood Avenue, Hayward, CA 94544-7085, phone 800-624-7892, fax 510-489-4367
2. Pitney-Bowes, Inc., Walter H. Wheeler Jr. Drive, Stamford, CT 06926-0001, phone 203-356-5000
3. Postalia, Inc., 1980 University Lane, Lisle, IL 60532-2152, phone 708-241-9090, fax 708-241-9091
4. Ascom Hasler Mailing Systems, 19 Forest Parkway, Shelton, CT 06484-0903, phone 203-926-1087

Usually, the decision to rent a postage meter is based on the volume and variety of business mail rather than the size of a company. But many businesses that mail as few as ten items a week use postage meters for the following reasons:

• Meter imprints look more professional than postage stamps.
• Meters eliminate the necessity of keeping a supply of stamps, thus reducing the number of trips to the post office.
• Meters facilitate close tracking of postal and shipping costs.
• Metering mail is faster than moistening stamps and applying them. Some models can be attached to special bases that moisten and seal envelopes as they imprint postage.
• Metered mail is processed by the USPS more quickly than stamped mail.
• Meters store postage and dispense it in exact amounts as needed.

Meters will print postage directly on envelopes that do not exceed certain dimensions, usually those up to 2¼ inches thick. For larger items, the machines will print the postage on prepasted tape, which is then affixed to the envelope or package. Some meters will print an advertising logo or slogan next to the postage imprint. Electronic models can be programmed with several advertising messages and reprogrammed as needed. The newest electronic meters feature automatic date setting, but older models require a manual date change each day.

Electronic postage meters are replacing earlier, mechanical versions. These newer models are less likely to break down and offer many enhanced functions. Deluxe versions are designed to interface with electronic postal scales that provide cost comparisons by calculating postage for commercial carriers (such as United Parcel Service and Federal Express) as well as different USPS mailing rates. These scales offer a "best way" key that automatically calculates the least expensive option.

Meters hold $100 to $10,000 of postage, depending on the model. Business managers determine the amount of postage needed based on their meter models, mailing needs, and cash management systems. For convenience, most firms store enough postage to last several weeks or months, subject to the USPS requirement that meters be reset at least once every three months (this is a security measure). Meter manufacturers or their authorized dealers are responsible for inspecting meters on a regular basis to guard against meter fraud.

Older postage meters must be taken to a post office for resetting. An office employee usually takes the meter and a company check to pay for postage, and a USPS worker resets the meter, storing the new amount of postage in it. In some areas, for a fee, the USPS will send an employee to an office at an appointed time to reset the meter. Ask local post office personnel about the availability of this service.

Some newer electronic meters can be reset by calling the manufacturer. An automated message system or a customer service representative asks for information about the meter, and then provides an access code that is punched into the meter to reset it. Still newer technology allows use of a computer modem to dial the manufacturer and reset the meter, all in one step. But in most cases, money to pay for the postage must be deposited with the USPS before a meter can be reset electronically. One manufacturer, Neopost, does not require that funds be deposited in a postal account. Instead, Neopost advances the postage and then immediately debits the client's bank account electronically and deposits that amount with the USPS.

Businesses with a large volume of mail and packages often invest in sophisticated metered-mail systems that produce detailed records and handle complex mailings with ease. For smaller firms, a postage meter complemented by an electronic scale may be sufficient, or just a postage meter and a regular postal scale may do.

PREPARING METERED MAIL

Post the following reminders near your postage meter to ensure correct and efficient use:

- Change the date on the meter each day.
- Apply the correct amount of postage. Check scales daily for accuracy and read postage rate charts carefully.
- Check for clear, readable meter imprints.
- Use fluorescent ink—this speeds processing by USPS equipment.
- Face all metered mail in the same direction for faster processing.

Mail Houses, Letter Shops, and Commercial Mail/Parcel Centers

Mail houses and letter shops prepare mailings to meet USPS requirements and then deliver them to USPS facilities. Small business mailings may be combined to qualify for volume discounts, thus allowing clients to use the mail service's bulk-mailing permit instead of buying their own. Check the yellow pages under "Mailing Services" or ask post office personnel for a list of USPS mailing partners in your area. USPS Postal Business Center personnel can also help you find local suppliers of these services.

Commercial mail and parcel centers are retail businesses at which you may purchase stamps (at no extra charge), ship packages, arrange for overnight deliveries, rent a postal box, make photocopies, and send or receive faxes. If you are willing to pay for the convenience of having packages wrapped and labeled as well as mailed, these services are also available. Some commercial mail and parcel centers offer other mailing services similar to those provided by USPS mailing partners.

There are about 9,500 of these businesses in the United States, including several large franchises and many independent operations. They are often located in suburban strip malls and downtown business centers. Look in the yellow pages under "Mailing Services" to find those near you. Some cater to small businesses and home-office workers. Visit conveniently located stores, compare their services and prices, and talk with the owner-operators about your needs. The home offices of some large U.S. franchises follow:

- Mail Boxes Etc., 6060 Cornerstone Court West, San Diego, CA 92121, phone 619-455-8800
- Pak Mail Centers of America, 3033 South Parker Road, Suite 1200, Aurora CO 80014, phone 303-752-3500
- Postal Annex, 9050 Friars Road, San Diego, CA 92108, phone 619-563-4800
- PostNet Franchise Headquarters, 2501 Green Valley Parkway #101, Henderson, NV 89014, phone 702-792-7115
- Amailcenter Franchise Corporation, 2030 Lake Forest Drive, Suite B2, Lake Forest, CA 92630, phone 714-837-4151

USPS Postal Business Centers can help you find local mailing services. To learn more about Business Center services and to locate the nearest center, contact your local post office or call the National Customer Support Center at 800-238-3150.

Commercial Package Delivery Services

United Parcel Service (UPS) is probably the best-known commercial package delivery service. Many businesses have used UPS services exclusively for years when shipping packages and merchandise, mainly because of lower rates for many items than those charged by the U.S. Postal Service. A UPS driver will stop at your business daily to pick up packages for a low weekly fee. One-time pickup service is also available for a small fee. UPS also offers worldwide package delivery services. Call 800-742-5877 for information on domestic and international shipping rates or to schedule pickups.

There are a number of excellent package/cargo shipment services available. The following table can be used as a quick reference guide for contacting the larger carriers about specific rates and services.

Company	*Toll-free number*	*Same day*	*Next A.M.*	*Next P.M.*	*2–3 day*	*Door-to-door pickup and delivery*
Airborne Express	800-247-2676		X	X	X	X
American Airlines	800-443-7300	X	X	X	X	X*
Associated Global Systems	800-645-8300	X	X	X	X	X
Burlington Air Express	800-225-5229	X*	X	X	X	X
Continental Airlines	800-421-2456	X	X	X	X	X*
Delta Airlines DASH (up to 70 pounds)	800-638-7333	X*	X*	X*	X*	X*
DHL Worldwide	800-272-7345	X	X			X
Emery Worldwide	800-443-6379		X	X	X	X
Federal Express	800-238-5355		X	X	X	X
Roadway Express	800-257-2837	X	X	X	X	X*
Roadway Package Service	800-762-3725				X	X*
Sky Courier (affiliate of Airborne Express)	800-336-3344	X*	X*	X*		X*
Sonic Air (division of UPS)	800-782-7892	X	X	X	X	X
TNT Express Worldwide	800-368-3400 (for same or next day service, call 800-677-4444)	X	X	X	X	X
TWA	800-892-2746	X	X	X	X	X
United Airlines	800-825-3788	X	X	X	X	X*
United Parcel Service (UPS)	800-742-5877		X*	X*	X*	X*
US Airways	800-428-4322	X	X	X	X	X*
U.S. Postal Service Express Mail	800-222-1811		X*	X	X	X (Note that mail sent to another country is transferred to that country's postal system for delivery, so the USPS cannot guarantee foreign deliveries.)

* Denotes a service that is available for domestic shipments only.

When It Must Be There Tomorrow (Or Today)

There are many air express mail services, and more seem to appear daily as businesses become increasingly dependent on rapid service. An "Air Cargo Report" in the May 9, 1996, issue of *Business Consumer Guide* magazine compared several of the largest delivery services in terms of cost, efficiency, and reliability. Some of their recommendations follow:

Company	Toll-free number	Recommended for
Airborne Express	800-247-2676	Overnight delivery of less than 3 pounds and next-afternoon delivery of packages weighing 5 pounds or less
Burlington Air Express	800-225-5229	Next day delivery of packages weighing 90 to 150 pounds
DHL Worldwide	800-272-7345	Fast document delivery and overseas shipments; competitive rates and the ability to clear packages through customs quickly are features
Federal Express	800-238-5355	Delivery of letters or small packages to Europe via International Priority Service; although Federal Express has set the standards for the industry, its prices are often quite high compared with those of other firms
U.S. Postal Service	800-222-1811	All deliveries to P.O. boxes and APO/FPO addresses; also, the best choice for Sunday and holiday deliveries

However, the report also suggests that using one firm for all of your shipping needs may be most economical, as a number of companies offer discounts based on volume.

Air Express Service Features

Most air express services:

- specialize in delivery of packages that weigh less than 100 pounds—for heavier air shipments, you may need to contact an air freight company such as Emery Worldwide or Burlington Air Express.
- charge flat rates based on weight, time of delivery, and special services required to pick up and deliver packages on schedule (the destination's distance from the shipping point is not a major pricing factor). However, surcharges for other services may surprise you. (See Air Express Service Limitations, on the next page.)
- offer lower rates for next-day deliveries than for same-day services, and lowest rates on second-day deliveries.
- charge less for packages brought to their offices by the customer, and more to provide pickup services. (Opening an account with the carrier sometimes qualifies customers for lower pickup charges. For example, UPS will provide every-business-day pickups for a flat weekly fee.)
- offer software that lets you track packages from your own computer. (For those who must frequently account for the whereabouts of packages, this can be very convenient.)
- track packages for customers at no extra charge.
- insure your air express packages at rates ranging from 25 cents to 50 cents per $100 of declared value.

In addition, several major services have drop boxes for labeled and prepaid packages. FedEx has about 30,000 drop boxes worldwide, and USPS Express Mail may be placed in special drop boxes or in regular USPS mailboxes.

Federal Express offers a special service called FedEx Ship, which is free software designed for small and occasional shippers. It can be used to schedule FedEx deliveries electronically, and also to prepare and print bar coded FedEx labels on plain paper. (A label is placed in a see-through pouch supplied by FedEx; the pouch is attached to the package.) The software also saves keystrokes by enabling you to import addresses from database software. Subscribers to America Online can download the software. Others may contact FedEx, 2005 Corporate Avenue, Memphis, TN 38132, phone 901-369-3600, to request FedEx Ship software.

Air Express Service Limitations

Even in a major metropolitan area such as Los Angeles, a hefty charge may be added to have a package picked up from an office a long way from the airport. Most express services are based near airports, so a driver may spend hours in traffic, driving to your office for the package and then back to the airport. Of course, that driving time must also be considered in the delivery schedule. For instance, if it takes an hour and a half to drive from your office to the airport, an air express service that advertises delivery within four to seven hours probably cannot get your package from Los Angeles to New York in that length of time, as three hours will be required just for your package to be picked up and taken to the airport.

None of the major air express services will cite specific thresholds for volume discounts. Home-based businesses are least likely to qualify, but any firm should be able to open a corporate account. Talk to carriers about your shipping needs and compare their prices—some may offer programs tailored to small businesses or infrequent shippers.

Most air express carriers (except the USPS) charge more to deliver on Saturday. And only USPS Express Mail packages can be delivered to post office boxes—all other services deliver to street addresses only. If bad weather grounds flights, delivery-time guarantees are null (read the fine print). But forces of nature notwithstanding, the air express industry has an excellent track record for secure and reliable service, even under daunting weather conditions.

Same-Day Services

Same-day delivery is the fastest growing market in the package-delivery industry. It is available from many domestic air express services, and even some international ones. Some airlines offer their own same-day express services. In addition, most surface courier and messenger services will arrange airport-to-airport and even door-to-door same-day deliveries.

Most same-day services rely on commercial flights to transport packages, with rates currently beginning at about $150. Large-volume customers receive discounts. Some carriers, such as Emery Worldwide's Expedite Service, will even arrange for charter flights when commercial flights are not available at the right time and place. Of course, such special services can be very expensive, but they are used frequently to deliver parts or documents that represent substantial business income if delivered immediately. Videotapes, magnetic tapes, computer disks, business proposals, and film are items often sent by express cargo.

Airlines offering same-day deliveries include American, Continental, Delta, TWA, United, and US Airways. Check the yellow pages under "Air Cargo and Package Express Services" for airline cargo services in your area. For airline express cargo counter-to-counter services, there is no need to reserve space in advance. Just call the airline to learn when the next flight leaves for your package's destination, then drop off the package at the airport ticket counter. Each carrier sets its own deadlines for leaving packages, but most require that you leave the package from 30 minutes to 1½ hours before flight departure. Some airlines provide domestic door-to-door courier services for an additional charge. However, more lead time is required; that is, you must have the package ready sooner if you want pickup and delivery services.

Recent changes in Federal Aviation Administration regulations require that airlines inspect all package/cargo shipments. The paperwork for inspections must be completed at the airport before the shipment is sent. This means that even though door-to-door pickup and delivery services are available, a representative of your firm must accompany each shipment to the airport. Therefore, the pickup service would be useful only for large shipments that office personnel cannot transport to the airport easily. Also, some airline companies do not provide door-to-door delivery services abroad due to international customs requirements. In such cases, package recipients are responsible for claiming shipments at the airline counter and clearing them through customs.

In general, airlines charge flat rates for express cargo services based on weight ranges. Prices start at about $50 for counter-to-counter service and over $100 for door-to-door service. TWA provides special envelopes (13 inches by 17 inches) that can hold up to 2.2 pounds for a flat rate, less than $45 at the time of this publication. There are dimension and weight limits for packages accepted for express cargo service, with maximum acceptable weights of 70 to 100 pounds, depending on the airline. Most airlines do not guarantee same-day international package service, and some will only guarantee arrival within two to three days.

Overnight (Next-Day) Deliveries

Few, if any, air express services deliver packages overnight to every destination in the United States. Generally, next-day morning deliveries are guaranteed only to major metropolitan areas. Overnight packages may not arrive at rural destinations until afternoon. For sparsely populated, remote regions, most express agencies guarantee only second-day deliveries.

Packages can be shipped from the United States to most destinations in Canada overnight. Service to Mexico fluctuates. Many overnight delivery firms offer service to Europe, but their coverage varies. In the past, DHL has supplied overnight delivery to more foreign destinations than other services, but this may be changing as new competitors enter the market. Most air express carriers offer two-day international service as well, and all offer assistance with customs declarations. Some air freight companies offer overnight services for small packages up to very large pieces, such as huge parts for manufacturing equipment.

USPS Express Mail

The USPS offers Express Mail same-day, next-day, and second-day delivery services within the United States. Some international services are also available, but delivery times are not guaranteed for international Express Mail as they are for domestic deliveries. Special Express Mail postage stamps or postal meter imprints may be used. The USPS will also open a corporate Express Mail account for your business with a minimum deposit of $100.

Same-day Express Mail is relatively inexpensive, but geographically limited to airport-based USPS facilities. (Ask your local postmaster for the location nearest you.) Door-to-door service is not available—your package must be taken to the nearest USPS airport facility at least an hour and a half in advance of the commercial flight to be used for its transport. When the package is dropped off, USPS staff can verify the time that your package will arrive at its destination airport and be released; you can then tell the recipient when to pick it up.

Most post offices accept Express Mail until 5:00 P.M. for next-day delivery. The USPS guarantees delivery by noon the next day to most addresses, and by 3:00 P.M. to the remainder. Express Mail packages can also be sent post office to post office, meaning the addressee can pick up the package at a local post office as early as 10:00 A.M.

Express Mail labels and packaging materials are free at your local post office. There are several options for mailing these letters or packages. They can be taken to the local post office, dropped in an Express Mail box, placed in your mailbox, or handed to your mail carrier. Of course, Express Mail postage must be prepaid (stamped or metered) unless the item is mailed at a post office customer counter. For an extra fee, the USPS will send a mail carrier to pick up your prepaid Express Mail package. There is no extra charge for Saturday Express Mail delivery, and only USPS Express Mail can be delivered to post office boxes, as mentioned previously.

IS OVERNIGHT DELIVERY REALLY NECESSARY?
A MONEY-SAVING STRATEGY

Before investing heavily in same-day or next-day delivery services, be sure they are really necessary. If a document must arrive the next day or within two days, a guaranteed service is essential. But suppose you have a document ready on Monday that must arrive at its destination

> by Thursday. If you copy the document and send it by USPS first-class mail on Monday, chances are it will arrive on Wednesday. (Fifty percent of all first-class mail arrives within two days.) On Wednesday, you can check with the recipient to see if the document has arrived. If not, the copy you retained can still be sent by an overnight delivery service to make the Thursday deadline. This strategy will save money in the long run, as many overnight delivery charges will be avoided.

Courier and Messenger Services

There are 8,000 to 10,000 surface messenger and courier businesses operating in the United States. Most serve a particular area or region, and many operate 24 hours a day. These firms often prefer to set up accounts for clients, running a credit check before establishing an account. When selecting a messenger service, ask for references. Check with the references about the service's record for on-time deliveries. Compare prices, but give extra weight to a reputation for courteous, reliable, professional service. In time, the personnel at a good messenger service will become familiar with your company's routine pickups, deliveries, and special needs, so that lengthy explanations are not necessary each time a delivery is scheduled. All of these agencies specialize in speedy local deliveries by car, van, or even bicycle. Regular and rush services are generally available.

Instant Correspondence

Just the Fax

For businesspeople with constant deadlines, fax machines are wonderful aids in meeting deadlines and cutting turnaround time. Messages can be sent and responses received almost instantaneously, at a much lower cost than the price of mail, messengers, or shipping. Faxing enhances your company's competitive standing by letting you respond immediately to requests for information from customers, suppliers, and colleagues. It also simplifies communications with clients and associates in other time zones, because the sender and receiver need not be in at the same time. Thanks to fax machines, it is usually no longer necessary for New Yorkers to be in their offices before dawn or after midnight to get urgent messages to colleagues in Berlin or Tokyo by telephoning them. (*See also* Communications Applications, page 153; Fax Machines, page 158; and Advantages and Disadvantages of Computer Faxing, page 159.)

Tips on Sending and Receiving Faxes

Each fax transmitted ties up two fax machines—the sender's and the recipient's. It also costs money, especially for long distance. Lengthy documents use a lot of the recipient's fax paper and ink supply. So use these tips to make the most of facsimile technology via fax machine or computer modem:

- Keep faxes short to avoid tying up machines and incurring unnecessary phone charges. It is especially important to be brief when sending a fax via computer modem, because faxes are saved as cumbersome graphics files instead of text files.
- Use a cover sheet when faxing to a large organization so the fax can be delivered promptly to the right person.
- Omit the cover sheet when faxing to a small business to save time, paper, and ink. Just make sure the addressee's name and your own are typed or written clearly at the top of the first page, that is, "To Sheree Bykofsky from Karen Kneipp." Also include the total number of pages being faxed (the date, time, sending and receiving fax numbers will be printed automatically by your fax machine).
- Leave generous margins (at least 1 inch) on each side of data to be faxed. Otherwise, some of your message may be omitted. Fax machines are like copiers—they do not copy every millimeter of a page. Handwritten notes in the margins may not be complete on the receiver's copy. If your document lacks sufficient margins or has notes written in the margins, reduce each page before faxing to make sure all of the information is transmitted.
- Reduce oversized documents before sending them. (Some fax machines will automatically scan and reduce oversized pages for you.)
- Check to make sure you have dialed the correct number if your fax machine automatically redials a number that is busy. Someone may be spared the annoyance of having your machine repeatedly try a telephone number and tie up a line that is not even a fax number.
- Number the pages being faxed, starting with "1," even if you are sending only part of a document with pages that were already numbered. This will make it easier for the recipient to put pages in order and check to see if any are missing.
- To avoid paper jams, make a copy of your document first. Do not put wrinkled, curled, rolled, or torn documents through the fax machine. Carbon paper, coated paper, and onionskin can also cause problems.
- Remove paper clips and staples before faxing.
- Read the owner's manual to learn the maximum number of sheets your machine's feeder can handle, and never exceed it.
- Check for incoming messages often and clear the paper tray to prevent paper jams. Make sure there is always plenty of paper in the machine so it will not run out in mid-message.

Confirming Transmission

Both fax machines and computer fax programs generate activity reports to confirm that a fax has been delivered or that there were problems in transmission. A typical report indicates the date and time of transmission, the receiving machine's number, the duration of the call, the number of pages sent, and that transmission was completed, or the reason it was not. A simple way to confirm that a fax message has been received is to ask the recipient to call you. Include the request in your cover sheet, or take advantage of your machine's *call reservation* feature, which delivers a call-back message with the fax.

FAX ETIQUETTE

1. Promise to fax something only when you intend to do so, and send it promptly.
2. Send lengthy faxes after hours if possible, so your transmission will not tie up the receiver's line (and your own) during business hours.
3. Keep faxes as short as possible.
4. Remember that fax messages are business correspondence. Proofread them carefully to eliminate grammar, spelling, and typographic errors.
5. Use the same standards of formality in faxes that are appropriate for other business letters. Avoid the temptation to be informal or casual just because you are sending a quick message.
6. Make sure handwritten notes are legible before faxing them.
7. Be considerate when sending faxes late at night to salespeople, consultants, or small business owners. A home-based professional or someone who is traveling may be awakened when the phone or fax machine receives your message. Ask first, just to be safe, and send faxes earlier in the evening if necessary.

Fax Cover Sheets

Cover sheets say something about your company and ensure that messages are delivered to the right people. To project a professional image and facilitate delivery, make sure your cover sheet includes the following:

• the sender's name, company name, address, and telephone and fax numbers
• the name, company name, and department of the recipient
• the number of pages being transmitted, including the cover sheet
• the person to contact if a transmission problem occurs
• any special instructions to the recipient
• an indication such as "c:" if the fax is being sent to more than one person

When designing your cover sheet, use a clear, legible, large typeface. Avoid using graphics, screens, or fancy borders, as they do not always transmit well. A small black-and-white reproduction of the company logo may be used, but remember that graphics take more transmission time, increasing the cost of each message. Graphics also require extra computer file space when sent via modem. Your company letterhead may make a suitable cover sheet if it is clear and easy to reproduce (*see* Figure 1.1).

FAX Transmittal

Ascher, Barkin, and Chase, Ltd.
555 West Avenue
Cincinnati, OH 66444
(215) 555-7436 fax (215) 555-6347 voice

To:

Company Name:
Department:
Fax Number:

From:

Subject:

Date Sent:

Time Sent:

Number of pages, including cover sheet:

Please call Anne Romero at (215) 555-6347 if there are any problems with this transmission.

Figure 1.1 Fax cover sheet

ELIMINATING JUNK FAXES

If your business receives unwanted advertisements by fax, your lines may be busy when important messages are waiting for transmission. Never agree to publish your number in a fax directory, as unscrupulous advertisers may exploit such listings. Use your machine's password function to block transmissions from fax machines with unfamiliar numbers.

The law is on your side. The Federal Communications Commission's (FCC) Telephone Consumer Protection Act of 1992 bans unsolicited advertisements via fax. It also requires that all sales faxes clearly indicate the sender's name and fax number. Every faxed advertisement must include a telephone number that recipients can call to prevent future transmissions from that source or on that subject.

How Important Is a Hard Copy?

There are several reasons to keep a paper copy of important faxes. First, mailing a hard copy is an excellent way to make sure the message is delivered. This also enhances the legal status of a faxed message. Attorneys seem to agree that a signed, faxed document is legally binding, but following up with a mailed original and keeping one in your files may be wise. It is also advisable to file a copy of the transmission report for important documents in case it is necessary to prove that the information was sent by a certain date and time.

Routine correspondence faxed directly from your computer need not be retained in paper form, however. The computer file is available for review, and printing a file copy may be a waste of paper and storage space. Faxing by computer should be used to reduce the amount of paper stored in your office, not to increase it. (*See also* The Paperless Office, page 155.)

Getting the Most for Your Money with Advanced Fax Features

Using all of your fax machine's capabilities is the best way to keep productivity up and telephone bills down. Read the owner's manual or call product support to learn how to take advantage of special features such as those listed below.

1. *Delayed transmission* allows you to schedule the time that a document will be sent. The unit automatically faxes a document at a time you have specified.
2. *Polling* lets your machine call others to request incoming faxes. For example, if you are expecting sales reports from 50 field representatives, your machine can be programmed to call their machines during the night so that all 50 reports are received without tying up your fax line during the workday.
3. *Broadcasting* is designed for faxing the same message to dozens, hundreds, or thousands of fax machines. The information to be faxed is merged with a database of recipients' names and fax numbers. This facilitates sending updated price lists, special promotional offers, or newsletters to an enormous pool of recipients. Remember to follow FCC regulations when faxing advertisements, sending them only to customers who want to receive them. Keep promotional material brief as a courtesy to others and to lower your costs.

When to Use a Fax Service Bureau

It may be more economical to let a fax service bureau handle large fax broadcasts to hundreds or thousands of recipients. This is a creative way to distribute company press releases to local, regional, or national media; deliver weekly newsletters to branch managers and field representatives; or send price changes to regular customers.

When you use a fax service bureau, it is only necessary to supply the document and a disk of fax numbers to be contacted. The service company can send your document to as many as 12,000 locations per hour. A bureau can also set up a fax-on-demand program for your firm to handle routine requests for information about products or services.

Hiring a fax service bureau for large projects has several advantages over using the office fax equipment:

- *Advanced technology.* A good service agency will have the latest in fax technology for fast, professional transmittals. This may save your firm the expense of continuously upgrading its fax equipment.
- *Lower cost.* Service bureaus usually receive discount telephone rates due to their large volume of calls. These savings will be passed along to you. Fax bureaus typically charge customers by the page or by the second.
- *Reduced use of company phone lines.* An enormous broadcast or a fax-on-demand service will severely tax your office phone system. A service bureau can dedicate as many as 200 phone lines to your project; this will also result in faster transmittal.
- *Efficiency.* Using a fax bureau for large projects frees your staff to focus on duties other than mastering the intricacies of fax broadcasting.
- *On-line capability.* Professional fax services are already connected to the information highway, so they can broadcast information faster than your company can establish an on-line address.

To locate a fax service bureau, look in the yellow pages under "Fax Transmission Services" or in a telecommunications trade journal under "Facsimile Marketing."

Keeping Messages Secure

Sending a fax is like mailing a postcard. Unless steps are taken to safeguard the message, it may be read by several people before reaching the addressee. Information sent via fax modem can be more secure, as it goes straight into the recipient's computer. Networked computers may mean public messages, however.

To ensure that confidential incoming faxes are read only by those for whom they are intended, locate the company fax machine in a secure area. Delegate fax checking and delivery services to an employee known for discretion. Establish procedures for prompt fax delivery in specially marked envelopes that keep the contents private. In a large business with centralized fax operations, it may be necessary to use fax equipment with individual mailbox capabilities. Messages addressed to a mailbox are stored in memory, but are not printed until the mailbox user inputs a retrieval identification number.

When faxing highly confidential information to someone else, make sure the recipient is aware that privileged data is on its way. Unless you are certain of the other party's security measures, call first to ensure that he or she will be standing by to receive the document. Double-check the fax number and dial it carefully to avoid sending sensitive information to a wrong number. If you are broadcasting sensitive documents to other fax machines or computers within your firm, check the broadcast list carefully before faxing. Be sure to delete any fax numbers outside the company. (The *Wall Street Journal* routinely receives internal marketing and financial reports from companies that have mistakenly included the paper's number in a fax broadcast intended for company personnel only. On several occasions, these unintentionally faxed documents have resulted in *Journal* articles that were an unpleasant surprise to the targeted companies.)

E-Mail

A recent survey reported that 75 percent of business telephone calls result in the caller's failure to reach the desired party. Playing telephone tag consumes valuable time that could be used for more profitable activities. Traditional postal mailings take days to be delivered; messenger, courier, and overnight delivery services are costly; and long-distance faxes can be quite expensive. Given these limitations, many professionals have found that E-mail (electronic mail) is the best way to send important messages quickly.

Using E-mail is simple. A message is typed or scanned into a computer that is connected to one of many service provider networks such as CompuServe or America Online. When the message is ready to be sent, the recipient's electronic address is entered; with a click of the mouse button, the mail is sent to the addressee's electronic mailbox. (Mailboxes are actually segments of memory in giant mainframe computers.)

E-mail services are often furnished at no extra charge by service providers who charge a monthly fee for several hours access to the network. Extra hours are billed at a flat rate, and E-mail services are provided as part of the regular service. Some providers offer unlimited access for a larger monthly fee. There are no long-distance fees for E-mail, no matter where a message is sent. And most service networks also furnish access to the Internet, a worldwide network linking many smaller networks. Thus, a user can send E-mail to anyone in the world who has Internet access, even though their basic service providers are not the same. (Some services do charge a fee for E-mail sent via Internet to another network's subscribers.)

Some useful features of E-mail include the following:

- the ability to send one E-mail message to several different recipients with no added cost or time.
- the auto-response option, which automatically addresses the recipient's response to E-mail after just one keystroke.
- the convenience of picking up mail even when you are away from the office by logging on to the service provider from your home or laptop computer.

E-mail works best when these simple rules are followed:

- Check for messages at least twice per day.
- Be concise. E-mail encourages brevity; in fact, there is a limit on the length of messages sent. Longer and more detailed messages are best suited for letters or faxes.
- Ask for the E-mail addresses of your customers and other business contacts, and make sure they have yours.

- Compose and proofread messages before connecting to your service provider's network. This saves money by not wasting your monthly basic-fee network access hours.
- Do not use underlining, boldface, or italics in E-mail. Messages are transmitted as ASCII characters, so those prepared with word-processing software should be saved as text-only characters before transmitting. Most newer software programs offer this option.
- Avoid using graphics in E-mail. They take a lot of transmission time and may not print clearly when received.
- Remember that E-mail messages can be intercepted easily by your boss, a co-worker, or computer hackers anywhere in the world unless an encryption device is used. To be safe, avoid sending highly confidential information via E-mail. (*See also* Communications Applications, page 153.)

Sources of Further Information

Organizations

Associated Mail and Parcel Centers, 705 School Street, Napa, CA 94559, phone 800-365-2672, fax 800-390-2672.

The Mailer Education Center offers seminars about current USPS services. For a free catalog of course descriptions, sites, and dates, write P.O. Box 836, Windsor, CT 06006-0836, or call 800-877-7843.

Messenger Courier Association of America, 1101 15th Street NW, Suite 202, Washington, DC 20005, phone 202-785-3298.

Books and Literature

Bredin, Alice. *The Virtual Office Survival Handbook.* New York: John Wiley & Sons, 1996.

Business Mailers Review is a biweekly, independent newsletter covering the U.S. Postal Service, private carriers, and suppliers. A one-year subscription in the United States, Canada, and Mexico costs $279. Contact *Business Mailers Review,* 1616 North Fort Myer Drive, Suite 1000, Arlington, VA 22209, phone 800-424-2908. (In Virginia, call 703-528-1244.) You may also fax your request to 703-528-4926, or use the E-mail address: mailer@pasha.com.

The *Domestic Mail Manual* is the bible of the U.S. Postal Service. It describes USPS services and mail classifications in detail. For a yearly subscription, contact the Superintendent of Documents, U.S. Government Printing Office, Washington, DC 20402-9371. Or consult the copy available for public use at your local post office. For businesses that make frequent international mailings or shipments, the *International Mail Manual* (available through the same sources) is very helpful.

Fishman, Daniel, and Elliott King. *The Book of Fax: An Impartial Guide to Buying and Using Facsimile Machines.* Chapel Hill, NC: Ventana Press, 1995.

The *Mailer's Software Catalogue* lists software available from many manufacturers. To request a copy, call 800-800-MAIL.

MailGram is a free newsletter covering direct mail marketing from a small-business perspective. It is published by PR Graphics, 4679 West Chester Pike, Newtown Square, PA 19073, phone 800-432-9870, fax 610-359-9840.

Mailing and Shipping Technology is a magazine for industry professionals. Write 2701 East Washington Avenue, Madison, WI 53704, or call 608-241-8777, fax 608-241-8666.

Memo to Mailers is a USPS newsletter that keeps customers apprised of new services and regulatory activities. For a free subscription, write to: Editor, *Memo to Mailers,* U.S. Postal Service, Washington, DC 20260-3122.

Passport is a free quarterly newsletter from the USPS covering international mail services. Contact WorldPost Services, USPS, P.O. Box 23793, Washington, DC 20026-3793.

On-Line Resources

Federal Express *http://www.fedex.com*

Four11 Corporation's worldwide listings of E-mail addresses, fax numbers, and telephone numbers *http://www.411.com*

Institute of Management and Administration's Mail Center Management Report Site *http://www.ioma.com/ioma/mcmr*

Mail Boxes, Etc. *http://www.mbe.com*

United Parcel Service *http://www.ups*

United States Postal Service *http://www.usps.gov*

2

Communicating

Written Communications

First Draft: Basics of Good Composition

Written communications reflect on the employees and the firms they represent. Although many executives take great care to dress and act professionally, some do not realize the negative impact of poorly written correspondence on clients and associates. The recipient visualizes the sender and mentally hears the writer's voice when reading a document, so professional tone, impeccable grammar, and attractive appearance are crucial. Consider the following elements of composition to see if your writing passes muster.

Setting the Right Tone

The tone of a letter or report should be chosen to produce the desired reaction in its reader(s). To ensure a businesslike response from recipients of your business communications, avoid sounding emotional. Even when writing a collection letter, there is nothing to be gained by sounding angry. The object of such a letter is to let its recipient know what actions will be taken if overdue bills are not paid. A display of anger may indicate that you are unsure of your firm's ability to collect, thus weakening your position instead of strengthening it.

A professional approach should also be maintained when your purpose is to sell a product or service. By all means, be positive and make the description interesting, but avoid gushing foolishly. The recipient assumes you are enthusiastic about your product—the point is to present facts that make the reader want to try it. As prospective customers usually do not know you, the information presented will not interest them unless it contains good reasons to buy the product, stated in an objective manner. Even a request for charitable donations should be businesslike. Its content may be designed to produce an emotional response in the reader, but you and your firm do not want to be perceived as overly sentimental or sappy.

Keep the tone of each document consistent. If you begin a collection letter in a stern manner, inserting a personal or light comment at the end would be inconsistent. It may also undo the letter's purpose. This tendency to undo previous statements is a common fault of business writers. It often results from a sense that the letter sounds too harsh. If this is the case, rewrite the letter until you are satisfied that its tone is appropriate to the situation. Do not add inconsistent remarks at the end.

Whatever the substance of your correspondence, be sure that your expectations of the recipient are reasonable. Allow plenty of time for delivery, as mail may be delayed. Action on your letter may be postponed because the recipient is out of town when it arrives, or has other urgent business to finish before responding.

Most important, remember that the purpose of company correspondence is to do business. If a long-standing professional relationship becomes friendly, you may lighten the tone of your communications. Never forget, though, that the acquaintance is based on shared business concerns. Always stay within the boundaries of good sense and good taste in business writing.

AVOIDING GENDER BIAS IN FORMAL WRITING

Many business professionals still struggle with the rules for writing grammatically correct documents with gender-fair language. A common mistake is to use *they, their,* and *theirs* inappropriately, substituting these generic plural pronouns for the singular, gender-specific terms *he, she, his, her,* and *hers.* For instance, an employee handbook states, "Each employee should sign their own time sheet every day," or a memo concludes, "Anyone requesting special consideration must present their reasons in writing." This usage is not acceptable in formal business writing, but there are ways to accomplish the same purpose:

- Substitute articles (*a, an,* or *the*) or other modifiers for gender-specific pronouns. "Each employee should sign a personal time sheet every day." "All requests for special consideration must be presented in writing."
- Rewrite the sentence with generic plural pronouns, but change the rest of the sentence so that their use is grammatically correct. "All employees should sign their own time sheets every day." "All department members requesting special consideration must present their reasons in writing."
- Use double pronouns: *he/she* or *s/he, him/her,* and *his/hers.* Most writers try to avoid this, as it can be cumbersome.
- Alternate feminine and masculine gender-specific pronouns in long documents, using *she/her/hers* in one section of a manual or report and *he/his* in the next.
- Use a second-person perspective. This was once considered unacceptable for formal writing but it is used increasingly due to its simplicity. "Sign your own time sheet every day." "If you feel that you deserve special consideration, present your reasons in writing."

Of course, it is still appropriate to use gender-specific pronouns when you know or can assume gender, as in "Committee Chairperson Mary Nolan stated her goals for the coming quarter" or "Each Riverdale Men's Club participant brought a prospective member to the meeting and introduced him to the group."

Cutting the Fat: How to Be Concise

Business language should be straightforward, not cluttered with flowery prose or pseudointellectual jargon. Clearly expressed statements in plain language are much better than stilted language, trite expressions, or strings of long words. Rather than creating an impression of intelligence and professionalism, complex sentences and esoteric terms just confuse the reader.

Write to convey information, not to fill pages. The purpose of a communication should dictate its length. For instance, a letter is usually one part of an ongoing conversation—one participant's opening remarks or response to previous comments from the recipient. It should be just long enough to say what needs to be said. If the message can be stated in one paragraph, do so and close the letter. If several pages are necessary to supply the requested information, reread them carefully to eliminate redundancies and needless elaborations.

Review the following suggestions before writing your next memo or letter.

- Outline (mentally or on paper) the information to be included before beginning to write. Following an outline prevents digression into unrelated matters and reduces the possibility of forgetting important data.
- Organize the information in all but the briefest messages by summarizing, elaborating, then summarizing again. State major points in the opening paragraph, then explain, clarify, and elaborate on each in subsequent sections. Close with another summary of the issues, followed by a request for desired action.
- Use the active voice as much as possible to make your meaning clear. Write, "I learned recently that . . ." instead of "I was notified recently that . . ." Using the active voice also makes statements more concise.
- Use abbreviations and acronyms after the first mention of complex names or titles. A parenthetical explanation should follow the first use of such terms, unless you are sure the reader is familiar with them.

Proofreading Your Work

Proofreading is a skill that should be cultivated by everyone who writes business correspondence. Employing this skill is the only way to ensure that embarrassing mistakes do not leave your office. No one likes the sinking feeling that occurs when errors are found in file copies long after the originals have been mailed. (See Figure 2.1 for basic proofreaders' marks.)

First, check to see that the text is correctly placed on the page. In a letter, extra space should be evenly distributed before and after the date line and after the closing. Of course, the distribution does not need to be exact, but make sure the body of the letter is not too far from the top or bottom of the page. All written documents should have top, bottom, left, and right margins of at least 1 inch. When letterhead information begins at the left margin, that left margin should be used for the entire letter. If the heading extends across the page, as many printed headings do, the letter's right margin should also be consistent with that of the letterhead.

Next, skim the entire letter or report, checking for obvious typographical errors. Also note whether words and lines are evenly spaced. Then read the text again for clarity and comprehension. Look for grammatical errors. Check for parallel construction within sentences, and see that coordinate ideas in lists are expressed similarly.

Finally, verify that names, addresses, numbers, and other information in the letter are correct. If tables or charts are included, have another person check your

Definition	Symbol	Example
Move to the right	]	] Page 1
Move to the left	[	[All's well that ends well
Center	][	] Contents[
Begin new paragraph	¶	¶ Now that we have settled
No new paragraph	no¶	no ¶ However, this does not show
Leave text as it was	(stet)	We are seeking ac̈commodation _(stet)_
Insert	∧ or ∨	I forgot to add the ∧word _lost_
Add a space	#	connected̬words
Close up the space	⌒	sub⌒mit the forms
Delete	ϑ	at this ~~present~~ time
Delete and close up	⌀	The company lost it⌒s contract
Transpose	∩	the ⁀waiter ⁀singing
Capitalize	≡	Ms. e̲mily Smith
All caps	≣ CAPS	Headline̲
Lowercase	/ lc	The /tem you requested
Small caps	= sc	8:00 am̲
Italicize	___ ital	The editorial in the Wall Street Journal
Bold	〰 BOLD	Never leave bags unattended
Spell out the word	(sp)	The office ordered (2) chairs. _sp_
Insert period	⊙	tomorrow⊙ From there, we will
Insert comma	⌄	paper clips⌄rubber bands, and tape
Insert quotation marks	⌄⌄	She said, Let's go for it⌄
Insert hyphen	\=\	a fly\=\by\=\night business
Insert parentheses	( )	The Small Business Administration (SBA) has

Figure 2.1 Proofreaders' marks

proofreading. Carefully written correspondence enhances the recipient's perception that you and your firm are reliable and trustworthy, but only if your facts are correct.

Formatting Business Letters

Most business letters contain eight parts: the heading, date line, inside address, salutation, body, complimentary closing, signature line, and initials. A reference line is optional, and notations such as "c:" and "Enclosures" depend on the contents of each letter. It is important to understand the purpose and correct placement of each element to make sure your correspondence looks professional.

There are several types of formats used for business letters, including *block style, modified block style, semi-block style,* and *simplified style.* These terms refer to the placement of the elements within the letter. In block or full block style, all items are flush with the left margin with no paragraph indentations; date, closing, and signature to the right of center and other items at the left margin with no paragraph indentations constitute modified block; modified block with indented paragraphs is semi-block style; all items at the left margin with no salutation or closing and no paragraph indentations indicate simplified style. A review of the parts of a letter follows, beginning at the top of a typical letter and continuing down the page, with a definition and discussion of each part. Figures 2.2 to 2.10 also illustrate standard business letter formats.

Heading (letterhead). Even small businesses usually have letterhead stationery, with the company name, address, telephone and fax numbers printed at the top. (E-mail addresses may also be included in heading.) Sometimes the names of company officers, corporate subsidiaries, and other vital statistics appear here. This information can be presented in any number of ways, from text and complex graphics with company logos to simple text. The design of its letterhead communicates volumes about a company before the reader reads a single word on the page. (*See also* Choosing the Right Business Cards and Letterhead, page 366.) The letterhead design appears only on the first page of correspondence. Subsequent pages are blank (they are called *second pages* by printing specialists). If your business does not have printed stationery, create a heading by typing the company name, address, phone and fax numbers, centered, about an inch from the top of the first page of each letter.

Date Line. The current date should be typed two to four lines below the heading or letterhead, depending on the length of the letter and optimal placement on the page. The date line may be flush left (block style) or it may be aligned with the closing and signature line, beginning at the center of the page (modified and semi-block styles). When the company letterhead has its name and address centered at the top of the page, however, the date may be centered under the letterhead address, with the closing and signature line beginning at the center (modified or semi-block style with centered date), as this is usually more attractive than an off-center date line with a centered letterhead. If the heading (letterhead) is flush left, the date usually looks best flush left also. It is customary in the United States to put the month first, then the day, and finally the year (May 1, 1997). European and military forms place the day first, followed by the month and then the year, without a comma separating the month and year (1 May 1997). In either style, the name of the month should never be abbreviated.

Inside Address. The recipient's address is placed four to eight lines below the date line. Again, this varies according to letter length and optimal placement on the page. If the receiver's name and title are known, include them in the address. It is optional to use Mr., Miss, Mrs., or Ms. on the inside address. Whatever the choice, the selection should remain constant throughout the letter. Consult the list entitled Proper Forms of Address for Officials and Degreed Professionals, page 37, when in doubt about the correct way to address people with special titles. Note that it is incorrect to address a physician, for example, as "Dr. Jane Doe, M.D." Either "Dr. Jane Doe" or "Jane Doe, M.D." is correct. Do not abbreviate corporation, city, or state names in the inside address. (Follow the guidelines in Using the U.S. Postal Service, page 2, for addressing envelopes for fastest delivery.)

Reference Line (optional). If included, this line is usually typed two lines below the inside address, flush left, but it may be centered. Sometimes reference information is typed in all capitals or in a bold font to be sure that it draws the reader's attention. The purpose is to provide a summary of the letter's contents for busy executives who write and receive volumes of correspondence daily. This line is also helpful for clerical staff who file correspondence. A reference line usually begins, "RE:" or "Re:" and may be more than one line in length; however, it should be as brief as possible. Large corporations often include reference lines in correspondence, especially when many letters are exchanged between the sender and recipient.

Salutation. This is the greeting, which is always typed at the left margin on the second line below the recipient's address, or the reference line if that is included. In business correspondence, a colon always follows the salutation, even when the recipient's first name is used ("Dear Mr. Smith:" or "Dear Robert:").

Body. The main portion of the letter begins on the second line below the salutation. This spacing never varies. Single-space the body unless the letter is only two or three lines long, in which case double-spacing creates a more professional appearance. Always double-space between paragraphs. Indenting paragraphs is optional, but if indentation is used, the first line of each paragraph should be indented five spaces.

Complimentary Closing. A complimentary closing is typed on the second line beneath the body of the letter. This spacing also never varies. It may be typed flush with the left margin, or it may begin at the center of the page (modified block and semi-block styles). The closing is followed by a comma. Standard professional closings include "Respectfully," "Very truly yours," "Sincerely," "Cordially," "Best wishes," and "Regards." Some latitude is permissible when choosing the complimentary closing, but it is best to use one of these standard phrases. Many firms require a certain closing on all correspondence, but some leave the choice to individual letter writers.

Signature Line. This is typed on the fourth line below the complimentary closing. An extra space or two may be included for writers with very large signatures, but otherwise, this spacing is standard. The signature line is aligned with the complimentary closing. It consists of the sender's full name followed by any professional abbreviations such as "C.P.A." or "M.D." No title is used before the sender's name, as the signature line is the typed version of the person's signature, and titles such as "Mr." or "Dr." are usually not part of a signature. Often, the sender's company title is placed on the first line under the signature line. This is not necessary when the sender's name and title are included in the heading or letterhead. In fact, the full name alone may be used, without titles such as "C.P.A.," if the letterhead includes the full professional title of the sender. In large corporations, the sender's direct telephone extension number may be typed beneath the signature line if it is not part of the letterhead.

Many busy executives authorize their assistants or clerical staff to sign correspondence for them in their absence or when there is a large volume of mail to be sent. This can be done in one of two ways. The sender's name can be signed, followed by a slash and the signer's initials, or the signer may sign his/her own name, with a slash before it. This is common practice for routine correspondence in some firms, but it is best for most documents to be signed by the sender, especially those documents containing crucial or sensitive information.

Initials. The sender's initials are typed in capitals, followed by a slash (/) or colon and the typist's initials, which are lowercase ("RJH:kb"). There are no spaces within this line. When the typist and sender are the same person, this line may be omitted, or just a slash followed by the sender's lowercase initials may be used ("/rjh"). The primary purpose of this information is to identify the typist for the sender's records. If a high-level executive's signature appears on the letter but it was prepared by a middle manager whose name does not appear, the writer's initials may also be included in this line. They are uppercase and placed between the signer's initials and those of the typist ("DB:RJH:kb").

Enclosure Notation. The enclosure notation may be very brief ("Enc." or "Encl."), or it may be spelled out ("Enclosure"). It is used when other materials are being sent with the letter, and is typed directly beneath the sender's initials. Some firms use the word "Attachment" instead of "Enclosure," but this should be substituted only if the enclosed material is stapled or clipped to the letter. The enclosure line may list (briefly) the materials included ("Enclosures: Proposal dated 1/18/97 and letter dated 2/3/97"), or the number of items or pages enclosed may be specified: "Enclosures (3)" or "Enclosure (4 pages)."

Copy Notation. This is included when a copy of the letter is being sent to another person or persons. The copy notation's purpose is to let the recipient know that others will see the letter and to keep a record of all recipients for the sender's files. Many firms still use the copy notation "cc:" although this is rather dated, because it means "carbon copy" or "courtesy copy." A more modern equivalent is just "c:" and the copy recipient's name. When the writer does not want the recipient to know that a copy is being sent to someone else, the notation "bc:" ("blind copy") and the copy recipient's name are typed on the sender's file copy only. If enclosures are also being copied to someone else, the copy notation may include that information ("c: Dolores Crissman with 2 enclosures" or "c: Dolores Crissman w/enc.").

PROPER FORMS OF ADDRESS FOR OFFICIALS AND DEGREED PROFESSIONALS

Business correspondence sometimes includes letters to people with professional titles, government officials, military personnel, or clergy. Take care to address them correctly, and begin each letter with the appropriate salutation. The following list may be helpful:

TYPE OF OFFICIAL	LETTER ADDRESS	SALUTATION
Government Officials		
Ambassador (foreign)	His (Her) Excellency John (Jane) S. Doe The Ambassador of . . . (*mailing address*)	Excellency *or* Dear Mr. (Madam) Ambassador
Ambassador (U.S.)	The Honorable John (Jane) S. Doe Ambassador of the United States American Embassy (*mailing address*)	Dear Mr. (Madam) Ambassador
Attorney General (U.S.)	The Honorable John (Jane) S. Doe Attorney General (*mailing address*)	Sir (Madam) *or* Dear Mr. (Madam) Attorney General
Cabinet member	The Honorable John (Jane) S. Doe Secretary of . . . (*mailing address*)	Dear Mr. (Madam) Secretary
Chief Justice of the Supreme Court	The Honorable John (Jane) S. Doe The Chief Justice of the United States The Supreme Court of the United States (*mailing address*)	Sir (Madam) *or* Dear Mr. (Madam) Chief Justice
Commissioner or Director of a government bureau	The Honorable John (Jane) S. Doe Commissioner (Director) of . . . (*mailing address*)	Dear Mr. (Mrs./Ms.) Doe
District Attorney	The Honorable John (Jane) S. Doe District Attorney (*mailing address*)	Dear Mr. (Mrs./Ms.) Doe

TYPE OF OFFICIAL	LETTER ADDRESS	SALUTATION
Government Officials		
Governor	The Honorable John (Jane) S. Doe Governor of . . . (*mailing address*)	Dear Governor Doe
Judge	The Honorable John (Jane) S. Doe Judge of the (*name of court*) (*mailing address*)	Dear Judge Doe
Legislator (state)	The Honorable John (Jane) S. Doe (*mailing address*)	Dear Senator Doe *or* Sir (Madam) *or* Dear Mr. (Mrs./Ms.) Doe
Mayor	The Honorable John (Jane) S. Doe Mayor of . . . (*mailing address*)	Dear Mayor Doe
President of the United States	The Honorable John (Jane) S. Doe President of the United States The White House 3600 Pennsylvania Avenue Washington, DC 20001	Mr. (Madam) President *or* Dear Mr. (Madam) President
Prime Minister	His (Her) Excellency John (Jane) S. Doe Prime Minister of . . . (*mailing address*)	Excellency *or* Dear Mr. (Madam) Prime Minister
Representative (U.S.)	The Honorable John (Jane) S. Doe United States House of Representatives (*mailing address*)	Dear Representative Doe *or* Sir (Madam) *or* Dear Mr. (Mrs./Ms.) Doe
Secretary-General of the United Nations	His (Her) Excellency John (Jane) S. Doe Secretary-General of the United Nations (*mailing address*)	Dear Mr. (Madam) Secretary-General

TYPE OF OFFICIAL	LETTER ADDRESS	SALUTATION
Government Officials		
Senator (U.S.)	The Honorable John (Jane) S. Doe United States Senate (*mailing address*)	Dear Senator Doe *or* Sir (Madam) *or* Dear Mr. (Mrs./Ms.) Doe

Religious Officials

Many clergy have doctoral degrees listed after their names. These may alter the proper saluation (for example, The Reverend Jane S. Doe, D.D.; Dear Dr. Doe). *Roman Catholic clergy often list a religious order after the name, with no change in the salutation (for example,* The Reverend John S. Doe, S.J.; Dear Father Doe). *A rule of thumb for use of the word* Reverend: *It almost never stands alone—usually, it is preceded by* The (*for example,* The Reverend John S. Doe *is correct, but* Dear Reverend Doe *is not correct. Some customary Roman Catholic saluations* (Reverend Father) *do use* Reverend *without* The, *but such usage is not customary for other clergy.*

Bishop (or Archbishop) (Roman Catholic)	The Most Reverend John S. Doe, Bishop (Archbishop) of . . . (*mailing address*)	Your Excellency *or* Dear Bishop (Archbishop) Doe
Bishop (or Presiding Bishop) (Episcopal)	The Right (Most) Reverend John (Jane) S. Doe, Bishop (Presiding Bishop) of . . . (*mailing address*)	Dear Bishop Doe
Minister (Protestant)	The Reverend John (Jane) S. Doe (*name of church*) (*mailing address*)	Dear Mr. (Mrs., Ms.) Doe *or* Dear Father Doe (*the feminine equivalent of "Father" has not yet been established— "Dear Reverend Doe" is often used, but is actually incorrect*)

TYPE OF OFFICIAL	LETTER ADDRESS	SALUTATION
Religious Officials		
Monk/male religious community member (Episcopal)	Brother John Doe *or* Brother Michael Luke (*use given name or religious name*) (*name of church or community*) (*mailing address*)	Dear Brother John *or* Dear Brother Michael Luke *or* Dear Brother
Monk/male religious community member (Roman Catholic)	Brother Michael Luke (*use religious name, not given name*) (*name of church or community*) (*mailing address*)	Dear Brother Michael Luke *or* Dear Brother
Nun/female religious community member (Episcopal)	Sister Jane Doe *or* Sister Michael (*use given name or religious name*) (*name of church or community*) (*mailing address*)	Dear Sister Jane *or* Dear Sister Michael *or* Dear Sister
Nun/female religious community member (Roman Catholic)	Sister Mary Theresa (*use religious name, not given name*) (*name of church or community*) (*mailing address*)	Dear Sister Mary Theresa *or* Dear Sister
Priest (Episcopal)	The Reverend John (Jane) S. Doe (*title, such as* Rector *or* Curate, *and name of church or community*) (*mailing address*)	Dear Mr. (Mrs., Ms.) Doe
Priest (Roman Catholic)	The Reverend John Doe (*name of church or community*) (*mailing address*)	Reverend Father *or* Dear Father Doe
Rabbi	Rabbi John (Jane) S. Doe (*name of synagogue*) (*mailing address*)	Dear Rabbi Doe

TYPE OF OFFICIAL	LETTER ADDRESS	SALUTATION

Military Officials

Members of the U.S. armed forces are addressed by full rank only in the address portion of correspondence. In salutations, a shortened title is used, as shown below. Note that it is proper to abbreviate the armed forces branch following a comma after the name in the address. USCG is the abbreviation for United States Coast Guard, USA for United States Army, and so on.

Brigadier General	Brigadier General
	    John (Jane) S.
	    Doe,
	USA (USAF, USMC)
	(*mailing address*)
		Dear General Doe

Lieutenant Colonel	Lieutenant Colonel
	    John (Jane) S.
	    Doe,
	USA (USAF, USMC)
	(*mailing address*)
		Dear Colonel

Degreed Professionals

When addressing correspondence to someone whose name is followed by an abbreviation for a professional degree or other designation, either the abbreviation following the name or a courtesy title preceding the name is used—never both, as shown below. A courtesy title is used in the saluation.

Attorney	Mr. (Mrs., Ms.) John
	    (Jane) S. Doe
	Attorney-at-Law
	(*mailing address*)
		Dear Mr. (Mrs., Ms.)
		    Doe

Certified Public
    Accountant
	John (Jane) S. Doe,
	    C.P.A.
	(*mailing address*)
		Dear Mr. (Mrs., Ms.)
		    Doe

Chiropractor	John (Jane) S. Doe,
	    D.C. *or*
	Dr. John (Jane) S.
	    Doe
	(*mailing address*)
		Dear Dr. Doe

Dentist	John (Jane) S. Doe,
	    D.D.S. *or*
	Dr. John (Jane) S.
	    Doe
	(*mailing address*)
		Dear Dr. Doe

TYPE OF OFFICIAL	LETTER ADDRESS	SALUTATION
Degreed Professionals		
Physician	John (Jane) S. Doe, M.D. *or* Dr. John (Jane) S. Doe (*mailing address*)	Dear Dr. Doe
Physician (osteopathic)	John (Jane) S. Doe, D.O. *or* Dr. John (Jane) S. Doe (*mailing address*)	Dear Dr. Doe
Psychiatrist	John (Jane) S. Doe, M.D. *or* Dr. John (Jane) S. Doe (*mailing address*)	Dear Dr. Doe
Psychologist or other holder of Ph.D.	John (Jane) S. Doe, Ph.D *or* Dr. John (Jane) S. Doe (*mailing address*)	Dear Dr. Doe
Social Worker	John (Jane) S. Doe, M.S.W. *or* Mr. (Mrs., Ms.) John (Jane) S. Doe (*mailing address*)	Dear Mr. (Mrs., Ms.) Doe
Veterinarian	John (Jane) S. Doe, D.V.M. *or* Dr. John (Jane) S. Doe (*mailing address*)	Dear Dr. Doe

Using Word-Processing Templates to Format Documents

Most newer word-processing applications include a number of preformatted templates that make it easy to set up many different types of documents easily. In WordPerfect 6.1, for example, a list of optional templates—including *blank document, legal, letter, memo, resume,* and *report*—appears each time the user begins to type a new document. If the letter template is selected, a series of illustrations appear, allowing the typist to view and choose from several different letter formats such as block or semi-block style. Then a series of query boxes appears, asking for the sender's address (optional, as preprinted letterhead may be used), recipient's address, salutation, and other parts of the letter, including the body, closing, signature line, initials, and copy/enclosure notations. The typist fills in each box that appears, and the word processor creates a beautifully formatted letter.

A customized template can be created if the existing formats are not exactly what the writer prefers. It is even possible to eliminate buying costly stationery for the office by creating a custom template that includes the company letterhead and printing documents on heavy bond paper with a good-quality laser jet or bubble jet printer. With color printing capabilities, many special effects can be created to give correspondence a more professional appearance. Similarly, office memorandums, reports, and presentations may be designed via the use of templates that are now included with most word-processing software. (*See also* Word Processing Applications and Desktop Publishing Programs, page 150, *and* Desktop Publishing—Professional Design at Your Fingertips, page 375.)

Types of Business Letters

Even with advances in computer technology and electronic mail, letters are still a common means of business communication. Correspondence often comprises a large segment of office overhead owing to the costs of stationery, postage, clerical labor, printing, copying, filing, and executive work time spent composing documents. Letters (and memos) provide or request information while building or maintaining relationships. This twofold purpose makes accuracy and clarity essential.

Most firms establish a standardized format for company letters, which may include only the basic layout (block style is increasingly popular) or extend to salutations and closings that are company trademarks. Guide and form letters save valuable time and creative energy, especially as computers and memory typewriters make it easy to mass-produce similar documents. However, many individual letters must still be written each day, as standardized responses are not feasible for most correspondence.

Guide Letters. These include some standard parts and some original sections composed to fit individual situations. For example, the same introductory and concluding statements or paragraphs may be used in responding to customer complaints and in responding to praise. Both letters could begin, "Thank you for your comments about the new line of office products we introduced recently. Our goal is customer satisfaction, so your opinions are very valuable to us." In response to praise, some paragraphs might be added to indicate that other customers also seem to like the new line, or some additional interesting facts about the products might be discussed. In response to complaints about products, specifics of the firm's return/replacement policy might be addressed, or suggestions about proper care and use of the product explained. In conclusion, another general paragraph could be used, such as, "We appreciate your business and want to offer the best office products available. Your comments are always welcome, as they help us meet your needs."

Form Letters. These are used when the same response covers situations that occur frequently, such as a basic cover letter replying to requests for information about a product or service. The letter is stored in a computer or memory typewriter, with coded stops to insert the date, name and address, salutation, and other variable data. As form letters are used so often, care should be used in their initial composition. It is not unusual for a new secretary or executive to spot grammatical errors or outdated expressions in form letters that have been used for years. Others may have used them so often that little thought is given to their contents' meaning, and their origins are lost in antiquity. For this reason, it is wise to review form letters occasionally, updating and revising them as necessary to ensure that they enhance the company's image. Remember that most recipients have not read this material before, so they will read it more carefully than an employee who sends the same letter a hundred times each month.

Some of the sample letters shown in Figures 2.2 to 2.10 may be effective form letters for your firm. Review them to identify those that could be useful. (Any part of these samples may be retyped verbatim for use as business correspondence only, without further permission from the publisher.)

Writing Memos

Written communications within the office often take the form of memos (memorandums). These may be brief notes or lengthy reports and internal proposals. The tone and level of formality used depend on the subject matter and the relationship between sender and recipient, just as in business letters. Again, language that is stilted or too casual should be avoided.

Memos announce new policies, confirm appointments, assign work duties, reiterate rules and regulations, offer suggestions, propose new projects, request information, compliment work well done, reprimand employees, report progress, and communicate a variety of other information. They may inform, confirm, direct, follow up, express appreciation, or convey disappointment.

Because memos are an important record of interoffice communications, the same rules of composition recommended for letters should be applied.

1. The tone of a memo should be chosen to produce the desired response in its reader(s). A professional, objective approach is essential.
2. The tone should be consistent from beginning to end.
3. The sender's expectations of the recipient must be reasonable.
4. The information conveyed or questions asked should be stated clearly, in plain language.
5. The facts to be included should be outlined before composition begins, to prevent digression into unrelated matters or inclusion of too much detail.
6. The rules of good grammar should be followed.
7. The memo should be proofread carefully, and all facts checked for accuracy, before it is sent.
8. The standard company memorandum format should be followed, if such a format has been established.

If your firm does not have a standard memorandum format, consider using the format illustrated in Figure 2.2. Note that copy notations may also be used on

Ascher, Barkin, and Chase, Ltd.
555 West Avenue
Cincinnati, OH 66444
(215) 555-6347 voice
(215) 555-7436 fax

January 10, 1998

Mr. John Doe, Managing Director
Smith & Doe, Inc.
2626 Fairfield Avenue
Wichita, KS 67218

Dear Mr. Doe:

Thank you for your letter of January 3, 1998, in which you requested further
information on our lines of software for laser printers. I have forwarded your
letter to Edward Johnson, our representative in the Wichita area. He will
contact you shortly to answer any questions you might have on the product. If it
appears that our line will suit your needs, Mr. Johnson will make arrangements
to provide a demonstration at your convenience.

Sincerely,
Joan S. Barkin

Joan S. Barkin
Vice President

JSB:ar

c: Edward Johnson

Figure 2.2 Letter acknowledging receipt of correspondence (block style)

Senior Partners:
Robert J. Ascher
Joan S. Barkin
J. Randall Chase

Ascher, Barkin, and
Chase, Ltd.
555 West Avenue
Cincinnati, OH 66444
(215) 555-6347 voice
(215) 555-7436 fax

Junior Partners:
Clarice D. Owens
Randall W. Chase

January 10, 1998

Mr. John Doe, Managing Director
Smith & Doe, Inc.
2626 Fairfield Avenue
Wichita, KS 67218

RE: Dougherty vs. Smith & Doe, Inc.

Dear Mr. Doe:

Please accept my apology for not sending the Dougherty pretrial
transcript sooner. I can only say that your copy of the transcript was
inadvertently filed instead of being mailed. I am embarrassed that your
phone call was necessary to bring our error to light.

Once again, I offer my regrets for our negligence. Please be
assured that keeping you informed of developments in your case is one of
our highest priorities. I have taken steps to see that such mistakes do not
happen again.

Please call me with any questions or concerns when you have
read the transcript. I will look forward to hearing from you soon.

Sincerely,
Joan S. Barkin

Joan S. Barkin, J.D., L.L.M.

JSB:ar
Enclosure

Figure 2.3 Letter of apology (semi-block style with date centered under letterhead)

Ascher, Barkin, and Chase, Ltd.
555 West Avenue
Cincinnati, OH 66444
(215) 555-6347 voice
(215) 555-7436 fax

Senior Partners:
  Robert J. Ascher
  Joan S. Barkin
  J. Randall Chase

Junior Partners:
  Clarice D. Owens
  Randall W. Chase

January 10, 1998

Mr. John Doe, Managing Director
Smith & Doe, Inc.
2626 Fairfield Avenue
Wichita, KS 67218

RE: Anne Collins Romero

Dear Mr. Doe:

I am happy to recommend Anne Romero for the position of Office Manager with your firm. She has been employed by our firm since June 1993, and has served as my personal secretary for the past two years.

Anne is a loyal and dedicated employee. She has excellent organizational and clerical skills. Since April 1996, Anne has supervised the work of five typists in our office, and a marked improvement in their performance and productivity has been noted. Her subordinates seem to like and respect her very much. A number of our clients have also commented on her pleasant personality, professional manner, and helpful attitude.

We will miss Anne very much when she and her family relocate to Wichita. I am confident that she will be successful in any position she undertakes, and that you will be more than satisfied with her work if she accepts your offer of employment.

Sincerely,

Joan S. Barkin

Joan S. Barkin

JSB:ar

c: Anne Collins Romero

Figure 2.4 Letter of recommendation (semi-block style with date centered under letterhead)

Smith & Doe, Inc.
2626 Fairfield Avenue
Wichita, KS 67218
(316) 686-8043 voice
(316) 686-1179 fax

February 11, 1998

Mr. Joseph Davenport, Store Manager
Office Supplies and Equipment Unlimited
1915 East Sunset Drive
Wichita, KS 67207

Dear Mr. Davenport:

In November, we purchased three Model 313 computers from you. Your representative, Mr. Cole, assured us that the equipment would work well with our existing printers. Information in your brochure also indicated that the Model 313 system is compatible with our Ace Laser Jet printers (Ace Model 1436).

The computers have not performed well with our printers, despite your company's assurances. In fact, we have called your service department for assistance at least twice weekly since buying the new computers. Service representatives have made five visits to our office, stating each time that the computer-printer interface problems were finally solved. Unfortunately, we continue to have difficulties. We have incurred substantial added expenses during the past three months due to these problems, which have resulted in clerical overtime as well as the costs of having several lengthy documents printed elsewhere.

We are now requesting a refund of the full purchase price of $4,250 for the three Model 313 computer systems. Please arrange to have a check for this amount delivered to our office as soon as possible. We will have the computers packed and ready to be picked up when your representative arrives with our refund.

Please contact our company president, Mr. John Doe, if you have any questions concerning this matter.

Sincerely,

Anne C. Romero

Anne C. Romero
Office Manager

/acr

c: Mr. John Doe

Figure 2.5 Letter of complaint (block style)

Smith & Doe, Inc.   **2626 Fairfield Avenue**   **Wichita, KS 67218**

(316) 686-8043 voice
(316) 686-1179 fax

January 10, 1998

Ms. Dolores Crissman
Midwestern Credit Bureau
One Jackson Place
Wichita, KS 67208

RE: Credit Status of Smith & Doe, Inc.

Dear Ms. Crissman:

We were recently contacted by a financial officer at our firm's bank, who informed us that a routine credit check on our business had revealed some disturbing information. A report from your company indicated that our account with Marshall-Jones, Inc., a firm based in Chicago, is 120 days overdue. This is not correct.

We are completely up-to-date in our payments to Marshall-Jones, and have been for the past year. Enclosed are photocopies of their monthly statements for the past six months and the canceled checks confirming receipt of our payments. Please correct your records accordingly and send us a copy of our updated credit report.

Thank you for your help in this matter.

Sincerely,

John C. Doe

John C. Doe
Financial Director

JCD/ar
Enclosures

c: Mr. Bill Standish, Fourth National Bank of Wichita (with enclosures)

Figure 2.6 Letter to credit bureau (semi-block style)

Smith & Doe, Inc.   **2626 Fairfield Avenue**   **Wichita, KS 67218**

(316) 686-8043 voice
(316) 686-1179 fax

January 10, 1998

Mr. George Winfield
Midstate Marketing Associates
19253 St. Charles Avenue, Suite 403
Wichita, KS 67216

RE: Your Overdue Account No. 32-446-11175

Dear Mr. Winfield:

As you have ignored several requests for payment of your past due account, we must insist that you send us a check in the amount of $1,157.50 immediately. This total includes $757.50 that is more than 120 days overdue, as well as $400.00 for supplies we delivered in December, as detailed on the enclosed statement.

Unless we receive full payment within five business days, we will turn your account over to a collection agency. We would regret the necessity of doing so, as this would jeopardize your credit rating. We will also be forced to terminate our business relationship.

Please send us your check now to avoid future unpleasantness. If you have already mailed your payment, call us on receipt of this letter to ensure that it has been received.

Sincerely,

John C. Doe

John C. Doe
Financial Director

JCD/ar
Enclosure

Figure 2.7 Collection letter (block style)

Smith & Doe, Inc.   **2626 Fairfield Avenue**   **Wichita, KS 67218**

(316) 686-8043 voice
(316) 686-1179 fax

January 10, 1998

Mr. George Winfield
Midstate Marketing Associates
19253 St. Charles Avenue, Suite 403
Wichita, KS 67216

RE: Application for Credit

Thank you for your application for credit.

We regret that we are unable to open a credit account for your firm at this time. This difficult decision was made due to conflicting information we received concerning your credit history.

We will be pleased to review your application at a later date, should you request it. Many businesses experience temporary financial difficulties that are resolved within a few months, and we would certainly like to extend credit as soon as your situation is resolved.

In the meantime, we hope to continue to serve you as we have during the past six months. Please continue to send a check with each order, to ensure immediate delivery.

John C. Doe

John C. Doe
Financial Director

JCD/ar

Figure 2.8 Letter denying credit (simplified style)

Smith & Doe, Inc.   **2626 Fairfield Avenue**   **Wichita, KS 67218**

(316) 686-8043 voice
(316) 686-1179 fax

January 10, 1998

Ms. Martha Trimble, Marketing Director
New Age Marketing, Inc.
1715 O'Rourke Lane
Wichita, KS 67216

Dear Martha:

I certainly enjoyed our conversation at the Dallas trade convention last week. Your description of New Age's increased productivity from graphics technology was of great interest to me.

As I mentioned, Smith & Doe has recently acquired the distribution rights to a new, state-of-the-art graphics software program that is so advanced, it must be seen to be believed. Called Special F-X, it was specifically designed with marketing agencies in mind. The enclosed brochure will give you some idea of its possibilities.

If you would like to see what Special F-X can do for New Age Marketing, I would be happy to demonstrate its capabilities to you and your staff. I will call you next week to talk about scheduling a demonstration.

Cordially,
Victoria Swanson

Victoria Swanson
Software Division Director

VS/dj
c: Terry Swanson, Sales Manager

Enclosure

Figure 2.9 Follow-up sales letter (modified block style)

Smith & Doe, Inc.
2626 Fairfield Avenue
Wichita, KS 67218
(316) 686-8043 voice
(316) 686-1179 fax

January 10, 1998

Steven F. Ball, Ph.D., Clinical Director
New Beginnings Center for Life Change
Post Office Drawer 19316
Wichita, KS 67278-19316

RE: Interactive Psychological Testing Software Proposal

Dear Dr. Ball:

Our proposal to supply and install an interactive psychological testing software package is enclosed. As you requested, we have included a breakdown of the software purchase price for each of the nine computer systems described in your request for proposal letter dated December 13, 1997. Should you choose to accept our proposal, we will install the software at no charge, so a breakdown of installation charges is not included.

If our proposal is accepted, we would also like to have one of our professional trainers demonstrate software operation for your clerical and/or professional staff, at no charge. This could be very helpful to them, as they will need to show each new client how to use the self-testing programs. A group training session could be held in our office or at your location.

Thank you for allowing us to bid on this project. Your plans to use interactive psychological testing software are exciting and innovative, and we would be pleased to assist New Beginnings in this venture.

I look forward to hearing from you concerning our proposal.

Sincerely,
Victoria Swanson

Victoria Swanson
Software Division Director

VS/dj
Enclosure

Figure 2.10 Proposal transmittal letter (modified block style with date centered under letterhead)

memos, indicating that copies are being sent to other departments or persons, as well as those addressed. A signature line is usually not included. Instead, the sender may initial or sign the memo next to his/her name, at the top. The signatures of sender and recipient should be included if the memorandum format is used to document supervisor/employee counseling sessions, reprimands, other personnel actions (*see* Problem-Solving Measures, page 255), or any formal agreement between a supervisor or a manager and an employee. (*See also* Using Word-Processing Templates to Format Documents, page 42.)

Producing Reports

Many businesspeople find it necessary to write formal reports as part of their professional duties. There are many different formats available, and the style should be dictated by (1) the established company report design, if any; (2) the importance of the topic covered; (3) the length of the material presented; and (4) the potential recipients/users of the report. For example, a lengthy document such as an annual report to stockholders usually has a title page and table of contents, and may be

```
                    Smith & Doe, Inc.
                  2626 Fairfield Avenue
                    Wichita, KS 67218
                  (316) 686-8043 voice
                  (316) 686-1179 fax


                      MEMORANDUM


     TO:      Projects Department
     FROM:    Monica Kelvin
     DATE:    January 14, 1998
     RE:      Sales of New Flotation Devices

     In November 1997, a new flotation device was introduced into our pool
     equipment line. A last-minute change in the product was made in an
     attempt to provide the safest and most attractive product on the
     market. An unexpected manufacturing problem resulted from the
     change in design, delaying shipment to all retail outlets.

     We sent a letter of explanation to each store manager, hoping to
     save our advance orders and to increase customer confidence in
     future products. The response to our letters was excellent. All of
     the retailers indicated that they will accept later shipment dates.
     They were enthusiastic enough about the new equipment to reconfirm
     all advance orders. Some even increased the size of their original
     orders.

     With the new orders we are receiving daily, it appears that this year's
     profits will exceed our goals.


     MK:dc


     c: Marketing Department
        John Sonoma
        Martha Rovier
```

Figure 2.11 Memorandum

divided into chapters with several levels of subheadings. Charts, graphs, tables, and figures can be included to illustrate the text. Sample pages of a typical business report are shown in Figures 2.12, 2.13, 2.14, and 2.15.

A good word-processing program that has spreadsheet and database functions makes it easy to produce professional tables and graphs for reports. Automatic indexing, cross-referencing, and table of contents production are other valuable word-processing aids for report writers. One aspect of report writing that is often overlooked is the importance of correctly citing the sources of previously published information used. Using the correct format for citations can seem overwhelming due to the wealth of data now available on CD-ROMs, the Internet, and videotapes, in addition to traditional print media. But some word-processing applications with automated report templates will even create appropriate citations via a fill-in-the-blank process that is simple to use. Help is also available in *The Chicago Manual of Style,* which includes detailed examples of the correct way to document any type of source. (*See also* Using Word-Processing Templates to Format Docu-

```
┌─────────────────────────────────────────┐
│                                          │
│                                          │
│                                          │
│          Market Research Report          │
│                                          │
│                                          │
│                                          │
│                August 1999               │
│                                          │
│                                          │
│                                          │
│    Prepared for the Product Development Division │
│             of Lionel Industries, Inc.   │
│                                          │
│                                          │
│                    by                    │
│            Georgette Stephenson          │
│                                          │
│                                          │
│                                          │
│                                          │
│                                          │
│                                          │
└─────────────────────────────────────────┘
```

Figure 2.12 Business report—title page

ments, page 42, and Desktop Publishing—Professional Design at Your Fingertips, page 375.)

Creating Proposals

Proposals may be addressed to potential clients or to others within the company. Client proposals delineate the price to be charged for specific projects (see Figure 2.16). Internal proposals usually recommend changes in office policies/procedures, new ways to use existing resources, or development of new projects. An internal proposal is written by an employee or department head for approval by a superior (see Figure 2.17).

The first paragraph of a well-written proposal states the reason the plan is being submitted. An unsolicited proposal must include information to establish that a problem exists and that there is a solution for it. A proposal prepared at the recipient's request need only mention the work that is to be done. The body of the document describes ways to solve the problem, specifying expenditures, time involved, material and equipment needed, an operations schedule, and personnel needs.

Concluding paragraphs may mention the firm's previous successes with similar projects and express appreciation for the opportunity to submit the proposal. An

Table of Contents

Figure 2.13 Business report—table of contents

offer to provide additional data or schedule a meeting to discuss the proposal is usually included.

Organizing Information in Sales Proposals

The first objective in writing a sales proposal is to discern the potential customer's needs. Only then can you form a plan to satisfy those needs. You must also determine your main competitors for the client's business. Compare your company's strengths against the competition; then emphasize your firm's advantages in the proposal.

Tailor the information to fit those who will decide which proposal to accept.

Market Research Report

Introduction and Overview

A survey of soft drink consumers in the Denver area was undertaken with the purpose of determining the appropriateness of this region for the introduction of a new soft drink product. Market analysis began in April 1999, and was concluded on June 30, 1999.

Development of Survey Instruments

Under the leadership of Peter F. Jameson, Ph.D., two discrete questionnaires were written. Both incorporated a multiple-choice question and answer method, and each was composed of 20 questions. However, there were several differences between Questionnaire A and Questionnaire B. (A copy of each is attached to this report, as Appendix A and Appendix B, respectively.)

Questionnaire A was intended for use with the under-25 age group, whereas B was to be used with older consumers. Thus, Questionnaire A contained a number of items that focused on peer pressure and the likelihood of choosing a soft drink based on others' opinions. On the other hand, Questionnaire B included several questions about health issues (caloric content and concerns about caffeine, aspartame, dyes, and other chemical ingredients).

Both survey instruments were designed for researchers to read each item aloud to individual survey participants and to record their responses. Despite the extra time and cost of such individual administration, this was deemed the best method of obtaining accurate results, as participants' reading comprehension levels were not a factor.

During the survey development process, the items in Questionnaire A were reviewed by three college students, two post-college working 24-year-olds, five non-college-educated 19- to 24-year-olds, two high school students, three junior high students, and two elementary school students. (This group consisted of 10 males and 7 females.) Questions were revised on the basis of these subjects' ability to comprehend what was asked, the level of interest shown in answering questions, and suggestions made by subjects regarding better ways to state each item.

Questionnaire B was reviewed during development by 17 adults—two males and two females from each of the following age groups: age 25–34, age 35–44, age 45–54, and age 55–70. One 78-year-old woman was also include in this group. As with Questionnaire A,

1

Figure 2.14 Business report—first page

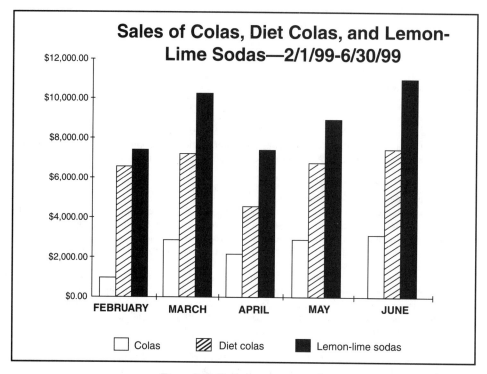

Figure 2.15 Business report—graph

For example, if the client's decision maker is an expert on the proposed subject, the data may be quite technical, with little explanation of the basics. But if the recipient is not so knowledgeable, it would be wise to include a summary that explains the proposed idea thoroughly. A glossary of technical terms may even be included, if this would be helpful.

When preparing unsolicited sales proposals, time and effort can be saved by sending a fairly brief document at first, with a query as to whether the company is interested in your services. If a positive response is received, a more detailed study of a potential client's needs can be undertaken.

Rapid Note-Taking Techniques

Shorthand is still a very useful skill, although it is no longer required for most clerical workers. Even small firms usually have dictating equipment, which is more convenient for the executive as well as easier for the typist. But shorthand can be utilized in many other ways. Even with a tape recorder in place, someone must usually take notes during meetings to outline major themes (a word-for-word transcription from tape is not appropriate for most meeting minutes). Jotting down

Klein Associates
19 East 47th Street
New York, NY 10017
(212) 453-1121 voice
(212) 453-1122 fax

PROPOSAL
TO REMODEL THE INTERIOR
COMMON SPACES OF XYZ COMPANY

Submitted To: XYZ Company—Mrs. Nora Walker, Office Manager
Submitted By: Klein Associates—Kenneth Rollins, Sales Director
Date Submitted: January 15, 1998

Klein Associates proposes to remodel the interior common spaces of XYZ Company, 658 East 63rd Street, at a total cost of $3,500. The area to be remodeled is approximately 50 feet wide by 100 feet long. The following installations will be provided in the quantities, sizes, and prices specified:

3 wrought-iron benches at $200 each	$ 600
2 wall murals (3 ft. by 5 ft.) at $250 each	$ 500
4 cafe table-and-chair sets at $150 each	$ 600
Area carpeting at $15 per yard (50 square yards)	$ 750
Cost of materials	$2,450
Labor	$1,050
Total Cost	$3,500

All materials will be guaranteed against defects for a period of 90 days, with this warranty beginning upon completion of the job. The prices quoted in this proposal are valid until March 1, 1998.

We appreciate the opportunity to submit this proposal to XYZ Company. Klein Associates has served clients in the New York area since 1983. Our interior remodeling projects have been featured in *New York* magazine and in the *New York Times*. We have also received accolades from satisfied customers, including Brooks Brothers and the Eric Goldman Company.

We are confident that you and your employees will be pleased with our work. Please call us for additional information or to schedule a meeting.

KR/dj

Figure 2.16 Proposal

XYZ Company
658 East 63rd Street
New York, NY 10017
(212) 533-4426 voice
(212) 533-4429 fax

PROPOSAL
TO RESTRUCTURE SUPERVISION OF CLERICAL
AND BOOKKEEPING EMPLOYEES

Submitted To: Mr. Raleigh Wood, President
Submitted By: Mrs. Nora Walker, Office Manager; Mrs. Gina Reinhold, Personnel Director
Date Submitted: January 25, 1998

Due to the rapid growth of XYZ Company in the past two years, a number of new office positions
have been created and personnel hired to fill them. It is no longer practical for all of these workers
to be supervised by the Office Manager. We are proposing that responsibility for supervision of
clerical and bookkeeping staff be reassigned to each division director, with the Office Manager
retaining supervision of Administrative staff only, as follows:

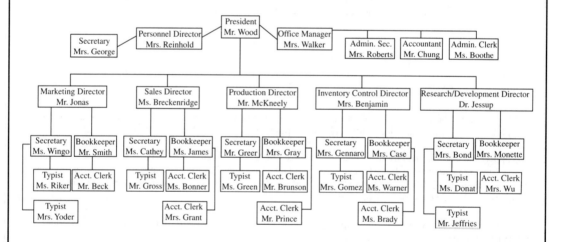

This proposed reorganization should enhance overall efficiency and promote teamwork
within divisions. Of course, the Personnel Director and Office Manager will continue to provide
general oversight of employee concerns and office procedures, respectively. We will also be happy
to assist the division directors in making the transition smoothly.

Nora Walker
Gina Reinhold

NRW:GBR:jr

Figure 2.17 Internal proposal

long phone messages in shorthand, to be rewritten or read back later, is also very useful. And last-minute instructions can be noted easily, with no forgotten details after the fact.

There are several shorthand methods now in use:

1. The Pitman method uses consonant symbols that are geometrical and derived from circle segments. Consonants with similar sounds are paired and distinguished by shading (the use of heavy lines). Vowels are disjoined and are indicated by light or heavy dots or dashes. The position of symbols (above, through, or under a line) determines the meaning of the words.

2. The Gregg method is based on segments of an ellipse or oval, representing the natural slope of longhand writing. Vowels are joined according to their natural order of pronunciation in words. Shading (use of heavy lines) is eliminated, and obtuse angles of more than 90 degrees are not used.

3. Century 21 Shorthand uses some of the same alphabetic strokes as the Gregg method, as well as primary alphabetic symbols. Its name is a reminder that it is a fairly new system, originating in 1974.

4. P.S. or Personal Shorthand uses the alphabet but no symbols, so this method can be used at the computer, as well as when writing by hand.

For the many office workers who have no knowledge of shorthand, here are a few suggestions to help get the important points on paper, fast:

- Use a handheld tape recorder whenever possible.
- Jot down quick notes (dates, times, who was speaking, and the counter number on the tape recorder) about the most important issues discussed.
- Never let writing take the place of comprehension.
- Never let note-taking become more important than your participation in the meeting (unless you are present solely for the purpose of taking the minutes).
- Remember that a word-for-word transcription is not needed.
- Concentrate on large issues, not minor details.
- Transcribe your notes as soon as possible after the meeting. If the notes are for your own records, transfer essential dates and other information to your day planner immediately. Rewrite notes on assigned tasks right away, while you can still remember details you did not have time to write down.
- Learn to abbreviate words used frequently in your business.

COMMON BUSINESS ABBREVIATIONS

accountant	acct.	group	grp.
administrator	admin.	guild	gld.
affiliate	aff.	incorporated	inc.
agency	agcy.	industry	ind.
also known as	aka	institute	inst.
associate	assoc.	insurance	ins.
attorney	atty.	league	lge.
branch manager	brm.	legal	leg.
brothers	bros.	limited	ltd.
building	bldg.	manager	mgr.
center	ctr.	manufacturing	mfg.
certified financial planner	CFP	market	mkt.
certified public accountant	CPA	meeting	mtg.
chief executive officer	CEO	not sufficient funds	NSF
committee	cte.	organization	org.
company	co.	partner	ptr.
consultant	cons.	power of attorney	POA
corporation	corp.	president	pres.
court	ct.	product	prod.
department	dept.	profit sharing	prs.
deputy	dpy.	realtor	rltr.
development	dev.	retired	ret.
director	dir.	senior	sr.
doing business as	dba	service	svc.
endorser	end.	society	soc.
equipment	equip.	subdivision	subdiv.
escrow	esc.	subsidiary	sub.
establishment	estab.	trademark	TM
estate	est.	trading as	t/a
executive	exec.	treasurer	treas.
federal	fed.	trust account	TRA
finance	fin.	trustee	ttee.
floor	flr.	very important person	VIP
foundation	fndtn.	vice president	v.p.
government	govt.		

Oral Communications

Public Speaking: You Can Do It

For most of us, public speaking is not easy. Studies have shown that most people rate speaking in public as one of their biggest fears—some say it is more frightening than the thought of dying. One of the most important goals of public speaking is to establish a rapport with the audience. This means connecting with listeners in a way that gains their attention, trust, and respect. To achieve the correct pace and tone for your presentation, be sensitive to the mood of the occasion. For example, complimenting the sponsoring organization or thanking key members for the opportunity to speak will usually make an audience more receptive to your point of view.

Preparing a Dynamic Oral Presentation

Preparation is the key to successful public appearances, as any veteran speaker knows. Follow these steps to prepare an effective oral presentation:

1. Analyze your audience. Make sure the members you want to reach have an equal understanding of the topic. If necessary, direct the speech to those whose agreement is most important. If there are two very different levels of understanding in the group, consider giving two presentations—one to give basic knowledge and background, and a second to describe your plan of action.

2. Consider your tactics. If your presentation offers a concept that involves change, making an emotional impact will help get your point across. As people often feel threatened by change and therefore resist it, present even the most cut-and-dried data with enough emotion to counteract that resistance. Pure logic alone will not convince your audience. Give examples that touch their lives to illustrate the effects of your proposal, as reasoning fueled by emotion is a powerful combination. For instance:

   (a) *Fear* can be a healthy motivator when it inspires action. Present illustrations that convert your listeners' fear of change into fear of losing something they value unless they make the changes you are suggesting.

   (b) *Hope of personal gain* is a major influence on individual and company decisions. Convince listeners that they can benefit by following your lead. They will then act to avoid a sense of loss from passing up the advantages you are offering.

   (c) *Belonging* is very important to most of us. If possible, use testimonials from people your listeners admire to build support for your ideas. And remember that most organizational activities require group action. Try to put across your ideas to group leaders so that others will follow their example.

   (d) A *sense of individuality* is also motivational, and it need not contradict the desire to belong. Suggest that your ideas may not appeal to everyone, because it takes strong, courageous individuals to act on their personal convictions. This establishes an attractive group (a vague set of brave, heroic right-minded thinkers) in listeners' minds, so that in some way acting as you suggest will make them a part of that elite company.

   (e) *Pride* is a powerful instigator. Pride of self, of place, and in work help to establish an emotional base for your presentation.

3. Allow adequate time to prepare your presentation, and schedule it for a time when key people can be present.

4. Organize your information in a logical, coherent order. Include only what the audience needs to know to understand your point.

5. Get your facts straight. Make sure you will not be embarrassed by having someone say, for example, "The studies you quoted are several years old. Newer research has shown just the opposite."

6. Tell the truth. Someone may challenge your information, so never lie or shade the truth. In-depth research should reveal plenty of facts to support your position; in our data-driven world, studies supporting almost any hypothesis can be located with ease. If there is a great deal of evidence opposing your ideas, say so—and then quote an equal number of surveys to support them.

7. Know your subject. Others present may know a great deal about the general field, but make sure you are an authority on the points you are presenting.

8. State your objective. Tell listeners why you are making this speech and what you hope to accomplish.

9. Delineate the parameters of the presentation. Outline the subjects to be covered, then mention briefly any important issues that will not be discussed and explain why, if pertinent.

10. Develop a central theme in presenting the problem, need, or issue.

11. Provide a method of evaluation, and define what a successful outcome would be.

12. Conclude the presentation by asking the audience to take action based on the facts you have presented.

PRACTICE MAKES PERFECT

When preparing a speech, you may choose to write the script word for word, to use an outline, to make note cards, or to memorize it completely. The less experienced the speaker, the more extensive the script should be. The best plan is have your opening statements committed to memory. This gives you an air of confidence and makes for a more exciting beginning. Practice reading the speech aloud several times before the actual presentation. This will help you become familiar with the major points and allow you to feel natural when presenting them.

Recording or videotaping your practice sessions can be very helpful. Notice any nervous or repetitive mannerisms such as touching your hair or shifting your weight from foot to foot. These are distracting and should be kept to a minimum. Practice moving with a purpose, to emphasize your points. Let what you do punctuate what you say.

Listen objectively to the volume and pitch of your voice. (It is probably not as bad as it sounds—most of us hate the sound of our own voices.) Few presenters speak too loudly; most do not speak loudly enough. But a high-pitched whine is not the answer. Try lowering the pitch and raising the volume to compensate for any loss of projection when pitch is lowered. Also pay attention to your diction. Is it clear and precise? This is especially important when a speech involves the use of technical terms that may be new to some listeners.

Many experienced speakers would do well to record their talks and review them. Some would be amazed at the number of times they repeat themselves, use hackneyed words or phrases, and say "uh" or "ah." Listen for speech patterns that are distracting and unappealing, and practice until you have eliminated them.

Visit the place where you will give the presentation, and consider the physical environment. Is the room too hot or too cold? How are the acoustics—will everyone be able to hear you? Is the lighting adequate? Will you be visible to everyone? Is the seating comfortable enough for the duration of your speech? Will a microphone be available? If so, what type? (If possible, practice saying a few words in the room where you will speak, or at least try to check the microphone before the meeting starts. Repeating the first part of a speech after a chorus of we-can't-hear-you's is not a good way to start.)

Plan your wardrobe ahead of time, too. Avoid dangling, clanking jewelry, which can be annoying, especially if amplified through a public-address system. Wear something comfortable that you can move around in easily. Wear what makes you look good and feel free. And be sure to empty your trouser pockets before your presentation if you are one of those people who tend to jingle pocket change nervously.

Making Contact

Here are some tips on connecting with your listeners and stating your views effectively:

- Introduce yourself. If the audience is unfamiliar with your background, tell them who you are, but briefly. They want your qualifications, not your life history.
- Engage the group with a smile, an opening story, or dramatic visual aids— something that will attract their attention.
- Impress them with your ideas, not your words. Avoid stilted language and needless repetition.
- Be natural.
- Identify with those who may find your ideas hard to accept. Never preach— empathize with problems and offer solutions.
- Use humor appropriately, but be certain your witticisms will not offend others. If a funny story or comment is used to open your talk and put everyone at ease, make sure it has some bearing on the situation or topic. Then get down to business. You may be a natural comedian, but your main objective is not to entertain. Even if your speech is enjoyed by all, it will not be a success if they focus on you instead of your topic.
- Empathize with your audience. Put yourself in their shoes, especially when advocating changes that will strongly affect them. Remember that people fear and resist change, even when it is positive; choose what you say carefully.
- Make eye contact. Never underestimate the power of nonverbal communication. Your facial expressions, tone of voice, and body language can undo the effect of your comments unless they reinforce your stated convictions. Making eye contact may be daunting, but it establishes a personal bond between speaker and audience that cannot be duplicated by any other form of communication. Try not to look

over people's heads and talk to the back of the room. Eye contact with individuals can actually calm you and make you feel more confident. (After all, your audience probably consists of people who are very similar to you.)

- Pace your audience. To see if they are under your spell, lean your head to one side slightly as you speak, and then lean it to the other side. Watch their reactions as you do this. If you are truly connecting with them, a few members of the group will unconsciously tilt their heads to the side, mirroring your movements. If you do not see evidence of a strong connection, drop back a little—that is, move back into a more empathetic mode to establish contact. Then check again to see how the audience is responding before moving forward too quickly.
- Pace yourself. If you rush through your presentation just so it will soon be over, all your efforts may be wasted. On the other hand, repeating yourself or elaborating on tangents wastes valuable time that should be spent making important points. Stay with your prepared script. Always be aware that busy people are giving you their time—make it worth their while to listen.
- Use visual aids to make your presentation more interesting and memorable. Remember that one picture is worth a thousand words.
- Show enthusiasm for your subject. If you appear bored or indifferent, your audience will certainly follow your lead.
- Pay attention to enunciation and diction. Be sure to check the pronunciation of names or unfamiliar words well in advance.
- Keep going, no matter what happens. If some technical mishap occurs, do not panic, freeze, or blame anyone (including yourself). Even if you make a big blunder during the presentation, simply correct the error and continue.
- Use nervous energy to propel you through the speech, but keep it under control. Our bodies supply adrenaline to help us survive desperate situations. If public speaking is a crisis for you, your body may provide such an overload that it is necessary to calm yourself. Try to channel the extra charge into mental alertness and concentration rather than let it turn into physical agitation and anxiety.
- Continue to project energy and enthusiasm throughout the talk and even when you leave the podium. Take the last couple of minutes to summarize the salient points of your speech. Then announce that you are concluding your speech, and do so, ending it with conviction. Take your seat in a confident manner, assured that the presentation was a job well done.

Staying Cool, Calm, and Collected

Even with the best preparation, you may still be nervous when the time for your talk arrives. Here are some ways to overcome anxiety before and during a speech:

1. Get plenty of rest before the big occasion, and try to schedule a light workday with time for a last-minute rehearsal.
2. Take a few slow deep breaths just before taking your place in front of the group. Nervousness causes shallow, rapid breathing. Breathing slowly and deeply produces the opposite effect.

3. Keep a mint handy or make sure there is water nearby. If you have a dry mouth, incessantly clearing your throat will not help matters. Drinking milk will coat your throat, but not in a productive way. Coffee can tighten your throat.

4. Make a hand gesture, stroll across the stage, or take some other physical action if your body begins to feels stiff or immobile. Sometimes your face may even start to feel numb, as though it might suddenly spasm. Move your head as you walk across the stage, or make a broad gesture that involves head movement.

Chairing a Meeting

Formal meetings usually follow parliamentary procedure, with the chairperson recognizing each person who wishes to speak. Less formal meetings may not be so structured, but when a chairperson has been designated, it is usually because someone needs to keep order. Planning is a key element of successful meetings; developing an agenda is important. In the agenda, include a list of topics to be covered. Arrange them in a logical order and then, for a formal meeting, present the list to those who are present.

A good chairperson stays firmly in charge of a meeting without being aggressive. It is his or her responsibility to:

- identify the problem
- make sure minority views are expressed to foster more inclusive solutions
- bring to light disagreements within the group and lead the meeting toward resolution of those differences
- ask stimulating questions to provoke discussion
- divide problems into smaller issues

In 1876 Henry Martyn Robert defined the responsibilities of a chairperson in his *Rules of Order* as follows: "It is the duty of the chairman, and his function, to preserve order and to take care that the proceedings are conducted in a proper manner, and that the sense of the meeting is properly ascertained with regard to any question which is properly before the meeting." Common pitfalls of chairing meetings include usurping meeting time by talking too much; failing to move the meeting forward by allowing others to talk too much; and rushing through the meeting, thereby preventing solutions from being discussed.

The leader controls a meeting and is responsible for keeping the pace lively. If the discussion moves off-topic, the chairperson leads the group back to focal points. Good facilitators know when to allow a discussion to continue so that all pertinent aspects of a problem are discussed and when it is time to move on to another topic. The goal is to ensure that each item on the agenda receives adequate coverage without needless repetition or disintegration into an exchange of trivial remarks.

To preserve a sense of democracy in meetings, it is important to control the vocal minority. There are often a few people who will try to dominate a discussion. The leader must know who they are and channel their contributions. This can be done in two ways: by soliciting other viewpoints, and by wrapping up that part of the discussion and moving on to the next. One of the roles of the chairperson is to encourage the quieter people present to state their views. If their reticence results from lower status within the organization, ask for their comments. Make them feel that their opinions are valuable.

Effective leaders also control the length of time permitted for each topic of discussion. It may be helpful to determine in advance how much time to allot for each item. It is sometimes advisable to announce these time goals at the start of the meeting and to occasionally remind those present that time is passing quickly. After a topic has been duly covered, the chairperson should summarize salient points and present a conclusion. When a vote is required, the group participates in that conclusion. (*See also* Making the Most of Meetings, page 213.)

Introducing a Speaker

The responsibilities of introducing a speaker include presenting that person in the best light, investing a sense of confidence in his or her abilities, and creating an atmosphere of respect. The first task is to get the audience's attention. They may be just entering the meeting room or they may be chatting in small groups, so the leader must direct their attention to the front of the room. A skillful introduction primes the audience so that the speaker steps up to address attentive and receptive listeners.

When a speaker is not well known, the purpose of the introduction is to establish and confirm his or her credentials, credibility, and reputation. A good introduction can elevate an unknown speaker's status with the audience. If you are not familiar with the person's background or topic, talk with him or her before preparing your script, making note of professional accomplishments and a few personal details that will interest the audience. It may be best to have the speaker write a script for the introduction, but try to spend a few minutes getting to know the person before attempting to tell an audience who this speaker is.

A dynamic and effective introduction will convince the audience that this is the right person to provide advice, facts, or technical information to this group. Excellent speakers can overcome botched introductions, but vague, silly, or inaccurate remarks by an emcee can create unnecessary hurdles. Above all, the introduction should create a positive attitude about the person who will soon have everyone's attention.

The keys to effective introductions include the following:

1. *Enthusiasm on the part of the person making the introduction,* to create excitement and positive anticipation.
2. *Reasons as to why the speaker is qualified to address this group on this subject.* The introduction should inform the audience about the speaker's knowledge of the subject, mentioning practical experience such as books written, education, special honors, and professional skills.

3. *Establishment of a connection between the speaker and the audience,* by relating personal or professional information that encourages a feeling of comradeship. Remarks about community affiliations, hometown origin, hobbies, family ties, or unusual career experiences are usually well received.

The length of an introduction is important, too. It should not be sloughed off with a flippant remark such as, "Here is a person who needs no introduction . . . ," but should be planned, concise, and to the point. When introducing someone, remember that you are not giving the speech—you are only preparing the audience for what is to come. Close your introduction by reiterating the subject of the talk and the speaker's name. Then turn the meeting over to the speaker and leave the stage. Professional protocol usually requires staying in the room to observe and control the meeting as well as to provide any technical assistance requested by the speaker.

Setting Up Training Programs, Seminars, and Workshops

The purpose of a seminar, workshop, or training program is to teach a specialized subject. Speakers or leaders must have credentials that convince attendees of their expertise in the field. Their reputation and the topics to be covered will determine a program's attendance and success. Employers must perceive that sessions will be beneficial enough to justify the time taken from work and the cost of the workshop. The most profitable seminars are those that appeal to clients, employees, and employers. The length of these programs can vary, generally running from a half day to five days. Weekend seminars are popular due to their convenience, and a great deal of information can be imparted in two and a half days.

The basic design is generally a series of lectures accompanied by literature and visual aids. Other extracurricular assistance may take the form of seminar-related exercises or planned hands-on experience following the sessions. Specialized information, not routine knowledge obtained in the normal course of business, must be presented. People seem to react more positively to seminars that provide in-depth coverage of specific subjects; broader offerings are not as well attended. Keep in mind that the subject matter presented must warrant the relatively high cost of the event—simply rehashing facts everyone knows will not justify the expense. On the other hand, esoteric topics of interest to only a tiny group may not draw a large enough audience to be worthwhile.

The best bet is to provide information not easily accessible to the largest number of prospective attendees. Ask these questions when deciding on the topic of a seminar:

1. What are some problems common to people working in this field?
2. How can a seminar or workshop address this problem?
3. What unique and helpful information or experiences can be offered?

4. How will the seminar be useful to participants, personally and professionally?

5. What topics will appeal to employers, encouraging them to pay for their employees to attend?

Publicizing the workshop is important. Is it to be a public offering with open registration and events or an in-house program designed just for your firm and its clients? To successfully market the seminar, you must design it to interest those who should attend. Then the agenda will dictate marketing strategy and sales methods. (*See also* Sponsoring Community Events and Educational Workshops, page 370.)

Advance registration with payment is a good idea for three reasons. It conveys the idea that space is limited and that response is high, making the event seem more attractive and cutting down on last-minute decisions not to attend. It provides a base of operating capital. And it permits sponsors to gear expenses toward estimated turnout. Seminar producers often charge more at the door, giving advance registrants a lower rate. Some guarantee a refund if cancellation occurs within a specified period of time prior to the event, usually one or two weeks. If your firm sponsors seminars regularly, it is more prudent to offer rain checks for future programs in lieu of refunds.

It is important to remember that a seminar is a type of group consultation. Fees are being paid for services to be provided. A conference or workshop must deliver the goods as advertised, or the sponsoring organization will lose face and weaken its chances of attracting participants to future events.

Meeting One-on-One

In one-on-one meetings, being assertive but not aggressive is essential. The four components of effective communication (words, voice, eye contact, and body language) are scrutinized more closely in private conferences than in large group proceedings. Follow these suggestions for successful personal meetings:

- Open the discussion in a friendly manner.
- Encourage the other person to talk, and listen carefully. (Planning your next remark instead of paying attention is not careful listening.)
- Respond to the other person's comments in a way that shows you were listening. Do not just continue with a prepared speech. Make it clear that you are trying to see the other point of view.
- Be alert to positive and negative reactions, and be ready to explain if misunderstandings occur.
- Acknowledge your own faults before making critical remarks about others, unless you are a supervisor meeting with a subordinate for disciplinary purposes. In this instance, discussing your own shortcomings may weaken the message you need to convey, giving the impression that you are to blame for the worker's poor

performance or that no changes are necessary because you sympathize with the situation.
- Be brief. A meandering presentation will not win respect or encourage agreement.
- Disagree by rebutting the other person's ideas. Never launch a personal attack.
- Accept comments and even criticisms graciously.

If you are in the superior position during a one-on-one meeting, take care to put the other person at ease. Making the reason for getting together clear when scheduling the talk or asking the other party to come to your office. State your case, make your point, and then allow the other person to speak freely. Try not to let phone calls or other staff interrupt, and give your full attention to the discussion. Conclude by asking if anything else remains to be said, restating your main points, and thanking the other person for meeting with you.

If you are in the subordinate position, you can make this a successful meeting even though you are not in total control. Remember that it is your superior's job to direct your work. When there is disagreement on how to handle a project, someone must decide which approach to take. Most of us prefer our own ideas and methods to those of others, so your supervisor may say, "Your ideas are good, but I like my own better. I want you to do it my way." That is the prerogative of management. Supervisors who always allow staff to follow their own instincts do not remain supervisors for very long. Accept management decisions with good grace after presenting your ideas in a confident, professional manner.

Planning what to say is important. Decide what the best possible outcome would be from your point of view. Then consider what the other person hopes to achieve by talking with you. Will you need to persuade, to recommend, to inform? What compromises are you willing to make? Organize your thoughts and present them coherently.

Make eye contact and watch your body language. Sitting stiffly with arms folded sends a powerful message that your mind is closed and you are on the defensive. Relax; lean forward slightly from time to time, indicating that the other person's comments are very important and you do not want to miss a single word. Take time to consider your response before answering a question, then answer to the best of your ability. Tell the truth, and give details as necessary. Vagueness is not a virtue, but neither is verbosity.

Keep your tone of voice professional. If you display anger by talking loudly, the meeting is over for all practical purposes, and you have lost an opportunity to achieve your goal. Be alert to signs of anger from the other person, and maintain control of your own emotions even if you are personally attacked or unjustly accused. You need not back down in order to maintain control; just make sure you try to understand how the other person sees things; then restate your position without rancor if your views have not changed.

Above all, be flexible in your approach. Planning ahead and anticipating what the other person wants will not guarantee the outcome. No one can completely understand what is in another's mind, so base your responses on what the other person says and does rather than on assumptions about his or her underlying motives and objectives. (*See also* How to Handle Meetings with Your Boss, page 214; and Negotiations, page 351.)

Telephone Tips

We have come a long way since Alexander Graham Bell successfully transmitted the first interoffice call to Mr. Watson. The telephone is such an omnipresent part of life that many of us give little thought to our speech and behavior patterns in phone conversations. An examination of your current habits and a review of good telephone manners may be warranted.

Telephone Etiquette

1. Say, "May I put you on hold for a moment, please?" if you are interrupted during a call. Wait for a response before pressing the "hold" button. When you return to the caller, apologize for the interruption. (Sometimes when you ask permission to put someone on hold, the other person will say, "No, you may not; I'm in a hurry." If this happens, apologize for the interruption and continue the conversation, unless a genuine emergency is waiting on another line.)

2. Finish eating or drinking before making calls. Although the telephone's microphone is small, it amplifies every sound. Callers can usually hear the small pauses and inhaling sounds that accompany cigarette smoking, and gum-chewing is very annoying. Also, there are a few places that are off-limits for business calls, even on a portable phone—restroom noises can be heard very clearly by the other party.

3. If this is your office policy, answer coworkers' phones when they are away from their desks and take accurate and complete messages. Treat their callers as you do your own. If you are rushing to make a deadline, have someone else take your calls and let others know you are not available to answer their phones.

4. End conversations politely. If you get involved with a chatty caller, nicely explain that you are due at an appointment or have another phone call to make. The caller will usually understand and let you go about your business.

5. Limit personal calls. People do need to check in with spouses, children, and sometimes friends, but do not take advantage of the situation. As with business calls, treat coworkers' family and friends as though they were your own when taking messages.

6. Make only work-related long-distance calls on company lines—never charge personal calls to the company.

7. Keep business calls as brief as possible, except when public relations duties dictate a leisurely chat. The other person is very busy, just as you are, and both of your firms will benefit from using telephone time wisely. Remember that coworkers may be waiting for an open line, or clients may be trying to call. Busy signals may mean lost income.

INFORMATION, PLEASE

Many people have learned to use the telephone directory in recent years due to the imposition of fees for routine directory assistance calls. But there are still a number of excellent services provided at no charge. A particularly helpful business resource is AT&T's toll-free directory assistance service.

For example, suppose you want to contact a manufacturing firm called Happy Hunting Sporting Goods. You know that it has an 800 number for customer service, as you have used it in the past, but you cannot locate it now. Or perhaps you think the company may have an 800 number and would like to save your firm money by using it. Just dial 800-555-1212 and ask for Happy Hunting Sporting Goods' toll-free number. Maybe a friend recently told you about a great restaurant in Denver named The Donner Party Gourmet Grill, and you want to reserve a table for a business luncheon during your trip next week. Dial 800-555-1212 and ask if there is a toll-free listing for the restaurant. You may be surprised to learn how many businesses have toll-free numbers.

AT&T publishes its *Toll-Free National 800 Directory (Business Buyer's Guide)* annually, listing over 120,000 toll-free business numbers nationwide in traditional yellow pages format. If you need a hotel reservation in a small town in Oklahoma but have no idea what hotels are there, look in the *800 Directory*'s yellow pages. There may be a chain hotel or an independent facility listed in the "Hotels, Motels & Resorts By State" listings.

Making and Taking Calls

When calling:

- Speak clearly and slowly, in a pleasant tone.
- Identify yourself and your company immediately: "Hello, this is Danielle Smith of ABC Technologies. May I please speak to Ron Parker?"
- Use a courtesy title until the other person invites you to use his or her first name.
- Ask if the other person has a few moments before beginning an involved discussion.
- Have other calls held during the conversation. It is very rude to call someone and then put that person on hold.
- Leave a message if you reach an answering machine, briefly stating the date, time, and purpose of your call. If you do not receive a return phone call within a reasonable time, call back. There may have been an equipment problem or someone else may have retrieved your message by mistake.

When answering:

- Answer calls within two or three rings.
- Give the name of the company. If it is your personal line, give your name as well: "DEF Supplies; good morning—this is Ron Parker." Avoid long, drawn-out responses, however. Most people find it annoying to wait through an interminable

message such as "Harker, Jones, McMahon, Jamison, and Merchant, Corporate Taxation Section; good morning, this is Adelaide Rutabaker; how may I be of assistance?" Your objective is to identify yourself and the firm in a pleasant, helpful manner, not to make callers wait (and pay long-distance charges) for this sort of spiel. "Law Offices—Ms. Rutabaker" is a much better response. Many office managers insist on the inclusion of greetings such as "good morning," "good afternoon," "season's greetings," or a company slogan ("Ace Auto Parts—always the lowest prices in town") in addition to the company, department, employee's name, and a phrase offering assistance. Such responses often produce the opposite of the desired effect by irritating busy callers. A pleasant "Ace Auto Parts—this is John" would convey the needed information and let the parties get on with the purpose of the call.

- Ask your assistant and coworkers to say, "Ms. Smith is in a meeting; may I take a message?" when you are out of the office or not taking calls.
- Have your assistant screen calls by saying, "I will see if Ms. Smith is available; may I say who is calling?" This response is appropriate even when a caller asks if you are in the office, as it avoids answering the question directly. If necessary, the statement can be repeated verbatim in a pleasant, professional manner, and only a confirmed boor could take offense at the evasion.
- Ask: "May I put you on hold?" before doing so, even if three other lines are ringing at once. If you must keep the caller holding, say, "I'm sorry to keep you holding," and explain the situation. Then ask, "Do you wish to continue holding?"

SPECIAL TELEPHONE SERVICES FOR THE HEARING IMPAIRED

Telephone equipment that allows reception and transmission of calls on-screen, in typed format, called a Text Telephone Device (TDD), is available for businesspeople with hearing problems. If your firm has hearing-impaired employees or customers, check with your local telephone company or equipment provider for more information. TDD users may call 800-855-1155 for details about equipment and AT&T's Telecommunications for the Deaf service. The service provides special assistance to hearing-impaired persons placing local, long-distance, collect, third-party, credit card, and other operator-assisted calls.

Domestic Area Codes (United States, Canada, Bermuda, Puerto Rico, Virgin Islands, and Other Caribbean Islands)

This numerical list of area codes is provided for use in quickly identifying the locations of area codes. For example, a telephone message may include just the caller's name and number. If you do not recognize the caller's name and would like to know where the call originated, use this list to locate the area code quickly. (A complete alphabetical list of area codes is usually included in local telephone directories.)

201 Northeastern New Jersey
202 District of Columbia
   (Washington, DC)
203 Western Connecticut
204 Manitoba, Canada
205 Northern Alabama
206 Seattle/Richmond area,
   Washington
207 Maine
208 Idaho
209 Central California
210 San Antonio, Texas
212 Manhattan, New York
213 Los Angeles, California
214 Dallas, Texas
215 Philadelphia, Pennsylvania
216 Cleveland metropolitan area,
   Ohio
217 Central Illinois
218 Northern Minnesota
219 Northern Indiana
228 Mississippi, except Jackson
240 Western Maryland
242 Bahamas
246 Barbados
248 Oakland County, Michigan
250 British Columbia, Canada
253 Northwestern Washington
   State
254 Eastern central Texas
264 Anguilla
268 Antigua and Barbuda
281 Houston, Texas
284 British Virgin Islands
301 Western Maryland
302 Delaware
303 Denver/Boulder area, Colorado
304 West Virginia
305 Miami, Florida
306 Saskatchewan, Canada
307 Wyoming
308 Western Nebraska
309 Northwestern Illinois
310 Southern California
312 Chicago, Illinois
313 Detroit, Michigan
314 St. Louis, Missouri
315 Northwestern New York State

316 Southern Kansas
317 Indianapolis, Indiana
318 Northern and western Louisiana
319 Eastern Iowa
320 Minneapolis and central
   Minnesota
330 Northeastern Ohio
334 Southern Alabama
340 U.S. Virgin Islands
345 Cayman Islands
352 Gainesville, Florida
360 Southwestern Washington State
401 Rhode Island
402 Eastern Nebraska
403 Alberta, Canada
404 Atlanta, Georgia
405 Central and western Oklahoma
406 Montana
407 Eastern central Florida
408 Western central California
409 Southeastern Texas
410 Eastern Maryland
412 Southwestern Pennsylvania
413 Western Massachusetts
414 Milwaukee area, Wisconsin
415 San Francisco area, California
416 Toronto, Ontario, Canada
417 Southwestern Missouri
418 Québec City, Quebec, Canada
419 Northwestern Ohio
423 Eastern Tennessee
425 Northwestern Washington
440 Northern central Ohio
441 Bermuda
443 Eastern Maryland
450 Quebec, Canada
456 Inbound international calls
473 Grenada
500 Personal communications services
501 Little Rock and northwestern
   Arkansas
502 Western Kentucky
503 Northwestern Oregon
504 Southeastern Louisiana
505 New Mexico
506 New Brunswick, Canada
507 Southern Minnesota
508 Northeastern Massachusetts

509 Eastern Washington State
510 Northwestern central California
512 Southern central Texas
513 Southwestern Ohio
514 Montreal, Quebec, Canada
515 Central Iowa
516 Long Island, New York
517 Central Michigan
518 Northeastern New York State
519 Southwestern Ontario, Canada
520 Arizona, except Phoenix
530 Northern central California
540 Western Virginia
541 Oregon, except northwestern area
561 Southeastern Florida
562 West Los Angeles, California
573 Eastern Missouri
601 Jackson, Mississippi
602 Phoenix, Arizona
603 New Hampshire
604 Vancouver, British Columbia, Canada
605 South Dakota
606 Eastern Kentucky
607 Southern central New York State
608 Southwestern Wisconsin
609 Southern New Jersey
610 Southeastern Pennsylvania, except Philadelphia
612 St. Paul/Minneapolis, Minnesota
613 Eastern Ontario, Canada
614 Central and southeastern Ohio
615 Northern central Tennessee
616 Western Michigan
617 Boston metropolitan area, Massachusetts
618 Southern Illinois
619 San Diego area, California
630 Chicago area, Illinois
649 Turks and Caicos Islands
650 Western central California
664 Montserrat

670 Commonwealth of Northern Mariana Islands
671 Guam
701 North Dakota
702 Nevada
703 Northern Virginia
704 Western North Carolina
705 Central Ontario, Canada
706 Northern Georgia
707 Northwestern California
708 Chicago area, Illinois
709 Newfoundland, Canada
710 U.S. Government
712 Western Iowa
713 Houston, Texas
714 Southwestern California
715 Northern Wisconsin
716 Western New York State
717 Eastern Pennsylvania
718 The Bronx, Brooklyn, Queens, and Staten Island, New York
719 Southeastern Colorado
724 Southwestern Pennsylvania
732 Central New Jersey
734 Southeastern Michigan, except Detroit
757 Eastern Virginia
758 St. Lucia
760 Southeastern California
765 Central Indiana, except Indianapolis metropolitan area
767 Commonwealth of Dominica
770 Northwestern Atlanta, Georgia, and surrounding area
773 Chicago area, Illinois
781 Boston area, Massachusetts, excluding Boston metropolitan area
784 St. Vincent and the Grenadines
785 Northern Kansas except Kansas City
787 Puerto Rico
800 Toll-free service numbers
801 Utah
802 Vermont
803 Northern central South Carolina
804 Central Virginia

805 Southwestern California
806 Northwestern Texas
807 Northwestern Ontario, Canada
808 Hawaii
809 Caribbean Islands
810 Northeastern Michigan
812 Southern Indiana
813 Western central Florida
814 Western Pennsylvania
815 Northern Illinois except Chicago area
816 Northwestern Missouri
817 Arlington/Fort Worth metropolitan area, Texas
818 Pasadena area, southern California
819 Sherbrooke, Quebec, Canada
830 Southwestern Texas
843 Coastal South Carolina
847 Chicago area, Illinois
860 Eastern Connecticut
864 Northwestern South Carolina
867 Yukon and Northwest Territories, Canada
868 Trinidad and Tobago
869 St. Kitts/Nevis
870 Arkansas, except Little Rock and northwest
876 Jamaica
880, 881 Toll-free calls originating from Canada or the Caribbean to the U.S. (caller pays the international portion of call)
888 Expansion of toll-free 800-type numbers
900 Commercial calls with added charges

901 Western Tennessee
902 Nova Scotia and Prince Edward Island, Canada
903 Northeastern Texas
904 Northern Florida
905 Southeastern Ontario, except Toronto, Canada
906 Northwestern Michigan
907 Alaska
908 Northwestern central New Jersey
909 Western central California
910 Central North Carolina
912 Southern Georgia
913 Kansas City, Kansas
914 Southeastern New York State
915 Western Texas
916 Northern central California
917 Cellular phones and pagers in New York City
918 Northeastern Oklahoma
919 Eastern North Carolina
920 Southeastern Wisconsin, except Milwaukee area
925 Northwestern central California
931 Southern central Tennessee
937 Dayton, Ohio
940 Northern central Texas
941 Southern Florida
949 Southwestern California
954 Southeastern Florida
956 Southwestern Texas
970 Western and northeastern Colorado, except the Denver/Boulder area
972 Dallas, Texas
973 Northwestern New Jersey
978 Southeastern Massachusetts

International Calls

Calls to Canada, Bermuda, Puerto Rico, and many Caribbean islands are considered domestic calls. These numbers are reached by dialing 1 + the area code + the local number, just as though you were calling any other U.S. number. In the following list, the area codes of such places are listed as their country codes with the exception of Canada, for which state (city) codes are listed. International calls are placed by dialing 011 (the international call dial prefix) + the country code + the city code (if necessary) + the local telephone number. Or you may call an international operator by dialing 00.

Some international calls cannot be dialed direct. If the country you wish to call does not appear on the following abridged list, consult an international operator. (AT&T publishes a complete directory of international country and city codes, the *International Telecommunications Guide,* which can be requested by calling 102880.) To get information or directory assistance for another country, dial 00 for an international operator. The operator will contact an English-speaking operator in the country you wish to call.

All of the preceding dialing instructions pertain to using AT&T long-distance services. Other long-distance carriers may require other procedures for domestic and/or international calls.

International Country and City Codes

Country and country code (*not necessary to dial 011 when calling from North America)	Major cities and city codes (**no city codes necessary)	Time difference in hours from U.S. eastern standard time
Albania 355	Durres 52, Elbassan 545, Korce 824, Shkoder 224, Tirana 42	+6
Algeria 213	Adrar 7, Ain Defla 3, Bejaia 5, Guerrar 9	+6
American Samoa 684	**	−6
Andorra 376	**	+6
Angola 244	Luanda 2, all other points**	+6
Anguilla 264*	**	+1
Antarctica (Casey Base) 67212	**	+3
Antarctica (Scott Base) 672	**	+3
Antigua and Barbuda 268*	**	+1
Argentina 54	Babia Blanca 91, Buenos Aires 1, Córdoba 51, Corrientes 783, La Plata 21, Mar Del Plata 23, Mendoza 61, Merlo 220, Posadas 752, Resistencia 722, Rio Cuatro 586, Rosario 41, San Juan 64, San Rafael 627, Santa Fe 42, Tandil 293	+2
Armenia 374	**	+9
Aruba 297	All points 8	+1
Ascension Island 247	**	+5
Australia 61	Adelaide 8, Ballarat 53, Brisbane 7, Canberra 6, Darwin 89, Geelong 52, Gold Coast 75, Hobart 02, Launceston 03, Melbourne 3, Newcastle 49, Perth 9, Sydney 2, Toowoomba 76, Townsville 77, Wollongong 42	+13/+14.5/+15
Austria 43	Bludenz 5552, Graz 316, Innsbruck 512, Kitzbuhel 5356, Klagenfurt 463, Krems An Der Donau 2732, Linz Donau 70, Neunkirchen Niederosterreich 2635, St. Polten 2742, Salzburg 662, Vienna 1, Villach 4242, Wels 7242, Wiener Neustadt 2622	+6

(continued)

Country and country code (*not necessary to dial 011 when calling from North America)	Major cities and city codes (**no city codes necessary)	Time difference in hours from U.S. eastern standard time
Azerbaijan 994	Baku 12, Daskasan 216, Sumgayit 164	+9
Bahamas 242*	**	0
Bahrain 973	**	+8
Bangladesh 880	Barisal 431, Bogra 51, Chittagong 31, Comilla 81, Dhaka 2, Khulna 41, Maulabi Bazar 861, Mymensingh 91, Narayangon 671, Rajshaki 721, Sylhet 821	+11
Barbados 246*	**	+1
Belarus 375	Loev 2347, Minsk 172, Mogilev 222	+8
Belgium 32	Antwerp 3, Bruges 50, Brussels 2, Charleroi 71, Courtrai 56, Ghent 9, Hasselt 11, La Louviere 64, Leuven 16, Libramont 61, Liege 41, Malines 15, Mons 65, Namur 81, Ostend 59, Verviers 87	+6
Belize 501	Belize City 2, Belmopan 8, Benque Viejo Del Carmen 93, Corozal Town 4, Dangriga 5, Independence 6, Orange Walk 3, Punta Gorda 7, San Ignacio 92, Stan Creek 5	−1
Benin 229	**	+6
Bermuda 441	**	+1
Bhutan 975	**	+11
Bolivia 591	Cochabamba 42, Cotoga 388, Guayaramerin 855, La Belgica 923, La Paz 2, Mineros 984, Montero 92, Oruro 52, Portachuelo 924, Saavedra 924, Santa Cruz 3, Sucre 64, Trinidad 46, Warnes 923	+1
Bosnia and Herzegovina 387	Mostar 88, Sarajevo 71, Zenica 72	+6
Botswana 267	Jwaneng 380, Kanye 340, Lobatse 330, Mahalapye 410, Mochudi 377, Molepolole 320, Orapa 270, Palapye 420, Serowe 430	+7
Brazil 55	Belém 91, Belo Horizonte 31, Brasília 61, Curitiba 41, Fortaleza 85, Goiania 62, Niteroi 21, Pelotas 532, Porto Alegre 51, Recife 81, Rio de Janeiro 21, Salvador 71, Santo Andre 11, Santos 132, São Paulo 11, Vitoria 27	+1/+2
British Virgin Islands 284*	**	+1
Brunei 673	Bandar Seri Begawan 2, Kuala Belait 3, Mumong 3, Tutong 4	+13
Bulgaria 359	Kardjali 361, Pazardjik 34, Plovdiv 32, Sofia 2, Varna 52	+7
Burkina Faso 226	**	+5
Burma *see* Myanmar		

(*continued*)

Country and country code (*not necessary to dial 011 when calling from North America)	Major cities and city codes (**no city codes necessary)	Time difference in hours from U.S. eastern standard time
Burundi 257	Bujumbura 2, Buruchi 50, Gitega 40, Muyinga 30, Rutana 50	+7
Cambodia 855	Phnom Penh 23	+12
Cameroon 237	**	+6
Canada 1*—do not use country code when dialing from North America; use state code as area code	No city codes; state codes are listed with relevant city names in parentheses: Alberta 403, British Columbia 250, British Columbia (Vancouver) 604, Manitoba 204, New Brunswick 506, Newfoundland 709, Nova Scotia 902, Ontario (London) 519, Ontario (North Bay) 705, Ontario (Ottawa) 613, Ontario (Thunder Bay) 807, Ontario (Toronto metropolitan area) 416, Ontario (Niagara Falls) 905, Prince Edward Island 902, Quebec (Montreal urban area) 514, Quebec (Quebec City) 418, Quebec (Sherbrooke) 819, Quebec (other areas) 450, Saskatchewan 306, Yukon and Northwest Territories 867	−1/−2/−3/0/+1/+1.5
Cape Verde Islands 238*	**	+1
Cayman Islands 345*	**	0
Central African Republic 236	**	+6
Chad 235	Abeche**, Faya**, Moundou 69, N'djamena 51, Sarh**	+6
Chile 56	Chiguayante 41, Concepcion 41, La Serena 51, Penco 41, Recreo 32, San Bernardo 2, Santiago 2, Talcahuano 41, Valparaiso 32, Vina del Mar 32	+1
China 86	Beijing (Peking) 10, Fuzhou 591, Guangzhou (Canton) 20, Shanghai 21	+13
Christmas Island 672	Christmas 4	+5
CNMI *see* Mariana Islands		
Cocos Islands 672	Cocos 3	+5
Colombia 57	Armenia 67, Barranquilla 58, Bogota 1, Bucaramanga 76, Cali 2, Cartagena 5, Cartago 656, Cucuta 75, Giradot 834, Ibague 82, Manizales 68, Medellin 4, Neiva 88, Palmira 22, Pereira 63, Santa Marta 54	0
Comoros 269	**	+8
Congo 242	**	+6
Cook Islands 682	**	−5
Costa Rica 506	**	−1
Côte d'Ivoire *see* Ivory Coast		
Croatia 385	Dubrovnik 20, Rijeka 51, Split 21, Zagreb 41	+6

(*continued*)

Country and country code (*not necessary to dial 011 when calling from North America)	Major cities and city codes (**no city codes necessary)	Time difference in hours from U.S. eastern standard time
Cuba 53	Havana City 7, Santiago de Cuba Santia 226	0
Cyprus 357	Famagusta 392, Kyrenia 581, Larnaca 4, Lefkonico 3, Limassol 5, Nicosia 2, Paphos 6, Platres 5, Polis 6	+7
Czech Republic 42	Brno 5, Havirov 6994, Ostrava 69, Prague 2	+6
Denmark 45	**	+6
Djibouti 253	**	+8
Dominica 767*	**	+1
Dominican Republic 809*	**	+1
Ecuador 593	Ambato 3, Cayambe 2, Cuenca 7, Esmeraldas 6, Guayaquil 4, Ibarra 6, Loja 7, Machachi 2, Machala 7, Manta 4, Portoviejo 5, Quevedo 5, Quito 2, Salinas 4, Santo Domingo 2, Tulcan 6	0
Egypt 20	Alexandria 3, Aswan 97, Asyut 88, Benha 13, Cairo 2, Damanhour 5, El Mahallah (El Kubra) 43, El Mansoura 50, Luxor 95, Port Said 66, Shebin El Kom 48, Sohag 93, Tanta 40	+7
El Salvador 503	**	−1
England *see* United Kingdom		
Equatorial Guinea 240	Bata 8, Malabo 9, Qaliub 2	+6
Eritrea 291	Asmara 1, Makale 1, Massawa 1	+8
Estonia 372	Rakvere 32, Tallinn 2, Tartu 7	+7
Ethiopia 251	Addis Ababa 1, Akaki 1, Awassa 6, Debre Zeit 1, Dire Dawa 5, Harra 5, Jimma 7, Nazareth 2, Shashemene 6	+8
Faroe Islands 298	**	+5
Falkland Islands 500	**	+1
Fiji Islands 679	**	+17
Finland 358	Espoo-Esbo 09, Helsinki 09, Joensuu 013, Jyvaskyla 014, Kuopio 017, Lahti 03, Lappeenranta 05, Oulu 08, Pori 02, Tampere-Tammerfors 03, Turku-Abo 02, Uleaborg 08, Vaasa 06, Vanda-Vantaa 09	+7
France 33	Aix-en-Provence 4, Bordeaux 5, Cannes**, Chauvigny 5, Cherbourg 2, Grenoble 4, Lourdes 5, Lyon**, Marseille 4, Monaco 4, Nice 4, Paris 1, Rouen 2, Toulouse**, Tours 2	+6
French Antilles, including Martinique, St. Barthélemy, and St. Martin 596	**	+1
French Guiana 594	**	+2

(*continued*)

Country and country code (*not necessary to dial 011 when calling from North America)	Major cities and city codes (**no city codes necessary)	Time difference in hours from U.S. eastern standard time
French Polynesia, including Moorea and Tahiti 689	**	−5
Gabon 241	**	+6
Gambia 220	**	+5
Georgia 995	Suhumi 881, Tbilisi 883	+9
Germany 49	Bad Homburg 6172, Berlin 30, Bonn 228, Bremen 421, Cologne (Köln) 221, Cottbus 355, Dresden 351, Düsseldorf 211, Erfurt 361, Essen 201, Frankfurt am Main (west) 69, Frankfurt an der Oder (east) 335, Gera 365, Halle 345, Hamburg 50, Heidelberg 6221, Karl-Stadt 9353, Koblenz 261, Leipzig 341, Magdeburg 391, Mannheim 621, Munich 89, Neubrandenburg 395, Nurnberg 911, Potsdam 331, Rostock 381, Saal 38223, Schwerin 385, Stuttgart 711, Wiesbaden 611	+6
Ghana 233	Accra 21, Koforidua 81, Kumasi 51, Takoradi 31	+5
Gibraltar 350	**	+6
Great Britain *see* United Kingdom		
Greece 30	Argos 751, Athens (Athinai) 1, Corfu (Kerkyra) 661, Corinth 741, Iraklion (Kritis) 81, Kavala 51, Larissa 41, Patrai 61, Piraeus Pireefs 1, Rodos 241, Salonica (Thessaloniki) 31, Sparti 731, Tripolis 71, Volos 421, Zagora 426	+7
Greenland 299	Godthaab 2, all other points**	0/+1/+2/+3/+4
Grenada, including Carriacou 473*	**	+1
Guadeloupe 590	Basse-Terre 81, Capesterre 86, Gosier 84, Grand Bourg 97, Jarry 26, Pointe-à-Pitre 8 or 9	+1
Guam 671*	**	+15
Guatemala 502	Guatemala City 2, all other points 9	−1
Guinea 224	Conakry 4, Faranah 81, Kindia 61, Labe 51, Mamou 68	+5
Guinea-Bissau 245	**	+5
Guyana 592	Anna Regina 71, Bartica 5, Beteryerwaging 20, Georgetown 2, Ituni 41, Linden 4, Mabaruma 77, Mahaica 28, Mahaicony 21, New Amersterdam 3, New Hope 66, Rosignol 30, Timehri 61, Vreed-En-Hoop 64, Whim 37	+2
Haiti 509	**	0
Honduras 504	**	−1

(continued)

Country and country code (*not necessary to dial 011 when calling from North America)	Major cities and city codes (**no city codes necessary)	Time difference in hours from U.S. eastern standard time
Hong Kong 852	All points 2	+13
Hungary 36	Abasar 37, Balatonaliga 84, Budapest 1, Dorgicse 80, Fertoboz 99, Gyongyos 37, Gyor 96, Kaposvar 82, Kazincbarcika 48, Komlo 72, Miskolc 46, Nagykanizsa 93, Szekesfehervar 22, Szolnok 56, Varpalota 80, Veszprem 80, Zalaegerszeg 92	+6
Iceland 354	Akureyri 6, Hafnarfjorour 1, Husavik 6, Keflavik Naval Base 2, Rein 6, Reykjavik**, Reyoarjorour 7, Sandgeroi 2, Selfoss 8, Siglufjorour 6, Stokkseyri 8, Suoavik 4, Talknafjorour 4, Varma 1, Vik 8	+5
India 91	Ahmedabad 79, Amritsar 183, Bangalore 80, Baroda 265, Bhopal 755, Bombay 22, Calcutta 33, Chandigarh 172, Hyderabad 40, Jaipur 141, Jullundur 181, Kanpur 512, Madras 44, New Delhi 11, Poona 212, Surat 261	+10.5
Indonesia 62	Bandung 22, Cirebon 231, Denpasar (Bali) 361, Jakarta 21, Madiun 351, Malang 341, Medan 61, Padang 751, Palembang 711, Sekurang 778, Semarang 24, Solo 271, Surabaya 31, Tanjungkarang 721, Yogyakarta 274	+12/+13/+14
Iran 98	Abadan 631, Ahwaz 61, Arak 861, Esfahan 31, Ghazvin 281, Ghome 251, Hamadan 81, Karadj 261, Kerman 341, Mashad 51, Rasht 231, Rezaiyeh 441, Shiraz 71, Tabriz 41, Tehran 21	+8.5
Iraq 964	Baghdad 1, Basra 40, Kerbela 32, Kirkuk 50, Mousil 60, Najaf 33	+8
Ireland, Republic of 353	Arklow 402, Cork 21, Dingle 66, Donegal 72, 73, 74, or 75, Drogheda 41, Dublin 1, Dundalk 42, Ennis 65, Galway 91, Kildare 45, Killarney 64, Limerick 61, Sligo 71, Tipperary 62, Tralee 66, Tullamore 502, Waterford 51, Wexford 53	+5
Israel 972	Afula 6, Ako 4, Ashkelon 7, Bat Yam 3, Beer Sheva 7, Dimona 7, Hadera 6, Haifa 4, Holon 3, Jerusalem 2, Nazareth 6, Netania 9, Ramat Gan 3, Rehovot 8, Tel Aviv 3, Tiberias 6, Tsefat 6	+7

(*continued*)

Country and country code (*not necessary to dial 011 when calling from North America)	Major cities and city codes (**no city codes necessary)	Time difference in hours from U.S. eastern standard time
Italy 39	Bari 80, Bologna 51, Brindisi 831, Capri 81, Como 31, Florence 55, Genoa 10, Milan 2, Naples 81, Padova 49, Palermo 91, Pisa 50, Rome 6, Torino 11, Trieste 40, Venice 41, Verona 45, Vatican City 6	+6
Ivory Coast (Côte d'Ivoire) 225	**	+5
Jamaica 876*	**	0
Japan, including Okinawa 81	Chiba 43, Fuchu (Tokyo) 423, Hiroshima 82, Kawasaki (Kanagawa) 44, Kobe 78, Kyoto 75, Nagasaki 958, Nagoya 52, Naha (Okinawa) 98, Osaka 6, Sapporo 11, Sasebo 956, Tachikawa (Tokyo) 425, Tokyo 3, Yokohama 45, Yokosuka (Kanagawa) 468	+14
Jordan 962	Amman 6, Aqaba 3, Irbid 2, Jerash 4, Karak 3, Maa'n 3, Mafruq 4, Ramtha 2, Sueeleh 6, Sult 5, Zerqa 9	+7
Kazakhstan 7	Alma-Ata 3272, Chimkent 325, Guryev 312, Petropavlovsk 315	+11
Kenya 254	Anmer 2845, Bamburi 11, Embakasi 2, Gigiri 2, Kabete 2, Karen 2882, Kiambu 154, Kikuyu 154, Kisumu 35, Langata 2, Mombasa 11, Nairobi 2, Nakuru 37, Shanzu 11, Thika 151, Uthiru 2	+8
Kiribati 686	**	+17
Korea, North 850	Pyong Yang 2	+14
Korea, South 82	Chuncheon 361, Chung Ju 431, Icheon 336, Inchon 32, Kwangju (Gwangju) 62, Masan 551, Osan 339, Pohang 562, Pusan (Busan) 51, Seoul 2, Suwon (Suweon) 331, Taegu (Daegu) 53, Uijongbu 351, Ulsan 522, Wonju (Weonju) 371	+14
Kuwait 965	**	+8
Kyrgyzstan 7	Osh 33222	+8
Laos 856	Vientiane 21, all other points**	+12
Latvia 371	Daugavpils 54, Jelgava 30, Liepaja 34, Riga 2, Ventspils 36	+7
Lebanon 961	Beirut 1, Tripoli 6, Zahle 8	+7
Lesotho 266	**	+7
Liberia 231	**	+5
Libya 218	Angelat 282, Benghazi 61, Benina 63, Derna 81, Misuratha 51, Sabratha 24, Sebha 71, Taigura 26, Tripoli 2133, Tripoli International Airport 22, Zawai 23, Zuara 25	+6

(*continued*)

Country and country code (*not necessary to dial 011 when calling from North America*)	Major cities and city codes (**no city codes necessary*)	Time difference in hours from U.S. eastern standard time
Liechtenstein 41	**	+6
Lithuania 370	Kaunas 7, Klaipeda 6, Panevezys 54, Siauliai 1, Vilnius 2	+7
Luxembourg 352	**	+6
Macau 853	**	+13
Macedonia 389	Asamati 96, Bitola 97, Gostivar 94, Kicevo 95, Krusevo 98, Lozovo 92, Skopje 91	+6
Madagascar 261	Antalaha 8, Antananarivo 2, Diego Suarez 8, Fianarantsoa 7, Moramanga 4, Tamatave 5	+8
Malawi 265	Domasi 531, Likuni 766, Luchenza 477, Makwasa 474, Mulanje 465, Namadzi 534, Njuli 664, Thondwe 533, Thornwood 486, all other points**	+7
Malaysia 60	Alor Star 4, Baranang 3, Broga 3, Cheras 3, Dengil 3, Ipoh 5, Johor Bahru 7, Kajang 3, Kepala Batas 4, Kuala Lumpur 3, Machang 97, Maran 95, Port Dickson 6, Semenyih 3, Seremban 6, Sungei Besi 3, Sungei Renggam 3	+13
Maldives 960	**	+10
Mali 223	**	+5
Malta 356	**	+6
Mariana Islands (Commonwealth of Northern Mariana Islands or CNMI), including Saipan 670*	Saipan Airport 2348, all other points**	+15
Marshall Islands 692	Ebeye 329, Majuro 625	+17
Mauritania 222	**	+5
Mauritius 230	**	+5
Mayotte 269	**	+8
Mexico 52	Acapulco 74, Cancun 98, Celaya 461, Chihuahua 14, Ciudad Juarez 16, Culiacan 67, Guadalajara 3, Hermosillo 62, Merida 99, Mexico City 5, Monterrey 8, Puebla 22, Puerto Vallarta 322, San Luis Potosi 48, Tampico 12, Tijuana 66, Torreon 17, Veracruz 29	−3/−2/−1
Micronesia 691	Kosrae 370, Pohnpei 320, Truk 330, Yap 350	+15
Moldova 373	Benderi 32, Kishinev 2	+7
Monaco 377	**	+6
Mongolia 976	Ulan Bator 1	+13

(*continued*)

Country and country code (*not necessary to dial 011 when calling from North America)	Major cities and city codes (**no city codes necessary)	Time difference in hours from U.S. eastern standard time
Montserrat 664*	**	+1
Morocco 212	Agadir 88, Beni-Mellal 348, Berrechid 2, Casablanca 2, El Jadida 334, Fez 5, Kenitra 73, Marrakech 4, Meknes 55, Mohammedia 332, Nador 660, Oujda 668, Rabat 7 and 77, Tanger (Tangiers) 99, Tetouan 996	+5
Mozambique 258	Beira 3, Chimolo 51, Chokwe 21, Maputo 1, Matola 4, Nampula 6, Quelimane 4, Tete 52, Xai-Xai 22	+7
Myanmar (Burma) 95	Bassein 42, Mandalay 2, Monywa 71, Prome 53, Yangon (Rangoon) 1	+11.5
Namibia 264	Gobabis 681, Grootfontein 6731, Industria 61, Keetmanshoop 631, Luderitz 6331, Mariental 661, Okahandja 6228, Olympia 61, Otjiwarongo 651, Pioneerspark 61, Swakopmund 641, Tsumeb 671, Windhoek 61, Windhoek Airport 626	+7
Nauru 674	**	+17
Nepal 977	Bhaktapur 1, Dhangadi 91, Gorkha 64, Kathmandu 1, Nepalgunj 81	+10.5
The Netherlands 31	Amsterdam 20, Arnhem 85, Eindhoven 40, Groningen 50, Haarlem 23, The Hague 70, Heemstede 23, Hillegersberg 10, Hoensbroek 45, Hoogkerk 50, Hoogvliet 10, Loosduinen 70, Nijmegen 80, Oud Zuilen 30, Rotterdam 10, Utrecht 30	+6
Netherlands Antilles 599	Bonaire 7, Curacao 9, Saba 46, St. Eustatius 38, St. Maarten 5	+1
New Caledonia 687	**	+16
New Zealand, including Chatham Island 64	Auckland 9, Christchurch 3, Dunedin 3, Hamilton 7, Hastings 6, Invercargill 3, Napier 6, Nelson 3, New Plymouth 6, Palmerston North 6, Rotorua 7, Tauranga 7, Timaru 3, Wanganui 6, Wellington 4, Whangarei 9	+17
Nicaragua 505	Boaco 54, Chinandega 341, Diriamba 4222, Esteli 71, Granada 55, Jinotepe 41 and 4122, Leon 311, Managua 2, Masatepe 44, Masaya 52, Nandaime 4522, Rivas 46, San Juan Del Sur 4682, San Marcos, Tipitapa 53	−1
Niger 227	**	+6
Nigeria 234	Badagry 1, Kaduna 62, Lagos 1, Port Hartcourt 84	+6
Niue Island 683	**	+6
Norfolk Island 672	All points 3	+16.5

(*continued*)

Country and country code (*not necessary to dial 011 when calling from North America)	Major cities and city codes (**no city codes necessary)	Time difference in hours from U.S. eastern standard time
Northern Ireland *see* United Kingdom		
North Korea *see* Korea, North		
Norway, including Svalbard 47	**	+6
Okinawa *see* Japan		
Oman 968	**	+9
Pakistan 92	Abbotabad 5921, Bahawaipur 621, Faisalabad 411, Gujranwala 431, Hyderabad 221, Islamabad 51, Karachi 21, Lahore 42, Multan 61, Okara 442, Peshawar 521, Quetta 81, Sahiwal 441, Sargodha 451, Sialkot 432, Sukkur 71	+10
Palau 680	**	+14
Panama 507	**	0
Papua New Guinea, including Admiralty Islands, Bougainville, New Britain, and New Ireland 675	**	+15
Paraguay 595	Asunción 21, Ayolas 72, Capiata 28, Concepción 31, Coronel Bogado 74, Coronel Oviedo 521, Encarnacion 71, Hernandarias 63, Ita 24, Pedro J. Caballero 36, Pilar 86, San Antonio 27, San Ignacio 82, Stroessner—Ciudad Pte. 61, Stroessner—Villarrica 541, Stroessner—Villeta 25	+1
Peru 51	Arequipa 54, Ayacucho 6491, Callao 14, Chiclayo 74, Chimbote 44, Cuzco 84, Huancavelica 6495, Huancayo 64, Ica 34, Iquitos 94, Lima 14, Piura 74, Tacna 54, Trujillo 44	0
The Philippines 63	Angeles 455, Bacolad 34, Baguio City 74, Cebu City 32, Dagupan 75, Davao 82, Iloilo City 33, Lucena 42, Manila 2, San Fernando—La Union 72, San Fernando—San Pablo 93, San Fernando—Subic Bay 47, San Fernando—Tarlac City 452	+13
Poland 48	Bialystok 85, Bydgoszcz 52, Crakow 12, Gdansk 58, Gdynia 58, Katowice 3, Lodz 42, Lublin 81, Olsztyn 89, Poznan 61, Radom 48, Sopot 58, Torun 56, Warsaw 22	+6

(*continued*)

Country and country code (*not necessary to dial 011 when calling from North America)	Major cities and city codes (**no city codes necessary)	Time difference in hours from U.S. eastern standard time
Portugal, including Azores and Madeira Islands 351	Almada 1, Angra Do Heroismo 95, Barreiro 1, Braga 53, Caldas Da Rainha 62, Coimbra 39, Estoril 1, Evora 66, Faro 89, Lajes Air Force Base 95, Lisbon 1, Madalena 92, Madeira Islands 91, Motijo 1, Ponta Delgada 96, Porto 2, Santa Cruz 92, Setubal 65, Velas 95, Vila Do Porto 96	+6
Puerto Rico 787*	**	+1
Qatar 974	**	+8
Réunion Island 262	**	+9
Romania 40	Arad 57, Bacau 34, Brasov 68, Bucharest 0, Cluj-Napoca 64, Constanta 41, Craiova 51, Galati 36, Iasi 32, Oradea 59, Pitesti 48, Ploiesti 44, Satu-Mare 61, Sibiu 69, Timisoara 56, Tirgu Mures 65	+7
Russia 7	Magadan 413, Moscow 095, St. Petersburg 812	+8 to +17
Rwanda 250	**	+7
St. Helena 290	**	+5
St. Kitts/Nevis 869*	**	+1
St. Lucia 758*	**	+1
St. Pierre and Miquelon 508	**	+2
St. Vincent and the Grenadines, including Bequia, Mustique, Palm Island, and Union Island 784*	**	+1
San Marino 378	All points 549	+6
São Tomé 239	**	+5
Saudi Arabia 966	Abha 7, Abqaiq 3, Al Khobar 3, Al Markazi 2, Al Ulaya 1, Damman 3, Dhahran (Aramco) 3, Hofuf 3, Jeddah 2, Khamis Mushait 7, Makkah (Mecca) 2, Medina 4, Najran 7, Qatif 3, Riyadh 1, Taif 2, Yenbu 4	+8
Scotland *see* United Kingdom		
Senegal 221	**	+5
Serbia *see* Yugoslavia		
Seychelles 248	**	+9
Sierra Leone 232	Freetown 22, all other points**	+5
Singapore 65	**	+13
Slovak Republic 42	Bratislava 7, Presov 91	+6
Slovenia 386	Ljubljana 61, Maribor 62	+6
Solomon Islands 677	**	+16

(*continued*)

Country and country code (*not necessary to dial 011 when calling from North America*)	Major cities and city codes (**no city codes necessary*)	Time difference in hours from U.S. eastern standard time
South Africa 27	Bloemfontein 51, Cape Town 21, De Aar 571, Durban 31, East London 431, Gordons Bay 24, Johannesburg 11, La Lucia 31, Pietermaritzburg 331, Port Elizabeth 41, Pretoria 12, Sasolburg 16, Somerset West 24, Uitenhage 41, Welkom 57	+7
South Korea *see* Korea, South		
Spain, including Balearic Islands and Canary Islands 34	Barcelona 3, Bilbao 4, Cadiz 56, Ceuta 56, Granada 58, Igualada 3, Las Palmas de Gran Canaria 28, Leon 87, Madrid 1, Malaga 5, Melilla 52, Palma de Mallorca 71, Pamplona 48, Santa Cruz de Tenerife 22, Sandander 42, Seville 5, Torremolinos 52, Valencia 6	+6
Sri Lanka 94	Ambalangoda 97, Colombo Central 1, Galle 9, Havelock Town 1, Kandy 8, Katugastota 8, Kotte 1, Maradana 1, Matara 41, Negombo 31, Panadura 34, Trincomalee 26	+10.5
Suriname 597	**	+2
Swaziland 268	Villaverde de Guadalimar 67, all other points**	+7
Sweden 46	Alingsas 322, Boras 33, Boteborg 31, Eskilstuna 16, Gamleby 493, Helsingborg 42, Karlstad 54, Linkoping 13, Lund 46, Malmo 40, Norrkoping 11, Stockholm 8, Sundsvall 60, Trelleborg 410, Uppsala 18, Vasteras 21	+6
Switzerland 41	Baden 56, Basel 61, Berne 31, Davos 81, Fribourg 37, Geneva 22, Interlaken 36, Lausanne 21, Lucerne 41, Lugano 91, Montreux 21, Neuchatel 38, St. Gallen 71, St. Moritz 82, Winterthur 52, Zurich 1	+6
Syria 963	Aleppo 21, Banias 43, Damascus 11, Deir Ezzor 51, Gableh 491, Halab 21, Hama 33, Hasake 52, Homs 31, Idleb 23, Jebleh 41, Jisr Shogoor 441, Kamishly 53, Kerdaha 492, Kuneitra 141, Lattakia 412, Nebek 12, Rakka 22, Safita 32, Sweida 16, Tartous 43, Yabroud 192, Zabadani 131	+7
Tahiti *see* French Polynesia		

(*continued*)

Country and country code (*not necessary to dial 011 when calling from North America)	Major cities and city codes (**no city codes necessary)	Time difference in hours from U.S. eastern standard time
Taiwan 886	Changhua 4, Chunan 37, Chunghsing-Hsintsun 49, Chungli 3, Fengyuan 4, Hsiaying 6, Hualien 38, Kaohsiung 7, Keelung 2, Lotung 39, Pingtung 8, Taichung 4, Tainan 6, Taipei 2, Taitung 89, Taoyuan 3	+13
Tajikistan 7	Dushanbe 3772	+11
Tanzania 255	Dar Es Salaam 51, Dodoma 61, Mwanza 68, Tanga 53	+8
Thailand 66	Bangkok 2, Burirum 44, Chanthaburi 39, Chiang Mai 53, Chiang Rai 54, Kamphaengphet 55, Lampang 54, Nakhon Sawan 56, Nong Khai 42, Pattani 73, Pattaya 38, Ratchaburi 32, Saraburi 36, Tak 55, Ubon Ratchathani 45	+12
Togo 228	**	+5
Tonga Islands 676	**	+18
Trinidad and Tobago 868*	**	+1
Tunisia 216	Agareb 4, Beja 8, Bizerte 2, Carthage 1, Chebba 4, Gabes 5, Gafsa 6, Haffouz 7, Hamman-Sousse 3, Kairouan 7, Kef 8, Khenis 3, Medenine 5, Tabarka 8, Tozeur 6, Tunis 1	+6
Turkey 90	Adana 322, Ankara 312, Antalya 242, Bursa 224, Eskisehir 222, Gaziantep 851, Istanbul Asya 216, Istnabul Avrupa 212, Izmir 232, Izmit 262, Kayseri, 352, Konya 332, Malatya 422, Samsun 362	+7
Turkmenistan 7	Ashkhabad 3632, Chardzhou 378	+10
Turks and Caicos Islands 649*	**	0
Tuvalu 688	**	+17
Uganda 256	Entebbe 42, Jinja 43, Kampala 41, Kyambogo 41	+8
Ukraine 380	Kharkov 572, Kiev 44, L'viv 322	+7
United Arab Emirates 971	Abu Dhabi 2, Ajman 6, Al Ain 3, Aweer 58, Dhayd 6, Dibba 9, Dubai 4, Falaj-al-Moalla 6, Fujairah 9, Khawanij 487, Ras-al-Khaimah 7, Sharjah 6, Tarif 88, Umm-al-Qaiwain 6	+9
United Kingdom, including the Channel Islands, England, Isle of Man, Northern Ireland, Scotland, and Wales 44	Belfast 1232, Birmingham 121, Bournemouth 1202, Cardiff 1222, Durham 191, Edinburgh 131, Glasgow 141, Gloucester 1452, Ipswich 1473, Liverpool 151, London (inner) 171, London (outer) 181, Manchester 161, Nottingham 115, Prestwick 1292, Sheffield 114, Southampton 1703	+5

(continued)

Country and country code (*not necessary to dial 011 when calling from North America)	Major cities and city codes (**no city codes necessary)	Time difference in hours from U.S. eastern standard time
Uruguay 598	Canelones 32, Florida 352, Las Piedras 324, Maldonado 42, Mercedes 532, Minas 442, Montevideo 2, Paysandu 722, Punta Del Este 42, San Jose 342, San Jose De Carrasco 38	+2
U.S. Virgin Islands 340*	**	+1
Uzbekistan 7	Karshi 375, Samarkand 3662, Tashkent 3712	+10
Vanuatu 678	**	+16
Vatican City 6, 39		+6
Venezuela 58	Barcelona 81, Barquisimeto 51, Cabimas 64, Caracas 2, Ciudad Bolivar 85, Coro 68, Cumana 93, Los Teques 32, Maiquetia 31, Maracaibo 61, Maracay 43, Maturin 91, Merida 74, Puerto Cabello 42, San Cristobal 76, Valencia 41	+1
Vietnam 84	Hanoi 4, Ho Chi Minh City 8	+12
Virgin Islands, British 284*	**	+1
Virgin Islands, U.S. 340*	**	+1
Wales *see* United Kingdom		
Wallis and Futuna Islands 681	**	+17
Western Samoa 685	**	−6
Yemen 967	Aden 2, Almahrah 5, Amran 7, Sana'a 1, Taiz 4, Yarim 4, Zabid 3	+8
Yukon and Northwest Territories *see* Canada		
Zaire 243	Kinshasa 12, Lubumbashi 2	+7
Zambia 260	Chingola 2, Kitwe 2, Luanshya 2, Lusaka 1, Ndola 2	+7
Zimbabwe 263	Bulawayo 9, Harare 4, Mutare 20	+7

Teleconferencing

The cost of a teleconference call is usually less than the expense of getting several people from different cities into the same room for a meeting. Most telephone systems have teleconferencing capabilities (*see* Speakerphones/Teleconferencing, page 165), or teleconferences can be arranged through an operator—check the telephone directory for instructions. Charges vary according to number of telephones connected, distances involved, and conference length.

Schedule and confirm a teleconference just as you would a meeting. Remember to take time differences into account. Make sure all participants have an agenda for the meeting, which is faxed or mailed in advance. It is usually best for one person to chair the teleconference, keeping the discussion focused and making sure that everyone has a chance to talk.

Voice Mail, Answering Machines, and Answering Services

Most businesspeople have a system for taking messages when they are away from their phones. Remember that callers form an impression of you and your company from the tone and efficiency of your message system, just as they do when someone actually answers the phone.

Voice Mail. Many office telephone systems have voice mail capabilities, and local telephone companies also offer this service. One advantage of this service is that you do not need to worry about equipment breakdown because messages are handled via computer (*see* Voice Mail Options, page 169); mail can be checked and outgoing messages changed from any Touch-Tone phone.

Answering Machines. These are still used by many small firms and home-based businesses. Equipment reliability is the most important factor to consider, so buy a good-quality machine. Important features include message pickup from remote locations and variable number of rings before the machine answers. Record a brief, professional message. Write it down first and record it once or twice for practice so you can review it for needed improvements. As when answering the phone in person, keep your answering machine's automated response brief and pleasant.

Answering Services. An answering service is a message center at a location other than your office. Make sure the one you choose has courteous, professional operators who identify you and your firm when answering. (Place calls to your own number occasionally to evaluate the service.) Always leave a number where you can be reached in case of emergency, and remember to notify the service each time you leave the office. You can call an answering service from any location to retrieve messages.

PROFESSIONAL VOICE MAIL MESSAGES

Whether you use an answering machine or voice mail, the content and quality of your message to callers says volumes about you and your business. Answer every call pleasantly and in a professional manner—remember that the caller may be a customer or an important business contact. When a machine answers the phone, its message should be even more positive, if possible, because the caller will be disappointed that the person called is not available.

Messages should reflect the general level of formality that is usual for a business. Examples of typical voice mail messages follow:

- *In a large corporate law firm*—"Jones, Smith, & Green Legal Offices. This is Jane Absher. I cannot take your call at this time, so please leave your name, number, and a brief message. I will return your call as soon as possible."
- *In a public relations firm known for its humorous ad campaigns*—"Hi, this is Roxanne Draper. Sorry I can't answer your call—I'm talking to

Oprah about one of my clients. Please leave your number, and I'll get back with you."

- *In a small, home-based business*—"Cathy's Catering Service. I'm sorry that I can't take your call at the moment, but I'll return it as soon as possible. Please leave your name, number, and a brief message after the tone."
- *In a small, home-based business without a separate business telephone line*—"This is the Eldridge residence, home of Cathy's Catering Service. Please leave your name, number, and a brief message, and we'll return your call."

Sometimes it is necessary to include more lengthy information in a voice mail or answering machine message:

- "This is John Parrish. I will be out of the office until Monday, November 1st. Please call my associate, Georgia Kaplan, at (314) 686-8043 if you need immediate assistance, or leave me a message and I'll contact you when I return."
- "You have reached the Sanders & Knowles Publishing Group. Our new offices are located at 416 Avalon Place, Baton Rouge, Louisiana 70808. We are in the office from 9 to 6, Monday through Friday. Please leave your name, number, and a brief message, and we will return your call during office hours."

Record the message several times and listen to it critically. Be sure that you do not speak too quickly, and that the words are clear. Ask an associate to critique it, too, and re-record it until you are satisfied that it gives a positive impression of you and your business.

Sources of Further Information

Organizations

The Grammar Hotline answers questions about punctuation, spelling, writing, and grammar. Send a stamped, self-addressed envelope to Tidewater Community College Writing Center, 1700 College Crescent, Virginia Beach, VA 23456, for a list of Grammar Hotline numbers.

Books and Literature

Bower, Sharon Anthony. *Painless Public Speaking.* New York: Prentice-Hall, Inc., 1981.

The Chicago Manual of Style, Fourteenth Edition. Chicago: University of Chicago Press, 1993.

The Complete Book of Contemporary Business Letters. Ridgefield, CT: Round Lake Publishing Co., 1996.

Jeffries, James, and Jefferson Bates. *The Executive's Guide to Meetings and Conferences.* New York: McGraw-Hill, 1989.

Langhoff, June. *Telecom Made Easy: Money-Saving Profit-Building Solutions for Home Businesses, Telecommuters and Small Organizations.* Newport, RI: Aegis Publishing Group, 1995.

Maggio, Rosalie. *How to Say It: Choice Words, Phrases, Sentences, and Paragraphs for Every Situation.* Englewood Cliffs, NJ: Prentice Hall, 1990.

Merriam-Webster's Collegiate Dictionary, Tenth Edition. Springfield, MA: Merriam-Webster, Inc., 1993.

Meuse, Leonard F., Jr. *Succeeding at Business and Technical Presentation.* New York: John Wiley & Sons, 1990.

The New York Public Library Writer's Guide to Style and Usage. New York: HarperCollins, 1994.

Seekings, David. *How to Organize Effective Conferences and Meetings.* New York: Nichols Publishing, 1989.

Shertzer, Margaret. *The Elements of Grammar.* New York: Collier Books/Macmillan Publishing Co., 1986.

Strunk, William, Jr., and E. B. White. *The Elements of Style.* 3rd ed. New York: Macmillan Publishing Co., 1979.

On-Line Resources

Local and long-distance carriers:
Ameritech *http://www.ameritech.com*
AT&T *http://www.att.com*
Bell Atlantic *http://www.bell-atl.com*
Bell South *http://www.bellsouth.com*
MCI *http://www.mci.com*
Nynex *http://www.nynex.com*
Pacific Telesis *http://www.pacbell.com*
Southwestern Bell *http://www.sbc.com*
Sprint *http://www.sprintlink.net*
U.S. West *http://www.uswest.com*

The Broadband Telephony Buyer's Guide *http://www.indra.com/unicom*

Telephone directories:
AT&T's Toll-Free Directory *http://www.tollfree.attnet/dir800*
AT&T's white pages, yellow pages, domestic and international listings *http://www.att.com/directory* or *http://www.555-1212.com*
Bell Communications' North American Numbering Plan for area code changes, lists, and information *http://www.bellcore.com/NANP*
Four11 Corporation's worldwide listings of telephone numbers, fax numbers, and E-mail addresses *http://www.411.com*

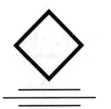

3

The Office
Environment

Office Design and Planning

Optimizing the Work Space for Productivity

To make the most of your office space, look at all aspects of the work environment as a whole. Furniture, equipment, communication systems, architecture, heating, lighting, and employees should all play important roles in the organization of your office. Consider the following:

- Efficiency—Place copy machines, file cabinets, fax machines, and computer stations nearest those who use them most. Group employee desks and offices so that those who work together are close to each other. Poor arrangement of workers and materials leads to excessive traffic and wasted time.
- Safety—Make sure walkways are clear and workers have enough room to move without knocking into furniture, equipment, or each other (*see* Accident Prevention, page 110). A cluttered or improperly designed office could be dangerous.
- Comfort—Avoid crowding too many employees into one space. Give workers enough personal space to operate. Comfortable office furniture is also very important in promoting a healthy work environment (*see* Avoiding Work-Related Injuries and Illnesses, page 112). Environmental factors such as temperature, noise, and lighting can have profound effects on productivity and should be carefully regulated. Try to put noisy equipment where it will not disturb workers, and make sure unshaded windows do not create too much light or heat. Keep in mind employees' proximity and convenient access to restrooms and the lounge.
- Attractiveness—Create a bright and friendly work space to raise worker morale. Artwork, plants, and an aesthetically pleasing layout may help business, too, if customers and associates visit.
- Space efficiency—Remember the importance of adequate space for each employee, but try to use the entire office space without wasted room. To maximize floor space, use walls sparingly, group desks together, and install shelves above desks instead of using freestanding units. Eliminate the clutter of old files and books by storing all records and materials not essential to daily operations. Fill corners and other empty spaces with plants or recycling boxes.
- Special needs of employees with disabilities—Many disabled people have the appropriate skills, experience, training, and/or education to perform essential job functions with some type of accommodation such as a voice-activated computer or customized work space. In businesses with 15 or more employees, the Americans with Disabilities Act (ADA) protects qualified job applicants and employees with physical disorders such as cosmetic disfigurement or loss of limb (as well as those with mental and psychological disorders) from discrimination based solely on their disabilities. The ADA also details the accommodations that businesses with 15 or more employees must make for disabled employees when they move into new facilities or renovate their existing space. Although there are many exceptions to the overall need to make office space accessible to the handicapped,

anyone who is considering a move or a renovation should get expert advice on the mandates of the act. Whether or not an office has disabled employees at present, it is wise to design the workplace so that special accommodations can be added easily when necessary. Wheelchair-accessible restrooms, hallways, doorways, and entrances should be included, as handicapped clients will appreciate these amenities, too. (To contact the U.S. Department of Justice for more information about the ADA, *see* Sources of Further Information, Office Planning, page 127.)

Attractive plants can enhance the office atmosphere, but they do require a certain amount of care and expertise to keep them healthy. If greenery is an important part of the decor, consider hiring a service to provide the plants and maintain them. This eliminates the possibility of wasting money on expensive flora only to see it wither and die, or adding plant care to an overburdened employee's chores. Of course, many workers enjoy bringing small plants for their own work spaces and should be encouraged to do so.

CHANGES IN OFFICE-PLANNING ASSUMPTIONS

With the advent of personal computers and the increase in white-collar occupations, workplaces have changed. More people work together in teams, using shared facilities and fewer individual pieces of furniture. Groups of employees work together in meeting rooms, conference areas, or even cafeterias. The emphasis has changed from exclusive space (for important members of the hierarchy) to shared space, and from a single work space for each worker to multiple work spaces for groups or teams. Pleasant settings are viewed as tools to increase productivity, not as privileges reserved for top-level executives.

Employees must be flexible in their response to changing business demands. This may mean that individuals or groups will need to move from one place to another. Moves are easier to handle by moving people only, rather than people and furniture. Such moves require establishing universal workstations, with adjustable work surfaces, seating, and cable support.

Ironically, as dependence on office technology increases, individual space decreases, although employees often need more space for their equipment than they did in the past. This requires resourcefulness on the part of space planners, who must identify cost-effective ways of maximizing space while maintaining employee comfort.

Open Office Plans

Because of their efficiency, open plans are commonly found in today's large offices. Thin, movable partitions are used to separate workstations, as opposed to the wall-enclosed offices of closed plans. Open plans save space, are less expensive to install and maintain, and easy to rearrange. They also make supervising workers easier and create an appearance of order and worker democracy. Critics of open offices say they do not offer sufficient privacy for staff, who are unable to control outside noise, distractions, temperature, and overhead lighting. In addition, employee morale may suffer if rows of identical, windowless cubicles are included. Despite their shortcomings, plans that are at least partially open (for example, with workstations in the center and closed executive offices on the periphery) are a practical necessity in many offices today.

Worker-Designed Offices

Asking for workers' input on office design is a positive and effective gesture on the part of management. It makes good business sense—after all, who knows better what works in an office than the people who work there? Employees will also appreciate an employer's concern for their opinions. Staff can be asked to make suggestions on office layout and be allowed to choose their own chairs and desks. With increased worker satisfaction and efficiency, worker-designed offices are sure to improve productivity.

Office Sizes

In the past, office sizes were easy to determine: division vice presidents had large corner offices, CEOs were housed in grand suites on the top floor, and humbler workers had desks or cubicles in a central area. To a certain extent, office size and position are still determined by a worker's position in the company hierarchy. However, the new emphasis on cross-functional teamwork and employee communication is beginning to produce changes in this area.

For example, private offices once averaged 12 by 14 feet (168 square feet); now a private office is more likely to be 10 by 12 feet (120 square feet). Some of the space eliminated from private offices is used to enlarge communal spaces such as supply and storage areas, conference rooms, and dining/employee lounge areas. The remaining space has disappeared completely, as the overall square footage of offices has dropped by as much as 25 percent due to corporate downsizing. Similarly, open cubicles have gotten smaller. Workstations were once 70 to 80 square feet in size, but now average only 60 to 70 square feet.

This decrease in office size relates to two factors. Real estate has become very expensive, so resources must be allocated more efficiently. And managers realize that larger offices are not necessarily more productive ones. However, offices cannot get much smaller or there will be no room for people to work in them. Use these guidelines to plan enough space for all employees to work efficiently:

- A work area at least 27 inches wide and 14 inches deep is necessary for each worker. (This does not include the space required for equipment such as computers, printers, and fax machines.) Most desks are 60 to 72 inches long and 30 inches deep, which should provide an adequate amount of work space.
- A desk chair requires 36 inches of space behind it for room to pull it out and sit down.

- A minimum space of 24 inches is needed for workers to pass behind or between pieces of furniture.
- A seated person takes up about 20 inches with the chair pulled up to the desk.
- U-shaped and L-shaped work spaces are most efficient. A compact L-shaped arrangement occupies about 5 feet along one wall and 6 feet in the other direction.

COMPUTERS THAT ENHANCE OFFICE DECOR

Just as colorful IBM Selectric typewriters made a hit in the 1970s, desktop computers in interesting shapes and hues may soon be available for business and home use. Smaller components and attractive furniture are already making the cold gray computer setup a thing of the past, and many future hardware offerings will be designed as much for attractiveness as functionality. In fact, Sony's purple-and-gray personal computer may be on the market any day. Look for other companies to follow with systems in rainbow colors.

Using a Floor Plan to Design an Office Space

Depending on the size, shape, and furniture requirements of your office space, you may decide to save the expense of hiring an interior design firm and create a floor plan on your own. Begin by studying the office space closely. Determine how much space each worker and all office machines will need. Also decide whether you will have an open plan, walled offices, or a combination of both; then determine which employees will have private offices and where walls must be erected. Remember to ask for input from workers who will use the space.

Once you have a basic structural layout, the easiest way to design an office floor plan is to start with a scale model. If you have access to building blueprints, use them, or make your own scale drawing. Use your computer to create a professional-looking floor plan (*see* Presentation and Graphics Programs, page 153), or draw one by hand as described below.

First, measure all wall dimensions of the office space with a tape measure. Measure irregularly shaped rooms carefully, as accuracy is important. Next, use standard grid paper (with ¼-inch boxes), a pencil, and a ruler to draw the dimensions of the room on a scale of 1 foot to ¼ inch. Each grid box will then correspond to one square foot of office space. Be sure to include all doors, closets, windows (noting height as well as width), recesses, and any other features built into the space. When you finish, make several copies of the drawing to use in designing the floor plan.

On a thicker sheet of grid paper, using the same 1-foot-to-¼ inch scale, draw the outlines (overhead view) of all furniture and equipment that the office will contain. Include desks, tables, bookcases, large plants, and freestanding office equipment such as copiers and water coolers. It is important to estimate furniture size correctly, so you may wish to use the following standard furniture dimensions for accuracy.

Desks and case goods	Dimensions in inches (width × depth × height unless otherwise noted)
Double pedestal desk, one or two box drawers and one file drawer in each pedestal	72 × 36 × 29–30 with conference overhang on all four sides; 60 × 30 × 30 without overhang
Single pedestal desk, two drawers in pedestal	72 × 36 × 29–30
Storage credenza, two drawers on each side, central storage area with doors and shelf	72 × 24 × 29–30
Kneespace credenza, two box drawers and two file drawers	72 × 21 × 29
Overhead storage unit	72 × 15 × 36
Lateral file, two drawers	36 × 20–21 × 29–29½
Bookcase, three shelves	36 × 14 × 48–51
Bookcase, five shelves	36 × 15 × 76
Typing return	48 × 24 × 27
Bridge return	48 × 24 × 29–30

Computer furniture	Dimensions in inches (width × depth × height unless otherwise noted)
Computer desk with adjustable keyboard platform (desk only; hutch dimensions are given separately, below)	60 × 30 × 29½ (keyboard height adjusts from 22¾–29½)
Hutch (mounts on work surface such as a computer desk)	56 × 15 × 32
Task desk	48 or 60 × 30 × 29½
Adjustable height workstation	36, 48, or 60 × 30 × 22–29
Mobile computer table	45 × 24 × 26½
Printer stand	30 × 24 × 26½

Modular components and panels	Dimensions in inches (width × depth × height unless otherwise noted)
Workstation	48 or 60 × 28 × 30
Corner workstation (L configuration)	65 × 39 × 30
Ninety-degree corner connector	28 × 28 × 30
Mobile file pedestal	15½ × 22 × 28
Privacy panel (to be mounted on workstation)	20–23 × 30, 36, 48, 60, 66, 72, or 80 (height × width)
Office panel (straight screen panel)	42 × 30, 48, or 60 (height × width)
	60 × 30, 36, 48, 60, or 72 (height × width)
	72 × 36, 48, or 60 (height × width)
Work surface	36 × 24 (width × depth)
	48 × 24 (width × depth)
	60 × 24 (width × depth)
	60 × 30 (width × depth)
	72 × 30 (width × depth)
Hanging file storage	16½ × 18 × 18½
Adjustable keyboard drawer	23 × 12 × 4
Overhead cabinet	36, 48, or 60 × 13 × 13
Corner table (connects two work surfaces)	48 × 24 × 30
Overhead open shelving	36, 48, or 60 × 12 × 12
Counter top	30, 36, 48, or 60 × 12 (width × depth)
Peninsula work surface	72 × 30 × 30
Mobile pedestal file	16½ × 18½ × 28¾

When you have drawn scale replicas of all furniture to be placed in the office, carefully cut out these shapes and lay them on a copy of the office layout. Arrange furniture and equipment to make the best use of space. When you arrive at a possible floor plan, trace the cutout shapes onto the office layout (Figure 3.1). If you wish to experiment with other floor plans, use the extra copies of the layout to do so. When you have created a number of possible floor plans, decide which one is best and use it to install the furniture and equipment.

Lighting the Office

Lighting is perhaps the most important environmental consideration in an office—after all, very little work is done in the dark. It affects all other environmental factors such as heating, energy, design, and acoustics. And, because lighting is relatively inexpensive (in comparison to heating and cooling, for example), high-quality lights are a cost-effective investment that will improve the work atmosphere markedly. There are several considerations to keep in mind when designing an office lighting system:

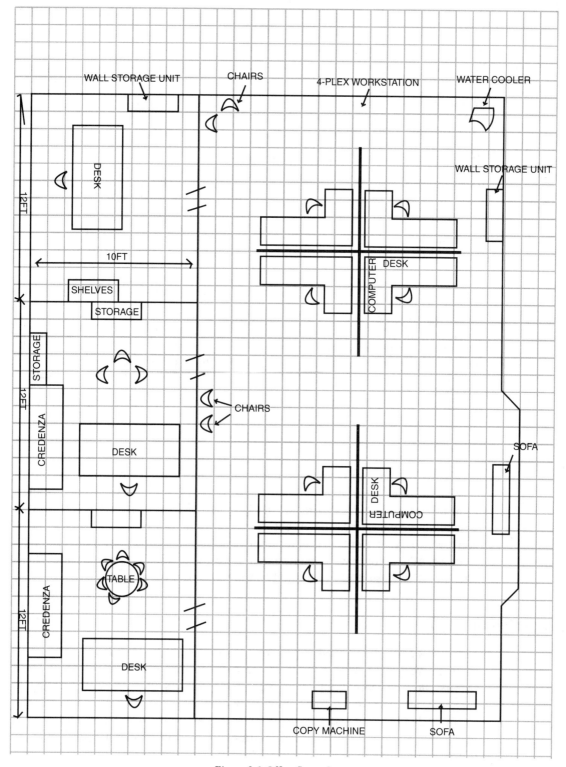

Figure 3.1 Office floor plan

- Natural and artificial light—The best working environments combine electrical lighting with natural light (sunlight). A well-designed office will feature windows or skylights to use natural light and minimize glare. Although artificial lighting is sufficient in most offices, research is proving that natural light benefits health, mood, and general well being.
- Direct and indirect light—Properly lit offices will also feature a combination of direct and indirect light. Direct lighting provides workers with most of the light needed to do specific tasks (hence the term *task lighting* for desk lamps and other direct light sources). Indirect light or *ambient light,* such as shaded room lamps or diffused ceiling lights, provides general comfort light that is shadow-free.
- Adjustable lighting—Office lighting, particularly task lighting, should be adjustable so workers can regulate the direction and intensity of the light, as the type and amount of light needed depends on the job at hand. In addition, ambient lighting that adjusts to varying amounts of natural outside light in the office can be cost- and work-efficient. Sensors that adjust light automatically are available.
- Brightness—Increased brightness enhances productivity, but too bright lights can hurt the eyes. General recommendations for the light required in office work, given in *foot-candles* (a measurement of the amount of illumination on a surface), follow:

Reading: 20–200 foot-candles (fc), depending on the print size and decipherability of material to be read
Computer work: 15–40fc
Drafting and design desks: 50–200fc, depending on the material being used
Conference rooms: 20–50fc
Copy room: 20–50fc
Mail room: 50–150fc
Stairs, halls, and elevators: 5–15fc

- Glare—To avoid glare, arrange lighting so that it stays out of the direct line of vision. Do this by shielding lights, shading windows, and using low-reflective work surfaces. Avoid direct overhead lighting as well.
- Fluorescent lighting—Fluorescent lights are common in offices due to their energy efficiency, low cost, and low levels of heat emission, but many people are not enthusiastic about them because of claims (largely unsubstantiated) that fluorescent bulbs cause rashes or skin cancer. Others find fluorescent lights cold and complain that their flicker and hum are annoying and distracting. Nevertheless, the continued popularity of fluorescent lighting seems to indicate that its benefits outweigh its shortcomings.
- Quality and color—Light quality can be as important as quantity. It should be *full-spectrum* (containing the full range of colors and near-ultraviolet rays) to imitate the nourishing properties of sunlight. Too much time spent in *deprived-spectrum* light may cause fatigue or depression. Light color also affects the appearance of the entire environment. Good office lighting flatters skin tones and enhances office decor.

It may be easiest to use a simple list of the major pros and cons associated with different types of lighting, as follows:

Type of light	Advantages	Disadvantages
Tungsten—warm, yellowish light (traditional incandescent light bulbs)	Widely available; inexpensive	Needs frequent replacement; generates excessive heat; uses energy inefficiently
Halogen—cool, crisp light	Whiter and brighter than tungsten, with a sparkling quality; good for display areas and decorative lighting	Expensive; some types require a transformer; these generate heat and need UV filters
Fluorescent	Uses the least amount of energy; inexpensive	Can alter appearance of colors and make surroundings seem dull; sometimes flickers; often makes humming noises

ENERGY-EFFICIENT LIGHTING

There are several ways to achieve energy efficiency in office lighting. One is to install energy-efficient fixtures, bulbs, or tubes throughout the office. Initially, new fixtures may cost more than standard ones, but will soon pay for themselves in reduced costs. Even standard overhead trough lighting, with fluorescent tubes and plastic baffles or lenses, can be made more efficient if narrower tubes and better ballasts are installed. (Ballasts convert incoming current into the range used by fluorescents.)

Maintenance is an important factor in efficient lighting. Dirty, dusty lenses and bulbs cut down significantly on the illumination provided by fixtures. Simple, regular cleaning is essential. Experts at General Electric recommend cleaning bulbs and tubes at least once per year. Plastic lenses should be wiped with a damp cloth. Louver panels or baffles should be removed and dipped into a detergent solution, then allowed to dry before being replaced. (Never wipe a lighting fixture with a damp cloth while the fixture is energized.)

Timely bulb and tube replacement is also important to maintaining an efficient office lighting system. Replace all bulbs and tubes on a set schedule, rather than one by one as they burn out. This reduces labor costs for replacement and eliminates the need for inventory of replacement bulbs or tubes.

Moving with a Minimum of Headaches

Finding the Right Moving Company

The best way to find a dependable moving company is through professional referral. Ask friends and business associates who have moved recently to recommend movers;

then call several promising companies. Explain your moving needs and give dates. Make a separate appointment to meet with a representative from each firm, showing each your office and the new location so he or she can see exactly what will be involved in the move. Provide each company with a detailed, written explanation of your requirements, including the number of trained moving supervisors you expect to be present and the duration of lunch breaks for their workers. Ask each firm to submit a proposal outlining a moving plan and its cost, with a reference list of businesses the firm has moved recently. Indicate a reasonable deadline for their proposals.

Evaluate proposals to decide which company will best get the job done to your satisfaction. Use an objective system, such as a checklist or graded evaluation sheet, to judge which mover best meets your needs. Rate each firm's proposed strategy, schedule, equipment, workforce, guarantee against damage, experience/reputation, and price, by asking these questions:

1. What is the proposed strategy or plan? (That is, how would each company approach the move?) What steps will be taken to ensure that all furniture and materials are moved to the correct floors and offices? How will tasks be organized?

2. How does each firm's proposed schedule (dates and hours) suit your needs? Will movers work at night, on a weekend, or stay after hours to finish the move, if necessary, at no additional cost? Does the time schedule conflict as little as possible with normal office work?

3. What tools and transportation would each company use? Are they effective and reliable?

4. Will enough workers be used to get the job done? Are they properly trained and supervised?

5. What precautions does the company take to protect office furniture, equipment, and facilities from damage? What guarantees and insurance are provided?

6. Can you trust the company to do a good job? How have they performed in the past?

7. Is the price reasonable? Does it include everything, including supplies? Is it guaranteed not to exceed a certain amount?

When you have narrowed the choice to one or two firms, check their references and call the Better Business Bureau to see if any complaints have been filed against them. Then tour their offices. Are they clean, efficient, and well organized? Does their equipment (dollies, trucks, etc.) appear to be in good shape? Do you feel comfortable with their organization and their attitude?

After making a decision on hiring a mover, accept that company's proposal, in writing, and get a contract that lists all dates, agreements, and arrangements. Read it carefully and have your attorney review it as well. Write to the companies you did not choose and thank them for submitting their proposals.

How a Realtor Can Help

A commercial real estate agent can be very helpful in finding new office space. The realtor will work with you to determine your location, space, and facility needs, then find available offices for your consideration. Appointments with property owners and managers will be made. The agent will act as a liaison with them in getting questions answered and requirements met. Finally, the realtor will help negotiate a lease to the satisfaction of both parties.

Use professional referrals to find real estate agents, or look in the yellow pages. Realtors' contingency-based fees may seem large, as they are usually a percentage of your new office's yearly rent. However, a good agent may save your firm money in the long run by finding office space that meets present and future needs.

Organizing, Packing, and Helping Employees Settle In

Moving workers to a new office can be relatively painless if the move is properly organized. Make sure office employees understand all moving procedures and what will be expected of them. Provide complete instructions that explain packing, labeling, and the schedule of moving activities.

Labeling. The foundation of a successful move is the labeling system. All furniture, equipment, and packed boxes should be labeled to show whose items are inside and to which floor and office they should be delivered. Develop a standard system for labeling that all workers use and understand. This will keep the move orderly and make the transition into new space as smooth as possible.

Before the Move. About two weeks before moving day, have employees clean out their desks, cabinets, and shelves, disposing of any unnecessary materials. During the week before moving day, they should begin packing. Have them take home all personal items, such as pictures and decorations, for safekeeping until after the move. All nonessential files, supplies, and equipment should be packed in boxes to be moved prior to the actual moving day. Cartons should be packed securely and clearly labeled. Employees should also keep an inventory of the contents of each box. Once emptied, desk drawers and cabinets should be locked, with keys taped to the furniture or stored in a safe place.

On Moving Day. Any essential files and equipment left unpacked should be packed on moving day. Follow the packing and labeling procedures already established.

After the Move. Arrange to have a small staff of movers around the office for a day or two following the move to relocate equipment and furniture if necessary. Employees may bring their personal items back to the office, set up their equipment, and restock desks and cabinets. The most important materials should be unpacked first, with inventory checks to ensure that everything has arrived safely. As boxes are emptied, they should be collapsed and stacked in a central location for cleanup. Have the moving company collect boxes and trash after all materials have been unpacked and arranged.

A WORD ABOUT STORAGE

It is always a good idea to move nonessential materials, such as old files and records, to safekeeping in storage. Storage space usually costs less per square foot than office space, so cleaning out the office while packing to move will help you make the most efficient use of your new space. Make sure the storage space is safe (well guarded, locked, and fireproof), accessible (open 24 hours a day), and convenient (located near the office). Check the yellow pages to find storage facilities near you, and inspect the space before signing a rental agreement.

How to Move and Avoid a Temporary Business Shutdown

Some business owners find it impossible to move without shutting down operations for at least a day or two. Good planning and organization will minimize lost business time, but a work interruption can be avoided in many cases. Work stoppages are costly and may affect the rhythm of an efficiently run organization for some time to come. If possible, schedule the move for the slowest part of the week, in the slowest week of the month, during the slowest month of the year. Consider moving one part of the business at a time, if that will allow operations to continue.

Plan moving activities to reduce any inconvenience to your clients or customers. Complete large projects or deliveries before the move is scheduled. Notify customers and suppliers as far in advance as possible, then move quickly when the time comes. Also, consider your staff. When is the best time to move the most essential workers? Plan around those who affect the largest part of operations, but keep all employees informed of moving plans and schedules. Everyone will appreciate being told what to expect, and miscommunications affecting business may be avoided.

Office Safety and Health

Fire: Are You Prepared?

Is your office prepared to handle a fire? The local fire department can help institute a complete fire safety program in your office. They will check on compliance with local fire codes, which cover everything from building construction materials and fire exits to emergency communication systems and maximum room occupancy. In addition, the Occupational Safety and Health Administration (OSHA) sets regulations to ensure that workers are properly protected. Begin evaluating fire-readiness by making sure your business is equipped with fire extinguishers, smoke detectors, fire alarms, and automatic sprinklers or other fire suppression devices.

1. Fire extinguishers must be stationed within 75 feet of all workers, and in any area especially susceptible to fire (such as a workshop where flammable chemicals arc used). Keep extinguishers in good working condition and have them inspected

regularly. All employees should know how to use them—make training and regular reinforcement a part of your fire safety program.

2. Smoke detectors must be placed throughout the office. Because most fires do not begin in main work areas, it is not sufficient to put them only in the busiest parts of the office. Also install them in seldom visited areas such as ventilation systems and remote storage closets.

3. Automatic fire alarms should be connected directly to the local fire station. Like smoke detectors, they should be placed in remote areas as well as heavily trafficked zones. Alarms must be loud enough for workers to hear throughout the office, with a distinct sound that is easily recognized. Manual fire alarms should also be accessible to all workers.

4. A sprinkler system or other fire suppression system is usually mandatory in all commercial buildings. The size and type required depends on office size and use, and will probably be specified in the local fire code. Sprinklers should be installed in the ceiling (or above a false ceiling). Fire suppression systems begin automatically, so signs should be posted to warn workers of the danger if hazardous substances are emitted when they are operating.

Fire Prevention

In addition to proper emergency equipment, any office fully protected from fire will have a complete fire prevention plan. Make available to all workers a detailed, written plan that covers every aspect of fire safety, including information about office dangers, operating and cleanup procedures for hazardous areas, and employee smoking regulations. Fire prevention also includes using safe materials in the office. Buy flame-resistant furniture and supplies—ask for a manufacturer's affidavit. Keep excess paper and other highly flammable materials to a minimum, and store these in fire-resistant cabinets. Plastics, which give off toxic fumes when burning, should be kept to a minimum as well (for example, use metal wastepaper baskets).

Interested and reliable workers may be designated as fire wardens, to take responsibility for keeping the total fire safety plan in order. Fire wardens should check fire extinguishers, alarms, sprinklers, exits, and emergency lights at least weekly. They also play an important role in orchestrating the office's evacuation plan in case of an actual fire.

Emergency Evacuation Planning

Although a good fire prevention program lessens the likelihood of an office fire, it still makes sense to plan for the worst. A detailed evacuation plan should be included in the employee handbook. Maps of the evacuation route should be posted at all fire exits, and quarterly fire drills should be held. Plan an evacuation route that directs workers to properly marked fire exits for the quickest and safest escape. Keep fire exits unlocked and clear of debris at all times. Elevators should not be used to escape a fire—they will be grounded on the first floor. Coordinate the evacuation routes for each floor of a building to avoid overcrowding in stairwells or halls.

If an evacuation becomes necessary, communication is of the utmost importance. The people least informed are most likely to panic during an emergency. Use a loudspeaker to communicate important information to workers. Fire wardens on each floor should lead the evacuation by maintaining order and directing people to proper fire exits. They are also in charge of handling any emergency equipment that is needed, although workers should not attempt to fight a fire unless it is necessary in order to evacuate safely. Before leaving the building, wardens or other previously appointed searchers should check lounges, bathrooms, and offices to make sure everyone has evacuated. Wardens also provide assistance to people with disabilities.

For more information on creating a complete emergency evacuation plan, contact your local fire department. (*See also* Sources of Further Information, Fire Safety, page 124.)

Security: *Preventing On-Site Theft and Other Crimes*

There are many ways to protect your business from crime. You can choose an alarm system, security guards, a surveillance system, two-way mirrors, unbreakable glass, I.D. cards, access cards, lights, locks, buzzers, or a combination of these. To decide which security measures are appropriate for your firm, the most important factors to consider are the types of equipment and property to be protected, and the crimes to which your office is most vulnerable.

What do you want to protect? Do you have expensive machinery and equipment at risk of theft? Does your company store sensitive information such as trade secrets? Does the office contain product inventory that could be stolen? In addition, keep in mind that security measures are not just for the protection of financial interests, but also to ensure the safety of workers. Consider the security concerns of employees a priority. Is your office vulnerable to burglary, customer theft, arson, computer sabotage, employee theft, or crimes such as rape, robbery, and assault? Is there any reason to think your office might be targeted for a bombing, kidnapping, or other terrorist threat? The type of security you choose should address all possibilities for on-site crime.

Despite the importance of office security, turning your office into a fortress can be self-defeating. Employees should not feel as though they are under suspicion. Security measures may cause resentment if they are perceived as evidence of management's distrust of staff. On the other hand, a lax attitude toward office crime will encourage workers (and others) to take advantage of the company. Take reasonable steps to ensure safety, but avoid paranoia.

Conferring with local police may be a good place to begin the development of a good office crime prevention strategy. At your request, officers will inspect the premises and suggest appropriate security measures. With their help, you can examine every aspect of your office, from company procedures to building architecture, in order to determine where security weaknesses may invite crime.

Here are some basic security principles to consider:

- A security alarm system to protect the office during off-hours may be necessary. Even if you decide against this, post alarm signs on doors and windows claiming that you do have such a system in place. This kind of empty warning may be enough to deter potential burglars.
- The best defense against theft is a secure office building. Doors and windows should be locked and unbreakable, particularly on the ground floor. Also, make sure a burglar cannot easily climb an outside wall to find an easier entrance on an upper floor or the roof.
- Security guards can be very effective in deterring crime. Remember, though, that one token guard cannot be held responsible for an entire building, particularly if proper surveillance equipment is not present.
- Opportunities for crime can be reduced by limiting access to the office. If necessary, require workers to carry I.D. or access cards, have all visitors sign in, and limit access to security-sensitive areas. Establish a system to ensure that the security manager knows who has office keys, who knows the office security code, and who is arriving early or staying late.

Hiring a Security Company

As concern over crime rises, the security industry is expanding to meet the demand for protection. But as more good security companies appear, unqualified agencies increase as well. Some larger businesses handle their own security by directly employing security guards. This alternative gives companies greater control over security arrangements, but also costs more than hiring a security company. Investigate the options closely, just as you would when buying any other product or service.

- Find out as much as possible about how the security company operates. What are the strategies and procedures used to deter crime? How does the company train guards and other employees? How organized does it appear? Are representatives open to discussing these issues?
- Ask the company to provide references from other clients. Call those businesses to inquire about the strengths and weaknesses of the security operation and their level of satisfaction with the firm's services.
- Call the Better Business Bureau or another consumer organization to see if the company has any complaints or litigation against it on file.
- Ask about their insurance coverage and workers' compensation history.
- Inquire about their applicant-screening process. Are the police, work, and driving records of prospective security guards checked? Are drug tests performed? Some states do not have licensing requirements for guards, so make sure the company checks applicants thoroughly. Clearly, it would defeat the purpose to entrust your facility to a guard with a criminal record.
- Visit a site the security company protects without giving them advance notice. Watch the guards—do they appear professional and well trained? Are they polite

to workers and visitors? Do they seem able to recognize a suspicious situation and handle it effectively? Are they properly equipped and adequately staffed?

• Compare a variety of prices and services to find the most cost-effective company, although money should not be the determining factor in your decision.

The close examination of your security company should not end once it is hired. A member of your staff should be appointed to supervise and coordinate crime prevention efforts. Keep thorough records to determine the effectiveness of the security company's services.

To locate security companies in your area, check the yellow pages under "Guard and Patrol Services" or "Security Services." (*See also* Sources of Further Information, Security, page 127.)

Employee Theft

Unfortunately, employee theft is a common problem that is often difficult to detect. It can be limited to pilfering office supplies or extend to embezzlement and employee-assisted burglaries. Business owners frequently find it hard to believe that their own workers would steal from them, so they refuse to take needed measures to prevent such losses. However, wise managers realize that some personnel find ways to rationalize petty theft. A worker may not consider it stealing to make personal long-distance calls on business phones, or to use company postage for personal mail. Perhaps an employee is dissatisfied at work and seeks revenge. Some may feel that they should be paid higher wages and think of stealing as a way of getting what the company owes them. Employees also steal due to real or perceived economic need, or just because theft gives them a feeling of power. Studies show that people with social or emotional problems are more likely to steal.

Theft by staff is not limited to petty stealing by lower-level workers. The white-collar crimes of management and executives can be much more damaging and costly to a company. These may also result from perceived economic need or may be rooted in dissatisfaction/resentment, carelessness/irresponsibility with personal and company funds, or simple greed. The greater independence and authority given to white-collar employees allow them more opportunities to steal.

Preventing in-house crime should be considered part of your overall security system. Though policing workers can be difficult and counterproductive in extreme degrees, there are a number of strategies to reduce employee theft without establishing an atmosphere of distrust.

1. Establish review procedures for inventory, income, and money disbursements to detect any misuse of funds. The tighter and more institutionalized procedures become, the less opportunity there is to abuse them.

2. Set a firm policy on the consequences to employees who are caught stealing, and communicate it effectively. Some employers allow their workers to take supplies home or make personal toll calls from the office. Make it clear to everyone if such use of company resources is not allowed in your firm.

3. Follow the policy firmly whenever employee theft is discovered. Reinforce the seriousness of the offense by telling workers when someone is caught stealing.

Let staff members know what disciplinary action has been taken. (There is no need to mention names, however.)

4. Encourage a general acceptance of the policy by all workers so that an employer/ employee rift is not created.

5. Consider the pros and cons before using lie detector tests or drug tests to check employee integrity. These may sometimes indicate a worker's propensity for theft, but do not necessarily prove wrongdoing. Such measures often produce great resentment among staff.

6. Promote worker satisfaction by encouraging open communication between employees and management. An employee who feels as though he or she is part of a work family will be less likely to act against company interests.

7. Set a good example at the top. Workers may follow the lead of a supervisor when stealing. A unified policy, applied equally to managers and other employees, will send a clear message to all workers.

Terrorism and Angry Employees: The New Office Menace

Incidents of terrorism by militant groups and individuals are a disturbing part of modern life. Violent crimes by disgruntled employees have become a leading cause of work-related deaths. Serious measures are needed to ensure employees' safety from unstable coworkers and outsiders. Managers should take steps to prevent office violence and be prepared to cope with it if prevention efforts fail.

Preventing Employee Violence

Company owners and managers can lower the probability of employee violence against coworkers by being alert to conditions that predispose workers to hurt or threaten others. Several preventive measures can reduce the likelihood of violent crime in your office.

Recognize the Signs of Disgruntled, Violence-Prone Workers. Pay attention to things employees do and say, as these often reveal violent impulses. The typical disgruntled worker is male and between 30 and 40 years old. Workers who display several of the following characteristics could be a danger to coworkers:

- dissatisfaction with management or work conditions
- paranoia
- explosive tendencies (quick anger and threatening remarks)
- social maladjustment, especially a lonely lifestyle
- depression
- abnormal vulnerability to stress
- low self-esteem
- attention-seeking behavior
- history of psychological problems
- history of bad work experiences

- unstable family life
- drug and/or alcohol abuse
- fascination with guns, other weapons, and the military
- financial problems

Use Safe Hiring Procedures. Eliminate potentially dangerous employees by screening applicants carefully. Look for the characteristics noted above during initial job interviews. Conduct background checks of past employment, crime records, driving records, and credit reports. Psychological testing is also an effective tool, but it can raise problems if the questions asked are too personal. For instance, it is generally unacceptable to ask specifically about an applicant's family or health, though general questions such as "What makes you angry?" are allowed. Check with your state labor board to make sure your employee screening procedures are legal.

Create a Healthy Work Environment. Promote communication between coworkers and between staff and management. Encourage workers to express any concerns, including fear of other employees. Programs such as drug/alcohol abuse treatment and psychological counseling should be available, either in-house (for large companies) or as part of a health-care plan. Create an atmosphere in which employees feel good about themselves and their jobs. Remember that work is a primary source of self-esteem and security for many people; try not to disrupt that sense of well-being.

Train Supervisors to Discipline and Terminate Employees with Care and Compassion. Worker violence frequently erupts after a negative work report or firing. Reduce the possibilities for violence by handling problems before they become insurmountable, with the focus on problem solving rather than punishment. Managers must clearly delineate behavior that needs correction, but they should also offer support to employees who are experiencing difficulties. (Of course, workers must also be willing to recognize and rectify problems.) A special level of compassion should be shown by management when an employee must be fired, with precautions to be sure the worker's legal rights are not violated (*see* Safe Firing Procedures, page 257). Any decision to terminate an employee should be final. If you fear a violent reaction, ask the worker to leave the premises and do not allow him or her to return.

Take Proper Security Precautions. Without turning the workplace into a police state, take steps to limit the possibilities for violent eruptions. (*See also* How to Solve Personnel Problems, page 253.)

Handling Terrorism

Terrorism may be directed at an entire company with the intention of hurting business; it may be focused on one particular individual; or it may be random. Although it is unpredictable, office terrorism frequently originates with current or past employees. It can take many forms—including bombings and kidnappings—and steps should be taken to prepare for all possibilities.

In business settings, kidnappers usually aim to extort money. Therefore, executives are the most likely targets. If you feel that you are at risk, some precautions may be necessary. Avoid drawing attention to yourself outside the office. Vary your schedule and routes to work so your location is not predictable at certain times each day. Carry a cellular phone in case of emergency, and consider hiring a bodyguard if you perceive a real and immediate danger. Becoming fearful is not necessary, but take any threats seriously.

The opportunity for terrorists to plant bombs in an office is limited by proper surveillance and security measures. Security personnel should be aware of everyone coming in and out of the building at all times, as well as any materials brought in or taken out. Nevertheless, offices should have a complete evacuation plan in case of emergency. If a bomb is threatened or suspected, employees should be told immediately (either by voice communication or alarm) to exit the building in a safe and orderly manner. They should go to a point far enough away to be out of danger from an explosion. The premises must be checked to make sure everyone has evacuated. Inform law enforcement officials, and have the gas and electricity turned off.

Staff should not search for a suspected bomb, but if one is found, no one should touch it. All search and recovery efforts are best handled by experienced professionals such as the police, the fire department, or federal agents. You can help, though, by providing necessary information about the building. Do not reenter the office until law enforcement agents determine that it is safe.

If your office receives a bomb threat or someone speaks to a kidnapper on the phone, take the call seriously and inform security immediately. Write down the caller's exact words, voice characteristics (rough, loud, deep, foreign accent), language (expressions, obscenities), manner (calm, angry, incoherent), and degree of familiarity with the office. Listen for background noises during the call and report them to the authorities. Such details will help investigators find the perpetrators. If the caller makes a bomb threat, try to find out when the bomb will explode, where it is, why it has been planted, and who is calling. (*See also* Security: Preventing On-Site Theft and Other Crimes, page 105.)

Accident Prevention

Office workers do face occupational hazards, although much more attention is given to protecting factory workers from accidental injury. Working in a safe environment is everyone's right, and all employees can help to promote safety. Make sure your employees understand and use basic precautions against job-related accidents.

Floors

- Keep walkways clear of boxes, chairs, and other obstructions.
- Tape down all exposed wiring so that people cannot trip over electrical cords, computer cables, and phone lines.

- Be careful when walking on slippery floors or stairs. Place warning signs on wet and slippery floors, especially while they are being washed or waxed.
- Retrieve dropped items (such as pencils or paper) that can make a floor slippery. Clean up spills immediately.
- Avoid using thick carpeting on office floors—it can be difficult to walk on, causing trips and falls.
- Keep mats at outside doors to avoid tracked-in snow or rain that may cause a hazard.

High Shelves and Storage Areas

- Avoid climbing on chairs or boxes to reach items. Instead, use a ladder tall enough to let you reach the desired height without stretching or standing on the top rung. Make sure the ladder is stable before climbing.
- Store heavy boxes and large objects on lower shelves. If these must be kept on high shelves, make sure they are firmly in place and not likely to fall.

Furniture, Office Machinery, and Electrical Outlets

- Keep file cabinets and drawers closed when not in use.
- Avoid buying furniture with sharp or protruding corners.
- Ground all electrical machinery and appliances properly.
- Install plenty of electrical outlets so that overloading does not occur.
- Unplug electrical equipment carefully—never jerk a plug from the wall.
- Keep dangling jewelry, hair, neckties, and loose clothing away from moving machinery.
- Know all procedures before operating machinery and proceed carefully.
- Maintain office equipment and facilities in good working condition.
- Never operate dangerous machinery when you are tired or feeling sick.
- Use proper protective gear when operating dangerous machinery.

Encouraging Employees to Avoid Accidents

Managers should take the lead in developing an accident-free workplace. You can create a positive, safety-conscious atmosphere by displaying office safety posters, such as those provided by the Occupational Safety and Health Administration (OSHA). Depending on the size and type of business, you may be required to institute a complete office safety program with goals, training, reinforcement, and reports to OSHA. Workers should be familiar with a detailed emergency plan covering all sorts of accidents. Establishing a clear chain of command will help to avoid injuries caused by miscommunication. A comfortable office environment (not crowded, excessively warm, or dimly lit) will also promote safety. Managers may also want to think twice before hiring someone with a history of accidental injuries.

Each employee should be expected to promote office safety by following all safety rules and reminding fellow workers to take proper safety measures. Assignments can be paced to avoid stress and overwork resulting in sloppy, reckless work habits. These safety tips may help workers avoid accidental injury:

- Stay alert, positive, and focused on work.
- Avoid boisterous horseplay.
- Operate only those machines and equipment that you have been authorized and trained to use.
- Familiarize yourself with building codes and OSHA regulations. If your office is not complying with them, you have the right to point out areas of noncompliance to management. If the problems are not remedied, you may complain to an OSHA office.

Avoiding Work-Related Injuries and Illnesses

In addition to avoiding accidents by removing safety hazards from the office, office managers should try to prevent health problems stemming from improper lifting, poor posture at desks/computers, and long hours of staring at computer screens. Office workers are filing more and more disability and workers' compensation claims for back injuries and stress-related illnesses. The time and money spent on accident prevention is minor in comparison with the possible consequences of ignoring safety rules. Some suggestions for avoiding office accidents are detailed in the following sections.

Lifting Heavy Objects Safely

Learn proper lifting techniques. Never use your back to lift heavy materials. Instead, stand close to the object, spread your feet, and bend your knees. Keep your back straight and get a good grip, then lift with your leg muscles. When carrying the object, keep your body straight. Use your feet to turn, not your waist. Set the object down in the same way that it was picked up, keeping your back straight.

Repetitive Strain Injuries and Carpal Tunnel Syndrome

Body strains caused by repeated actions are known as repetitive strain injuries (RSI). Office workers, especially those who spend many hours typing or sorting mail, are particularly prone to an RSI called carpal tunnel syndrome (CTS). The carpal tunnel is the wrist area where muscles, tendons, nerves, and blood vessels pass into the hand. CTS occurs when repeated bending forward of the wrist compresses the carpal tunnel nerves while simultaneous finger movements exert muscles. It is characterized by irritation, tingling, numbness, or even severe pain in the hand and fingers.

An office worker can avoid CTS by sitting with the back upright, arms parallel to the floor, and wrists straight (*see* Office Chairs and Workstation Posture, page 113). Regular breaks should be taken to reduce the strain of repetition. For typists, a more ergonomically sound keyboard than the standard "QWERTY" setup (such as a Dvorak or Klockenberg keyboard) can minimize stress, too.

If CTS is diagnosed, immediate attention should be given to prevent worsening of the condition. The syndrome usually begins in one finger and spreads; if allowed to advance, CTS may become incurable and lead to muscle weakness, loss of coordination, and atrophy. Anti-inflammatory drugs or surgery sometimes help. The best treatment for mild cases is to let hands and wrists rest and recuperate naturally. Modifying behaviors that cause CTS and taking a break from repetitive activities can do wonders.

Another repetitive strain injury experienced by office workers is cubital tunnel syndrome. This is due to compression of nerves in the elbow's cubital tunnel from bending the elbow sharply while typing. Sufferers experience aching in the elbow and shooting pains in the hand. Extending the elbow regularly and cushioning it may relieve cubital tunnel syndrome, as will a change in body position and rest. Advanced cases may require drugs or surgery.

Office Chairs and Workstation Posture

Chairs are probably the most important type of equipment in an office, affecting employee comfort, productivity, and health. Take special care in selecting the right chair for each worker's needs (*see* Chairs, page 178). Good posture is important, too, and a properly adjusted chair will encourage its occupant to sit correctly. Adjust the chair, keyboard position, or desk height until the following optimal posture points are automatic:

1. Hips should be fully back in the chair and bent at 90 degrees to form a straight line up through the shoulders and ears.
2. Elbows should be bent about 90 degrees for typing, with wrists straight.
3. Upper arms should be perpendicular and lower arms parallel to the floor.
4. Knees should be bent about 90 degrees, with plenty of legroom under the desk.
5. Feet should be flat on the floor or on a footrest.

Using Video Display Terminals Safely

As computers have become a major part of today's office environment, their use has raised health concerns. The main user complaint associated with computer screens, or video display terminals (VDTs), is eyestrain. Workers who spend long periods in front of a VDT may experience eye irritation, fatigue, blurred vision, or headaches. These symptoms are attributable to many factors, including office lighting, screen brightness and color settings, VDT position, and body positioning. These tips can help to lessen the strain caused by hours of computer use.

1. Arrange lighting to avoid a glare on the computer screen. To do this, adjust task lighting (*see* Lighting the Office, page 97) so it does not shine directly onto the

screen. Turn the VDT away from windows or install a nonreflective screen to reduce sunlight glare.

2. Adjust the levels of contrast, brightness, and color on the VDT to comfortable settings. Too much or too little contrast and brightness will strain the eyes. An easy-to-read middle ground is best.

3. Position the VDT so that the top of the screen is no higher than seated eye level. If you are referring to a written document while typing, keep the screen and the document close together and at the same distance from your eyes. This will keep eye movement and refocusing to a minimum.

4. Seat yourself at the right distance from your VDT—about an arm's length (15 to 25 inches) away. If you are more comfortable at a shorter or longer distance, make sure your eyes are not under strain.

5. Take frequent breaks to rest your eyes, at least 15 minutes every two hours. Take a longer break after four or five hours of work. Remember that your eyes (and body) need a rest from the strain of looking at the screen and performing repetitive motions. Playing computer games during breaks will not provide the needed relief.

RADIATION AND VDTs

Video display terminals emit small amounts of X-rays and electromagnetic fields, both of which are dangerous at high levels of exposure. This has prompted concern that VDTs may lead to the development of cataracts or cause birth defects if used by pregnant women. However, tests have shown no basis for such fears. The amounts of radiation emitted by VDTs are far below OSHA standards for safe radiation levels.

Sick Building Syndrome

About one in every three buildings in the United States exhibits signs of sick building syndrome (SBS). This means that millions of people work in unhealthy offices each day. Workers in SBS buildings may experience headaches, feelings of fatigue or irritability, nausea, depression, burning eyes, rashes, infections, burning noses and throats, and/or joint pain. In severe cases, SBS leads to cancer. Estimates put the cost to business at $60 to $100 million per year in medical expenses and lost productivity.

A number of factors contribute to sick building syndrome:

• recirculated air in buildings with ventilation systems that do not bring in enough fresh outdoor air

• loss of negative ionization in air trapped in ducts; this deprives the building's occupants of needed endocrine system stimulation and results in diminished alertness and harmful bacterial growth

• the cumulative effects of small amounts of air pollutants such as ammonia, asbestos, benzene, carbon dioxide, carbon monoxide, dust, ethanol, formaldehyde,

fungi, lead, methanol, nitrogen oxide, ozone, paint fumes, PCBs (polychlorinated biphenyls), pesticides, radon, sulfur oxide, toluene, trichloroethane, and vinyl chloride
- other, harder to define consequences of spending many hours each day in an unnatural indoor environment (for example, sunlight deprivation can cause depression in susceptible individuals)

Unfortunately, there is no easy cure for SBS. Addressing the problem in a large building requires time and money. If many workers experience symptoms related to SBS, however, there are a number of ways to improve the situation. First, conduct a detailed health survey of all workers to determine the general symptoms experienced, the types of employees who become ill, and the concentration of incidences in certain areas. This will narrow the list of factors that may be causing problems.

Next, give the building manager your findings. The problem may be easily corrected via adjustments to the ventilation system or the removal of known pollutants from the building. If this does not remedy the problem, call a government agency such as OSHA or its research arm, NIOSH (the National Institute of Occupational Safety and Health). An investigator from one of these agencies can inspect your building to find out the steps needed to remedy the situation. It may be necessary to hire an air quality specialist to study the building and recommend ways to cure sick building syndrome.

Some procedures to use at the first signs of SBS include the following:

- Clean the entire heating, ventilation, and air-conditioning (HVAC) system to eliminate molds, fungi, and bacteria.
- Replace the ventilation system.
- Install air filters.
- Install a negative ion generator in the HVAC system.
- Rid the building of smoke, aerosol sprays, and perfumes that contribute to air pollution.
- Replace carpet, which traps pollutants, with flooring, which can be cleaned more thoroughly.
- Examine all machines, furniture, stored chemicals, and cleaning materials to determine their effect on air quality.

If these measures do not solve the problem, you may want to consider moving your business to another building rather than undertake costly investigation and renovation procedures. The air inside any building is affected by outside air quality, so there is little anyone can do to improve inside air when a building is in a heavily polluted area. In such cases, moving is the only alternative.

First Aid in the Office

Everyone in the office needs to be familiar with basic first-aid procedures. Employers should give special training and refresher courses to staff involved in hazardous work. General office workers at least should be required to read a first-aid manual as part of their orientation process. It can be included as part of the employee handbook, with copies available in each work area for quick reference (*see* Creating a Policies and Procedures Manual, page 189). The manual should provide detailed instructions on handling basic medical emergencies—falls, cuts, burns, poisoning, electrical shock, and heat exhaustion are just a few.

In addition, instructions and diagrams describing more complex emergency procedures (such as the Heimlich maneuver, mouth-to-mouth resuscitation, cardiopulmonary resuscitation, and checking vital signs) should be posted in employee lounges and cafeterias. Also post telephone numbers for emergency medical and ambulance services, the local hospital information service, and poison control centers.

A well-stocked first-aid kit (*see* Contents of an Office First-Aid Kit, below) is essential to every workplace. Complete, easily accessible records of every employee's medical history should be available at a moment's notice. Workers with serious medical conditions (such as diabetes, heart disease, or epilepsy) would be wise to inform colleagues of their health problems and provide instructions on how to help if necessary. Employers should respect an employee's right to keep medical conditions confidential while fostering an environment that encourages openness and understanding to facilitate lifesaving responses in emergency situations. Both managers and employees can lessen the likelihood of emergencies by promoting safe, healthy work habits in the office (*see* Accident Prevention, page 110, and Avoiding Work-Related Injuries and Illnesses, page 112).

When a serious medical condition or injury incapacitates a staff member, priority should be given to: (a) maintaining breathing and circulation; (b) preventing blood loss, shock, and further injury; and (c) getting professional medical help. All office employees should be prepared for medical emergencies long before they occur. Proper first-aid procedures can save lives and speed recuperation from illnesses and injuries. The Heimlich maneuver and mouth-to-mouth resuscitation are techniques that anyone can learn with training and a little practice; however, CPR (cardiopulmonary resuscitation) is more difficult and may injure the victim if inexpertly applied. A local YMCA, emergency medical service, hospital, or Red Cross chapter can provide more information on first aid in the office. Or contact your regional OSHA office (*see* How to Contact OSHA, page 125). For a list of national organizations offering first-aid courses and information, *see* First-Aid Training, page 125.

Contents of an Office First-Aid Kit

When assembling an office first-aid kit, consider the number of workers in the office and any special medical problems in your staff. If your type of business predisposes employees to a certain kind of risk, stock appropriate supplies. Despite rigorous prevention efforts, some injuries may be more likely to occur in certain businesses. For example, in a printing firm, a large supply of finger bandages and antiseptic ointment may be needed for paper cuts incurred during constant paper sorting and handling. A company in which many workers use computers all day might stock extra bottles of eyedrops to soothe tired eyes. Design your first-aid kit to suit your own office's specific needs, but be sure to include the following basic supplies:

- first-aid handbook detailing a variety of emergency procedures
- adhesive bandages in assorted sizes and shapes (at least 100)
- fabric bandages (at least one roll)
- soft gauze bandages
- hypoallergenic first-aid tape (one roll)
- antiseptic wipes
- cotton balls
- sterile eye pads
- ophthalmic irrigating solution
- eyedropper
- sterile sponges
- clean towels
- antiseptic soap
- first-aid cream (one tube)
- burn cream
- cold pack
- nonprescription pain-relief pills
- small paper cups
- rubbing alcohol
- smelling salts
- blunt-nosed scissors
- tweezers
- measuring spoon set
- splints
- thermometer
- disposable rubber gloves
- sterile mouth protectors (to form a hygienic barrier between resuscitator and victim during mouth-to-mouth breathing)

Before undertaking a first-aid training program or stocking supplies, it is a good idea to see if your business must meet certain OSHA requirements in this area. Your regional OSHA office can supply a vast amount of information on first-aid training, equipment, and supplies. (*See also* The ABCs of OSHA, page 118, and Sources of Further Information, How to Contact OSHA, page 125.)

Workers' Compensation

Legislation creating workers' compensation originated in 1911, when the rise of industry made fair handling of work-related injuries a growing necessity. Any worker injured on the job (or as a result of work conditions) is entitled to workers' compensation, no matter who was at fault. Workers' compensation generally covers medical care, wage replacement (usually two-thirds of normal wages), severance pay, benefits, and rehabilitation costs. When a work-related death occurs, burial expenses and income benefits to families are also provided. The no-fault aspect of workers' compensation is important because it saves workers, employers, and the judicial system the cost and time required for lawsuits. It also encourages employer openness and accountability. And, because companies pay for workers' compensation via insurance premiums, owners and managers are more likely to stress safety in the workplace in order to reduce operating costs.

Workers' compensation is administered separately by each state, so specific regulations vary. Depending on the state, companies may provide workers' compensation through private insurance, through state programs such as state-approved insurance companies, or through self-insurance. Most states provide similar benefits that continue until an injured worker is fully recovered. Additional benefits are available for permanent injuries.

To lower workers' compensation costs, a business owner or manager should try to make the workplace as safe as possible. It is also advisable to purchase the most complete, cost-effective insurance program available. In addition, injured employees should be encouraged to return to work as soon as they have recovered. Finding ways to keep injured workers involved with the company may prevent them from seeing themselves as permanently disabled.

Claim-filing procedures vary from state to state. In general, any injury requiring a physician's care must be filed with the insurance company or workers' compensation office. An authorized supervisor or manager should fill out forms and send them to the proper office as soon as possible. Some work-related injuries must also be filed with OSHA (see the next section).

For more information on Worker's Compensation, contact your state's Department of Labor or the Office of Workers' Compensation.

The ABCs of OSHA

The U.S. Department of Labor established the Occupational Safety and Health Administration (OSHA) in 1970 with these goals: to reduce workplace hazards; to set legally enforceable health and safety standards in industry; to provide a system for reporting work-related injuries and illnesses; and to help businesses comply with regulations through free consultation, programs, training, and publications. OSHA regulations cover everything from safe walking surfaces to fire protection, from welding safety to compressed air equipment usage. The five OSHA regulation volumes (*General Industry; Maritime; Construction; Regulation and Procedures;* and *Field Operations*) are exhaustive and extremely specific.

Record Keeping and Reporting

Companies falling under OSHA jurisdiction must report every work-related illness and most injuries to the appropriate OSHA office. The primary forms for record keeping and reporting are Form 200, Log and Summary of Occupational Injuries and Illnesses (used to provide a brief description of and information about an illness or injury), and Form 101, Supplementary Record of Occupational Injuries and Illnesses (to provide more detailed information, such as the names of people involved and the circumstances surrounding an incident).

Businesses are exempt from federal record keeping, unless otherwise notified, if they have no more than ten full- or part-time employees at any time during a given year. Companies with Standard Industrial Classifications 55 to 65, 67, 72, 73, 78, 81 to 84, or 86 to 89 are exempt from regular OSHA-reporting procedures, but must follow OSHA standards. Many states have their own OSHA offices with separate record keeping regulations. Companies that achieve positive results (lower rates of illness and accident) by voluntarily implementing safety and health programs are eligible for lower workers' compensation insurance costs.

Training and Consultation

OSHA offers training courses in occupational safety and health at its Training Institute in Des Plaines, Illinois, and at some regional offices. Free consultation services are also available to managers seeking professional assistance in improving safety operations. You can request a consultation by phoning or writing your regional OSHA office (*see* Sources of Further Information, How to Contact OSHA, page 125). The consultation includes an initial conference with management and a walk-through inspection with input from workers. The consultant then compiles a report and recommends ways for the company to improve occupational safety and health. In a final meeting between management and consultant, the parties agree on and set a timetable for improvements. OSHA will conduct one or more progress checks to see if improvements are made according to the timetable. Consultations, unlike inspections, are confidential and do not result in citations if corrections are made. A business may qualify for a one-year exemption from OSHA inspections by requesting a consultation and complying with recommendations.

Inspections, Citations, and Fines

OSHA compliance officers are entitled to enter and inspect any business under OSHA jurisdiction without warning during regular work hours after obtaining the proper warrant. When an OSHA officer arrives, management should ask to see a picture I.D. and the warrant, and also inquire about the purpose of the inspection. An employee representative should accompany the officer on the inspection tour.

Inspections usually occur in high-hazard industries. OSHA gives these priorities to inspections: (1) areas with the most potential for serious injury or illness; (2) areas where accidents have already occurred; (3) areas for which employee complaints have been filed; and (4) general inspections.

OSHA compliance officers follow a standardized procedure during inspections. First, an officer researches the company's health/safety history and the hazards of that particular industry. Then a warrant to conduct the inspection is obtained. The compliance representative then goes to the workplace and holds an opening conference with management. After this initial conference, the actual walk-through inspection is conducted. In a closing conference with management, the officer explains OSHA's initial findings and advises the manager of any citations that will be recommended. (Inspectors make recommendations on citations for noncompliance, but they do not make final decisions as to what citations and fines will be levied.) Finally, the compliance officer makes an agreement with management on penalties for hazards and the corrections that will be made.

After the OSHA officer's report is filed, the area OSHA director decides whether to give a citation and fine. Citations specify the violated OSHA regulations and set a date by which hazards must be rectified. The business is required to post any citations in the workplace at the site where violations were cited for a minimum of three days or until the unsafe conditions are corrected. Penalties range from $1,000 to $10,000. These may be challenged by the business owner or manager. Challenges are sent to an independent review board, and a business is not required to make corrections until the review of its challenge is complete. The review process sometimes takes several years.

Filing Complaints

Employers may not discriminate against workers who file complaints with OSHA about workplace hazards, and employees may request confidentiality when reporting unsafe conditions. To file a complaint, a worker must complete a required form that is available at OSHA offices. To report life-threatening workplace hazards, call 800-321-OSHA (800-321-6742), the national 24-hour hotline. This number is to be used only for life-threatening situations—lesser complaints and questions should be directed to the regional OSHA office.

A complaint should describe violations and negligence as specifically as possible and supply all available evidence. OSHA gives priority to complaints in this order: (1) those indicating immediate, life-threatening danger, which are investigated within 24 hours; (2) those concerned with serious hazards, addressed within 3 days; and (3) less serious situations, investigated within 20 working days. All other types of complaints are addressed by correspondence.

For addresses and phone numbers of OSHA's national and regional offices, *see* Sources of Further Information, How to Contact OSHA, page 125. You may also call the OSHA-approved state safety and health administrations in Arizona, Arkansas, California, Connecticut, Hawaii, Indiana, Iowa, Kentucky, Maryland, Michigan, Minnesota, Nevada, New Mexico, New York, North Carolina, Oregon, South Carolina, Tennessee, Utah, Vermont, Virginia, the Virgin Islands, Washington, and Wyoming.

EMPLOYER/EMPLOYEE RIGHTS AND RESPONSIBILITIES UNDER OSHA REGULATIONS

The following is an overview of privileges and obligations established by OSHA. For specific questions and concerns, contact your regional OSHA office.

EMPLOYEE RIGHTS INCLUDE THE FOLLOWING:

- having a safe workplace
- refusing to work in an unsafe workplace
- having access to OSHA standards in the workplace
- requesting safety and health information from an employer
- seeing company records and observing how hazardous materials are monitored
- requesting an OSHA inspection or filing a complaint without fear of employment discrimination or retribution
- having complaints to OSHA kept confidential from an employer
- requesting information from OSHA or NIOSH
- having an employee representative accompany the OSHA agent during an inspection
- answering the questions of OSHA inspectors freely
- objecting to OSHA citations
- being informed of employer actions dealing with OSHA regulations

EMPLOYEES ALSO HAVE CERTAIN RESPONSIBILITIES:

- compliance with OSHA regulations
- reading OSHA posters displayed in the workplace
- cooperating with OSHA inspections
- following an employer's safety and health rules
- reporting hazards to a supervisor
- reporting work-related illnesses or injuries to a supervisor

AN EMPLOYER'S RIGHTS INCLUDE THE FOLLOWING:

- retaining the confidentiality of any trade secrets observed by OSHA compliance officers during inspections
- requesting OSHA consultations
- seeing proper identification and necessary warrants when inspectors arrive, being informed of the reason for an inspection, and having opening and closing conferences with inspectors
- contesting citations and penalties
- applying for a variance of OSHA regulations

EMPLOYERS ALSO HAVE CERTAIN RESPONSIBILITIES:

- providing a safe workplace
- informing workers of OSHA standards
- informing workers of hazards and providing safety training
- displaying OSHA posters listing rights and responsibilities
- making OSHA regulations and safety records available for employee review

Is Smoking an Issue?

Office smoking policies should be set with fairness toward all workers—smokers and nonsmokers. As in other sensitive areas of personnel administration, a good business manager will consider all workers' feelings and concerns about smoking rather than base decisions solely on personal preferences. Whatever your position on office smoking, avoid characterizing smokers or nonsmokers by personal habits that may not affect job performance.

In most offices, the mounting evidence of secondhand smoke's dangers has resulted in policies that contain smoking to designated enclosed areas or prohibit it completely. There are a number of reasons to limit or ban smoking in the office:

- Your business may be violating local ordinances, state laws, and/or OSHA regulations if smoking is not restricted. Many states now have general laws banning or restricting smoking in public places; some require that employers enforce policies protecting nonsmokers. Also, numerous local ordinances against smoking have been enacted in recent years.
- The American Lung Association estimates that smoking costs businesses $38 billion annually in lost work time and medical costs. Some studies have suggested that smokers have a 35 to 40 percent higher rate of absenteeism and tend to be less productive than nonsmokers. Nonsmokers report distractions and health problems as a result of coworkers' smoking. Some have even won disability and workers' compensation benefits as a result of secondhand smoke exposure in the workplace.
- Smoking has been shown to cause cancer, heart disease, lung disease, and emphysema. It also exacerbates many other health problems.
- Uncontained smoke contributes to poor air quality throughout the building.
- Smoking is a fire hazard.
- Offices are harder to keep clean when smoking is permitted. Smoke produces a hard-to-remove film on ceilings, walls, glass, and other surfaces.

Setting Policy

It may be best to ban smoking in the office completely, and it is legal for an employer to do so. A growing number of businesses are smoke-free, and many others are rapidly heading in that direction. But it is important to consider everyone's interests before enacting a strict no-smoking policy. Some valued employees or members of management may be longtime smokers who are very resistant to change. If smoking will be allowed in certain areas, these must be enclosed, with direct ventilation to the outside and a separate ventilation system from the rest of the building.

Take a positive approach when developing an office smoking policy by integrating it with an overall employee health program. Get everyone to participate in making the rules. Provide health education and encouragement to employees who want to quit smoking. Make smoking-cessation treatment programs available to anyone who wants to use them. If your workplace is unionized, consult with the union when developing a policy to minimize objections later. Research the issue to make sure the policy is fair and legal before making it effective. The American Lung Association offers model company smoking policies to help. (Most telephone directories have toll-free state and local American Lung Association chapter listings.)

Distribute copies of the new policy to all workers before it goes into effect. Begin by putting up "No Smoking" or "Smoke-Free Workplace" signs and removing ashtrays and cigarette machines from smoke-free areas. Set a timetable for implementing the policy, and enforce it. Finally, treat violations of office smoking policy in the same way other company rule violations are handled. Let workers know that this is a serious issue and that employees who break the rules will not go unnoticed.

For a list of organizations that offer information on developing smoking policies, *see* Sources of Further Information, Office Health and Safety, page 129.

Keeping Our Global Office Clean

Setting Up an Office Recycling Program

Most offices use large amounts of paper, cardboard, and plastic, all of which are recyclable. Starting a recycling program at work is a good idea, not only to conserve natural resources, but also because recycling makes good business sense. Most states have incentives such as tax deductions and credits for companies that recycle. Your business can even make money by selling used materials to recycling centers.

Finding a Recycling Center

To locate a recycling company that will pick up recyclables, call several garbage companies. You may also contact city, county, or state agencies listed in the yellow pages under "Public Works," "Environmental Services," "Sanitation," "Waste Disposal," or "Recycling." Or check the yellow pages for listings under some of the same headings. Contact one or more centers for information on pickup schedules and the types of materials accepted (white and colored paper? cardboard? glossy paper? newspapers? glass? aluminum?). Also ask how materials must be sorted, cleaned, and packaged to be accepted, and whether the center pays for recyclables collected. Choose a recycling center based on service, convenience, and cost; then arrange for pickups. The center may supply your office with collection bins, bags, and other materials.

Getting the Program Started

Let everyone in the office know about the program. Post reminders explaining sorting procedures, listing materials to include, and noting pickup schedule. Notify the office cleaning service or custodians so they will not dispose of recyclables when emptying trash and garbage. Ask for volunteers to oversee the recycling program. Appoint at least one person on each floor of the building to make sure the program runs smoothly and pickups are made as scheduled.

Place collection bins in convenient, centrally located spots. It makes sense to put aluminum can bins in employee lounges and near soda machines. The main paper bin might be located near the copy machine. Label bins prominently so employees will not use them as trash receptacles by mistake. Put a small paper collection bin in each private office or near each group of desks. Recycling coordinators should make sure employees empty their individual paper bins into the main one regularly.

If your office makes money by recycling, allow employees to decide how it will be spent. Possibilities include giving the money to charity, setting up a scholarship, using it for office parties, or buying something to be used by everyone, such as a microwave oven.

Conserving Natural Resources

In conjunction with recycling efforts, office workers should be encouraged to protect the environment by conserving materials. There are a number of ways to do this, such as buying recycled supplies. Paper, envelopes, boxes, tissues, and paper towels can all be made from recycled materials. The person responsible for purchasing office supplies can request that recycled materials be used to fill orders. If toner cartridge refills are available for copy machines and printers, use them—they usually cost less than replacement cartridges, anyway. Ask a local computer dealer for details, or call the American Cartridge Recycling Association at 305-539-0701. Decrease office waste by using less paper: Use cloth instead of paper towels, a sugar dispenser instead of packets, and washable coffee mugs instead of paper or styrofoam cups. Also, reuse scrap paper for scratch pads or as packing material. (*See also* Sources of Further Information, Recycling, page 129.)

Sources of Further Information

Organizations

Fire Safety

National Association of Fire Equipment Distributors
401 North Michigan Avenue
Chicago, IL 60611
Phone 312-644-6610

National Burglar and Fire Alarm Association
7101 Wisconsin Avenue, Suite 901
Bethesda, MD 20814
Phone 301-907-3202

National Fire Protection Association
One Batterymarch Park, P.O. Box 9101
Quincy, MA 02269
Phone 617-770-3000

National Fire Sprinkler Association
429 South Locust Street
Sycamore, IL 60178
Phone 815-895-5521

First-Aid Training

American Medical Association
515 North State Street
Chicago, IL 60610

American National Red Cross
17th and D Street NW
Washington, DC 20006

National Association of Emergency Medical Technicians
9140 Ward Parkway
Kansas City, MO 64114

How to Contact OSHA

Write to Occupational Safety and Health Administration, Department of Labor, 200 Constitution Avenue NW, Washington, DC 20210. To report life-threatening workplace hazards, call 800-321-OSHA (800-321-6742), the national 24-hour hotline; to request publications, call 202-219-9667; for general information, call 202-523-3148 or contact your regional OSHA office:

Region I—Connecticut, Maine, Massachusetts, New Hampshire, Rhode Island, Vermont
133 Portland Street, First Floor,
Boston, MA 02114
Phone 617-565-7164

Region II—New Jersey, New York, Puerto Rico, Virgin Islands
201 Varick Street
New York, NY 10014
Phone 212-337-2378

Region III—Delaware, District of Columbia, Maryland, Pennsylvania, Virginia, West Virginia
Gateway Building, Suite 2100
3535 Market Street
Philadelphia, PA 19104
Phone 215-596-1201

Region IV—Alabama, Florida, Georgia, Kentucky, Mississippi, North Carolina, South Carolina, Tennessee
1375 Peachtree Street NE, Suite 587
Atlanta, GA 30367
Phone 404-347-3573

Region V—Illinois, Indiana, Michigan, Minnesota, Ohio, Wisconsin
230 Dearborn Street
Chicago, IL 60604
Phone 312-353-2220

Region VI—Arkansas, Louisiana, New Mexico, Oklahoma, Texas
525 Griffin Street
Dallas, TX 75202
Phone 214-767-4731

Region VII—Iowa, Kansas, Missouri, Nebraska
911 Walnut Street
Kansas City, MO 64106
Phone 816-426-5861

Region VIII—Colorado, Montana, North Dakota, South Dakota, Utah, Wyoming
1961 Stout Street
Denver, CO 80294
Phone 303-844-3061

Region IX—American Samoa, Arizona, California, Guam, Hawaii, Nevada, Trust Territories of the Pacific
71 Stevenson Street
San Francisco, CA 94105
Phone 415-744-6670

Region X—Alaska, Idaho, Oregon, Washington
1111 Third Avenue
Seattle, WA 98101
Phone 206-553-5930

Office Design and Furniture

American Furniture Manufacturers Association
P.O. Box HP-7
High Point, NC 27261
Phone 919-884-5000

American Institute of Architects
1735 New York Avenue NW
Washington, DC 20006
Phone 202-626-7300

American Institute of Building Design
991 Post Road E
Westport, CT 06880
Phone 203-227-3640

American Society of Furniture Designers
P.O. Box 2688
High Point, NC 27261
Phone 910-884-4074

American Society of Interior Designers
608 Massachusetts Avenue NE
Washington, DC 20002
Phone 202-546-3480

Building Owners and Managers Association International
1201 New York Avenue NW, Suite 300
Washington, DC 20005
Phone 202-408-2662

Business and Institutional Furniture Manufacturers Association
2680 Horizon SE, Suite A1
Grand Rapids, MI 49546
Phone 616-285-3963

Business Products Industry Association Retail Office Furniture Dealer Division
301 North Fairfax Street
Alexandria, VA 22314
Phone 703-549-9040

Interior Design Society
P.O. Box 2396
High Point, NC 27261
Phone 800-888-9590

Society of Industrial and Office Realtors
700 11th Street NW, Suite 510
Washington, DC 20001-4511
Phone 202-737-1150

Office Health and Safety

Association for Repetitive Motion Syndromes
P.O. Box 514
Santa Rosa, CA 95402
Phone 707-571-0397

Center for Clean Air Policy
444 North Capitol Street, Suite 602
Washington, DC 20001
Phone 202-624-7709

Citizens for a Better Environment
407 South Dearborn, Suite 1775
Chicago, IL 60605
Phone 312-939-1530

For more information on developing an office smoking policy, call your local American Lung Association or one of the following organizations:
Indoor Air Office, Environmental Protection Agency, 202-475-7174
Office on Smoking and Health, Centers for Disease Control, 404-488-5705
National Cancer Institute, 800-4-CANCER

Office Lighting

American Lighting Association
P.O. Box 580168
2050 Stemmons Freeway
Dallas, TX 75258
Phone 214-698-9898

Illuminating Engineering Society of North America
120 Wall Street, 17th Floor
New York, NY 10005
Phone 212-248-5000

International Association of Lighting Designers
18 East 16th Street, Suite 208
New York, NY 10003
Phone 212-206-1281

Office Planning

Office of the Americans with Disabilities Act (ADA)
Civil Rights Division
U.S. Department of Justice
P.O. Box 66118
Washington, DC 20035-6118
Phone 202-514-0301 (voice) or 202-514-0381 (TDD)

Recycling

American Cartridge Recycling Association
Phone 305-539-0701

American Paper Institute
260 Madison Avenue
New York, NY 10016
Phone 212-340-0650

Earth Care Paper Company
Phone 608-256-5522 for a copy of the booklet
Office Paper Recycling

Environmental Protection Agency—Office of Solid Waste
401 M Street SW
Washington, DC 20460
Phone 800-424-9346 for brochures

Keep America Beautiful
Nine West Broad Street
Stamford, CT 06902
Phone 203-323-8987

National Recycling Coalition
1101 30th Street NW, Suite 305
Washington, DC 20007
Phone 202-625-6406

Security

American Society for Industrial Security
155 North Fort Meyer Drive, Suite 1200
Arlington, VA 22209
Phone 703-522-5800

International Association of Professional Security Consultants
13819-G Walsingham Road, Suite 350
Largo, FL 34644
Phone 813-596-6696

National Alarm Association of America
P.O. Box 3409
Dayton, OH 45401
Phone 800-283-6285

National Burglar and Fire Alarm Association
7101 Wisconsin Avenue
Bethesda, MD 20814
Phone 301-907-3202

National Council of Investigation and Security Services
P.O. Box 449
Severna Park, MD 21146
Phone 800-445-8408

Books and Literature

The Americans with Disabilities Act: Questions and Answers is a brochure published jointly by the Equal Employment Opportunity Commissions and the Department of Justice, Civil Rights Division, in August 1996.

Becker, Franklin, and Fritz Steele. *Workplace by Design: Mapping the High Performance Workscape.* New York: Jossey-Bass, 1995.

Bredin, Alice. *The Virtual Office Survival Handbook.* New York: John Wiley & Sons, 1996.

Dickson, Ron. *Smooth Moves: How to Successfully Relocate a Company.* Fairfax, VA: National Moving and Storage Association. Call 703-934-9111 to request a copy, or write to the National Moving and Storage Association, 11150 Main Street, Suite 402, Fairfax, VA 22030.

Evan Terry Associates, *Americans with Disabilities Act Facilities Compliance: A Practical Guide.* New York: John Wiley & Sons, 1993.

Evan Terry Associates, *Pocket Guide to the ADA.* New York: John Wiley & Sons, 1997.

Kanarek, Lisa. *Organizing Your Home Office for Success.* New York: Plume Books, 1993.

Pascarelli, Emil, and Deborah Quilter. *Repetitive Strain Injury: A Computer User's Guide.* New York: John Wiley & Sons, 1994.

On-Line Resources

First-Aid Training

The American Medical Association *http://www.ama-assn.org*

Office Design and Security

Information on numerous aspects of planning, design, safety, and related topics.
http://www.abuildnet.com
http://www.build.com
The Lighting Research Center (Rensselaer Polytechnic Institute) *http://www.lrc.rpi.edu*
On-line interior design firm listings *http://www.abuildnet.com/design.html*

Office Health and Safety

ErgoWeb, devoted to ergonomic concerns *http://tucker.mech.utah.edu*
The Office of Workers' Compensation *http://dol.gov/dol/esa/public/owcp org.htm*
The U.S. Occupational Safety and Health Administration *http://www.osha.gov*

Recycling

Keep America Beautiful *http://www.kab.org/garbage.html*

4

Office Equipment and Supplies

The selection of machines and equipment for your office may require a substantial investment of time and funds. So choose machines with features that increase productivity and give a good return on your investment. Equipment that can be upgraded may cost more, but will often save the cost of buying new machines later. When the quality of several models is comparable, consider value-added extras such as customer service, warranties, cost of supplies, and operating costs. Include employees who will use the machines in the selection process, as they probably know best which features are necessary and which will save time and money.

To Lease or Buy?

Traditionally, most companies have purchased equipment with cash or financed it with bank loans. Now, many businesses lease office machines, especially computer or medical equipment and other items that become obsolete rapidly.

Operating leases are one type of lease. You pay a flat monthly fee, but when the term of the lease is over, ownership of the equipment reverts to the lessor. The lessee has the option of purchasing the equipment at fair market value or continuing to rent. Operating leases offer flexibility, allowing you to upgrade to newer equipment at the end of the lease. *Capital leasing* resembles a home mortgage or lease/purchase agreement, in that the payments you make go toward purchasing the equipment.

The two types of leases differ in the way they are regarded by the Internal Revenue Service (IRS). With operating leases, you may deduct payments as expenses, but you may not depreciate the equipment. For capital leases, it is the opposite—you may deduct for depreciation, but not for payments. Rates are typically tied to the Treasury bill rate; terms are tied to IRS depreciation schedules, ranging from 12 to 84 months.

How do you decide whether to lease or buy? Begin by considering your cash flow, tax situation, anticipated needs, and length of time you plan to use the equipment. You may have little cash on hand and limited credit, or you may wish to keep your lines of credit open for other purchases. With a lease, your initial cash outlay is small. If the equipment you need is likely to become obsolete quickly, you should probably lease it. By leasing, you will have the option of upgrading if your needs change; also, you can often lease more sophisticated, expensive equipment than you can afford to buy.

Negotiate terms before signing a lease. Look for leases that allow the most flexibility, particularly if you are leasing high-tech equipment. For example, be sure that your lease contract spells out options for upgrades. You should be able to choose among new or used upgrade components made by any manufacturer and supplied by any vendor. The leasing company should agree to finance any upgrades. Make sure that your contract allows you to return leased equipment with like-for-like parts rather than the original parts. This is particularly important in the computer industry, where there are many equivalent products and the preference is to replace components rather than to repair them.

Leasing equipment has some financial disadvantages. Lessors may impose penalties if equipment is returned early. The lessee usually pays all taxes, service charges, insurance, and maintenance costs for leased equipment. You may pay nearly the full cost of the leased equipment, plus interest, over the length of a lease.

You may lease equipment through a bank, a captive leasing company (a subsidiary of a manufacturer), an independent leasing company, or directly from a lessor. Your vendor is an important partner in your business. Select one on the basis of flexibility, stability, services offered, and knowledge.

- Appraise flexibility in terms of willingness to make changes to the lease, custom tailor solutions to your needs, and offer creative financing solutions.
- Check into a vendor's financial status and number of years in business.
- Look for value-added services that include electronic asset management to keep track of high-tech leased equipment and disaster recovery programs, which plan for what-if scenarios such as floods or fires.
- Be sure lessors have a firm command of the capabilities of equipment you lease.
- Use knowledgeable people in your own firm to evaluate a vendor's expertise.
- Check out independent leasing companies, which often have the best prices, as they provide equipment from a range of manufacturers.
- Make sure that any used equipment you lease is certified as eligible for maintenance.

When to Buy

Unless you expect to use the equipment for 12 months or less, you should not lease small-ticket items such as individual personal computers (PCs), printers, or terminals unless multiple quantities are needed. Leasing will cost more than outright purchase in the long run. However, items such as copiers (particularly color copiers), audiovisual equipment, and phone systems may be better leased. Here are some important questions to ask before buying:

- How long has the vendor been in business?
- Can the vendor supply you with a list of satisfied customers as references?
- What kind of technical support does the company offer? Does it suit your needs?
- Does the vendor guarantee a quick response to your calls with questions or problems?
- Is the vendor an authorized dealer?

BUYING USED OFFICE EQUIPMENT

When you are on a budget, setting up an office can seem tremendously expensive. Everything at the showroom or office supply store seems to cost hundreds of thousands of dollars. However, office equipment such as copiers and fax machines may be bought used and reconditioned. There is a market for used furniture; some companies even specialize in reconditioning furniture, panels, and other office items. You can have wall panels that are like new at a considerably lower cost, for example.

Advantages

Popular, tried-and-true models are frequently available. Staff may already be familiar with the equipment, so training courses may not be necessary. And the price is usually right.

Disadvantages

Customer support and manufacturers' warranties are often unavailable for secondhand equipment. You may also have difficulty finding replacement parts if a machine uses proprietary elements and/or the maker has gone out of business. Some manufacturers refuse to work on outdated equipment, so you may need to find an independent repair service for older models. Before buying used equipment of any kind, try it out to make sure that it works. Line up vendor or service support before making a purchase. Arrange for a written warranty or maintenance contract without preconditions. Look for a popular model to ensure future availability of parts and backup equipment.

Service and Warranties

Service and maintenance considerations vary with different types of equipment. Most office equipment (particularly electronic equipment) is sturdier and more reliable today than it was years ago. Items like fax machines, modems, and laser printers may be tricky to operate, causing user problems, but they seldom break down. Therefore, it is generally more cost effective to buy quality equipment with the longest warranty offered than to pay extra for a service contract or extended warranty. Copy machines are an exception to this rule—service is critical in this area. Expect your dealer to supply a good service contract or extended warranty.

Computer Hardware and Software

Getting the right computer(s) for your business requires time and comparison shopping to find the best value. Choices abound in the market. You can select from general purpose desktop systems at a fairly low price; more powerful systems for desktop publishing, computer-aided design, and graphics; and portable laptop or notebook computers to use when traveling.

IBM-Compatible PC or Apple Macintosh?

What type of computer should you buy? The vast majority of computers on the market are known as IBM compatibles, PC compatibles, or PC clones, because they use the DOS (disk operating system)-based architecture originally developed for the IBM PC (personal computer). A significant minority, however, are made by Apple Computers and use an entirely different operating system known as Macintosh ("Mac" for short). When first introduced, PC clones were inexpensive but hard to use; Macs cost more, but were easier to learn, especially for graphics. That is no longer true. Most IBM compatibles now come with Microsoft Windows 95, a graphical user interface (GUI) that incorporates many of the same features that make Macs easy to operate. And Apple now manufactures some less expensive versions of the Macintosh, the Performas. Prices are comparable to those of PC clones.

Some differences remain. Macintosh software tends to be more expensive than Windows-based software. And although Windows makes using a PC clone much easier than using DOS alone, the combined Windows/DOS system has yet to achieve the ease and simplicity of the Macintosh. If you are buying a computer system for the first time, you may want to try both types of computers before making a decision. Of course, if you or others in your office are experienced Mac or IBM-compatible users, the choice may be obvious. Also consider compatibilities between your firm's computers and those of branch offices or clients with whom you exchange data; that is, if your corporate office uses Macintosh computers, you may want to use them as well.

Apple's new Power PC offers a much-needed compromise for Macintosh users, given that PC compatibles dominate the marketplace and business world. This model has a Pentium microprocessor equivalent to those in the fastest PC clones and allows use of IBM-compatible software as well as Macintosh programs.

COMPUTERESE FOR THE COMPUTER ILLITERATE

Data and speed measurement terms

bit	*bi*nary dig*it,* either a zero or a one; the smallest unit in computer information handling
bps or *baud rate*	*b*its *p*er *s*econd or *b*auds *p*er *s*econd, the speed at which data are transmitted from a computer across telephone lines via a modem
byte	the basic unit of data storage, a number of consecutive binary digits that are acted upon as a unit, a byte represents one character and there are usually eight bits in a byte
cpi	*c*haracters *p*er *i*nch (term used in word-processing applications)
cps	*c*haracters *p*er *s*econd (term used in describing printer speed)

dpi	*d*ots *p*er *i*nch, a measurement of the inking density of a printer (the higher the dpi, the better the print quality)
gigabyte	approximately 1 billion (1,073,741,824) bytes
K or *KB*	kilobyte, approximately 1,000 (1,024) bytes
Kbps	kilobytes per second
M, MB, or *meg*	megabyte, approximately 1 million (1,048,576) bytes, primary and secondary memory (RAM and magnetic media) are measured in kilobytes, megabytes, and gigabytes.

Other terms

ANSI	*A*merican *N*ational *S*tandards *I*nstitute, one of the standard formats for representing characters on a computer (*see ASCII*)
application	the use of technology to achieve a specific objective; software programs are often referred to as applications (for example, word-processing applications or accounting applications)
architecture	the grand scheme or design of a system; for example, database architecture, client/server architecture, PC-based architecture, or integrated architecture
archival	a medium that is readable and/or writable for an extended period (such as years or centuries)
ASCII	*A*merican *S*tandard *C*ode for *I*nformation *I*nterchange, a standard computer character format that is often used for files to be shared between programs (*see ANSI*)
ATM	*a*synchronous *t*ransfer *m*ode, a step beyond local area networks
AUTOEXEC.BAT	a small file read by MS-DOS as a computer starts up; it contains information about programs and is run at start-up
BIOS	*b*asic *i*nput/*o*utput *s*ystem; acts as an intermediary between an operating system and the computer's hardware
bundle	a package that includes several products for one price; for example, a computer with a CD-ROM drive, printer, monitor, keyboard, cables, software, and one or more CD-ROMs
bus interface	an electronic pathway between CPUs and input/output devices such as disk drives or CD-ROMs

COMPUTERESE (continued)

Other Terms

cache	a holding area for data that allows the system to match data transfer rates and presentation speed requirements
CD-I	Compact Disc-Interactive; an interactive multimedia system developed by Philips and Sony that connects to a television and stereo audio system
CD-R	*CD*-recordable players and media that allow users to create a CD-ROM, written from the PC as if it were a magnetic disk drive; the end product cannot be erased or written over; also known as *WORM* CDs (*see WORM*)
CD-ROM	compact disc-read-only memory, a laser-encoded optical memory storage medium
CD-ROM drive	a computer peripheral that plays CD-ROMs
CHKDSK	DOS command to scan the disk in a specified drive and display a status report that shows errors on the disk
CHKDSK/F	DOS command to scan a disk for errors and fix any errors found
client/server technology	pertaining to a network in which the *server* is a host or central computer and the *clients* are individual PCs connected to it, performing separate tasks; the server (which may be a mainframe, a minicomputer, or a large PC) manages generic functions for a whole organization; this technology makes system maintenance relatively simple but may cause security problems, as access to a single PC generally means access to the entire system
compatible	describes different hardware devices that use the same software programs
CONFIG.SYS	a file read by MS-DOS as the computer starts up; it contains information about how a user wants certain computer features to be identified and used
contact manager	a sophisticated PIM (personal information manager) that may include features such as automatic dialing of phone numbers, recording of dates and details of client contacts, E-mail, and word processing (*see PIM*)

controller	a specialized processor that controls the flow of data between a computer and one or more peripheral devices
CPU	central processing unit (the heart of a personal computer), which contains the chips that allow a computer to perform its functions
data	the basic elements of information that may be processed or produced by a computer (the preferred pronunciation is "dayta")
database	a list of information such as names, addresses, telephone numbers, inventory lists, test scores, or any other type of information that needs to be sorted and updated; database software applications simplify using and keeping such records
decode	convert information from machine- or computer-readable format
default	a standard setting or action taken by hardware or software when the user has not specified otherwise
desktop publishing	the process of creating and printing "camera-ready" documents (that is, documents that are ready to be reproduced for distribution) by using a computer, printer, and special software; often used to produce materials such as company brochures and newsletters
device driver	a program containing the instructions necessary for a computer to control a peripheral device, such as a mouse or CD-ROM drive
disc	preferred term for reference to optical storage media such as CD-Audio, CD-I, CD-ROM, videodisc, or WORM
disk	preferred term for reference to magnetic media, such as floppy and hard disks
DOS	disk operating system, a microcomputer operating system developed in 1980 by Seattle Computer Products and later purchased by Microsoft Corporation; it was developed for use in the original IBM PC as PC-DOS; as MS-DOS (Microsoft DOS), it is the dominant operating system for PC-compatible computers (DOS is pronounced "dahss")

COMPUTERESE (continued)

double-speed (2X) drive	CD-ROM drive that reads certain kinds of data faster than the standard requires (155 KB/sec); triple-speed and quadruple-speed disks (3X and 4X) are now common
drive	a computer device that reads information from storage media, such as floppy disks and CD-ROMs
drive bay	the opening in a computer chassis designed to hold a floppy drive, hard drive, CD-ROM drive, tape drive, or other device
EDI	*e*lectronic *d*ata *i*nterchange, the transfer of paper-based processing to electronic processing, similar to electronic funds transfer (EFT); examples include purchasing, billing, and receivables processes
E-mail	*e*lectronic *m*ail, used to send messages and files from one computer to another via a network (local or worldwide)
encode	convert information into machine- or computer-readable format
executable	in MS-DOS, a file with the extension ".EXE," which denotes a program that carries out commands; files with the extensions ".BAT" and ".COM" are also referred to as executable files
expansion slot	an internal connection on a PC motherboard that can accept a printed circuit board
FAT	*f*ile *a*llocation *t*able, part of the MS-DOS operating system that keeps track of the location of files on a disk
file server	a component of a local area network that stores information for use by clients or workstations (*see client/server technology*)
floppy disk	a flexible plastic magnetic storage unit inserted into a slot on the computer for storage and retrieval of data; termed *floppy* as opposed to the *hard* disk located inside the computer
format	an established system standard in which data are stored; disks must be formatted before data can be saved on them, but

	there are only a few types of formats and many floppy disks are sold already formatted; formatting a disk (including a hard drive) erases all previously recorded information, so users should be careful when using the format command
fragmentation	storing parts of a file in disparate available space on a disk rather than contiguously; too much fragmentation on a hard disk makes the computer take longer to find data, so the disk should be defragmented occasionally
groupware	software shared by several people, such as Lotus Notes
GUI	*gr*aphical *us*er *i*nterface, a layer of software that lets users interact with the computer by choosing items from the screen, usually by clicking or double-clicking with a mouse; the Macintosh Finder and Microsoft Windows are examples of GUIs (*see icon*)
hierarchical file system	used in the Macintosh platform for a directory structure that employs a graphical metaphor of folders containing files or additional folders; Macintosh interface elements—color icons—are embedded with file structure information, accessed by double-clicking with the mouse; analogous to the directories and subdirectories of MS-DOS–based hardware
html	*h*yper*t*ext *m*arkup *l*anguage, the standard computer language for desktop publishing programs; used in many Internet Web sites due to its readability and attractive appearance
IBM compatible	computers of the same type as an IBM PC, but made by various other companies; these use the same kinds of hardware and software that are accepted by IBM PCs, and are the predominant type of personal computer used in homes and businesses; Apple (Macintosh) computers have a strong following but are not so numerous; also known as *PC clones* and *PC compatibles*

COMPUTERESE (continued)

IBM PC	the original personal computer manufactured by International Business Machines Corporation in 1981; the term "PC" has since become generic
icon	a pictorial representation of a function or task, used in GUIs such as Windows and Apple Macintosh Finder
interface	the link between two pieces of disparate equipment, such as a CPU and a peripheral device; also, a method of translating data from computer to user
LAN	*l*ocal *a*rea *n*etwork, a system connecting two or more personal computers for shared resources and communication
LED	*l*ight-*e*mitting *d*iode, a type of crystal employed in creating informational displays on electronic equipment
Macintosh	familiar name for non-IBM-compatible computers made by Apple Computer, Inc.; *Macintosh* actually refers to the central processing unit and its operating system; monitors and other hardware may just say "Apple"; these computers have long been recommended for novices, as they were much simpler to operate than IBM compatibles until very recently (*see Macintosh OS 7.5*)
Macintosh OS 7.5	often referred to as "System 7.5"; the most recent version of the Macintosh operating system used in Apple computers
magnetic medium	any agent used to store data via variations in magnetic polarity; usually floppy disks, hard disks, and tape
magneto-optical	an information storage medium that is magnetically sensitive only at high temperatures; a laser heats a small spot, which allows a magnet to change its polarity; the medium is stable at normal temperatures; magneto-optical discs can be erased and re-recorded
menu	a list of on-screen options presented by a software program during its operation, usually enclosed in a box; the desired option is selected via use of the mouse or keyboard

Microsoft Windows	a GUI operating environment developed by Microsoft for IBM compatibles with the MS-DOS operating system; it features a system of program icons for quick point-and-shoot use with a mouse; Windows 95 is the first version of this program that is an operating system in its own right
modem	a device that enables the computer to communicate with fax machines, the Internet, and other computers via connection to a telephone line; may be *internal* (located inside the central processing unit) or *external* (attached to the computer)
monitor	the video screen on which computer data are displayed
mouse	a palm-sized gadget used to move the cursor around on the monitor, with buttons that are clicked to choose desired options after the cursor is positioned on them; usually black or gray with a long matching cord (its "tail") connecting it to the central processing unit
MS-DOS	*M*icro*s*oft *d*isk *o*perating *s*ystem (now used interchangeably with *DOS*)
multimedia	any application that combines text, graphics, audio, or video files
network interface card (NIC)	add-in circuit board that allows a PC to be connected to a local area network
network license	a license from a software vendor that allows an application to be shared by many users via a network
neural network	a network model designed to mimic the way the brain works; neural networks are used by Wall Street firms to predict market prices by detecting patterns in what was once thought to be random data
OCR	*o*ptical *c*haracter *r*ecognition, software that translates graphics files (such as those transmitted by fax modem) into files readable by a word-processing application
open system	computer architecture featuring broad connectivity of different brands of software and hardware, such as the UNIX design
operating system	a computer program that runs the computer and handles data traffic between disks and memory

COMPUTERESE (continued)

OS/2 Warp	an operating system for IBM compatibles that is much less widely used than DOS or DOS plus Windows
PC	personal computer
PC clone	initially a derogatory term for IBM-compatible computers made by companies other than IBM; this phrase no longer has negative connotations, as many competent computer companies now manufacture such equipment (*see IBM compatible*)
PC compatible	*see IBM compatible*
peer-to-peer	a type of LAN that treats all workstations connected to it as equals and does not require a file server to hold shared files
peripherals	all additional hardware components that are external to the CPU, including keyboards, monitors, disk drives, printers, modems, and mice
PIM	*personal information manager*, a simplified database application for personal use that usually includes an address and phone book and scheduling and calendar features
platform	a type of computer or operating environment; for example, Macintosh, DOS/Windows, CD-I, and Sega are different platforms
proprietary	a device or program designed and owned by a particular manufacturer or vendor, as opposed to a standard
RAM	*random access memory*, in which a computer stores (temporarily) any data retrieved from the hard drive or a floppy disk; changes made in this information will be lost when the computer is turned off unless the changes have been saved to a drive or disk
retrieval engine	a program that finds and presents data to the user
RISC	*reduced instruction set computing*, a chip technology that reduces the number of instructions required to perform a function, resulting in increased processing speed
ROM	*read-only memory*, used to store information such as the BIOS system; these data are not lost when a computer is turned off

RSI	repetitive *s*train *i*njury, such as carpal tunnel syndrome, which may result from improper posture while using a computer for long periods
SCSI	*s*mall *c*omputer *s*ystems *i*nterface (pronounced "scuzzy"), a standard interface used to connect peripheral devices to a computer
search engine	*see retrieval engine*
sector	a physical data block of a medium such as a hard drive or CD-ROM
sound board	a device required by a DOS-based computer to access digital sound; the device usually takes the form of an add-in board inserted in the computer
spreadsheet	a computer file designed to perform mathematical calculations on a set of data (for example, a payroll spreadsheet file may automatically calculate gross wages when the number of hours worked and hourly pay amounts have been entered); spreadsheet software applications can be used to create spreadsheets for many different accounting and budgeting functions
System 7.5	*see Macintosh OS 7.5*
UNIX	an operating system that is somewhat independent of hardware brands; UNIX is an example of open system architecture
UPS	*u*ninterruptible *p*ower *s*upply, which allows for smooth system shutdown in a power failure without loss of data
WAN	*w*ide *a*rea *n*etwork that connects two or more personal computers
WORM	*w*rite *o*nce-*r*ead *m*any, a type of permanent optical storage that allows the user to record information on a blank disc; information may be added until the disc is full, but not erased or changed

Basic Desktop Systems

When deciding on a computer, there are three critical performance standards to consider: system memory or *random access memory* (*RAM*), clock speed, and microprocessor chip speed. RAM is measured in megabytes (MBs or "megs"). Clock speed, or system speed—the speed at which the computer actually computes—is measured in megahertz (MHz). The frequency at which the microprocessor chip operates is also measured in MHz, and currently available models have processor speeds of 75 MHz to 166 MHz. When purchasing a new system, make sure the chip's speed is at least 133 MHz for best performance.

Ten years ago, a new IBM-compatible central processing unit contained a 286 MHz microprocessor chip. Subsequently, the 386 chip and the 486 chip were developed. Then the Pentium chip was advertised as faster than the 486. New PCs contain a 586 microprocessor chip (which is a Pentium chip), and an even faster 600-level version may soon be on the market. Apple equivalents of the 586 are the Power PC models.

A desktop computer system usually consists of a *central processing unit* (*CPU*), a monitor, a keyboard, and an input/output device such as a mouse. The CPU contains a motherboard, a hard drive, one or two floppy disk drives (Macs use only 3½-inch disks; PCs both 3½- and 5¼-inch disks), and three to eight expansion slots for PC peripherals or SCSI devices (*see* Computerese for the Computer Illiterate, page 134, for definitions of *SCSI* and other unfamiliar terms). The newer CPUs are available in traditional desktop, minitower, and tower configurations, rather than just the horizontal desktop versions of the past. Minitower and tower CPUs may require the rearrangement of existing computer furniture components to accommodate their height, but these generally allow for more expansion options as their cases are larger than the horizontal versions (towers have the largest cases).

The *motherboard* is the internal board that connects the CPU to all the other components. The *hard drive* or *hard disk* is the internal disk drive that does most of the work. It is where all software, operating programs, and data files are stored. The size of the hard drive is important, as software and files constantly require additional storage. A 250 MB hard drive was once considered large, but 1-gigabyte drives (four times as big) are becoming common. Get the largest hard drive you can afford.

RAM is another important type of memory. It allows you to open files and run software; it is also measured in megabytes. New systems usually come with 8 to 16 MB of base RAM, and even more (24 MB, for instance) will be standard in future hardware. Again, when buying a new system, buy as much RAM as your budget will allow. Although Windows 95 is advertised to run with only 8 MB of RAM, it requires 16 MB for best operation, so you may want to consider adding additional RAM to older PCs that will continue to be used in the office. At about $300 to $400 for an additional 8 MB, it may be worth the investment to keep older equipment usable.

Monitors come in a variety of sizes, from 12 to 21 inches (measured diagonally, as television screens are). Color monitors are standard now. When buying a monitor, make sure that you see it in operation. Images should be clear and sharp, without fuzziness. Currently, a 0.28mm dot pitch, 17-inch monitor with 1,024 by 768 dpi resolution is best to reduce eyestrain.

Keyboards come in several different styles. The standard PC or Mac keyboard is of the type known as "IBM extended," with function keys across the top, the regular QWERTY keyboard below, and a number keypad and cursor keys to the right. This format is also available in angled versions designed to prevent or reduce the potential for repetitive strain injuries. There is also a new Windows 95 keyboard that allows access to the "Start" button without reaching for the mouse.

The *mouse* is usually a separate device with its own cable, connected to the keyboard or the CPU, although some keyboards have a built-in mouse or trackball. The mouse allows you to move the cursor around on the screen and to select files and software programs more easily than by using the keyboard.

BACKING UP THE HARD DRIVE

Despite the sophistication of office computer equipment and software (and sometimes because of it), accidents can happen, especially when a number of different employees have access to equipment. Safeguarding valuable information is simple with a large-capacity tape backup drive. Some are currently available for as little as $150. The advantage to using a tape backup drive is that it requires no supervision (that is, no taking out one floppy disk and inserting another), so it can be set up to save the contents of the entire hard drive when the office day ends and left to do its work after hours. The backup process may only take a few minutes, depending on the amount of information on the hard drive, so information can be backed up at other times during the day if desired, but the overnight backup is generally more time efficient.

Remember that computers are machines with many parts that can fail. It is not uncommon for even a brand-new system to crash and lose all stored data due to a defective hard drive, a problem with the power supply module, or some other mechanical difficulty. In the absence of a tape backup drive, it is best to copy critical information to floppy disks periodically to prevent loss of data. This can be accomplished in an organized manner with each large file directory stored on a separate, labeled disk once a week or month. A less time-consuming alternative is to keep a blank floppy disk in the computer whenever you are working with important files and to copy those files to the disk before exiting. If you work with the same files each day, just label a set of disks "daily backup." These can be formatted and reused over and over.

Portable Computers

Desktop computer systems are the mainstays of the business computing world—sturdy, functional, and long-lasting. But they must be left in the office at the end of the day. Portable computers are useful for anyone who takes work home or needs a computer on business trips. Notebook or laptop computers have all the capabilities of desktop models but cost more because of the technology required to make components smaller and lighter. Models in the standard notebook category (above 5 pounds in weight) offer everything a desktop system does: an internal hard drive (available in sizes up to and over 1 gigabyte), a 3½-inch internal floppy drive, a screen, and a keyboard, albeit miniature. Frequent travelers may want to investigate a new line of rugged notebook models recently introduced by FieldWorks Inc.; these include a 9.5-pound notebook in a rubberized magnesium alloy frame that is advertised to withstand being dropped several feet. In fact, this model is so sturdy that U.S. Special Forces parachuting into hostile territory are now provided with FieldWorks notebooks and special instrumentation to help them locate missile guidance systems.

Smaller models (under 5 pounds), known as subnotebooks, often sacrifice the internal floppy drive to lower weight. Many laptops also come with built-in modems so they can be used as fax machines while you are on the road. A laptop may be plugged into an outlet using an AC power adapter or use battery power. Most have room for two internal batteries (giving four to six hours of operation); large, brick-sized external batteries may be purchased and installed for additional independent computing time.

As technology advances, more options in portability are being made available. Xybernaut Corporation's new Mobile Assistant model weighs only about 3 pounds and is designed to be worn attached to a belt around the waist. A headband supports a small monitor that is positioned just in front of the user's right eye, and a wristband keyboard is available. With voice-recognition software, however, data can be entered or retrieved through verbal commands, leaving both hands free.

The drawbacks of portable computers include high prices, comparatively small screens, and downsized keyboards. Some people find it difficult to switch back and forth from a laptop keyboard to a regular keyboard because the layout is different and seems very crowded in some models. However, if a portable computer is essential to your work, there are some (expensive) new devices that can make a laptop the only computer you need. A *docking station* can be used to connect your portable to a full-sized monitor, keyboard, printer, and other peripherals at your desk. CD-ROM drives, modem connections, and hard drives are available with some higher priced docking stations. In these, plugging in your laptop adds more memory and automatically connects its modem, too. With a docking station, you need not own a desktop central processing unit at all—just plug in your laptop to complete the desktop system. At present, the total price for a high-quality laptop computer, monitor, docking station, and other components of such a system is more than the price of an excellent new desktop system and a moderately priced portable computer.

For anyone operating on a shoestring, there is a much less expensive way to connect your laptop and desktop computers. If you have a good desktop system already, but need a portable as well, consider networking the two via cable. The modems can be cross-linked, too, so that software and stored documents can be accessed by either computer and information transferred easily between them. (*See also* Taking Presentations on the Road, page 162, and Taking the Office with You via Portable Computer, page 406.)

Printers

There are three basic types of printers:

1. *Dot matrix,* which are inexpensive, functional, and best for printing multipart forms. Current models offer 24-pin printing heads and near-letter-quality printing.

2. *Ink jet/bubble jet,* which produce a laser look (including color printing, if desired) at more affordable prices than laser jet printers. They are fairly rugged, can print up to nine pages per minute (faster than some laser printers), and are available in portable models for use while traveling.

3. *Laser,* which produce fast, crisp pages (up to 12 pages per minute, 300 to 1200 dpi, with 600 dpi fairly standard). But you do pay for them—often twice as much as for ink jet or bubble jet models. Color laser printers are even more expensive.

When choosing a printer, think about operating costs and how much printing you will do in terms of pages per month. Supplies for different types of printers vary widely in cost. Dot matrix printers use ribbons that cost $6 to $10 each, ink jet printers use ink cartridges at an average cost of $25 to print about 250 pages, and laser printers use expensive toner cartridges at about $100 each to print approximately 4,000 pages. Also, get the biggest, deepest document tray available to avoid refilling it constantly. It is worth paying extra for a 500-sheet paper tray if you do a lot of printing.

MULTIFUNCTIONAL PERIPHERALS

Recent technological advances have made possible almost instantaneous information processing and transmission. However, the number of gadgets required to take advantage of communications wizardry sometimes threatens to fill the entire office. For those who prefer some clear space on the desk top, one multifunctional peripheral such as Lexmark's Medley 4X for Windows replaces three essential tools—the fax machine, copier, and high-quality color printer. Doing it all from one piece of equipment is the wave of the future.

Optional Computer Hardware

Scanners

Even if they are not needed for graphic or desktop printing purposes, scanners provide a good way to store nonelectronic documents (*see* The Paperless Office, page 155). You can scan a page into your computer and then use optical character recognition (OCR) software to translate it into a word-processing document. In addition, new devices combine scanner, OCR, speaker, and voice-recognition technology (*see* Speakers and Microphones, page 148) for the visually impaired, enabling them to have printed matter read aloud via computer. Documents can also be created orally and edited.

Flatbed scanners work almost like copiers: Put the page down on the glass, close the top, and the scanner performs its function. Handheld scanners are least expensive. These can be run along a document to scan it into the computer, but are limited by the size of the scanning head. Sheet-fed scanners work more like a fax machine, with sheets of paper fed one at a time. Scanners take up little space, and most are designed to go between the monitor and CPU.

Modems

A modem is necessary to send electronic mail and transfer files via the Internet as well as to fax via computer and use voice mail. The modem must be connected to a telephone line and that line is not available for telephone calls when the modem is in use. For this reason, it is best to set aside one telephone line for modem use only so that telephone calls and modem usage can occur simultaneously. Otherwise, callers will get a busy signal whenever the modem is in use, and faxes, E-mail, and Internet access have to wait until a line is free before proceeding.

There are *internal modems,* installed within a computer in an expansion card slot; *external modems,* which plug into a serial port; and *PC card modems,* which are external modems for portable computers. (Portable computers can also use internal modems.) The standard speed for modems now is 28.8 Kbps using standard analog phone lines; faster transmission requires digital connections. Internal and external modems work in about the same way. Internal modems save desk space, but external modems have the advantage of external diagnostic LED status lights to indicate that the modem is working.

CD-ROM Drives

It is debatable whether purchasing a new computer without an internal CD-ROM is optional for most business uses, as the biggest and best software applications and research databases (such as encyclopedias) are much easier to use and install with CD-ROMs. Also, because of the amounts of data included, some applications may soon be available only on compact disks.

If you are considering adding a CD-ROM drive to existing equipment, internal and external versions are available. External drives are easier to install, but internal drives take up less space. A triple-speed (3x) drive is the current standard, though six-speed drives will soon be available. CD-ROM disks hold a lot of data—up to 650 MB. Many experts predict that they will soon replace floppy disks as the software storage medium of choice. As programs get bigger, installing them from a single CD-ROM rather than 12 to 20 floppy disks certainly seems attractive. CD-ROMs also can hold a great deal of reference materials, saving space on shelves full of dictionaries, encyclopedias, and atlases (*see* CD-ROMs for Reference, page 457).

Speakers and Microphones

Speakers and microphones are now standard accessories that are included with most new desktop computers sold as complete systems. Voice-recognition software is being introduced and upgraded, too, so that giving voice commands and/or dictation may soon replace keyboard-mouse combinations for many applications. Hands-free computer operation is invaluable for employees with limited typing skills as well as for those with physical handicaps.

Infrared (IrDA) Ports and Compatible Devices

Infrared (IrDA) ports are also standard on most new desktop systems. IrDA technology enables the user to connect a portable computer, printer, keyboard, or other IrDA-compatible device to the desktop CPU without plugging in a cable. A busy executive returning to the office from a trip can transfer files from a laptop computer directly to the desktop CPU just by placing the laptop in "view" of the IrDA port and issuing a few simple commands. Wireless remote keyboards are also convenient, as they allow the user to reposition the keyboard more easily by eliminating the cord.

Operating Systems

A computer's operating system (OS) is the basic software that must be installed before the computer can read and use other software applications. The operating system you choose will be determined largely by your choice of an IBM-compatible or Apple computer, and will in turn determine what other software can be used on your computer. As noted above, IBM PCs and PC clones generally use DOS (alone or with Microsoft Windows or another GUI) and Apple computers use Macintosh OS.

DOS (MS-DOS)

If you purchase IBM PCs or compatibles for your office, you will probably want to use MS-DOS as the basic operating system. Most users prefer to use DOS in conjunction with a GUI such as Windows 95; this makes it much easier for computer novices to load and use a number of software applications. DOS offers many useful features to optimize computer performance, such as the CHKDSK and CHKDSK/F commands, which tell the system to scan a disk for errors and correct them.

IBM OS/2 Warp

OS/2 is the other operating system for IBM compatibles, much less widely used than DOS or DOS plus Windows. OS/2 features multitasking—the ability to run more than one task at a time, such as spell-checking one section of a document while writing another. Because software developers have not created many OS/2-based applications, software tends to be more expensive and less varied than applications designed for use with DOS, DOS plus Windows, or Windows 95. However, OS/2 can run Windows applications by incorporating Windows into the OS/2 Warp environment or by creating an interface that will run the application. IBM sells OS/2 Warp with a bundle of software written especially for the OS/2 environment, making it a bargain to acquire.

Macintosh OS 7.5

Known simply as System 7.5, this is the most recent version of the Macintosh operating system. Though it is easier to use and install than DOS plus Windows or OS/2, System 7.5 lacks their multitasking capabilities. However, it offers the Macintosh features of long file names, ease of viewing files within folders, and ease of moving files from one folder to another. System 7.5 requires eight MB of RAM for best operation.

Windows 95

Windows 95, released in August 1995, was the first version of Windows to be a true operating system. In addition to being widely available, Windows 95 (with or without its current upgrade, Windows 97) offers multitasking. Memory management is better than in earlier versions, meaning that applications are less likely to fail while performing complex tasks. The new plug-and-play standard makes it easier to install peripherals. You may also name your files whatever you wish rather than being restricted to eight-character names with three-character extensions. Windows 95 requires 8 MB of RAM (16 MB is better) and a 486 microprocessor; however, it runs best on a computer with a 586 chip. Many applications are still available for its predecessor, Windows 3.1. However, as Windows 95 and faster microprocessors become standard, Windows 3.1 applications will become more and more outmoded.

Software Programs for Offices

Most basic computer systems come preloaded with much of the software necessary for office use. The most important software categories for businesses are word processing, accounting, spreadsheet, database, communications, presentation, networking, and utility applications, in addition to suites that incorporate most or all of the categories.

Word Processing Applications and Desktop Publishing Programs

Word-processing applications are the most basic and extensively developed software for personal computers, and are essential to most offices. Corel WordPerfect and Microsoft Word are the most used word processors for both Windows and Macintosh users (the latest Windows and Macintosh versions are almost indistinguishable in terms of function, and can even share files). Other favorites are Word Pro 96 for Windows 95 (the newest version of Lotus AmiPro) and Claris for Macintosh. Some word-processing applications include spreadsheets and database functions, even though they are not complete suites. Most also handle mail merge functions, allowing users to produce mass mailings and print individually addressed form letters and envelopes. The best Windows- and Macintosh-based programs can be customized to suit the way you work. You may change icons, buttons, and tool bars to display the functions you use most.

File management differs among operating systems and word-processing programs. The Macintosh still has great file management capabilities—you may name files anything you want, and it is easy to create hierarchical nests of files displayed by icon or name; applications designed to work with Windows 95 incorporate similar file management strategies. WordPerfect 7 and Word Pro 96 are best in this regard, but Microsoft Word for Windows 95 has made improvements since the last version. Word also offers excellent on-screen help—it lets you type a question in plain English and responds with the necessary instructions and a list of related help topics. Its automatic correction features and automatic formatting are also easy to use. Most major word-processing applications feature automatic correction, spell-checking, and formatting, all of which are wonderful office aids (*see* Using Word-Processing Templates to Format Documents, page 42).

For those who prefer DOS-based applications (without Windows), the most useful word-processing applications are Software Publishing Corporation's Professional Write and the more recent versions of WordPerfect for DOS. WordPerfect 6.1 for DOS includes the features that made WordPerfect 5.1 so popular with DOS-only users, as well as fax and electronic mail capabilities.

Of course, the more advanced word-processing programs include all of the features needed to produce excellent desktop publications; however, it is often simpler to use an application designed for the purpose. Microsoft Publisher is probably the easiest program to use, especially for those who are just learning to use the computer or setting up a newsletter or brochure for the first time. QuarkXPress offers more options and advanced features for experienced publishers. Adobe PageMaker 6.0 for Windows combines the power of QuarkXPress with the ease of using Microsoft Publisher, so it is currently a very popular product. (*See also* Desktop Publishing—Professional Design at Your Fingertips, page 375.)

Accounting Packages

Computers with good accounting software can play a key role in money management for any business, large or small (*see* Understanding Computer Financial Software, page 337). One of the most popular accounting software applications is Peachtree Accounting 3.0 for Windows, which features a tutorial that can help even a novice set up company finances. It also offers payroll and inventory capabilities. QuickBooks 3.0 for Mac (Intuit) and Quicken Deluxe 5.0 for Windows/Quicken 6.0 for Mac are excellent choices for businesses that do not have inventory-tracking needs; they are also good choices for personal accounting.

Large firms that require powerful accounting applications usually employ an installer or accountant with programming expertise to modify a standard accounting package to suit the firm's needs. Look for a flexible package that employs industry-standard technology and can be tailored to meet your requirements.

Spreadsheets

The most popular spreadsheet applications are Microsoft Excel, Lotus 1-2-3, and Corel's Quattro Pro, which are fairly equal in features and usability. Each is available as part of an office suite package and each has its advantages. Excel offers Wizards (automated aids) and looks and functions much like Microsoft Word, so if you are a Word user, you will find Excel easy to learn. Lotus 1-2-3 calculates imaginary scenarios well. Quattro Pro is the least expensive of the three, yet matches Excel and 1-2-3 almost feature for feature. It also has better graphics capabilities and good links to outside database applications. All three require hefty amounts of RAM to run properly.

Databases

From customer names and addresses to inventory records and accounting details, the information contained in databases may be vital to a company's existence. Most businesses have made the leap to computerized databases in lieu of keeping records on paper or index cards. Keeping such data on the computer makes it easier to access and update, rendering your business more profitable and stable in the long run.

Database programs range from sophisticated to simple. Relational databases can pull information from different files and combine data in many different ways. Other programs are more like electronic versions of the familiar Rolodex address file. Two sophisticated database programs are Lotus Approach (part of Lotus Smart-Suite) and FileMaker Pro from Claris (a special feature allows you to swap files between the Windows and Macintosh versions). Both programs offer relational power but are not too complicated for the average user. You can prepare reports, work with several different databases at once, and have your choice of automated outlet templates, such as mailing labels.

To create a personal database (of sales prospects, for example), many executives rely on a *personal information manager* (*PIM*) or a *contact manager.* PIMs are generally for individual use, incorporating an address and phone book, scheduling features, and calendars—some of the most popular ones include Lotus Organizer, Starfish Sidekick, and Day-Timer Organizer. However, contact managers are rapidly replacing PIMs due to their expanded capacity for organizing and transmitting data. Anyone whose livelihood depends on business contacts will appreciate such advanced features as follow-up call scheduling, faxing, E-mailing, and printable contact histories. GoldMine for Windows 95 (GoldMine Software) is probably the most powerful contact manager currently available, but it takes more effort to learn than older favorites, such as ACT! from Symantec and Now Up-to-Date (for Macintosh and Windows), which are both available in updated versions. ACT! can store a contact history, including details of conversations; schedule meetings; dial phone numbers; connect to E-mail; and help in writing letters, memos, and reports, using a built-in word processor with 30 templates.

Databases, contact managers, and PIMs require commitment from the user in proportion to the amount and importance of the data they contain, as it takes time to input necessary information and keep it up to date. However, the time invested to become familiar with a contact manager's operations, in particular, can produce excellent results for busy people. A complex database may need a full-time manager.

Communications Applications

Communications software allows E-mailing, faxing, and transferring files via modem to remote computers or from laptop to desktop PCs. Fax programs send and receive faxes, convert received faxes to word-processing documents, forward received faxes to other numbers, and even help to design a fax cover sheet. FaxWorks, WinFax Pro 4.0 for Windows, and Fax Pro 1.5.3 for Mac are some current favorites. An advantage offered by E-Mail Connection for Windows (by ConnectSoft) and Claris Emailer for Mac is a one-stop mail center for all your E-mail messages, even though you may have several different addresses on more than one on-line service.

Another burgeoning software classification helps users find what they need on the Internet using such applications as Netscape Navigator Personal Edition 1.2 for Windows. Rated by *Home Office Computing* magazine ("Editors' Picks," January 1996) as "a near-perfect all-in-one Internet solution," this application can make life on the Web much easier and save on-line time as well.

One of the most exciting developments in computer technology has been the evolution of programs that make voice communications over the Internet possible. Conversations take place in "real time"—that is, at a normal conversational speed—and users can talk to anyone in the world with no long-distance charges, paying only the standard Internet access fee and any local phone charges. Programs such as Internet Phone for Windows (VocalTech) and NetPhone (Electrical Magic) promise to revolutionize long-distance business communications.

Presentation and Graphics Programs

Presentation software offers sharp charts and graphics for slide shows on a computer screen, images for an overhead projector, and electronic transmission to clients, in addition to printed materials. Lotus Freelance Graphics 96 for Windows 95 is an excellent program, as is Microsoft's PowerPoint 4.0 for Mac users. Some business graphics programs also have presentation features, and their specialty is megacollections of shapes, designs, clip art, figures, and fancy text fonts, with superior drawing and painting capabilities. Use these to enhance desktop publications, create flowcharts, or create an office floor plan (*see* Using a Floor Plan to Design an Office Space, page 95). Applications such as Visio 4.0 for Windows 95, JASC's Paint Shop Pro 3.11 for Windows, and ClarisImpact 2.0 and SuperPaint 3.5 for Mac provide versatility of design and ease of use. CorelDraw 6 for Windows 95 is a huge program—it comes on three CD-ROMs—that probably offers more drawing, desktop publishing, and presentation capabilities than most offices need. It is a wonderful tool for those who rely on computer-generated illustrations. Adobe Illustrator 5.5 for Mac continues to be a favorite with professional artists.

Networking Software

Linking a group of individual computers in a network offers a number of benefits, including the ability to share files, software, and peripheral devices such as printers and modems. Simple networks connect individual computers, whereas more complex networks use *client/server architecture* in which a *server* (central computer) manages generic functions for the network. *Clients* (individual PCs) are connected to the server. Networking gives each client PC access to a modem, printer, and other peripherals installed in the server. A local area network (LAN) or wide area network (WAN) allows a computer linked to the server to access any file on it, just as anyone can open a drawer in a central file cabinet and pull out a folder. On many simple networks, you can also gain access to files on the hard drive of any client computer unless those files are password protected. Workgroup programs are software applications that help coworkers use a network. They enhance tasks such as group scheduling and contact management (very useful for a sales force), or time and billing management for attorneys, accountants, and other professionals. Newer technology even allows two users at different PCs to work on the same document at once.

Lotus Notes, Microsoft Exchange Server, Face to Face by Crosswise, and FormFlow from Symantec are all currently popular. It is important to note that many networking applications specialize in certain types of information sharing, so the primary needs of a business will determine the choice of groupware. For those with many needs and many employees, Lotus Notes may be the right choice, as it seems to do just about everything.

Utilities

Utilities programs include optical character recognition (OCR) packages for use with scanners, voice-recognition software, and project management software, as well as applications such as Norton Utilities 95 for Windows 95 and Norton Utilities 3.1 for Mac. Even computer novices can use a utilities program to scan for viruses and keep stored information in good working order by defragmenting files, undeleting files (almost everyone occasionally deletes something and then regrets it), and performing a number of other helpful maneuvers. The two leading manufacturers of utilities software, Symantec and Central Point, have now merged and continue to produce the most useful applications of this type.

A program to uninstall applications, such as Microhelp's UnInstaller 3 for Windows, is also a good investment for those who still use Windows 3.1, as Windows tends to install new applications by putting files in many different locations, including directories of shared files. This makes it very difficult to hunt and search for all files when manually deleting an application from the hard drive and often results in incompletely removed programs or the wrong files being accidentally deleted. Windows 95 includes an uninstall program, so a separate program is not needed.

Suites

Applications packages that include word-processing, graphics, database, spreadsheet, and accounting programs are known as *suites*. Suites such as Microsoft Office

7, Corel WordPerfect Suite for Windows 95, and Lotus SmartSuite 96 are generally more powerful and take up more disk space than word-processing applications alone (for instance, Microsoft Works, WordPerfect, or Lotus Word Pro 96). However, installing a suite allows the user to switch easily among applications that look and feel similar and share information between applications. Also, the total disk space used is less than or comparable to what would be required to install individual programs to handle each set of tasks.

New computer systems usually come preloaded with a number of useful software packages. If you are purchasing new equipment, consider the software included with each model as one of its more important features.

(*See also* Using Word-Processing Templates to Format Documents, page 42; Computers That Enhance Office Decor, page 95; Understanding Computer Financial Software, page 337; Using Legal Software Packages to Prepare Basic Legal Documents, page 351; Taking the Office with You via Portable Computer, page 406; CD-ROMs for Reference, page 457.)

THE PAPERLESS OFFICE

When personal computers began to spread throughout the business world, it seemed that the widely heralded paperless office would soon become a reality. Instead, there seems to be more paper around the office than ever before, as new technology (word-processing software, laser printers, copiers, and fax machines) makes it easier to produce, revise, and distribute reams of text, graphics, and data. Sometimes information is printed and filed just because the computer user is afraid something will happen to the computer file or that the information will not be found when needed again (*see* How Important Is a Hard Copy?, page 24).

If you have problems locating computer files, develop a better system for saving them. Computer storage capabilities include hard drives—now available in 1 gigabyte or more—tape drives, cartridge drives, and optical drives, all designed to hold vast quantities of information for easy access. Document and image management software will help you find files when you need them (*see* Organizing Documents Stored on Computer, page 196).

Once again, the paperless office is rumored to be imminent—and this time, the rumor may prove true. This is due to the development and use of networks, E-mail, computer faxing, inexpensive scanning technology, and CD-ROM storage. If your office uses some of this technology each day, you may be closer to taming the paper tiger than you think.

E-mail software allows individual PC users to send text messages to other users on the Internet via a modem. (And remember, with a LAN or other network, only the main computer must have a modem.) Electronic messages can be sent, or files transferred, to colleagues or clients without leaving your desk and without making copies.

Faxing from a fax machine requires a paper document that is scanned by the machine. To avoid printing a computer file just so it can be faxed, use fax software and your modem to fax directly from your computer to another computer or fax machine. This saves time, too.

CD-ROM technology has recently become an important element in business. Because of their high storage capacity, CD-ROMs are ideal for storing reference materials such as a tax law library—a single CD-ROM holds enough information to fill several shelves in printed form. And with the new WORM CDs, it may soon be common practice for businesses to save correspondence, reports, and other text files on CDs rather than in file cabinets.

Scanners convert paper documents into graphics files, which can then be converted into text files by OCR software. (Text files take up less space and can be edited.) Thus, scanners allow conversion of paper into computer files to be stored on a computer's hard drive, so even incoming correspondence may be filed electronically. Coming technology will let users store huge amounts of data on CD-ROMs made in their own offices, reducing several file cabinets full of documents to a single disk.

Buying and Selling Used Computer Equipment and Software

Even though computer prices have come down in recent years, an office computer system is still a significant expenditure. Software, too, may cost hundreds of dollars. Selling your older computer equipment and/or buying used PCs and programs may give your business the computing power it needs at a substantial savings. Remember, computer hardware and software are constantly being upgraded. You may not need the latest version or the fastest chip. Check the classified ads or find a broker (check the yellow pages under "Computer Equipment—Used") to help sell your existing equipment or buy someone else's. Some brokers take a commission; others list equipment for sale. Some do both. Many offer information on the most popular systems and the state of the market, for a fee.

Although you have decided that your present computer equipment is not sufficient for your needs, it may be just what a first-time computer user or high-school student is looking for. But you must be prepared to sell it for a lot less than its original purchase price, because computers depreciate quickly. You may have paid thousands of dollars for a PC system that is worth only hundreds now. (Apple computers tend to hold their value better than IBM-compatible models.) Just as you know that the trade-in value of an older car will not be sufficient to purchase a much newer model (even if the newer model is also used), you cannot expect your outdated PC to bring in enough cash for an upgraded model. Read ads in computer magazines, newspapers, and shoppers' weeklies to see what others are charging for models similar to yours, and advertise it accordingly. You may also consider donating it to a nonprofit organization for good will and tax deduction purposes.

Evaluating Secondhand Equipment

- Check the *BIOS* (basic input/output system) of a used computer to ensure that it is from a reliable company such as Compaq, Phoenix, or AMI.
- Turn the machine on and leave it on for a while when you are looking it over. Some problems show up only after the machine is warm.
- Run a CHKDSK command on a DOS-based machine.
- Run some of your favorite software (bring the disks with you) to see how well they work.
- Test the keys on the keyboard to see if they stick.
- Open the CPU box and look for melted or obviously broken components. Dust is not something to be concerned about.
- Test the printer, if the system has one, to make sure that it works. Print a couple of pages of text and graphics with your own software to see how well the printer and software interface. Check on availability of printer ribbons or cartridges for older models.
- Try a used CPU with your own monitor and keyboard if you are not buying a complete system. If you cannot do so, make sure the CPU can be returned if it does not interface well with your other hardware.
- Be sure to get all necessary documentation about setting the jumper switches for the system—otherwise you risk damaging the motherboard if you decide to upgrade the system by adding a better video card or an internal fax modem.
- Make sure used software has transferable licenses, then call the manufacturer for transfer instructions. Most require a letter signed by the previous owner transferring ownership of the product and giving the serial number. This is necessary only if the seller has registered the software by sending a postcard, fax, or E-mail after the original purchase.
- Get the manual and all original disks (CD-ROMs and floppies) for used software. If the seller will not give them to you, it is not a legitimate transfer and you should not make the purchase.
- Find out if this equipment or software version is known for problems by checking on-line forums, calling the manufacturer, or asking a computer expert or knowledgeable friend.

New and faster microprocessor chips are being developed continuously. IBM-compatible pre-586 Pentium chip models run at 70 to 90 MHz, faster than the 486-based models that operate at 33 to 60 MHz. Apple's Quadra, Performa, and PowerBook models are comparable in speed to IBM-compatible 486s, and its PowerPC models operate at Pentium speeds. Some users will find the 486, Quadra, or Performa models adequate for present needs, as a lot of commercial software still runs well on these machines. But this is changing rapidly. In general, the older a computer model is, the slower its speed will be. Buying an older computer may result in slower, less efficient operations due to its inability to run new software programs with advanced time-saving features. So think carefully about the speed needed for software applications you may want to purchase in the future.

Copiers and Fax Machines

Copiers

Copiers offer a range of features, from collating and stapling to reducing, enlarging, darkening, and lightening. Some have settings for reproducing photographic images. Look for one with lots of automated features and large paper trays or drawers to reduce time spent loading paper. If you make a lot of two-sided or odd-sized copies, you will want advanced paper handling features such as an automatic document feeder, which lets you place lengthy documents in the feeder to be fed automatically into the copier. (This is a big time-saver for staff.) To produce high-volume reports, a machine with a multiple-bin sorter is essential. A stapling feature is also a big time-saver for staff.

Copy speed is another important factor to consider. Keep in mind that the page-per-minute speed usually quoted is for single-sided copies. Ask for the duplexing rate if most of your copies are two-sided.

Before selecting a copier, you should know the amounts and types of copies your office needs. Determine copy volume by reading the meter on your present machine and dividing that figure by the number of months it has been in use, or check your maintenance contract. Some machines are designed for heavy use and produce thousands of copies without jamming or requiring routine maintenance; others are more economical for small offices with low copy volume. Unnecessarily high per-copy costs and maintenance problems can result from acquiring a machine that is too sophisticated for your needs or not rugged enough to handle the office copy volume.

Many business managers lease copy machines or buy used copiers. Remember to check on the availability of service/maintenance contracts, parts, and supplies, if you are thinking about buying an older model machine.

Fax Machines

Buying a good fax machine does not mean buying the least expensive one with the features you need. The cost of operating the machine may also be a significant expense. The most important factors to consider are print quality, document feed quality, and cost per copy.

Print Quality. For the best print quality, choose a fax machine that offers a resolution of 300 dots per inch (dpi) or more; superfine function, which increases the clarity of images sent; and image smoothing, which enhances received images. If your office will transmit photographs frequently, select a machine that offers many gray scales. Low-end machines offer 16 different scales (shades) of gray, whereas high-end machines print up to 128 different shades. Keep in mind that superfine function and gray scales enhance print quality but also slow transmission time.

Document Feed Quality. A fax machine is no time-saver if you must hand-feed documents or refeed misfed pages. Look for a sturdy, reliable model with an automatic feed tray that handles lengthy documents without jamming. Consumer guides will alert you to those that perform smoothly.

Cost per Copy. The manufacturer's suggested retail price is only one aspect of the cost of operating a fax machine. Far more pertinent to your budget is the cost per copy, which is a function of transmission time plus material costs. Be sure to evaluate each machine's transmission speed and the cost of equipment such as paper and ink cartridges or ribbons. If your office sends lengthy long-distance faxes, high-speed transmission (14.4 Kbps or higher) features may save money. But remember that it takes two machines, one to send and one to receive, and the slower partner always sets the pace. Although many fax models advertise high transmission speeds, there are still many 9.6-Kbps fax machines in operation. Until these are replaced, those that transmit at 14.4 or 28.8 Kbps will be forced to match their slower speed. However, if you fax frequently to offices with a high-speed machine, a fast model at your location may pay for itself in lowered phone bills.

Types of Fax Machines

Fax machines come in four types: thermal, ink jet, laser, and LED (the last three are similar to computer printers). Thermal faxes use heat-sensitive paper that is expensive, although the machine itself is not. Maintenance is simple: Replace the paper when it runs out. Thermal paper is slick, curly, and fades over time. If staff members copy thermal-paper faxes before filing them, a plain-paper fax machine will save money despite its higher initial cost.

Ink jet, laser, and LED fax machines use plain paper (the type used in copy machines) and ink or toner cartridges that must be replaced when they run out. Cartridges cost $25 to $100, depending on the type of machine.

Making a Decision

If your office sends and receives fewer than 20 fax pages per day, there is no need to invest in the most expensive technology. But a top-of-the-line model will be worth the investment if 40 or more pages are faxed daily. Consumer guides such as *What to Buy for Business: The Independent Consumer Guide to Office Equipment* can help you decide. Remember to make sure that important features work when communicating with any other fax machine, as many advanced features operate only between compatible machines from the same manufacturer.

ADVANTAGES AND DISADVANTAGES OF COMPUTER FAXING

Fax technology is becoming multifunctional. New models can print, copy, fax, and scan images. Users control faxing from personal computers and choose whether to send and receive through an external fax machine or an internal computer fax modem. Industry standards are being developed for computer accessories that will drive and connect many different pieces of office equipment, making them all part of a computer-based communications system. At present, internal computer fax modems have both pros and cons.

Advantages

- Image resolution is higher because text and graphics are generated directly from disk.
- Faxes are more secure because messages go directly to their recipients.
- Documents can be faxed without interrupting other work, as a fax modem can send or receive while you do other tasks on your computer.
- Paper jams cannot interrupt messages because your computer sends/receives directly to/from the other fax machine or computer. No printing is necessary unless you want paper copies for your files.

Disadvantages

- A computer can only receive messages when it is on.
- Messages can consume large amounts of hard disk space.
- Items such as drawings, handwritten notes, completed forms, and signed documents must be converted to computer files via optical scanner before being sent.

Typewriters (When They're Still Necessary)

Typewriters still hold their own in a few areas, despite being surpassed by computers for most tasks. Using a typewriter is much faster and easier than persuading a computer to create an individual mailing label, address a few envelopes, or fill in multipart and preprinted forms correctly. You must set up a word-processing application to print labels or envelopes and then reconfigure the printer to accept them. Compared with the simplicity of rolling a label or envelope into a typewriter and typing the address, use of a computer and printer requires a lot of effort for one or two items. Completing preprinted forms on a computer printer takes skillful preparation to make sure the information goes into the correct spaces, whereas it is very easy to do this with a typewriter. And only dot-matrix printers can be used to print on multipart forms. (Laser, ink jet, and bubble jet printers spray ink on the paper, which will not produce an image on second and third copies. Only dot-matrix printers actually type text onto the page.)

Typewriter users may be less likely to succumb to repetitive strain injuries such as tendinitis and carpal tunnel syndrome. Typewriters have springy keyboards, cushioning the fingertips, and rows of keys are set successively higher. This leads to healthier positioning of the hands, wrists, and arms, with more support from the upper body, than does the use of a flat computer keyboard. Electric typewriters also require a pause every few minutes to insert a new sheet of paper. The motions used to insert paper flex the wrist, hand, and fingers, giving them a break from their typing position. (These benefits are not always part of typing on electronic or word-processing models because they function as computers do—many pages of data can be entered without stopping to roll paper into the carriage and print.)

If you do use a typewriter for minor tasks, make sure that it is properly serviced. Office supply stores usually still service electric typewriters, although they may sell only electronic versions. If you do not have either, look for a heavy-duty desktop model rather than a lightweight portable. Remember, too, that electric typewriters are sturdy pieces of machinery, built to last for many years, and electronic models are also very reliable. You may want to consider buying a used model.

Audiovisual Equipment and VCRs

Overhead and Slide Projectors

With the advent of presentation software for the personal computer, it seemed likely that slide and overhead projectors would disappear completely. However, PCs and printers have created new uses for this older equipment. Now users can produce high-quality images on a computer and create slides or transparencies by printing them on transparent acetate film with a laser printer.

Overhead projectors are either *reflective* or *transmissive.* Reflective models work on the principle of shining light from overhead onto a mirrored base that reflects the light back through a lens. Transmissive models have a light source in the base with the lens overhead on an arm.

There are other reasons for the continued popularity of slide and overhead projectors. They are fairly portable, and presentations may be edited easily by removing one slide or sheet and replacing it with another. Unlike video equipment or PCs, overhead and slide projectors require minimal technical ability. Carousel slide projectors, in fact, have changed very little since Kodak first introduced them in 1962. Current models offer very fast slide changes, random slide access, and automatic lamp changes. Overhead projectors are also used as light sources for *liquid crystal display* (LCD) panels.

LCD Panels and Projectors

Using an LCD panel with an overhead projector is now common for presentations and training courses, even though a panel costs several thousand dollars. Certain advantages make LCD panels and projectors popular, including time and money saved by not waiting for slide or transparency production and ease of creating dynamic presentations (even with a portable computer). LCD panels can be connected to PCs or videotape players, projecting video sequences and computer graphics onto a big screen so they are visible to large gatherings.

LCD panels are available in two types: *passive matrix* and the newer *active matrix* (for video projection and animation). Active matrix screens are more expensive, but they give vivid and accurate color representation as well as good text and graphic images. Even if your presentations will not include moving images, they will look best, especially complex images, on an active matrix screen. Active matrix screens show details passive matrix screens cannot. However, if price is important, a passive matrix screen probably will suffice for images such as two-dimensional graphs and line drawings. Monochrome screens are also available; they are fine for showing static images such as spreadsheets or database searches. (They cannot handle moving images at all.)

Reflective overhead projectors will not work with LCD panels; only transmissive models can be used. To get the best projected image, an overhead projector with a very bright light is needed, as only 20 percent of the light gets through a passive matrix panel and just 2 to 3 percent through an active matrix panel. So choose an overhead projector with a clear lens (not glare-free or cream-colored), as these transmit more light.

The type of bulb used in your projector is also important. Metal halide arc lamps and quartz halogen bulbs produce white light, which creates the best projected image. Overhead projectors with halide lamps cost more (over $2,000) and the bulbs may be hard to replace. However, they are best for LCD panel use, as they give the brightest light. Quartz halogen bulbs are relatively inexpensive and may produce a bright enough light when used with the correct lens. But sharp projections may require a metal halide projector, especially in settings with a lot of ambient light.

An LCD projector is a stand-alone unit that comes with its own internal light source, audio speakers, and sometimes a built-in computer for creating presentations. LCD projectors cost more than panels and are rather unwieldy. Panels are easier to take with you for giving presentations while traveling.

TAKING PRESENTATIONS ON THE ROAD

There is no longer any need to take a monitor or projector along for computer-generated presentations in remote locations. A recent innovation for business travelers is a computer device that allows use of a laptop computer in conjunction with almost any regular television as its monitor. The device is attached to the laptop's serial port and then plugged into the television. In addition to its usefulness for presentations, this gadget also permits use of a hotel room television as a monitor, so that laptop convenience can be combined with the viewing ease of a full-sized monitor. Call Consumer Technology Northwest (800-356-3983) for more information about its Presenter adaptors.

Videotape Players and Recorders

VCRs (from videocassette recorders, their original name) have many uses in the business world, from training sessions to public relations releases. There is no need to buy a machine that costs more than $500 unless you will use it to edit videotapes, but very inexpensive (less than $300) machines often lack features such as stereo sound. They may also produce fuzzy images. A VCR in the $300 to $400 price range can still supply sharp images and useful features.

Look for a model with four video heads for the best picture. (More than four does not mean a better picture, however, as the fifth head is an erase head that allows you to patch two frames together without distortion. Unless you are creating or editing tapes, the fifth head will not be needed.) Four-head models also provide the best images in slow motion and freeze-frame modes, and usually have additional features such as extended power backup to store clock and timer data during electrical outages.

A unit with stereo capability is a good choice for showing training tapes. To get the full effect, you will also need a stereo television. For high-fidelity playback, a VCR must have two audio heads. When shopping, make sure that the salesperson is not including the audio heads in the count when describing a VCR as a four-head model.

Other features include *jog-shuttle control,* which advances or rewinds the tape in a variety of speeds, from frame-by-frame to fast-forward; *go-to,* which finds and advances the tape to a blank spot for recording; and *VCR-Plus*—a foolproof way to tape a television program by entering the short code listed with each show in program guides.

Telephones

Basic Telephone Systems

Broadly speaking, there are five types of telephone systems:

1. *KSU* (key service unit) *systems* include the key service unit itself (a box that holds the power supply, switches, and central processing unit); the phones (which are proprietary and must be of the same type); and an add-on board for special features. Generally speaking, if the phone on your desk has a lighted button for each incoming line, you are using a KSU system. The advantage is that you can easily tell which lines are in use. These systems support three to a hundred users. Everyone has access to all phone lines, so there is no need for a receptionist to answer calls other than for screening purposes.

2. *KSU-less systems* are very easy to install. These are plugged into existing RJ-14 (two-line) or RJ-11 (one-line) jacks, in any number of configurations. No special wiring is required; just plug them in and they are ready to use. All features are built into each unit, so they are called "smart phones" because there is no installation or configuration of a central unit. They do require a source of electrical power to run the electronics and will not work during power outages. Usually, KSU-less systems accommodate only two to four incoming lines and four to eight extensions, so they are best in small offices or home-based businesses.

3. *PBXs* (private branch exchanges), *PABXs* (private automatic branch exchanges), and *EPABXs* (electronic private automatic branch exchanges) were once available only to companies with over 50 employees. Smaller versions are now on the market. A PBX is easy to spot—you usually dial "9" to get an outside line. PBX systems offer more flexibility than KSUs, allowing you to add phone, fax, and modem lines easily and give different features to different extensions. A PBX system also permits use of any type of phone—you need not purchase proprietary equipment from the system manufacturer. However, a PBX does require a full-time receptionist to field incoming calls.

4. *Hybrid systems* combine KSU and PBX technology, so you may use your own single-line phones as extensions rather than proprietary equipment. In a hybrid system, some phones without all lines connected to them can be used, unlike a KSU system. Depending on the system, a receptionist is optional.

5. *Centrex systems* are available for lease from your local phone company. They offer a range of services without requiring special phones or proprietary equipment. Centrex systems are extremely flexible; you may configure each station differently and have just a few lines or thousands of them. Calls come in directly to each line, so there is no need for a full-time receptionist.

USEFUL OFFICE PHONE OPTIONS

automatic call distribution	lets you program phone groups so incoming calls go to available stations according to the length of time a station has been idle
call accounting codes	permit entering a numerical code to charge calls to a certain department or project—useful for keeping track of calls for billing
caller I.D.	displays the phone number and sometimes the name of each caller; this service is provided by the phone company; a caller I.D. attachment is necessary
call forwarding	lets you forward incoming calls to another extension
call transfer	allows transferring calls to ring on another line, so the transferor need not wait with the caller on hold to see if the other party picks up
conferencing	lets you add another party to a call already in progress
distinctive ringing	causes calls to ring in an identifiable pattern, depending on whether they originate from an inside or outside line
intercom	allows you to call another extension without dialing the full phone number

paging	permits use of the phone system to make announcements, either through individual speakers on each phone or through amplified speakers
privacy/do not disturb	allows you to dial a code or press a button to keep from being interrupted while on a call
redial	allows you to ring the last number called by pressing one button instead of dialing the number again; also known as *last number redial*
speed dial	lets you program your phone to call frequently used numbers by entering a brief numerical code for each of them

Cordless Phones

Cordless phones allow you the freedom of walking around while talking. These phones consist of a base station (which must be connected to both a source of electrical power and a telephone jack) and a portable handset, which is like a regular phone handset except that it contains a battery to provide the power for each conversation. The base station recharges the battery, so it is best to replace the handset after each use. The handset's battery life is measured in talk time (time spent in conversation) and standby time (length of time the phone holds a charge when not in use). Talk time ranges from a few to several hours; standby time may be as long as 14 days.

Radio waves carry conversations between the base station and the handset, thus eliminating the need for a cord. Usually an antenna on the handset receives the radio waves, but some models use your hand and arm for an antenna. The new generation of cordless phones include 900 MHz digital transmission to keep calls private. Their transmission distance is also much improved; for example, Uniden's 900 MHz Extend-A-Phone handset will operate at least a half mile from the base station. Many handset models automatically turn on and hang up when picked up or placed down in the base station. A paging feature is useful for locating the handset when you have forgotten where you left it.

Speakerphones/Teleconferencing

Speakerphones are half duplex, which means that only one caller can speak at a time (if both speak at once, words or phrases are clipped off). A teleconferencing device operates in full duplex sound (the unit transmits and receives at both ends of the line simultaneously) over normal phone wires. It can be plugged into a regular telephone line. The phone is then plugged into the teleconferencing device, so you do not need a separate phone. At present, there is no way to get rid of the tunnel sound effect that seems characteristic of most calls on speakerphones. The sound results from the microphone being physically distant from the sound source, and occurs even when teleconferencing devices are added.

For information on scheduling and placing teleconference calls, *see* Teleconferencing, page 87.

Cellular Phones

With a cellular phone (cellphone), you can go almost anywhere without missing a call, but the service can be expensive. Start-up fees range up to $50, depending on the special offers available, so check around. Basic service charges range from $15 to $60 per month. There is also a small fee per local call—incoming and outgoing—and also long-distance charges. Per-call fees vary according to time of day. The most expensive (peak) time usually is weekdays, 7:00 A.M. to 7:00 P.M. In addition, if you travel to another city and use your cellphone there, per-day and per-call roaming fees will apply.

Although cellphones are very convenient, be aware that they provide little or no security. Although high-end phones have voice encryption features that use sophisticated algorithms to protect your calls by switching frequencies, mid-range and lower-end phones do not. You can use a scrambler, which converts your signal into coded gibberish, if the person you are calling has a matching descrambler. Another security option is to purchase a digital cellphone that will transmit your signal in binary format as digitized pulses. Standard analog format mimics the waveform patterns of human speech and is much easier to pick up on a scanner. Of course, digital cellphones cost more, but the added security may be worth the extra money. Digital service should soon be available in all areas of the country.

A new PCM (personal call manager) by SoloPoint Communications sets up an interface between your cellphone and office or home phone. The SoloCall SmartCenter lets you listen to calls on your office/home line just as though you were screening calls by listening to answering machine messages before picking up. (Callers do not know that you are listening.) To talk with the caller, just punch a number and the call is connected to your cellphone. The PCM can also be programmed to accept calls from only those people you want to talk with and to take messages from everyone else. It can also switch a caller back to your office answering machine after you have finished talking to leave a recorded reminder—for instance, when you are driving and cannot take down a number or write a note. The PCM can be programmed via your desktop computer with Windows-compatible software or by Touch-Tone phone after you have left the office. Call SoloPoint at 408-364-8850 for more information.

There are three basic types of cellular phones: mobile phones installed permanently in the car, transportables that work in the car but may be taken with you, and handheld portables.

1. *Mobile phones* (car phones) consist of three parts: an electronic box mounted in the vehicle; the antenna, mounted on the rear window or roof for best recep-

tion; and a handset. Hands-free calls can be made via a microphone clipped to the sun visor and a speaker in the handset cradle.

2. *Transportable phones* are similar to mobile phones, but also may be used away from the car. An optional book-sized kit, which must be taken out of the car with the phone, consists of a three-watt transceiver, rechargeable batteries, and an antenna.

3. *Portable (handheld) phones* fit in a shirt pocket or handbag. These weigh from 3 to 11 ounces. Due to their small size, portable phones are less powerful than mobile phones, resulting in occasional interruptions or static on the line. These phones are powered by batteries and battery life is measured in talk time and standby time, as in cordless phones. Talk time ranges from 30 minutes to 3 hours depending on the model. Standby time is 6 to 30 hours.

USEFUL CELLULAR PHONE OPTIONS

A/B switching	see DualNAM capability
automatic credit card dialing	saves time and money if you make many long-distance calls
battery level meter	shows how much power remains in your battery, via a graphic display
call timer	comes in several versions, such as a call-in-progress timer, a cumulative timer, and a last-call timer; time is displayed on the LED/LCD window common to all cellphone designs
DTMF	dual-tone multifrequency (the cellphone version of Touch-Tone dialing); allows use of your cellphone for calls requiring tone codes, such as credit-card calls and calls to check your voice mail
dual mode	lets you switch between digital and analog features when using a digital cellphone in an area where only analog service is available
DualNAM capability	allows registration for home service in two cities, so you save money by not having to pay roaming charges (NAM stands for numeric assignment modules); this is particularly helpful if you travel frequently between two different cities; A/B switching simplifies switching between carriers, which is useful with the DualNAM feature when you are roaming

USEFUL CELLULAR PHONE OPTIONS (continued)

electronic volume control	controls volume separately on the earpiece, ringer, and keypad
lock	keeps unauthorized persons from using your cellphone
memory	holds 30 to 100 or more phone numbers that can be speed-dialed using a one-, two-, or three-digit code; some phones have alphanumeric memory, so you can access stored numbers with a letter code if you prefer
missed call counter	lets you know if calls were received while the phone was in standby mode; this feature is particularly handy if you have voice mail
ring tone selection	permits selection of a distinctive ringing pattern for your phone; some pocket phones can be set to vibrate when you get a call, instead of ringing
scratchpad	stores phone numbers in temporary memory
signal level meter	shows the strength of your cellular signal

Pagers

Many businesspeople depend on pagers for vital contacts. Often, people who spend a great deal of time away from their desks use pagers in conjunction with cellular phones. They ask frequent callers to page; once a caller's number shows up on the pager's display, they use their phones. This saves the cellular phone's battery, which would run out if the phone had to be left on to receive calls.

There are three type of pagers:

1. Tone/voice pagers, which receive and transmit voice messages.

2. Digital pagers, which send an audible or vibratory alert signal and then display the phone number of the person calling.

3. Alphanumeric pagers, which receive and display messages composed of words as well as numbers.

Each type of pager has its advantages. Tone/voice pagers let the caller transmit a message just as though speaking into an answering machine. But the message will be audible to anyone in the vicinity of the pager when it is received. For this reason, digital pagers are preferable for those who often receive messages while in meetings or public places. Alphanumeric pagers provide both the privacy and the capacity to send more than just a phone number, as anyone with E-mail access can send a short message.

Voice Mail Options

Voice mail is a computerized messaging system that directs calls to various voice mailboxes. Callers may leave messages, listen to announcements, select from a menu of options, be transferred to another number, or request transfer to an operator, all by pressing keys on the keypad. Voice mail works in one of two ways: via on-premise voice mail equipment or off-premise service from a phone company or third-party provider.

Basic voice mail features include the following:

- Caller message control—Gives callers the option of reviewing, editing, or erasing and re-recording messages before they are sent.
- Date/time stamp—Gives the date and time of each message when you press a button.
- Future delivery—Lets you record a message to yourself to remind you of an upcoming event.
- Mailbox extension—Creates separate private mailboxes on a single line so every person using that line can have an individual mailbox.
- Mailbox security—Keeps messages private by securing your voice mailbox with a personal password.
- Message annotation—Allows you to add a voice note to any message received in your voice mailbox, then saves the message for yourself or forwards it to other mailboxes within your system.
- Message reviewing options—Lets you listen to messages in any order; save some messages while deleting others; reply immediately to a message sender; and forward messages to other voice mailboxes.
- Message sending options—Permits specification of a certain delivery time for a message.
- Message waiting notification—Alerts you, by a special dial tone, that you have messages waiting. Some systems offer a message lamp or a blinking icon.
- Messaging—Lets you send messages to other people on the same voice mail system by recording a message when you call in from outside and then sending it to any voice mailbox within the system. This saves on time and long-distance charges.
- Multiple greetings—Permits you to record and store more than one outgoing message, and allows you to change from one message to another.
- Outcall notification—Lets you program the system to page you at another number.
- Urgent/private message handling—Allows a caller to mark a message urgent so you will hear it first, no matter where it is in the message queue. Or the message can be marked private, so it cannot be accessed without a password.

(*See also* Telephone Tips, page 68, for information about answering machines, answering services, and special telephone equipment for the hearing impaired.)

Long-Distance Telephone Services

Offering clients the option of calling your business toll-free is becoming a must in today's competitive business world. In fact, so many companies have added this feature that a new area code (888) has been designated for this service. Establishing a toll-free number usually means that your business will pay a flat rate for a certain number of hours of incoming and outgoing long-distance calls each month. A surcharge applies to time increments over the basic time allotment. Most long-distance service providers can set up a toll-free number for you, so check with several to determine the best rates available. There are some interesting options to consider, such as the 880 or 881 toll-free numbers that let customers from other countries call your office and share the expense with you (they pay only the international portion of the charges).

It is also important to compare prices for outgoing calls, calling cards, and other basic long-distance services. Faxing and computer data transfers via modem have resulted in increased long-distance payments for most firms, although savings in mail and copier costs may offset these to some extent. For a list of long-distance service providers and contact information, *see* Long-Distance Service Providers, page 182.

Toll-Free Service and Support Numbers for Office Equipment Manufacturers

Computers, Peripherals, Printers, Fax Machines, and Copiers

Adobe Systems: 800-833-6687
  Desktop publishing and graphics/paint software
Apple Computer, Inc.: 800-538-9696
  Computer systems (desktop and portable), printers, monitors, and personal digital assistants
AST Computer Inc.: 800-876-4278
  Computer systems (desktop and portable)
Brother International: 800-276-7746
  Computer printers and fax machines
Canon: 800-652-2666
  Computer printers, copiers, multifunctional peripherals, and fax machines
Citizen America: 800-477-4683
  Portable computer printers
Claris Corporation: 800-325-2747
  Business software
Compaq: 800-345-1518
  Computer systems (desktop and portable)
Consumer Technology Northwest: 800-356-3983
  Presenter devices to connect laptop to a television
Corel: 800-772-6735
  Software applications, including all versions of WordPerfect

Dell Computer Corp.: 800-613-3355
  Computer systems (desktop and portable)
Epson America: 800-289-3776
  Computer systems (notebooks), printers, and fax machines
Gateway 2000: 800-846-2000
  Computer systems (desktop and portable)
Hewlett-Packard Co.: 800-752-0900
  Computer printers, scanners, multifunctional peripherals, and calculators
IBM: 800-426-2968
  Computer systems (desktop and portable), printers, copiers, and personal digital assistants
Intuit: 800-816-8025
  Accounting and other software
Iomega: 800-697-8833
  ZIP Drive backup device
JASC: 800-622-2793
  Graphics/paint software
Konica: 800-256-6422
  Computer printers and copiers
Kyocera Electronics Inc.: 800-232-6797
  Computer printers and copiers
Lanier Information Services: 800-708-7088
  Multifunctional computer peripherals
Lexmark International Inc.: 800-891-0331
  Ink jet computer printers
Lexmark International, Inc.: 800-358-5835
  Multifunctional color copier/fax/printer
Microsoft: 800-426-9400
  Software and operating systems
Mita Copystar America: 800-222-6482
  Copiers
Murata Business Systems: 800-543-4636
  Fax machines and pagers
NEC America: 800-632-4636
  Computer systems (desktop), printers, monitors, and fax machines
Netscape: 800-320-2099
  Netscape Internet Navigator
Nokia: 800-296-6542
  Display products
Novell: 800-451-5151
  Software
Okidata: 800-654-3282
  Computer printers, multifunction peripherals, and fax machines
Panasonic: 800-742-8086
  Computer printers, monitors, fax machines, and telephone answering machines

Peachtree Software: 800-247-3224
  Accounting software
Quark: 800-788-7835
  Desktop publishing software
Ricoh: 800-637-4264
  Copiers and fax machines
Sharp Electronics: 800-237-4277
  Copiers, fax machines, computer printers, and personal digital assistants
Sony: 800-352-7669
  Computer monitors
Symantec: 800-441-7234
  Norton Utilities and other software applications
Tektronix Inc.: 800-835-6100
  Computer printers
Texas Instruments: 800-527-3500
  Computer systems (desktop and portable)
Toshiba: 800-334-3445
  Computer systems (portable), fax machines, printers, and copiers
Visio Corporation: 800-248-4746
  Graphics/presentation software
Xerox: 800-862-6567
  Copiers
Zenith Data Systems: 800-533-0331
  Computer workstations

Telephone Equipment

AT&T: 800-283-4918
Ericsson: 800-227-3663
Nokia: 800-666-5553
Northern Telecom: 800-842-7439
Sony: 800-937-7669
TMC: 800-862-1638
Uniden: 800-297-1023
VTech: 800-624-5688

Office Supplies

Years ago, the only source of office supplies and equipment was the corner stationer, who purchased materials from distributors/wholesalers and then sold them to businesses at a considerable markup. In response, many businesses developed purchasing departments to get the best prices on supplies. But purchasing departments can be bureaucratic and slow, with requisitions sometimes taking weeks to fill. And employees' preferences for certain brands or types of supplies may be ignored if big purchasing departments order only the least expensive brands available, in bulk.

Now, many business managers, freelancers, and telecommuters have discovered office superstores, which offer lower prices and a wide selection of supplies. Corporate purchasing cards, available to businesses of any size, make it easier for employees to shop for supplies at discount prices. Ordering from warehouse catalogs, either via mail or on-line, is another widely used means of buying supplies.

Superstores

Superstores (such as Staples, Office Depot, BizMart, and OfficeMax) have several advantages over the corner stationer: lower prices; a wide range of stock; and services such as delivery, assembly, and copying. Superstores have better prices because they buy directly from manufacturers, eliminating some of the retail markup. They are usually open on evenings and weekends, which is convenient for people who work at home.

These stores offer two methods of buying supplies: shopping in the store or ordering from a catalog (a method often preferred by larger companies). Many chains offer regular delivery arrangements so that companies can have necessary items restocked without having to place orders.

In addition to the usual office supplies such as paper, pens, and printer ribbons, superstores also offer high-tech items and furniture. Check their selection of computers, fax machines, printers, desks, chairs, case goods, and file cabinets.

Corporate Purchasing Cards

Using corporate credit cards is a good way to avoid setting up a purchasing department while decreasing the time required for requisitioning office supplies. Credit cards can help your business save money, as they can be used to reduce the cost of processing orders. A corporate purchasing card is similar to a consumer credit card, but it is issued to individuals at the request of a corporation. The corporation identifies each employee who is authorized to use the card, and may also specify that an employee can use a card only to purchase items in particular product categories or at certain stores. Restrictions are flexible; cards can be tailored to individual projects to keep budgets in line and help in tracking expenses. Individual employees receive statements detailing their purchases, but only one employee or department gets the consolidated bill, which is paid with a single check.

Corporate purchasing cards remove the burden of dealing with invoices and requisitions for small-ticket items in large companies with purchasing departments. For smaller firms, credit cards provide an easy way to buy and keep track of supplies at a relatively low cost.

Catalogs

Most purchasers of office supplies can locate all necessary items in a catalog without spending time going to a store to examine the options. It is much simpler to look in the catalog index, turn to the right page, and call in an order. The supplies are delivered within a few days, and sometimes same-day service is available.

New variations on the printed catalog are electronic and on-line catalogs. Electronic catalogs (issued on floppy disks or CD-ROMs) are easy to update, so customers are less likely to order unavailable or out-of-date items. Also, catalogs can be issued quickly, as there is no wait for them to be printed. They can even be updated daily when new products become available or old ones are discontinued, so that current information is always provided. On-line catalogs are accessed via computer modem.

Electronic catalogs are particularly well-suited to high-tech office equipment, which changes rapidly due to technological advances. In addition, some electronic furniture catalogs include computer-assisted drawing programs, allowing customers to create an office floor plan to see if new furniture will fit in existing space (*see* Using a Floor Plan to Design an Office Space, page 95).

When deciding on a catalog supplier, look for telephone support, cost of delivery, delivery time, and a generous return policy. Many suppliers provide toll-free numbers and customer support lines. Some catalog merchants offer free regular shipping (two to four business days) if the cost of an order is over a certain amount. Others ship large orders overnight at no extra charge, and some provide free pickup of returned items. You should expect full credit on all returns. (*See* Sources of Further Information, Office Supply Sources, page 183, for a list of office supply catalogs, and Office Supply Websites, page 184, for on-line services.)

BASIC OFFICE SUPPLY CHECKLIST

Desk accessories

- ☐ Address card file/business card file
- ☐ Appointment book
- ☐ Binder clips
- ☐ Calculator
- ☐ Calendar
- ☐ Calendar holder
- ☐ Copy holder (for typists)
- ☐ Day planner
- ☐ Desk pad
- ☐ Glue
- ☐ Letter/legal trays (in/out trays)
- ☐ Letter opener
- ☐ Memo holder
- ☐ Paper clip holder
- ☐ Paper clips—small
- ☐ Paper clips—large
- ☐ Paste
- ☐ Pencil sharpener
- ☐ Pencil tray
- ☐ Pen holder
- ☐ Rubber bands
- ☐ Rubber stamp pad
- ☐ Rubber stamps
- ☐ Scissors
- ☐ Stamp dispenser
- ☐ Stapler
- ☐ Staple remover
- ☐ Staples
- ☐ Tape (cellophane)
- ☐ Tape (masking)
- ☐ Tape dispenser
- ☐ Utility dish (for paper clips, pens, pencils, and other small items)
- ☐ Wall planner
- ☐ Wastebasket

Filing supplies

- ☐ Expanding (accordion) files
- ☐ File folder labels
- ☐ File folders
- ☐ File guides
- ☐ Hanging file labels
- ☐ Hanging files

- ☐ Index card files
- ☐ Index cards
- ☐ Index tabs
- ☐ Report covers
- ☐ Ring binders
- ☐ Storage cartons

Paper supplies

- ☐ Adhesive notes
- ☐ Copy paper—colored
- ☐ Copy paper—legal size
- ☐ Copy paper—letter size
- ☐ Copy paper—oversized
- ☐ Letterhead
- ☐ Letterhead envelopes
- ☐ Letterhead second sheets
- ☐ Notepads

- ☐ Plain bond typing paper
- ☐ Plain envelopes—#6 3/4
- ☐ Plain envelopes—#10
- ☐ Printer paper
- ☐ Ruled letter/legal tablets
- ☐ Scratch pads
- ☐ Steno pads
- ☐ Telephone message pads
- ☐ Thermal fax paper
- ☐ Window envelopes

Writing utensils

- ☐ Ballpoint pens
- ☐ Correction fluid
- ☐ Dry-erase markers
- ☐ Erasers
- ☐ Felt-tipped pens
- ☐ Fountain pens
- ☐ Highlighters
- ☐ Ink

- ☐ Marking crayons
- ☐ Mechanical pencils
- ☐ Pencils
- ☐ Permanent markers
- ☐ Refill lead for mechanical pencils
- ☐ Refills for pens
- ☐ Roller ball pens

Toner, cartridges, and ribbons

- ☐ Calculator ribbons
- ☐ Drum cartridges (copiers)
- ☐ Ink cartridges (ink jet/ bubble jet printers)
- ☐ Printer ribbons (dot matrix printers)
- ☐ Printhead cartridges (ink jet/bubble jet printers)

- ☐ Toner cartridges (laser printers)
- ☐ Toner/developer cartridges (copiers)
- ☐ Typewriter correction ribbons
- ☐ Typewriter printwheels/type elements
- ☐ Typewriter ribbons

BASIC OFFICE SUPPLY CHECKLIST (continued)

Computer supplies

☐ Connection cables for peripherals
☐ Data storage tapes/ cartridges
☐ Disk holders
☐ Disk labels
☐ Extension cords
☐ Floppy disks

☐ Keyboard dust covers
☐ Media storage files
☐ Mouse pads
☐ Optical discs
☐ Printer cables—bidirectional
☐ Printer cables—standard
☐ Printer dust covers
☐ Surge suppressors

Mailing supplies

☐ Address labels for envelopes—fan-fold style (for dot matrix printers)
☐ Address labels for envelopes—roll style (for typing or hand- addressing)
☐ Address labels for envelopes—sheets (for laser or ink jet printers)

☐ Address labels (4″ × 3″) for packages
☐ Booklet envelopes
☐ Catalog envelopes (without clasps)—various sizes
☐ Clasp envelopes—various sizes
☐ Interoffice envelopes

Audiovisual equipment

☐ Carousel trays (slide projectors)
☐ Head-cleaning kit (VCRs)
☐ Projection screen
☐ Replacement lamps (projectors)

☐ Slide film
☐ Slide holders
☐ Transparency film
☐ Videotape cases
☐ Videotape cassettes
☐ Videotape labels

Office Furniture

Desks and Case Goods

The desk is the single most important piece of equipment in the office. Buying a desk for an office was once a straightforward procedure: A top-ranking senior executive got a large desk of gleaming, polished wood, with matching case goods; middle managers were furnished with wood and metal or laminate furniture; secretaries had metal or laminate exclusively. But with the arrival of personal computers, the restructuring of corporations, and increased workforce mobility, office furniture selection is no longer based solely on the user's corporate rank. Function, durability, and cost are also important.

A standard office suite consists of a desk, lateral files, storage credenzas, and shelving (either freestanding bookshelves or surface-mounted bookshelf hutches). Credenzas can supply cabinet space or an additional work area (knee-space credenzas).

Functionality means selecting furniture according to its primary use. Is it strictly a work table or does the occupant need to impress visitors? Must it fit into a corporate image, or can the user express an individual preference? If appearance is important, wood usually makes the best impression. However, laminates and metal surfaces are often more durable and may be quite attractive. These are available with high-gloss finishes, a variety of edge shapes and trims, and a wide range of colors. In addition, laminate and metal items are generally less expensive than wood.

Technology is another consideration. A desk must provide sufficient wire management capabilities to accommodate cables and wiring for telephones, fax machines, personal computers, monitors, and printers. Even the most traditional-looking desks and case goods now offer effective cable management. Wire management is important not only for safety and visual reasons, but also to improve efficiency. Cables that come unplugged or are hard to reach slow down productivity. Look for desks with sliding tops and large-capacity channels beneath, and consider those with hollow legs to bring wires from the desk top to floor-level power sources.

Flexibility is also important. Desks must support a range of functions, from working at a computer terminal to reading reports, talking on the telephone, or preparing documents. Modular designs are most adaptable. For example, desks may come with removable or replaceable tops for adjustability of height and angle. Designs that can accept typing returns (to create L- or U-shaped work areas) and adjustable keyboard drawers are also highly flexible and functional.

Computer and Systems Furniture

Systems furniture includes work surfaces, file cabinets, shelving, and organizational devices connected to panel systems that provide both space planning and privacy. First widely used in the 1960s, systems furniture is flexible, affordable, and still very much an integral part of the open office landscape. It works well with modern electronic equipment. Units can be configured to handle networked computers, printers, and fax machines, with raceways for cables and wiring and adjustable shelving for keyboards and printers.

When buying computer and systems furniture, consider the following:

• Make sure your office plan is technology-friendly. Wire management for electronic equipment should be incorporated into your furniture's design, accommodating power, networking, and space requirements of current and future equipment such as computers, telephones, and fax machines.

- Purchase office panels with bottom raceways, as these are best for electrical systems with many wires and circuits. Add another tier of raceways for separate voice and data lines. Vertical wire management is another consideration—make sure it is convenient and accessible. At points where cables reach the work surface, flush-mounted channels with pull-up covers should keep wiring out of sight but easily accessible.
- Choose designs that accommodate specific technology, yet offer flexibility—for example, a computer table that includes extra shelves for speakers, supply storage, a printer, and CD-ROMs or disks.
- Insist on computer tables with sliding or articulated shelves for keyboards, and adjustable mouse trays. These not only conserve surface space, but also reduce the risk of repetitive strain injuries (*see* Avoiding Work-Related Injuries and Illnesses, page 112). Proper keyboard height is 26½ to 29½ inches, which is lower than the standard desk height of 30 inches.

(*See also* Optimizing the Work Space for Productivity, page 92, and the standard office furniture dimensions listed on pages 96 and 97.)

Chairs

Proper chairs are important. An average office worker spends nearly eight hours a day sitting at a desk, which means the chair gets almost continuous use. Thus, it is crucial to find chairs that incorporate features such as lumbar support, seat-height adjustment, tilt-lock control, and a stable base.

Sitting in one position for a long time can result in poor posture and inhibit blood circulation, causing severe back pain. Back pain is the second most common reason given for missed work days (influenza is the first). According to the National Center for Health Statistics, one-fifth of all back ailments are reported while people are at work, and back ailments account for one-fourth of all lost productivity. The search for comfortable, ergonomically correct work chairs becomes even more important when these statistics are considered. No one wants to risk musculoskeletal injuries that could lead to long-term pain and lost productivity and income.

Here are some suggestions on what to look for when purchasing office chairs:

- Chairs should be adjustable to adapt to a wide range of body types. Some chairs now come in different sizes and widths and can be configured to suit individuals. Users should be able to move the backrest forward, reducing the depth of the seat, so that people with shorter legs can rest their feet flat on the floor or on a footrest while still getting proper back support. A backrest that can be adjusted forward and backward supports individual spinal curvatures and the worker's full body weight, thus relieving stress on the lower back. Otherwise, the lower back ends up supporting the weight of the entire upper body.
- Seat height must be adjustable. The average chair has a range of about 5 inches, which should be adequate in most cases. Proper seat height varies with each employee. When seated, the feet should rest comfortably on the floor or on a footrest. This reduces pressure on the underside of the thighs.
- Armrests should be height-adjustable and preferably removable.

- The seat should have a soft front edge (sometimes called a waterfall edge) to relieve pressure on the underside of the thighs. Pressure can cause poor circulation and pains in the legs and lower back. Seats should also be comfortably padded and made of materials that absorb perspiration.
- The back-tilt angle should also be adjustable. Although it is important that the chair back stay in an upright position while the user is working, a seated person should be able to lean back occasionally to relieve strain on the back muscles.
- Chairs should have a five-point base to prevent tipping, and castor locks to keep chairs with wheels in place.

When purchasing chairs for the office, allow each worker to test a variety of chairs and select the one that is most comfortable. Different workers will value different features, according to body type and the best type of chair for individual work assignments. Single-task workers can select from executive chairs, dedicated-task chairs, and stools. Others need chairs that meet changing job requirements if they spend part of the day working at computers and the rest of their time reading, preparing documentation, and making phone calls. Keep in mind the following recommendations from the American National Standards Institute/Human Factors and Ergonomics Society:

- A chair should allow the user to sit comfortably upright, with arms hanging straight down from the shoulders and elbows bent at a 90-degree angle.
- A worker should be able to sit upright on the chair with knees bent at a 90-degree angle and feet flat on the floor or a footrest.
- A chair should support the occupant's back when he or she is seated in an upright position.

In addition, the Occupational Safety and Health Administration is developing workplace ergonomic standards to reduce the risk of repetitive strain injuries. Individual states have also put their own standards into place. The most significant are the California standards, which state that seat pans must be height- and depth-adjustable, backrests must provide adjustable lumbar support, and arm supports must be adjustable or removable. (*See also* The ABCs of OSHA, page 118; Worker-Designed Offices, page 94.)

File Cabinets, Storage Cartons, and Shelving

Despite the arrival of the personal computer and expectations of paperless offices to come, the need to store and shelve paper records and reference materials is still with us. File cabinets, whether upright or lateral, are the method of choice for storing current materials in unbound form. Archival materials and inactive records may be stored in file boxes. Bound materials, such as three-ring binders or books, can be stored upright on shelves.

File Cabinets

File cabinets are available in several types (*see* File Drawers and Sizes, page 192). When buying cabinets, look for steel ball-bearing glides or nylon rollers, so that drawers pull out smoothly, and adjustable leveling glides to keep drawers level when extended. Business records should be kept in fireproof or fire-resistant file cabinets. Taller files should have pull-out shelves and automatic safety interlocks to guard against tipping over when more than one drawer is pulled open. Side-to-side rails for hanging files are standard. You may also want to consider file drawers that offer both side-to-side and front-to-back configurations for hanging file folders, for increased flexibility in storing odd or oversized items.

Files can be made of wood, laminate-covered particle board, or metal. Lateral files and storage credenzas (which include cabinet space as well as file drawers) are often available as part of an office furniture suite, to match desks and other case goods. Rolling file carts, for temporary use or for home offices, are also available. Some resemble ordinary two-drawer vertical file cabinets on wheels; others have open sides or tops and may be made of wood, coated wire, or even wicker.

File Folders. File folders are now offered in several different materials. The thickness of file folder stock is measured in *points* (the thicker the file material, the more durable). Common weights are 9½-point, medium weight; 11-point, heavyweight; 18-point, tag stock; and 25-point, pressboard. Manila is the familiar cream-colored file folder stock; it is the most widely used and typically comes in 9½-point and 11-point weights. Some file folders that are good for heavy use are made of Kraft paper, which is usually 11-point weight. Pressboard file folders, with cloth gusseted bottoms, are the strongest (20- or 25-point) folders available, and designed to withstand active handling. Plastic file folders are also durable and designed to take rough handling. They are water-repellent and resistant to fraying, stains, tearing, and creasing.

Folders are also described in terms of their *cut,* which is the width of the tab at the top edge. A one-third-cut folder has a tab one-third the width of the folder, for example. Straight-cut folders have tabs equal to the width of the file folder. Other styles include one-half-cut, one-fifth-cut, and two-fifths-cut.

Storage Cartons and File Boxes

Because paper stored en masse is heavy and bulky, file storage boxes need to be strong. Therefore, the most durable types have double- or triple-wall corrugated construction, sometimes with metal or plastic corner and lip reinforcement. Some may also have plastic rim baffles to prevent dust from entering. A storage box may have a separate lift-off top or may close with flaps, often secured with a string latch. For ease of handling, they often have cut-in holes for your hands or plastic grips on each end. Some can be stored within a metal framework or on shelves for better access.

Shelving

Records, books, and reference materials can be stored in wood or metal bookcases or on shelving systems. Bookcases, which generally stand alone (not attached to the walls, floor, or ceiling), may have fixed or adjustable shelves. Adjustable shelves are useful if materials vary in size.

Because it is strong, industrial and commercial metal shelving is often used to hold records, which tend to be heavy. The perforated metal uprights are reinforced with x-braces. Frames may be fastened to the floor or walls for greater stability. Wall-hung shelves often use an angle-and-bracket system, with the angle clipping onto the upright perforated bracket. This is known as clip shelving.

Sources of Further Information

Organizations

American Furniture Manufacturers Association
P.O. Box HP-7
High Point, NC 27261
Phone 919-884-5000

Business and Institutional Furniture Manufacturers Association
2680 Horizon Drive, Suite A1
Grand Rapids, MI 49546-7500
Phone 616-285-3963

Business Products Industry Association, Retail Office Furniture Dealer Division
301 North Fairfax Street
Alexandria, VA 22314
Phone 703-549-9040

National Federation of Independent Businesses
600 Maryland Avenue SW
Washington, DC 20024
Write for details about their bimonthly magazine and other literature on business topics.

SOS Help Center, an on-line computer information service with a parts database (invaluable for older model computer owners) and links to the technical-support Web sites of all major computer manufacturers.
Phone 800-300-2199 or access *http://www.torch-usa.com, torchusa@ultranet.com* for subscription information.

Books and Literature

In addition to the references listed under specific headings below, the following are excellent references for information about many different types of office equipment and supplies:

Consumer Reports—For subscription information, write Consumers Union of the U.S., Inc., 101 Truman Avenue, Yonkers, NY 10703.

Consumers Digest—For subscription information, write Consumers Digest, 5705 North Lincoln Avenue, Chicago, IL 60659.

Buying and Leasing Office Equipment

Contino, Richard M. *Handbook of Equipment Leasing: The Legal, Financial, Accounting & Business Knowledge Needed to Do Any Type of Lease Arrangement.* New York: AMACOM Division, American Management Association, 1989.

Derrick, John. *The Office Equipment Advisor.* Pleasantville, NY: What to Buy, Inc., 1995.

Harding, Michael, and Mary Lu. *Purchasing.* New York: Barron's Business Library, 1991.

What to Buy for Business: The Independent Consumer Guide to Office Equipment. Pleasantville, NY: What to Buy, Inc., annual. (Call or write: What to Buy, Inc., One Rebecca Lane, Pleasantville, NY 10570, phone 914-741-1525 or fax 914-741-1367.)

Computer Hardware and Software

Bott, Ed. *Using Windows 95.* Carmel, IN: Que, Inc., 1995.

Computer Shopper, MacWeek, and *PC Magazine.* New York: (One Park Avenue, New York, NY 10016) Ziff-Davis Publishing.

Home Office Computing. New York: Scholastic, Inc. (411 Lafayette Street, New York, NY 10003, phone 800-228-7812).

Steinberg, Gene. *Using the Macintosh.* Special ed. Carmel, IN: Que, Inc., 1994.

Copiers and Fax Machines

Consumer guides published by What to Buy, Inc., such as *The Plain Paper Fax Guide, The Low-Volume Copier Guide and Budget Fax Overview,* and *What to Buy for Business: The Independent Consumer Guide to Office Equipment.* (Call or write: What to Buy, Inc., One Rebecca Lane, Pleasantville, NY 10570, phone 914-741-1525 or fax 914-741-1367.)

Fishman, Daniel, and Elliott King. *The Book of Fax: An Impartial Guide to Buying and Using Facsimile Machines.* Chapel Hill, NC: Ventana Press, 1995.

Furniture

Kanarek, Lisa. *Organizing Your Home Office for Success.* New York: Plume Books, 1993.

Ostrom, Lee T. *Creating the Ergonomically Sound Workplace.* San Francisco: Jossey-Bass Publishers, 1983.

Long-Distance Service Providers

Amnex 800-287-2646

AT&T 800-222-0400

Cable & Wireless 800-486-8686

Frontier 800-836-7000

INS 800-469-4000

LCI 800-860-1020

LDDS WorldCom 800-264-1000

MCI 800-950-5555

Network Phoenix 800-800-3002

One Star 800-950-4357

Sprint 800-877-4646

UniDial Communications/Solutions 800-832-7999

U.S. Long Distance 800-460-1111

Office Supply Sources

Global Computer Supplies 800-845-6225

Modern Service Office Supplies 800-672-6767

Office Depot 800-685-8800

OfficeMax 800-788-8080

Penny Wise 800-942-3311

Staples 800-333-3330

Viking Office Products 800-421-1222

Small Business Equipment

Attard, Janet. *The Home Office and Small Business Answer Book.* New York: Henry Holt, 1993.

Edwards, Paul, and Sarah Edwards. *Working from Home.* 4th ed. Los Angeles: Tarcher/ Putnam, 1994.

Storage

Diamond, Susan Z. *Records Management: A Practical Guide.* 3rd ed. New York: AMACOM Division, American Management Association, 1995.

Telephones/Communication Equipment

Langhoff, June. *Telecom Made Easy: Money-Saving Profit-Building Solutions for Home Businesses, Telecommuters and Small Organizations.* Newport, RI: Aegis Publishing Group, 1995.

Mobile Office. Boulder, CO: Cowles Business Media (P.O. Box 5727, Boulder, CO 80322, phone 800-271-1218).

NetGuide magazine, which features reviews of over 100 Internet sites monthly. CMP Media, Inc. (600 Community Drive, Manhasset, NY 11030, phone 800-829-0421).

On-Line Resources

Computer Equipment Websites

An excellent explanation and comparison of OS/2 Warp vs. Windows 95 *http://www.austin. ibm.com/pspinfo/os2vschg.html*

Egghead Software *http://www.egghead.com*

Macintosh software *http://www.apple.com http://www.ambrosiasw.com*

Online Used Computer Swap *http://www.creativelement.com/swap*

SOS Help Center, an on-line computer information service with a parts database and links to the technical-support Web sites of all major computer manufacturers. *http://www.torch-usa.com/torchusa@ultranet.com*

The Used Software Exchange *http://www.midwinter.com/usox*

Windows software *http://www.windows95.com*

Office Supply Web Sites

Boise Cascade *http://www.bc.com*

EZ Office Supplies, Inc. *http://www.eezz.com*

Norton Office Supplies *http://www.inovatec.com/nortons*

Office Depot *http://www.datadoc.com/dde/odepot.htm*

OfficeMax *http://www.officemax.com*

Office Papers & Supplies *http://www.papermax.com*

5

Office Systems

Office Policies and Procedures

One of the first directives given to most new employees is, "Read the company policies and procedures manual." Such a manual generally describes company objectives and management guidelines to help employees reach those objectives. A *policy* has been defined as "a definite course of performance or guiding principle adopted for the sake of expediency, facility, and circumspection, to influence and determine both immediate action and long-term decisions or endeavors" (Koontz, O'Donnell, and Weihrich, *Essentials of Management*). *Procedures* are established to carry out the policies that have been determined by management.

Defining Office Policies

Philosophy of Management

The policies of an organization originate with the company's *philosophy of management*. Management philosophies differ widely, even when comparing two firms of similar size in the same field of endeavor. For example, the owners or managers of Company A might have a policy of promoting people from within, whereas the policy of Company B might be to recruit employees, especially middle managers, from outside. The philosophy of management and resulting company policies are determined by a combination of several factors:

- the company's relationship, if any, to social and political organizations
- the types of people who are owners, managers, and employees of the business
- the internal relationships between employees and managers
- the history of the business
- the ethical and moral framework of the organization's managers, employees, customers, and suppliers
- the environment—local, regional, national, and/or international—in which the organization functions
- the economic and financial climate in which the organization functions
- the professional, commercial, or industrial milieu that interacts with the organization's operations
- the organization's relationship to government agencies and bureaus—local, regional, state, or federal

Company Objectives

Policies are closely related to the objectives of an organization. Objectives state what is to be done; policies determine the nature of actions to be taken. Like objectives, policies may be general or specific, flexible or inflexible, idealistic or realistic, and narrow or broad in scope.

Policies:

- are general statements that serve to guide employee actions
- limit decisions to those that are consistent with, and will contribute to, company objectives
- help employees decide how to resolve issues before they become problems
- describe typical situations covered, making it unnecessary to reevaluate similar situations each time they occur
- permit managers to delegate authority in specific instances yet still maintain control over their subordinates
- encompass areas of practice that require nominal degrees of judgment and interpretation by employees
- are more often described in ideological, hypothetical, or theoretical phrases than in specific, hard-line terms

Work Areas Most Affected by Policies

Company policies influence every segment of an organization's operations, including its manufacturing facilities, production lines, warehouses, sales outlets, recreational facilities, grounds and transportation services, and, of course, the office itself. However, the work and desired attitudes of personnel in some departments are more affected by policies than others.

Personnel. Policies established for recruiting, hiring, firing, and on-the-job conduct are often quite specific, leaving little margin for discretionary action. The dictates of the job market and the problems of finding suitable personnel often result in strong personnel and employment policies.

Administration. Policies related to financial matters, particularly investments and accounting, are usually well established from the start due to governmental regulations and monetary restrictions. Fiscal policies may be very firm, with little flexibility, as ignoring them could result in fines or penalties.

Marketing and Sales. Policies governing the relationships between company representatives and the public are crucial to business success. Thus, sales and service policies must be clear-cut and precise to enhance company image and ensure customer satisfaction.

Office Procedures

Office procedures are systems and routines that are fundamental to company efficiency and productivity. They vary in type, complexity, and number, according to the size and nature of a business as well as many other factors. Office management is essentially a service role that involves establishing procedures that meet a number of criteria:

1. Procedures must be realistic and workable.

2. They must be uniform throughout the company, except when the work of a department or an individual necessitates special consideration. (For example, most staff members may be required to take a lunch break from noon to 1:00 P.M. daily so that the office is fully staffed during busy morning and afternoon hours. The decision to let sales personnel stagger their lunch hours, with only departmental approval, could cause resentment among other staff. If everyone knows that this exception is based on the need for salespeople to be available at all times to handle emergency orders, other workers will be less likely to complain.)

3. They must meet Equal Employment Opportunity standards (*see* Fair Play: Eliminating Employment Discrimination, page 228).

4. They must be enforced for a stated and reasonable period of time before review and revision.

5. They must be clear-cut and readily communicated to all levels of management and personnel.

Management Responsibilities

Office management involves planning and administering a number of procedural areas. These may include the following responsibilities:

1. *Formulating the structure and avenues of communication for all office systems, procedures, and related realms of performance.* Office procedures are integral elements in any organization plan, whether for a commercial enterprise or a nonprofit institution. As such, they should be outlined and described in annual reports as well as in the articles of incorporation.

2. *Supervising clerical employees and their work.* This includes coordination with management as well as with related departments such as personnel and administration.

3. *Determining specifications for all standard office accessories, such as desks, filing cabinets, chairs, computers, calculators, reference books, copiers, stationery, and office supplies.* Standardization is important for two reasons: It simplifies the indoctrination of new employees to accepted uses of office space and equipment, and it helps to reduce overhead by facilitating the purchase of furniture, equipment, and supplies in bulk, at discount prices.

4. *Administering all communications systems and policies, including correspondence, telephones, answering systems, fax machines, and electronic mail.* An essential element in communications planning is installing equipment and developing procedures to ensure confidentiality and security of business records and trade secrets.

5. *Planning, implementing, and monitoring accounting/bookkeeping functions, filing, and other forms of record keeping.* The goals of management in this respect are (a) to establish uniform procedures that increase office efficiency; (b) to expedite employee training and orientation programs on record keeping; and

(c) to ensure compliance with financial and government regulations concerning records such as annual reports, tax returns, board meeting minutes, research, and legal proceedings.

6. *Controlling the physical and aesthetic designs and configurations of offices, including furniture, equipment, heat, air-conditioning, and lighting* (*see* Office Design and Planning, page 92). Uniformity enhances efficiency and assists in projecting the desired company image. It also provides a suitable environment for all personnel on an equitable basis.

7. *Coordinating functions and interactions within and between departments* (for example, setting up procedures for communication between clerical personnel and employees of divisions who use their services and/or equipment, such as copiers).

8. *Planning special events* (such as seminars, training programs, and public tours) *that require the use of selected office space and systems for short-term occupancy to avoid disruption of essential office routines.*

Creating a Policies and Procedures Manual

A company policies and procedures manual is imperative for most businesses— Occupational Safety and Health Administration (OSHA) regulations require an employee manual with certain inclusions, updated at regular intervals (*see* The ABCs of OSHA, page 118). Due to increasing employee/employer litigation, the company policies and procedures manual should be carefully researched and written. Grievance procedures, anti-harassment policies, incident-reporting methods, employee assistance programs, security measures, benefits eligibility, and overtime/compensatory pay are some of the most important areas to be covered. Clarity and attention to detail are most important. The language and terminology used should be easily understood by lower level employees as well as professional and technical staff.

If responsibility for writing the manual is delegated to a middle manager such as the office or personnel manager, top management should review and approve its contents before distribution. In a large company with many employees, it may also be wise to have an attorney review it. In fact, the process of creating or updating the company manual may require more time and research than a manager can afford. Many firms now employ consultants to help in the process. Computer software is also available to help in this and other human resource management areas. The Sources of Further Information section on page 210 also lists some excellent resources from experts in the field.

Most policies and procedures manuals contain a number of sections in a format that has become standard. The following information may be used as a general guide for creating your manual.

Title Page. The first page should have the title "Office Procedures Manual," followed by the company's name, mailing address, phone number, date of manual publication, and name/title of the person to whom inquiries should be made.

Statement of Responsibility. This may be included on the title page or on a separate page immediately following it. The statement of responsibility gives the name of the committee or manager responsible for delineating office procedures and the basis for authority to do so.

Statement of Purpose. The approved, stated objective of the publication should be brief and affirmative, printed either on a separate page or at the top of the "Contents" page. A typical statement of purpose follows:

> *This statement of office procedures for the American Distribution Corporation has been prepared and approved by management as an expression of the company's policies and practices in regard to the conduct of business, including the establishment of offices, facilities, employer/employee responsibilities and relationships, and interactions with clients, customers, and the general public. This document is not a legal instrument, but rather an official expression of management's desires and plans for the establishment of a sound and productive working environment for its personnel, as well as the means by which company objectives shall be attained. Policies and procedures are subject to change, as management deems necessary, by distribution of an updated and revised version of this manual.*

Contents Page. This page should briefly list the eight categories of procedures delineated in the previous section. Such categories may differ from one company to another depending on the organization's size and complexity. Subject areas may be listed in order of importance or by the order in which they are most logically considered in the company's structure.

Review of Procedures. Each procedure should be described as briefly as possible, but in as much detail as necessary to be clear. Language and style should be appropriate for understanding by all employees. Some procedures are more complicated than others and will need more space.

Adding Visual Interest

As employees will be expected to read and refer to the company policies and procedures manual as needed, it should be made as attractive and visually interesting as possible. The type font used should be clear and large enough to be read easily. Desktop publishing software, with its wide varieties of fonts, layouts, and graphic designs, can be used to make your manual attractive and readable rather than dull and uninteresting. Some textual descriptions of office procedures can be enhanced and clarified by the addition of illustrations, sketches, or charts. For example, the section on office decor may include line drawings of the types of furniture to be used, fabric swatches showing acceptable color schemes, and floor plans to indicate the most effective uses of space. The personnel supervision section may include an organizational chart showing the chain of command. Many manuals contain an office floor plan showing escape routes and exits to be used in case of fire or other emergency (*see* Emergency Evacuation Planning, page 104).

Publication and Distribution

Typical manuals range from professionally printed booklets to photocopied pages in report folders. The former are generally produced only by large corporations, as printing costs may be high. In smaller businesses, the company handbook is more often produced in-house. The number of copies required depends on the size of the business. Copies of the policies and procedures manual are usually distributed to owners and managers, employees, legal advisers, and business consultants. Extra copies are required for placement in each departmental office, in the company files, and for distribution to workers yet to be hired. Actively involved shareholders may also receive copies.

CONTACTING EMPLOYEES IN EMERGENCIES

Sometimes it is necessary to contact employees during nonbusiness hours to notify them of special circumstances such as office closings due to bad weather. In a small firm, this is usually no problem if the office manager has an updated list of all employees' home telephone numbers. In a large company, however, one person could not make all of the necessary calls, so a system would have to be developed to handle such situations. Often the first employees notified call three others (chain calling). Supervisory personnel may be given the responsibility of maintaining contact lists for the employees they oversee, with the expectation that they will make the necessary calls if the need arises. Heads of large departments may choose someone to routinely update all contact lists and ensure that supervisory staff have them by mailing copies to supervisors' homes. Whatever the system used, forethought and planning will make a big difference in the company's handling of unusual situations.

Order from Chaos: How to Organize Your Files

"Developing an organizational and filing system is not a talent that evolves naturally. It's a skill that must be learned," says Terri Lonier, lecturer and consultant, in her practical book, *Working Solo*. Your filing problems will not be solved automatically just because records are now saved on computer. They may even be exacerbated, because computer users tend to communicate more often than they did before the days of automation, and many responses come back in the form of mail and other papers (*see* Software Programs for Offices, page 150, and The Paperless Office, page 155, for information on managing computer files).

To avoid being overwhelmed by paperwork and filing, follow these professional tips:

1. Establish a designated place and time to review incoming mail.
2. Never file incoming mail simply to get it out of the way. Deal with each piece of correspondence the first time it crosses your desk. If you must delay action on certain incoming items, place them in an active desk file in order of priority, marked with dates to follow through (*see* Handling the Mail, page 197).

3. Be ruthless—learn to use your wastebasket.
4. Use a system of colored self-stick dots for each item in your active desk file: red for most urgent, yellow for pressing, and blue for a slight deferral.
5. If you receive a lot of junk mail, prepare a form letter and mail it to the senders with clear instructions to take you off their lists.
6. Stifle the urge to make a lot of photocopies.

If chaos still reigns, chances are that your office layout should be rearranged to handle paperwork more efficiently. Determine how much time and space you need for each step in the organization of your paperwork and where to locate each item being processed. Piling papers on top of papers does not improve efficiency. Office supply stores offer many types of paperwork organizers, so find some products to help you sort papers in a logical manner.

File Drawers and Sizes

The most convenient piece of equipment for managing clutter and disorder is the filing cabinet, which can accommodate either letter- or legal-sized documents. There are a wide variety of choices, with size, quality, price, ease of operation, style, and color to be considered.

Vertical Files. These are the type that most people picture when the term *file cabinet* is used. They are available in standard sizes with two to six drawers or shelves, and are designed to protect files to varying extents. Many are impervious to fire, water, and theft. Check drawer depth, the quality of sliding mechanisms, frame sturdiness, solidarity and contour comfort of handles, and the ease with which drawers can be accessed. (For example, if you will place frequently used files in each drawer of the cabinet, consider whether stooping or stretching to reach bottom and top drawers will be inconvenient.)

Lateral Files. These store files from side to side, rather than from front to back. They are wider than vertical cabinets, but not as deep; they do not protrude from the wall as far as vertical files. Files are generally easier to access than in vertical cabinets, and each drawer holds many more files. Thus, when a drawer is opened, more files are available for easy reference. Getting files from the top drawer is much easier (even for short people) than with vertical files because all files are equally accessible when the drawer is opened. (Instead of stretching to reach far back into the cabinet for the last files in a drawer, you just walk to the end of the drawer to get them.) Bottom drawers still require stooping, but again, all files in the drawer are completely in view and accessible. Two-drawer cabinets may provide a much-needed extra work surface, as they are table height. Some lateral files have drawers sized to hold blueprints or other large documents flat. These are called *flat files* and usually have a number of shallow drawers.

Open-Front Files. If filing and retrieving papers are substantial activities in your work, you might consider an open-front cabinet. These are best described as the type used in medical offices, where they are in constant use as patients come and go. Open-front cabinets allow you to read the labels on all folders quickly and easily, but have the drawback of necessitating special folders and hangers.

Shelf Files. These are similar to open-front cabinets, but offer doors that pull out to enclose files when not in use; they can be locked for security purposes.

Open-File Carts. Because they are mobile and can be moved into many floor positions, these are useful for work in progress when constant reference is needed or considerable quantities of files are being reorganized. Open-file carts, available in a variety of sizes and types, are most useful for large offices where space is not at a premium.

File Storage Containers. The most common are cardboard boxes that can be stored in a closet. These containers are also available in plastic, and come in several styles and sizes. Prices usually depend on the sturdiness of the box. Some are designed with drawers that pull out for easy access.

Types of Filing Systems

When setting up or reorganizing your office, consider the pros and cons of several different types of filing systems. Some are appropriate for large central filing systems that a number of different workers use daily. Simpler systems are more often used for sets of files maintained by a small office or an individual employee. Listed below are the most common office filing systems and a description of each.

Name Files. Generally, the quickest and easiest method of filing is to classify material according to the name of the client or company it concerns, and to file each folder alphabetically. When this system is used, no index list is necessary. Material within folders is usually filed chronologically, with the latest entries on top. In the case of extensive correspondence with an individual or organization, you may want to separate folders into periods by dates, using folders imprinted with tabs for that purpose. Examples of name files are "Acme Office Supplies" (supplier company file) and "Walters, George" (client file). It may be necessary to include a "Miscellaneous" subject file for each letter of the alphabet, for one-time correspondence with persons or firms. (For instance, if John Smith writes to you about services you do not offer, that letter and a copy of your response may be clipped together and filed in the "Miscellaneous" *S* folder.) Place miscellaneous folders behind the last name folder for each letter.

Subject Files. When material does not lend itself to classification by name, you will find it more convenient to maintain subject files. Select the subject headings carefully, using the word(s) most commonly associated with the material in each file. Subject headings must be significant, specific, and technically correct to avoid confusion. Noun titles should be used when feasible. If several different words or phrases apply, use a file index list with cross-references to refer users back to major entries. Maintenance of a file index is one of the main disadvantages of subject files, but it is usually necessary. (For example, you may have difficulty remembering exact subject categories when there are a large number of files. A "Specifications—Products" file may have been created several months ago, but now that you need to file new specifications, you are looking for a file named "Product Specifications." You will not find the file by searching through the *P*s in the file drawer, but the cross-index will have a listing in the *P*s such as "Product Specifications: see Specifications—Products.") Again, it may be useful to add a "Miscellaneous" file for each letter of the alphabet for one-of-a-kind documents that do not fit any of the major subject headings. Subject files are usually in alphabetical order.

Combined Name and Subject Files. This combined system offers the advantages of both. First, decide what subject categories to use. Then set up hanging files with labels of different colors for different subjects. Individual name folders are then alphabetized within each subject area; color-coded file folder labels make it easy to refile them. (For example, hanging files may be used for subject categories such as "Clients" or "Product Specifications," with individual client or product folders alphabetized within each hanging file. Client file folders and product file folders can be separated at a glance if all client files have red labels and all product files, blue ones.) Retrieval will also be simpler if a cross-reference system is used for subject headings. Depending on the size and complexity of the whole set of files, the cross-index can also associate names with related subjects, and vice versa. Also, a whole drawer, rather than hanging files, may be used for each subject, with subject titles placed on color-coded file drawer labels. Particle-board file dividers can also substitute for hanging files when several subjects fit in one drawer, with color-coded subject labels on the dividers.

Subject-Duplex Files. If your files are expanding steadily and you must keep track of many subjects and names, you may find it best to identify materials by subject and number. Subject headings are given a base number, such as 100 for client files, 200 for product specifications, and so on. Individual name folders within each subject are then given auxiliary numbers, such as 100.1 or 100.2. Folders are filed in numerical sequence. Using this type of system requires a related numerical file index that lists all names and subjects alphabetically and also numerically by code numbers.

Creating File Indexes

A cross-reference file index is simple to create. In a history teacher's office, a file containing American presidents' biographical sketches could be labeled "American Presidents." The cross-reference file index might contain an alphabetical cross-reference for each president, chronological cross-references for the last two centuries, and alphabetical cross-references to political party affiliations. A numerical file index for subject-duplex files is even simpler, as it is just a list of numbers with the subject file categories next to them and the numbers/names of individual files listed under each subject category.

File indexes require constant updating to be helpful. In the past, indexes were kept in card files or notebooks. As most offices now use computers, keeping an index on computer makes quick updates relatively simple. An updated printout is usually placed in the very front of the top file drawer.

In addition to being used as a cross-reference guide for large subject files, a file index may also be used to catalog locations of reference materials and objects too large to include in standard filing cabinets, such as maps, blueprints, or artwork. However, if your office has many oversized or bulky items, such as videotapes, cabinets designed specifically for them can be purchased.

Closed Files

Closed files may be organized by any of the previously listed systems. They are often kept chronologically, with cross-references to names, events, and other topics pertinent to their subject matter. Seldom used reference files may be kept in storage containers in a storage area. Records of past business transactions, old correspondence, former clients, or discontinued products may also be packed away. Be sure that storage containers are clearly labeled according to contents and dates. Store only those records that must be kept, and remember that they are being stored because you may need to retrieve them someday. Make it as easy as possible to find those files later.

Tickler Files

Tickler files are created to remind the user of work that must be done periodically or by a certain date. They are available in a variety of dimensions, capacities, and types. Tabs may list months, days, weeks, or even hours. A tickler card file is 3½ inches by 5 inches in size, with 12 monthly sections, each of which has 31 subsections for each day of that month. Memos are made on cards or slips and placed in chronological order behind each monthly divider. A correspondence tickler file may be set up in an accordion file or desk file drawer, with sections for each day of the month or each month of the year. These are often easiest to use, as a copy of the most recent correspondence concerning an event can be placed in the tickler file under a date well in advance of the deadline necessary for action. A handwritten note can be made on the tickler file copy, but often, just seeing the memo or letter again will remind the user of necessary follow-up procedures.

Tickler files have numerous purposes, the most common being to alert users to take action on matters such as the following:

- sending reminders of scheduled meetings, conferences, seminars, and other events
- making follow-up calls or sending correspondence concerning earlier business negotiations and ongoing projects
- reordering key supplies or having equipment checked
- submitting tax payments or returns
- paying insurance premiums that are due or renewing policies
- making other regularly scheduled payments
- recognizing business anniversaries or milestones
- acknowledging employee or departmental achievements
- submitting required reports

File Placement and Storage

After choosing a filing system and the cabinets needed to store files, the next step is deciding where to locate each set of files within the office. It is usually impossible to place all active files within arm's reach, even in a small office. It may be helpful to rank each set of materials by its frequency of use. Then locate the files as follows:

- Those ranked "1" (used daily) should be within arm's reach of your desk or working area—in your desk's file drawer, perhaps.
- Those ranked "2" (used at least once per week) may be farther away, yet still within your immediate office space.
- Those ranked "3" (used monthly) may be kept in a file room or other area near your office.
- Those ranked "4" (used only once every two or three months) and "5" (recently closed) can be relegated to a general company file or storage area that is accessible but not within your immediate area.
- All other files should be sent to remote storage or discarded. (For legal guidelines on setting the length of time to keep different types of records, *see* Record Keeping: How Much Is Enough? page 357.)

When planning storage space, review all areas of the office that can be converted with minimal effort. Many ingenious devices are available to turn corners, closets, and stairwells into storage nooks and cubbyholes. These may be used to organize and store binders, periodicals, newsletters, books, and tapes for easy access. For example, magazines can be filed upright, in chronological order, by placing them in an open-style holder designed for this purpose. Newsletters and reports are often filed in ring binders. You may want to install several small bookshelves, rather than one large one, so that books used frequently can be placed over or near your desk.

Organizing Documents Stored on Computer

Developing a logical system for naming and organizing computer files is just as important as an orderly procedure for paper files. In many offices, each PC user tends to name files by an idiosyncratic system that may be difficult or impossible for others to decipher. Recent improvements in the most popular word-processing programs have included a new capacity for longer file names so that users are no longer restricted to eight-character titles, but a predefined system is still necessary to ensure that files can be located quickly and easily.

Two common mistakes in computer filing are the failure to create appropriate directories and subdirectories for document storage and the use of cryptic abbreviations that have little meaning weeks or months later. Another error is saving several letters, memos, or other correspondence as one multipage document. For example, a typist may open a new document when the first letter is typed to the ABC Roofing Company and then add all subsequent ABC Roofing letters to the end of that same document, ending up with a 50-page computer file called "ABCROOF.LTR." Each time a new letter is written or an old one sought for review, this long document must be opened and navigated.

To set up computer files efficiently, give some thought to the major categories of correspondence, reports, presentations, and other items that will be retained in memory. The same types of filing systems used for paper files may be employed. Remember that the term *file* is rather misleading in computer terminology, as a file is one discrete item or document rather than a "folder" storing a number of related items. (Each letter or memo, for example, will be a separate file.) A *directory* is the "drawer" in which files are stored, and *subdirectories* are the "folders" for closely related documents (files).

Frequent correspondence or reports with the same subject are usually the most difficult to distinguish without using long file names. Although word processors now offer document summary features for a synopsis of content that can be displayed in addition to the file name, filling in the summary information can be time-consuming. Also, when a list of documents is shown on screen, extra-long file names and/or file summaries take up so much room that the screen can display only a few files at once. The user must scroll through the list to locate the desired file. Keeping file names short and arranging them in appropriate subdirectories often results in easier retrieval.

For example, the secretary for a busy wholesale liquor distributorship could create directories named *customer, forecast, complain,* and *interofc.* In the *customer* directory, subdirectories called *restaurt, clubs,* and *parties* may be created. Then another subdirectory for each restaurant customer would be added under the *restaurt* subdirectory, such as *bogarts, olivegar, bennigan, redlobst,* and so forth. If monthly invoices for each customer are prepared, the December 1996 invoice for Bogart's Beef Palace would be saved under the file name *dec96.inv.* A letter thanking Mrs. Bogart for her continued patronage could be named *thanks.ltr.* If correspondence is frequent on several different topics, related letters could be further subdivided into topical groups—for example, a subdirectory called *thanks* for routine "thank you for your continued patronage" letters, with the August 21, 1998, letter named *aug21.98,* and so on. The most important aspect of computer filing is to create file, subdirectory, and directory names that tell the viewer what is in that document at a glance. In large firms, an officewide system of naming and saving files may be necessary, especially if a network is used to link PCs and files are accessed by many different employees.

Handling the Mail

Efficient mail-handling procedures are vital to any organization's communications network. Larger businesses have mail rooms to sort incoming mail by department and individual recipient. Even in smaller firms, someone is usually designated to sort and distribute the mail to *IN* boxes on people's desks. Once these were modest receptacles containing a few short memos, reports, and letters. Today the formerly innocuous *IN* box is often a major threat to office efficiency, groaning with formidable stacks of paper that can devastate a daily work schedule. This is due to the ever increasing output of copy machines and computer printers, the escalating use of fax machines, and a tremendous rise in direct-mail marketing.

Dumping your *IN* box and its contents into the wastebasket is not an option, attractive though this may seem. At least some of the mail you receive daily is important and must be reviewed. So, how do you tame the monster? Procrastination is a common response to the stacks of correspondence, bills, catalogs, requests for donations, and complaints received by businesspeople daily. To avoid being drowned by the deluge, schedule a regular time each day to review incoming mail and develop a routine for handling it efficiently.

For information on outgoing mail-handling procedures, *see* Chapter 1, Getting It There.

Turning an *IN*-Box Nightmare into a Dream

The following suggestions will help organize your incoming mail-handling procedures:

1. Arrange labeled receptacles to receive sorted mail.
   (a) Use stacked legal- or letter-sized trays or receptacles as necessary to handle a typical day's mail.
   (b) Label one tray for correspondence you must answer or act on; one for items to be filed; one for items to be routed to other staff; and one for useful materials (magazines, catalogs, reference information) to be scanned in leisure moments. (Tuck some of these items under an arm or in your briefcase when leaving the office. Read them while commuting or waiting in line during errands—see item 11 in the following section on time management.)
2. Sort mail according to the classifications already established.
   (a) Read each first-class letter, marking it for routing, filing, action, or response.
   (b) Note the dates/times of meetings and events mentioned in correspondence in your appointment calendar or day planner (*see* Day Planners, page 201).
   (c) Review and approve invoices as you open them, then route them for payment.
   (d) Discard junk mail immediately.
3. Deal with the items set aside for response or action.
   (a) Prepare responses immediately to requests for decisions or information you can readily supply.
   (b) Take necessary actions on other correspondence.
   (c) Attach brief notes to any correspondence that cannot be handled immediately, noting the deadline for response or action as well as what must be done. Mark your day planner accordingly, or place the letter in your correspondence tickler file.

4. Keep an adequate supply of paper clips, self-stick notes, rubber bands, highlighters, and staples at hand when reviewing the mail.

Time Management

It has been said that time is our scarcest resource. Office efficiency depends on organizing, planning, and acting on priorities to keep this precious commodity from being wasted. The following suggestions can help you use your time wisely:

1. *Be positive.* Although your workload may seem overwhelming, believe that you can do it. This attitude is an essential tool to meeting any challenge.

2. *Set goals and keep them clearly in mind.* Write down your goals, which may be anything from learning Spanish to increasing office productivity by 20 percent. Many successful businesspeople testify to the magic of goal setting, and especially to the power of putting those goals on paper. Keeping your objectives at the forefront of consciousness helps you to see the forest, not just the trees, and encourages productivity.

3. *Take time to plan each day and make a "to do" list.* Break down each goal into the tasks that must be done to accomplish it, and make a list of the tasks you need to accomplish each day. Use a day planner or personal organizer for this purpose, listing your appointments, tasks, deadlines, and social activities.

4. *Set priorities.* Assign realistic priorities to the items on your "to do" list, ranking them from most important to least pressing. You can do this by rewriting the list or by using numbers or letters. Give first priority to things that absolutely must be done before any other tasks. If you end with ten first-priority items, you should probably move everything listed under other priorities to another day. Then go back and look at your ten must-do items again. Is it realistic to expect to get them all done? If not, make some of them a lower priority and/or move them to another day.

5. *Allow yourself to fail, but do not set yourself up to do so.* In scheduling daily activities, allow extra time in case something goes wrong. Make contingency plans to cover yourself.

6. *Note your accomplishments.* As you complete each task, check it off your list.

7. *Delegate, delegate, delegate.* Even if you do not have subordinates or an assistant, you can probably think of ways to delegate tasks. Maybe you can arrange to have a colleague alternate attending daily meetings with you, so that each of you is free during meeting time every other day. (Scanning someone else's notes will usually tell you all that you need to know about what occurred in a meeting. Your boss may agree to this arrangement when convinced that the time saved will make you and your partner more productive.) Make sure all tasks on your list are duties that must be handled by you.

8. *Reduce interruptions.* Life is full of well-meaning people who are out to steal your time. If your phone calls can be answered by another person or screened by an answering machine, you can return calls when you are ready to do so. To avoid entrapment in interminable calls or one-on-one meetings, begin the exchange by letting the person know you are very busy and have only a moment to spare. When you are ready to end a conversation, say so politely. If people tend to drop into your office just to chat, talk with them briefly, then stand up to signal that you must get back to your work. (This is powerful body language.) Mention a deadline you are trying to meet, then walk to your door and open it if your visitor still shows no sign of leaving. You can even make a trip to the coffee machine or rest room if necessary, just to get the visitor to follow you out of your office.

9. *Never say "yes" when you want to say "no."* Obviously, some tasks are not negotiable. However, if you are constantly approached by others to help them with projects such as volunteer fund-raisers, you may need to be more assertive. Do you really want to do these things, or are you just afraid to say no? Remember, your time is precious, and you must safeguard it. Say "no" politely, of course, but do it without guilt.

10. *Start your day the night before.* Make a mental note of things to do tomorrow and do whatever you can to make it easier, such as picking up cleaning or making one more phone call today. Choose tomorrow's clothing before retiring, and get a good night's sleep.

11. *Turn commute time and waiting time into saved time.* Instead of bemoaning the hours spent driving, on the bus, or waiting in line at the bank, make that time work for you. Carry a pocket-sized notebook and pen or a microcassette recorder. Dictate memos, record brilliant insights, or note things you must remember to do. Or use that time to read correspondence, minutes of meetings, or professional articles. If you are an audio learner, you may also consider listening to books on tape or learning a foreign language by using a portable stereo system.

Wall Planners

Wall planners are useful office tools that remind all staff members of important events, company deadlines, upcoming meetings, work schedules, and holidays. They should be displayed prominently in common areas and used as an adjunct to interoffice communications. In addition, wall planners can boost office morale if deadlines are marked off as they are met and if comments noting individual staff accomplishments are noted. Most important, wall planners should reduce reliance on excuses such as "I forgot" or "Nobody told me."

There are several sizes and types of wall planners available. Some are made of paper, with a single month in large print displayed on each page and the whole year shown in miniature. Events and deadlines for the month are filled in, and the old page is thrown away when a new month begins. Another type of wall planner has a laminated surface that can be written on with wipe-off dry markers. This type of planner consists of a generic calendar page with days and dates to be written in each month. Scheduled events are filled in as well, and all is wiped clean at month's end.

One or more members of the office staff, such as the office manager or executive assistant, should be designated to fill in events on the office wall planner. It should be placed in an area that is physically and visually accessible. All employees should be aware that they are responsible for checking it and noting important events.

Day Planners

If used properly, a day planner can be the most valuable time management tool that money can buy. It lets you keep all essential information in one portable place so your time is not wasted looking for scraps of paper with important phone numbers or project notes. You can use a day planner to make prioritized daily task lists, write down long-term goals, schedule appointments, take notes at meetings, and refer to essential business information and addresses and telephone numbers.

Day planners come in a variety of sizes, formats, and price ranges, but most have the same essential elements. These include a refillable binder for new calendar pages (usually two pages per day, divided into time increments), spaces for task lists, notepaper, and an address/telephone directory. A removable, clear plastic ruler or sheet marks the current day's pages. Many have tab-divided sections that you can customize to track and organize various projects.

Depending on the day planner you choose, there may be additional sections for extensive note-taking, business card sleeves, receipt pockets, a pen/pencil holder, and even a place for your checkbook. Clear plastic sleeves or zippered pockets may also be provided for items such as postage stamps, paper clips, and adhesive notes (to flag important pages in your planner); city or public transportation maps and schedules; and train, plane, or theater tickets. Some day planners have a variety of reference sections such as minidictionaries for bad spellers, tables of weights and measures, maps, calorie counters, and area code directories. Blank forms for exercise/workout logs, expense account records, meeting agendas, and mileage logs may also be included. In addition, you can usually purchase blank pages or even order customized forms.

To get the most from a day planner, you must use it faithfully, every day. It should take only a few minutes to write down daily objectives, set priorities for them, and note the day's appointments and deadlines. Refer to your planner often during the day, and check off each item as it is completed. Make sure all items are either checked off by day's end or moved onto the next day so they are not forgotten. At the end of each day, permanently transfer crucial information to an easily accessible place. For example, if you jotted down meeting notes or a new contact's address and phone number, be sure to transfer that information to your office Rolodex or the correct project file. Some planners are equipped with monthly indexes at the front of each month's pages (you can make your own with a blank, lined page). These should be used to quickly find calendar pages with vital information by listing a page's date and a memo such as "directions to meeting with Mr. X" or "conversation with Ms. Y re office politics." Then it will not be necessary to search each calendar page to find those notes later.

When a day planner is used appropriately, it becomes an indispensable cache of vital information. Make sure that your name, address, and telephone number are prominently displayed on the outside cover, inside cover, or front page. Then, if your day planner is lost or misplaced, the kind soul who finds it can return it to you.

Appointment Calendars

An appointment calendar may be used alone or in conjunction with a day planner. It is often the tool of an assistant or secretary who is responsible for scheduling and tracking appointments. In that case, it is critical to ensure that the appointments in your day planner are the same as those in your secretary's appointment calendar. Any changes in either should immediately be communicated and noted. If your appointment calendar goes with you everywhere, remember to put your name, address, and phone number in it in case it is lost.

When making entries, clearly note the name of the person you are meeting (and the name of the person's assistant or secretary, if appropriate), the time and address of the meeting (including brief directions and parking instructions if necessary), and the telephone number of the meeting place. Confirm each appointment the day before it is scheduled, or at least check a few hours in advance. This will prevent your showing up for a meeting only to learn that the other person has either forgotten or written down the wrong date. Make a notation on your appointment calendar, such as a circled "C," to show that the meeting has been confirmed. Because individual schedules are constantly changing, it may be advisable to use a pencil to write in your calendar. Otherwise, a messy, illegible jumble of crossed-out entries could cause you to miss an important meeting.

Appointment calendars are available in a variety of sizes and formats, from pocket-sized to desk-sized. Some offer a view of the entire month or week. Others devote one or two pages to each day, with each hour broken into 15-minute increments. Many are designed for individual use, but some are available with separate columns for several executives' appointments. This is ideal for an assistant or secretary who schedules appointments for more than one staff member.

Incoming/Outgoing Telephone Logs

If your job requires spending a lot of time on the telephone, an incoming/outgoing telephone logbook can help you manage and organize your workload. In it, you can record all calls made and received. A review of your log will show just how much of your time is devoted to calls, answering the question, "Where did the day go?" (A log of necessary calls and their duration may also help to convince your boss that you need an assistant.)

A typical log has pages on the left for incoming calls and pages on the right for outgoing ones. Note each call received on the left side as you are greeting the caller, or when you receive a phone message slip from your assistant. As you return or initiate calls, enter them on the outgoing call page. Also, check off returned calls by their corresponding incoming calls on the left page. This system is extremely useful for following up on business calls and avoiding searches for lost message slips.

If you handle a high volume of calls, a telephone log is a useful tool for office assistants or secretaries who are responsible for reminding you to return calls or for initiating your calls. At the end of each day, there is a clear, organized record of all calls received, returned, and initiated. The next morning, you can see at a glance which calls were not returned by the previous day's end.

A telephone log can also be used to track billable or tax-deductible telephone expenses for a particular project or client. As calls come in, you or your assistant can note the client, project, or case name next to each incoming or outgoing call, as well as the amount of time spent on the call. Your monthly telephone bills will be easier to reconcile, too. (*See also* Databases, page 152, and Communications Applications, page 153, for information on organizing business contact information and telephone numbers via computer software.)

WHAT DAY WILL THAT BE? (PERPETUAL CALENDAR)

Occasionally it is helpful to know the day of the week on which an event far in the future will occur or the weekday on which something happened 30 years ago. The perpetual calendar provides that information. Our 12-month, 7-day-a-week yearly calendar has only 14 variations. For instance, in a year that begins with January 1 on a Sunday, subsequent weekdays for that year will fall according to just two different patterns: the pattern for a leap year, and the pattern for a regular year. The same is true for years beginning on the other six days of the week.

The perpetual calendar is a year-by-year list of all years since our modern calendar began. It shows which of the 14 yearly variations applies to each year. For your convenience, the perpetual calendar for 150 years (1901 to 2050) is included below. Figure 5.1 contains the yearly calendars numbered 1 through 14. To find the day of the week of a past or future date, locate that year on the list of years; then note the number following the year. Find the yearly calendar corresponding to that number in Figure 5.1 and use it to learn the day on which any date occurred or will occur.

1901 . . . 3	1909 . . . 6	1917 . . . 2	1925 . . . 5
1902 . . . 4	1910 . . . 7	1918 . . . 3	1926 . . . 6
1903 . . . 5	1911 . . . 1	1919 . . . 4	1927 . . . 7
1904 . . . 13	1912 . . . 9	1920 . . . 12	1928 . . . 8
1905 . . . 1	1913 . . . 4	1921 . . . 7	1929 . . . 3
1906 . . . 2	1914 . . . 5	1922 . . . 1	1930 . . . 4
1907 . . . 3	1915 . . . 6	1923 . . . 2	1931 . . . 5
1908 . . . 11	1916 . . . 14	1924 . . . 10	1932 . . . 13

1933 . . . 1	1963 . . . 3	1993 . . . 6	2023 . . . 1
1934 . . . 2	1964 . . . 11	1994 . . . 7	2024 . . . 9
1935 . . . 3	1965 . . . 6	1995 . . . 1	2025 . . . 4
1936 . . . 11	1966 . . . 7	1996 . . . 9	2026 . . . 5
1937 . . . 6	1967 . . . 1	1997 . . . 4	2027 . . . 6
1938 . . . 7	1968 . . . 9	1998 . . . 5	2028 . . . 14
1939 . . . 1	1969 . . . 4	1999 . . . 6	2029 . . . 2
1940 . . . 9	1970 . . . 5	2000 . . . 14	2030 . . . 3
1941 . . . 4	1971 . . . 6	2001 . . . 2	2031 . . . 4
1942 . . . 5	1972 . . . 14	2002 . . . 3	2032 . . . 12
1943 . . . 6	1973 . . . 2	2003 . . . 4	2033 . . . 7
1944 . . . 14	1974 . . . 3	2004 . . . 12	2034 . . . 1
1945 . . . 2	1975 . . . 4	2005 . . . 7	2035 . . . 2
1946 . . . 3	1976 . . . 12	2006 . . . 1	2036 . . . 10
1947 . . . 4	1977 . . . 7	2007 . . . 2	2037 . . . 5
1948 . . . 12	1978 . . . 1	2008 . . . 10	2038 . . . 6
1949 . . . 7	1979 . . . 2	2009 . . . 5	2039 . . . 7
1950 . . . 1	1980 . . . 10	2010 . . . 6	2040 . . . 8
1951 . . . 2	1981 . . . 5	2011 . . . 7	2041 . . . 3
1952 . . . 10	1982 . . . 6	2012 . . . 8	2042 . . . 4
1953 . . . 5	1983 . . . 7	2013 . . . 3	2043 . . . 5
1954 . . . 6	1984 . . . 8	2014 . . . 4	2044 . . . 13
1955 . . . 7	1985 . . . 3	2015 . . . 5	2045 . . . 1
1956 . . . 8	1986 . . . 4	2016 . . . 13	2046 . . . 2
1957 . . . 3	1987 . . . 5	2017 . . . 1	2047 . . . 3
1958 . . . 4	1988 . . . 13	2018 . . . 2	2048 . . . 11
1959 . . . 5	1989 . . . 1	2019 . . . 3	2049 . . . 6
1960 . . . 13	1990 . . . 2	2020 . . . 11	2050 . . . 7
1961 . . . 1	1991 . . . 3	2021 . . . 6	
1962 . . . 2	1992 . . . 11	2022 . . . 7	

Logging Activities and Inventory

In the business sense, a *log* is a record of equipment or performance that is kept for administrative and control purposes. It is used to enhance understanding of conditions or situations. When activities are logged daily, a record of your business operations and functions is created. This can be useful in several ways. Incoming and outgoing telephone logs were described in a previous section, but logs can also be useful in other ways:

- as a record for reference when writing progress reports
- as substantiation for tax returns and claims
- as a means of comparing profits and losses when operating procedures are changed from one period to another
- as insurance against overlooking the importance of recording certain basic functions

Inventory Logging

An inventory log is essential for any company that produces, distributes, or markets products to ensure that an adequate supply of goods is kept in stock. A log may be needed to maintain office supplies that must be readily available, especially in larger firms. Only careful logging and record keeping can determine whether your organization is adequately stocked and how often supplies must be replenished to avoid shortages and operational delays. The main purpose of inventory logging is to ensure that supplies and stocks are efficiently replaced at a cost in keeping with their importance to your business. When turnover rates and averages are calculated via a log, inventory maintenance costs can be compared with income produced from sales and distribution of products. If results show a costly inventory and a discouragingly low level of profits from sales, inventory purchasing and storing procedures may be to blame, not your sales force.

Logging is indispensable for detecting and preventing losses due to employee theft, burglary, spoilage, or erosion (such as liquids that evaporate or powders that cake). It is critical for keeping track of supplies such as food items and drugs, which may become harmful as they deteriorate. Routine logging also acts as a hedge against errors in incoming supply lists or tabulations of withdrawals.

The most common inventory logging system keeps a running account of each item listed in the inventory via index cards or a computer database. A typical log is shown in Figure 5.2. To be complete, a log may also include a chronological rundown of amounts used internally, sold, or distributed to others; goods replaced by better quality items; and items discarded due to deterioration or damage. In a large company, the rundown would include a record of the department responsible for ordering or selling goods or an accounting of inventory amounts used by each department.

Ordering and Keeping Track of Supplies

Complementary to the inventory logging system, and equally essential, is the system used for ordering and purchasing all inventory items. The ordering procedure provides practical data for more effective evaluation of inventory logs. A comparison of the costs of competitive brands and the frequency with which they must be purchased can help management answer the question, "Which brand gives us the most for our money in the long run?"

Few situations are more exasperating than arriving at work, enthusiastic and ready to tackle an important assignment, only to find that the office has run out of something you need to work on the project. The last ink cartridge for your printer has just run dry, there is no paper for the copy machine, or someone has taken your last unused floppy disk.

A universal complaint of office workers is that they do not have enough storage room. If you are among the protesters, evaluate your supply requirements in terms

Figure 5.1 Perpetual calendar—the 14 alternating variations

10 **11** **12**

13 **14**

Figure 5.1 (*Continued*)

of shelf life. You may find that the problem is not lack of space, but misplaced priorities. Stock items should be purchased and stored according to a chronological system based on the time lag between storage and use. Otherwise, an 18-month supply of letterhead and envelopes may be taking up space that should be used for a larger supply of copy paper.

How do you solve this problem? Make a list of all items needed for office functions and procedures. Then estimate the amount of each that is used during a given period, such as a month or a quarter. Base the time period on your proximity to sources of supply and the time allowance needed to ensure delivery. Many items are now available for same- or next-day delivery, so it is safe to keep only enough supplies for a short time, as there is no danger of running out and having to wait for an order to arrive. More storage space can be allocated for hard-to-get essentials

```
┌─────────────────────────────────────────────────┐
│              INVENTORY LOG                        │
│   Description of item: _____  │
│   Safe shelf life: _____  │
│   Reorder schedule: _____  │
│   Time required to obtain: _____   │
│   Normal ordering quantity or amount: _____    │
│   Maximum or minimum extremes: _____      │
│   Amount or quantity ordered: _____      │
│   Date ordered: _____  Date received: _____   │
│                                                   │
└─────────────────────────────────────────────────┘
```

Figure 5.2 Inventory log

or for large amounts of bulky supplies (like copy paper) that are used very quickly. If you work in a remote area and must rely on mail-order sources, you may need more leeway and thus more storage space.

One argument cited for overstocking is that buying in large quantities is necessary to obtain discounts or take advantage of special sales. But real savings are small and discounts are available almost for the asking. Are the savings worth using limited office space for extra storage? Superstores and warehouses selling office staples at minimal prices have spread rapidly across the United States, partly due to the rapid increase in computer, fax machine, and copier use (*see* Office Supplies, page 172, for more information).

As with salable inventory stock, many types of office supplies deteriorate rapidly. Examples are inks, glues, and other liquids that evaporate; envelopes and labels that become tacky; colored paper that fades; and metal paper clips or fasteners that rust. Make sure supplies are kept in spaces that are dry and never too hot or cold, and remember that many supplies will deteriorate even in the best conditions.

Using Flowcharts to Track Projects

Flowcharts are diagrams depicting the order and movement of activities. For example, they may be used to show the progress of an ongoing project and the employees/departments involved in it. Flowcharts can illustrate tangible processes, such as the steps required to build a product on an assembly line, or abstractions, such as corporate profits and losses.

First used in the chemicals industry to portray the literal flow of substances being blended, flowcharts were gradually adapted to other applications. They are

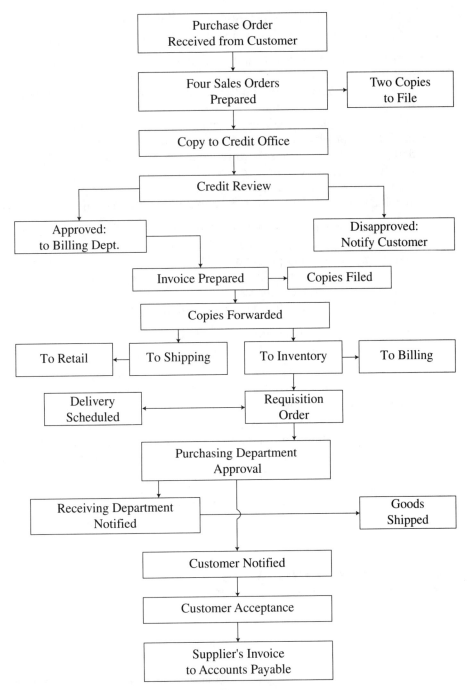

Figure 5.3 Inventory control flowchart

useful tools for defining and clarifying procedures and can be valuable aids in the problem-solving process. Today flowcharts are used for diverse purposes:

- depicting the transportation and distribution of goods among several checkpoints and locations
- training technicians to dismantle, repair, and reassemble a complicated piece of equipment
- designing computer programs or communicating programming descriptions
- providing an overview of the relationship between manufacturing processes
- depicting the steps necessary to research, write, edit, design, and print a manual
- tracing the creation of a product, from its initial design through research, development, testing, and production
- keeping track of inventories of products, materials, and supplies (see Figure 5.3)

The use of flowcharts is not limited to large companies or complex technological procedures. A speaker may sketch a simple diagram to help the audience visualize the steps in a marketing program. Desktop publishing now allows quick creation of professional flowcharts to illustrate complex processes and concepts for presentation at meetings and conferences.

How do you make a flowchart? Just follow these steps:

1. Select an activity or function to illustrate.
2. List all elements involved in the procedure, grouping activities that are closely related.
3. Sort the elements into chronological or sequential order.
4. Write the name of each element or step in a box.
5. Design boxes of different shapes to represent each step of the procedure. In a complex procedure, one shape may be used for all individual tasks in one part of the process and other shapes for other parts. (For example, use a triangle for each stage of the design process, a square for research steps, circle for development, octagon for testing stages, and oblong for production procedures.)
6. Connect the boxes with lines to show how processes are related.
7. Draw arrows to portray the sequential or chronological flow of events.

Sources of Further Information

Organizations

American Management Association
135 West 50th Street, New York, NY 10020
Offers publications and seminars on office efficiency.

Center for Entrepreneurial Management
180 Varick Street, New York, NY 10014

Publishes newsletter, Success *magazine, and literature on office management.*

National Federation of Independent Businesses
600 Maryland Avenue SW, Washington, DC 20024
Publishes bimonthly magazine and literature on business topics.

Books and Literature

Attard, Janet. *The Home Office and Small Business Answer Book.* New York: Henry Holt, 1993.

Cox, William N. *How to Prepare a Personnel Policy Manual.* New York: Bullet Publishing, 1995.

Derrick, John. *The Office Equipment Advisor.* New York: Business, Inc., 1993.

DeVries, Mary. *Professional Secretary's Encyclopedic Dictionary.* Englewood Cliffs, NJ: Prentice Hall, 1989.

Diamond, Susan Z. *Records Management: A Practical Guide.* 3rd ed. New York: AMACOM Division, American Management Association, 1995.

Edwards, Paul, and Sarah Edwards. *Working from Home.* 4th ed. Los Angeles: Tarcher/Putnam, 1994.

Ehrenfeld, Tom. "The (Handbook) Handbook." *Inc.,* Vol. 15, November 1, 1993.

Hemphill, Barbara. *Taming the Paper Tiger: Organizing the Paper in Your Life.* Washington, DC: Kiplinger Books, 1992.

Kanarek, Lisa. *Organizing Your Home Office for Success.* New York: Plume Books, 1993.

Koontz, Harold, Cyril O'Donnell, and Heinz Weihrich. *Essentials of Management.* 3rd ed. New York: McGraw-Hill, 1982.

Lonier, Terri. *Working Solo.* New Paltz, NY: Portico Press, 1994.

Mark, Teri J., and Jane M. Owens. "Comparing Apples to Oranges: Methods for Evaluating and Selecting Records Management Software." *Records Management Quarterly,* Vol. 30, January 1, 1996.

Mims, Julian. "Writing for Results." *Records Management Quarterly,* Vol. 29, January 1, 1995.

Rosenbaum, Alvin. *The Complete Home Office: Planning Your Work Space for Maximum Efficiency.* New York: Viking Press, 1995.

On-Line Resources

Hard at Work, a Web site that features on-line help for office management issues as well as publications, seminars, and other aids for human resources specialists
http://www.hard@work.com

Work Force Online, another excellent source of on-line assistance for people management
http://www.workforceonline.com

6

People: The Office's Most Valuable Asset

Managing Superiors, Subordinates, and Peers

Everyone has a boss, or so the saying goes. Even the chief executive officer (CEO) of a huge corporation is accountable to customers and/or stockholders. The best managers set a good example for employees by interacting with their own superiors appropriately and earning the respect of subordinates. Suggestions in the following sections may be useful to management and workers in establishing, maintaining, and respecting an effective chain of command.

MAKING THE MOST OF MEETINGS

Meetings serve many functions, among them planning, training, problem solving, and progress reporting. All meetings have a common purpose, however—the communication of necessary information. Important points to remember when planning meetings are:

- Formal conferences can be more effective than informal communications because they offer an opportunity for better organization, stricter attention, and clearer definition of the group affected by the subject at hand. But—
- A casual discussion at lunch or during a down moment in the office may be more effective than a formal meeting, as inspired and creative ideas are often generated in an atmosphere of comfort and informality.
- A common management error is to include everyone in regular staff meetings and attempt to cover all necessary topics at one time, sometimes reflecting the concern that lower-level workers will feel left out if they are not included. However, when staff have been subjected to many interminable meetings covering topics of interest to only a few, most would be happy to be uninformed about such matters.
- Successful meetings require planning and direction from beginning to end. Include as many different viewpoints from as many different departments as practical, but keep the number of participants to ten or fewer if possible.

To ensure that the time spent in meetings is necessary and productive, ask yourself these questions when planning each conference:

- Are daily or weekly staff meetings truly productive? If not, reduce them to an as-needed basis.
- Can some topics be covered better in smaller groups, with only those immediately concerned present? Or—
- Can some meetings be combined to save time?
- Are the participants only those employees who are necessary and interested in the subject at hand?

(*See also* Chairing a Meeting, page 63, and Meeting One-on-One, page 66.)

Satisfying Superiors

First, realize that your superiors are human, with hopes, fears, and dreams that are probably similar to yours, though their approach to work situations may be very different. Then remember that you must comply with their decisions and expectations. If you can persuade a superior to try a different approach, that is well and good, but you are expected to follow instructions until those are changed. To promote a good working relationship with your supervisor(s), follow these suggestions:

- Understand what is expected of you.
- Try to see things from your supervisor's perspective.
- Learn all of the ways that your boss communicates, including body language and what is implied as well as what is explicitly stated.
- Emulate the work ethics and practices of your superiors.
- Keep your supervisor(s) informed of your work and achievements.
- Accept their suggestions and criticism gracefully, even if you feel that these are unnecessary or undeserved, and use them to make positive changes.
- Never criticize, contradict, or embarrass your boss in front of others.
- Support a superior's decisions in public, then express your contrary opinions diplomatically in private.
- Be assertive and honest, but never on the attack.
- Stay out of conflicts between your supervisors and their superiors.
- Never go over your superior's head unless you have discussed the matter with him or her first and are sure that the situation justifies your actions.

How to Handle Meetings with Your Boss

Careful planning is necessary to ensure that your ideas will be given the respect and attention they deserve. Before deciding on an approach, examine your motives carefully. The boss will be interested in your ideas only if they contribute to the success of the company. Although your main goal is probably to promote your own interests (this is the primary motivation behind most human acts), your presentation must show that what you propose will serve the company goal of making money.

For example, suppose you have asked for a meeting because you are concerned about company morale following a recent announcement that no raises or bonuses will be forthcoming this year. Employee turnover has risen sharply, and personnel who remain are angry or depressed. Of course, you are concerned about your own employment security and salary as well as the emotional climate within the workplace. Remember that the owner or manager is a person, too, with personal security at stake, and that cutbacks have been made in order to protect company profits, to ensure that business operations can continue. Approach the situation armed with facts illustrating the poor quality of products and services being produced due to employee discontent and the resulting loss of business because of dissatisfied customers. Never make the emotional welfare of employees the focus of the conversation; this is relevant only as it pertains to business goals.

If the boss has requested a meeting, ask what the topic of discussion is to be. Then prepare as though you had proposed the meeting, concentrating on a positive approach. Never take a defensive stance; try to remain objective and concentrate on presenting facts, even if your work is being criticized. If you are at fault, admit it; then ask for suggestions to help you improve.

Always be prepared with solutions to each problem you present. If you have requested the meeting, begin by stating that there is a problem and that you would like to propose a solution. Even when difficulties seem insurmountable, we usually have some sense of what the solution could be. Your goal in the meeting will be to detail ways to achieve that solution, not to lay a problem at the boss's feet and walk away. Whether you are a vice president or a line employee, your superior has placed certain job responsibilities in your hands. Your suggestions on solving problems should be expected and appreciated.

Remember that the boss is the boss, and that his or her decisions are final. The solutions you present may be rejected in favor of strategies preferred by your superior. Accept this gracefully as the prerogative of management. If you were in the other person's shoes, you, too, might prefer your own ideas and solutions to those presented by others.

EVALUATION DO'S AND DON'TS FOR SUBORDINATES

Do

Approach each evaluation with a positive attitude, even if you suspect that your supervisor is displeased with some aspect of your work. Take the attitude that the purpose of the meeting is to help you improve your work.

Accept justified criticism by taking responsibility for mistakes or poor performance. Do not attempt to excuse your behavior by blaming others. Instead, state that you are aware that your work needs improvement, and list specific steps you are taking to correct past errors.

Talk with your supervisor frequently (not just at formal evaluations) about your work. Ask for feedback on your performance and suggestions on ways to improve.

Keep the details of your interview confidential. Do not discuss specifics with other employees. You should expect your supervisor to keep details of the meeting private; discussing them with others puts your boss in the position of not being able to respond to others' reactions to your version of events.

Tell your supervisor frankly about any problems you are having, whether these concern interactions with other employees, other employees' work (only as it affects your ability to perform), or your need for more direction, assistance, or training.

Listen to what your supervisor has to say and be open to criticism or suggestions. If you disagree with any points discussed, say so in a calm, respectful manner. Then, if a compromise is not reached, remember that your supervisor has the last word and accept direction gracefully.

Communicate your loyalty to company goals and your desire to succeed. Thank your supervisor for supporting you and helping you improve your work.

Don't

Assume that you must be on the defensive. You may find yourself making excuses for behavior that the boss had no intention of criticizing.

Accuse your supervisor of favoritism toward others or unfair bias against you unless you have very good reason to do so. If you feel that you must discuss such issues, approach the subject with a statement such as, "Sometimes I feel that you criticize my work because you dislike me rather than because my work is truly unsatisfactory." Because your statement reveals a feeling of vulnerability, not anger, your boss is likely to respond by honestly considering his or her own behavior and motives (at this moment and in future interactions with you) rather than immediately becoming defensive and viewing your comments as excuses for poor performance.

Criticize your supervisor harshly. Your supervisor's performance is also at issue here, as the quality of your work reflects on this person's ability to supervise you effectively. If there are areas in which you need more assistance, direction, or support, discuss them by offering specific suggestions about what you need to do a good job. Instead of criticizing your supervisor's failure to provide support in the past, state that you know he or she is busy and has many other concerns, and take responsibility for requesting help or direction in the future.

Argue about issues that represent personal idiosyncracies, as everyone has these. For example, if your supervisor is compulsively neat and criticizes your messy office, diplomatically state that you envy those whose desks are neat, but that you seem to need everything in arm's reach to work efficiently. Ask for a compromise—would your supervisor be satisfied to see your desk organized, straightened, or completely clean at the end of each workday? (You can always sweep everything into an empty file drawer or cabinet at the end of the day, if necessary.)

Make empty threats or place your job in jeopardy by emotional outbursts in reaction to criticism. Never threaten to resign rather than complying with your supervisor's demands unless you have given this serious consideration before the evaluation and intend to follow through if necessary. It may indeed be time for you to move on, but threatening to resign opens the door for your boss to accept your resignation, leaving you with no job and no recourse to unemployment or the severance benefits that may accompany involuntary termination.

Threaten to go over your supervisor's head about the results of an evaluation unless the situation is extremely serious and there is no other solution to your problem. Realize that you may not receive the desired support from above, that your supervisor will probably continue to be your supervisor even if your evaluation results are reversed on appeal, and that the aftermath may be more unpleasant for you than for your boss.

Supervising Subordinates

Although managers should not view their employees as children or assume a parental role in directing their activities, good supervisory skills do have a lot in common with the characteristics of good parents. Most supervisors and employees would probably agree that confidence, consistency, courtesy, and compassion—in addition to thorough job knowledge—are the most important qualities of good supervisors. Check your own performance in the following areas:

- Be sure subordinates understand what you expect from them in their work and behavior.
- Be as courteous to subordinates as to superiors.
- Be open and approachable.
- Appreciate good work and give proper credit.
- Reprimand subordinates in private, not in the presence of others.
- Earn subordinates' loyalty and cooperation by not taking advantage of them.
- Listen to their ideas and concerns.
- Learn what motivates them most effectively.
- Delegate, delegate, delegate!
- Never play favorites, take sides, or encourage dissension.
- Make decisions without being aggressive or wielding your authority unnecessarily.
- Be an effective decision maker by taking all factors into account before making a pronouncement.
- Communicate your decisions and those of your superiors in a firm manner.

Constantly examine your own actions to be sure they are fair. If an employee expresses concern about unfair treatment, ask a peer or your own superior for an objective review of your actions to be sure of your motives, and take steps to correct any inappropriate behavior.

When someone publicly challenges your authority or openly refuses to take direction from you, state that you have taken everything into consideration and that this is your decision. Then let everyone know that insubordination will not be tolerated. Ask the recalcitrant employee to step into your office. Do not allow subordinates to draw you into arguments in public, and never make disciplinary threats in public. You may empathize with a worker's frustration by saying, "I know that this is not what you wanted and that you are disappointed with my decision, but you are a professional and I expect your cooperation and full compliance with my decision."

Let your subordinates know that you are not interested in hearing excuses for bad behavior. This does not mean that you should not ask an employee to describe any extenuating circumstances that may have caused poor job performance. But when a problem *behavior* (such as chronic lateness, constant criticism of others, or habitual disrespect and insubordination) is the issue, asking the person to justify it is a waste of time. The point to be made is that there is no excuse for such behavior and it must stop.

Sometimes managers must reverse or reconsider previously announced decisions. When subsequent developments necessitate such changes, communicate these in the same firm, confident manner that was used to issue the original decision. Even though some workers may have predicted this outcome, you are their supervisor and it was appropriate for you to decide on the original approach based on the facts of the situation. Now that new data is available, you are revising procedures in light of that information, not because your original decision was in error.

Delegating Duties

Effective delegation is a balancing act. A manager who delegates too little usually wastes valuable time on work that could be handled by others while neglecting the executive planning and decision making that are crucial to business success. At the other extreme is the manager who gives too much authority to subordinates and loses control of the organization. Successful delegation uses all the resources and talents at your disposal, but it ensures that your team works at maximum efficiency.

Managers can find many reasons not to entrust responsibilities to others. A common excuse given is that the work is too important to delegate. The problem with this "if you want it done right, do it yourself" approach is that one person cannot do everything just to make sure the work is done well—employees are hired because there is more work than one person can do. Managers are there to see that the work is done, not to do it all themselves. An executive who refuses to delegate responsibility and authority is not fulfilling the most important requirement of a management position, and may be replaced by someone who knows how to manage. This negates another reason frequently given for refusal to delegate—the fear of becoming expendable if subordinates take on important tasks. In most businesses, supervisors who know how to delegate are those considered first for promotions and raises.

Time and energy are required to train subordinates and evaluate their work, but these are among the primary functions of management. An executive who says, "I can do it faster myself than I can show someone else how to do it" is forgetting an important aspect of assigning responsibility to others. The fact is, teaching someone else to do a job and then turning it over means one less task for the manager in the future. This frees time for training employees to do other tasks and for evaluating their work. Conversely, a subordinate's job consists of doing the duties assigned by the manager. Your employees were not hired to do whatever they please; they were hired to do the work you assign them.

The real reason for not assigning a task to someone else may be that you do not understand the work well enough to explain it. Remember that you only need to know what must be accomplished in order to delegate duties. If the employee's task is something you have never done and know nothing about, doing it yourself will mean finding someone to teach you, or teaching yourself to do it. It will be just as easy to help a subordinate figure it out. The best approach in this instance may be to have another, more experienced worker train your employee. Another approach is to explain the purpose of the task and allow your subordinate to decide how it should be done. Stress that part of the assignment is finding the best way to do it. State that you will check on the progress being made and will offer suggestions as needed until the job is satisfactorily completed; then be sure to do so.

Most employees respond with enthusiasm when given some leeway to develop their own work methods. Trust your staff enough to challenge them in this manner—the show of confidence will boost their self-image. Some managers rigidly insist that there is only one way to do a job right, limiting the opportunities to improve performance by delegating only to those who will never suggest changes. Others give work to subordinates that they should do themselves. This is usually due to laziness, the desire to avoid unpleasant tasks and decisions, or lack of confidence in their own ability to do the job. After assigning their duties to others, they hope to escape personal responsibility for poor decisions by blaming their staff if things go wrong. (When their own superiors learn who has been making the decisions and actually doing the managerial work, these managers may find that they are indeed expendable.)

Good supervisors delegate work and authority to maximize workplace efficiency, not to minimize their own workloads. Manageable tasks should be assigned to an entire team of capable workers, along with the leeway for them to learn, to grow in their jobs, and to find satisfaction in their achievements.

Communicating Your Expectations. Communication is the key to effective delegation. The person to whom you assign each duty must clearly understand the following:

- the results expected
- the assignment of responsibility for those results
- the standards for doing the job well
- the reason the task is important and necessary
- the consequences of not doing the task or not doing it satisfactorily
- the level of authority being given with the assignment

SIX STEPS TO EFFECTIVE DELEGATION

1. *Define the task.* Whether you are designing a complex flowchart or just making a "to do" list, you must know what needs to be done before taking action to accomplish it.

2. *Assign responsibility.* Consider the skills, strengths, interests, experience, and present workloads of your employees when deciding which worker should be assigned a specific task. Give workers opportunities to learn new skills occasionally instead of always giving them jobs they already know how to do.

3. *Explain the task.* Tell your subordinate why a job must be done and your expectations for the results. Suggest methods based on the worker's level of ability, independence, initiative, and need for training, but be open to new ideas from your subordinate.

4. *Design a plan for accomplishing task objectives.* Again, depending on the individual worker, arrange for necessary tools and resources, help to establish priorities, and set a reasonable schedule for completion of the work.

5. *Check the worker's progress.* Stay involved as much as necessary to ensure that the work is being accomplished, but do not intrude on the worker's ability to perform.

6. *Give credit for work well done.* When the job is done, evaluate results with the worker. Praise him or her for success, and note any areas of needed improvement.

Evaluating Employees

Regular employee evaluations ensure peak performance in the office. They also help to determine promotions and raises and document unsatisfactory work that may lead to demotion or dismissal. Evaluations can be seen as a positive step toward problem solving and motivation if emphasis is placed on reinforcing good work and making sure it continues.

An evaluation may be formal, with a defined system of criteria and ratings, or informal. Regardless of the approach used, it is essential that employees know in advance what is expected of them and how they will be evaluated. The system must be fair in the eyes of the staff. Standards and criteria should be applied evenly and consistently.

Just as in the educational system, the primary purpose of an employee report card is not to punish poor performance. The intention should be to document areas of excellence and those that need improvement, with the goal of helping an employee become more successful at work. Unless evaluations are viewed in this manner, they will be dreaded by managers and staff alike. Worker resentment will result in an unwillingness to accept evaluation results and make needed changes, rendering the process useless and even destructive.

Viewing evaluations as tools to improve performance should not obscure the fact that job security, promotions, and raises depend on satisfactory work. Workers with poor evaluations must be told that supervisors will observe them to see if needed changes are being made. They should understand that subsequent evaluations must indicate satisfactory progress and performance, and the consequences of failure to improve. Dates for reevaluation and minimum standards for improvement should be included. Management must then follow through by dismissing, demoting, or suspending workers who fail to achieve the minimum standards set forth.

Factors to consider in employee evaluations:

• attitude	• job knowledge	• communication skills
• quality of work	• initiative	• judgment
• quantity of work	• leadership abilities	• flexibility
• dependability	• efficiency	• cooperation
• punctuality/attendance	• creativity	• interpersonal relations

The evaluation process should be constant and ongoing in order to achieve desired results. Therefore, it is best to schedule formal appraisals at least once a year. When an evaluation shows serious flaws in performance, a schedule for reappraisal at shorter intervals should be established. Managers may also schedule extra performance reviews to recognize achievement or target problems. Additional evaluations may also be helpful when a transfer, promotion, or resignation causes change or confusion.

The Evaluation Interview. Prepare for an evaluation by reviewing the employee's job requirements and performance history. Allow the employee a chance to prepare as well by notifying him or her of the date and time of the interview. (Sometimes, you may even ask the employee to give some thought to certain issues and be prepared to suggest alternatives to current procedures.) Make a list of points to cover, and include an opportunity for the worker to bring up other issues when you have completed your agenda. Conduct the interview in a quiet, private setting to encourage open communication on both sides. As the supervisor, your responsibilities during the meeting include the following:

- explaining the purpose of the evaluation
- discussing general performance standards and expectations of the employee
- detailing the results of your evaluation on each aspect of the worker's performance, with an explanation of the criteria used
- encouraging comments and questions from the employee on each issue discussed
- listening carefully to comments, answering questions fully, and considering the worker's concerns about performance criteria and requests for additional training, assistance, direction, or support
- summarizing the discussion of each issue by restating the problem to be solved with the employee's input noted
- reiterating performance objectives and criteria, noting any changes you will make as a result of the worker's comments; reemphasizing criteria that will not be changed despite the employee's input
- responding to requests for assistance, training, or direction by delineating specific actions you will take to satisfy the needs expressed, or explaining why the requested assistance, training, or direction will not be provided
- specifying the date of the next evaluation
- delineating the actions you will take at the next evaluation if performance criteria are met, exceeded, or not met satisfactorily
- discussing the effects of evaluation results on the worker's salary and/or job status, if applicable
- signing and having the employee sign a summary of points discussed and solutions agreed upon

Evaluation Documentation. Although reference has been made to informal evaluations, managers are advised to prepare written documentation of every evaluation interview or supervisory conference with an employee. In today's litigious society, this is necessary to protect the company, the supervisor, and the rights of employees. Even if all points discussed in an evaluation interview are positive and the worker receives a glowing report, results should be documented briefly and signed by the supervisor and the employee, with original signed copies for the personnel file and the employee.

Documentation should include the following:

- names of those present (usually just the supervisor and the employee, but sometimes a supervisor will ask the personnel manager to be present if serious performance flaws must be discussed)
- date of the evaluation
- reason for the evaluation (for example, regularly scheduled review, promotion, demotion, transfer/change of job title, change of supervisor, counseling session due to a specific problem, termination)
- results of the evaluation (a list of factors considered—attitude, quality of work, etc., as noted previously—with a rating such as "excellent," "good," "average," or "unsatisfactory" for each)
- effects of the evaluation on employee status (placed on probation, removed from probation, promoted, demoted, salary increased, salary decreased, title changed, etc.)
- date of the next evaluation
- employee objectives to be reached before the next evaluation, if applicable (such as specific performance standards that must be met to avoid disciplinary action or to achieve a desired promotion)
- supervisory objectives to be reached before the next evaluation (for example, providing agreed-upon training for the employee, reducing the employee's workload by hiring an assistant, or redistributing work)
- action to be taken if employee performance objectives are met satisfactorily by the next evaluation (such as promotion, salary increase, removal from probationary status)
- action to be taken if employee performance objectives are not met satisfactorily by the next evaluation (such as placement on probationary status, demotion, salary decrease, termination)

The evaluation summary may be a form that is completed by the supervisor during the interview, with a space for the employee to write comments when signing it. Or it may take the form of a memorandum that is prepared by the supervisor after the interview, with the employee returning to the supervisor's office to review the document, add comments in the space provided, sign, and receive his or her copy.

EVALUATION DO'S AND DON'TS FOR SUPERVISORS

Do
Explain the process completely to encourage positive attitudes about evaluations from everyone involved.

Use specific examples to document and support evaluation results.

Make evaluations an ongoing process by taking notes of employee performance throughout the year rather than just for a few days before regularly scheduled evaluations.

Encourage employees to express their concerns openly during evaluations and at any time, with the understanding that any questions about your decisions should be asked in private.

Keep all evaluation interviews confidential except when it is necessary to review results with your own superiors.

Concentrate on solving the largest problems, not on nitpicking or laying blame.

Focus on performance criteria to be met, not personal characteristics that have no real bearing on performance.

Listen to what employees have to say and be open to their ideas.

Communicate your desire to see workers succeed.

Make your decisions clear and emphasize that they are to be followed, after considering any issues the employee wants to discuss.

Don't

Allow evaluations to reflect personal favoritism or bias toward subordinates.

Pass personal judgment on workers due to performance deficiencies— keep the focus on work, not personalities.

Participate in further discussion (or arguments) about your decisions once you have carefully considered the employee's comments and responded to them.

Ask for excuses to explain bad behavior.

Threaten disciplinary actions that you do not have the authority to take.

Cooperating with Peers

In the final analysis, the respect of one's peers may be a more accurate indication of job performance than the opinions of superiors or subordinates. After all, peers are workers who occupy similar positions in terms of level of authority, personal workload, training, experience, and compensation. They face similar stresses and can appreciate the difficulties that must be overcome to achieve success. Good relationships with same-level coworkers are facilitated by the following:

- communicating openly and effectively
- being patient, helpful, and friendly
- showing sensitivity to cultural and personal differences
- expressing admiration for others' good work
- borrowing good ideas (with the originator's permission) to improve your performance, and expressing your appreciation for useful tips
- sharing your own successful methods freely
- choosing positive, enthusiastic team players as your personal support system
- competing in a healthy, friendly manner, with the attitude that overall company success is more important than individual achievements

- isolating personal conflicts so that work is not affected by them
- keeping confidences confidential

RESPONDING TO RUMORS

Office gossip is one of the most powerful and potentially destructive forces in the workplace. Do your part to reduce the harmful effects of hearsay by refusing to spread rumors. When others pass on juicy tidbits, respond in a skeptical manner with statements such as, "I would have to see that to believe it" or "Someone must be pulling your leg." Gently reminding rumormongers of others' feelings may cause them to think twice about what they are saying. For instance, you can say, "I would certainly hate for someone to be saying that sort of thing about me" in a manner that conveys genuine concern for the subject of gossip rather than a judgmental attitude toward the news bearer. If this does not stop the problem, use a stronger statement, such as, "I would rather have Jane tell me such personal things herself if she wants me to know them." Try not to make enemies by sounding preachy or morally superior, but do remind others that gossip can hurt or destroy lives and careers, so it is not an innocent pastime.

Teamwork Strategies

When you are part of a team, use these suggestions to help your company reach its goals with top efficiency:

- Understand each group member's work style and personal goals, as well as the role each plays in accomplishing the firm's objectives.
- Have confidence in the ability of each team member to do assigned tasks.
- Trust coworkers and subordinates to have the best intentions and promote the success of the entire group. Inspire them to trust you, too.
- Foster a noncompetitive atmosphere within the group so that all share successes and failures.
- Reach a consensus on the goals, plans, procedures, and individual jobs of the team.
- Encourage group comradeship, consideration, cooperation, and loyalty.
- Communicate effectively with all members to define, confront, and solve problems.
- Concentrate on group efficiency—the goal of a team is to produce more as a group than individuals could accomplish by working separately.

If you are asked to function as a team leader, win your colleagues' support by the following:

- knowing the strengths and weaknesses of team members and using that knowledge to create better group interaction
- discouraging internal strife by not playing favorites
- promoting unity by involving everyone in important roles
- developing camaraderie through positive activities and a healthy work environment

- creating group interdependence so that success requires everyone's cooperation
- challenging group members to high achievement by setting a good example
- recognizing the accomplishments of individuals as well as the entire group

---

THE WISDOM OF THE GURUS: MANAGEMENT EXPERTS IN THEIR OWN WORDS

"Hire the best. Pay them fairly. Communicate frequently. Provide challenges and rewards. Believe in them. Get out of their way—they'll knock your socks off."

"First and foremost as a manager or supervisor . . . your job is to get things done through other people. . . . You are paid to manage, not perform every task."

"The manager who supports the boss—the manager whom the boss can rely on and trust—is the one who will be given the most freedom and the least supervision."

"A wage earner goes home when it's 'quitting time.' A manager leaves when the work is done—or takes it home."

Mary Ann Allison and Eric Allison
Managing Up, Managing Down

"Development . . . is a matter of human energies rather than of economic wealth. And the generation and direction of human energies is the task of management. Management is the mover and development is a consequence."

"[W]hen a variety of tasks have all to be performed in cooperation, synchronization, and communication, a business needs managers and a management. Otherwise, things go out of control; plans fail to turn into action; or worse, different parts of the plans get going at different speeds, different times, and with different objectives and goals, and the favor of the 'boss' becomes more important than performance."

"The good time users among managers spend many more hours on their communications up than on their communications down. They tend to have good communication down, but they seem to obtain these as an effortless by-product. They do not talk to their subordinates about their problems, but they know how to make the subordinates talk about theirs."

Peter Drucker
People and Performance

"The productivity of work is not the responsibility of the worker but of the manager."

Peter Drucker
Management in Turbulent Times

"The man who delegates responsibilities for running the company, without knowing the intimate details of what is involved, runs the enormous risk of rendering himself superfluous."

"The best way to inspire people to superior performance is to convince them by everything you do and by your everyday attitude that you are wholeheartedly supporting them."

"It is much more difficult to measure non-performance than performance. Performance stands out like a ton of diamonds. Non-performance can almost always be explained away."

"[T]he most important element in establishing a happy, prosperous atmosphere [is] an insistence upon open, free, and honest communications up and down the ranks of our management structure."

Harold Geneen
Managing

"The output of a manager is the output of the organizational units under his supervision or influence."

"There is an especially efficient way to get information, much neglected by most managers. That is to visit a particular place in the company and observe what's going on there."

"[T]he information most useful to me . . . comes from quick, and often casual verbal exchanges. This usually reaches a manager much faster than anything written down. And usually the more timely the information is, the more valuable it is."

"Just as you would not permit a fellow employee to steal a piece of office equipment . . . you shouldn't let anyone walk away with the time of his fellow managers."

Andrew S. Grove
High Output Management

"Once somebody asked me to identify the single most useful management technique that I learned through my years of managing. My answer was: the practice of regularly scheduled *one-on-one* meetings."

"[F]or most of us being pushed *too* hard and crowded into a corner is counterproductive. Great honesty is seldom helpful without empathetic compassion, skillfully expressed in private, by someone assumed to care about the other person's well-being."

"Power . . . means the ability to get things done, to mobilize resources, and to draw on what is necessary to accomplish goals."

"Individuals who are *repeatedly* persuasive in meetings are rarely those who come armed with prepared speeches. Rather, they are individuals who can see other points of view and create compromises or new solutions, who can hold their views in suspension while permitting themselves to remain a part of the process—then intervene at the right point to guide the discussion to shore. They tend to choose words and images that *integrate* concerns in the group's thinking. The key is to find common ground and take others' points and use them creatively."

" 'Acceptance time' is a powerful antidote to conflict in Japanese organizations. The things a person believes in are often more important belongings than physical possessions. . . . Even less compelling beliefs reach back into a person's past and forward into his future. When new ideas or facts come along, however compelling they may be, it is felt that people need time to let go gradually of the old before they can accept the new."

Richard Tanner Pascale and Anthony G. Athos
The Art of Japanese Management

"Applaud the new, rough-cut or not, and yawn at even good performance that involves no bold moves and no fast-paced experiments."

"Celebrate what you want to see more of."

Tom Peters
Thriving On Chaos

"Before you take on the counseling role, ask yourself if the situation really calls for it . . . give the individual a reasonable chance to turn things around under his or her own power, with your wholehearted support, without your interference. Counseling is *not* meddling— 'involvement without the right or an invitation.' Too soon is as disastrous as too late. You have the right to counsel only when you're invited, or performance problems threaten to undermine an individual's ability to contribute over time in spite of conscientious education and coaching."

"The brand of leadership we propose has a simple base of MBWA (Managing By Wandering Around). To 'wander,' with customers and vendors and our own people, is to be in touch with the first vibrations of the new."

Tom Peters and Nancy Austin
A Passion for Excellence

"[Well-managed modern organizations] treat everyone as a source of creative input. What's most interesting is that they cannot be described as either democratically or autocratically managed. Their managers define the boundaries, and their people figure out the best way to do the job within those boundaries. The management style is an astonishing combination of direction and empowerment. They give up tight control in order to gain control over what counts: results."

"Politics can be good or bad. Few things get done without a power base. Hence many of our finest managers are closet politicians. . . . Those that make things happen are politically skilled and understand the use of power."

"There was a time when people were 'factors of production' managed little differently from machines or capital. No more. The best people will not tolerate it. And if that way of managing ever generated productivity, it has the reverse effect today. While capital and machines either are or can be managed toward sameness, people are individuals. They must be managed that way."

Robert H. Waterman
The Renewal Factor

"If you don't do it excellently, don't do it at all. Because if it's not excellent it won't be profitable or fun, and if you're not in business for fun or profit, what the hell are you doing there?"

Robert Townsend
in *Business Speak* by Suzette Haden Elgin

"If two men on the job agree all the time, then one is useless. If they disagree all the time, then both are useless."

Darryl F. Zanuck
in *Business Speak* by Suzette Haden Elgin

Fair Play: Eliminating Employment Discrimination

The Equal Employment Opportunity Commission (EEOC) is a federal agency that defines and enforces laws concerning employment discrimination. These laws apply to any business employing at least 15 persons each workday for 20 or more weeks of the current or past year. Only private clubs, certain departments of the District of Columbia, and Native American tribes (as employers) are exempt. A company may not discriminate against an employee for suing it under these laws or for helping someone else to do so—by testifying in court, for example. Employers can promote fair employment practices by training managers and employers to recognize and avoid discriminatory statements and acts. EEOC regulations should be prominently posted with reminders that violations are actionable.

General Prohibitions

It is against federal law to fire, refuse to hire, or deny anyone proper compensation, work conditions, job training, or privileges based on age, race, religion, gender, or national origin. An employer or company can also be sued for limiting, segregating, or classifying employees or job applicants by any of these five characteristics if such classification deprives any of them of work opportunities or status in the workplace. When there are other reasons for segregating employees, the company can be found guilty of illegal discrimination if a worker proves that such classification was even partly based on age, race, religion, gender, or national origin.

Special Circumstances: Religion, Gender, and National Origin as Job Qualifications

Intentional discrimination as a business necessity (for example, claiming that clients will not talk to black people) is not a viable defense in court. However, the law recognizes that sometimes religion, gender, or national origin can be an actual qualification for a job. Perhaps the position is running a Jewish community center, or a women's rights organization; being Jewish or a woman, respectively, might help the person to do a better job. It is important to note that legally race can never be considered a qualification for a job.

Employees with Disabilities

People with disabilities are also protected from job discrimination. An employer must make accommodations for a worker with disabilities if the business is financially able to do so and the worker is otherwise qualified. Employment criteria that tend to screen out people with disabilities are illegal. HIV-positive people are protected as disabled. So are individuals who have been successfully rehabilitated from illegal drug habits and those who are enrolled in alcohol/drug treatment programs and are no longer using illegal drugs or drinking inappropriately. However, current users of illegal drugs are not protected, and discrimination against them is not actionable. Drug testing is not considered to be discrimination, and it is legal. (*See also* Optimizing the Work Space for Productivity, page 92.)

Older Workers

Age discrimination laws apply to fewer employers. Federal law prohibits employers of 20 or more persons from age-based discrimination against workers aged 40 to 70 with regard to hiring or firing decisions, wages, work conditions, privileges, or employment referrals. As with other forms of EEOC-defined discrimination, employers may not segregate or limit such workers in any way that might affect their opportunities or job status. Forcing someone to retire is also illegal unless the person is 65 or older, holds an executive or other high-ranking position, and is entitled to retirement benefits totaling at least $44,000.

Gender and Pregnancy Considerations

Gender discrimination laws require that men and women be paid equally for doing the same work. Pregnancy must be treated like any other temporary health condition, with the same leave and benefits as for any illness. The Family and Medical Leave Act, though not an EEOC law, prohibits discrimination against pregnant women in hiring or firing. It also makes forced maternity leave illegal if the woman is able to work during pregnancy and wants to do so.

Discrimination Not Covered by the EEOC

The EEOC does not regulate discrimination due to sexual orientation, and there are no current federal laws banning such discrimination. However, some cities and states prohibit discrimination against lesbians, homosexuals, and bisexuals, and some gay employees have won damages when suing their employers. Even in a city or state where such discrimination is not prohibited, it may sometimes be possible to bring suit successfully if gay employees can prove that discrimination against them is gender-based.

Where to Get Help

If you think you may be a victim of any of the previously mentioned kinds of discrimination, are unsure about whether you or your company could be sued, or wish to get more information on EEOC procedures, call the Equal Employment Opportunity Commission toll-free at 800-669-3362. To find the EEOC office nearest you, call 800-669-4000. On both of these lines, information is given in English and in Spanish. Your state attorney general's office and local human rights/civil rights commissions may also be of help. Some other national organizations that provide information and assistance in dealing with discrimination are listed in the Sources of Further Information section at the end of this chapter.

HOW TO RECOGNIZE AND TRANSCEND THE GLASS CEILING

The "glass ceiling" is a figurative name for an artificial, though very real, barrier that keeps women from attaining truly equal employment opportunities in mid- and upper-level management. To a lesser extent, the term also refers to similar barriers that tend to stop minority workers' advancement at even lower levels. Regardless of its intended victims, the glass ceiling hurts everyone: employees, employers, the entire country. Depriving employees of advancement based on gender or ethnicity not only denies them fair recognition; it can also prevent the achievement of maximum productivity.

Many factors contribute to creating glass ceilings in offices—some obvious, others less so. The problem often goes beyond individual attitudes and into the entire institutional structure of a company. Job promotions, for example, are often based on subtle systems of networking and word of mouth that put those less entrenched in an organization—usually women and minorities—at a disadvantage. To eliminate these unfair practices, managers must be conscious of the glass ceiling and committed to removing it. Steps toward remediation include the following:

- giving equal consideration to all applicants for promotions
- keeping detailed performance records of all workers and reviewing them closely when making decisions about promotions
- announcing and posting all advancement opportunities to all workers instead of relying on networking to inform interested employees
- developing a formal system of promotion based on objective standards that are applied equally to every worker by every supervisor in the company
- focusing on developing worker potential rather than continuing traditions
- making lower-level positions leading to management—such as sales positions—available to all employees and applicants, rather than placing women or minorities in only those jobs that offer limited opportunity for advancement
- soliciting referrals and recommendations for management positions from women and minorities as well as from male staff members
- being purposeful in considering women and minorities for promotions from the beginning of their employment, as future members of management are often identified early
- making it clear to any executive search firms hired that the company is interested in providing equal employment opportunities for everyone
- including the company's Equal Employment Opportunity director in management promotion decisions rather than just entry-level hiring
- reviewing the company's promotions system constantly to ensure its fairness and objectivity

Two divisions of the U.S. Department of Labor are particularly helpful to those with questions about shattering the glass ceiling. These are the Office of Federal Contract Compliance Programs–Employment

Standards Administration, and the Women's Bureau. They can be reached at the addresses and phone numbers listed at the end of this chapter in Sources of Further Information, page 277 (national offices) or at the locations given under U.S. Department of Labor Regional Offices, page 279.

Defining and Dealing with Sexual Harassment

Sexual harassment on the job has plagued working women (and men) for centuries. Businesses are now addressing it as a serious problem with potential legal consequences for companies that overlook or ignore its existence. Since Anita Hill's public accusation that Clarence Thomas—her former boss and a nominee for the position of Supreme Court justice—had sexually harassed her, the topic has been more openly discussed. As serious as the problem is, institutions have been finding increasingly effective ways to address it.

Types of Sexual Harassment

Quid Pro Quo

Legally, there are two categories of sexual harassment. The first is called *quid pro quo* harassment, a Latin phrase meaning "this for that." It is defined as making employment, salary, promotions, or other benefits contingent on a worker's submission to sexual advances or behavior. Sexual advances include asking for sexual activity; sexual behavior is unwanted touching or looking. Firing or demoting an employee for refusing to acquiesce to sexual demands is an obvious example. Quid pro quo harassment can be identified and prosecuted more easily than harassment based on a hostile working environment.

Hostile Working Environment

The second category of sexual harassment involves the creation of a *hostile working environment*. This is defined as sexual behavior that makes an employee's work environment intimidating or abusive; it may also affect the worker's job performance. Factors contributing to a hostile environment include frequent sexually offensive language (written or spoken) and any display of sexual material. Some examples of behavior that could create a hostile environment include constant unwelcome advances, comments about a woman's breasts, and taunts about a person's sexual reputation.

An employee can sue a superior for sexual harassment, but not a coworker. However, the company and/or its managers can be sued for knowingly allowing harassment by a coworker if the existence of a hostile work environment can be proved. Many employers have taken steps to prevent such behavior and the problems it causes, which include an uncomfortable work environment and possible law-suits.

Preventing Problems Through Company Policy

The best way for a company to prevent sexual harassment is to have a clear internal policy against it while making sure all staff members know and understand the policy. This is accomplished via educational workshops, prominently posted reminders of prohibitions against offensive behavior, and company newsletters. Strong policies encourage victims to come forward; this is in the best interests of the company, as 10 percent of sexual targets leave their jobs. About 50 percent try to ignore the problem, but experience a 10 percent drop in productivity. In addition to its effects on the target of harassment, a hostile environment can affect the job performance of perpetrators and witnesses as well.

A strong policy must be clear in its definition of harassment and explicit about the penalties. Examples of prohibited behavior should be included, along with a guarantee that complaints will be treated confidentially. The reporting/grievance procedure and review process, with neutral, well-trained third parties to conduct investigations, are also essential parts of a good policy. More than one person should be designated to receive complaints, and a system of regularly reviewing the workplace environment (via confidential worker surveys) is a good preventive measure. Employees must be assured that retaliation for accusations of harassment will not be tolerated.

Handling Complaints of Harassment

When a complaint is brought, it is important to have an objective party review the matter. Sometimes there is no one in the workplace who is accepted as impartial by all parties. In such cases, state Fair Employment Practices offices can often recommend professional investigators. In a good investigation, the employee bringing the complaint, the accused person, and witnesses are all interviewed. Evidence is carefully weighed, including the credibility of everyone involved. All parties should be told immediately about the investigation's results. If the reviewer finds that no harassment occurred, the person bringing charges should be told that there are other legal remedies beyond company review procedure, and that the complaint may be pursued further if the worker is not satisfied. Even if the matter ends with the company's investigation, it may be necessary to make changes in the workplace, separating the accuser and the accused.

If a charge of sexual harassment is found to be true, the company should immediately give a written apology to the victim. Then management should proceed with disciplinary action promptly and according to its written policy. It is advisable to place a written reprimand in the perpetrator's personnel file, in addition to any other sanctions. Possible disciplinary actions range from mandatory completion of sexual harassment training to termination.

Sometimes a complaint cannot be resolved internally and an employee takes it to court. Under federal law, sexual harassment is considered a form of sex (gender) discrimination, provided the perpetrator is a heterosexual man and the victim is a woman. Same-sex harassment is a controversial legal area—there have been some successful suits, but its legal definition is still much disputed. Harassment of men by female coworkers also occurs, but this has also proved difficult to define and remedy.

Getting All the Facts

Many states, counties, cities, and municipalities have their own laws concerning sexual harassment, in addition to federal mandates. To learn more about local ordinances, contact your regional EEOC office; a local civil, human rights, or women's issues department; your state attorney general's office; the Fair Employment Practices agency or Commission on the Status of Women in your area; or the local chapter of the National Organization for Women. If there is a law school nearby, it may sponsor a women's rights clinic. Some national organizations combating sexual harassment are included in the Sources of Further Information section at the end of this chapter, with addresses and phone numbers for easy reference.

IS YOUR WORK ENVIRONMENT HOSTILE?

To determine whether sexually abusive and intimidating behaviors are occurring in your office, ask the following questions:

- Do employees make potentially offensive comments about the physical appearance of other workers?
- Do staff members tell jokes that could be considered sexually offensive to anyone listening?
- Are sexually suggestive objects or photos (such as pinup calendars or "souvenirs" depicting nude or scantily clad people or obscene witticisms) on display in the office?
- Do employees make potentially unwanted sexual overtures by sending correspondence to or calling other employees?

Include questions of this type on confidential surveys for all workers to complete on a regular basis. If any of these situations do occur in your workplace, take immediate steps to make all employees aware of company policy on sexual harassment. Then survey again to determine if the problem has been eliminated.

Finding the Perfect Employee

Placing the Right Employment Ad

Successful staffing begins with finding the right employees. Of all recruitment methods, advertising is the most direct and basic. Effective advertising depends on including the right information and placing ads where they will attract the most qualified applicants. Ads should be accurate, so the first step is to have the position's supervisor conduct a job analysis and write a complete, specific job description on which to base the ad. (*See* Competitive Salaries, page 321, for a discussion of position titles and ways to avoid problems due to inaccurate or misleading job names.)

A good help-wanted ad makes the job sound attractive and creates an impression of the company in the reader's mind. Be aware of subtleties in tone and meaning—use language that reflects the company's ambience, whether that is formal, friendly, creative, or highly organized and efficient. Be as concise, specific, and descriptive as possible. Avoid using unnecessary gender-specific language or other terms that may imply illegal employment discrimination.

Most employment ads should include all of the following information:

1. *Position title*—Use bold type or all capital letters. This is usually placed at the head of the ad, as prospective applicants will look for it first, but it may be located in the body of the ad if it is sufficiently highlighted for quick recognition.

2. *Description of duties*—Explain the main responsibilities of the position and its role in the company.

3. *Education and/or experience*—List the degree(s), training, and amount of experience required or preferred. Include a statement such as "Must have MBA plus five years postgraduate experience to be considered" to discourage unqualified applicants, saving your time and theirs.

4. *Employee benefits*—Mention specific benefits only when those are particularly attractive, as in "Excellent health, life, dental, and disability insurance—employer pays half of premiums" or "Generous retirement and profit-sharing plans." Otherwise, a brief phrase such as "Excellent benefits" may be sufficient.

5. *Attractive features of the position*—List appealing facets of the job (level of authority, travel, high pay, flexible hours).

6. *Instructions on how to respond to the advertisement*—Ask applicants to mail or fax their résumés and provide the appropriate company official's name/title/ address and fax number (or the newspaper's address and code mailbox number for responses to anonymous ads). If respondents must call for appointments or stop by the office to pick up application forms, provide the company telephone number, address, and the name of the person to see. Also specify the hours during which calls or applications will be taken. Include instructions about references, samples of work, or other documentation that may be required.

7. *Deadline for responding and/or the date by which you would like to fill the position.*

8. *Equal employment opportunity*—Include the phrase "Equal Opportunity Employer" or "EOE" at the end of the ad.

9. *Optional information*—Use a company slogan or headline to capture readers' attention, if desired. You may want to ask each applicant to supply a salary history to help you determine his or her present career level. And you may want to indicate the starting salary if it is attractive or helps to indicate the level of experience sought.

Should you list the name of your company? You may want to exclude it (a) to keep other companies from knowing that your firm is hiring; (b) to discourage walk-in applicants or phone calls in lieu of the requested résumés by mail; (c) to prevent phone calls from applicants who have sent résumés but have not received a response; (d) to reduce applications from unqualified people who are simply attracted by the firm's prestigious name; and/or (e) to prevent resentment of your firm by those who applied but were not contacted for interviews. On the other hand, some very qualified applicants may not respond to anonymous ads because they fear the embarrassing possibility of applying to their current employers inadvertently. Also, your firm's good reputation may attract some excellent candidates who already hold good positions but would rather work for your company.

Interviewing Prospective Employees

A manager's ability to interview job candidates successfully increases the probability of recruiting the most-wanted applicants. The process provides an opportunity for the interviewer to assess a candidate's qualifications, goals, motivations, values, and communication skills. The manager must also use this time to acquaint desirable prospects with the character of the firm, company benefits, and challenges the job offers. Both parties should learn a great deal during the interview.

Screening Applicants

It is often necessary to screen applicants to limit the number of candidates interviewed. If an ad produces an overwhelming response, clerical staff may assist in the screening process by checking résumés or applications to see if the required training, education, and experience are listed. After the names of unqualified applicants are removed from consideration, a more in-depth screening by management may be required if there are still many candidates for the position. Sometimes it is easy to eliminate unsuitable prospects by scanning their applications. For example, if the position requires a lot of correspondence and report writing, checking résumés for grammar, punctuation, and fluency may narrow the field considerably. But remember that the screening process cannot take too much time or the best candidates may no longer be available when they are contacted for interviews.

Preparing for Interviews

With a good screening process, it should be possible to interview no more than eight candidates for a single position. If possible, spread the interviews out so that only three or four people are seen in one week. Otherwise, you may not have time to mentally process one applicant's strengths and weaknesses before interviewing another.

Preparation is crucial. The interviewer should come to the meeting with a clear idea of the characteristics the position requires, a prepared list of questions for the applicant, and a pad of paper to jot down notes and observations. Reserve a quiet, private location for interviews and have coffee and water available. Be familiar with an applicant's résumé or application before going into the meeting.

Characteristics to Consider. An important part of your preparation for interviews is listing the most important qualifications for the position. For example, does this job require in-depth technical knowledge and the ability to work with minimal training and supervision? Or is it more important for this employee to be outgoing and personable and inspire confidence in clients? (Sometimes the best employees are those who learn quickly and take direction well rather than those who have the most technical knowledge.) Listing desirable qualities in order of their priority will help you find the best person for the job. It can help to avoid being swept away by a charismatic candidate if charm is not one of the most important qualifications for the position. By the same token, your priority list will remind you that applicants who lack interview polish should not be eliminated from consideration for a position that does not require a lot of public contact. Some characteristics to consider when making your list of priorities:

- technical knowledge
- level of ambition
- verbal communication skills
- written communication skills
- listening skills
- personal ethics
- positive attitude
- loyalty to the company
- confidence, poise, and maturity
- proper dress and grooming
- leadership skills
- creativity
- flexibility
- willingness and ability to learn
- independence and initiative
- discretion and ability to maintain confidentiality

Of course, many of these characteristics cannot be discerned in an interview, no matter how thorough your questions or how astute your observations. But a good interviewer can form an impression of a candidate's strengths and weaknesses in important areas by asking questions such as those listed below. Former employers and business associates may also provide useful information during reference checks if your questions are phrased correctly.

Questions to Ask. Prepare a list of questions that will allow the candidate to speak freely so that you can evaluate communication skills. Use similar questions for all applicants. Avoid asking for information that is covered in the application or résumé—this is an opportunity to learn more. Your queries should be easy to understand and relevant to the position being filled. Appropriate questions cover specifics of the candidate's work experience, education, skills, and career goals.

They should elicit answers that will indicate personality and attitudes. Typical questions might include the following:

- What is your best quality/greatest strength?
- What do you like most about yourself?
- What do others seem to like best about you?
- What do you dislike about yourself?
- What personality traits cause the most problems for you?
- What do others criticize most about you?
- What makes you angry?
- How do you act when you are angry?
- How do you respond when others are angry with you?
- What is most important to you about any job that you consider?
- What is least important?
- What do you like most about your current job?
- What do you like least about it?
- Why do you want to leave your current job?

Legal Considerations. Anyone in a position to interview job candidates should be familiar with the requirements of the Equal Employment Opportunity Commission with regard to interviewing and hiring procedures. A number of laws—including the Civil Rights Act, Age Discrimination in Employment Act, Privacy Act, Vocational Rehabilitation Act, and Freedom of Information Act—include provisions that affect the interviewing process. Questions asked cannot imply discrimination based on race, color, religion, physical disability, national origin, marital status, number or ages of children, arrest record, or economic status. In addition, questions that imply discrimination based on height, weight, language skills, or education level are illegal unless directly relevant to the job. Contact the EEOC for more information (*see* Fair Play: Eliminating Employment Discrimination, page 228), and consider attending a training seminar or workshop on EEOC compliance to ensure that your interviewing techniques are appropriate.

Conducting Interviews

Set a comfortable tone with a few conversational pleasantries, but avoid wasting a lot of time. Explain the interviewing procedure, then move on to the questions you have prepared. Listen carefully as you allow the candidate to answer questions completely. Take notes of your observations and impressions, jotting down any statements that particularly impress or concern you. You may want to use a checklist to rate areas such as eye contact and verbal skills, but it is best to avoid judging people strictly on a point system. Making notes on a copy of your questions list (with spaces beneath each question) is usually better. Just be sure that note taking does not become so important that you miss subtle cues requiring close observation.

As you watch the candidate's body language, be conscious of your own. Keep your facial expressions and comments noncommittal so the interviewee cannot read your reactions. This is important—not to deceive the person, but to make sure his or her responses are honest rather than adjusted to a perception of what pleases you. Invite candidates to ask their own questions, but maintain control of the interview by directing the conversation and keeping it within a time limit. When the time is up, thank the person and see the candidate out. Then jot down final impressions and note areas of concern to address in a second interview if this candidate is one of your top choices.

Checking References

Checking applicants' references before making final hiring decisions can prevent problems later, when an employee's serious flaws can cause tremendous loss of time and money. Also, if an employee proves to be violent or dangerously incompetent, an employer can be judged negligent for not properly checking the employee's references. Unfortunately, reference checking has become complicated in this age of litigation. Past employers are reluctant to give information that could affect a candidate's future because they fear lawsuits in reprisal for negative comments, so reference checks often provide little information. Knowing what to ask and how to ask it will enhance your chances of getting useful data.

Do not waste time with personal references, and assume that any references the candidate has provided will be favorable. The most unbiased and accurate references come from past supervisors. During interviews, ask candidates to notify their previous employers that you will be calling for references. (Never call a current employer without the candidate's consent.) You may ask candidates to sign a permission slip allowing you to call their former employers, though this may not make past employers any more willing to speak openly.

When calling, it is important to establish a rapport. Supervisors are often instructed to provide only the candidate's name, job title, and dates of employment; but if you can ensure confidentiality and inspire trust, references may willingly reveal more. The best questions will not directly challenge the candidate's competence but will subtly reveal the supervisor's attitude about the former worker. Listen carefully for implications and read between the lines of pat phrases. Refer to the notes from your interview with the candidate and add relevant statements from the supervisor to your data.

Key questions to ask during a reference check include the following:

- How would you describe the quality of the candidate's work?
- What sort of responsibilities does this person handle best?
- How well do you think the candidate would perform these duties? (Briefly describe the position to be filled.)
- Why did the candidate leave your company?
- Would you rehire this person?
- Should we have any reservations about hiring this applicant?
- What training methods were most successful with this candidate at your firm?

- How did this person work with others? Did the candidate have a good attendance record?
- Is there anything else we should know about this person?

Making a Decision

When all initial interviews have been completed, you may want to schedule second interviews for the best candidates. Most hiring decisions can be made after one or two meetings with a prospective employee; third interviews are seldom justified. If you are still unsure which person to hire after second interviews, your expectations may need an adjustment. Or it could be that none of the finalists is appropriate. In such cases, you may want to start the entire process again or reevaluate the position. (For instance, would a higher starting salary attract more qualified applicants?) Maybe the employment advertisement should be rewritten in an effort to attract a different group of applicants.

TEN FACTORS TO CONSIDER BEFORE HIRING SOMEONE

1. Does the candidate possess the necessary professional skills?
2. Does he/she inspire confidence?
3. Does this applicant seem to be enthusiastic about the job?
4. Is this someone who will grow in the job and stay with the company?
5. Is the candidate trainable; can he/she learn new skills?
6. Will this person work well with others?
7. Is the candidate able to take direction?
8. Does this applicant possess leadership skills?
9. How well will the candidate's personality and attitudes fit into the overall organizational culture of the company?
10. Could a more qualified candidate be found by extending the job search?

The Employment Application

Résumés are requested for most professional office positions, with application forms sometimes used to provide information in a standardized format for quick review. Generic forms are available in office supply stores. However, you will probably want to design a company form if your firm uses them regularly.

Before designing an application form, collect samples used by similar companies. Note the features you want to include and those that are not needed. Examine the types of questions and wording used. It is legal to ask the gender, race, marital status, and religion of applicants, although it is illegal to use this information in determining employment. If you have reason to request this information on the application, make the personal information section detachable so that an interviewer will not see it when examining the application. Include a statement on the form reminding applicants that they are entitled to withhold any information that could be used to discriminate against them.

Application forms vary according to individual business needs, but most request the following information:

1. *Personal data:* name, Social Security number, address, telephone number, birth date

2. *Educational history:* names of all schools attended, including high schools, business or technical schools, colleges, and graduate schools; school locations; dates attended; majors/courses; grade point averages; graduation dates; degrees earned; honors/awards received

3. *Employment history:* name, address, and telephone number of each previous employer; title of each position held and a description of the duties of that position; beginning and ending dates of employment; salary; supervisor's name; reason for leaving; military experience, if any

4. *Professional references:* name, title, company, address, phone number

5. *Other information specific to the position:* relevant skills, willingness to relocate or travel, date available for work

The company's letterhead should be used at the top of the form (perhaps in miniature to save space). Remember to include a line for the date of application, usually just after the letterhead. Most firms now include a signature line at the end of the form for the applicant to certify that the information given is correct and to grant permission for the prospective employer to contact former employers for references. (*See* Figure 6.1 for an example of a standard employment application.)

Using Temporary Employment Services

Temporary employment agencies supply workers to client companies on a short-term basis for a fee. Businesses of every size and type may benefit by using temporary workers to replace employees who are sick or on leave or to provide extra help during busy seasons and for special projects. In recent years, the changing lifestyles and increased mobility of office professionals have made temporary work very attractive to many highly skilled people. Someone new to an area or between jobs may take several short assignments for immediate income instead of taking the first job that is offered. Temporary assignments often turn into permanent job offers, too, when a top-notch worker impresses an employer and is asked to stay with the company.

Teachers, graduate students, and other seasonally occupied personnel may also sign with temporary employment services to earn extra money during summer and holiday seasons. As many permanent office workers schedule vacations during these periods, the largest number of highly qualified workers may be available when your office needs them most. Other typical temporaries include parents of small children who work only when extra money is needed, retired workers (often highly skilled

XYZ Company

658 East 63rd Street, New York, NY 10017

APPLICATION FOR EMPLOYMENT

(212)533-4426 voice/(212) 533-4429 fax

Date of application: _____

PERSONAL INFORMATION

Last	First	Middle initial	Date of birth	Social security number
Address	City	Zip	Telephone (Day)	Evening

CURRENT EMPLOYMENT

Position desired	Full time ☐ Part time ☐	Desired salary	Willing to relocate?	Date available to begin work
Currently employed?	Present employer			

May we contact your current employer?   If yes, address and phone number of current employer and name of your supervisor
Yes ☐ No ☐

EDUCATION

High school—name and location	Dates attended	Date graduated or date highest grade completed	Diploma/degree received
College or university—name and location	Dates attended	Date graduated or number of years attended	Diploma/degree received
College or university—name and location	Dates attended	Date graduated or number of years attended	Diploma/degree received
Trade, business, or other school—name and location	Dates attended	Date graduated or number of years attended	Diploma/degree received

EMPLOYMENT HISTORY(List most recent first.)

Employer	Position held
Address	Duties
Phone	Salary
Employed from (date) To (date)	Reason for leaving
Employer	Position held
Address	Duties
Phone	Salary
Employed from (date) To (date)	Reason for leaving
Employer	Position held
Address	Duties
Phone	Salary
Employed from (date) To (date)	Reason for leaving

OTHER AREAS OF EXPERIENCE/EXPERTISE

Special study or training

Foreign languages read/spoken

U.S. military service	Rank	Present membership in National Guard or Reserves

BUSINESS/PROFESSIONAL REFERENCES

1. Name	Relationship	Mailing Address	Phone
2. Name	Relationship	Mailing Address	Phone
3. Name	Relationship	Mailing Address	Phone

May we contact your present and former employers? ☐ Yes ☐ No

I certify that all information given in this application is true and correct. _____

Applicant's signature   Date

Figure 6.1 Employment application

and experienced) who enjoy working occasionally, and people who like the freedom and adventure of moving from assignment to assignment.

Finding the Right Temporary Service

Many reputable temporary services are available. Some are branches of regular employment agencies, and some deal strictly with temporary workers. Check the yellow pages under "Temporary Services" and "Employment Contractors." Any service you consider using should do the following:

* belong to the National Association of Temporary Services (119 South St. Asaph Street, Alexandria, VA 22314, phone 703-549-6287)
* provide the names of other client firms as references
* perform background checks on all workers
* test workers to determine their skills and knowledge of office equipment and procedures
* provide training as needed to enhance workers' versatility and competence
* evaluate workers after each assignment by contacting client firms for feedback on worker performance
* provide your company with a written contract or service agreement
* specialize in supplying the types of workers you need

Determining an agency's specialty is important. For instance, a temporary employment agency may place more unskilled manual laborers or medical personnel than office workers, although its advertisements list all types of positions. (This is not to imply that such ads are fraudulent—just that some firms handle a large number of office assignments and others do not. The ads often indicate every type of placement available through an agency.) The best way to find the right service is to call several agencies, then visit their offices. If you visit late on a Friday afternoon, you may see a number of temporary workers stopping by to turn in time sheets for the week; some may drop them into a mail slot just after closing time. This will give you a chance to observe the types of workers usually employed by an agency. Another way to locate the right agency is to call the personnel managers of businesses similar to yours and ask which temporary services they have used and found satisfactory. Most will be happy to share this information with you.

The Pros and Cons of Using Temporary Workers

As in other areas of business management, there are advantages and disadvantages to weigh if you are thinking of using a temporary employment service. The most important considerations are noted below.

Pros
1. Competent workers can be on the job within a few hours at most, depending on the degree of expertise required.

2. The time and expense involved in recruiting, screening, interviewing, and checking on prospective employees are eliminated.

3. The paperwork usually associated with hiring new employees (applications, W-4 forms/payroll information, health insurance enrollment, workers' compensation and Social Security payments) is also eliminated, as these workers are employed and paid by the temporary service, not the client company.

4. Workers who are unsatisfactory or no longer needed can be discharged at any time by calling the temporary agency to request a replacement or an end to the service agreement; the paperwork and unpleasantness usually associated with terminations and layoffs are avoided. (Most workers are quickly reassigned to other positions, anyway.)

5. Managers and personnel directors may find excellent candidates for permanent positions in temporaries who perform well and seem to fit in with the company. If a client firm and temporary worker want to make their arrangement permanent, the temporary employment service collects a fee for making the match. This happens so often that the terms are specified in the client company's service agreement as well as each temporary worker's contract with the agency.

6. Temporary service representatives make it their business to learn as much as possible about a client firm's special needs and to find just the right worker for each assignment.

Cons

1. Temporary workers cannot be expected to demonstrate the company loyalty and dedication that are expected of permanent employees.

2. The time spent training and orienting temporary workers to office procedures is lost when those workers move on.

3. Highly skilled workers (clerical or professional) may not be available when needed.

4. A constant influx of temporary workers can be disruptive to the flow of business.

5. The hourly cost of using temporary employees may be higher than the expenses associated with regular staff, as the employment agency's commission is included in the hourly fee.

6. Certain businesses (law offices, medical corporations, even insurance firms) may have confidential information that cannot be entrusted to temporary staff.

CONFIDENTIALITY CONCERNS

The confidentiality issue must be carefully considered with respect to temporary employees. For example, a physician trusts office workers not to divulge patients' medical data—their continued employment is contingent on their discretion. Patients know that clerical staff must have access to their medical records in order to make lab appointments, file insurance claims, and provide other necessary services. But most patients would not want a constant stream of temporary workers to have access to their files. The use of five different temporaries during one year would mean that five more people have learned the intimate details of patients' physical and financial situations. Even if the temporary workers are as discreet as the regular staff, this invasion of privacy is usually not justified. When confidential information is involved, a better solution to short-term personnel shortages is to pay regular staff overtime to cover for others during vacations or to ask retired employees to fill in.

Making the Necessary Arrangements

Before calling a temporary employment agency to request services, determine the skills and experience required for the positions to be filled, the number of workers needed, and the length of time that the temporary workers will be used. Arrange for someone who is familiar with the work to provide job orientation and supervision for temporary workers. When you talk with the employment agency representative, describe your company's business and provide directions to your office. Give the name of the person who will supervise the worker. Then tell your employees that a temporary worker has been hired and ask them to make the new person feel comfortable. Prepare the desk or office to be used so that work can begin smoothly and promptly. Make sure necessary instructions are given when the worker arrives, and that the workload assigned is manageable.

Other Temporary Solutions

Highly skilled managers and professionals with at least ten years of experience can be located for short-term consultant positions by calling the Association of Part-Time Professionals (703-734-7975). Many companies are now turning to this form of employment to satisfy temporary personnel needs. National associations of consultants also supply contact information for professionals in many fields (*see* Consultants: A Directory of Resources, page 275). Companies known as *job shops* can be used for discrete tasks such as mass mailings. Yellow pages listings for the appropriate industry should supply some firms for consideration. Trade organizations may also have information on local job shops.

Innovative Staffing Strategies

The past three decades have produced major lifestyle changes for most U.S. employees, and many businesses have responded by introducing staffing programs to accommodate these. The widespread increase in single-parent and two-income households, worker mobility, and urbanization are all factors affecting the workplace. Technological advances assist employers and employees by facilitating communication, record keeping, and home-based work activities. Flexible work schedules and the employment of consultants or part-time workers are important staffing options in today's world.

Alternative Work Schedules

Alternatives to the traditional 40-hour workweek share several positive aspects. They tend to reduce absenteeism and employee turnover by increasing workers' job satisfaction. Personnel problems such as chronic lateness decrease, too, when staff are allowed more flexibility in choosing their own work schedules. Productivity may also rise subsequent to the implementation of some of these programs. Qualified workers may be easier to recruit at average or lower-end salaries when attractive scheduling alternatives are offered. But documented successes do not mean that all or any of these alternatives are right for every company.

Managers should carefully consider the impact of such programs on the costs of doing business (overhead, administrative, and payroll expenses) as well as their effect on productivity (work flow, efficiency, and ease of employee supervision) and customer service. For example, utility bills are higher for offices that are open longer hours, and security costs may increase, too. Payroll computation can be more complex if everyone works a different schedule, and problems such as appropriate compensation on holidays may arise. Picture this compressed workweek scenario: Worker A normally works 4 hours on Tuesdays and 12 hours on Wednesdays, Thursdays, and Fridays—8:00 A.M. to 9:00 P.M. with an hour for lunch. Worker B normally works 12 hours on Mondays, Tuesdays, and Wednesdays and 4 hours on Thursdays (8:00 A.M. to noon). What happens when the office closes at noon on Thursday, Christmas Eve? Should Worker A receive 20 hours of holiday pay and Worker B no holiday pay at all, as the office is open all 40 hours of Worker B's normal schedule, but only 20 hours of Worker A's? Such situations occur frequently, and compensation policies must be established in advance to ensure fairness to everyone.

Another potential problem is that employees on flexible schedules are not always present to fill in or help out when coworkers are sick, on breaks, or overloaded with work. Yet they may have time on their hands when colleagues have gone home, customers are not calling, or supervisors are not present to redistribute the workload. In addition, longer hours can lower productivity on 10- or 12-hour days. Employees are also more likely to acquire second jobs when permitted to choose their own work hours, with the attendant difficulties of divided loyalties, overwork, and burnout. And when everyone is not working the same schedule, time may be lost due to interoffice communication difficulties—information needed at 6:00 P.M. from another worker cannot be obtained until that person arrives at noon the next day, for example.

Because there are so many factors to consider, implementation of alternative work schedules is often begun on a trial basis. This gives management an opportunity to observe effects on business operations before making a final decision. Employees are encouraged to work efficiently and keep productivity high in order to keep the privilege of setting their own schedules. The most frequently used options are listed below.

The Compressed Workweek

Since the 1970s, many companies have allowed full-time employees to squeeze a 40-hour workweek into less than the traditional five days. Compressed workweeks commonly involve four 10-hour days, four 9-hour days plus one half day, or even three 12-hour days (for a 36-hour week). This allows greater flexibility for workers who have young children or aged parents to tend, reducing absenteeism resulting from responsibilities at home. But it also provides more opportunities for staff to find second jobs. Although this program is very popular with employees and attractive to job applicants, the disadvantages noted above may outweigh the positive effects of implementation.

Flextime

A German innovation from the late 1960s, flextime (or flexitime) caught on quickly in American companies. It lets employees vary their schedules as needed or set their own regular schedules with the stipulation that a predetermined number of hours will be worked per week or per day. Managers may establish *core time* each day or on several days, meaning that attendance is mandatory during those hours. Core time is usually scheduled during peak customer service hours and for regular staff meetings. *Flex bands* are periods when attendance is optional, often at the beginning and end of each day. Flextime has been shown to reduce lateness, absenteeism, and personnel turnover and also to increase worker productivity and satisfaction. However, individual business needs and supervisory and administrative difficulties must be considered.

Consultants and Part-Time Employees

Administrative costs can be reduced by employing workers on a part-time or consultant basis, with benefits such as vacations, health insurance, sick leave, holiday pay, and employer Social Security contributions reduced or eliminated. These programs may be used alone, together, or in conjunction with other staffing plans to fulfill specific business requirements.

Consultants

Professional staff may be contracted on an hourly or per-job basis, or to fulfill designated responsibilities for a fixed salary, working whatever schedule is necessary to fulfill contract requirements. For example, a small firm may contract an accountant to handle its books, taxes, and payroll for an established monthly fee. Or a consultant may be hired for an hourly fee (usually with predetermined maximum billable hours) to perform specialized duties such as first-aid training for new employees. Such professionals are considered self-employed for tax purposes, with the employer paying the agreed-upon gross wages with no tax, Social Security, or other deductions taken out. This simplifies accounting procedures and can cost less than providing the usual employee benefits for regular employees.

Part-Time Employees

Permanent part-timers can satisfy a number of business needs in small companies and large corporations, too. For instance, part-time clerical staff may answer the telephone and relay customer service needs when normal office hours are over (at night, on weekends, and on holidays) in a wholesale food/drink business, with route salesmen on call for emergency deliveries and service. Part-time receptionists can also be used by large firms with many regular workers on flexible schedules to handle calls after regular hours. Often the applicants for such jobs have full-time duties (with benefits) elsewhere, so part-time employers may not need to furnish health insurance, vacation, or retirement options. Employing part-timers eliminates complicated scheduling plans to cover positions that must be manned at all times when the office is open.

In *job sharing,* a traditionally full-time position is shared by two permanent part-time employees who divide job responsibilities or share the same duties but work at different times. Sometimes each pair member works more than 20 hours per week. For employers, the main benefit of this program is its attractiveness to highly skilled, career-oriented persons who do not want to work full time, widening the pool of available good workers. Valuable employees of retirement age or beginning their parenting years may be retained in this manner. Other typical applicants for job-sharing positions are graduate students and nonprofessional workers who are attending college part time. For managers, the challenge of job sharing is to coordinate the work of one job between two people. Accountability, cooperation, and supervision can be problems. There may also be additional costs involved in hiring two people to fill one position: more payroll taxes, insurance, and benefits. If each person works more than 20 hours per week, the position will cost more than paying one full-time worker. However, when there is too much work for one full-time employee but not enough for two, job sharing is a good option. Some of the extra costs of job sharing may be avoided by employing part-time workers as consultants, on an hourly or per-job basis.

Virtual (Home-Based) Staff

With recent developments in technology, the virtual office is becoming a reality for many workers. Fax machines, the Internet, E-mail, teleconferencing, and same-day courier services provide the necessary links to office systems. One big benefit of using home-based staff is the savings on office space, furniture, and equipment, as virtual commuters provide their own. Virtual staff members may be employed full time or part time, as regular employees or consultants. They may work out of their homes 100 percent of the time or come to the office for meetings and other scheduled functions. This area of employment is growing rapidly, as it satisfies many workers' desire to create their own schedules and set their own pace. Employers have also found that personnel problems such as personality conflicts, tardiness, absenteeism, and too frequent gabfests are drastically reduced by the use of virtual staff.

Interns

College students working toward business degrees are often encouraged or required to perform supervised internships to gain practical experience. Using interns is a low-cost alternative to hiring part-time employees and may bring fresh insights and ideas into the firm. Providing internship slots is a good source of public relations, marking your business as community oriented. It also lends an aura of prestige from the confidence placed in your company by university faculty who consider it a good training site for budding business executives. Contact the National Society for Experimental Education, a professional association of employers, educators, and career counselors involved in promoting the development of business internships, for more information on developing internships at your work site. (*See* Sources of Further Information, Staffing Solutions, page 278, for contact information.)

Other Considerations

In addition to weighing the pros and cons of any staffing innovation, employers should check with the local Wage and Hour Division of the U.S. Department of Labor for guidelines on wage and hour laws that may affect alternative staffing programs, especially for lower paid workers. Guidelines cover required breaks and lunch periods per number of hours worked, which may preclude some of the more extreme compressed workweek and flextime schedules. The Employment Standards Administration of the Office of Federal Contract Compliance Programs can also provide needed information in this area (*see* U.S. Department of Labor Regional Offices, page 307, for the address and telephone number). To ensure that employment contracts are legal, have an experienced attorney prepare or check consultant agreements for part-time or professional workers. An excellent guide to using the new workforce is *Managing Contingent Workers: How to Reap the Benefits and Reduce the Risks* by Stanley Nollen and Helen Axel; this publication offers practical advice on the pros, cons, and legal considerations involved. (*See also* Sources of Further Information, Staffing Solutions, page 278, for helpful organizations and contact information.)

SMART STAFFING

When hiring new employees and assigning their duties, keep these points in mind:

Diversity: Resist the temptation to hire people who act and think just as you do. Look for workers from varying backgrounds and experiences to provide different ideas and perspectives.

Skills: Hire workers according to the needs of the business, and place them in roles that provide opportunities to use individual skills.

Teamwork: Assign people who work well together to the same work teams. Observe coworker interactions and workplace dynamics closely and make changes as necessary.

The overall picture: Choose employees who will fit into and complement the corporate culture of your firm.

Communication: Be sure that all workers understand their roles and where they fit into the company hierarchy and organizational structure.

Employee Benefits

Most employers provide workers with several types of benefits in addition to their wages. These extras make a big difference in an organization's ability to recruit and retain the best employees. Usually, large firms offer good benefit packages with liberal amounts of paid time off, partial payment of health and life insurance premiums, contributions to employee retirement programs, and bonuses or pay incentives (*see* Employee Compensation Plans, page 321). Small businesses often struggle just to pay the required Social Security taxes and workers' compensation premiums for each employee, and may not pay their staff for time not worked.

The following sections discuss points to consider when setting office policy for paid time off and unpaid family/medical leave requirements mandated by federal and state laws. Options for providing day-care assistance to employees for children and elderly family members are also discussed.

Vacations, Holidays, and Sick Leave

Paid leave is not legally mandated except in government agencies and in companies with union contracts, but most firms with full-time employees include paid leave as part of employee benefits. A firm's investment in this area may pay for itself when employees return from leave rested and with renewed enthusiasm for work. Some health-conscious firms even allow employees to use company time for sports and fitness programs. Although too much time off can cause work disruptions and hurt productivity, well-managed leave programs can improve productivity, lessen stress, and increase worker satisfaction.

The office policies and procedures manual should include a section on paid leave that addresses each of the following areas.

Vacations (Annual Leave). Many firms enact a system based on length of employment so that vacation and sick leave amounts increase with seniority. For example, an employee who has been with the firm less than five years may be granted two weeks of vacation and two weeks of sick leave each year. After five years of employment, three weeks of vacation and sick leave may be given, and four weeks after ten years of service. Four to six weeks of paid leave is a reasonable limit for the most senior employees.

Sick Leave. Sick leave may be offered at a rate comparable to each employee's vacation leave, based on longevity with the firm. Smaller businesses sometimes use a *reasonable sick leave* policy, with pay for sick days left to the discretion of each worker's supervisor. Sick leave is granted as needed with no set maximum for each year. If an employee has been absent due to illness for an excessive amount of time, the supervisor may disallow further sick leave payments. This type of sick leave policy should be used with caution, as it sets the stage for charges of unfair treatment and discrimination.

Personal Days. Some companies allow employees to take off two or three days each year for any reason, in addition to paid vacations, holidays, and sick days.

Funeral Leave and Leave for Jury or Reserve Duty. Employers may give their workers paid leave to attend funerals of close family members. Some firms pay workers a regular salary when they are on leave for jury or reserve duty, with the requirement that pay received for that duty be given to the employer. Others require that employees use vacation or personal leave for these situations. Details should be fully explained if special leave is given.

Disposition of Unused Leave. A written policy should explain whether vacation and sick leave can be accumulated indefinitely or whether leave is forfeited when not used within a certain length of time. It should also note whether employees who resign or are terminated will be paid for unused leave.

Procedures for Requesting Leave. Guidelines for vacation and sick leave requests should specify the amount of advance notice to be given when scheduling vacations and should explain how conflicting requests will be handled, by seniority or by date of request. The procedures for requesting sick leave and supplying necessary documentation (such as a physician's statement) are essential. Instructions on turning in leave requests, whether to a supervisor or personnel office, should also be included.

Restrictions on Scheduling Vacations. Certain types of businesses need all of their employees during busy times of the year. For instance, an accounting firm may have a policy limiting vacations to months when tax deadlines are not looming. Any time periods when vacations cannot be scheduled should be explained.

Paid Holidays. Many U.S. businesses are closed on major holidays such as New Year's Day, President's Day, Memorial Day, July Fourth, Labor Day, Thanksgiving Day, and Christmas Day. Workers are usually paid regular wages when offices close for holidays. Generous employers may also include Good Friday, national election days, Veterans Day, the day after Thanksgiving, Christmas Eve, and New Year's Eve as paid holidays. Businesses that never close usually pay extra wages (holiday pay) to those who must work on major holidays. In addition, workers may be given the option of receiving holiday pay on their own ethnic or religious holidays, such as Rosh Hashannah and Yom Kippur or the Chinese New Year, in lieu of payment for Christian holidays (such as Christmas and Good Friday) that they do not observe.

A list of days that the office will be closed and a notice as to whether workers will be paid should be included in the policies and procedures manual.

Federal and State Requirements for Family and Medical Leave

The federal Family and Medical Leave Act of 1993 guarantees leave from work in cases of personal or family medical emergency. The law applies to all public agencies and to companies with 50 or more employees working within 75 miles of each other. Such organizations must provide up to 12 weeks of *unpaid* leave per year to any worker whose personal or family emergency requires hospital care or continuing medical treatment, if the employee has worked for the firm one or more years and has worked at least 1,250 hours in the past year.

The act states that an employee's job is protected—that is, the same position or one with equivalent pay, benefits, and status must be made available to the worker on his or her return from family or medical leave. Provisions for continuing health insurance during such leave are also included. For more information, call or write the Office of Federal Contract Compliance Programs, Employment Standards Administration (*see* Employment Discrimination—General Information, page 277, for the address and telephone number).

Most states have legislation that works with or supersedes federal family and medical leave requirements. The amount of leave allowed and characteristics of affected companies (the number of employees necessary to make the law applicable) vary by state. Most states specify that family or medical leave should be available for pregnancy, childbirth, adoption, and serious medical conditions of a worker or the worker's child, spouse, or parent.

Any employee who has been denied the mandated family/medical leave has the right to file a complaint with the local Wage and Hour Division of the U.S. Department of Labor (*see* U.S. Department of Labor Regional Offices, page 279, for contact information). Complaints must be filed within a certain time period, with documentation. A worker who suspects that leave has been unfairly denied should first check the company policies and procedures manual and follow listed procedures for filing a grievance within the company. If this does not produce satisfactory results, the next step is to talk with a union representative when applicable. Nonunion employees should talk with other workers to determine whether they have also been denied legally mandated family/medical leave. In that case, a group complaint can be filed. An attorney or legal aid agency may be needed to prepare a viable complaint.

Child-Care and Elder-Care Services

The need for competent and convenient child care has risen as women and single parents have become a major part of the workforce. As the number of senior citizens rises, the demand for elder care is also increasing. Family care is consistently listed by workers as a benefit that contributes significantly to job satisfaction, so it is in a company's best interest to help employees balance work and family responsibilities. Although providing a complete day-care package is often beyond the means of smaller companies, all employers can address these growing concerns in some way.

From the most complex and costly option to the simplest and least expensive alternative, the choices include the following:

1. *Establishing a child-care/adult-care center at work.* On-site care administered by the company involves huge financial, organizational, and legal concerns, so it is viable only for large corporations with many employees and proper facilities. For workers, this is probably the most convenient alternative. Coordinated child- and elder-care programs are particularly beneficial to participants, as children and senior citizens can profit from time spent together.

2. *Sponsoring a child-care/adult-care center.* Off-site family care contracted by the company is also expensive, but it involves fewer administrative concerns. Care providers may be schools with extended programs, churches, day-care centers, senior citizen "drop-in" centers, and retirement homes.

3. *Joining a consortium.* Consortiums can be formed with other companies to lower family-care costs by pooling resources to set up day-care facilities. Contracting with established day-care programs may also be more affordable via consortium membership.

4. *Providing financial assistance to workers.* Pretax family-care pay vouchers can make it easier for workers to pay for needed day care. For more information on setting up this system, contact the Administration for Children, Youth, and Families—Office of Human Development Services, U.S. Department of Health and Human Services (*see* Family Care, page 278). Ask about the Dependent Care Assistance Plan.

5. *Allowing alternative scheduling.* Programs allowing flextime, job sharing, a compressed workweek, part-time schedules, and home-based jobs permit workers the flexibility needed to be productive employees while caring for their family members.

6. *Providing information.* Referrals to good family-care programs near the office can be very helpful for new employees, new parents, and those who have recently taken responsibility for aged relatives. If no other assistance can be offered, providing an up-to-date list of reputable facilities, their hours of operation, and fees charged will be helpful.

Note that the first four options raise questions of company liability. To minimize the risks to children and elders and reduce potential legal problems, consider only fully licensed and insured programs. Areas of concern include transportation (arranging for drivers and vehicles), food preparation, physical facilities, and caregivers themselves. Day-care staff should be hired carefully, with proper screening, education, and medical training; in addition, enough workers must always be present to provide adequate supervision of those in their care. For the company's protection, develop written policies and guidelines for such family-care programs and require employees to sign reasonable disclaimers of company liability. *See also* Sources of Further Information, Family Care Resources, page 278, for addresses and phone numbers of government agencies and other organizations to contact for information and assistance on day-care programs.

How to Solve Personnel Problems

Although employees are a company's most important resource, it is important to remember that all workers, at every level, are human beings—and when people are involved, problems are sure to occur. Good managers know that solving them is one of their most important responsibilities, and that each decision made will affect workers' morale, efficiency, and productivity. They also know that the best strategy is to act immediately before a problem gets worse. Before taking any action, however, it is necessary to understand exactly what is causing the difficulty.

Defining the Problem

Most personnel problems fall within one of the following categories:

- incompetence
- laziness
- insubordination
- personality conflicts
- theft or other illegal activities
- chronic substance abuse
- violations of company policy
- excessive absenteeism
- chronic tardiness
- gossiping
- shifting blame
- undermining others' accomplishments
- bickering
- lying

Answering the following questions will help to clarify the issues:

- Is the problem real, or is it just a misperception or miscommunication that can be remedied immediately by clarifying minor issues?
- Is the problem something different than what it initially appeared to be? Has it been observed firsthand by the manager, or is it evidenced in the results it has produced?
- How big is the problem? Is it a continuing occurrence? Is it disruptive to the office? Is it hurting business?
- Does the problem come from outside the company, or is it strictly an internal difficulty?
- Do the employees involved understand that what they are doing is wrong? Do they know what the correct behavior would be? Do they understand the consequences of their actions?
- Can the situation be resolved at this level of management, or will the authority of a higher-up be necessary?

The answers to these questions will provide the framework for determining appropriate solutions that adhere to company policy. The information obtained will also be necessary for documentation of actions, especially when legal issues must be considered.

Managing Employees

It is not a manager's responsibility to parent workers or teach them to be better people, but to solve problems for the sake of the company. However, even problem employees may have some strengths that offset their weaknesses. Approaching difficulties as potential learning experiences for workers can improve their performance in the long run. The first rule of problem solving is to focus on the solution rather than expend too much energy assigning blame.

This does not preclude assigning responsibility where it is due. When the problem has been clearly defined, it may be appropriate to discuss obvious shortcomings privately with each employee involved. Delineate problem areas, set goals and dates for further review, and explain the consequences of failure to improve (*see* Evaluating Employees, page 220). Then move on to the solution and keep the focus positive.

Remember that a wise manager does the following:

- approaches workers directly
- treats everyone fairly and equally
- remains open to workers' concerns and suggestions
- stays sensitive to the egos and emotions at play during all interactions
- avoids getting involved in employees' personal and family issues
- recognizes that some problems are beyond his/her control

Dispute Resolution

Coworker disputes, though common, are dangerous because they involve delicate interpersonal relations that can explode and disrupt an entire office. A manager must be prepared to mediate such situations quickly, objectively, and in ways that prevent future difficulties. Here are some guidelines for definitive responses to bickering, backbiting, blame shifting, gossiping, and undermining of others' work:

- Make sure that everyone involved understands the importance of working together and resolving disputes—and the consequences if problems continue.
- Recognize the signs of a dispute—low morale, tension, complaints, and decreased productivity.
- Keep the dispute isolated to the original workers involved by taking action at the first signs of trouble.
- Give the parties an opportunity to resolve their dispute without assistance by letting them know that the problem has been noticed and will be addressed by management if not resolved immediately.

- Watch for change, then meet with the warring parties if they do not resolve their difficulties.
- Provide a comfortable atmosphere for the parties to discuss their concerns with each other.
- Insist on openness and complete communication.
- Mediate discussions objectively, without pronouncing judgment.
- Teach workers to handle disputes without involving others, both through training and by example.
- Focus on agreements, then try to find positive results from disputes.

If attempts at dispute resolution are unsuccessful, further steps are necessary. The company's best interests are the primary concern, so maximum efficiency and productivity are the main goal. Everyone involved should clearly understand that this goal will be reached by whatever means are necessary. Options to consider:

- bringing the parties together to work on a task to encourage comradeship and teamwork
- separating those involved by moving desks, rearranging work teams, or reassigning duties
- reviewing productivity requirements, deadlines, and job coordination to be sure that there is no basis for further conflict

Problem-Solving Measures

A manager's reaction to a workplace problem should be appropriate and fall within company policy. Be flexible, though, and consider extenuating circumstances. Always keep your boss or supervisor informed of your actions, some of which may require consultation with the personnel or legal department. Make sure your superiors are in agreement with the measures to be taken. If you must discipline, use a preset system of progressive discipline in which sanctions become more severe as a problem continues. The following guidelines may be helpful:

First action: Talk directly with workers, making them aware that you have observed the problem, and offer some solutions.

Second action: Warn the persons involved (orally) that the problem has not been resolved, stating the corrections that are needed and the consequences of allowing the situation to continue.

Third action: Provide counseling and training to correct the problem.

Fourth action: Issue a written warning, formally outlining the problem and the previous steps that have been taken to address it. State that previous efforts have been unsuccessful and that notice is being given of changes that must be made. Set reevaluation dates for review, and clearly define the consequences of failure to correct the problem.

Fifth action: Reprimand the persons involved via memos placed in permanent personnel files.

Sixth action: Suspend the parties without pay for a period predetermined by company policy.

Seventh action: Terminate the worker(s) responsible for the continuing problem.

Once the situation has advanced past the first action, it is important to keep records of every action taken. You may be forced to show documentation of a performance problem if a termination is contested legally. Write down the time, date, and location of each relevant instance, and the rules that were violated. Record only objective facts and observations, not accusations or assumptions. Also record the steps taken (discussions, counseling, oral and written warnings), where and when each step occurred, and the persons present at each incident or discussion. Include a summary of points made during counseling sessions, concerns expressed by each party, agreements made, and the results (positive or negative). When the fourth stage is reached, a copy of the written warning and all prior documentation should be sent to the personnel department, with a copy retained for the manager's records. It is best to have the employee sign a statement acknowledging receipt of the warning and agreeing to the problem-solving measures that have been delineated.

Termination should be viewed as the last resort in solving personnel problems. Alternatives to firing include the following:

- counseling
- further training
- transfer to a more suitable job
- restructuring duties
- reducing employee work hours to limit or isolate problems

Making Sure the Problem Is Resolved

Monitor each problem situation to ensure that those involved are making the requested changes. If problems persist, reconsider the situation and the measures taken. Perhaps it is a larger issue than it seemed originally, or maybe the agreed-upon solution was not entirely appropriate or adequate.

When All Else Fails: Firing an Employee

When no feasible alternative can be found, there is no choice but to terminate the employee(s) responsible for the continuing difficulties. Firing an employee is one of the most unpleasant and stressful management tasks. In addition to legal, administrative, and company policy issues, there is a strong emotional component that touches everyone in the office. It is common for the terminating supervisor to feel guilt and worry about staff reactions. However, the company will benefit if the firing is appropriate, and a terminated employee may even be well served by separation from the firm.

A variety of performance problems may warrant termination:

- dishonesty, disrespect, or betrayal of confidence
- blatant and extreme insubordination or refusal to perform reasonable tasks
- lack of productivity or poor work quality due to sloppiness or laziness

- illegal activities such as stealing, bribery, accepting kickbacks, sexual harassment, or physical assault
- chronic absenteeism
- recurring drug or alcohol abuse that affects job performance

When faced with terminating an employee, the supervisor must be sure to act in a fair and legal manner, as described below.

Safe Firing Procedures

The United States has a long-standing tradition of following the *employment at will* doctrine, which allows an employer to fire a worker at any time, with or without reason. This doctrine still exists in theory, but there are many exceptions and limitations to the policy in today's business world. Antidiscrimination laws dictate that employees cannot be fired because of age, gender, race, religion, ethnic origin, or physical disability (*see* Fair Play: Eliminating Employment Discrimination, page 228). In addition, workers are protected if they do the following:

- protest against, report on, or refuse to participate in illegal company activities
- attempt to form a union or file discrimination charges
- are chosen for jury duty

Union and personal contracts, as well as some implied contracts, also limit an employer's right to fire workers.

Following these suggestions may help to prevent lawsuits resulting from illegal termination procedures:

- Allow sufficient time to remedy a problem via other alternatives.
- Weigh options carefully.
- Obtain legal advice in situations that are not clear-cut, especially if circumstances indicate immediate termination without prior warning and documentation.
- In large firms, reach agreement among the company owner(s), manager(s), and personnel director before any action is taken.
- In situations with underlying issues such as obvious personal animosity between a supervisor and employee, have a higher-up handle all aspects to avoid charges of unfair practices.

When all factors have been considered and an objective decision to terminate has been made, a manager should take the necessary action with no indication of personal reservations or fear of consequences. As noted previously, all actions leading to termination should be clearly documented. Company liability can be reduced by complete personnel files that include specific records of private meetings with the employee, memos defining the problem, oral and written warnings, previous disciplinary actions, agreements on corrective measures, employment contracts, and results of performance evaluations. It may also be necessary to prove that employment standards are objective, appropriate, fair, and applied equally to all workers.

The Termination Interview

When the time comes to fire a worker, the individual must be treated with respect and consideration. Although it is not a manager's responsibility to comfort employees who have failed to perform adequately, a compassionate approach is best for several reasons. Workplace morale may be adversely affected by overly harsh termination procedures, as fired employees often talk to former coworkers. Making an effort to preserve the affected person's self-esteem and trying to calm fears about the future may also prevent violent outbursts and retaliations (*see* Terrorism and Angry Employees: The New Office Menace, page 108). And perhaps the most important reason to terminate with kindness is the knowledge that everyone makes mistakes, so that a manager forced to fire someone will feel better afterward if the deed is done as gently as possible.

During the interview, a manager should not express guilt or misgivings about his or her own past actions, training procedures, office politics, or decisions that have been made. Neither should sorrow at losing the employee be communicated. Such statements could provide ammunition for legal appeals. The decision to terminate should be stated directly and firmly, with a brief review of events leading to this conclusion. Judgmental remarks about the employee's behavior, character, or performance should be avoided.

Termination interviews should always be held in person. (If an employee is being fired for job desertion, ask for a meeting by writing or phoning. Only when the worker refuses to meet or does not respond to these attempts should notification be delivered by phone or letter.) A private conference between supervisor and employee is usually held, but it is sometimes advisable to have a personnel department representative present. If possible, schedule the effective date at the best time of the day, week, month, or year to minimize the employee's pain and embarrassment. Keep the meeting short and directed. Explain why the decision has been made in clear and professional terms. Be prepared for any reaction, from laughter to tears to violent anger. If you fear violence, have a security guard nearby or even in the room in extreme situations. Allow the fired employee to ask questions, but make it clear that the decision is final. Arrange for the return of all company property, including I.D. cards, credit cards, access cards, keys, and books or computer disks containing company secrets.

When all questions have been asked and answered, proceed to details of the company's severance program, which should be specified as part of office policy. Although this type of program is not legally mandated, severance programs help fired employees recover, improve office morale, and contribute to a positive company image (*see* Severance Packages, page 325). Packages may include the following:

- severance pay, which is often the regular salary for two weeks, one month, or another specified period after termination (some firms allow one week of severance pay for each year with the company)
- counseling, to help the terminated worker cope and restore his or her confidence
- outplacement assistance, which can include use of secretarial services to prepare résumés, use of an office to conduct a job search, or other assistance with résumé preparation and interviewing skills

- health insurance benefits, with a specified duration and explanation of the cost to the employee, if the company has paid part of the premiums previously but will no longer do so

There are certain federal requirements concerning the continuation of health insurance benefits for employees who retire, resign, or are terminated. Such benefits are provided at no cost to the employer, as a worker must pay the full premium when requesting such continuation of benefits. For more information, call the Federal Information Center at 800-688-9889 and ask for the address and phone number of the U.S. Pension and Welfare Benefits Administration's regional office for your area.

Documentation

All terminations should be documented fully and immediately. Details of the termination interview are important, so carefully note each point made in the discussion, as well as observations of the employee's reactions.

Stress Management

Stress management should not be viewed merely as an employee's problem. If workers are under serious strain on the job, this will be manifested throughout the office in lower productivity, decreased efficiency, and increased tension. Therefore, both management and staff should take steps to relieve stress from routine office pressures, seasonal or short-term increases in workloads, and out-of-the-ordinary occurrences.

What Management Can Do to Reduce Stress

To prevent or reduce unnecessary stress and provide a more relaxed, productive workplace, managers can do the following:

- Provide stress management training and counseling. Offer programs to help managers and workers identify the signs of stress and learn how to deal with them. Also, provide access to a counselor, whether in the office or out. Note, though, that maintaining some level of stress can be beneficial in promoting good work.
- Set realistic deadlines and standards for employee performance.
- Alter job assignments as necessary to distribute responsibilities equally throughout the workforce.
- Create a system for allowing extra time off when workloads and stress levels have been unusually high.
- Allow workers to express uncertainty and/or frustration without fear of retaliation by establishing an open-door policy to encourage private communication of such issues to supervisors.

- Respond to legitimate overwork concerns by setting priorities for work to be done, so that employees understand what is absolutely necessary and what can be neglected if not everything can be completed.
- Show special appreciation for employees who have worked hard and well during stressful periods.
- Provide stress-relief activities such as company softball tournaments, weekly staff get-togethers, and access to health club facilities.

How Employees Can Cope with Office Pressures

Workers can probably do more to manage their own stress levels effectively than management can. Employees who want to improve in this area should do the following:

- Practice better time management to avoid overwork caused by procrastination or time wasted on unimportant details.
- Get organized by setting goals and priorities daily and for the long term.
- Take the time to understand tasks fully before beginning them.
- Practice stress-relief techniques such as meditation, yoga, or other relaxation exercises.
- Take small breaks for relaxation exercises or just a five-minute stroll outside the office.
- Express concerns and frustrations in an appropriate manner to the appropriate supervisory person, rather than complain to coworkers who can do nothing to alleviate the situation.
- Develop positive relationships with coworkers, as negative personal interactions are a major contributor to stress and hamper team efforts.
- Maintain a healthy lifestyle by exercising, eating properly, avoiding drug or alcohol abuse, and getting enough rest. Allow for needed leisure time after stressful work situations.
- Accept some stress as a normal part of work, channeling it into a positive sense of competitiveness, motivation, and initiative that will improve work performance.
- Ask supervisory personnel to set priorities for work to be accomplished, and then follow those priorities.

Workers are sometimes reluctant to tell their supervisors that they are overworked because they fear this will make them seem incompetent. Communicating legitimate concerns may be the best way to improve chronic stress, however. Sometimes confiding in coworkers, counselors, friends, or family can help to release stress, but this should not be substituted for open communication with supervisory personnel.

Office Etiquette

Office Politics: Playing for Everyone to Win

Though it often has a negative connotation, politics is a natural and unavoidable part of office life. The trick is doing it well while maintaining high ethical standards.

Good workers can use politics to sell their ideas, promote their achievements, and gain authority. But those with less noble intentions can also use politics to win a level of control that is dangerous to the company and damaging to the work environment. Office politics should be used sparingly and aimed at benefiting the entire company. Here are some appropriate political strategies:

- Earn the trust of coworkers by honest, ethical words and practices.
- Cultivate a positive image by being successful, cooperative, and supportive of others, as the best way to present a good image is to deserve it.
- Build alliances by cultivating work relationships with people who have similar or complementary interests—there is power in coalitions that are based on honesty and geared toward positive goals, and simple favors done for others will usually be repaid.
- Be subtle, as a casual comment is often more persuasive than a formal presentation.
- Practice patience, and observe others carefully to gain an understanding of organizational interactions.
- Notice how others communicate, and use this knowledge to facilitate understanding and cooperation.
- Observe which ideas work and which do not, and how the most successful people in the organization present their proposals.
- Learn about existing alliances between others, and act accordingly.
- Know who the decision makers are, and who has access to needed information and resources.
- Avoid flexing authority unnecessarily, as this results in resentment and dissension.
- Know when to compromise, and stay focused on the ultimate end: results.
- Remember that good negotiating skills are the key to influencing change.
- Be open to others' ideas.
- Recognize the political ploys used by others, and seek to understand the reasons for their attempts to influence decisions.
- Judge others by the quality of their ideas and achievements, not by personal idiosyncrasies.
- Play fairly, and always be sure that any information used to persuade others is correct and appropriate for such use.
- Use politics to achieve personal goals only when these will also benefit the company.
- Focus on real achievement rather than impressing others, as political moves are not a substitution for hard work.

AVOIDING OFFICE MINEFIELDS

Office etiquette is constantly changing as social mores evolve and old-fashioned rules become irrelevant. It is sometimes difficult to know how to approach a person or situation, and even harder to ensure that personal reactions are appropriate when others create problems. The following scenarios may provide some ideas on handling sticky situations with finesse and grace:

1. A supervisor calls you "honey" or "sweetie" in front of other staff members and you find it demeaning. What can you do? First, try to determine if he or she intends this as an insult, or if your superior is simply not using good sense. Even if such endearments are not malicious, you need not accept them. In private, convey your desire to be addressed in a more professional manner.

2. A personnel representative from another company calls to request information on one of your employees. Should you fax it to that person? Not without the employee's written permission, as anyone near the fax machine on the receiving end may see the transmittal.

3. Your coworker or supervisor is a chain smoker who ignores the "No Smoking" signs in your office or building. What do you do? The likelihood of this situation is lessening as more and more offices ban or limit smoking, but the problem still occurs. Try not to be a crusader in your request for smoke-free air, and avoid putting the smoker on the defensive. With all of the current health information available about the hazards of smoking, it is likely that many confirmed smokers truly want to quit but have not yet found the strength to do so. Approach the subject without making judgments or giving advice, perhaps with a gentle reminder that there is no ashtray in the office because smoking is prohibited in the area. Suggest alternatives such as a clean-air machine or smokeless ashtray in the smoker's personal area.

Dressing the Part

In the business world, first impressions can make the difference between ultimate success and failure, so professional dress and grooming are very important. The main concerns should be quality, tastefulness, good fit, neat appearance, and comfort. Some companies have dress codes, but most firms rely on traditional, unwritten clothing standards. Suits are the norm in many professional offices, but personnel in more creative businesses (such as entertainment companies) tend to dress more casually.

In recent years, many companies have adopted "casual Fridays." Companies expect their staff to come to work in traditional professional dress from Monday to Thursday; on Friday, however, employees are given more flexibility. On these casual Fridays, suits are not required, and men and women can dress down. It is not uncommon, in certain companies, to see staff members in jeans and sneakers. In other workplaces, such dress might be frowned upon. When in doubt, the safest course is to emulate colleagues in comparable positions, dressing at least as formally as they do.

For those who do not trust their own clothes sense, experienced salespeople in better quality stores can often provide assistance in choosing professional clothing and clothing appropriate for casual Fridays. The following guidelines may be helpful, as they represent traditional formal office dress standards.

For Men

Suits. Dark blues and grays convey the most authority—muted plaids and pinstripes are fine, too—but browns and blacks are not recommended. Suit styles should never be too trendy. They may be single- or double-breasted, with or without side vents, and with or without cuffed trousers. A suit jacket should be worn to formal meetings, when leaving the office, and when talking with a superior. Keep the jacket buttoned when standing; unbutton it when sitting.

Shirts. Smooth cotton, long-sleeved white shirts are best, but pinstripes or pastels may also be worn.

Ties. Good quality fabrics and conservative colors and patterns are best—silk with diagonal stripes, small dots, or subtle repeated prints. Handkerchiefs are not required, but one may be worn in the breast pocket as an accessory.

Shoes and Socks. Lace-up, polished leather shoes should be worn, in either black or brown. They may be plain-toed or wingtip. Dark socks that do not droop are appropriate; they must be long enough to keep the legs covered when they are crossed.

Accessories. A dark, one-inch-wide belt with a brass buckle is the conservative choice. A watch that is simple and of good quality is best. Avoid wearing any jewelry other than a wedding band and tasteful cuff links.

Grooming. Hair and nails must be clean, short, and neat; facial hair is frowned upon in more conservative settings. Of course, an antiperspirant is crucial, and only a mild cologne should be used.

For Women

Suits. Long-sleeved, matched skirt suits in a conventional cut are most formal, although pantsuits and long-sleeved dresses are acceptable in many offices. Dark blue and gray are the best colors, but black, brown, dark green, and burgundy are also common. Skirts should be a relatively conservative, fashionable length.

Blouses. White, long-sleeved blouses with conservative necklines are a good choice with dark suits, but other colors are acceptable.

Shoes and Hosiery. Dark leather (not suede), closed-toe, medium-heeled pumps are best. Boots, spike heels, and flats should not be worn unless the office atmosphere is informal. Aching feet can make a day seem very long, so styles that look professional, fit well, and feel comfortable are essential. Shoes with run-down heels or scuff marks should either be repaired or left at home.

Accessories. Scarves and simple jewelry add interest to professional clothing and can soften the severity of dark suits. Earrings should be in small, tasteful, classic styles (not dangling or hooped). Necklaces and pins of pearls, gold, or silver are nice. Watches should be small, simple, and of good quality (analog, not digital). Wedding and engagement rings may be worn, but wearing several rings or rings with large settings is not strictly professional.

Grooming. Hairstyles should be neat, easy to manage, and conservatively styled—not too big, too short, or too long. Long hair can be tied back or pinned up in a classic style. Only moderate amounts of makeup and mild perfumes are appropriate for the office, and extreme nail lengths are in bad taste. Nail polish in clear, natural, or subdued colors is best.

MINDING YOUR MANNERS

In your workspace

- Respect the space and privacy of others by not dropping in too often or staying too long.
- Keep your voice low when talking to others or on the telephone, particularly if you work in an open office.
- Ask neighbors if your music will bother them before turning it on or use headphones.
- Smoke only in areas set aside for that purpose.
- Decorate your office, cubicle, or desk in a tasteful manner.
- Be courteous to everyone, regardless of their status in the office hierarchy.
- Avoid hugs, kisses, or other affectionate touching, except on rare occasions.

At the copy machine

- Interrupt lengthy copying sessions by letting those with small jobs make their copies before you finish.
- Refill the paper supply if you use a lot of paper.
- Take care of all problems you encounter or report them to the maintenance person; never just walk away from a jammed machine.

In the kitchen or employee lounge

- Clean up after yourself and put uneaten food away.
- Get your own coffee and lunch instead of asking subordinates to bring it to you.
- Respect others' food and personal items; if you would like to borrow something, ask first.
- Refill the coffeepot if it is empty.

Employee Dating: Pros, Cons, and Setting Policy

Dating coworkers was once strictly taboo, but in most offices it is now recognized that personal relationships are inevitable, natural, and quite common. The question is not "Should it be allowed?" but "How should it be handled?" There are advantages and disadvantages of employee dating for both staff and management to consider.

Benefits of Employee Dating

Here are some of the positive aspects of intimate relationships between coworkers:

- added excitement in the workplace
- improved teamwork and productivity

- a more relaxed and friendly atmosphere
- increased stability and reduced turnover
- relief of tension

Potential Problems with Employee Dating

There may also be problems with employees who are romantically involved, such as:

- emotional distractions that reduce productivity
- damaged working relationships when personal associations end badly
- complication of office interactions
- bias and favoritism
- tension due to romantic competition
- conflicts of interest

Setting Policy

A company's policy on employee dating will depend on a number of factors, including its corporate culture, traditions, history, demographics, business type, location, and the manager's personal values. More informal and creative companies, and those that have many young employees, tend to set more liberal policies, but some conservative firms prohibit such relationships. Some managers choose to deal with the issue on a case-by-case basis, neither encouraging nor discouraging dating unless a couple's personal issues become disruptive. Problem situations may include extramarital affairs that are demoralizing to observers, supervisor/subordinate dating that results in preferred treatment of a subordinate, sexual harassment, and extracurricular involvements that involve sexual politics.

Setting a formal policy that applies equally to everyone will make the position of management clear. It is legal to prohibit disruptive relationships at work, but if an employer's actions are challenged in court, there must be evidence to prove that the relationship was adversely affecting the workplace. Company policy can legally forbid the employment of married couples in the same office, especially when one spouse would be in the other's direct line of supervision. But it is against the law to intrude on employees' privacy, so prohibiting discreet relationships that do not cause problems may be unwise.

An appropriately written dating policy should do the following:

- explain how and why certain relationships can become disruptive
- delineate specific behaviors that define problematic relationships
- specify how disruptive associations will be handled (*see* How to Solve Personnel Problems, page 253)
- state that it will apply equally to all employees
- include an acknowledgment of employees' right to privacy

Other Work Relationships That May Be Problematic

- mentor/apprentice, if work guidance relationships between executives and younger workers are misunderstood by one of the parties involved or by others in the office

- boss/secretary, if the pair act overly familiar with each other or get involved in each other's personal lives
- close friends, if the relationship alienates others or causes rumors to circulate
- married couples, if they flaunt affection, give each other special treatment, shut out others, or fight openly
- competing coworkers, if the competition undermines the company and causes polarization
- familial ties, if there is favoritism or a sense that the relative does not deserve his or her position or expects the relationship to forestall disciplinary action for incompetence. (*See also* Office Policies and Procedures, page 186.)

Business Gift Guidelines

Gifts from Managers to Employees

Giving gifts to employees is an effective way of communicating appreciation for their efforts. The size and type of gift is up to the individual manager or supervisor, but usually depends on factors such as number of employees, employer/employee relations, and corporate culture. For instance, in a business with many employees it is not likely that a birthday gift for each will fit the company budget. Of course, individual supervisors may choose to buy gifts for subordinates or coworkers with their personal funds if their team is small and close-knit; however, this can quickly become a financial burden if employees begin to expect such gifts and no company funds are forthcoming.

Here are some ideas for inexpensive presents that convey appreciation and thoughtfulness without overburdening the company budget:

- For each employee's birthday, give a card, flowers, balloons, or a small gift of comparable value (a pen, candy, or fruit basket).
- For personal milestones, give a card or appropriate gift such as a savings bond for a new baby or crystal for a wedding.
- For work-related events such as 10- or 20-year anniversaries, retirement, or attained sales goals, give a gold watch, a clock, a plaque, or a savings bond.
- For Thanksgiving and/or Christmas, give turkeys or hams for holiday meals.
- For Christmas, a cash bonus is customary. It is also nice to give small gifts to personal secretaries or assistants.
- For Secretaries' Day, give flowers and/or a small gift.

Workers can also pool funds for employee gifts from the entire staff. These gifts may have more personal significance to the recipients but should not be viewed as substitutes for gifts from management.

Gifts for the Boss

Customs vary widely in different companies, so it is best to ask coworkers about their usual practices in advance of special occasions. This will eliminate the embarrassment of being the only sales associate who does not give the sales manager a gift, or the equally awkward scenario that occurs when a gift is unexpected and its purpose is misunderstood. In many firms, employees are not expected to give presents to their superiors, but a holiday or birthday card is almost always appreciated. Even when it is not customary, gifts are usually acceptable, too, if a personal relationship exists between the worker and supervisor.

Gifts for Clients and Associates

Gifts to business colleagues are never an obligation, but a unique gift that shows personal consideration can make a lasting impression. The intention may be to show appreciation for the client's business or to commemorate an anniversary, milestone, or special occasion. To avoid any appearance of bribery, gifts should not be expensive (no more than $75). The item should be tasteful, of good quality, attractively wrapped, and contain a personal note. The following ideas should help:

- sample products from the company
- practical business tools, such as calendars or calculators, bearing the giver's company logo
- books on relevant subjects or of particular interest to the recipient
- tickets to a performance or sporting event
- items purchased while traveling
- items that are indigenous to your area, such as local foods or crafts, for clients in other parts of the country or world
- cards or flowers

OFFICE PARTIES

Office parties are occasions for colleagues to relax and interact on an informal basis. A defined policy or set of rules is probably not necessary if everyone understands that drunkenness, improper sexual activity, and destruction of property will not be excused. Just in case, though, it may be best to hold parties at another location, as this will probably help to set a more comfortable tone. All improper behavior should be clearly discouraged and any dangerous or illegal activities forbidden, as in any work situation. Most employees will recognize that their behavior at office parties makes an impression on management and will act accordingly. Occasional behavioral problems should be handled discreetly. Arrangements for safe transportation should be available to anyone who has been drinking. Everyone present should remember that even though the purpose of an office party is to have fun, it is also a work-related activity. The embarrassing consequences of foolish behavior at such functions can damage or destroy a promising career.

Handling and Defusing Corporate Crises

The most crucial management skills come into play during a workplace crisis. Successful crisis managers must handle public relations, human resources, operations, legal issues, and any number of unpredictable factors. Sometimes crises are uncontrollable, but often they can be anticipated, with coping strategies outlined in advance. The manner in which such situations are handled can markedly influence a manager's career path.

Defining a Crisis

First, it is necessary to understand what constitutes a crisis. A situation is a crisis when it is at risk of (a) escalating in seriousness; (b) interfering with business operations; (c) hurting the company physically or financially; (d) damaging the company's image; or (e) leading to a government or media investigation. Many different types of situations qualify as crises: rumors, industrial accidents, product recalls, strikes, the sudden death of a staff member, on-site crimes, and more. A crisis management plan should cover all of these possibilities and others specific to the company.

Developing a Crisis Plan

Prepare for crises by making a list of previous crises within the company or similar businesses, estimating the likelihood of recurrence, and then identifying other possible areas of vulnerability. Then rank these crises from most likely and most serious to least probable and least destructive. Analyze past incidents to determine if they were handled successfully; then consider alternative methods of handling such situations. Appoint a crisis team to be in charge during unusual situations, explaining what will be expected of each team member and the consequences of responding incorrectly. Make provisions for planned crisis simulations, if appropriate.

During a Crisis

Recognize the seriousness of the situation, and try to isolate it so that normal work can continue while the crisis team handles the problem. Make sound decisions based on the crisis plan. Proper management includes the following:

- notifying the proper people
- meeting with the crisis team to collect information and plan action
- establishing a "crisis room" to centralize necessary tools and information
- identifying one qualified spokesperson to channel information outside the company to ensure its consistency and truthfulness

• dealing with inquiries and reactions from employees, stockholders, citizens of the community, the media, and government agencies by being helpful but protective of the company

After a Crisis

Thank those who played a role in managing the crisis, and recognize outstanding contributions. Take some time to recover, then evaluate management of the situation to determine its effect on cost, public opinion, media coverage, and crisis team performance. Modify the crisis management plan as necessary so that any recurrence can be handled more successfully.

What To Do If You Are Fired

For most people, the sudden loss of a job is a traumatic experience. Fear of financial insecurity is usually compounded by feelings of embarrassment, depression, and rage, resulting in a badly damaged sense of self-worth. Being fired at some time in a lifetime of working is an experience common to many people, but this does not seem to register during those first terrible moments, hours, and days of joblessness. Here are some suggestions that can make a bad time a little easier.

First, it is important not to leave work on a bad note. When you receive the news of your termination, do not storm out of the office or threaten anyone. Instead, take a few minutes in private to absorb the shock and compose yourself. After you have become calm, ask to discuss your severance benefits. As you will probably still be very shaken, avoid making major decisions immediately (on lump sum versus weekly payments, for instance). Be especially cautious about signing anything right away, or setting a final work date if given that option. State that you would like to consider the alternatives before making any decisions, and that you will notify management of your choices on the next working day. (Even if you will not be in the office on that day, arrangements can be made by telephone and documents signed and delivered by mail or fax to prevent an embarrassing return.) If you must notify clients of your impending departure and turn projects over to other staff members, do so quickly, quietly, and with dignity. Invariably, one or more colleagues will appear to express their regrets that you are leaving. Avoid discussing the details of your termination, as this will only slow your departure and will almost certainly upset you further. You may want to leave the office immediately and return for your personal belongings when others have gone home for the day, with a personal friend, spouse, or relative accompanying you for emotional support.

The real coping process will begin after you leave the office and reach the safety of your home. Allow yourself some time to experience the shock and accept what has happened. Keep lines of communication open with people close to you. Talk to your spouse, family, friends, or a counselor about your emotions. Do not allow feelings of failure to dominate your thinking, even if the termination resulted from your own errors in judgment or performance. In such a situation, accept responsibility for the loss of your job and determine to benefit from the experience, but realize that a failure at work does not make your whole life a failure. As media magnate and Atlanta Braves owner Ted Turner once said, "If you never made a mistake, you never made anything" (from *Business Speak* by Suzette Haden Elgin). Just think: Someone as successful as Mr. Turner knows how it feels to make mistakes, and considers them a necessary part of creating your place in life. View this event as a life experience that can lead to positive results and new opportunities.

Stay active physically and mentally, and make the most of your enforced leisure. In addition to beginning a job search and planning your next career move, get plenty of exercise and spend extra time with family and friends. It may reassure you to write a budget plan that reduces household spending during the time that you will not have a regular income. You can also investigate temporary work assignments within your professional area, or even in lower level positions than those you would consider taking on a permanent basis. This can help to alleviate financial worries and give you time to recoup emotionally before plunging into the job market. In fact, temporary assignments within or outside of your specialty could lead to permanent employment by providing opportunities to demonstrate your skills and making new business contacts at the same time (*see* Using Temporary Employment Services, page 240).

STARTING YOUR OWN BUSINESS BY WORKING AT HOME

The U.S. Bureau of Labor Statistics reported that about 10 million Americans were self-employed in 1994, and just over half of them worked at home. Other surveys have revealed an incredible diversity in home-based businesses, from T-shirt sales to dog training to construction work and consulting. The numbers are evenly divided between male and female workers, 44 percent of whom have college degrees. Interestingly, only 55 percent of respondents to a 1995 study owned home computers, and only 23 percent had fax machines.

If you have a home computer and an Internet address, check the employment possibilities that are posted daily on bulletin boards in your field of business. Perhaps this is the time to begin a home-based business of your own.

Negotiating a Severance Agreement

Companies offer severance benefits to ease financial pressures for terminated workers while they look for new jobs. Although there are no legal requirements for such arrangements, you are entitled to compensation if others in your company have received it or if it is part of company policy. Many organizations do not have firm policies on severance pay and other benefits, which means that these are negotiable. Get the facts before accepting anything; learn all of the factors on which management bases its severance agreements. You may wish to consult an attorney, but first give your superiors a chance to be fair. It is in the company's best interest, as well as yours, because compassionate termination arrangements contribute to a positive community image and enhance employee morale. And in this litigious society, your boss is probably eager to avoid any grounds for a wrongful termination suit, so she or he will not want to deny your reasonable requests. Expect some compassion from management and use it to your advantage when negotiating.

Get the agreement in writing, including a detailed explanation of the reason for your termination, and do not sign anything until you have read it and understood it completely. The severance package should contain the following:

- *Severance pay,* including the amount, type, and dates of payment, and how this sum was calculated. Will the pay continue for the specified period even if you find another job right away? Do you have the option of taking it in a lump sum instead of several installments?
- *Other benefits,* such as health, life, and disability insurance, stock options, pension plan contributions, and unused vacation days. Federal law mandates that employers meeting certain qualifications must make health insurance group benefits available to employees who leave the company for any reason, for a certain period of time, even though the firm is not required to pay any part of the premiums.
- *Career development assistance,* which could take the form of career counseling; assistance with networking, interview skills, and résumé preparation; provision of references; retraining; or the use of secretarial staff and office machines to help in your job search.
- *Personal counseling/therapy,* which may be offered at company expense in some situations, if this is necessary to help you through this difficult time.

Unemployment Benefits

Terminated employees who do not receive severance pay are often eligible for unemployment benefits. To file a claim, go to a state job service or employment office as soon as possible and carefully fill out the necessary forms. To ensure that you receive the full amount to which you are entitled, research your state's unemployment legislation and procedures so that you know exactly what to expect.

In most cases, workers are entitled to 26 weeks of benefits at about 50 percent of their previous salary. You will be ineligible if you were fired for misconduct (committing crimes or sabotaging the company), if you resigned voluntarily (unless you can prove that you left because conditions were unbearable), or if you are receiving severance pay from the firm. In addition, you are eligible for benefits only if you are actively pursuing job opportunities and have not refused reasonable job offers. Be patient while waiting for your unemployment benefits to be processed, and remember that you may appeal the benefit amount if you are not paid the maximum allowable at your previous salary level.

Wrongful Termination Suits

Anyone who has been fired for reasons that are not legally justified can sue for damages, unless an agreement not to do so was part of an accepted severance contract. But such suits are costly, time-consuming, and difficult to win. A lawsuit opens the employee's work record to close scrutiny, and details of the proceedings become part of the public record. This can hurt the worker's chances of finding a new job. Before making a decision to take legal action, it is advisable to consult an attorney who is an expert in the field of employment laws and EEOC (Equal Employment Opportunity Commission) guidelines. (*See also* Severance Packages, page 325.)

Directory of Executive Recruiters and Their Specialties

Top Executive Recruiting Firms

Firms That Work on Retainer Only

Boyden
364 Elwood Avenue
Hawthorne, NY 10532
914-747-0093
Other offices: Atlanta, Chicago, Houston, Morristown (NJ), New York, Pittsburgh, Washington, others worldwide
Salary minimum: $90,000

DHR International Inc.
10 South Riverside Plaza, Suite 2220
Chicago, IL 60606
312-782-1581
Other offices: Dallas, Fort Lauderdale, Kansas City (MO), Los Angeles, Mexico City, New York, Upper Montclair (NJ)
Salary minimum: $60,000

Egon Zehnder International, Inc.
55 East 59th Street, 14th Floor
New York, NY 10022
212-838-9199
Other offices: Atlanta, Chicago, Los Angeles, San Francisco, others worldwide
Salary minimum: $125,000

Heidrick & Struggles, Inc.
233 South Wacker Drive, Suite 7000
Chicago, IL 60606
312-496-1000
Other offices: Atlanta, Boston, Cleveland, Dallas, Greenwich (CT), Houston, Jacksonville (FL), Los Angeles, Menlo Park (CA), New York, San Francisco, Vienna (VA), Washington (DC), others worldwide
Salary minimum: $100,000

Korn/Ferry International
237 Park Avenue
New York, NY 10017
212-687-1834
Other offices: Atlanta, Boston, Chicago, Dallas, Houston, Los Angeles, Menlo Park (CA), Miami, Minneapolis, Newport Beach (CA), Philadelphia, Princeton (NJ), San Francisco, Seattle, Stamford (CT), Washington, others worldwide
Salary minimum: $100,000

Lamalie Amrop International
200 Park Avenue, Suite 3100
New York, NY 10166

212-953-7900
Other offices: Atlanta, Chicago,
    Cleveland, Dallas, Houston, Tampa
    (FL), others worldwide
Salary minimum: $100,000

Paul Ray Berndtson
301 Commerce Street, Suite 2300
Ft. Worth, TX 76102
817-334-0500
Other offices: Atlanta, Chicago,
    Dallas, Irvine (CA), Los Angeles,
    New York, others worldwide
Salary minimum: $90,000

Russell Reynolds Associates, Inc.
200 Park Avenue
New York, NY 10166
212-351-2000
Other offices: Atlanta, Boston,
    Chicago, Dallas, Houston, Los
    Angeles, Menlo Park (CA),
    Minneapolis, New York, San
    Francisco, Washington, others
    worldwide
Salary minimum: $100,000

Sanford Rose Associates International
265 South Main Street, Suite 100
Akron, OH 44308
330-762-7162
Other offices: 51 throughout the
    United States

Specialties: Varies by office; also
    works on contingency
Salary minimum: Varies by office

Schweichler Associates Inc.
200 Tamal Vista, Suite 100, Building
    200
Corte Madera, CA 94925
415-924-7200
Specialties: Communications, high
    technology, manufacturing
Salary minimum: $125,000

SpencerStuart
277 Park Avenue 29th Floor
New York, NY 10172
212-336-0200
Other offices: Atlanta, Dallas,
    Houston, Los Angeles, Menlo Park
    (CA), Philadelphia, San Francisco,
    Stamford (CT), others worldwide
Salary minimum: $150,000

Ward Howell International, Inc.
99 Park Avenue, 20th Floor
New York, NY 10016-1699
212-687-3730
Other offices: Atlanta, Barrington
    (IL), Chicago, Dallas, Encino (CA),
    Houston, Phoenix, Stamford (CT),
    others worldwide
Salary minimum: $75,000

Firms That Work on a Contingency Basis

Dunhill Personnel Systems, Inc.
100 Woodbury Road
Woodbury, NY 11797
516-952-3000
Other offices: 180 throughout the
    United States
Specialties: Computers,
    environment, finance, health

care, manufacturing,
    service industries
Salary minimum: $25, 000

Fox-Morris Associates, Inc.
1617 JFK Boulevard, Suite 210
Philadelphia, PA 19103
215-561-6300

Other offices: Atlanta, Baltimore,
Charlotte (NC), Cleveland, Dallas,
New York, Orange (CA),
Pittsburgh, Rutherford (NJ), State
College (PA), Winston-Salem (NC)
Salary minimum: $50,000

Management Recruiters International
Inc.
200 Public Square, 31st Floor
Cleveland, OH 44144-2301
216-696-1122
Other offices: over 700 throughout the
United States
Salary minimum: $45,000

Romac International, Inc.
120 Hyde Park Place, Suite 200
Tampa, FL 33606
813-258-8855
Other offices: Andover (MA), Atlanta,
Boston, Dallas, Fort Lauderdale,
Houston, Louisville (KY), Miami,
Minneapolis, Orlando (FL),
Pittsburgh, Raleigh (NC), San
Francisco, Wayne (PA), Wellesley
(MA)
Specialties: Accounting, banking,
computers, health care,
pharmaceuticals, technology
Salary minimum: $15,000

Sales Consultants
200 Public Square, 31st Floor
Cleveland, OH 44114-2302
216-696-1122
Other offices: 162 throughout the
United States
Specialties: Sales, all industries
Salary minimum: $30,000

Search West Inc.
2049 Century Park East, Suite 650
Los Angeles, CA 90067
310-284-8888
Other offices: Ontario (CA), Orange
(CA), San Francisco, Westlake
Village (CA)
Specialties: Biotechnology, finance,
health care, high technology,
insurance, service industries
Salary minimum: $35,000

Source Services Corp.
5580 LBJ Freeway, Suite 300
Dallas, TX 75240
214-972-3002
Other offices: Over 40 throughout the
United States
Specialties: Computers, engineering,
finance
Salary minimum: None

Executive Recruiter Organizations

Association of Executive Search
Consultants
500 Fifth Avenue, Suite 930
New York, NY 10110
212-398-9556

International Association of
Corporate & Professional Recruiters
1001 Greenbay Road, Suite 308
Winnetka, IL 60093
847-441-1644

National Association of Executive
Recruiters
625 N. Michigan Avenue, Suite 600
Chicago, IL 60611
312-867-1060

National Association of Personnel
Consultants
3133 Mt. Vernon Avenue
Alexandria, VA 22305
703-684-0180

Consultants: A Directory of Resources

Associations of Consultants

Busy managers often prefer to use consultants to provide information and guidance in areas such as employee benefits, legal issues, real estate, accounting, and marketing. The firms listed in this section offer consulting services that may be of interest to your business.

American Association of Healthcare
  Consultants (includes American
  Association of Hospital Consultants)
11208 Waples Mill Road
Fairfax, VA 22202
703-691-2242

American Association of Insurance
  Management Consultants
P.O. Box 3517
Bloomington, IL 61701
309-828-8851

American Association of Political
  Consultants
900 2nd Street NE, Suite 217
Washington, DC 20002
202-371-9585

American Association of Professional
  Consultants
12300 107th Terrace
Overland Park, KS 66210
913-498-0505

American Consultants League
1290 North Palm Avenue
Sarasota, FL 34236
941-952-9290

American Consulting Engineers
  Council
1015 15th Street NW, Suite 802
Washington, DC 20002
202-347-7474

American Institute of Certified Public
  Accountants
Management Services Division
1211 Avenue of the Americas
New York, NY 10036
212-596-6200

American Society of Consulting
  Planners
122 South Michigan Avenue, Suite
  1600
Chicago, IL 60603
312-786-6371

Association of Executive Search
  Consultants
500 Fifth Avenue, Suite 930
New York, NY 10110-0900
212-398-9556

Association of Image Consultants
  International
1000 Connecticut Avenue NW, Suite 9
Washington, DC 20036
301-371-9021/800-383-8831

Association of Internal Management
  Consultants
7960-B Soquel Drive, Suite 296
Aptos, CA 95003
408-662-9890

Association of Outplacement
  Consulting Firms International

1200 19th Street NW, Suite 300
Washington, DC 20036
202-857-1185

Association of Professional Material
  Handling Consultants
8720 Red Oak Boulevard, Suite 224
Charlotte, NC 28217
704-676-1184

Council of Consulting Organizations
(includes the Association of
  Management Consulting Firms and
  the Institute of Management
  Consultants)
521 Fifth Avenue, 35th Floor
New York, NY 10175
212-697-9693

Independent Computer Consultants
  Association
11131 South Towne Square, Suite 5
St. Louis, MO 63123
314-892-1675/800-774-4222

Institute of Certified Financial
  Planners
3801 E. Florida Avenue, Suite 708
Denver, CO 80210
303-759-4900

Institute of Certified Professional
  Business Consultants
330 South Wells Street, Suite 1422
Chicago, IL 60606
312-360-0384/800-447-1684

Institute of Tax Consultants
7500 212th Street SW, Suite 205
Edmonds, WA 98026
206-774-3521

International College of Real Estate
  Consulting Professionals
297 Dakota Street

Le Sueur, MN 56058
507-665-6280

National Association of Computer
  Consultant Businesses
1250 Connecticut Avenue NW, Suite
  700
Washington, DC 20036
202-637-6483

National Association of Management
  Consultants
4200 Wisconsin Avenue NW, Suite 106
Washington, DC 20016
202-466-1601

National Association of Personnel
  Consultants
3133 Mt. Vernon Avenue
Alexandria, VA 22305
703-684-0180

National Institute of Certified Moving
  Consultants
11150 Main Street, Suite 402
Fairfax, VA 22030
703-934-9111

National Society of Environmental
  Consultants
303 West Cyprus
San Antonio, TX 78212
800-486-3676

Occupational Program Consultants
  Association
3010 Fairview Park Drive
Falls Church, VA 22042
703-205-6796

Professional and Technical
  Consultants Association
P.O. Box 4143
Mountain View, CA 94040
415-903-8305

Society of Risk Management
   Consultants
300 Park Avenue
New York, NY 10022
800-765-SRMC

Consultant Referrals

Consultants' Network
57 West 89th Street
New York, NY 10024
212-799-5239

National Consultants Referrals Inc.
8445 Camino Santa Fe, #207
San Diego, CA 92121
619-552-0111/800-221-3104

Sources of Further Information

Organizations

Employment Discrimination—General Information

**Equal Employment Opportunity Commission
(EEOC)**
Publications Unit
2401 E Street NW
Washington, DC 20507
Phone 800-669-3362 (TDD 800-669-3302)
Phone 800-669-4000 for the nearest EEOC office.

Office of Federal Contract Compliance Programs
Employment Standards Administration
U.S. Department of Labor
Washington, DC 20210
Phone 202-219-9475

**National Employment Lawyers Association
(NELA)**
600 Harrison Street, Suite 535
San Francisco, CA 94107
Phone 212-603-6491

Employment Discrimination—Gender; Sexual Harassment

**To request EEOC guidelines on sexual
harassment, phone or write:**
Equal Employment Opportunity Commission
Publications Unit
2401 E Street NW
Washington, DC 20507
Phone 202-634-1947

Fund for the Feminist Majority
Sexual harassment hotline
Phone 703-522-2501

National Women's Law Center
11 DuPont Circle NW, Suite 800

Washington, DC 20036
Phone 202-588-5180

**9 to 5, The National Association of Working
Women**
Job problems hotline
Phone 800-522-0925, fax 212-226-1066

**NOW Legal Defense and Education
Fund**
99 Hudson Street, 12th Floor
New York, NY 10013
Phone 212-925-6635

U.S. Department of Labor, Women's Bureau
200 Constitution Avenue NW
Washington, DC 20210
Phone 202-219-6593 or 800-827-5335
(TDD 800-326-2577)

Women Employed
22 West Monroe, Suite 1400

Chicago, IL 60603
Phone 312-782-3902

Women's Legal Defense Fund
1875 Connecticut Avenue, Suite 710
Washington, DC 20009
Phone 202-986-2600

Employment Discrimination—Racial

NAACP Legal Defense and Education Fund
99 Hudson Street
New York, NY 10013
Phone 212-219-1900

Family Care

Administration for Children, Youth, and Families
Office of Human Development Services
U.S. Department of Health and Human Services
P.O. Box 1182
Washington, DC 20013
Phone 202-245-0354

Administration on Aging
Department of Health and Human Services
200 Independence Ave SW
Washington, DC 20201
Phone 202-245-0724

American Association of Retired People
1909 K Street NW
Washington, DC 20049
Phone 202-872-4700

Child Care Info Exchange
P.O. Box 2890
Redmond, WA 98073
Phone 206-883-9394

Children of Aging Parents
2761 Trenton Road
Levittown, PA 19056
Phone 215-945-6900

National Child Care Association
920 Green Street
Conyers, GA 30207
Phone 800-543-7161

Local agencies may be located by checking the yellow pages for offices listed under "Child Care/Children's Services," "Family Services," "Department of Child Care," or "Commission on Aging." Local, state, and federal listings can also be found in the white or blue pages under similar headings.

Staffing Solutions

Families and Work Institute
330 Seventh Avenue
New York, NY 10001
Phone 212-465-2044
Fax 212-465-8637

National Association of Temporary Services
119 South St. Asaph Street
Alexandria, VA 22314
Phone 703-549-6287

The National Society for Experiential Education
3509 Haworth Drive, Suite 207
Raleigh, NC 27609
Phone 919-787-3263

U.S. Department of Labor Regional Offices

Each regional Department of Labor office houses a division of the Employment Standards Administration, which includes an Office of Federal Contract Compliance Programs (OFCCP), an Office of Workers' Compensation Programs (OWCP), and a Wage and Hour Division. In the following list, the main address for each regional office and its Public Affairs telephone number is listed, with telephone numbers also given for OFCCP, OWCP, and the Wage and Hour Division.

Region I—Connecticut, Maine, Massachusetts, New Hampshire, Rhode Island, and Vermont
U.S. Department of Labor
JFK Federal Building
Boston, MA 02203
Office of Public Affairs: phone 617-565-2072
Office of Federal Contract Compliance Programs: phone 617-565-2055
Office of Workers' Compensation Programs: phone 617-565-2102
Wage and Hour Division: phone 617-565-2066

Region II—New York, New Jersey, Puerto Rico, and the Virgin Islands
U.S. Department of Labor
201 Varick Street
New York, NY 10014
Office of Public Affairs: phone 212-337-2319
Office of Federal Contract Compliance Programs: phone 212-337-2007
Office of Workers' Compensation Programs: phone 212-337-2033
Wage and Hour Division: phone 212-337-2000

Region III—Delaware, District of Columbia, Maryland, Pennsylvania, Virginia, and West Virginia
U.S. Department of Labor
3535 Market Street
Philadelphia, PA 19104
Office of Public Affairs: phone 215-596-1139
Office of Federal Contract Compliance Programs: phone 215-596-6168
Office of Workers' Compensation Programs: phone 215-596-1181
Wage and Hour Division: phone 215-596-1185

Region IV—Alabama, Florida, Georgia, Kentucky, Mississippi, North Carolina, South Carolina, and Tennessee
U.S. Department of Labor
1371 Peachtree Street NE
Atlanta, GA 30367
Office of Public Affairs: phone 404-562-2080
Office of Federal Contract Compliance Programs: phone 404-347-3200
Office of Workers' Compensation Programs: phone 904-232-3426 (administered by the Florida OWCP office at present as there is currently no Region IV Regional Director for OWCP)
Wage and Hour Division: phone 404-562-2080

Region V—Illinois, Indiana, Michigan, Minnesota, Ohio, and Wisconsin
U.S. Department of Labor
230 South Dearborn Street
Chicago, IL 60604
Office of Public Affairs: phone 312-353-4807
Office of Federal Contract Compliance Programs: phone 312-353-0335
Office of Workers' Compensation Programs: phone 312-886-5883
Wage and Hour Division: phone 312-353-7280

Region VI—Arkansas, Louisiana, New Mexico, Oklahoma, and Texas
U.S. Department of Labor
525 Griffin Street
Dallas, TX 75202
Office of Public Affairs: phone 214-767-4777
Office of Federal Contract Compliance Programs: phone 214-767-2804
Office of Workers' Compensation Programs: phone 214-767-4713
Wage and Hour Division: phone 214-767-6895

Region VII—Iowa, Kansas, Missouri, and Nebraska
U.S. Department of Labor
City Center Square
1100 Main Street
Kansas City, MO 64105
Office of Public Affairs: phone 816-426-5481
Office of Federal Contract Compliance Programs: phone 816-374-6035
Office of Workers' Compensation Programs: phone 816-426-2723
Wage and Hour Division: phone 816-426-5386

Region VIII—Colorado, Montana, North Dakota, South Dakota, Utah, and Wyoming
U.S. Department of Labor
1801 California Street
Denver, CO 80202
Office of Public Affairs: phone 303-844-1300
Office of Federal Contract Compliance Programs: phone 303-844-1210
Office of Workers' Compensation Programs: phone 303-844-1310
Wage and Hour Division: phone 303-844-4406

Region IX—Arizona, California, Guam, Hawaii, and Nevada
U.S. Department of Labor
71 Stevenson Street
San Francisco, CA 94119
Office of Public Affairs: phone 415-975-4740

Office of Federal Contract Compliance Programs: phone 415-975-4720
Office of Workers' Compensation Programs: phone 415-744-6749
Wage and Hour Division: phone 415-744-6625

Region X—Alaska, Idaho, Oregon, and Washington
U.S. Department of Labor
1111 Third Avenue
Seattle, WA 98101
Office of Public Affairs: phone 206-553-7620
Office of Federal Contract Compliance Programs: phone 206-553-4508
Office of Workers' Compensation Programs: phone 206-553-5521
Wage and Hour Division: phone 206-553-4482

Books and Literature

Allison, Mary Ann, and Eric Allison. *Managing Up, Managing Down.* New York: Cornerstone Library, 1984.

The Directory of Executive Recruiters, 1995. Contact Kennedy Publications, 603-585-6544, to order a copy.

Drucker, Peter. *Management in Turbulent Times.* New York: Harper & Row, 1980.

Drucker, Peter. *People and Performance.* New York: Harper & Row, 1977.

Ehrenfeld, Tom. "The (Handbook) Handbook." *Inc.,* Vol. 15. November 1, 1993.

Elgin, Suzette Haden. *Business Speak.* New York: McGraw-Hill, 1995.

Geneen, Harold. *Managing.* Garden City, NY: Doubleday, 1984.

Grove, Andrew S. *High Output Management.* New York: Random House, 1983.

Grove, Andrew S. *One-On-One With Andy Grove.* New York: G. P. Putnam's Sons, 1987.

Lord, Mary. "Top Schools." *U.S. News & World Report,* Vol. 122. March 10, 1997.

Mainiero, Lisa A. *Office Romance: Love, Power, & Sex in the Workplace.* New York: Rawson Associates, 1989.

Manigan, Colleen. "The Graveyard Shift." *Public Management,* Vol. 76. April 1, 1994.

Mark, Teri J., and Jane M. Owens. "Comparing Apples to Oranges: Methods for Evaluating and Selecting Records Management Software." *Records Management Quarterly,* Vol. 30. January 1, 1996.

Nollen, Stanley, and Helen Axel. *Managing Contingent Workers: How to Reap the Benefits and Reduce the Risks.* New York: AMACOM Division, American Management Association, 1996.

Pascale, Richard Tanner, and Anthony G. Athos. *The Art of Japanese Management.* New York: Simon & Schuster, 1981.

Peters, Tom. *Thriving On Chaos.* New York: Knopf, 1987.

Peters, Tom, and Nancy Austin. *A Passion for Excellence.* New York: Random House, 1985.

Sexual Harassment: A Handbook for Managers and Supervisors. Philadelphia: Haimes Associates. To order a copy, send $2 with your request to Haimes Associates, 708 South Washington Square, Philadelphia, PA 19106, phone 215-922-1617.

Waterman, Robert H. *The Renewal Factor.* New York: Bantam, 1987.

On-Line Resources

America's Job Bank, an on-line career service sponsored by the U.S. Public Employment Service
http://www.ajb.dni.us

Hard at Work, a web site that features on-line help for office management issues as well as publications, seminars, and other aids for human resource specialists
http://www.hard@work.com

Online Career Center, a database of help-wanted ads and instructions on responding to them or placing ads for vacant positions in your business
http://www.occ.com

U.S. Department of Health and Human Resources, which offers a wealth of information and contact options for questions about family care, health issues, employee assistance, and more
http://www.os.dhhs.gov

U.S. Department of Labor's home page, which will direct you to web sites for OSHA, the Office of Federal Contract Compliance Programs, the Office of Workers' Compensation Programs, the Employment Standards Administration, the Small Business Administration, the Wage and Hour Division, and other Department of Labor agencies
http://www.dol.gov

U.S. Social Security Administration
http://www.ssa.gov

Work Force Online, another excellent source of on-line assistance for employee management
http://www.workforceonline.com

7

Finances
and Formulas

Proprietorships, Partnerships, and Corporations

If you are just starting a company, you must decide whether to organize it as a sole proprietorship or some type of partnership or corporation. The structure you choose will have an impact on record keeping, payment of taxes, and company decision making.

In a *sole proprietorship,* there is no legal distinction between the company and its owner, who is personally responsible for debts incurred by the company. For tax purposes, the owner and the business are one entity. There is an accounting distinction between the owner and the business, however, as personal debts and assets of the owner are not included in the company's financial statements.

A *partnership* is an unincorporated business owned by two or more people or business entities. In a *general partnership,* all partners share management responsibilities for business operations. They also share ownership of business assets and the obligation to pay the partnership's debts or liabilities. There is no limit to the amount of risk borne by each general partner; that is, each partner is liable for the total debts of the business, and must use personal assets to pay those debts if necessary.

A *limited partnership* includes one or more *limited partners* who, in return for their investment, receive a share of the profits or losses. Limited partners are liable only for the amount of money they have invested in the business, and their personal assets are not at risk. In a limited partnership, there are one or more general partners who manage the business on a day-to-day basis. Although limited partners do not participate in everyday management, the partnership agreement often stipulates that they must be consulted on major decisions—for example, selling all or most of the partnership's assets usually requires the consent of limited partners. As in general partnerships, general partners are personally liable for the debts of the business.

Partnerships as business entities are not subject to income tax. Each partner receives a proportionate share of the business income, expenses, and credits, and includes those on personal income tax returns. Partnerships usually have a limited term of business; that is, the partnership agreement stipulates a time period for the existence of the partnership.

A *corporation* is a legal entity that is separate from its owners. Ownership is represented by shares of stock. Stockholders are not personally liable for debts of the business unless they have chosen to co-sign or guarantee the corporation's debts or obligations. Corporation owners (shareholders) risk only the amounts that they have invested in the business. In *closely held corporations,* shares are owned by a limited number of individuals. Limitations are usually placed on the transferability of stock in the company. This gives the owners control over the sale of stock; in other words, each owner has a say about who may buy stock and become an owner. *Public corporations,* conversely, sell specified amounts of stock to the public.

Anyone can become an owner of the corporation by purchasing stock. An *initial public offering* is one way in which stock is made available to the public. The Securities and Exchange Commission (SEC) regulates the public stock trade and establishes requirements for going public. Expert advice is recommended to ensure compliance with all SEC requirements.

Limited liability companies (LLCs) and *limited liability partnerships* (LLPs) are partnership-corporation hybrids, offering some of the advantages of each. Generally, LLCs and LLPs limit owners' liability, as in a corporation, but operate as partnerships for tax purposes. There is an art to setting up and using these organizations, and the compromises involved must be carefully considered. If an LLC or LLP is not set up correctly, the owners could be liable as though they were in a partnership although the business pays taxes as a corporation—a potentially disastrous situation. So the decision to form an LLC or LLP should be made only after consulting an attorney who specializes in this field. Limited liability companies cannot be formed in some states.

S corporations constitute a business structure that is attractive to many smaller companies. Here, owners have limited liability, but pay no corporate income tax. Instead, they report their share of company profits on their personal tax returns. This eliminates the possibility of double taxation. However, S corporation rules allow limited fringe benefits and no more than 35 stockholders. The amount of company profits and your personal tax bracket will determine whether this type of incorporation would benefit your business.

There are advantages and disadvantages to each type of business organization. Incorporating is expensive, with yearly fees to be paid in addition to legal and registration fees involved in setting up the corporation. However, many unincorporated businesses could benefit from the advantages of incorporation. Often, sole proprietors or partners do not understand the tax benefits of corporations. For example, when a business is incorporated, health insurance premiums for its owners become business expense tax deductions for the corporation. Due to the high cost of health insurance for an individual or small group of owners, this tax advantage may offset the initial and yearly costs of incorporation. Owners may then enjoy limited liability and other advantages of incorporation as well as good medical coverage, with incorporation and insurance often costing no more than insurance premiums alone for an unincorporated owner.

Incorporation necessitates the provision of workers' compensation and unemployment insurance coverage for company owners as well as other employees; in unincorporated businesses, owners are not considered employees, and only employees must be covered. Premiums for these protections are determined by income level as well as occupation, so an owner's coverage may be costly compared with that of other workers if the business involves physical risk (for example, construction work). In less risky occupations, though, the security afforded by these two benefits can be very important to small business owners.

Because it is a business entity separate from its owners, a corporation continues to exist after an owner dies or leaves the business. Shares in the business are transferable from one person or business entity to another. In unincorporated firms, transferability of ownership is usually more limited. The complexity of these and other factors involved render expert guidance essential for owners to make the right decision about the form a business will take. (*See also* Incorporating a Business, page 347, and Taxation by Classification, page 302.)

The ABCs of Accounting

Fundamentals

Accounting is the process of recording and summarizing business and financial transactions and analyzing and reporting business results. Within the broad category of accounting are three subcategories. *Management accounting* involves interpretation of financial information to aid in managing a company. *Tax accounting* is the specialized field that deals with tax planning and the preparation of tax returns. *Financial accounting* is the process of maintaining information about the financial resources, obligations, and activities of an organization. Anyone involved in a business should have general knowledge of the basic principles of financial accounting. Small business owners should have a thorough understanding of the details of the accounting process.

Although maintaining financial records may seem complex and mundane, good record keeping is a key to success in any business venture, large or small. It allows you to keep track of the financial variations of your business. By regularly reviewing financial records, you can discover trouble spots before they become severe enough to threaten the survival of your business. You can then take corrective measures to avert serious problems.

Basic Terms

An *asset* is anything a business owns that has monetary value. Examples of assets include cash, supplies, amounts owed by customers, land, buildings, furniture, and equipment. The last four are referred to as *fixed assets*—the resources a business owns that are not intended for resale. A *liability* is anything a business owes to others, including loans, accounts payable, taxes payable, and payroll payable. *Capital* (the owner's equity or net worth) is the owner's claim on assets after liabilities are subtracted. *Revenue* is income received by a business as payment for its products or services. *Expenses* are the costs of operating a business, such as payroll and utility bills. An *income statement* provides information about revenue and expenses for an accounting period. A *balance sheet* is like a snapshot of the financial state of a business. It reports the total assets, liabilities, and capital of a business as of a given date. An income statement and a balance sheet are parts of a company's *financial statements*, which are required for a number of different business operations (*see* Why Financial Statements Are Necessary, page 289).

The Basic Equation

The difference between what the owner owns (assets) and what the owner owes (liabilities) is the capital (net worth) of the business. In accounting, this is expressed by the basic equation:

$$Assets = Liabilities + Capital$$

This accounting equation is used to ensure that a business's books are in balance. At the end of a business year, for example, revenue and expense accounts are closed out by totaling revenue and expenses, subtracting total expenses from total revenue, and adding the net (final) figure to the owner's capital. This enables the business to begin the new year (or new accounting period) with zero balances in the revenue and expense accounts, so that the company has a fresh start in calculating net profit.

The Income Statement

As stated previously, an *income statement* (also called a *profit and loss statement*) provides information about revenues, expenses, and profits or losses during a given accounting period. A simple income statement includes two columns, one showing figures for the current month and one showing year-to-date figures:

	Current Month	*Year to Date*
Sales	$2,000	$13,000
Cost of sales	1,200	7,560
	$ 800	$ 5,440
Other operating costs	300	2,040
Pretax income	$ 500	$ 3,400
Income taxes	150	1,133
Net income	$ 350	$ 2,267

More complex income statements might include a breakdown under cost of sales to show beginning inventory, purchases, and ending inventory. Operating expenses also might include details such as salaries, advertising, insurance costs, supplies, and equipment depreciation.

The Balance Sheet

As its name indicates, a *balance sheet* contains two sides that must be equal (in balance). The left side shows assets such as cash, accounts receivable, inventories, and fixed assets. The right side shows liabilities such as accounts payable, loans, and taxes payable; it also includes capital. A simple balance sheet might look like this:

	Assets			*Liabilities and Capital*	
Cash	$ 300		Accounts payable	$ 300
Receivables	900		Notes payable	300
Fixed assets	600		Mortgage payable	600
				$1,200
			Owner's equity	600
	$1,800			$1,800

The Accounting System

The financial activities of a business are organized by an accounting system. This system keeps track of every piece of financial information related to the business, including the sale and purchase of merchandise; invoicing and accounts receivable; accounts payable; payroll; tax payments; and financial statements. To keep track of all these items, financial information must be collected and recorded using either a manual or computer system. Collecting and recording such information is called *bookkeeping.*

Bookkeeping consists of several components. The first is the *journal,* a diary in which daily transactions are first recorded. Each journal entry shows (1) the date of the transaction, (2) the amount of money involved, (3) a brief description of the transaction, and (4) the asset, liability, capital, revenue, or expense account affected by the transaction.

After a transaction is entered in the journal, it is posted to the correct account in the ledger. An *account* is a record that keeps track of all transactions affecting one type of asset, liability, capital, income, or expense. A *ledger* is the book or file in which transactions for several accounts are recorded. *Posting* a transaction simply means transferring it from the journal to the appropriate ledger. The book in which all account information is recorded is called the *general ledger.* All business transactions are entered on the corresponding ledger sheet in the general ledger.

The size and type of business determine the accounts that are necessary. It is often helpful to assign numbers to accounts when setting up an accounting system. A typical numbering system would number liability accounts 200 to 299, with accounts payable as number 205 and accrued payroll as 210. Any numbering system can be used. The list of account numbers is called the *chart of accounts.*

Double-Entry Bookkeeping. Because accounting operates on the principle of keeping the basic equation in balance (*Assets = Liabilities + Capital*), each transaction recorded in the general ledger includes two entries (a *double entry*). This makes sense if you remember that every transaction involves exchanging one thing for another.

Each account has two sides: the *debit* or left side of the account, and the *credit* or right side of the account. Try not to think of debits and credits as increases and decreases. Whether a debit or credit increases or decreases an account depends on the type of account involved. Asset accounts usually have debit balances. Increases to asset accounts are recorded as debits, and decreases are recorded as credits. This is easy to remember by noting that assets are on the left side of the basic equation, and debits (increases) to asset accounts are recorded on the left side of the account.

Liability and capital (owner's equity) accounts usually have credit balances. Increases to liability accounts are recorded as credits and decreases are recorded as debits. To remember this, note that liabilities and capital are on the right side of the basic equation, and credits (increases) to these accounts are recorded on the right side of the account.

The Trial Balance. An account is said to be *in balance* when the sum of all debits equals the sum of all credits. A *trial balance* (which should be done at the end of each accounting period) simply means adding up all debit account balances and all credit account balances to ensure that they are equal. If they are not equal, an error was made in bookkeeping that should be located as soon as possible. Common errors that keep an account from balancing are posting an item to the wrong side of the account, or posting a transaction in only one account, rather than performing the required double entry.

Generally Accepted Accounting Principles (GAAP). When reading a financial report or a company's annual report, you will probably see *GAAP* mentioned. GAAP are the universal rules or framework for determining information to be included in financial statements and the ways in which the information will be presented. GAAP ensure that all financial statements are written in the same language so that they can be read more easily.

Cash versus Accrual Accounting

The two most popular accounting methods are the *cash* and *accrual systems*. Many small businesses operate on a cash basis, which means that revenue and expenses are recognized only when payment is actually made or received. A business operating on a cash basis would not record a sale made on credit as paid until the customer actually pays the bill. Unpaid invoices would not be recorded as expenses until the business pays the invoices. The cash method is relatively simple.

Businesses with large amounts of payables may benefit from the accrual accounting method. The accrual system recognizes revenues and expenses at the time they are incurred, even if payment has not been received from a customer or bills have not been paid by the business. The accrual method provides a more accurate picture of business profitability at any given time than does the cash method.

There are a number of accounting methods that are hybrids of the cash and accrual systems. The Internal Revenue Service (IRS) generally requires that businesses dealing in inventories (such as retail outlets) use the accrual method. Owners of other types of companies may choose almost any accounting method as long as the firm's financial operations are accurately reported. However, it is necessary for a business to use one accounting method consistently. If an owner decides to change accounting methods after reporting use of another method on previous tax returns, written approval must be obtained from the IRS.

Why Financial Statements Are Necessary

Financial statements are summarized reports that provide basic financial information about a company. The three most important financial statements are the income statement, the balance sheet, and the statement of changes in financial position. Any circumstances that are not apparent in the financial statements should be explained in the notes to the financial statements. (For example, special circumstances surrounding outstanding loans, assets, or accounting methods should be included if these affect the company's financial position but are not immediately apparent in the financial statements.) A statement of changes in financial condition shows any increase or decrease in working capital from beginning to end of an accounting period. It lists the sources and uses of funds and helps to establish a budget and to determine whether additional capital is needed. This statement is not always necessary. However, creditors, potential investors, or the IRS may occasionally request it.

Small business owners may be tempted to ignore the need to prepare financial statements, but they will find that they are required on certain occasions. Your company's financial statements will be needed in order for the business to do the following:

- Apply for a loan—Many financial institutions require copies of current and past financial statements from small business owners. Creditors may also request periodic statements after a loan is granted to monitor the success of the business.
- File an insurance claim—When a business files an insurance claim, its financial statements (particularly the balance sheet) are needed to verify the value of fixed assets.
- Prepare tax returns—Much of the information in financial statements is necessary to calculate state and federal taxes.
- Meet state requirements—Many states require that corporations provide annual financial statements to stockholders.
- Comply with an audit—If creditors, partners, or major shareholders ask for an audit of the business, financial statements will be requested.

Financial statements should fully explain the financial condition of a business. Therefore, regular analyses of financial statements can pinpoint problems such as declining sales, high operating expenses, or excessive fixed assets. By comparing statements from different periods, business owners can make necessary corrections to avoid financial crises.

BUSINESS ARITHMETIC

Converting fractions to decimal numbers: Using $\frac{8}{9}$ as an example, convert the fraction to a decimal by dividing the numerator by the denominator:

$$\frac{8}{9} = 8 \div 9 = .8889$$

Converting decimal numbers to fractions: To change a decimal number into a fraction, round the decimal number to two figures at the right of the decimal, then use the decimal number as the fraction's numerator and use 100 as its denominator:

$$.16 = \frac{16}{100}$$

$$.8889 = .89 = \frac{89}{100}$$

$$.50 = \frac{50}{100}$$

Reducing fractions: To reduce a fraction to its simplest form, divide its numerator and its denominator by the largest whole number that will go into each of them evenly, without a remainder:

$$\frac{16}{100} = \frac{4}{25} \ (16 \div 4 = 4; \text{ and } 100 \div 4 = 25)$$

$$\frac{89}{100} = \frac{89}{100} \ (\text{simple fraction; cannot be reduced})$$

$$\frac{50}{100} = \frac{1}{2} \ (50 \div 50 = 1; \text{ and } 100 \div 50 = 2)$$

Converting decimal numbers to percentages: Shift the decimal two places to the right (multiply by 100):

$$.63 \times 100 = 63\%$$
$$1.03 \times 100 = 103\%$$
$$.286 \times 100 = 28.6\%$$

If there are not enough digits in the number to move the decimal two places to the right, add a zero to the right of the decimal number before moving the decimal:

$$.9 = .90 = 90. \text{ (or } 90.0) = 90\%$$

Converting fractions to percentages: First, convert the fraction to a decimal number, then multiply the result by 100 by moving the decimal two places to the right:

$$\frac{8}{9} = 8 \div 9 = .8889 \quad .8889 \times 100 = 88.89\%$$

Converting percentages to decimal numbers: First, put a decimal after the number, then divide by 100 by moving the decimal two places to the left:

$$63\% = 63 \div 100 = .63$$
$$103\% = 103 \div 100 = 1.03$$

If there is already a decimal in the percentage number, just move it two spaces to the left:

$$28.6\% = 28.6 \div 100 = .286$$

Using conversion tables: You may want to keep handy a conversion table that lists the most common fractions, percentages, and decimals for quick reference.

	Conversion table	
Fraction	**Percentage**	**Decimal**
$\frac{1}{2}$	50	.5
$\frac{1}{3}$	33.33	.3333
$\frac{1}{4}$	25	.25
$\frac{1}{5}$	20	.20
$\frac{1}{6}$	16.67	.1667
$\frac{1}{7}$	14.29	.1429
$\frac{1}{8}$	12.5	.125
$\frac{1}{9}$	11.11	.1111
$\frac{1}{10}$	10	.1
$\frac{1}{11}$	9.09	.0909
$\frac{1}{12}$	8.33	.0833
$\frac{1}{13}$	7.69	.0769
$\frac{1}{14}$	7.14	.0714
$\frac{1}{15}$	6.67	.0667

Computing averages: To average two or more numbers, add them together and divide their sum by the number of units being averaged. For example, if your company has five locations that employ 12, 21, 32, 64, and 11 people, respectively, you can get the average number of employees per location as follows:

$$12 + 21 + 32 + 64 + 11 = 140; 140 \div 5 = 28$$
(28 is the average number of employees per location)

Calculating percentage of change: When dealing with averages, business managers often want to report average sales, increases/decreases, and the percentage of change during a stated period of time. To calculate the percentage of change, find the average for the figures involved; then use that average to compute the percentage of that average that is represented by increases or decreases. The following example shows how to figure average sales per month, the percentage of change (increase) each month, and the average monthly increase for a company's sales over a three-month period:

Average Monthly Sales

August sales	$ 75,000
September sales	85,000
October sales	95,000
Total sales	$255,000

$255,000 ÷ 3 = $85,000
(total sales ÷ number of months = average monthly sales)

Percentage of Change (Percentage Increase)

August over July increase (assuming July sales were $70,000):

$75,000 − $70,000 = $5,000   (August sales − July sales = amount of increase)

$5,000 ÷ 70,000 = .0714 = 7.14%   (increase ÷ July sales = percentage of increase)

September over August increase:
$85,000 − $75,000 = $10,000   (September sales − August sales = amount of increase)

$10,000 ÷ $75,000 = .1333 = 13.3%   (increase ÷ August sales = percentage of increase)

October over September increase:
$95,000 − $85,000 = $10,000   (October sales − September sales = amount of increase)

$10,000 ÷ $85,000 = .1176 = 11.76%   (increase ÷ September sales = percentage of increase)

Average Monthly Increase

$5,000 + $10,000 + $10,000 = $25,000   (August increase + September increase + October increase = sum of monthly increases for this three-month period)

$25,000 ÷ 3 months = $8,333.33   (sum of monthly increases ÷ number of months = average monthly increase)

Accounts Payable

Paying on Time

With organization and planning, the never-ending flood of bills for your office can be paid quickly, efficiently, and on time. First, establish an understanding with your various vendors. Ask what their terms of payment are (on receipt, 10 days, 30 days, etc.). You may be able to negotiate different, more convenient terms for your business depending on how often you want to write checks. A high volume of bills may necessitate check writing once a week, whereas a lower volume may allow you to write checks less often. Paying bills in groups is a fast and efficient way of managing payables, so batch invoices as much as possible. Take note of any discounts that are applicable if payment is made by a certain date, and take advantage of them. Of course, some vendors, such as utility companies, have less flexible due dates. Note those due dates on your calendar or in a tickler file to avoid late fees.

If cash flow should present a problem in paying invoices on time, be sure to call your vendors and let them know. Do not avoid the situation or refuse to take vendors' phone calls. Give your vendors a projected date by which you plan to make full payment and, if possible, offer to pay a portion of the outstanding balance by the original due date. This practice will improve your chances of maintaining good credit.

Keeping Up with Invoices

Set up a filing system that will take the chaos out of managing payables. Open invoices (invoices to be paid) should be filed alphabetically in a temporary file. An alphabetical accordion file works well for this. Check any previous balances shown to make sure they have not already been paid. Avoid making duplicate payments by insisting on paying only original invoices. Paying faxed or photocopied invoices increases your risk of paying an invoice twice. Also, copies of invoices will not pass the scrutiny of an IRS or accounting firm audit.

Check the accuracy of each invoice. If your company has various department heads and personnel who make purchases, set up files of open invoices to be approved by each department. Make sure all bills are verified and approved via the initials or signature of an appropriate staff member. A more efficient way to verify an invoice's accuracy is to use a purchase order system. All invoices should be signed or initialed by a company official (perhaps someone who also signs company checks), even if purchase orders are used. This will be important if your company is audited; it also protects the bookkeeper or accountant from inadvertently paying for unauthorized purchases.

For items that require payment at the time of purchase, use check request forms containing blanks for vendor and purchase information. (These should be completed by the employees who are purchasing items.) Like invoices, check request forms should be initialed or signed by the appropriate company official before checks are cut. When a check is presented for payment, get an original receipt or invoice from the vendor and attach this to the signed check request.

Use an "Approved" file or basket for ready-to-be-paid bills that are waiting for manual check writing or computer check entry. The bookkeeper or accountant should write a numerical account code on the face of the invoice, if your company's accounting system requires this.

Making Purchase Orders Work for You

Using a purchase order (p.o.) system is one of the best ways to track and control expenditures. Numbered p.o. forms can be obtained at many office supply stores or can be ordered to include your company's billing address and whatever vendor and purchase information your office requires. Purchase orders do the following:

- *Make it easier to anticipate and track the costs of running your business.* With a completed, detailed p.o. in hand before the bill arrives, the bookkeeper or accountant can determine the cash flow necessary to keep the business financially afloat. Knowing in advance what money is committed takes the surprise out of paying bills and also allows for planning for growth, changes, and other expenditures. Approved purchase orders (with paid bills, open invoices, and check requests) can be entered into your computer accounting system or calculated manually when you need to determine if the business or an individual department is staying on budget.

- *Help to control costs and prevent unauthorized purchases.* A staff member fills out a p.o. that details the quantity and cost per unit (or labor hour) of goods or services to be purchased. Then a company official who has financial authority approves it before an order is placed. Any questions about cost can be answered before the money is committed. Further, if it is made clear to all vendors that your company requires approved purchase orders for all purchases and will not pay invoices without them, staff members will be unable to place orders without the appropriate approvals.

- *Simplify the processing of invoices for payment.* As purchase orders are filled out and approved, file them alphabetically by vendor in an "Open Purchase Orders" file (an alphabetical accordion file works well for this). Send a copy to the vendor for confirmation. If your firm uses three-part p.o. forms, file the third copy in a numerical p.o. file that will give quick access to information about a particular p.o. by its number. Let vendors know that they should refer to p.o. numbers on their invoices. When bills are received, match each invoice with its corresponding open p.o. number(s). Also compare the goods/services and dollar amounts on the invoice with those on the purchase order(s). Question vendors about any discrepancies. If invoices match approved purchase orders, you may bypass the extra step of asking individual purchasers to verify invoice accuracy. When invoices are submitted for approval by company officials, a preapproved p.o. attached to each invoice eliminates the need for further information.

Setting Priorities for Payment

Develop a routine of opening the mail and stamping all bills to be paid with a "Received" date stamp. When you are ready to write checks, pay the oldest bills first—the ones received on the earliest dates. This will establish a chronological history of purchases, aid in tracking and planning costs, and facilitate good relationships with vendors. Give priority to paying independent contract labor, small or single-proprietor businesses, and reimbursement invoices first. These individuals and vendors may not have the type of cash flow that makes waiting for payment easy. They will appreciate prompt payment and be more likely to give you better deals on future goods and services.

REMEMBER THE IRS!

When paying independent contractors, be sure to note on each invoice whether the payment is subject to 1099 reporting. The IRS requires that businesses report amounts paid to independent contractors for labor or rentals if total payments to that contractor by that business exceed $600 during one year. (In most cases, 1099 forms do not need to be sent to incorporated businesses.) Reimbursements to individuals are not subject to 1099 reporting provided that such reimbursement requests are accompanied by original receipts. Keep a manual log or use a computer accounting program to track, by vendor, all payments that are subject to 1099 reporting. Ask new vendors if they are incorporated, and get a federal tax I.D. number or Social Security number for each. If a vendor is not incorporated and your payments to that vendor fit the 1099 guidelines, you must issue a 1099 by January 31 of the following year, and send a copy to the IRS. Also, note that having a federal I.D. number does not always mean that a company is incorporated.

When the Checks Are Ready to Mail

Once checks are written, confirm that the total amount of each check adds up to the total amount of all current invoices for that particular vendor. When checks have been signed and mailed, file each paid bill alphabetically in individual vendor files that are stored separately from open invoice files. Paid invoices for each vendor should be filed chronologically, with the most recently paid bills on top. If your checks are three-part forms, staple one copy of the check to the appropriate paid invoice(s). If your checks are one part only, write the check number, check amount, and check date on each paid invoice, or attach the paid invoice(s) to a photocopy of the check. This will facilitate accessing information on payment and purchase history. The third copy of three-part checks can be stored in a separate numerical check file, which gives a quick cross-reference to information on a particular check number.

Accounts Receivable

If your company allows customers to buy now and pay later, a billing procedure must be established. The keys to getting paid on time are making sure your customers understand the terms of payment and keeping accounts receivable up to date. There are many computer software programs available to simplify accounting procedures, and most firms now rely on some form of computer record keeping to aid in billing (*see* Understanding Computer Financial Software, page 337, and Software Programs for Offices, page 105).

Preparing Invoices

Invoices should be printed on a business letterhead and should include the following information: what was purchased, purchase date, amount of purchase, sales tax if applicable, invoice date, due date, and payment terms such as "Net 30" (meaning the total amount is due 30 days from the date of the invoice). Leave a space on the invoice for the customer's p.o. number.

Establish a numbering system for your invoices—any type will do. If you are just starting a business, you may want to select a number other than "1" for the first invoice. Many computer invoicing programs automatically number invoices.

Include a line on the invoice that indicates how the check should be written—for example, "Please make checks payable to XYZ Plumbing." Invoices should also list your firm's taxpayer identification number or Social Security number. You will need to decide whether to use invoices with two copies, one for the customer to keep and one to send back to you (the remittance copy), or whether to send just one copy for the customer to keep. When billing for services provided, indicate the hourly rate as well as the number of hours billed. Establish a method for rounding hourly work by the half or quarter hour. Figure 7.1 is an example of an invoice for goods, and Figure 7.2 shows a typical invoice for services.

Overdue Notices

Set up a procedure for dealing with late payments, then apply the procedure consistently to all customers. If a customer fails to pay by the due date, call and remind the individual or firm that payment is due; then send another invoice. Mark the invoice "Second notice, please remit payment immediately" or something similar.

Keep a record of every customer contact regarding late payments. If you make a telephone call, note the date and time of the call and what the customer said regarding payment. Photocopy all late notices. Consider sending second and third notices by certified mail so that the customer cannot claim that the notice was never received. These records will be crucial if legal action is necessary to get payment. (*See* Figure 7.3.)

Collection Agencies

Collection agencies specialize in collecting overdue payments. They often have staff who are trained in getting resistant customers to pay their bills. Most agencies charge a percentage of the amount collected. You may want to refer any account approaching 90 days overdue to a collection agency; when an account reaches that point, it is clearly a problem. An agency's likelihood of collecting payment increases according to how quickly an account is turned over to them.

Taking Legal Action

What if months pass and a customer still has not paid? If you prefer not to use a collection agency, you may consider taking the customer to small claims court.

Address City State Zip Phone Fax

TO: Name of Company

Address

City, State ZIP Code

INVOICE

TOTAL DUE $

REF NO.	QTY	DESCRIPTION	PRICE EACH	TOTAL

Salesperson ....

Purchase order number ....

Purchase order date ....

Purchaser name ....

Terms ....

Date shipped ....

Shipped via ....

FOB ....

Prepaid/Collect ....

Tax exempt ....

Reason ....

Exemption no. ....

Sold to:

Company name ....

Address ....

City, State Zip ....

Phone ....

Fax ....

Delivered ☐

Delivery address: ....

Shipped ☐

Shipping address:

Picked up by customer ☐

Please make checks payable to: Your Company Name

SUBTOTAL	
SHIPPING & HANDLING	
PAYMENTS	
PLEASE PAY THIS AMOUNT	$
TERMS: Net 30 days	

Figure 7.1 Invoice for goods

DATE OF INVOICE	

INVOICE:
WORK PERFORMED

LABOR

DATE	QUANT.	DESCRIPTION	PRICE	TOTAL
		TOTAL		$

MATERIALS

DATE	QUANT.	DESCRIPTION	PRICE	TOTAL
		TOTAL		$

TRAVEL AND MISCELLANEOUS

DATE	QUANT.	DESCRIPTION	PRICE	TOTAL
		TOTAL		$

INVOICE TOTALS

LABOR	
MATERIALS	
TRAVEL AND MISC.	
TOTAL DUE	

Figure 7.2 Invoice for services

Company Name

City State Zip Phone Fax

te

stomer Name
ddress
ty, State Zip

ear _____.

e have not received your payment for the following charges:

REF NO.	DATE	DESCRIPTION	AMOUNT	LATE FEES % RATE	LATE FEES AMOUNT	CHARGES PLUS LATE FEES

Total past due:	
New charges:	
Total now due:	

s you know, our credit policy requires full payment within 30 days of pickup or delivery. Please check your cords. If you have recently sent your payment, disregard this notice and accept our thanks. If you have not paid e full balance, however, please send the amount due promptly to:

our Company Name
ttention: Name of Credit Manager (if applicable)
ddress
ity, State Zip

incerely,

our Name
itle

N:sec

Figure 7.3 Overdue notice

Small claims regulations vary from state to state, but usually allow citizens to bring suits for amounts under $2,000. Use of an attorney is usually not justified in small claims actions, as the small claims system was created to provide court access to individuals not represented by attorneys. Court dates are usually available faster, and court costs lower, in small claims actions. Many states offer free small claims court advice by phone or in person. The people who provide this advice can help you complete the forms and make sure you meet all filing requirements. Prepare your case ahead of time, and when you go to court, take two extra copies of all related paperwork—one for the other party and one for the judge.

Payroll

A *payroll* is a record showing not only the gross salary or wages of each employee, but also tax withholdings, other deductions, and the net amount of pay for the payroll period—usually weekly, biweekly, semimonthly, or monthly. Other deductions may include contributions to savings accounts, profit-sharing increments, and insurance premiums. The simplest payrolls are weekly/biweekly for salaried employees or hourly workers whose hours do not vary with each pay period. In these cases, each employee's wages are the same every pay period except when rate of pay, exemption status, or deductions change. Semimonthly payrolls require figuring the payroll based on the number of workdays in each period, which varies according to the calendar. A record of vacation and sick leave earned and taken is usually also shown on the paycheck stub. This provides a regular update for each employee's information and review, as well as an organized record for the company.

Doing It Yourself

If your business is not very large, you may be able to handle the payroll essentials internally. Follow these steps when figuring the company payroll:

1. Determine all of the elements (such as those cited above) that are collectively part of the payroll. List them in order of priority, depending on the nature and extent of deductions and contributions in your particular business.
2. Know and comply with federal, state, and local laws regarding payroll. These include laws on taxes, insurance, wages and hours, and unemployment compensation. Failure to keep accurate payroll records in compliance with laws and regulations can result in severe penalties. It is especially important to understand and follow IRS guidelines for withholding, depositing, and reporting Social Security, Medicare, and income taxes.
3. Keep records of authorizations for adding new employees, terminations, transfers, and overtime.
4. Delineate procedures and design forms for timekeeping (the specification of work hours and pay periods).

5. Keep a payroll journal to reflect the actual makeup of each payroll, usually in columnar form showing the breakdown of all elements.

Computer software programs are now available to simplify payroll preparation (*see* Understanding Computer Financial Software, page 337).

Using a Payroll Service

Because of the complexity of laws relating to wages, withholding, work hours, and filing and reporting requirements, payroll managers must be experts in their field. Unless you are knowledgeable in this area or are willing to invest some time to learn the basics of payroll accounting, or have someone on staff who is experienced, you may want to consider turning the job over to a payroll service. The cost may be justified and even canceled out, as using a service conserves a manager's time for more remunerative pursuits, helps to avoid penalties for legal infractions, and eliminates many problems that can result from improper payroll accounting. The IRS is particularly strict about payroll taxes, for example, and reports that each year, one-third of all businesses must pay costly penalties due to errors in their payroll procedures.

Contracting for an outside payroll service should be considered if your payroll is complicated. Factors to consider are the use of part-time help, business dealings with contractors in other countries, flexible commissions for salespeople, regular moving expenses, an active recruitment program, acquisition of other companies, and changing economic or legislative situations in your area of business. In short, you should consider outside help unless your company's payroll pattern is steady and changes little from month to month and you have the staff and expertise to compute, record, and administer payrolls. Most payroll services guarantee payment of penalties resulting from their errors in processing a client's records. There are "Payroll Preparation Service" listings in the yellow pages, but also seek counsel from independent professionals in the fields of accounting, law, and management consulting.

Paying Taxes

Preparing tax returns and paying taxes involve filling out some additional forms for small business owners and self-employed people. Like everything else involved in running a business, the key to making tax preparation simple is keeping good records throughout the year. If you wait until April 1 and dump a pile of receipts on a tax preparer's desk, you will undoubtedly end up paying more taxes than if you had planned a tax strategy from the start and kept your records organized.

The IRS provides several publications on tax matters related to small businesses. Instead of waiting until tax time, you may want to request these publications and review the requirements immediately. Some helpful publications are Numbers 334, *Tax Guide for Small Business;* 463, *Travel, Entertainment, and Gift Expenses;* 534, *Depreciation;* 917, *Business Use of Car;* and 946, *How to Begin Depreciating Your*

Property. An order blank and mailing instructions are included in 1040 and 1040A instruction booklets, or check with your local IRS office.

Taxpayer Identification Numbers

The federal government requires that businesses use taxpayer I.D. numbers to report taxable income. The owner of a sole proprietorship can sometimes use his or her Social Security number as the tax identification number for the business. However, if salaries are paid or excise taxes are owed, a separate taxpayer identification number must be obtained from the IRS. Corporations are always required to use taxpayer I.D. numbers. Check with the IRS regarding current regulations, and check again if you make changes to your business structure. To obtain a taxpayer identification number, complete IRS Form SS-4 and return it to the address indicated on the form. Or call the number provided in the instructions for the SS-4 to apply for an I.D. number by telephone. Usually, a federal taxpayer I.D. number can be acquired in one day if you apply by phone.

Deductible Expenses

According to the IRS, an expense must be *ordinary* and *necessary* to qualify as a deduction. This means that the item must be something normally required by your type of business. It must also be of help to you in doing your job. Be careful about deducting personal living expenses as business expenses. Yes, it is ordinary and necessary for you to sleep and eat so you can do a good job at work, but the IRS usually does not view your apartment rent or grocery bills as deductible expenses of doing business.

Remember that small businesses can deduct most items used to run the business, including advertising/marketing expenses, postage, telephone answering services, legal fees, on-line information services, delivery services, business stationery, and office supplies. A percentage of the cost of meals at which clients are entertained is also deductible. The formula for calculating meal deductions is provided on Schedule C. The cost of subscriptions to trade journals and membership fees for some professional organizations can also be deducted. Check with the IRS to make sure your memberships qualify.

Be careful about taking the deduction for a home office. The IRS has very strict rules concerning qualifications for this deduction. Taking it can be a red flag that causes the IRS to review a return more carefully. As a rule, if your home office is not used exclusively for business purposes, the deduction may not be appropriate.

It is important to keep all receipts and record every business expense incurred. Expenses should be organized by category. A computer record keeping program can make this fairly simple. You may want to review Schedule C, *Profit or Loss from Business,* to determine the categories to be used to track your expenses.

Taxation by Classification

Unincorporated business owners record profits or losses on their personal income tax returns. Sole proprietors report profits or losses on Schedule C. Partners report profits or losses on their individual 1040 forms. Partnerships also must file Form 1065, *Partnership Return of Income.* Depending on the size and complexity of your business, as a sole proprietor or member of a partnership you may be able to prepare your own tax returns. But it would be helpful to have an accountant to call with questions.

The tax requirements for corporations vary according to the legal structure of the corporation. Usually, the corporation pays taxes on its profits. If a corporation shareholder receives salary or dividend income from the corporation, that income must be reported on his or her personal 1040. Taxes for corporations can be quite complex, and the assistance of a tax accountant is usually required.

The tax forms you must complete will depend on the organization of your business, your personal finances, and your family situation. Most small businesses will need at least the following forms:

- Form 1040
- Schedule C, *Profit or Loss from Business* (sole proprietorship); Schedule 1065, *Partnership Return of Income;* or Schedule 1120, *Corporation Income Tax Return*
- Schedule SE, for self-employment taxes
- Schedule 1040-ES, for estimated taxes for individuals
- Schedule 4562, for equipment depreciation and amortization
- Schedule E, for partnerships

Self-Employment Taxes

When you are employed by someone else, half of your required Social Security and Medicare taxes are withheld from your salary. Your employer pays the other half and sends the total Social Security/Medicare taxes to the IRS at least once per quarter, as required. When you are self-employed, either as a sole proprietor or a partner, you must pay both the employee's and employer's share of these taxes. This is referred to as the self-employment tax, and should not be confused with income taxes, which are another matter.

The self-employment tax is paid on your net earnings—the amount you earn after all business expenses are deducted. The instructions for calculating this tax are provided on Schedule SE. Some tax benefits of self-employment may be overlooked unless you consult a professional. For instance, the IRS allows you to deduct half of the self-employment tax from your adjusted gross income. This can result in substantial savings on your taxes.

Estimated Income Taxes

Self-employment also means taking responsibility for paying quarterly estimated income taxes to the IRS and your state tax authority. Failure to do so can result in penalties. To calculate how much you should pay, request Form 1040-ES from the IRS and the comparable form from your state tax authority. The requirements may change periodically, so review them carefully and complete the estimated tax worksheet provided with the form. Fill out the payment stub and send in your check. The payment dates for filing estimated taxes vary slightly each year, but payments for the prior quarter are due in the months of April, June, September, and January. (The January payment is for the last quarter of the previous year.) If your financial circumstances change during the year, you can recalculate your quarterly payments and increase or decrease them as necessary.

Taking the Automobile Deduction

When using a personal vehicle for business purposes, a company owner can deduct the costs of such use as a business expense. Either the standard mileage rate or the actual cost of operating your vehicle may be deducted. With the *standard mileage method,* a record is kept of the number of miles driven for business purposes. Then a flat rate per mile (established by the IRS) is deducted. The cost of parking, tolls, and automobile registration may also be deducted.

The *actual cost method* may result in a larger deduction. Record the number of miles driven for business purposes and the total number of miles driven for all purposes in a given year. Also record other automobile expenses such as batteries, insurance, oil changes, registration fees, repairs, gas, and depreciation. At the end of the year, use the business-miles-driven and total-miles-driven figures to calculate the percentage of vehicle use that was business-related. Multiply this percentage by total automobile expenses to determine the amount of your deduction.

There is one caveat to this: You cannot use the standard mileage method unless it is used the first year your car is driven for business purposes. If the standard mileage method is used for the first year, you may switch to the actual cost method the following year, but not vice versa.

Depreciation and Amortization

Calculating depreciation and amortization can be complicated but can save a great deal on taxes. Deducting part of a fixed asset's cost each year of its useful life is known as *depreciation.* Among the items usually depreciated are vehicles used for business purposes, computers, other expensive office equipment, and furniture. *Amortization* is similar, except that it involves intangible assets. *Intangible assets* are items such as patents, copyrights, franchises and licenses, and good will. For example, if you pay $200,000 to patent an invention, the amount is amortized over the useful life of the patent.

For both depreciation and amortization, the IRS provides guidelines for determining useful life. Review the relevant IRS publications and/or seek the advice of an experienced tax preparer before calculating these money-saving deductions.

Payroll, Sales, and Property Taxes

If your business has any employees, Social Security, Medicare, and federal/state income taxes must be withheld from their wages. These withholdings and the company's required contributions to Social Security and Medicare must be recorded and deposited according to IRS and state regulations (*see* Payroll, page 300).

If your firm sells taxable items, you must establish an accounting system that records sales taxes collected. These taxes are then paid to the appropriate state or local authority. Property taxes may also be due on land, vehicles, buildings, or other business assets. The requirements for paying sales and property taxes vary according to state, county, and city. Contact local authorities to ensure compliance with the regulations in your area.

Banking Basics

Choosing a Financial Institution

There are several different types of financial institutions available to serve business needs. Small company owners should check on special services for small businesses. Also, credit unions now offer many or all of the services formerly available only from banks. Membership is restricted to specifically defined groups of people, but if you are not a member, you may be eligible to join if you have a relative who has a membership. Credit unions may offer lower rates on loans/credit cards and pay higher rates on savings. Check with several financial institutions before making a choice.

The Company Checkbook

If you are a sole proprietor, there is no distinction between your business and personal funds. But you should have separate bank accounts for business and personal finances in order to track the financial condition of your business. Establish a business account and deposit any business income into the account. Use the account to pay all business expenses. Determine how much you will draw from the business for personal living expenses. At specified intervals, transfer the draw from the business account to your personal account. Be fair to yourself about the amount of your draw, but be disciplined as well. Business cash flow problems may be created by arbitrary decisions to withdraw extra sums for personal expenses such as vacations or large purchases. Also, you must remember to allocate a percentage of your draw to pay quarterly estimated income taxes.

The owner or manager of a small business must also decide whether any other employees will be authorized to write checks from the business account. If you have a bookkeeper or accountant who pays the company's bills, that person can be given authority to use the account or may just prepare checks for the owner/manager to sign. No matter what system is used, it is important to control the number of people who have access to company bank accounts.

Recording Checks and Balancing the Account

When recording a check in the checkbook or account register, note the invoice number and accounting code corresponding to the payment. Also note this information on the check itself (*see* Accounts Payable, page 292). A business checkbook is balanced in the same way as a personal account, and it must be tallied each month. Nothing will ruin your business reputation faster than writing checks for which you do not have sufficient funds; this could happen if you fail to balance the checkbook promptly to discover any errors. (Of course, you would never deliberately write checks unless you had enough money in the business account to cover them, as floating checks often sink.)

As with a personal checking account, you will receive a statement from the bank each month. Canceled checks or photocopies of them will accompany each statement. Some managers prefer to use dual-copy checks that automatically provide check copies for their records. Financial institutions refer to these as NCR (no copy required) checks. In any event, your canceled check or check copy is your record of payment for a bill or invoice.

The checking account statement will include a list of checks that were paid during the month. To balance the account, follow these steps:

1. Review the listed checks that were paid and mark those checks in your checkbook. As you mark them, verify that the amount listed on the statement matches what is on the check copy and the amount recorded in your checkbook. You may discover checks that were not recorded in your check register due to oversight. If so, enter them in the checkbook and subtract them from your checkbook balance.

2. Review the deposits listed on the statement and mark the corresponding deposits recorded in your checkbook. A note about deposit slips: Each time you make a deposit to your account, check the transaction record (your receipt) to make sure the deposit was entered correctly. Never put the receipt away without looking at it—check it immediately. If the amount recorded on the transaction receipt is incorrect, ask the teller who received your deposit to correct it. Business deposits often contain long lists of checks received as payment and/or large amounts of cash. The person who receives and records your deposit could make a mistake. Such an error is much easier to find and correct immediately than after days or weeks have passed. This double checking will also prevent the embarrassment of having your own checks returned due to insufficient funds when your records indicate that funds were in your account to cover them. Your financial institution may even require you to sign a receipt verifying the amount of each deposit; this is for your protection as well as theirs. Of course, you should retain the transaction receipt from each deposit for comparison with the deposit amounts shown on your monthly statement.

3. Read through the statement to see if there are any monthly fees, automatic deposits, or automatic withdrawals that are not listed in your check register. List them at this time. If your account is interest bearing (meaning interest is paid on the funds in your account at regular intervals), also record any interest earned and the date it was credited to your account. Some financial institutions add interest after each statement cycle; this means you should not add the interest to your account until after you have balanced it.

4. Add any deposits that were not credited to your account at the time the statement was printed (not listed on the statement and marked off in step 2). Then make a note of the total.

5. Turn the statement over. Most statements include a worksheet on the back to aid in balancing the checkbook. There should also be a place to list checks you have written that have not yet been received and paid by the bank. List all checks that were not marked in step 1, when you checked off those that were listed in the statement. After listing all of these checks, total the amounts.

6. Fill in the worksheet's reconciliation column, which should look something like this:

Ending Balance Shown on This Statement   _____

Add: Deposits Not Credited in This Statement   _____

                                       Total   _____

Subtract: Checks Outstanding (those shown in your

        checkbook but not on this statement)   _____

                               Balance   _____

The ending balance will be shown on the front of your statement. Write that amount on the line provided. Write the amount of total deposits not credited on this statement (from step 4) in the appropriate space. Enter the total amount of outstanding checks listed on the worksheet (step 5). Perform the necessary calculations. The final amount, or *balance,* should match the amount in your checkbook.

7. Make a note in your checkbook of the point at which your account balanced by highlighting the amount or circling it with a colored pen. When you are balancing the account the next month, it will help to know where to begin looking for an error.

If the balance on your worksheet does not match the balance in your checkbook, subtract the smaller figure from the larger one to get the difference. Look through your check register and the statement to see if the exact amount of the difference appears anywhere. If it does, see if the check or deposit in that amount was added or subtracted twice by mistake, or if a check was recorded as a deposit or vice versa. If this does not pinpoint the error, follow these suggestions to find the mistake:

- Verify that the amounts you listed as outstanding checks match what is in your checkbook. Then check to see if you totaled them correctly.
- Verify all subtractions and additions in your checkbook, beginning with the balance obtained after the previous month's statement was received. Check again to be sure that checks and deposits were recorded correctly and listed in the correct columns.
- Review your checkbook to make sure no checks or deposits were listed twice.
- Look for a transposition mistake if the amount of the error is evenly divisible by 9. Accidentally reversing the digits on either side of the decimal or completely reversing all digits will always result in a difference divisible by 9. For example, if you wrote $24.67 instead of $42.67, the difference between the correct amount

and the incorrect figure is $18.00. Recording an $8.79 check as $9.78 will result in a $.99 error.

If you still cannot locate an error, you may wish to visit your financial institution and have someone there assist you.

MAKING BUSINESS INVESTMENTS

Businesses are constantly faced with the need to *leverage* money—that is, to increase their purchasing and operational power by selecting investments that will keep pace with inflation and bring in additional funds. These may be short-term or long-term investments. Chances are your financial future will be determined by long-term investments, as short-term ventures are usually designed for professional investors rather than corporations. Unless you are knowledgeable and experienced in the investment field and have ample time to devote to financial matters, it is advisable to let a professional handle your investments for you. Smart money management starts with selecting the right people for the job. Here are some common types of investments to accomplish financial objectives for commercial and nonprofit organizations:

- Real estate—Many businesses flourish by purchasing rental properties such as offices and warehouses, thus guaranteeing a steady rental income that pays for certain company operations from month to month. Rental prices increase with inflation, so the income increases as inflation raises business expenses.
- Money market funds—These funds offer financial security, a reasonable return on your money, and a considerable amount of liquidity. They are basically mutual funds invested in short-term, interest-earning securities such as Treasury bills, government bonds, and certificates of deposit.
- Long-term securities—These require strong investment management to achieve the financial balance and goals you have in mind. Many factors must be considered: the degree of risk, the size and nature of your portfolio, the changing nature of business markets at home and abroad, the maturity dates of investments selected, and your overall financial objectives for growth or dividends.
- Commodities—Purchasing futures contracts in commodities is a volatile and tricky form of investment, not for the timid or inexperienced. Betting on the buying and selling of commodities such as livestock, coffee, or wheat is a precarious venture. However, this can be a lucrative type of investment for companies in fields related to commodities or when a great deal is known about certain commodities.
- Specialized investments—Many companies have made smart investments (usually long term) by using excess cash to purchase valuables such as precious metals, rare coins, gems, or antiques. This type of investment makes sense only if the owner or manager is very knowledgeable about the chosen area. Also, the business must be able to hold the items purchased for many months or years until their value has increased substantially.

Getting Outside Help with Finances

Financial accounting for a business is time-consuming even for an owner with an accounting background and years of experience. If you are just beginning a business and do not have accounting experience, you may save time and money by turning your accounting over to someone else. There are three types of professionals available to help you—bookkeepers, accountants, and CPAs (certified public accountants).

Bookkeepers, Accountants, and CPAs

Independent firms and individuals who provide bookkeeping services can be found in every city. *Bookkeepers* may have two- or four-year degrees from colleges or business schools. They also may be trained to set up and maintain accounting systems. Some bookkeepers do not have degrees but have learned bookkeeping from on-the-job experience and a few courses. Bookkeepers can help you keep your accounts up to date, but they are primarily trained to do the detailed work required to record transactions and balance accounts. They may not have the knowledge to help analyze your financial position or spot trouble before it becomes serious.

Accountants usually have college degrees in accounting and more knowledge than bookkeepers about the interpretation and analysis of financial data. They may be better trained to assist you in planning a financial strategy and keeping your business in sound financial shape. An accountant may focus on analyzing financial information by employing bookkeepers to do detailed record keeping for client accounts.

CPAs are accountants who have passed a rigorous state board examination. Applicants for CPA certification must also have a certain amount of experience in performing audits. (Most states require 500 hours of auditing experience.) A CPA designation granted by one state cannot be used in another state unless the person contacts the second state's Board of Accountancy and complies with their requirements for certification. In some states, such as California, only CPAs can call themselves accountants.

Whether to hire a bookkeeper, an accountant, or a CPA is a personal choice. Accountants and CPAs provide more comprehensive services, but they also charge more. If your business is fairly simple, a good bookkeeper may be all you need. Here are some basic guidelines for selecting the right person:

- Find out where and when the person was educated. Make sure the school has a good reputation. If you decide to use someone who has not been practicing very long, keep in mind that he or she may not have the experience to handle unusual financial situations.

- Ask other businesspeople to recommend accounting firms or individuals. Many accountants and bookkeepers specialize in certain types of businesses. It may be best to hire someone who already knows the intricacies of your type of operation.
- Bigger firms are not necessarily better. Large CPA firms have huge clients who get most of their attention. Small businesses are better served by small firms or individuals who can provide personal attention.

You should always be aware of the financial condition of your business, even though you have turned accounting tasks over to someone else, and you should have a basic understanding of accounting principles. Look at the financial records several times each month instead of just asking your accountant if everything is all right. As the owner or manager of a business, you are the primary person responsible for its financial status. (*See also* Accounting Firms, page 340, for information on contacting a number of nationwide services.)

On-Line Accounting and Banking Services

Local and national services with on-line capabilities are an excellent alternative to in-house accounting and financial procedures. Many accounting firms now offer on-line accounts payable/receivable, payroll, and tax accounting services (*see* On-Line Resources, page 342). For example, a small business manager may transmit payroll information to a service and receive data to print the checks within 24 hours. Payroll reports and tax records are returned to the client via computer.

Even the smallest financial institutions are now rushing to establish Internet websites and PC-based banking. Typical on-line services offered include access to account information, transfer of funds between accounts, automatic payroll tax deposits, loan/credit applications, and other cash management services. Some banks also feature on-line payroll accounting services and tax reporting. For instance, those banks can invoice a business's customers, receive its payments, and automatically deposit them to the business account; process accounts payable invoices by debiting the client's account and mailing the necessary payments; and process client payrolls by preparing paychecks and automatically transferring payroll tax deposits to government accounts.

At present, larger firms are more likely to use on-line financial and accounting services than one-person businesses or small partnerships. But many banking institutions are actively seeking small business clients and will provide, free of charge, all information and software necessary to establish an on-line account.

Expense Accounts—Tracking Yours and Theirs

Few functions in the business world have been subjected to more fraud, deceit, misunderstanding, and mismanagement than personal expense accounts. Yet the guidelines can (and should) be simple, the records accurate, and the enforcement of rules and restrictions completely effective.

Setting a Simple, Accurate, and Effective Policy

When establishing expense accounts, clarify the following issues and present your position in writing to all personnel involved:

1. Specify which employees (such as salespeople in the field) will receive cash advances for which they are accountable.
2. Specify which employees will be reimbursed for expenses they pay out of pocket.
3. List the kinds of out-of-pocket expenses that will and will not be covered by the company.
4. Pinpoint the maximum amounts permissible for each type of expense.
5. Provide expense report forms and detailed guidelines for reporting expenses, whether paid in advance or reimbursed after the fact.
6. Distribute to all participating employees reprints of applicable passages from IRS guidelines that describe deductible expenses and an employee's obligation to report business expenditures and reimbursements.
7. Establish policies limiting the types and amounts of expenses (meals and entertainment, for example) that employees may incur on behalf of clients or customers.
8. Require accurate documentation for all expense account transactions, including receipts, bills, credit card printouts, or other acceptable verification of amounts, dates, and recipients. Such documents should be of a type that would be acceptable to the IRS if submitted with tax records.
9. Maintain an expense account record for each employee for review and comparison if questions arise.

Keeping a Record of Travel Expenses

If trips are infrequent, a travel diary daily record can be kept by the traveler in an empty lined notebook. A page should be set up for each day of the trip, as shown in Figure 7.4. The name, address, and phone number of the hotel for that day should be included, with appointment times, locations, and agendas in the "TO DO" area, with space between scheduled meetings to jot down other activities that may occur. The "NOTES" area is for thoughts, reminders, observations, goals, or contacts' addresses and phone numbers. Only business expenses are recorded in the "SPENDING" area—personal expenditures can be recorded in the general expense log.

A general expense log can be kept in the travel diary. It should begin in the middle or back of the book. Each expense is listed as it occurs (in chronological order). The "Description of expense" column should be used to note the type of expense (meals, lodging, supplies, transportation other than rental car, entertainment, gifts, etc.). Of course, an "Exchange rate" column is not necessary for trips within the United States. Gasoline and car expense logs are also needed for business trips that involve the use of personal, company, or rental cars. The odometer reading

Travel Diary Daily Record

Date:

Purpose of trip:

Current location:

TO DO

Time   Location   Description of activity

NOTES

SPENDING

Daily budget:

meals: lodging: supplies:

transportation: entertainment: gifts:

other:

Total spending:

Figure 7.4 Travel diary daily record

at the beginning and end of the trip are included, as well as the cost of any repairs, parts, or supplies.

When a number of employees travel often on company business, standardized company travel expense forms are usually developed. The general expense log and gasoline/car expense logs can be combined into one form. A travel diary daily record may not be needed for short trips, but it can be useful for longer ones, as it is easily maintained and provides detailed information that can be transferred to standardized expense logs at the end of each trip.

REGARDING REIMBURSABLES

If your records are disorderly or inadequate, you may neglect to bill other companies for expenses incurred in doing business with them. Or you may overlook costs that could be listed as deductibles on your business income tax returns. Here are some tips for tracking reimbursable or deductible expenses that are often missed.

- Ask your telephone company and long-distance carrier about call accounting services that track phone calls and even rebill costs to clients, suppliers, and others who are frequently called. The extra service is usually free.
- Get into the habit of requesting receipts for everything, and persuade coworkers to do the same. Once this becomes a habit, it is not difficult, and it can pay big dividends.
- Maintain daily expense logs in all offices or departments, using them to flag expenses for which no receipt, bill, or other documentation has yet been received.
- Use credit cards or other charge services as much as possible so that others will do your record keeping for you. Such cards are interest free if the bills are paid on or before the due date each month.
- Make a list of the types of expenses that are likely to be overlooked during record keeping, reimbursement, and tax preparation. Make sure other key people in your company are also aware of these possible oversights.
- Focus on all expenditures in the expense category that are taxed substantially. If you do business in Europe, for example, you can recover all or part of the value-added taxes on hotel rooms, rental cars, meals, and even seminars. These can be as high as 18 percent or more. Setting up procedures to gain refunds from foreign government agencies can be well worth the effort.

Petty Cash

A *petty cash fund* is used to pay for small business expenses. It should be established with a fixed amount, and a specified employee should be given authority to disburse funds from it. When someone makes a purchase that can come out of petty cash (such as donuts for a staff meeting), a simple petty cash form should be completed by the purchaser. The form should indicate what is being purchased, the purpose of the item(s), and the amount of the expenditure. This form, with the purchase receipt attached, should be presented to the employee in charge of the petty cash fund. That employee should verify the amount, write the corresponding account number from the chart of accounts on the petty cash slip, and obtain the signature of the staff member who is submitting the form. A disbursement can then be made from the petty cash fund to reimburse the purchaser. Figure 7.5 shows a sample petty cash voucher.

When the funds in petty cash are depleted or reach a low balance, the employee in charge of the fund should balance the fund. This is done by totaling the receipts submitted and verifying that those receipts plus the cash balance in the fund equal the total (fixed) amount of the fund. The petty cash receipts can then be recorded in the ledger. A new check should be issued and cashed to bring petty cash up to its maximum (fixed) balance. A petty cash journal (such as the one in Figure 7.6) should be kept with the fund.

Maintaining the security of a petty cash fund is important. It can be a temptation to dishonest employees, and small losses add up. The best security measure is limiting the number of people authorized to make payments from petty cash. The

---

PETTY CASH VOUCHER

Date: _____   Voucher No. _____

FOR	*ACCOUNT DEBITED*	*ACCOUNT NO.*	*AMOUNT*

TOTAL _____

Approved by: _____

Received by: _____

Figure 7.5 Petty cash voucher

PETTY CASH JOURNAL

DATES FROM_____   TO_____   BALANCE ON HAND_____

Date	Voucher #	Account	Account #	Payee	Approved by	Total	Balance

TOTAL VOUCHER AMOUNT _____

Checked by: _____   TOTAL RECEIPTS _____

CASH ON HAND _____

OVERAGE/SHORTAGE _____

Approved by: _____   PETTY CASH REIMBURSEMENT _____

BALANCE FORWARD _____

Figure 7.6 Petty cash journal

fund should be kept in a locked safe or box, and only authorized staff should have access to the key or combination. Unannounced audits of the fund should be conducted periodically to verify that it is in balance. Like everything else concerning business finances, the owner or manager should maintain some control over the petty cash fund.

Inventory Tracking

Many businesses have substantial proportions of their budgets allocated to establishing and maintaining inventories of products, goods, materials, and operational supplies. Thus, accurate inventory tracking is essential. Sound inventory control can make the difference between profit and loss, and even determine whether a company stays in business. Inventory tracking is not just counting products in the stockroom or warehouse. It also affects many other areas of business, such as the system for purchasing products and supplies, timing of purchases, marketing and sales programs, calculation of taxable income and deductions, and security procedures to protect goods from theft and mismanagement.

The first requisite for sound inventory control is competent purchasing. Ordering of all items must be effectively planned, whether the stock is for distribution and sale or for company operations. Take into account seasonal variations, business growth or decline, and possible emergencies or other contingencies that could make certain commodities unavailable. Inventory tracking requires keen observation of recent and past business needs, as well as anticipation of future changes.

When ordered stock is received, take the following steps to ensure proper control:

- Check all items against their invoices to see if quantities are correct.
- Make sure the prices quoted and listed match.
- Check the totals against your original orders to make sure the item types and quantities match the listed specifications.
- Check or spot-check incoming items for damage or improper packaging.
- List and report any discrepancies to the supplier, conveyor, or agent without delay. If necessary, arrange for an immediate vendor inspection of all items/records in question.

Both functional and physical discrepancies may affect inventory tracking. In most businesses, record keeping and inventory handling occur in different locations, usually in separate departments under different supervisors. It is good business practice to have different persons handle actual inventory and inventory records. Therefore, coordination between departments is essential to effective inventory control.

In businesses that supply products to customers, similar checking and rechecking procedures should be followed when processing orders. Filling customer orders also involves invoice preparation, shipping and delivery schedules, and ordering items to replenish the stock that has been sold. Figure 5.3, page 209, is a procedural flowchart that delineates the steps involved in filling customer orders while maintaining inventory control.

Budgets

A *budget* is a formal statement of management's expectations regarding income, expenditures, sales, volume, inventories, personnel, and various transactions. It consists of projected revenue and expenses for a defined accounting period. A *departmental budget* covers the projected revenue and expenses for one specific unit of an organization, whereas a *master* or *comprehensive budget* gives projected figures for the business as a whole. The main components of a budget are the *projected income statement,* the *balance sheet,* and the *cash budget.*

When reading a budget, think of it as a tool for planning and control. At the start of an accounting period (generally a month, a quarter, six months, or a year), the budget is used as a plan—a guide to anticipating financial and monetary situations. At the end of the period, the budget serves as a control device to help management measure actual performance against the plan, with the goal of improving future performance.

Here are some steps typically involved in budget preparation:

1. A realistic sales forecast is developed, based on past records, ongoing organizational and operational changes, and a study of existing and projected market conditions.
2. Production volume or inventory-stocking expenses for the period are estimated. This is based on the sales forecast—which predicts the amount of products needed during the period based on forecasts of how many products will be sold—and necessary internal/external processing factors.
3. Production or inventory-stocking costs and all operational expenses (office overhead, payroll, marketing) are estimated. Factors such as expected price increases for supplies or production labor are taken into consideration.
4. Projected cash flow is calculated.
5. Projected financial statements are formulated.

Computer software programs can be very helpful in budget writing, especially if your office uses computer-based accounting procedures. Most financial software programs will readily produce the figures needed for budget creation, as the needed information is already present in the computer accounting records. (*See also* Understanding Computer Financial Software, page 337.)

Pricing Your Product or Service

The price charged for a product or service should meet two criteria. First, it must cover your costs of buying/producing/delivering an item, or all expenses—including management and employee wages—of supplying a service. Second, your price must be competitive; it must not be significantly higher or lower than the prices charged by other businesses in your area for a similar product or service. Before starting a business, evaluate the market, the need for your product or service, and prices offered by competitors. Only then can you determine whether your business can offer pricing that is competitive enough to attract customers and sufficient to cover necessary expenses.

There are several ways to calculate price, and establishing a consistent pricing formula is important. Consistency means that you need not rethink pricing strategy each time you begin selling a new product. Budgeting and accounting are also simpler, because a consistent pricing formula makes income and profit more predictable. The most common product pricing method is called *standard markup*. It is represented by the formula:

retail price = cost + markup

In this formula, markup is a predetermined percentage of the cost. (For example, many small retail businesses use a standard markup of 50 percent.) A similar approach uses the same formula, except that management considers what competitors are charging for similar products and adjusts the markup percentage to remain competitive.

When pricing products, you may want to consider using *odd-number pricing*. Studies have shown that pricing an item at $19.97 rather than $20 can increase sales, as some consumers perceive the price as closer to $19 than $20. However, studies have also shown that a more upscale clientele will be attracted by prices ending in zeros. So, if you want to emphasize the quality and exclusiveness of your products, use prices ending in zeros.

More complex pricing strategies require investigation of the potential market to learn what factors most affect customer decisions. For example, some customers are not looking for the lowest price. They may have already decided to buy something and be willing to pay a higher price to get other benefits, such as better service or free delivery. Another factor to consider is whether you will permit customers to use credit cards or charge accounts that you provide. Customers may be willing to pay slightly higher prices if they can buy on credit, and they often buy more items when using credit. If you do permit credit purchases, be sure to include your cost for providing such credit when you calculate prices (*see* Retail Businesses—How to Give Credit, page 328). Manufacturers must consider other factors when pricing products, such as direct costs, manufacturing costs, nonmanufacturing costs, and profits. Complex calculations and a great deal of knowledge about the manufacturing process are required.

Pricing a service is more difficult than pricing a product because you are selling an intangible item. One good method for setting a price is to determine how many employee hours are available to provide the service and how much you need to cover all expenses; then calculate your hourly rate accordingly. When calculating hours available to provide the service, include hours worked by your employees as well as their paid holidays, vacation time, and sick time. Also consider the fact that if you—the owner of the business—are providing the service, every work hour will not be available to do so. Some time must be used for bookkeeping, marketing, and other activities that do not actually earn money. Also, remember to subtract your own vacation and sick time, and be sure to include tax liability.

For example, if you are running a housecleaning business and you and two employees provide services, your calculations may look like this:

$ 2,400 cleaning supplies
  28,000 owner's salary
  13,000 employee A salary
  13,000 employee B salary
   2,000 employer's share of owner's self-employment taxes
   1,650 employer's share of both employees' Social Security taxes
   3,950 for workers' compensation, liability insurance, and miscellaneous expenses
$64,000 Total yearly expenses

5,120 = Total work hours available per year (2 employees × 40 hours × 49 weeks = 3,920 hours + owner × 25 hours × 48 weeks = 1,200 hours, for a total of 5,120 hours)

$12.50 = Lowest possible service price per hour ($64,000 ÷ 5,120 = $12.50)

In this example, the price per hour should be at least $12.50. You could round this number to $15 per hour or charge even more if the market will support a higher price. You would also want to find out what other businesses in your area that provide the same service are charging.

If your service offers something unique, you can certainly charge more than your competitors. For example, if you offer a service such as financial planning or massage therapy and your employees go to clients' homes or businesses instead of requiring them to come to your place of business, you can charge more for the convenience provided.

Projecting Cash Flow

A *cash flow projection,* or cash forecast, is a necessary tool for financial planning and management of a business. A projection shows all money coming in and going out; its most valuable function is identification of potential trouble spots. Its structure is a simple formula:

cash balance at the beginning of the month
+ receipts − disbursements = ending balance

The ending balance is a surplus if it is a positive figure and a shortfall if it is a negative figure. Of course, a surplus is the desired outcome.

The degree of detail in a cash flow projection depends on several factors, including the size of your company, the amount of financial activity during the period in question, and the kinds of items that qualify as receipts and disbursements. Sales figures alone, for example, can be misleading in a company that extends credit, since the payments for sales may not be received within the projected period. Check earlier cash flow records to determine how to calculate projections for your type of operation. For instance, if your business is seasonal or if receipts and disbursements vary substantially from month to month, adjust projections accordingly. Seasonal fluctuations tend to show up well in advance of seasonal peaks and valleys. You must determine the average amount of time lapse between receipt of revenues (that is, when your business actually receives payment for products or services) and dates of necessary disbursements (when your business must pay the expenses—such as wages and manufacturing costs—of supplying the products or services). Your company's purchases of inventory items, for example, depend on the cash available to pay for those stocks as well as the availability of supplies, delivery times, the time your firm will require to alter/repackage/produce/sell goods, and the size and nature of inventories essential to the business.

Another crucial factor in projecting cash flow is the type of payment arrangements you make with vendors. The figures in your books from month to month should accurately reflect such agreements—for example, whether suppliers/servicers require full or partial payment before processing your orders or sell to you on credit with varying financial terms.

In addition to regular operating costs such as wages, distribution, marketing, and utilities, a cash flow projection should also include payroll taxcs, sales taxes, and income taxes. Funds for unexpected or emergency situations must also be included. Expenditures that occur only yearly or quarterly can be easily forgotten in monthly cash flow calculations. Commonly overlooked items (such as insurance premiums, business gifts, entertainment, franchise fees, dues, professional fees, property assessments, and payment of dividends) can result in cash flow nightmares.

Forecasting Business Trends and Growth

Predicting the future of a business has been compared to forecasting the weather—even with advanced technology, meteorologists are often wrong. But a business seldom gets into trouble overnight, and there are many signs to indicate the possibilities of success or failure.

A key forecasting device is the ratio of current assets to current liabilities, sometimes known as the *quick ratio.* Divide total current assets by total current liabilities to obtain it. The results might look like this: 1.9:1 (or 1.9 to 1). A quick ratio is meaningless until it is compared with past ratios and then projected into the future. If the ratio of assets to liabilities is decreasing, such as a change from 1.9:1 to 1.4:1, your business is becoming less *liquid* (harder to convert assets into cash if necessary), and you can expect to have more difficulty in meeting financial obligations. If, on the other hand, you see that the asset figure is increasing in relation to the liability figure, your financial stability is improving.

A ratio change in either direction from one period to the next is not necessarily cause for concern or elation, as cash and liquidity patterns tend to fluctuate. Long-term patterns and trends must be evaluated. Pay special attention to periods that seemed positive but are shown as downtrends in long-term evaluation. Then determine the points at which changes up or down indicate major trends in your business rather than minor variations.

Employee Compensation Plans

Employee compensation programs play a vital role in the lives of employees and their families and have a marked influence on the popularity of a workplace. Today's workers expect good salaries and benefits, and substandard programs can seriously hinder management efforts to attract and retain the best personnel. Managers are often surprised to learn that competitive salaries are only the tip of the iceberg. For many workers, benefits such as flexible leave policies and health insurance are as important as actual wages earned.

Several components typify attractive employee compensation plans, including competitive salaries, incentive/bonus packages, insurance benefits, pension/retirement plans, generous severance packages, and liberal vacation/sick leave policies. Day-care programs for workers' children or aged parents may even be included. In addition, federal law mandates certain provisions for maternity and family leave (*see* Employee Benefits, page 249, for information on leave policies and family care programs).

The cost of each employee benefit program must be weighed against its likelihood of helping the firm reach productivity and profitability goals. When decisions have been reached on the benefits to be offered, a detailed explanation of each benefit should be included in the company's policies and procedures manual (*see* Creating a Policies and Procedures Manual, page 189, and Defining Office Policies, page 186).

Competitive Salaries

Determining salary levels is one of the most difficult decisions faced by management, regardless of a company's size. Some managers make the mistake of setting salaries at the lowest possible levels because they do not understand that employees view wages as a reflection of their individual and collective worth to the company.

To set attractive but realistic salary levels in a competitive market, list all applicable financial points of comparison. For example, if you own a retail business, you should know what other area retailers pay their employees, including office workers, stock clerks, and delivery persons, as well as salespeople. But remember the old adage that no two jobs are alike, and structure salaries accordingly. When comparing positions to determine competitive salary levels (whether the positions being compared are within your organization or in other firms), ask the following questions about each position:

- Is the job title accurate? Is the same job title used for two positions with very different responsibilities? If so, consider retitling the positions to avoid confusion. For instance, assume that starting pay for an "account representative" averages $35,000 per year in your area for salespeople who go out into the market and service accounts. In your firm, clerical staff who take phoned-in service orders may be called "account representatives." After a position analysis is done, you may decide to call these clerical workers "account clerks" to avoid confusion when advertising for new personnel. This will also forestall questions from your staff concerning their wages versus those of "account representatives" in other firms.
- Is there a minimum experience requirement for job applicants?
- Are there minimum education and training requirements?
- Does the job require a high level of natural skill that is not necessarily the result of training or experience?
- Does the job demand considerable responsibility and/or accountability?
- Is length of service a significant factor? (Perhaps the salary levels for similar jobs performed by seasonal, new, and long-term employees should be quite different, as long-term, regular employees are often more valuable due to their knowledge and experience. But this is not always true.)
- Does the job entail any undesirable drawbacks, such as disagreeable location, excess travel, or physical hardship?
- Are there possibilities for promotion to a higher level position?

A position analysis will not only enable you to set salaries at levels that are attractive and realistic, it will also provide the information needed to answer applicants' questions about a position. This is especially important if prospective employees question starting salaries that are lower than those offered by other companies for comparable-sounding positions.

Incentive and Bonus Packages

Stock option plans are a common means of allowing employees to share in the profits of a company. Some plans make automatic stock transfers to employees each year at no cost to workers. Length of service usually determines full ownership of the shares accumulated in this manner, so an employee must stay with the company a specified number of years before actually owning the shares. Workers may also be given the option of purchasing certain amounts of stock (usually based on annual salary) at the end of each year worked for the company. Some firms give pay bonuses at the end of the year based on an employee's length of service and salary level in addition to the amount of company profits for that year. The objective in offering such plans is motivating staff to work harder and stay with the company in order to increase its profits and share in them.

Tuition and educational benefits are also attractive incentives for many employees. These range from underwriting short-term seminars or outside training programs to partial or full reimbursement of college tuition. Some companies allow educational leave for staff to attend college classes applicable to their area of work (for example, a salesperson working on a marketing degree may be allowed to attend classes two mornings per week without losing pay or using vacation time).

Insurance Benefits

When employee insurance benefits are mentioned, health insurance is the first thing that comes to mind. Other types of insurance are also provided by many businesses to help workers protect themselves and their families against the financial losses caused by sudden death or long-term disability. Choosing the right insurance company to provide business coverage is important, so consider several before making a decision. A list of nationwide insurance firms and how to reach them is included in Sources of Further Information under Insurance Firms on page 341.

Health Insurance

In an age of steadily rising costs for medical care, most people cannot afford private health-care policies. They rely on group plans available at affordable premiums through their place of work. At one time, large corporations often paid the entire cost of health insurance for employees and their families, but this occurs less frequently now. An employer's decision to pay part, all, or none of employees' health insurance premiums is based on several factors. These include the number of employees, the company's financial health, the cost of other employee benefits, and benefits offered by other firms competing for good workers. If a small business owner elects not to pay any part of employees' premiums, workers may be allowed to decide which health insurance policy the firm should take. Workers will appreciate being included in this decision, as the choice will affect their coverage and premiums. For example, employees may be asked if they prefer coverage with relatively low premiums but larger deductibles and co-payments or a policy with higher premiums, lower deductibles, and smaller co-payments.

Paying a generous percentage of workers' health-care premiums may help to attract better qualified personnel. The quality of the insurance plan offered is also a key factor in reducing turnover. A plan that includes dental coverage may provide a competitive edge in recruiting and retaining employees. (Two factors have influenced the growing attractiveness of dental coverage: the escalating cost of dental care and an increased focus on the importance of preventing tooth decay and gum disease.)

There are certain federal requirements concerning the continuation of health insurance benefits for employees who retire, resign, or are terminated. Such benefits are provided at no cost to the employer, as a worker must pay the full premiums when requesting such continuation of benefits. For more information, call the Federal Information Center at 800-688-9889 and ask for the address and phone number of the U.S. Pension and Welfare Benefits Administration's regional office for your area.

Life and Disability Insurance

Life insurance premiums under a group insurance plan are usually much more affordable than individual, privately obtained policies. Some people with preexisting health problems may be accepted for group life insurance coverage although they have been turned down for private policies. Health-care policies may contain built-in disability provisions for employees who are unable to work for extended periods due to illness or nonwork-related accidents. Work-related accidents are usually covered by workers' compensation insurance (*see* Workers' Compensation, page 117).

Retirement Plans

Most companies see a clear advantage in trying to retain loyal employees for the long term, improving productivity and skills and avoiding turnover of personnel. Statistically, 70 percent of all employees in the United States retire before the age of 65. One reason is that Social Security benefits, when combined with other pension and retirement plans, provide the financial freedom for people with long service to enjoy a comfortable lifestyle after retirement. Also, many older people can supplement their retirement income with part-time employment without endangering Social Security benefits or paying heavy income taxes.

With this trend toward earlier retirement, many companies offer appealing retirement benefits in order to attract and retain good employees, especially as the future of Social Security benefits becomes more and more uncertain. Incorporated businesses may also set up other types of retirement benefits, such as profit-sharing or money-purchase plans.

There are two basic types of retirement plans. *Defined contribution plans* are those in which a certain percentage of an employee's salary is deposited in a pension fund. This set amount may be deducted from the employee's wages or contributed by the employer or shared by both. In a *defined benefit plan,* contributions are not static. They are based on actuarial projections of the retirement benefit to be paid and the worker's age. Age determines the number of years an employee can work for the company and, thus, the total projected contribution to the fund.

Some special types of retirement plans follow:

• Simplified Employee Pension (SEP) plans are defined contribution plans in which the owner makes all contributions to the fund. Contributions are typically based on a percentage of earnings or wages that each participant receives from the business. There are no annual pension fund tax returns to file with the IRS. Adopting the SEP is accomplished by filling out a one- or two-page form that does not have to be filed with the IRS. Although SEPs are very simple to set up and administer, there are some disadvantages, so review the participation requirements with a financial adviser.

• 401Ks—also called *cash plans* or *deferred arrangement plans*—make it possible for employees to place part of their wages in profit-sharing, stock-bonus, or pension plans. Income taxes on contributions are deferred until the money is actually withdrawn, so there is a limit to the amount of yearly contributions that qualify for tax deferment. Such salary-reduction plans are considered to be excellent long-term investments.

- Keoghs—for self-employed individuals and partnerships—were named for the U.S. congressman who proposed the legislation creating them. The maximum allowable yearly contribution to a Keogh is usually determined by the participant's earnings from the business. Withdrawals cannot be made before age 59½ without payment of substantial penalties except in certain limited situations.

Severance Packages

The amount of compensation paid to a terminated employee often depends on the circumstances of termination. Some workers must be laid off or forced to take early retirement because of business setbacks or other reasons. In such cases, compassionate employers usually feel that some form of termination pay is due. As mentioned previously, federal law also requires that group health insurance coverage be continued for a specified length of time, at the employee's expense, for any worker who requests it when leaving the company.

When a worker is terminated due to corporate reorganization or financial problems, and not for any failure on the part of the employee, it is very important to ensure that the individual's rights are not violated. Many companies, sensing a downtrend in their business or industry, anticipate monetary problems by promoting early retirement and providing certain benefits to people who take this option. From a company standpoint, it has become increasingly common to offer lump-sum settlements, avoiding future expenditures and a never-ending stream of paperwork and record keeping. Many people find this alternative appealing because they can pay off mortgages and other financial obligations and then step forward into retirement with a clean slate.

Even when employees are fired for cause (other than outright criminal activity), employers must be careful not to violate their rights. This is especially true if the reason for dismissal is a matter of management judgment, such as sloppy dress, inefficiency, or hostility toward a supervisor. Standard severance compensation is at least one week's wages.

No matter what the circumstances under which a worker leaves the company, an employer should apply termination policies that will avoid any future financial and/or legal entanglements. Severance policies must be consistent, applying equally to all individuals, whether they are young, single, and have few financial obligations, or older workers and straining to support their families. In addition to following legal mandates concerning terminations, managers should remember that compassionate severance packages will reflect well on the company and enhance its image in the community. (*See also* When All Else Fails: Firing an Employee, page 256.)

Understanding Insurance

Regardless of the size or complexity of your business, you will need to obtain certain types of insurance. A comprehensive insurance plan will protect you and your business from unexpected losses that can be caused by a variety of circumstances. The easiest way to purchase business insurance is to find a package policy that includes all of the coverage you need. Package policies eliminate much of the confusion and guesswork required to select separate plans for different types of coverage. When reviewing a package policy, ask to see the *Named Perils and Exclusions* list. Named perils include the types of losses covered by the policy; exclusions are losses not covered by the policy.

Insurance Deductibles

A *deductible* is the amount the insured person or company must pay when a loss occurs before the insurance takes effect. (If your policy has a $1,000 deductible and your business suffers a $5,000 loss from fire or theft, you will be required to absorb the first $1,000 of the loss; insurance will pay $4,000.) Often, there is a choice of deductibles—the higher the deductible, the lower the premium. Be sure to choose a deductible amount that your business can afford to cover if a loss occurs.

Property, Liability, and Medical Coverage

Property insurance usually covers the premises and contents of your property. Most businesses need protection against theft and fire. Many natural disasters are not covered under standard policies, so you may want to purchase specific coverage for earthquakes or floods if these are a problem in your area. Even if you do not own the building where your business is located, you will want to insure its contents. For instance, if you own a dry cleaning business, you will need insurance to cover damage or destruction of your equipment and furnishings as well as customers' clothing.

Liability and *medical insurance* policies cover injuries to other people or damage to their property that occurs on your property or as a result of your business operations. This is particularly important if your business often has people other than employees on site. If a customer is injured on your site, your medical policy will pay for it. If an injured person sues your business, liability coverage will pay for the company's legal defense and any compensation awarded. (This can vary depending on who is at fault for the accident, the state in which it occurs, and your particular policy.) Special considerations arise if your business does work for a client at his or her site. The client may require proof that your company has liability and workers' compensation insurance. The client company may also insist that its firm be made an *additional named insured* on your policy to protect it against losses or suits resulting from injury to one of your employees on its site.

Most states require that employers provide *workers' compensation insurance* to protect employees against on-the-job injuries. In some states, coverage is provided by a state fund. Each state's fund works differently. Usually, employers are required to contribute to the fund for each employee. If an employee is injured on the job, the state workers' compensation fund pays for medical costs and loss of income. In states without such a fund, employers must obtain coverage from independent carriers.

Automobile Insurance

Many states require that all vehicle owners carry *automobile insurance*. If your employees drive company vehicles, they should be covered on your policy for that vehicle. If employees use their own cars for business-related travel such as deliveries or errands, you should investigate *non-owned automobile coverage*. If employees frequently rent vehicles for business use, you should consider *hired automobile coverage*. Automobile insurance includes three categories of coverage: comprehensive, collision, and liability. *Comprehensive insurance* covers such items as theft and fire; *collision insurance* pays for damage to your vehicle in the event of an accident; the *liability* portion of your auto insurance covers injury or damage to other persons, vehicles, or property as the result of an accident in which your vehicle is involved. Insurance for property stored inside a vehicle, such as samples, tools, or merchandise, may require separate coverage.

Other Types of Coverage

If a natural disaster occurs and your business is unable to operate due to property damage and the time needed for repairs, *business interruption* or *loss of income insurance* covers continuing business expenses such as salaries, utilities, and taxes. *Disability insurance* replaces income that is lost due to an owner's long-term illness or injury. It can also pay for business overhead expenses while a sole proprietor recuperates from an illness or injury. This is similar to business interruption insurance except that it pays during periods of disability rather than during times when business operations are prevented due to a natural disaster. *Life insurance* for business owners is specifically designed to protect the business and its employees if the owner dies.

Your company may also need special insurance such as *computer coverage* (which can provide more protection than standard property coverage), *pollution and hazardous waste coverage*, or an *umbrella policy*. As the name implies, an umbrella policy covers a broad range of situations that can adversely affect your business.

Insurance prices and coverage differ greatly from one insurer to another. You will want to shop around to determine the company that can best meet your needs. The best way to be certain you have the necessary coverage is to locate an insurance agent who specializes in insurance for your type of business. Ask your business associates for referrals.

Risk Management

A business owner should do everything possible to prevent accidents resulting in costly litigation and insurance claims. The process of preventing claims is called *risk management.* If your business has many potential hazards, have an experienced risk manager evaluate the site and make suggestions for improving safety. Implement strict safety guidelines and require employees and customers to follow them (*see* Accident Prevention, page 110, and Avoiding Work-Related Injuries and Illnesses, page 112).

Credit and Loans

Credit allows individuals and businesses to complete transactions with the promise that payment will be made at a later date, in compliance with the terms of a credit agreement. There are two types of credit: purchase credit and loan credit. *Purchase credit* is extended by a business to individuals or other firms, allowing them to obtain services or merchandise by deferring payment. *Loan credit* gives borrowers access to cash from banks and other financial institutions.

Retail Businesses—How to Give Credit

Anyone who sells something must consider whether to allow purchases on credit. The simplest method for retail businesses is accepting major credit cards. To arrange this for your business, contact your bank or other financial institution and ask to meet with their credit card representative. You will be required to sign a contract stating that you will pay the bank a percentage of the total sale on each credit card transaction. This percentage may vary from one institution to another, so check with more than one firm and negotiate with credit representatives to get the best rate. You will be given the instructions and forms needed for customer credit card transactions by the institution you choose. Check with your accountant on setting up your books to include credit card purchases and a record of amounts paid to your bank for supplying the credit service. (Note: Paying a percentage of credit card sales to a financial institution means less profit for your business on each of those sales. For this reason, many businesses set prices higher to cover that percentage and give discounts to customers who pay cash. Some merchants do not allow customers to charge specially priced or sale items, as their profit margin is already lower on those.)

A second way to give credit is to establish your own credit system. Have your attorney draft a simple application and disclosure form. There are federal disclosure requirements, so be sure your lawyer is familiar with them. Disclosure requirements change constantly, but usually include providing specific details to borrowers about (1) the interest rate and how it is calculated; (2) whether there is a grace period after purchases are made, before interest begins accruing; (3) penalties for late payments and how they are calculated; and (4) annual fees charged to customers. You need not issue cards to customers—you can just require some form of identification when charges are made. This type of credit is more personal but also involves developing a billing system and dealing with delinquent accounts (*see* Accounts Receivable, page 295).

Checking Credit

Retail businesses and service companies should require completed credit applications before extending credit to individuals or firms (Figure 7.7). Call at least two of the credit references listed by an applicant to check payment records. If you anticipate doing credit checks on a lot of businesses, you may wish to use the services of Dun & Bradstreet or another national firm that collects and provides credit information on businesses. Services are usually available on a per credit check basis or by paying an annual fee. Using such an agency will save you the time and effort of checking credit references. You may also want to consider joining a local credit bureau to obtain information on the creditworthiness of potential customers. Most credit bureaus charge membership fees as well as a small fee for each credit check.

Obtaining Credit

As a business owner, there will undoubtedly be many instances in which you will want to purchase something from a supplier and pay for it later. The easiest way to do this is to obtain a credit card for your business and use the card whenever possible. If a supplier does not accept credit cards, inquire about obtaining credit and complete a credit application. You may want to register your business with a firm such as Dun & Bradstreet so that others can obtain credit information about your business.

Paying bills on time is one of the most important factors affecting your ability to obtain credit. If you are in a business that has a small circle of vendors and suppliers and your bills are not paid promptly, word will spread and you may be required to pay cash for all transactions.

Using a Business Credit Card

If you decide to open a credit card account for your business, make sure the credit limit is a reasonable one. Use the card for business purchases only, and make payments out of the business account. Avoid masking cash flow problems by charging too much, as you must pay interest and finance charges on the outstanding

The Curio Cabinet
1460 Park Lane Avenue
Boulder, Colorado 80312 (303) 468–1476

APPLICATION FOR CREDIT

NAME _____ PARENT COMPANY (IF SUBSIDIARY) _____

ADDRESS _____ PHONE _____

CITY, STATE, ZIP _____ FAX _____

TYPE OF BUSINESS _____ YEAR ESTABLISHED _____

AT PRESENT LOCATION SINCE _____ PURCHASE ORDER REQUIRED? _____

THE FOLLOWING INFORMATION MUST BE COMPLETED IN FULL. ALL INFORMATION WILL BE HELD IN STRICTEST CONFIDENCE.

COMPANY OFFICERS:

NAME AND TITLE _____

NAME AND TITLE _____

NAME AND TITLE _____

TAX EXEMPT STATUS? _____ (IF YES, PLEASE ENCLOSE LETTER OF EXEMPTION.)

CREDIT REFERENCES: (LIST ONLY THOSE WITH WHICH YOUR BUSINESS HAS CURRENT ACCOUNTS.)

1. FIRM NAME _____ PHONE _____ BUSINESS TYPE _____
   ADDRESS _____ CITY, STATE, ZIP _____

2. FIRM NAME _____ PHONE _____ BUSINESS TYPE _____
   ADDRESS _____ CITY, STATE, ZIP _____

3. FIRM NAME _____ PHONE _____ BUSINESS TYPE _____
   ADDRESS _____ CITY, STATE, ZIP _____

FINANCIAL INFORMATION:

BANK NAME _____ ACCT. NO. _____ PHONE _____

ADDRESS _____ CITY, STATE, ZIP _____

I(WE) CERTIFY THAT THE ABOVE INFORMATION IS TRUE AND CORRECT, AND THAT I (WE) CAN AND WILL COMPLY WITH YOUR CREDIT TERMS.

DATE _____ SIGNATURE _____

TITLE _____

Figure 7.7 Application for credit

balance. If your business relies excessively on a credit card without paying the full balance at least once per quarter, your business finances may need to be reevaluated. Large credit card balances will also affect your ability to secure loans for the business. Set up strict guidelines for all credit purchases, especially if more than one employee is authorized to use the account.

Business Loans

Many business owners find it necessary to apply for business loans at some point, whether their companies are new or have been operating for many years. Understanding where to go for a loan and what most lenders require will facilitate your loan negotiations. Financial institutions are in the business of lending. They want to make loans to people with solid businesses or good ideas that have been carefully developed. If you present your request for a business loan in a well-planned, professional manner and have a good credit history, it is likely that you will obtain the desired financial support.

Banks and credit unions are the most obvious sources of loans. Some financial institutions have stringent requirements for making business loans; some make a special effort to help small businesses and/or minority-based firms. If you are a small business owner, ask entrepreneurs in your area for recommendations. Commercial finance companies specialize in lending money to small and medium-sized manufacturers and wholesalers. You may qualify for a finance company loan if you are unable to obtain one from a bank or other financial institution. A third source of financing is the Small Business Administration (SBA), a federal government organization created in 1953 to help small businesses succeed and grow. SBA loans have some unusual requirements (for instance, you must be rejected by two private lenders before the SBA will consider your application), so visit the SBA office in your area to obtain literature about its loans.

Both business and personal loans fall into two major categories: secured and unsecured. A *secured loan* is one for which the borrower provides collateral to guarantee payment of the loan. The collateral can be a house, a car, or some other asset. If the loan is not paid, the lender has the legal right to seize the collateral and use it to pay the loan. An *unsecured loan* is provided simply on the basis of the borrower's creditworthiness. Unsecured loans are usually for smaller amounts than secured loans and their interest rate may be higher.

Lenders offer a wide variety of loan terms, so check with several to make sure you get the best interest rate and length of time to pay back the loan. Because they often lend to high-risk borrowers, finance companies generally charge higher interest rates than banks. Ask for brochures and disclosures that detail loan conditions and review them carefully.

Many loans are designed for specialized purposes, such as *accounts receivable loans, inventory loans,* and *retail sales financing.* Some of these are short-term loans designed for businesses that need extra funds to help with temporary cash flow problems. When talking with lenders, describe your business and its needs fully to see if any specialized loans are available to you.

What a Lender Requires from You

When a financial institution approves a loan, it is lending money that depositors have entrusted to the institution for safekeeping, so its officers must do their best to ensure that the money will be repaid. Depending on the lender's internal guidelines, the loan officer who interviews you will have the authority to make certain decisions about loans. At some financial institutions, applications are reviewed by a committee. The loan officer or committee will evaluate your probability of succeeding in business to determine your ability to repay a loan.

Most lenders ask business owners for a business plan, current business financial statements or projected financial statements, and personal financial statements (a list of personal assets and liabilities). The loan officer or committee will consider several factors when evaluating your loan application. For instance, lenders usually do not want to supply more than 50 percent of the capital needed to start a business. If you need a loan for more than 50 percent of the needed capital, you should look for other sources, such as a silent partner, or wait until you have saved at least half of the amount needed to start your business.

Loan evaluation also involves consideration of your type of business. The economic conditions affecting that business sector will be evaluated to determine whether a downturn is likely. The loan officer will also consider whether the business will offer a unique service or product line and whether excess competition may cause it to fail. The location of the business, its past growth and future potential, your financial management, and other internal procedures will also be evaluated.

MORTGAGE TABLE

To calculate monthly mortgage payments, divide the loan amount by $100,000. Locate the applicable rate of interest in the following table and note the figure in the column under the term of the loan. Multiply that figure by the result obtained when the loan amount was divided by $100,000. The final figure will be the mortgage payment.

Rate (%)	Length of mortgage in years					
	5	**10**	**15**	**20**	**25**	**30**
5.0	1,887.12	1,060.66	790.79	659.96	584.59	536.82
5.5	1,910.12	1,085.26	817.08	687.89	614.09	567.79
6.0	1,933.28	1,110.21	843.86	716.43	644.30	599.55
6.5	1,956.61	1,135.48	871.11	745.57	675.21	632.07
7.0	1,980.12	1,161.08	898.83	775.30	706.78	665.30
7.5	2,003.79	1,187.02	927.01	805.59	738.99	699.21

Rate (%)	Length of mortgage in years					
	5	**10**	**15**	**20**	**25**	**30**
8.0	2,027.64	1,213.28	955.65	836.44	771.82	733.76
8.5	2,051.65	1,239.86	984.74	867.82	805.23	768.91
9.0	2,075.84	1,266.76	1,014.27	899.73	839.20	804.62
9.5	2,100.19	1,293.98	1,044.22	932.13	873.70	840.85
10.0	2,124.70	1,321.51	1,074.61	965.02	908.70	877.57
10.5	2,149.39	1,349.35	1,105.40	998.38	944.18	914.74
11.0	2,174.24	1,377.50	1,136.60	1,032.19	980.11	952.32
11.5	2,199.26	1,405.95	1,168.19	1,066.43	1,016.47	990.29
12.0	2,224.44	1,434.71	1,200.17	1,101.09	1,053.22	1,028.61
12.5	2,249.79	1,463.76	1,232.52	1,136.14	1,090.35	1,067.26
13.0	2,275.31	1,493.11	1,265.24	1,171.58	1,127.84	1,106.20
13.5	2,300.98	1,522.74	1,298.32	1,207.37	1,165.64	1,145.41
14.0	2,326.83	1,552.66	1,331.74	1,243.52	1,203.76	1,184.87
14.5	2,352.83	1,582.87	1,365.50	1,280.00	1,242.16	1,224.56
15.0	2,378.99	1,613.35	1,399.59	1,316.79	1,280.83	1,264.44
15.5	2,405.32	1,644.11	1,433.99	1,353.88	1,319.75	1,304.52
16.0	2,431.81	1,675.13	1,468.70	1,391.26	1,358.89	1,344.76
16.5	2,458.45	1,706.42	1,503.71	1,428.90	1,398.24	1,385.15
17.0	2,485.26	1,737.98	1,539.00	1,466.80	1,437.80	1,425.68
17.5	2,512.22	1,769.79	1,574.58	1,504.94	1,477.53	1,466.33
18.0	2,539.34	1,801.85	1,610.42	1,543.31	1,517.43	1,507.09
18.5	2,566.62	1,834.17	1,646.52	1,581.90	1,557.48	1,547.94
19.0	2,594.06	1,866.72	1,682.88	1,620.68	1,597.68	1,588.89
19.5	2,621.64	1,899.52	1,719.47	1,659.66	1,638.01	1,629.92
20.0	2,649.39	1,932.56	1,756.30	1,698.82	1,678.45	1,671.02
20.5	2,677.29	1,965.82	1,793.35	1,738.15	1,719.01	1,712.18
21.0	2,705.34	1,999.32	1,830.61	1,777.64	1,759.66	1,753.40
21.5	2,733.54	2,033.03	1,868.08	1,817.28	1,800.41	1,794.67
22.0	2,761.89	2,066.97	1,905.76	1,857.06	1,841.24	1,835.98

Credit Checks

If your business is a sole proprietorship or partnership, the lender will conduct a thorough credit check on you and your partners, if any. This is because a sole proprietor is, in essence, personally borrowing money; in a partnership, the partners are borrowing money. Credit checks usually involve the services of a national credit rating company, such as TRW, Trans Union, or Equifax.

Potential lenders will review your credit history to determine your total amount of indebtedness. This helps them evaluate a prospective borrower's ability to repay a loan. Your credit report will show the institutions to which you owe money, outstanding balances, and monthly payments. If you are a cosigner or a joint borrower on any loan, that will also show on your credit report. Federal, state, and county judgments or liens and the status of any student loans are included, too. The credit report will show delinquencies of 30 days or more that have been reported by creditors. Bankruptcies will show on a credit history for seven to ten years, depending on the type of bankruptcy.

If you have delinquent items or a bankruptcy on your record, it is important to tell the truth about such items on the loan application and explain the circumstances fully. One 30-day delinquency probably will not cause your loan application to be denied, but several such items or longer periods of delinquency may cause difficulty.

When reviewing a loan application, many financial institutions will examine the prospective borrower's *debt ratio,* which is obtained by dividing total gross monthly income by total monthly expenses. The number obtained is the percentage of an applicant's income that is already committed to repaying other debts. Payments on the new loan being considered will be included in this calculation. An acceptable debt ratio depends on several factors, including the amount of money an applicant will have available after all bills are paid. This sum of money is called an applicant's *discretionary dollars,* the funds available for variable monthly expenses. The institution will determine the amount of discretionary dollars that an applicant must have available by considering how many people are supported by that amount and/or the cash flow needs of the business.

Counteroffers

Occasionally, a financial institution will make a counteroffer on a loan application. This may occur if the borrower does not have sufficient credit history for the institution to judge creditworthiness. If a counteroffer is made, this indicates that the lending institution wants to do business with you. Be willing to work with them to negotiate a loan that is acceptable to both parties.

INTEREST CHARTS

Fundamentally, almost all for-profit organizations depend on capitalization, which comes from two sources: equity and debt. Rarely is *equity* (money accumulated from sales of shares and/or products and services) sufficient to finance operations on a steady and reliable basis. Thus, a practical, balanced capitalization plan usually includes borrowing money from an outside source. This type of *debt* is good business when the use of borrowed funds generates more profits than the total interest payments due on the loan.

How do you chart interest rates and related costs to determine whether your organization is financially sound? Think of borrowing money as a form of rental, similar to rental expenses for office space, equipment, or warehouse facilities. Interest charting has three components: (1) the *principal* (total amount borrowed, whether received in a lump sum or predetermined increments); (2) the *rate* charged, expressed as a percentage of the principal; and (3) the *time/maturity factor,* calculated as the periods during which regular payments are due and the date on which the final payment must be made. Most interest charts are calculated in annual terms, as rates are traditionally defined on a 12-month scale. A simple way to chart interest is to use the formula

interest = principal × rate × time

In addition, the method of calculating interest depends on whether it is simple or compound. *Simple interest* is a charge based on the principal only. For example, if you purchase a computer that costs $5,000 and the supplier agrees to a simple interest rate of 14 percent with payment due in 12 months, you will owe $5,700 at the end of the year. Using the formula, *interest = principal × rate × time,* that would be $700 = $5,000 × .14 × 1 year. At the end of that year, you might again negotiate a simple interest rate by paying just the $700 interest due and agreeing to pay an additional $700 interest plus the $5,000 principal at the end of the second year. The second year's interest is calculated only on the original amount borrowed.

Compound interest is more common in deferred-payment agreements or loans contracted by businesses. It includes calculation of interest on interest as well as principal. Thus, in the preceding example, the figures would be similar for the first year, but different for the second. For the second year's calculations, the balance due at the end of the first year ($5,700) would be treated as the new principal base. To determine total compound interest on a loan, it is helpful to prepare an interest chart, as shown:

interest = principal × rate × time	*principal + interest = loan balance*
year 1: $ 700 = $5,000 × .14 × 1 year	$5,000 + $ 700 = $5,700
year 2: $ 798 = $5,700 × .14 × 1 year	$5,700 + $ 798 = $6,498
year 3: $ 910 = $6,498 × .14 × 1 year	$6,498 + $ 910 = $7,408
year 4: $1,037 = $7,408 × .14 × 1 year	$7,408 + $1,037 = $8,445
year 5: $1,182 = $8,445 × .14 × 1 year	$8,445 + $1,182 = $9,627

In this example, you would be paying $98 interest on interest the second year, as well as on the principal, and so on. Total compound interest at the end of the second year would be $1,498. By the end of the fifth year, compound interest would be $1,182 for that year alone. Compounding entails a substantial increase over periods longer than a year, even when payments are made regularly. (In the hypothetical example given, no payments were made during the five-year period, so that compound interest was calculated on the full amount of the principal and the yearly interest each year. Of course, you should subtract the total payments made during the year at each year's end before recalculating the new principal base for the next year.)

Preparing interest charts before making financial commitments is good business. You must ask yourself if the products, supplies, or services to be purchased are worth the steadily increasing amount of interest to be paid. Would it be better to do without them? Is there a less expensive means of financing what you need?

It may be to your advantage to calculate compound interest on a time period of less than one year, working with a fraction of the annual rate. As a year consists of 12 months, a yearly interest rate can be figured on a monthly basis by the formula

$$monthly\ rate = yearly\ rate \times \frac{1}{12}$$

For example, using a 14 percent annual rate, the effective compound interest rates for shorter periods would be as follows:

$$monthly\ rate = yearly\ rate \times \tfrac{1}{12}$$

$.0117 = .14 \times \tfrac{1}{12}$	(monthly interest rate = 1.17%)
$.0350 = .14 \times \tfrac{1}{12} \times 3$ months	(quarterly interest rate = 3.5%)
$.0700 = .14 \times \tfrac{1}{12} \times 6$ months	(semiannual interest rate = 7%)

Business Grants

A grant is money that need not be repaid, usually from a foundation or government agency. A brochure from the Small Business Administration describes business grants as "money that you are given to pursue a project and produce something that is beneficial for the greater good of society." In a sense, grants are repaid by a firm's use of the money to achieve objectives listed in the grant application. Billions of dollars in grants are available to businesses in the United States, from some 1,100 federal assistance programs and hundreds of others administered by state and regional agencies and private philanthropies. A business must specify a need that will benefit the public to qualify for a grant. Determine whether you can meet this basic criterion before beginning the application process.

The first step in obtaining a business grant is to learn what grants are available for your business. This is not an easy task, as there are so many different types of grants and so many agencies offering them. A good place to begin is to call or write the Federal Information Center, P.O. Box 600, Cumberland, MD 21501-600, phone 301-722-9098 (toll-free number: 800-688-9889). Ask for information about the center nearest you; it will have localized information and perhaps a database for computer searches. Other recommended sources of information are the *Catalog of Federal Domestic Assistance,* which is published annually (write the U.S. Government Printing Office, Superintendent of Documents, Washington, DC 20402) and *The Complete Guide to Getting a Grant* by Laurie Blum.

What are your chances of obtaining a grant? A recent survey indicated that, over a seven-year period, more than 15 percent of business research grant applications were approved. This does not seem to be a high approval rate until you consider that half of all grant applications are rejected due to sloppy or inadequate requests. The key is to write a grant proposal that presents your case in a positive manner, with a realistic appraisal of your needs and attention to detail. Suggestions for writing successful grant proposals are clearly spelled out in the resources suggested above. Here are a few tips:

1. Make sure your request is addressed to the right committee.
2. Ask for assistance in a positive way, not as though you are asking for charity.
3. Use a sales approach and be forceful, but not aggressive, in presenting your case. Be enthusiastic about your business or project.
4. Emphasize community benefits that would result from work made possible by a grant to your company. Bear in mind that your goals need not be totally altruistic. For example, you might describe how the grant would enable your business to produce better products for public consumption, and that new jobs would be created by the expansion made possible by a grant.
5. Mentally picture the recipients of your grant proposal and imagine their reactions to your reasoning. How would you respond to this proposal if you were on the grant committee?
6. Fine-tune the technical details in your proposal, following instructions from the grant committee carefully and making sure your facts are accurate. Get to the point of your application as quickly as possible, but make sure to include all necessary details.
7. Use a respectful tone and dignified style in your presentation. If you are uneasy about your writing skills, seek professional help. Such organizations as the Service Corps of Retired Executives (SCORE) can provide excellent advice at no cost. Call your local chamber of commerce to contact the SCORE in your area.
8. Try again if your first grant application is not approved—there is plenty of grant money available.

Understanding Computer Financial Software

With the help of computers, keeping track of financial information and other data is much simpler than in the past. Instead of entering numbers and balancing accounts manually, you can purchase software to do most of the work. Computers can simplify accounts receivable, invoicing, accounts payable, payroll, and many other bookkeeping functions, as well as store data such as customer information. Financial software comes in three basic types: accounting, spreadsheet, and database programs.

Accounting Programs

Accounting applications are preconfigured, specialized databases. Many are designed specifically for small businesses. These software packages come with templates for every type of financial record a business might need. (A *template* is a blank record already designed to arrange and calculate numbers for a certain type of financial function.) Accounting packages include templates for your general ledger, inventory, accounts receivable, accounts payable, purchase orders, invoicing, and payroll. Some also include templates for financial statements, bank account records, and budgeting. When choosing packaged software, find out if any are specifically designed for your type of business.

Payroll accounting programs such as Intuit QuickBooks 3.1 or QuickBooks Pro include yearly federal/state withholding schedule updates on disks or CD-ROMs. Once you have entered each employee's salary or rate of pay, tax withholding status, and deduction amounts/types, preparing a payroll means just inputting the amount of regular and overtime hours worked and various types of leave taken. The software will then determine each employee's gross pay; calculate, subtract, and record all tax withholdings and other deductions; keep a record of leave earned and taken; and present a completed payroll summary for your use in writing checks and making tax deposits. Some programs will print the checks for you.

Packaged accounting software also can be useful for keeping track of home finances. This type of software contains templates for home budgeting, bank account tracking, investment records, and tax records. Popular accounting programs for home use are Intuit Quicken Deluxe 5.0 for Windows/Quicken 6.0 for Mac and Managing Your Money by MECA.

Spreadsheet Programs

Spreadsheet programs are tools for compiling numbers and performing comparisons. With spreadsheets, you can instruct the computer to perform certain calculations to help you see the relationships between numbers. This software usually requires that you set up the desired type of spreadsheet before it can provide the information you want. Small business managers could use a spreadsheet to compare competitors' prices, for example. Some popular spreadsheet programs are Lotus 1-2-3, Microsoft Excel 7.0 for Windows 95/Excel 5.0 for Mac, and Corel Quattro Pro.

You probably use a database every day without thinking about it (the telephone directory, for example). A computer database can organize a variety of related information such as customers' names, addresses, phone numbers, and contact persons, as well as their most recent dates of purchase and types of merchandise bought. Database records can be programmed to automatically update information entered in another part of the same database, so that entering one customer invoice payment updates several different parts of that customer's record. A generic database software program can perform all of the functions included in accounting software packages. However, you must set up or create your own templates for each type of financial record needed.

Database Programs

Databases can also be valuable marketing tools. If your database keeps track of the types of merchandise each customer purchases, you can ask the computer to generate a list of all customers likely to be interested in a special sale on those products. A personalized letter can then be sent to just those customers. Popular database software includes Claris Filemaker Pro, Microsoft Access, Lotus Approach, and Corel Paradox, which is available as part of Corel's Professional Office suite or its OfficePro package. (Note that Corel now owns the WordPerfect word-processing programs that dominate the industry, so using Corel's financial software would make merging word-processing documents with financial records very easy if your office already uses WordPerfect.)

Choosing the Right Software

Selecting financial software depends on several factors. How much do you want to customize your software? How confident are you of your ability to learn the software? How much money can you spend? Do you want your financial software to interface (communicate) with other programs, such as word-processing software? Packaged accounting programs are usually less expensive than database programs, but they also provide less flexibility. With packaged software, use is limited to the record-keeping system provided. Be sure to find out how much a package can be customized to suit your needs. Database packages provide a great deal of flexibility, but also require more work. However, by using a database package, you can set up an accounting system to meet the special needs of your business.

Integrated systems (suites) are the most expensive and most flexible programs. They include spreadsheet, database, and word-processing programs. Such software packages have incredible capabilities to merge and incorporate data from all three programs, meeting virtually any financial or marketing need. Microsoft Office, Corel Professional Office, and Lotus SmartSuite are popular suites. (*See also* Software Programs for Offices, page 105.)

Sources of Further Information

Organizations

General Assistance

Chambers of commerce—Check with yours to see if there is a local Service Corps of Retired Executives (SCORE). SCORE members provide valuable business advice at no charge as a service to the community. Many chambers of commerce also have extensive reference libraries and business collections, and their staff members are skilled at helping to locate information.

Government agencies—Some exist solely to provide information to the public, and their employees can help you access a vast amount of information on almost every facet of U.S. life and business. They are often criticized by professionals and business executives for a disinterested or bureaucratic approach to problems. The key to getting results is doing your homework to determine which federal, state, or local agencies are likely to be most helpful to you.

Merchant confederations—These may or may not be affiliated with chambers of commerce or other national groups. They are composed mainly of regional or local members whose objective is to help each other in business.

Trade associations—Organized for almost every profession and field of business, these associations will usually respond to inquiries from nonmembers as well as members.

Accounting Firms

These companies are among the top accounting firms in the United States. One of them may be right for your business:

Arthur Andersen & Co.
1345 Avenue of the Americas
New York, NY 10105
Phone 212-708-4000

Baird, Kurtz & Dobson
901 East St. Louis Street
Springfield, MO 65806
Phone 417-865-8701

Coopers & Lybrand
1301 Avenue of the Americas
New York, NY 10019
Phone 212-259-1000

Deloitte & Touche
World Financial Center
New York, NY 10045
Phone 212-436-2000

Ernst & Young
787 Seventh Avenue
New York, NY 10019
Phone 212-773-3000

Grant Thornton
One Prudential Plaza
Chicago, IL 60601
Phone 312-856-0001

KPMG Peat Marwick
767 Fifth Avenue
New York, NY 10153
Phone 212-909-5000

McGladrey & Pullen
102 West Second Street
Davenport, IA 52801
Phone 319-324-0447

Moss Adams
1001 Fourth Avenue, Suite 2900
Seattle, WA 98154
Phone 206-223-1820

Plante & Moran
27400 Northwestern Highway
Southfield, MI 48034
Phone 810-220-0070

Insurance Firms

The following companies are among the largest and best-known providers of business insurance in the United States:

Aetna Life & Casualty
151 Farmington Avenue
Hartford, CT 06156
Phone 203-273-0123

Allstate Life
2775 Sanders Road
Northbrook, IL 60062
Phone 708-402-5000

Cigna
900 Cottage Grove Road
Hartford, CT 06152
Phone 203-726-6000

Equitable Life Assurance
787 Seventh Avenue
New York, NY 10019
Phone 212-554-1234

IDS Life
American Express Financial Advisers
733 Marquette Avenue
Minneapolis, MN 55402
Phone 612-671-3131

Jackson National Life
5901 Executive Drive
Lansing, MI 48911
Phone 517-394-3400

John Hancock Mutual Life
101 Huntington Avenue
Boston, MA 02199
Phone 617-572-6000

Lincoln National Life
1300 South Clinton Street
Fort Wayne, IN 46802
Phone 219-455-2000

Massachusetts Mutual Life
1295 State Street
Springfield, MA 01111
Phone 413-788-8411

Metropolitan Life Insurance
1 Madison Avenue
New York, NY 10010
Phone 212-578-2211

Mutual of New York
1740 Broadway
New York, NY 10019
Phone 212-708-2000

Nationwide Life
1 Nationwide Plaza
Columbus, OH 43215
Phone 614-249-7111

New York Life Insurance
51 Madison Avenue
New York, NY 10010
Phone 212-576-7000

Northwestern Mutual Life
720 East Wisconsin Avenue
Milwaukee, WI 53202
Phone 414-271-1444

Pacific Mutual Life
700 Newport Center Drive
Newport Beach, CA 92660
Phone 714-640-3011

Principal Mutual Life
711 High Street
Des Moines, IA 50392
Phone 515-247-5111

Prudential of America
751 Broad Street
Newark, NJ 07107
Phone 201-802-6000

Travelers
1 Tower Square
Hartford, CT 06183
Phone 203-277-0111

State Farm Life
1 State Farm Plaza
Bloomington, IL 61710
Phone 309-766-2311

Variable Annuity Life
2919 Allen Parkway
Houston, TX 77019
Phone 713-526-5251

The following associations may also be of help in selecting insurance coverage for your firm:

Insurance Fund Foundation
13555 SE 36th Street, Suite 105
Bellevue, WA 98006
Phone 206-747-6631

National Insurance Consumer
Helpline
Phone 800-942-4242

Insurance Information Institute
110 William Street
New York, NY 10038
Phone 212-669-9200

Risk and Insurance Management
Society
205 East 42nd Street
New York, NY 10017
Phone 212-286-9292

(*See also* Chapter 12, Business Resources, page 455, for a detailed list of organizations and how to contact them.)

Books and Literature

Edwards, Paul, and Sarah Edwards. *Working from Home.* 4th ed. Los Angeles: Tarcher/ Putnam, 1994.

Harper, Stephen C. *The McGraw-Hill Guide to Starting Your Own Business.* New York: McGraw-Hill, 1991.

Ragan, Robert C. *Step-by-Step Bookkeeping: The Complete Handbook for Small Business.* New York: Sterling Publishing, 1992.

Trade periodicals are published for almost every field of business and industry, even those that are very specialized. Most trade journals also provide free or low-cost services for subscribers seeking solutions to professional problems. Call the local library's reference desk for help in locating the one for you, or browse Web sites for your profession on the Internet. Periodicals of interest should be listed when a business database is queried about your specialty.

On-Line Resources

Accountant On Call service, a nationwide accounting firm
http://www.aocnet.com

Credit management information and support
http://www.creditworthy.com

Electronic Accountant service
http://www.electronicaccountant.com

H&R Block's Web site for information on frequently asked tax questions
http://hrblock/com.tax

North American Free Trade Agreement
gopher://cyfer.esusda.gov/ll/ace/policy/nafta

U.S. Bureau of Labor Statistics
http://stats.bls.gov:80/blshome.html

U.S. Department of Commerce Economic Data
gopher://una.hh.lib.umich.edu/ll/ebb

U.S. Department of the Treasury—Internal Revenue Service
http://irs.ustreas.gov

U.S. Federal Reserve Economic Data
http://www.stls.frb.org/fred

8

Legalities

Hiring the Right Attorney

This chapter is intended to provide an overview of some common legal issues facing business owners. For specific legal advice, it is best to consult a qualified attorney. In fact, most businesses require the services of an attorney for needs ranging from incorporation to contract preparation to trademark registration, so even a small company should secure the services of a good attorney. The first step in hiring a lawyer is to consider the present and future legal needs of the business so that the type and volume of legal work to be done can be estimated with reasonable accuracy. It is then useful to get recommendations from colleagues and friends, especially those who are in the same field of business with similar legal requirements. Ask which lawyers work well with people, and whether clients are usually satisfied with this firm or individual's work, remembering that laypeople are not always qualified to evaluate professionals and may overestimate an attorney's skills and success ratio. Also, clients who recommend legal firms often receive preferential treatment such as reduced fees or priority service. Thus, a recommendation may be colored by a client's self-interest.

Another possibility is to consider firms that provide accounting as well as legal services. Many CPAs are also attorneys or can recommend competent legal representatives. It may be best to secure the services of one firm to fill both needs (*see* Getting Outside Help with Finances, page 309).

On the other hand, there are advantages to having separate firms for each function. They may each serve as in-house auditors for the other, as accounting and legal functions often overlap. Law directories are also useful for getting more information about lawyers. *The Martindale-Hubbell Law Directory,* published annually, is available in most libraries; it is an excellent source of information about attorneys and their areas of expertise. A list of local lawyers can also be obtained from Legal Directories Publishing Company, Inc., Suite 201, 1314 Westwood Boulevard, Los Angeles, CA 90024. Another resource is your local law school. Law professors, rarely called on to recommend lawyers, can be quite knowledgeable and willing to help. The state bar association should be contacted to ensure that an attorney under consideration is properly licensed and has no record of disciplinary action.

A prospective attorney should be interviewed before the final decision is made to hire that individual or his or her firm. Lawyers who are not willing to be interviewed or who want to charge for this initial consultation should be approached with caution; however, a consultation fee may be worth the investment if other factors are promising or if only a few attorneys specialize in your field of business. Factors to consider during the interview include whether questions asked are relevant and whether the attorney appears interested in your business and legal concerns. Ask about the candidate's experience in dealing with similar situations and about past successes and failures.

When a decision has been made, a written fee agreement should be prepared before the attorney begins work. For most business matters, an hourly rate is customary, perhaps with contingent incentives (bonuses tied to success in meeting the company's objectives) or caps (limits to ensure that the attorney does not expend an inordinate amount of time on a case without prior approval from the business owner or manager). When a malpractice suit must be handled, the entire fee should be on a contingency basis.

It is also important to remember that one lawyer's experience may be ideal for some of your company's legal matters but not others. If a business's legal problems extend into different areas of law, several attorneys may be needed to handle the different situations. For this reason as well as basic courtesy, it is a good idea to write a diplomatic thank-you note to anyone who was interviewed but not hired so that this person may be contacted to fill other needs. Also, careful selection of an attorney should eliminate many problems in advance, but no strategy is foolproof. There may be unanticipated difficulties with the lawyer chosen by your business, necessitating reconsideration of other candidates in the future.

Business Licenses and Permits

Federal, state, and local governments require that new businesses obtain various licenses and permits before opening. It is very important to get the necessary licenses and permits as early as possible, as these may determine whether a certain type of business can be opened at the desired location. It is the owner's responsibility to secure the necessary documents and pay the required fees—not having the needed paperwork could result in fines. To find out what kind of licenses and permits you need, check with the local Small Business Administration office (call 800-827-5722 to find the nearest branch), your state's department of commerce, the local chamber of commerce, or trade associations. Start with local requirements, as city or county authorities will often provide valuable information about compliance with state and federal requirements.

Local Permits and Licenses. Many types of business are required to obtain fire safety and room occupancy permits, zoning permits, and building permits for renovations. Additional licenses may also be needed; for example, a food-related business will probably need a food and beverage license and a health department permit, as well.

State Licenses. Most business-related licenses are issued by state agencies. These include professional permits for lawyers, architects, doctors, nurses, pharmacists, accountants, funeral directors, real estate agents, tax preparers, mechanics, contractors, hairstylists, cosmetologists, and other skilled personnel. Obtaining these permits is typically the responsibility of the individual, but business owners should make sure job candidates are properly licensed before hiring them. Usually, a business must also have a tax registration and employer identification number, a sales tax license and resale permit (commercial), and workers' compensation and unemployment insurance. State licenses are also required to sell food, alcohol, or firearms; a permit for hazardous wastes and emissions may be issued by a state agency or multistate regional authority. Some states require a general license for any type of business. Of course, all business vehicles must have appropriate motor vehicle licenses and inspection stickers, and a special driver's license is required to operate certain types of vehicles.

Federal Requirements. Required federal licenses are limited to businesses selling or manufacturing alcohol, tobacco, or firearms; dealing with meat products or drugs; dispensing financial advice; engaging in interstate trucking; or broadcasting over radio or television. But most businesses need federal tax identification numbers (*see* Taxpayer Identification Numbers, page 302).

Incorporating a Business

There is no definitive answer to the question "Should I incorporate my business?" Before making a decision, it is best to consult an attorney who can explain all of the costs, risks, tax advantages, and legal restrictions that apply to each type of business organization to be considered. (*See also* Proprietorships, Partnerships, and Corporations, page 283, for an overview of the characteristics of common business structures.)

The main features of corporations include the following:

1. *Transferability of shares*—Ownership (shares) can be sold, transferred, or inherited without dissolving the corporation. A sole proprietorship or partnership no longer exists when an owner or partner dies or leaves the business.

2. *Centralized management*—It is often cost effective for corporations to provide benefits such as workers' compensation, health insurance, and retirement plans, as even the company's contributions to the owners' plans are tax-deductible if the owners are also salaried employees.

3. *Indefinite life*—A corporation's term of existence is not specified or tied to the original owners'/shareholders' continuing participation. This stability is reassuring to employees, customers, shareholders, and creditors. (Partnership agreements generally delineate a specified term of existence.)

4. *Liability protection*—A corporation is an entity completely separate from its owners' personal holdings and interests. The owners will not be held personally liable (their personal assets will not be at risk) for payment of the corporation's debts, taxes, or legal judgments.

Any business with two or more of these four characteristics should be incorporated, as the Internal Revenue Service (IRS) will tax it as a corporation. Some of the newer types of business structures, such as limited liability companies, offer some features of corporations, but not all. Therefore, it is important to follow the advice of a legal expert before deciding on the form your business will take.

There are also drawbacks associated with incorporation. The government regulates corporations' activities to ensure that their advantages are not misused—for example, a corporation owner who enjoys limited liability benefits without truly separating personal and corporate assets can be held liable for corporate debt. This is known as "piercing the corporate veil." There are legal and application fees involved in setting up a corporation. Also, more detailed record keeping is usually required for corporations than for unincorporated businesses. Small business owners may choose another option because of the complexities involved (*see* Proprietorships, Partnerships, and Corporations, page 283).

How to Incorporate

Before taking any action, it is advisable to enlist the help of an experienced lawyer and to check with the IRS for complete instructions. Several steps are usually necessary to form a corporation.

- Owners must determine the best state in which to incorporate. Typically, a company owner will choose the state in which the business is located, although a business that operates across state lines (and almost all do, theoretically) can be incorporated in any state. Some states, such as Delaware, offer better tax incentives than others.
- Articles of incorporation must be drafted. These articles establish the corporation and set the guidelines under which it will operate.
- Each investor must sign a shareholder's (subscription) agreement. This explains the purpose and structure of the corporation and how stocks will be distributed. A small business owner/employee will often sign an employment agreement outlining the responsibilities of the position and the compensation to be paid. Each shareholder may also sign a buy-sell agreement to restrict the sales of shares to outsiders to keep ownership of the corporation in the hands of its creators.
- A board of directors to oversee company operations should be elected at the first shareholders' meeting. Subsequent meetings are usually held once a year.
- The first board of directors' meeting should be held. At this first meeting, company officers—a president and vice president, at least—should be elected; corporate bylaws (company rules) adopted; a company bank account opened; and the first issue of stocks approved.
- Stocks must be formally issued. Each shareholder should get a certificate indicating his or her amount of shares (stock) in the company.
- A federal taxpayer identification number must be obtained. This registers the corporation with the Internal Revenue Service and allows the company to begin operations.

A new source of help for business owners planning to incorporate can be found on the Internet. A number of legal firms have established Web sites that offer the convenience of incorporation via on-line responses to queries and electronic transfers of needed documentation (*see* On-Line Resources, page 361).

Contracts

Essential Elements

Contracts are instrumental in many business dealings, such as buying and selling goods, leasing office space and equipment, and entering into a partnership or joint venture. A formal agreement can be simple or complex, but all contracts must contain two elements: the *consideration,* which is the money, goods, or other things of value exchanged; and the *acceptance,* an agreement between the parties.

When entering into a contract, particularly one that is complex and detailed, it is best to have an attorney's help. Because oral agreements are difficult to substantiate in disputes, written contracts are preferable and sometimes necessary (as in real estate deals, long-term agreements, and agreements involving large sums). Whether writing a contract yourself or having an attorney prepare it, make sure it is clear, complete, and concise. Use as little legal jargon as possible. The contract may take any form, but should contain the following elements:

- name, address, and complete identification (relevant background information) of each party
- dated signature of each party or the person legally authorized to sign for each
- all specifications of the agreement
- date the agreement will be fulfilled (for example, the date goods will be delivered and payment made)
- duration of the contract (how long it will remain in effect)
- warranty agreement explaining what will happen if one side cannot fulfill the terms of the contract
- conditions under which the parties can terminate or change the agreement
- arbitration agreement specifying how disputes will be settled and who will be responsible for legal costs
- indication of the state whose laws apply in the agreement

Other inclusions may be required for certain types of agreements and in certain states.

The Universal Commercial Code

The Universal Commercial Code (UCC) is a legal guideline for business contracts. It has been adopted, at least in part, by all states. It contains rules for contracts dealing with the sale of goods. The UCC provides that a contract is not valid if it has not been signed, if it has expired, if the offer has been revoked, or if a reasonable amount of time has passed without an agreement between the parties. A contract is also invalid if it involves illegal acts, if it was signed under duress, if the terms have been misrepresented, or if a legitimate mistake was made or misunderstanding occurred. Contracts found to be exceedingly unfair may be ruled invalid based on consumer protection laws or other legal considerations. All commercial business owners should be familiar with the UCC.

Employment Contracts

An employment contract is an agreement between employer and employee delineating the duties of the employee and the compensation to be paid by the employer. Though contracts are not necessary in most hiring situations, they can sometimes be important in clearly defining expectations. Inventors, writers, artists, and scientists are often bound by contracts that give ownership of their creative work to the companies employing them. Some employment contracts contain confidentiality and noncompete agreements to protect the company's business and trade secrets. In addition, companies often contract employees for defined periods of time. This ensures that time and money invested in training will not be wasted by employees who stay a brief time and then leave for a better position.

Any viable employment contract must conform to all applicable laws. Typical elements of such a contract include the following:

- delineation of salary and any bonuses or commissions to be paid; benefits such as health insurance and retirement plans; paid expenses (auto expenses, moving expenses, etc.); and stock options, if any
- complete description of the position, including title, authority, duties, and responsibilities
- work hours, vacation, sick leave, and holiday leave
- consent to relocate, if applicable
- duration of the contract or term of employment, and conditions for renewal
- whether the agreement continues if the business is sold
- conditions of contract termination, such as permanent disability, death, or bankruptcy of the business
- provisions for failure to perform, including firing and the severance package
- other conditions necessary and specific to the position
- specification of the state under whose laws the contract operates
- arbitration arrangement in case of dispute

Other agreements may be included in the employment contract or be made separately, such as a *noncompete agreement,* a *nondisclosure agreement,* and a *shop rights agreement.*

Noncompete Agreement. Companies often require employees to agree not to compete against the business while working for the company and/or after leaving the company. Those agreements extending beyond employment should be limited to a reasonable period of time and geographical area or they may be judged unfairly restrictive, and thus invalid.

Nondisclosure Agreement. Companies with trade secrets or other proprietary information may ask employees to respect the confidentiality of all information they learn about the company during employment, including data or product formulas, inventions, processes, financial information, and customer lists.

Shop Rights Agreement. By common law, inventions made on company time and with company tools belong to the company. A signed agreement is not necessary, but it helps to reinforce the concept and makes court disputes unnecessary.

Basic Legal Documents That Every Business Needs

Most business managers will need contracts, releases, and other legal agreements from time to time. If your firm uses such documents frequently, it may be worthwhile to purchase a number of legal forms and keep them on file for ready use. Forms may be bought in stationery and office supply stores. For contracts specific to your industry, contact trade organizations or ask other businesses with similar operations. Your local Small Business Administration office may also be of assistance. Sample forms can also be found in books such as *The Complete Book of Small Business Legal Forms* by Daniel Sitarz.

Using Legal Software Packages to Prepare Basic Legal Documents

Some routine legal documents can be prepared without an attorney's assistance by using one of several legal software applications now available. This is not to suggest that a business can forgo hiring an attorney altogether, but to offer an alternative to using preprinted legal forms for run-of-the-mill matters for which most companies do not require the services of an attorney. Such programs usually feature such documents as power of attorney, leases, promissory notes, employment agreements, and wills, with the added benefit of detailed instructions on executing them correctly (necessary signatures, notaries, and witnesses). The quality of these applications varies. One of the best currently available is Quicken Family Lawyer (Parsons Technology). Less comprehensive programs include Do-It-Yourself-Lawyer (Expert Software) and Managing Your Money's Personal Attorney (Meca Software).

Negotiations

There are several stages involved in business negotiations:

1. A working relationship is established.
2. The opening position of each party is stated.
3. Arguments and persuasion are exchanged between the parties.
4. Solutions or alternatives are proposed.
5. Concessions are made (or negotiations break down).
6. A final agreement is reached.

Many factors affect the course and outcome of negotiations. Recognizing these and preparing for them in advance are important. It may even be possible to manipulate some of them to suit your position. Consider the following:

- format of the negotiation (in person, by mail, or on the telephone)
- persons present (top executives or lower level staff)
- location of the meeting (your office, their office, neutral ground)
- time of day (morning, lunch, afternoon, evening)
- projected length of negotiation (several days, one day, an hour)
- deadline for needed agreement (how long you can wait for the deal to be made, and whether the other parties can out-wait you)
- seating arrangement of all parties at the table (facing each other as adversaries, on the same side, in an informal setting with no table at all)
- degree of formality to be maintained during the meeting
- negotiation style of the other party (competitive or cooperative)

Negotiator Styles

Learn as much as possible about the way your counterpart negotiates, and give some thought to your own style. *Competitive negotiators* attempt to get their way by being aggressive. They convey anger, resolution, and a feeling of tension. While this may intimidate their counterparts into agreement, more often it will alienate and antagonize the opposition and make negotiations difficult, if not impossible. *Cooperative negotiators* seek common ground and fair solutions. They attempt to reach agreement through trust, openness, and reciprocation. This style is more apt to result in effective negotiations, particularly if the other side is also cooperative. But too much willingness to concede will be construed as weakness and will be exploited by aggressive negotiators.

Negotiator Do's and Don'ts

Do:

- Ask for more than you expect to gain so there is room to compromise.
- Be confident and articulate.
- Tell the truth.
- Be fair and realistic.
- Show commitment and resolve.
- State your position in a persuasive manner.
- Prepare for negotiations by getting all of the facts, including advance research on the other side's situation and motives.
- Know your bottom line—the least attractive agreement acceptable.
- Prepare alternatives and possible solutions.
- Watch the opposition's body language.
- Use silence as a tool, listening more than talking.
- Get something in return for each concession made.
- Allow the other side to save face—to feel that they have also won.
- Get the agreement in writing, and have your side prepare the contract.

Don't:

- Be afraid to ask for what you want.
- Make empty claims, threats, or promises.
- Be predictable.
- Show disrespect or make insulting comments.
- Allow the other party to intimidate you.
- Be overly aggressive or adversarial.
- Play games.
- Give in too much or too easily.
- Reveal too much about your needs and motives.
- Be in a hurry to make a deal, when possible.
- Take "no" for an answer!

Protecting What You Have

Patents

Patents protect the rights of inventors to profits from their creations; that is, others cannot make, sell, or use a patented device for profit without the patent owner's permission. To qualify for a patent, an invention must be a useful working object, not just an idea or model; it must be clearly different from any other invention already in existence; and it must not be something that is obvious to anyone working in that particular field. A patent may also be granted for an improvement on an existing invention; for a new design of an existing invention, called a *design patent;* or for the production or discovery of a new variety of plant life, called a *plant patent.*

An invention must be patented within one year of its first use or marketing or its creator loses the right to patent it. It is not necessary to have a patent in order to market an invention, but doing so provides a legal basis for infringement lawsuits. Remember that a patent may be ruled invalid if it is misused or challenged in court.

Only the inventor can apply for a patent, which lasts for 17 years. Qualified patent attorneys can guide you through the patent process:

1. Filing a disclosure document. Though not required, it is a good idea to file a disclosure document for a small fee to the Patent and Trademark Office. By describing the creation through writing and drawings, a disclosure document establishes the invention's date of origin. The document will remain confidential for two years while you work on the patent application.

2. Performing a patent search. Preliminary research is crucial to make sure an invention is original and patentable. The patent application process is long and costly, and this step may save the expense of filing an application for a device that someone else has already registered. A patent lawyer or agent can do the search, or you may try to do it yourself (*see* Conducting a Patent Search, page 354).

3. Completing the application. When you are satisfied that your invention is patentable, obtain patent application forms and instructions by writing to the U.S. Patent and Trademark Office, Commissioner of Patents and Trademarks, Washington, DC 20231. Government Printing Office Publication No. 003-004-006-617, *General Information Concerning Patents,* offers valuable instructions (or call 703-308-4367 for general patent information). Your application should be as thorough as necessary, but also clear and concise. It will contain eight parts or sections:

(a) an abstract, giving the invention's background information

(b) specifications, describing how the invention works

(c) claims, defining the scope of the invention and explaining how it is original

(d) a declaration stating that you believe the invention to be original and that you are its inventor

(e) drawings of the invention—specific standards for drawings are described in the instructions

(f) the proper application fee, which varies depending on whether a company, an independent inventor, or a nonprofit organization is applying for the patent

(g) a transmittal letter documenting everything contained in the application package

(h) a self-addressed stamped postcard that the Patent and Trademark Office will send back to you, informing you that your application has been received and is being processed

4. Waiting for a response. After your case is reviewed, a letter will be sent from the Patent and Trademark Office accepting, rejecting, or requesting alterations in your application. If it is rejected, you may appeal. If clarifications or alterations in the application are requested, you will be given a number of months to resubmit it with the necessary changes. A second Patent Office action will follow, accepting or rejecting the revised application. If your invention is accepted for patenting, a *notice of allowance* will be sent, inviting you to send in the patent fee. The patent deed will be issued on receipt of the fee.

5. Maintaining the patent. The process does not end when a patent deed is granted. Patents must be administered through regular maintenance fees, by marking your invention with a notice (typically its patent number), and by informing the Patent Office if your patent right is sold. Also, it is your responsibility to ensure that your patent is not infringed upon, and to take legal action if it is.

CONDUCTING A PATENT SEARCH

Preliminary research is crucial to make sure an invention is original and patentable. The patent application process is long and costly, and thorough research may prevent the wasted expense of filing an application for a device that someone else has already registered. In addition, pre-searched applications are given a higher priority by the Patent and Trademark Office. For a thorough search, a competent patent lawyer or agent will charge a flat fee or about $50 per hour.

Of course, performing your own patent search may save considerable expense, but this can require large amounts of time to be sure that the search is complete. There is a U.S. Patent Depository Library in most states, and the Patent Public Search Room is in Arlington, Virginia. Use of these resources is free, although a fee may be charged for use of a computer search database, which can make the search much easier.

Copyrights

Copyrights are the equivalent of patents for original creations such as written works, movies, drama, dance, music, and visual art. It is illegal to use copyrighted material without permission for display, reproduction, distribution, adaptation, or performance. It is not necessary for material to be published in order to copyright it, but some creative works—such as ideas, methods, phrases, slogans, and names—cannot be copyrighted.

To obtain the proper registration forms for copyrighting, contact the U.S. Copyright Office, Publications Section LM-455, Library of Congress, Washington, DC 20559, phone 202-707-9100, or use Internet website *www.loc.gov*. For most business uses, Form TX or Form VA is appropriate. Form TX covers all nondramatic literary works, including textbooks, reference materials, catalogs, directories, advertising copy, and computer programs. Form VA includes visual arts such as graphics, photography, architectural blueprints, technical drawings, diagrams, and models. Form PA is used for works to be performed, such as movies, plays, and dance choreography. Form SR is for sound recordings.

Fill out the forms clearly and completely. In addition, send two copies of the work (a photo or sample pages if the work is too large to send), and include the applicable fee (currently $20, payable in check or money order). Send the form, fee, and copies of the work to: Register of Copyrights, Copyright Office, Library of Congress, Washington, DC 20559. The application will be processed in about three months. You will then receive a certificate of registration. It is customary to indicate that a work is copyrighted by including the symbol © or the word "copyright" followed by the owner's name and date of copyright. Although registration entitles you to sue for damages in infringement cases, it is up to you to find and prove any instance of misuse. Newly copyrighted works remain copyrighted for the entire life of the author plus 50 years. Works published before 1978 were copyrighted for 28 years, with the option to renew for another 47 years (75 years total, if the copyright was renewed).

Any business use of a copyrighted work requires advance permission from its creator unless such use is covered by the *doctrine of fair use*. This doctrine provides for certain instances in which copyrighted work can be quoted, excerpted, or reprinted without permission. Generally, up to 250 words of text from a work can be used without permission if such use is not intended to deprive the copyright holder of income from the work.

Although no concrete legal standards for what constitutes fair use have been defined, the following criteria should be used to determine whether a proposed usage would be considered fair use:

1. The use is not for profit.
2. The amount used is small in proportion to the whole original work (no more than a few paragraphs of a book, and less in shorter works).
3. The use does not diminish the value of the original, or adversely affect it in any other way.
4. The use accurately reflects the original work and does not quote passages out of context.
5. The original is not relied on too heavily in the secondary work in which it is used.

It may be best to consult a copyright attorney before using copyrighted material for business purposes if there is any doubt as to whether the doctrine of fair use is applicable.

Trademarks

Because a symbol or a name can be a company's most prized asset, trademarks provide important legal protection. It is not necessary to register a trademark in order to use it commercially. However, registration establishes your exclusive right to use it and provides a basis for lawsuits against anyone who uses it without permission. A trademark may be a name, symbol, logo, or device that identifies goods or services. It cannot be a slogan or just a surname, or be merely descriptive or generic. (Surnames and descriptive names may qualify for the Supplemental Trademark Register.) A trademark must not do the following:

• resemble another trademark too closely
• feature national, state, or municipal symbols (such as flags)
• misrepresent a service, product, or organization
• disparage any person or group
• feature the likeness or signature of a living person without that person's consent
• suggest a connection to someone or something, unless that connection truly exists
• be immoral or obscene

Before applying for trademark registration or beginning to use a trademark, check to see if it is already in use by conducting a trademark search. A professional trademark search service or lawyer can conduct the search for you, or you can do it yourself via a computer database such as Cassis. A Trademark Depository library in the major city nearest you will have the database available for your search. Hiring a trademark service will cost more but will provide a more complete search.

When you know that your trademark has not already been registered, call the Commissioner of Patents and Trademarks (703-557-5249) to request the necessary forms. (Or call 703-308-4367 for general trademark information. Ask for a copy of the booklet *Basic Facts About Trademarks,* which covers all of the specifics on trademark registration.) In addition to the registration form, the following should be included in your application:

- a drawing (in black ink on white paper) of the symbol, logo, or device
- three specimens showing how the mark is used (such as appearances on packages or in advertisements)
- the required fee, in a check or money order made out to the Commissioner of Patents and Trademarks

Send the completed application and enclosures to the Patent and Trademark Office, Commissioner of Patents and Trademarks, Washington, DC 20231. If the application is approved, your trademark will appear in a publication called the *Official Gazette.* Anyone opposing its registration has 30 days to file an objection for review by the Trial and Appeal Board. If there are no protests, you will receive a certificate of registration. (For information on the status of your application, call 703-305-8747.) Trademark registration lasts for as long as the trademark remains in use, though it may need to be renewed. Trademark registration is indicated by the ® symbol after the logo. The ™ marking indicates an unregistered trademark protected by common law only within its state of origin.

A WORD ABOUT TRADE SECRETS

Though business ideas, plans, formulas, processes, and methods are not patentable, they are often protected under common law as trade secrets. To qualify, a trade secret must be something worth protecting that you have actively sought to keep private (through nondisclosure agreements, for instance). You give up your right to a trade secret if you make the information available to anyone not bound by a nondisclosure agreement. Unlike patent laws, trade secret laws are not clearly defined and judgments remain highly subjective.

Record Keeping: How Much Is Enough?

The extent to which offices save documents depends on the specific needs of the business, government regulations, the advice of lawyers and accountants, and employees' reluctance to throw things away. Managers must balance the necessity of keeping required records with the need to keep the office clutter-free. Classify documents as necessary (those that must be retained), unnecessary (those to be discarded as soon as possible), and useful (those to be kept in off-site storage or in the office only as space allows).

Develop a standard office-wide system, based on legal needs and space concerns, of record storage or destruction. Good business practice includes shredding discarded materials that contain confidential information. Here are some general guidelines for paperwork that should be retained:

- Keep permanently: records of business accounts, property deeds and mortgages, insurance records, credit history, year-end financial statements, stock and bond records, employee contracts, medical and retirement plans, certificates of incorporation, company bylaws, minutes of shareholders' meetings, list of stockholders, trademark registrations, patent certificates, copyrights, canceled checks, receipts from important payments and purchases, accountants' audit reports, and property appraisals.

- Keep for eight years: expired contracts and leases, canceled checks relevant to taxes, expense records, payroll records, personnel records of former employees, inventories, purchase and sales records, accident reports and claims, tax returns.
- Keep for three to five years: correspondence, employment applications, internal audit reports.
- Keep for one year: monthly bank statements, deposit slips, all canceled checks, purchase orders, receiving sheets, stockroom withdrawal forms.

Although computer use can reduce the flow of paper and free some space in filing cabinets (*see* The Paperless Office, page 155), computer files must be protected from harm. Keep disks stored in a moderate climate and away from equipment that could cause data erasure. Make backup disks for all computer records and keep them safely locked away. With fax and scanner technology, even incoming correspondence and signed documents can now be stored on disk. But check with your attorney to be sure that original paper documents are retained as required.

Privacy, Security, and Safety of Information

It is best to keep private any commercially useful or valuable information, from personnel files, client lists, and financial records to patents, formulas, and processes. Effective protection of proprietary information requires a complete program that gives careful attention to all security issues in the office.

Develop a systematic approach to protecting business assets. Beyond the usual security procedures (controlling who has access to company records and what goes in and out of the office), managers must anticipate potential information leaks and take steps to prevent them. Employees, clients, consultants, contractors, and licensees are all possible sources of leaks. Begin by hiring people you believe to be trustworthy and honest. Explain the importance of keeping proprietary information private. Instruct staff on what information must be kept confidential and how to guard against outsiders seeking access to it. For instance, remind staff not to discuss such information in public places and to keep travel plans quiet. Have all workers sign a reasonable nondisclosure agreement that remains in effect even when an employee leaves the company. Restrict access to confidential information so that staff members are privy only to the information they need to do their jobs. If possible, divide knowledge of trade secrets among several trusted employees. Only top management should have comprehensive knowledge of valuable trade secrets.

Classify documents as not confidential (information that need not be protected), confidential (proprietary information that should be kept private), and most sensitive (key trade secrets). Stamp confidential and sensitive documents with a notice such as "CONFIDENTIAL—DO NOT COPY," indicating that unauthorized disclosure, reproduction, or use of the material is forbidden. Before publication, review written materials such as brochures, manuals, articles, and interviews about your company (even if written by staff members for internal distribution) to make sure that proprietary information is not included. When possible, legally protect valuable products and processes, logos, and original text with patents, trademarks, and copyrights. Shred all documents containing confidential information before discarding them.

The widespread use of computers has brought a new set of security concerns. Protect your company's computer records by installing an in-house system created by trustworthy programmers. There should be no access to the system from outside—that is, confidential files should not be kept on computers accessible by Internet, fax, or modems. Develop a system to control interoffice access, using encryption, key locks, frequently changed passwords, and removable hard drives. Lock up floppy disks and restrict the use of computers after hours.

Filing cabinets, desks, and storage areas containing confidential information should be locked. Photocopiers should be located in open, centralized areas with nondisclosure warnings posted nearby to reduce opportunities for secretly copying proprietary information. Instruct employees on proper telephone precautions, reminding them that callers are not always who they say they are, that some information should never be given on the phone, and that cellular phones should be used only for routine, nonconfidential calls. Have a trustworthy staff member monitor all outgoing faxes to make sure no secrets are being released.

Sources of Further Information

Organizations

Small Business Administration
Phone 800-827-5722 to locate the branch nearest you.

U.S. Copyright Office
Publications Section LM-455
Library of Congress
Washington, DC 20559
Phone 202-707-9100

U.S. Patent and Trademark Office
Commissioner of Patents and Trademarks
Washington, DC 20231
Internet Web site: *www.loc.gov*
Phone 703-308-4367 for questions regarding patents; 703-557-5249 regarding trademarks; or 703-305-8747 to check on trademark application status.

State Bar Association Directory

State	*Telephone Number*
Alabama	205-269-1515
Alaska	907-272-7469
Arizona	602-252-4804
Arkansas	501-375-4605
California	415-561-8200
Colorado	303-860-1115

Connecticut	203-721-0025
Delaware	302-658-5279
District of Columbia	202-223-6600 or 202-737-4700
Florida	904-561-5600
Georgia	404-527-8755
Hawaii	808-537-1868
Idaho	208-334-4500
Illinois	217-525-1760
Indiana	317-639-5465
Iowa	515-243-3179
Kansas	913-234-5696
Kentucky	502-564-3795
Louisiana	504-566-1600
Maine	207-622-7523
Maryland	410-685-7878
Massachusetts	617-542-3602
Michigan	517-372-9030
Minnesota	612-333-1183
Mississippi	601-948-4471
Missouri	314-635-4128
Montana	406-442-7660
Nebraska	402-475-7091
Nevada	702-382-2200
New Hampshire	603-224-6942
New Jersey	908-249-5000
New Mexico	505-842-6132
New York	518-463-3200
North Carolina	919-677-0561 or 919-828-4620
North Dakota	701-255-1404
Ohio	614-487-2050
Oklahoma	405-524-2365
Oregon	503-620-0222
Pennsylvania	717-238-6715
Puerto Rico	787-721-3358
Rhode Island	401-421-5740
South Carolina	803-799-6653
South Dakota	605-224-7554
Tennessee	615-383-7421
Texas	512-463-1400
U.S. Virgin Islands	340-778-7497
Utah	801-531-9077
Vermont	802-223-2020
Virginia	804-775-0500 or 804-644-0041
Washington	206-727-8200
West Virginia	304-558-2456 or 304-342-1474
Wisconsin	608-257-3838
Wyoming	307-632-9061

Books and Literature

Kubey, Craig. *You Don't Always Need a Lawyer.* Yonkers, NY: Consumer Reports Books, 1991.

Legal Directories Publishing Company, Inc. 1314 Westwood Boulevard, Suite 201, Los Angeles, CA 90024 (to order a legal directory).

The Martindale-Hubbell Law Directory. New Providence, NJ: Martindale-Hubbell, 1995 (published yearly).

Ross, Martin J., and Jeffrey Ross. *Handbook of Everyday Law.* 4th ed. New York: Harper & Row, 1981.

Sitarz, Daniel. *The Complete Book of Small Business Legal Forms.* Carbondale, IL: Nova Publishing Co., 1991.

Yates, Sharon Fass, ed. *The Reader's Digest Legal Question & Answer Book.* Pleasantville, NY: Reader's Digest, 1988.

On-Line Resources

Employee Relations Web Picks (recommended websites for information on employment law, labor relations, and more) *http://www.nyper.com*

The Consumer Law Page *http://seamless.com*

The WWLIA Legal Dictionary (part of the U.S. Legal Information Center website) *http://wwlia.org/diction.htm*

U.S. Legal Information Center *http://www.lia.org*

U.S. Patent & Trademark Office *http://www.uspto.gov*

9

Image: The Face Your Business Shows the World

Advertising for All Budgets

Advertising is a much more comprehensive and complex undertaking than most business managers realize. In brief, it is the art of attracting public attention to an organization's products, services, philosophies, policies, needs, or plans by means of paid communication through one or more media, such as newspapers, magazines, radio, TV, billboards, mailings, or displays. Advertising is multidimensional and can be perceived as (1) a form of generalized or specialized communication delivered to large or small audiences, and distinguished from other means of communicating by the fact that an advertiser pays a medium to deliver its message; (2) a component of economic systems in free-market countries where consumer preferences dictate what goods will be produced and which services will be available; (3) a means of financing the mass media by providing up to 75 percent of newspaper/magazine revenues and 95 percent of radio/TV revenues.

Large sums of money are not necessarily required to finance a campaign that will get results. Advertising can be successfully geared to small, home-based businesses as well as megacorporations. Ad agencies get their commissions from the medium in which ads are placed (for example, the newspaper, magazine, radio/TV station or network), not from the advertiser. So you can hire an agency to place ads for you, yet pay only the cost of the advertisement, not the agency's fee.

Fortunately, there are many inexpensive forms of advertising that are quite effective, including classified ads, shopper ads, direct mailings, spot radio commercials, and point-of-sale items.

- Place classified ads in newspapers, periodicals, or newsletters. Start your campaign with small test ads and gradually expand as they prove effective.
- Publish shopper ads in free tabloids that are distributed locally in shopping malls and other outlets. These are comparatively inexpensive.
- Consider using direct mail to advertise. This has the advantage of reaching only a selective group of prospective buyers for your products or services. Results can be evaluated at very little cost by starting with limited test mailings.
- Run spot radio commercials in local markets for quick results—they can be recorded and broadcast easily and inexpensively.
- Use point-of-sale items to help customers keep your business in mind. Advertise your company's name and products on posters, leaflets, business cards, order blanks, pens/pencils, or scratch pads (*see* Promoting Your Business, page 367).
- Investigate on-line advertising of products or services. This may be far less expensive than many other types of advertising—just be sure your computers and phone lines are ready to handle a big response (*see* On-Line Marketing, page 389).

Many businesses can reduce advertising costs by developing public relations campaigns and press releases that are interesting enough for the media to use at no charge. (*See also* Public Relations, page 369, and Writing a Press Release, page 371.)

Graphic Design and Logos

Graphic design plays a vital role in the success of many businesses because it helps to project the proper image, often more successfully than words or actions. The graphic design of an organization begins with the skillful application of forms, illustrations, colors, and typography to create a clear and effective image. Designers may make, review, discard, and remake the initial rendering several times until the basic design is satisfactory. The design is then refined for an application that is visible to the public.

Sometimes graphic design is so awkward and artless as to repulse rather than stimulate our inclination to use a product or service. "Much of what comes our way is just plain ugly," says Elizabeth Adler, an experienced design consultant, in *Print That Works.* "Brochures, newsletters, flyers, and ads regularly offend the eye with their aggressive design or downright junkiness." Good design motivates in a positive way and is often so natural and unobtrusive that it makes little or no conscious impact. It should enhance a company's image and communicate ideas, concepts, and objectives clearly to associates, customers, clients, and the public.

Ten Common Design Mistakes

The best examples of graphic design are tasteful, attractive, stylish, memorable, and capable of creating moods or triggering ideas. By contrast, poor design generates little response or, even worse, elicits hostile reactions. Here are ten common design mistakes to avoid:

1. sacrificing style and quality to get a bargain
2. preparing designs for various graphics in an organization without integrating them harmoniously
3. selecting colors that are too bright or unappealing
4. merging text and graphic elements in a way that makes the words hard to read and muddies or obscures the graphic images
5. making a design too large for the page or items on which it will be used, or using it too frequently so that it overpowers the message it should illustrate
6. creating designs that are too complex for the papers and inks that will be used to print them
7. ignoring current trends in public preferences regarding art, style, and composition
8. trying to save money by doing it yourself instead of hiring a competent, experienced designer for the job

9. using too many elements, which results in clutter and confusion
10. failing to coordinate the design phase with later phases of rendering and production

Logos with Clout

A *logo* (short for *logotype*) is a symbol used as a single, all-in-one visual representation of an organization or individual (see Figure 9.1). A logo is called a *trademark* when it is applied to a product or used as the emblem of a service. Logos are reproduced in advertising of all kinds, and often appear on company vehicles, uniforms, office signs, and stationery. Though it may look simple to the viewer, a good logo has several basic components:

• strong identity characteristics, such as an organization's initials or a symbol that stands for the type of business
• design that is powerful, but not blatant
• the ability to make a quick imprint on the viewer's memory

Figure 9.1 Logos

- uniqueness, so it does not infringe on competitors' rights
- adaptability for use in several forms and media with no loss of impact

Choosing the Right Business Cards and Letterhead

When you receive a letter or a salesperson gives you a business card, what is your reaction if the paper and print look cheap or the design is gaudy? What if the wording of a slogan is exaggerated or boastful? First impressions are important, and these inanimate representatives have not performed well for the individual or organization soliciting your business. On the other hand, a favorable reaction to cards or letters predisposes the receiver to respond in a positive manner.

If it is your responsibility to choose and order business cards or stationery, think of them as company representatives. They are as important as a businessperson's dress and speech in influencing potential customers or clients. Sometimes people who are meticulous about professional dress and grooming completely ignore the impression their printed communications make on others.

Business Cards

Almost everyone in business carries cards to use as identification or to give the firm's address and phone number to professional contacts. The standard card is 3½″ × 2″, and yours should not differ in size or shape unless there is a good reason for the variation. The imprint should be limited to your name in the center, your title and company name in the lower left corner, and your business address and phone number on the lower right. (E-mail addresses and fax numbers may be included in the address section.) A conservative block or roman typeface is preferable, engraved in black ink on quality parchment or white card stock. A trademark or logo is acceptable if it is not too large, but a slogan should not be imprinted unless it is very short and an inseparable part of the logo. If a brief message must be included, such as "50 Years of Community Service" or a listing of local affiliates, it should be on the back of the card.

Business cards play an even more important role in foreign corporate culture than they do in the United States. The procedure for exchanging cards is often rather formal (*see* Foreign Business Etiquette, page 417). Because this is such an important gesture, it is best to have cards printed in the local language for foreign business trips. An English translation can be included on the reverse side. Make sure that your business title is included on your cards even if you are self-employed, as this is a necessary formality abroad.

BUSINESS CARDS—AN AID IN KEEPING CURRENT ACCOUNTS AND ACQUIRING NEW ONES

A recent survey correlated printers' business card orders in 15 metropolitan areas with other indicators of financial growth and prosperity. The results indicated a substantial increase in business card orders overall, with new businesses responsible for only part of the expansion. Other important factors were the regional rates of recession and recovery. An increase in business card ordering seems to occur in areas in which weak economic conditions necessitate harder work by firms and individuals to maintain existing business accounts and acquire new ones. Increased unemployment rates also account for extra business card orders: Those who are seeking jobs have new cards printed to attach to résumés and give to prospective employers. On the other hand, cities that have largely recovered from a recession experience a plateau in business card sales.

Letterhead

Even if your business requires only a minimal amount of correspondence, suitable stationery is essential. It should be treated as a public relations tool. When letterhead is properly designed and used appropriately, letters and memos (or even postcards) can upgrade your professional image and promote business. Stationery need not be engraved or expensive, but it must have style and class. It should reflect the company image that your firm wants to promote. It is acceptable to use the company logo on letterhead, but the reproduction should be low key. Logo color and design should not overpower the content of a letter.

When planning and ordering business cards, letterhead, and other printed material that represents your firm, keep the design uniform. This will help to build the company identity. Businesses on a limited budget may use black-and-white stationery internally, with a modest supply of deluxe stationery for correspondence with clients and customers.

Promoting Your Business

The purpose of business promotion is to develop name recognition for your company and generate interest in its products and services. Promotion is less direct than advertising but can be very effective in building sales and a company image. It can take many forms, depending on budget and the targeted market. Discount coupons, two-for-one offers, free merchandise or services with purchase, rebates, direct mail fliers offering information and a chance to try products at a discount, invitations to a special sale, and contests with company products as prizes are effective promotional devices. (Research state laws on contests before planning one.) Coupons, brochures, fliers, and other printed matter can be professionally printed or desktop-published right in the office. The key is using well-designed, eye-catching materials that provide enough information to generate further interest.

Promotional Items

Giving away frequently used items (for example, pens, key chains, or calendars) is a good promotional strategy when items are imprinted with the company's name, logo, address, and phone number. Such items build name recognition and goodwill. Promoting your business and making its name known may mean hiring someone to put fliers, brochures, or coupons on windshields in parking lots or to attach rolled-up fliers to residential doorknobs. Higher priced options include buying space in a newspaper or shopper's weekly to publish coupons, or buying a mailing list and using the direct mail approach (*see* Direct-Mail Marketing, page 386).

Product Demonstrations

Sponsoring a party to demonstrate or explain the benefits of products or services is another way to promote your business. Free product samples, coupons, initial consultations, door prizes, or other giveaways can be offered as incentives to those who attend. If your budget precludes renting a public space for the event, parties can be held at an existing customer's home, with free or discounted products as incentives for the host. Attendees can be invited by the host, solicited through mailings, or both. Prospective new clients, additions to your mailing lists, and actual sales may result from promotional parties.

Trade Shows

Exhibiting at trade shows is a high-profile way to promote your company. Trade shows allow the introduction, display, and demonstration of merchandise or services. They provide an opportunity to meet and talk with hundreds or thousands of prospective customers and distributors. Fliers, brochures, small items, product samples, and discount coupons may be given away. Use trade shows to gather names and addresses for your mailing list, and build your company image via a striking display booth and informed, helpful staff to greet the public. Make the most of your investment by mailing advance information to clients and potential customers, inviting them to visit your booth. Set appointments by telephone with key people who may be too busy during the show to stop by your exhibit. Generate advance interest by letting the press know that your firm will be represented at the show, and what you have to offer. Send press releases and press kits to the media (*see* Writing a Press Release, page 371, and Creating a Press Kit, page 372).

Getting to Know Prospective Customers

Any promotional campaign will be more successful if the market is researched before planning a strategy. Who are the target customers or clients? Where do they live? How much money do they earn? What publications do they read? Conduct a survey (formal or informal) of current customers, learning as much about them as you can. In addition to providing information needed to keep existing clients satisfied, this will pinpoint the demographics of prospective clients. (It may also generate some ideas about groups who could use your products but who have not been aware of or attracted to your business.) Keep a record of clients' names, addresses, and telephone numbers and build a mailing list. Read trade publications and market research surveys to gather as much information as possible about the people you are trying to reach. (*See also* Consumer Surveys and Demographics, page 382.)

Public Relations

Public relations is the art of building a positive company image via the media—in the community, with existing clients, and with prospective customers. The idea is to let the world know what you do and how good you are at it. The coverage you want will be free advertising for your company, but information must be presented in a form that is newsworthy, educational, or entertaining, so that it will be attractive to the media.

Good Will Begins in the Office

On a very basic level, public relations starts within your company. If management is open and communicative with employees, promoting ethics, truthfulness, and good customer service, that positive image will be projected to the community and to your client base. Fostering good relations with suppliers is essential, too. Pay them on time and with a smile. Also, develop positive relationships with the company's financial institution; this will help your public image as well as make future loan approvals more likely. In addition, word will spread about the firm's reliability.

Talk to customers—find out how satisfied they are and what they want; join trade organizations and talk to colleagues. Learn what people in the community think about you and your company, and then decide on a public relations strategy. Do you want to build on a positive image that already exists, or to change negative perceptions of your business? Public relations activities can take many forms, so consider carefully which options would be best to promote the desired image.

Using the Press

The most basic method of obtaining media publicity is to use press releases and press kits (*see* Writing a Press Release, page 371, and Creating a Press Kit, page 372). These are essential tools in promoting upcoming company events. Get to know key people in the media, and learn which editors are most likely to accept the articles you would like to publish. Call newspapers, special interest magazines, trade publications, consumer magazines, television stations, and radio stations to find out who should receive your press releases and press kits. Then build a media list and use it, making sure to keep it updated. Are there consumer shows or business news forums on television or radio that may give positive exposure to your new product or service? Can an interview be arranged for someone in your firm to discuss a particular area of expertise, your company's imminent relocation, or an upcoming seminar that you are planning? Call the hosts of these shows and let them know that you would like to schedule an interview.

In addition to press releases and press kits, you may opt to write an article offering advice or how-to information relative to your field of expertise. Or you may conduct a customer survey and write an article to publish your findings. Send a query letter to the appropriate news editor, outlining the subject of your article, the advice/information you have to offer or the gist of your survey results, and why you are considered an authority on that subject.

Sponsoring Community Events and Educational Workshops

Another way to foster a positive company image is by sponsoring community activities such as a Little League team, complete with uniforms bearing your company name, or the local symphony or ballet. Your company may give a party to help raise money for a new hospital wing, or sponsor an essay-writing contest for local schoolchildren. Such activities benefit the community and associate your company's name with philanthropic pursuits. Company-sponsored educational seminars covering trends in your field are usually of interest to the business community and afford an opportunity to build your public image. Offering how-to workshops in which company representatives share their expertise is a good way to demonstrate professionalism and good will. Seminars and workshops can be lively panel discussions with a variety of speakers, or by-invitation-only meetings for customers and colleagues.

Remember that many company activities, from unveiling a new small business consultation service to holding an awards ceremony for a local fire-fighting hero, can become newsworthy events. Publicize all such events—including seminars, ceremonies, contributions, and sponsorship of charitable endeavors—by sending press releases to the appropriate editors and producers. Call media representatives once they have received your articles and offer to provide additional information or answer any questions they may have.

Responding to Hard-Earned Publicity

Be prepared for publicity! If your press releases or inquiries to talk show hosts are successful, you may be asked for an interview or for more information. Make sure you are well versed on the facts. Always tell the truth, even when it is unpleasant. If a situation occurs that could produce negative publicity for your firm, it is usually best to face the inevitable and release the bad news before others do. This allows you to present the facts in the best light possible, and gives you a chance to tell your side of the story.

When your press releases are published or broadcast or you are interviewed on a talk show, be sure to send a thank-you note to the news editor or show host. If there is unfavorable coverage, call the editor or producer and tell your side of the story calmly and clearly. Be careful to avoid arguments. If you have strong convictions about your company's mission and ethics and believe in its products or services, your confidence and certainty will be contagious.

Writing a Press Release

A press release is an effective public relations tool that when published affords your company free publicity and advertising. It consists of a page or two of well-written, newsworthy material (that is, information that is of interest to readers or viewers) announcing any event you want to publicize. The subject of your article may be the introduction of new products or services, the promotion or addition of a key employee, your firm's relocation to a new site, details on an upcoming workshop or educational seminar sponsored by your business, or a company picnic for children at a local orphanage. The possibilities are endless for press releases that will capture the interest of a news editor or producer.

When a press release is ready for publication, it is mailed to the news editors of targeted publications and the producers or hosts of radio/TV news programs and talk shows. To decide where a story should be sent, read local and national newspapers, magazines, and trade and consumer publications. Listen to radio and television news, informational broadcasts, and talk shows. Choose the most appropriate outlets for your story. Is it of local, regional, or national interest? Does it have wide appeal, or is it geared to a very specialized group? Read publication mastheads to see which editors handle articles such as yours. Then call each paper, journal, or television or radio station to confirm your choices.

Newsworthiness is only one aspect of a successful press release. Busy news editors often publish releases exactly as received, so your article must be well written. No matter how interesting the subject, an incoherent, poorly organized press release will probably be discarded as unusable. Write and rewrite each release. Make points in a clear and logical manner. Good grammar, proper punctuation, and perfect spelling are a must—nothing repels an editor more than poor spelling and grammar, turning your exciting news into wastebasket fodder.

Basic Rules of Composition

Adhere to the basic rules of composition. The first paragraph should cover journalistic basics: who, what, when, where, why, and how. Next, elaborate with interesting details. Finally, in the third paragraph, summarize major points and present conclusions. (This three-paragraph rule need not be followed if just one or two will suffice.) Each paragraph should have a topic sentence, or *lead,* that puts forth the most important information and introduces that paragraph's subject. Subsequent sentences should relate to the lead and further elaborate on that topic.

Press Release Form and Length

Form is important, too. Your company name, address, and telephone number should appear at the top of the page, or the release may be printed on company letterhead. At the very top of the press release, type "FOR IMMEDIATE RELEASE" in all capitals and underlined, either flush left or flush right. If the release should be printed on, before, or after a specific date, add that information to this line (for example, "FOR IMMEDIATE RELEASE ON OR AFTER 7/17/97"). Directly opposite this line, in capitals but not underlined, put "FOR FURTHER INFORMATION:" with the contact person's name and telephone number beneath it.

Next comes the headline. Make it snappy and eye-catching, and make sure it conveys the essence of your news. Type it in capitals, centered on the page and underlined. Skip two lines, and start the body of the release. Indent paragraphs and double-space the release, allowing sufficient margins for editors to jot down notes. The very first item on the first line of the body of the release should be the city from which you are writing, followed by a comma and the date. This item should be enclosed in parentheses.

Try to limit the release to one page, but if you do go over a page, type the following centered at the bottom of the page: --more--. To signify the end of the release, type one of the following: --30--, ###, or END. Figure 9.2 illustrates the correct press release format.

Adding Excitement

Now you have checked and rechecked your release for organization, coherence, correct grammar, and professional format. But something is still missing: excitement. Before working on it again, take a moment to feel your passion for the subject or to get excited about the event. Realize how important this information is. Pretend you are the reader; read it aloud, and imagine how it will sound when read on radio or TV. Will it catch a reader's or listener's interest? If not, rewrite sentences to make them bolder or more dramatic. Shorten long sentences and try to eliminate passive verb constructions. Use succinct, descriptive, visual language. Read it to a friend who writes well and ask for suggestions.

CREATING A PRESS KIT

A press kit is a group of nicely packaged publicity materials sent to newspapers, magazines, and radio/TV stations. A press release is the

The Curio Cabinet
1460 Park Lane Avenue
Boulder, Colorado 80312 (303) 468-1476

FOR IMMEDIATE RELEASE ON OR BEFORE 6/19/97

FOR FURTHER INFORMATION:
Mary Nolan, (303) 468-1476

ANTIQUE SHOW BENEFITS LITTLE LEAGUER

(Boulder, 6/21/97) The Curio Cabinet and the Park Lane Mall Merchants Association are sponsoring an antique show on Sunday, June 21, from 9:00 A.M. to 5:00 P.M. Refreshments, door prizes, and informative presentations by local antique dealers will highlight the event. Half of each antique dealer's profits from sales during the show will be donated to help pay for nine-year-old Bobby Landrum's costly medication for hemophilia. He requires daily injections of a special clotting agent to prevent crippling or life-threatening blood loss. Each person attending the show will be asked to donate $5.00 to the medical fund.

Curio Cabinet owner Mary Nolan said she learned of Bobby's plight when he signed up to play ball with the Curio Cubs, the Little League team she sponsors. Bobby's parents, Steve and Joan Landrum, talked with Ms. Nolan and coach Jim Wright about special precautions and emergency procedures before practice began. They mentioned that Bobby could not play ball or lead a normal life without medical treatment that costs $60,000 to $100,000 per year. The Landrums' health insurance pays 80 percent of expenses, but the family must pay the rest. Bobby is the youngest of four children, and both of his parents are teachers at a local junior high school. "We've used up our savings and taken a second mortgage on our home, but the situation is getting desperate," Steve explained. "We're afraid the time may come when we can't afford his medication."

Several antique dealers have volunteered to give talks on topics of interest to antique lovers, such as "Depression-Era Treasures," "Restoring Antique Furniture," and "Look What I Found in Grandma's Attic!" Antique jewelry, glass, furniture, books, and clothing, from commercial and private collections, will be on display in the Curio Cabinet and in the mall. Talks, prizes, and refreshment will be offered in the store. Activity schedules are available at area antique shops, the Curio Cabinet, and at the Mall Office.

###

Figure 9.2 Press release

most important element of your press kit, as it conveys the essence of your story. Other items in the kit add background information and visual interest. If you are seeking coverage by national media, include any previously published local articles relative to the story. Previous publications will lend credibility with news editors. Include 8″ × 10″ photos, such as one showing the photogenic new executive receiving a community service award and another of her speech at a town meeting. Include a short biography of the new executive and information about other company executives, if pertinent to the story. If your firm is planning an expansion that will create new jobs, include a copy or photo of plans for the new facility. If your story is about a new product, your kit may include a sheet of pertinent facts and information about the product, a sample product (if possible), and a list of well-known customers. A press kit for the press release in Figure 9.2 might include a picture of Bobby in his Little League uniform, smiling at the entrance of The Curio Cabinet. Background information in the press kit could be copies of monthly medical bills and published articles about hemophilia's effects and the high cost of treatment.

Write a cover letter briefly describing the event to be publicized. Affix typed captions, on label stock, to the back of each photo. Put the press kit into an attractive folder with inside pockets. Include a business card of the person to contact for more information. (Some folders have scored holders specifically for this purpose.) Send kits to the editors and producers you have decided are most likely to use it. Then follow up with calls to make sure the press kits were received and to offer your assistance if more information is needed.

Company Newsletters

Newsletters help to develop name recognition and credibility in the community by publicizing what your company does. They should include newsworthy items about your company's activities, history, growth, new products, key players, trends of the trade, and useful advice. Newsletters can be an essential vehicle of communication to employees and the public. As the name implies, the main purpose of this medium is to disseminate company news—not necessarily anything earthshaking or dramatic, but current facts that are of interest to readers. The most common mistake made in newsletter creation and development is focusing on format and design rather than content. As a result, many newsletters are clogged with irrelevant materials such as cartoons, light banter, or even recipes. The best newsletters contain useful facts and schedules of upcoming events, prompting readers to clip items or make a note of worthwhile tips or important dates.

The best, most informative newsletters:

- use simple, tasteful graphic designs, such as logos or emblems readily identified with the organization
- come out periodically on dates and times when recipients are likely to be unhurried and receptive to them
- are conveniently sized, usually 8½″ × 11″
- reach a deliberately selected group of people who are most likely to be interested in their subject matter
- contain ideas and suggestions that prompt discussions among readers and letters to the editor
- consist of eight pages or less, except for special editions on topics that merit in-depth coverage
- feature a masthead listing the editor and other contacts for readers with questions, suggestions, or potential news items
- are distributed to employees and interested others whose names and addresses are frequently reviewed and updated to keep the mailing list current and minimize wasted circulation costs

If you are involved in planning, editing, or writing a newsletter, remember its main purpose. It exists to communicate information about company events and activities. Helpful information (such as how-to articles) may also be included, but keep filler material to a minimum. A newsletter's primary purpose is not to entertain but to inform. Size and frequency of publication should depend on the amount of news available and financial considerations. Many newsletters are now produced at minimal cost with sophisticated desktop publishing software programs. Arrange the editorial format by priority and keep sections consistent from one issue to the next, although a section may be deleted when there is no newsworthy material to report. Readers look first for sections that are of most interest to them, so make it simple for them to find what they want.

DESKTOP PUBLISHING—PROFESSIONAL DESIGN AT YOUR FINGERTIPS

Desktop publishing is the process of creating camera-ready documents such as newsletters and brochures by using a computer, special software, and a printer. Sophisticated design and editing features are part of good desktop applications, making it possible to create professional documents of an infinite variety. Such programs are also used to create and edit attractive home pages (websites) on the Internet (*see* On-Line Marketing, page 389, for more information).

Detailed graphics and professional quality text are produced by hypertext markup language or html, an abbreviation that is very familiar to Internet users. This computer language is much more than a special font. Use of html allows a document publisher or website author to give certain words or phrases an additional meaning so that users can click the mouse on highlighted areas and thus connect to other sites. Html is also involved in the intra-office computer networking process.

There are a number of excellent desktop publishing software programs available and some software promoters offer intensive training in their use. If your business outsources production of newsletters, flyers, and brochures, a good software application and training in its use will save your firm money in the long run.

Joining Professional Organizations and Getting the Most from Membership

Everyone in business can probably benefit from membership in one or more professional organizations. There are more than 100,000 associations at federal, state, and regional levels, so it should not be difficult to find one that suits your needs and expectations. What can membership offer? Here are some examples:

- opportunities to meet and exchange ideas with others whose professional interests and goals are similar to yours
- conferences, seminars, and other programs to improve professional knowledge and skills
- group discounts and special courses in continuing education programs or schools
- periodicals, books, videotapes, CD-ROMs, and other literature and communications about your area of expertise

- group health and other insurance programs
- group discounts on purchases of professional equipment and supplies
- job search and transfer assistance
- opportunities to pool research or resources with other individuals and organizations

Finding the Right Group

How do you find a list of potential organizations and then choose the right one(s)? Visit your local library and ask to see a reference volume called the *Encyclopedia of Associations*. This directory is a comprehensive listing of thousands of organizations, tabulated and cross-indexed so you can quickly find those in your field. Each entry provides a description of the organization, its address and phone number, and usually the name of the current director or other contact person.

You may also contact your local chamber of commerce or a similar agency associated with business, industry, and the professions. Ask for suggestions about associations and societies in your field of interest. Members of the Service Corps of Retired Executives, which is closely associated with chamber of commerce offices, are usually knowledgeable about such matters.

Many professional organizations set up membership information booths and brochures at seminars and conferences on subjects of professional interest. Attending such events should provide opportunities to learn about some associations and interact with members. This can be very helpful when you are making a decision about which group to join. Business and professional journals often feature articles about membership organizations and include application forms. Many associations advertise in trade journals, and an inquiry to the editor may net some useful information.

Sources of Further Information

Organizations

Bilingual Business Cards

Advantage (all languages)
Phone 212-213-6464

Inlingua (all languages)
Phone 713-622-1516

Oriental Printing (Japanese, Chinese, Korean)
Phone 708-439-4822

Paramount Process Printing (all languages)
Phone 212-691-3700

Professional Image Consultant Firms

Achievement Concepts
1963 Cynthia Lane
P.O. Box 430

Merrick, NY 11566
Phone 516-868-5100

Communication Resources
Harvard Square
P.O. Box 537
Cambridge, MA 02238
Phone 617-332-4334

Conrad Communications
6 Black Birch Lane
Scarsdale, NY 10583
Phone 914-725-2360

Dale Carnegie & Associates
1475 Franklin Avenue
Garden City, NY 11530
Phone 800-231-5800

Kaufman Professional Image Consultants
233 South Sixth Street, Suite 702
Philadelphia, PA 19106
Phone 215-592-9709

Tracy Presentation Skills
2414 Londonderry Road, Suite 767
Alexandria, VA 22308
Phone 703-360-3222

Books and Literature

Adler, Elizabeth. *Print That Works.* Menlo Park, CA: Bull Publishing Company, 1991.

Cross, Wilbur. *Choices with Clout: How to Make Things Happen by Making the Right Decisions Every Day of Your Life.* New York: Berkley, 1995.

Cross, Wilbur. *Encyclopedia Dictionary of Business Terms.* Englewood Cliffs, NJ: Prentice Hall, Inc. 1995.

Encyclopedia of Associations. New York: Gale Research, 1996.

Kehrer, Daniel. *Save Yourself a Bundle.* New York: Simon & Schuster, 1994.

Linville, Christopher. *Strike It Rich.* West Nyack, NY: Parker Publishing, 1983.

Lonier, Terri. *Working Solo.* New Paltz, NY: Portico Press, 1994.

On-Line Resources

The University of Florida's Networked Writing Environment offers assistance and help for desktop publishers *http://www.ucet.ufl.edu/writing/htmhelp.htm*

Cool Stuff desktop publishing site *http://desktoppublishing.com*

10

Marketing for Growth

Defining and Researching the Competition

According to the Marketing Practices Division of the Federal Trade Commission, a common mistake in marketing is miscalculating the number and nature of competitors. So, you must first define your competition and then you must research it. The following sections help to differentiate between these steps, and suggest ways to cover all the bases.

Defining the Competition

Developing a merchandising plan can be confusing in any competitive market, and defining competitors by type and importance is essential. Companies competing for your customers or clients can be divided into two categories: *primary competitors,* those with products or services like yours, and *secondary competitors,* those that market products unlike yours but could take away some of your business. For example, a cruise line company's primary competitors are other cruise lines. Its secondary competitors are other types of travel operators who could lure prospective vacationers to their vacation services.

Make a list of primary competitors and a list of secondary ones. Next, arrange each list by priority, with the most successful businesses on top. This will make it easier to target sales, marketing, and advertising campaigns to be most effective. Put yourself in the place of your major competitors. Use their products and try their services; assign others in your company to do the same. What do they offer that is better than what your company currently delivers? If possible, contact their customers to obtain favorable or unfavorable reactions. Visit competitors' headquarters or locations where their products or services are sold to learn more about their strengths and weaknesses.

When visiting other businesses, observe their employees closely. Are they comparable to yours, more professional, more helpful, better educated, or more experienced? Make a habit of reading competitors' help wanted ads and fliers to see how they describe the kind of people they want to hire. As the saying goes, a company is its people, so defining a rival business includes knowing something about its employees.

Researching the Competition

Once you have an overview of your top primary and secondary competitors, there is still research to be done. You will have begun a research file while defining the nature of your competition, but now you must gather a different type of information. If a company under scrutiny is a public corporation, it will be easy to acquire a copy of its annual report; this will give details on profits, losses, and other financial information. Similar kinds of data can be gleaned from business articles such as those in *Consumer Reports, Business Week,* or *Advertising Age.* Other data will be found in third-party industrial and commercial reports such as financial summaries, or in newsletters published by numerous marketing services. Scan government publications in your business field for notifications of new products, trademark registrations, and patent applications of competitors.

Some of the most valuable research data can be accumulated through regular attendance at trade meetings and shows, where companies go out of their way to present product lines and introduce new services. You may also hear some revealing allusions to competitors' future marketing plans. By attending trade shows regularly, you will also gain insight into the stability of other companies, by observing whether their key people come back again and again or whether there are always new faces (evidence that their marketers are constantly moving on).

Market research also includes obtaining a thorough knowledge of the geographical area covered by your business and the competing firms that also cover that area. If you were not interested in geography at school, now is the time to change your attitude. Keep a simple, easy-to-read map of your marketing territory. Update it frequently by adding references to competitors' spheres of operations, noting areas where they are strongest and weakest. Then you can see at a glance where your company should focus its sales impact and extend its promotional campaigns.

ATTITUDE COUNTS

During the process of defining and researching your competition, remember the advice of Robert L. Davidson, an able and experienced marketing consultant. In his book *Contracting Your Services,* he wrote, "A long, long time ago, there was a saying that 'if you invent a better mousetrap, the world will beat a path to your door.' Forget it. There are a great many talented people in the world, many of whom can do what you do and do it equally well. Marketing is a way to elevate yourself above the general noise level, a way to be seen, heard, and called upon. Marketing is also a way to present your service where the demand and opportunities are greatest."

Evaluating the Competition

After defining and researching the competition, you are ready to evaluate its impact on your market. A good way to begin is by listing questions that should be answered by a review of the data that you have accumulated. Here are some examples to help get your list started:

- Is the market open for new competitors?
- Are there enough customers for all of us?
- Do we overlap with our competition in any product areas? Are there some differences in these areas that we can use to our advantage? What differences will work against us? Should we consider offering a different line of products, or a wider variety, or change our products in some other way to make us more competitive?

- Are any of our services similar to those of our competitors? Are ours different in any way that could give us an edge over the competition? If not, can we change or add to our services in some way so that we have an advantage?
- Are we concentrating on areas in which we have the greatest advantage over our competition (lower prices, faster delivery, better product knowledge, more accessible location, more convenient hours, etc.)?
- Can we improve the product or service areas in which we have the least advantage?
- Do we advertise in the same media that most of our competitors use?
- Are we taking steps to counter the advertising thrust of our strongest competitors? (Can everyone in our office sing our biggest competitor's jingle from their TV commercials? If so, can we develop an advertising campaign to make our company name just as memorable?) The competition advertises "the lowest prices in town," but our products are of a higher quality than theirs—does our advertising campaign reflect this?
- Do our prices compare favorably with theirs?
- Does our public image measure up to that of our strongest competitors? If not, why?
- Have we learned from the public relations mistakes of similar businesses?
- Is there any competitor with whom we would like to merge?
- Are our facilities comparable to those of our primary competitors?
- Have our competitors been in business longer than our firm has?
- Have several businesses of our type failed in the last few years?
- Can we garner the market share that we need in order to be profitable?
- Have we failed to attract certain types of prospects?

COMMON MARKETING BLUNDERS

The American Association of Advertising Agencies lists the following common blunders made by marketers:

1. ignoring the needs and tastes of customers by assuming their preferences are the same as the marketing manager's
2. misjudging the number of potential customers, clients, or patrons
3. failing to conduct surveys to determine customer preferences for new products and services and/or modifications of existing ones
4. miscalculating the size and nature of the competition
5. becoming complacent when sales are satisfactory rather than developing follow-up strategies
6. overlooking market trends that predict reductions in the demand for certain products, product groups, or services
7. using sales data for peak months as averages without taking into account seasonal declines
8. failing to grasp the implications of new product spin-offs from existing products that have established brand identities and loyal purchasers

9. cutting back on market research funds and projects when business seems to be moving favorably

10. expecting that last year's plans will suffice for next year

Marketing Plan Objectives

A successful marketing plan is designed to accomplish four basic objectives: attracting new customers, developing repeat business, creating a positive image, and outmaneuvering the competition. Each of these is important to the financial success of any business that has products or services to sell.

1. *Attracting new customers*—A constant influx of new customers is essential to business growth. New customers are necessary to replace those who have strayed and to build a larger sales base.

2. *Developing repeat business*—Regular customers are vital to the stability of a business. Their purchases provide a constant source of revenue; they are also likely to recommend your services or products to others. Never take them for granted, or they may become former customers. Communicate with them regularly to learn if their preferences are changing or if they have suggestions to improve your business.

3. *Creating a positive image*—Public perception of your company will influence customers' buying habits as much as any other marketing strategy. Keep your image polished at all times.

4. *Outmaneuvering the competition*—One of the few certainties in business is that competitors are always trying to lure your customers away, no matter what you do or how well you do it. Conversely, your goal must be to keep your current customers and to attract some away from the competition. The best marketing plan usually wins.

Consumer Surveys and Demographics

Consumer surveys range from a few hundred questionnaires filled out by customers at a small retail shop to sophisticated nationwide studies by research organizations like Nielsen, Information Resources, and Dun & Bradstreet. It would be too costly, and probably impossible, for a company with thousands of customers to interview all or a large percentage of them. However, consumer research techniques have been refined so that responses from a small cross section of customers reflect group preferences fairly accurately. This process of surveying a representative group is called *sampling.* Its widespread use in consumer research is based on the premise that sample group members have been chosen to be very similar to the larger group. For example, suppose that 38 percent of all hand lotions sold are bought by women over age 50, 30 percent by women aged 30 to 49, 20 percent by women aged 17 to 30, and 12 percent by men aged 30 to 50. Assume that about 200 customers will be surveyed. A representative cross section would consist of about 76 women over age 50, about 60 women in their thirties and forties, about 40 women in their teens and twenties, and about 24 men aged 30 to 50. Representative sampling techniques allow the assumption that the responses of the small group surveyed will closely approximate the responses that would be obtained if every consumer could be questioned. Well-designed surveys make it possible for a company to evaluate the market in terms of actual consumer needs, desires, attitudes, buying habits, and purchases.

Determining Your Targets

Targeted customers include those who already use your products or services, those who purchase from your competition, and those who are potential consumers—people who do not use this type of product at present but who might. For a successful marketing campaign, you must know what types of people comprise each of these groups; otherwise, your promotional strategies may not reach actual prospects. Make sure to focus on the right targets before beginning a promotion.

How do you line up your consumer/marketing targets? Before starting a list of potential consumers, rid yourself of the assumption that you already know what customers want because you know what current customers buy. The truth is that you cannot know exactly what they want until you ask them some questions. How many times have you gone from one store to another, looking for a certain type of product, only to settle for one that was not exactly what you had in mind? Marketers for the stores that did not get your business would not know why you did not purchase one of their products unless a clerk questioned you and gave them that information. And the marketing staff for the store where you finally made a purchase would be wrong in assuming that what you bought was exactly what you wanted. Realistically, most managers do not have time to conduct on-the-spot surveys of all customers, and most clerks have no incentive to do so.

To establish your targets, first get a visual impression of the geographic borders and zones of your marketing area. Then pinpoint demographic patterns that are relevant to your products or services. Surveys of teenagers will not help to increase sales of incontinence products for the elderly. (Yes, teenagers are potential incontinence product consumers, but it will be a long, long time before their preferences matter!) If you sell weight-loss products, your primary targets are obese people. Many types of demographic data can be acquired from federal, state, and local government agencies. These statistics may be supplemented or substantiated by marketing service organizations that have developed complex working prototypes based on race, family size, gender, income level, and other variables. If you hire an advertising agency, expect their help with sampling and surveys. Ask them to show you examples of programs created for companies similar to yours in size, extent, location, and sales objectives.

Survey Timing, Location, and Validity

As you proceed with the planning stage of a survey or sampling program, be sure to allow enough lead time. Lead time is most affected by the extent of the research required to pinpoint targets. A survey can be quick and simple if, for example, you are about to sell a new lure for salmon fishing in western rivers and have a specific type of customer in mind. Or it can be time-consuming and complex if the object is to determine who is likely to buy a new type of security alarm.

Choosing when and where to conduct a survey is also important, especially when seasonal products are its focus. Summer vacationers sunning themselves on a Florida beach are probably not the best choice for a survey on consumer preferences in snow boots. Nor would a swimwear manufacturer choose November as the best month to interview customers. The *validity* of data refers to whether the right questions were asked of the right people at the right time and in the right place, so that the information gathered is useful for its intended purpose.

Establishing Focus Groups

Marketing consultants are often asked how long the information from a survey remains accurate and how often customers change their preferences and brand loyalties. Many consumers do try different products from time to time in an effort to get more and spend less. Product preferences also change as family and life situations shift. But basic patterns of choice remain surprisingly constant. When meaningful changes occur, they usually do so over a gradual period of time as variations that can be recognized and accounted for in a marketing study. Occasionally, a disruption such as a natural disaster or economic recession will shake a local market to its core. Some marketing areas are more susceptible than others to economic downturns: real estate, automobiles, and luxury items are notable examples. But all business managers should be alert to signs of changing market conditions.

If you own or manage a large company, consider establishing a marketing *focus group.* The group consists of three to ten or more people who meet for individual and group interviews on a selected topic. A moderator is present to ask questions and motivate group discussions. Focus groups can alert management to warning signs of market downtrends that might otherwise go undetected. Professional marketers refer to this type of economic radar as a *regional marketing attitude,* and use such information to prepare for coming transitions in advance of any major changes. One of the problems many companies face is that managers may be isolated from marketplace realities due to their preoccupation with other aspects of business operations. A focus group can help by assisting with the development of surveys as well as by anticipating market changes.

Determining the Size of a Survey Sample

The size of a survey sample greatly affects the reliability of the information obtained. In a statistical sense, *reliability* refers to whether the same information would be obtained if similar questions were asked of a similar group of people under similar circumstances. In order to draw general conclusions from the responses of a sample group, the sample must be large enough to allow for individual differences of opinion. For example, a large toy manufacturer researching bathtub duck preferences of three-year-olds would want to get the opinions of more than five children. If three of the five liked yellow ducks, one wanted a black duck, and one was frightened by all ducks offered, it would be risky to assume that other groups of three-year-olds would indicate the same preferences. This hypothetical sample group is so small that if the responses of one or more group members are atypical, their reactions will skew (distort) the survey results. However, if 500 children are surveyed, and 180 to 220 of them are frightened by all ducks presented, the manufacturer could probably assume that 20 percent of three year olds will be afraid of all ducks being tested.

The sample size necessary to produce accurate information is dictated by several factors. Answer these questions to determine sample size: How uniform is the population to be studied? How much error can be tolerated? How stable or subject to change will responses be? What will the cost per person surveyed be? Will the information obtained result in sufficient profits to justify the dollars spent on a large sample? How much time should be allowed for the sampling? When should the project begin?

The more homogeneous the group of consumers being questioned and the larger the error that can be tolerated, the smaller the sample required. If all members of a sample were identical and would respond in exactly the same way, the questioning of a single individual would be adequate. But people are individuals, so there is usually some variation in their responses to any product or service. The good news is that even the largest samplings seldom require more than 2,000 respondents.

Demographic Considerations

In his *Encyclopedic Dictionary of Business Terms,* author Wilbur Cross defines *demographics* as "data that has been compiled and computed to present statistics about the makeup of population segments, specifically in regard to age, sex, education, location, income, ethnic background, and religious faith. Demography is the scientific study of the size, distribution, and composition of human populations . . . a branch of sociology that uses birth and death rates and related statistics to determine the characteristics of a population, discover patterns of change, and make predictions." The use of demographics in marketing has expanded tremendously in recent years because of the ease of compiling and accessing computer data. Several recent sociological trends influence most current marketing strategies:

- the growth of senior citizen/retirement populations
- an increased emphasis on minority groups and a growing demand for ethnic products and services
- the appearance of double-income families in which both parents earn substantial salaries and require full-time child-care services

The preferences of these population groups have become very important and cannot be ignored by marketers. Population shifts and the relocation of retailers to suburban shopping malls have changed commercial profiles drastically. All of these demographic factors should be taken into account when marketing plans are developed. Fortunately, a wealth of demographic data is available for use in planning advertising and promotional campaigns (*see* Demographic Data Sources: Organizations and Publications, page 392).

CUSTOMER-FRIENDLY MARKETING

In today's competitive marketplace, many businesses subscribe to the theory that the customer is always right. Unfortunately, customers are sometimes wrong, and the company is left holding the bag. A better approach is to know who your customers are and what they want, using formal and informal surveys to constantly update this information. Then, if problems occur, they can readily be solved to the customer's satisfaction without undue losses to the company. Accountability for the quality of products and services is vital.

Ask these questions to determine if your marketing strategy is designed to prevent complaints and amicably resolve those that inevitably occur.

- Are sales records studied to determine which types of consumers are repeat customers?
- Do we know why dissatisfied customers have been unhappy with our products or services?
- Have we often solved problems in such a way that the customer continues to do business with us? What were the details of those situations?
- Have we failed to resolve some problems adequately, resulting in lost customers? Have the same problems occurred frequently? Do we value the business of the types of clients typically involved? If so, what can we do to keep them?
- Is our customer relations program adequate and effective?
- Are our policies geared to keep good customers' business, even when they are wrong?
- Do we take steps to show our appreciation of repeat customers' business so that they are motivated to recommend our services to others?

Direct-Mail Marketing

Direct mail is a form of advertising in which a sales message is carried directly from advertisers to prospective buyers via prepared mailing lists. The Direct Mail Advertising Association defines this marketing tool as a means of communicating a message via printed materials sent directly to a select group of prospects. Think of direct mail as a package to be delivered to prospective customers. Each element of the package should be carefully prepared to meet your objectives. Then the whole package should be reviewed to see that its individual parts work well together and present your message clearly.

The main component of a direct mailing is a letter describing the product or service offered. Its language and style should be appropriate for the people to whom it is addressed. Include references to other enclosures, especially order blanks and instructions. Most direct mail letters encourage readers to prompt action if they are interested in advertised products. Graphic design and layout should clarify and draw attention to the text rather than just be decorative or interesting. Of course, all parts of the package should be attractive and look professional. Additional literature and illustrations may be enclosed to supplement information provided in the letter and promote positive action by the consumer. Order forms and instructions should be simple, making it easy for the recipient to respond. Preaddressed, postage-paid envelopes are essential.

Many direct mail marketers purchase mailing lists of specific types of customers. Before buying a mailing list, learn something about the people on it. Have they responded to previous mail by actually becoming customers or clients? How large were their orders? Ask the mailing list supplier these and other specific questions, because otherwise, your company will waste time and money on recipients who are not likely to buy your products.

If you are considering direct mail as a marketing strategy, the Direct Marketing Association is a good source of general information. Established in 1917, this organization has served thousands of companies involved in direct marketing. Its comprehensive database is easily accessible by modem, and its library features over 600 reference books and many trade publications. Seminars and conferences are also available to help direct mailers make the most of their medium. A number of other helpful organizations and publications are listed in Direct Mail Marketing Information: Organizations and Publications, page 392.

Telemarketing

Although telemarketing can be a useful marketing medium, it must be used with care. There are so many fraudulent telemarketing schemes that a special group, the Alliance Against Fraud in Telemarketing, has been formed to protect consumers. More than 70 groups are members of this Washington-based organization. Individual consumers are not the only victims of telephone fraud. Businesses have also been casualties of callers who convince managers to pay nonexistent "overdue" bills. Due to the suspicious atmosphere created by unscrupulous telemarketers, legitimate businesses with reputable sales plans can be vulnerable to consumer complaints and censure if their marketing approach is too aggressive or their claims are exaggerated. To avoid suspicion, telemarketers should refrain from making overstatements, offering discounts or prizes that sound too good to be true, or using exaggerated verbal inducements to make sales. Campaigns should be straightforward and consumer-oriented, with clearly articulated details and explanations.

When properly planned and administered, a telemarketing campaign can be a productive adjunct to other marketing strategies. The advantages of telephone sales include opportunities to do the following:

- communicate quickly and directly with prospective customers
- provide a personal approach
- determine a prospect's degree of interest and make the sale by emphasizing benefits with special appeal
- obtain the names of other prospects after a sale has been made
- determine whether a new product line or service is going to be popular (useful when test marketing)
- use automatic dialing and recorded messages to reach large numbers of prospective clients at a relatively low cost

A disadvantage of telemarketing is that the cost of making enough calls to generate one sale can be quite high. Using a *reseller* or *aggregator* can result in considerable savings. This individual or firm purchases blocks of long-distance telephone time at a discount, then resells the service in smaller allotments. For more information, contact the Telecommunications Resellers Association, a national association representing more than a hundred phone service resellers across the United States. Carriers such as AT&T, MCI, and Sprint also offer special telecommunications services such as temporary 800 numbers, a service that was not available a few years ago. Conducting a limited test within a small geographical area is another money-saving option, as this will help to determine whether a larger telemarketing campaign will be cost effective.

You can also obtain useful information from organizations established to police the industry. This step is recommended for telemarketers planning to offer large discounts or bonuses to telephone prospects. For example, it is important to understand the ethical implications of offering discounts to telephone contacts that are not given to other customers. This kind of information is available from organizations such as SprintGUARD, which has a phone fraud protection plan for small businesses and users of Sprint's 800-number service. The National Consumers League is another excellent source of information on the ethics and standards of telecommunications. Call for Action is an international network of more than 600 volunteers who work hot lines at radio and TV stations to assist, educate, and solve problems for small businesses victimized by fraudulent telemarketers.

The National Telecommunications and Information Administration (U.S. Department of Commerce) makes policy recommendations about telecommunications. It is also involved with making regulatory changes and setting professional standards. Staff members can be helpful in interpreting codes relating to issues of personal privacy that come into play when salespeople call customers at home. Your local phone company can supply you with practical information and recommendations for developing a productive telemarketing campaign. It will also alert you to any state or local restrictions and regulations that apply.

For the addresses and phone numbers of these organizations and a list of useful publications on telemarketing, *see* Telemarketing Assistance: Organizations and Publications, page 392.

On-Line Marketing

Creating a basic web page for your business can be very simple and may cost nothing if your on-line service includes a space for your website as part of the basic package. It is now estimated that as many as 30 million people use the Internet, and many more sign on daily. No special software or expertise is required to set up a page, but development of an on-line catalog with professional graphics may warrant the services of an experienced designer. Updating web page information is fast and easy, so your ads can always be current. Browse the Internet and look at the vast diversity of product information available, then set up your product description/price list/how-to-order information and get ready for a big response.

Tracking the Success of a Marketing Campaign

There are a number of ways to track the effectiveness of a marketing or promotional campaign. For example, if coupons are mailed to customers on a mailing list, you will want to keep records of how many coupons were mailed versus redeemed. Ask new customers or clients how they heard about your business. Was it through a mailing, a friend who attended a product demonstration party, or a giveaway with your company's name and address on it? Did they hear an ad on the radio, or see one in the newspaper? How many requests for more information were generated by your last mailing? How many of those requests turned into actual sales? Did the people who became customers as a result of a trade show promotion spend more money than those who were attracted by a direct mailing? By continually evaluating strategies, you will be able to spend promotional dollars wisely. Learning what customers liked and disliked about any marketing strategy will enable you to improve the next campaign and thus attract more new customers.

Selling Successfully

Twenty Ways to Make It Happen

Selling is an art. Although some people seem to be born with the ability to make any product enticing to others, most successful sales representatives have worked hard to perfect their skills. They have learned to take the active role in business transactions, convincing prospects to become buyers. Here are some tips to help you close those important deals:

1. Know your products or services well and be aware of both positive and negative aspects.
2. Learn what your competitors have to offer.
3. Have the pricing structure firmly in mind, including areas open to negotiation, discounts available, and any other factors that may affect prices.
4. Learn as much as you can about a prospect in advance.
5. If the buyer is a complete stranger, get some ideas about needs and preferences before making your sales pitch.
6. Be friendly, tactful, courteous, and dignified.
7. Update your information about your product and your competitors' products constantly to make sure you know what you are comparing.
8. Do your best to help each customer make the right choice if several alternatives are available. This will reduce later disappointments, returns, and refunds, and satisfied customers will ask for you next time.
9. Be firm and assertive when discussing the merits of your product, but never be overly aggressive.
10. Show genuine interest in the customer's needs.
11. Give your name and number to a prospect who wants time to think before buying, and try to arrange a time to meet again for the decision.
12. Suggest reasonable alternatives when price is an obvious blocking point.
13. Be thoroughly familiar with your company's policies on partial or delayed payments.
14. Have a ready list of satisfied buyers to give as references (with their permission, of course) if your product is expensive or technologically complex.
15. Provide warranties or service contracts when appropriate.
16. Use your time well. When the discussion has obviously reached a dead end, thank the customer for considering your product, offer your assistance for future needs, and move on to other prospects.
17. Be frank and ask appropriate questions if you and your customer seem to be miscommunicating. Look for the real meaning behind the other person's words. Learn something about body language, which can tell you what a customer does not say.
18. Suggest complementary products or services when a sale is satisfactorily completed.
19. Ask discreetly for names of others who may need your services, always taking the attitude that your job is to serve the public.

20. Recognize your customers when they return, calling them by name and referring to purchases they have made in the past.

Developing Your Sales Skills

Good salespeople seem to get better and better, even when they change products or employers. To sharpen your skills, take the attitude that you are always learning something new. Check your current performance to see if you are improving. Nurture your own interest in what you are selling by using the following self-improvement techniques. Your customers will reward you with increased enthusiasm for your product.

1. Learn one basic truth about selling at the start of each work week. Practice that technique all week; in just three months you will have perfected a dozen new sales tools.
2. Seek out successful salespeople for advice. Ignore the others.
3. Team up with a sales colleague for informal training sessions. Ask each other pointed questions about the pros and cons of what you are selling. Pretend you are prospective customers who are pushy or hostile and practice your sales techniques.
4. Visit retail stores, offices, or other outlets where your competitors are making their own sales presentations. When appropriate, request demonstrations. Use what you learn to make your own sales talks better.
5. Keep close track of your sales records—most and least successful—and concentrate your sales efforts at the times (days, hours, seasons) that show the most promise, based on your sales history. Use the other times for paperwork or to do needed research on your products or the competition.

KEEPING IN CONTACT WITH CLIENTS

Staying in contact with clients is a top priority for many successful salespeople. The object is to keep your name and business clearly in their minds. List customers in order of their importance, which is determined by the amount of business they represent at present and in the future. Anticipate their current needs, plans, and interest in your product or service. Keep in touch by sending them helpful information that shows your genuine interest in their fields of endeavor. If in doubt about how often to contact a client, err on the side of calling too much. Never let a client feel neglected.

When possible, enlist the aid of a third party who will speak well of your skills and services to the right people at the right times. In some instances, it may be helpful to talk with a client's customers. This can give you an idea of the client's strong points and shortcomings so you can be of service to all concerned.

Sources of Further Information

Demographic Data Sources: Organizations and Publications

Asian Americans Information Directory. New York: Gale Research, 1992. Covers more than 5,000 organizations concerned with Asian-American life.

Black Americans Information Directory. New York: Gale Research, 1991. Contains some 4,800 entries on organizations concerned with the interests of African-Americans.

Census Catalog and Guide. Published annually by the Superintendent of Documents, U.S. Government Printing Office. Describes demographic literature available, usually at no charge, from the U.S. government.

Consumer USA. New York: Gale Research, 1994. Profiles markets and major producers of consumer goods.

Database Search Service, ATA Services, Inc., 2200 Mill Road, Alexandria, VA 22314. Search and retrieval service, available to the public at a nominal charge, for all information contained in Federal Communications Commission database files.

Databased Marketing. New York: John Wiley & Sons, 1992. A manager's guide to marketing tools of the 21st century.

The Focus Group Directory. Published annually by the American Marketing Association, 250 South Wacker Drive, Chicago, IL 60606, phone 312-648-0536. Recommends ways to use focus groups for marketing.

Hispanic Americans Information Directory. New York: Gale Research, 1993. A guide for marketers interested in selling to Hispanic consumers.

Women's Information Directory. New York: Gale Research, 1995. A guide to more than 5,000 organizations that provide data about the purchasing habits of women of all ages.

Direct Mail Marketing Information: Organizations and Publications

Business to Business: Direct Marketing Resource Guide. Published by the Direct Marketing Association, 11 West 42nd Street, New York, NY 10036-8096, phone 212-768-7277. Constantly updated. Describes resources for assistance in direct mail marketing and selling.

The Complete Direct Mail List Handbook. New York: Prentice-Hall, Inc., 1988. Information on 35 mailing list categories. Recommendations on stimulating positive responses from prospective customers and clients.

Desktop Direct Marketing. New York: McGraw-Hill, 1993. Shows how to use computers to create and distribute personalized direct mail.

Direct Marketing Association, Inc., 11 West 42nd Street, New York, NY 10036-8096, phone 212-768-7277.

The Direct Marketing Handbook. New York: McGraw-Hill, 1994. An encyclopedia of information about direct mail by some of the industry's most successful practitioners.

The Handbook of International Direct Marketing. First published in 1992 by the European Direct Marketing Association. Reviews the world's top 40 markets. Useful for companies doing business in foreign markets.

Telemarketing Assistance: Organizations and Publications

Call for Action national headquarters, phone 202-537-0585. Assists with fraud prevention.

Crocker, Julie, ed. *Telemarketer's Guide to State Laws.* New York: Direct Marketing Association, published annually. A compilation of state laws concerning telemarketing, with a review of pending legislation and a state-by-state list of relevant telemarketing statutes.

Davidson, Robert L. *Contracting Your Services.* New York: John Wiley & Sons, 1990.

Kordahl, Eugene B., and Arnold L. Fishman. *Annual Guide to Telemarketing.* New York: Telemarketing, Inc., published annually. Reports on all phases and levels of telemarketing. Offers information on sales, costs, and suppliers; market profiles; domestic telemarketing service bureaus; and foreign summaries.

National Consumers League/Alliance Against Fraud in Telemarketing, phone 800-876-7060.

National Telecommunications and Information Administration, U.S. Department of Commerce, 14th Street and Constitution Avenue NW, Washington, DC 20230, phone 202-377-1551.

SprintGUARD telephone fraud protection plan, phone 800-877-7330.

Stone, Bob, and John Wyman. *Successful Telemarketing.* New York: NTC Publishing Group, 1992. A step-by-step guide to setting up and managing a telemarketing operation, with examples and case histories.

Telecommunications Resellers Association, phone 703-734-1225.

Marketing Consultants: Directories, Associations, and Publications

American Association of Advertising Agencies, 666 Third Avenue, New York, NY 10017, phone 212-682-2500.

American Management Association, 135 West 50th Street, New York, NY 10019, phone 212-586-8100.

American Marketing Association, 250 South Wacker Drive, Chicago, IL 60606, phone 312-648-0536.

Association of Management Consulting Firms, 521 Fifth Avenue, New York, NY 10175. Provides inquirers with lists of consultants in any specific field.

Consultants and Consulting Organizations Directory. New York: Gale Research, 1994. Lists more than 15,000 consultants and consulting firms in the United States and Canada, arranged by category and fields of expertise.

Consultants News. Kennedy Publications, Templeton Road, Fitzwilliam, NH 03447, phone 603-585-6544.

Database Search Service, ATA Services, Inc., 2200 Mill Road, Alexandria, VA 22314. Search and retrieval service, available to the public at a nominal charge, for all information contained in Federal Communications Commission database files.

Directory of Management Consultants. Published every other year by Kennedy Publications, Templeton Road, Fitzwilliam, NH 03447, phone 603-585-6544. Profiles more than 1,500 firms, indexed according to services offered, location, industry, and key executives.

Dun's Consultants Directory. Published annually by Dun & Bradstreet. Locates, identifies, and classifies top consulting firms in 200 specialties.

European Consultants Directory. New York: Gale Research, 1992. Updated regularly; useful for businesses operating in foreign and domestic markets.

Experts Contact Directory. New York: Gale Research, 1994. Lists expert professional contacts in business, government, and other areas, arranged by hundreds of subject fields.

Levinson, Jay Conrad. *Guerrilla Marketing Online Weapons.* Boston: Houghton. Mifflin Software Reference Division, 1996. An excellent source of information on virtual marketing.

Office of Consumer Affairs, U.S. Department of Commerce, 14th Street and Constitution Avenue NW, Washington, DC 20230. Consultations and technical assistance for businesses regarding consumer-related issues.

Telecommunications Resellers Association, P.O. Box 8361, McLean, VA 22106, phone 703-734-1225.

Other Recommended Reading for Marketing and Business Managers

Argenti, Paul. *The Portable MBA Desk Reference, An Essential Business Companion.* New York: John Wiley & Sons, 1994.

Bangs, David H., Jr., and Steve White. *The Business Planning Guide.* Dover, NH: Upstart Publishing Company, 1992.

Clancy, Kevin, and Robert Shulman. *Marketing Myths That Are Killing Business.* New York: McGraw-Hill, 1994.

Cross, Wilbur. *Growing Your Small Business Made Simple.* New York: Doubleday, 1993.

Daniels, Lorna M. *Business Information Sources.* Berkeley, CA: University of California Press, 1993 (updated regularly). One of the most comprehensive business guides available, with information on marketing and related fields and recommendations on consultants.

Godin, Seth, ed. *Business Almanac & Desk Reference.* Boston: Houghton Mifflin, 1994.

Internet Navigator: A New User's Guide to Network Exploration. New York: John Wiley & Sons, 1994. A useful guide to beginning a search on the Internet.

Kehrer, Daniel. *Saving Your Business a Bundle.* New York: Simon & Schuster, 1994.

McKenna, Shawn. *The Complete Guide to Regional Marketing.* Homewood, IL: Richard D. Irwin, Inc., 1992.

On-Line Resources

Great Website Design *http://www.unplug.com/great/begin.htm*

Marketing Communication *http://www1.usa1.com/~rblunt/market.html*

USDATA, an excellent market research database *http://www.usadata.com*

11

Travel

Planning a Business Trip

First Things First

An organized approach to planning your trip will prevent headaches later. The following details should be handled as soon as possible after scheduling a business trip:

- plane reservations and other transportation arrangements—rental cars, shuttles, transit passes; request special meal or seat selections if desired
- hotel reservations to suit business and personal needs such as conference rooms, safe-deposit boxes, smoking or nonsmoking accommodations, and particular locations
- special requirements for foreign travel:
  (1) a current passport (*see* Passports, page 400)
  (2) a visa, if required (*see* Visas, page 402)
  (3) any immunizations required or recommended (*see* Immunization Requirements for Foreign Travel, page 404)
  (4) an international driving permit, if needed (*see* International Driving Permits, page 403)
  (5) a carnet, if you take displays or samples with you (*see* Carnets, page 416)
  (6) a traveler's insurance policy, if your current insurance policy does not cover you and your belongings when you travel
  (7) a set of business cards in the language of the country you will visit, with an English translation on the reverse side
  (8) a bit of research to verify that your trip will not coincide with a foreign holiday that would complicate matters due to business and bank closures or local tourists crowding transportation, restaurants, and hotels (*see* Holidays Around the World, below)

HOLIDAYS AROUND THE WORLD

World holidays: New Year's Day (January 1)
North and South America: Columbus Day (October 12)
Europe, Latin America, Communist countries: May Day/Labor Day (May 1)
Christian holidays: Epiphany (Roman Catholic, January 6), Good Friday (spring), Easter Sunday and Monday (spring), Assumption (Roman Catholic, August 15), All Saints' Day (Roman Catholic, November 1), Immaculate Conception (Roman Catholic, December 8), Christmas (December 25)
Moslem holidays: Ramadan (early spring)

Argentina: Revolution Day (May 25), Malvinas Day (June 10), Flag Day (June 20), Independence Day (July 9), Anniversary of San Martín's Death (August 17)

Australia: Australia Day (last Monday in January), Veterans Day (April 25), Queen's Birthday (second Monday in June), Boxing Day (December 26)

Austria: National Day (October 26)

Belgium: National Day (July 21), Armistice Day (November 11), Dynasty Day (November 15)

Brazil: Carnival (four days before Ash Wednesday), Tiradentes Day (April 21), Labor Day (May 1), Independence Day (September 7), Feast of Brazil's Patron Saint (October 12), Proclamation of the Republic (November 15)

Canada: Victoria Day (May 22), Dominion Day (July 1), Labour Day (first Monday in September), Thanksgiving (second Monday in October), Remembrance Day (November 11), Boxing Day (December 26)

China: Chinese New Year (late January/early February), Chinese Youth Day (May 4), Communist Day (July 1), People's Liberation Army Day (August 8), National Day (October 1)

Denmark: Common Prayers Day (two weeks after Easter), Constitution Day (June 5)

Egypt: Eid al-Fitr (late spring), Evacuation Day (June 18), Revolution Day (July 23), Eid al-Adha (summer), Hijira (summer), Al-Ashoura (summer), the Prophet's Birthday (autumn), Victory Day (October 6)

France: Joan of Arc's Day (May 14), Bastille Day (July 14), Armistice Day (November 11)

Germany: German Unity Day (June 17)

Great Britain: Twelfth Night (January 5), Spring Bank Holiday (last Monday in May), Queen's Birthday (second Saturday in June), Summer Bank Holiday (last Monday in August), Guy Fawkes Day (November 5), Boxing Day (December 26)

Greece: Independence Day (March 25), National Day (October 28)

India: Republic Day (January 26), Holi (March), Ram Navami (March), Id-Ul-Fir (May), Muharram (August), Independence Day (August 15), Janamashtmi (September/October), Dussehra (October), Gandhi's Birthday (October 2), Diwali (October/November)

Ireland: St. Patrick's Day (March 17), June Bank Holiday (first Monday in June), August Bank Holiday (first Monday in August)

Israel: Purim (March), Passover (April), Holocaust Memorial Day (May), Remembrance Day (May), Independence Day (day after Remembrance Day), Shavuot (seven weeks after Passover), Rosh Hashana (September/October), Yom Kippur (10 days after Rosh Hashana), Sukkoth (five days after Yom Kippur), Shemini Atzeret (seven days after Sukkoth), Simchat Torah (day after Shemini Atzeret), Chanukah (December)

Italy: Liberation Day (April 25), Founding of the Republic Day (June 2), St. Gennaro (September 19), National Unity Day (November 4)

Japan: Genshi-Sai (January 3), Adults' Day (January 15), National Foundation Day (February 11), Emperor's Birthday (April 29), Constitution Memorial Day (May 3), Children's Day (May 5), Respect for the Aged Day (September 15), Culture Day (November 3), Labor Thanksgiving Day (November 23)

Kenya: Kenyatta Day (October 20), Jamhuri Day (December 12)

Korea: Independence Movement Day (March 1), the Buddha's Birthday (April 8), Children's Day (May 5), Memorial Day (June 6), Constitution Day (July 17), Liberation Day (August 15), Thanksgiving (September/ October), Armed Forces Day (October 1), National Foundation Day (October 3)

Mexico: Constitution Day (February 5), Benito Juarez's Birthday (March 21), Cinco de Mayo (May 5), Independence Day (September 6), Day of the Dead (November 1), Mexican Revolution Day (November 20), Feast of Mexico's Patron Saint (December 11 and 12)

Netherlands: Queen's Day (April 30), Liberation Day (May 5), St. Nicholas's Day (December 5)

Philippines: Bataan Day (April 19), Independence Day (June 12), National Heroes' Day (November 30), Rizal Day (December 30)

Portugal: Liberty Day (April 25), National Day (June 10), Proclamation of the Republic Day (October 5), Independence Day (December 1)

Russia: Victory over Fascism Day (May 9), Republic Day (June 12)

South Africa: Van Riebeeck Day (April 6), Republic Day (May 31), Settlers' Day (September 7), Kruger Day (second week in October), Public Holiday (December 17)

Spain: St. Joseph's Day (March 19), Victory Day (April 1), National Day (July 18)

Switzerland: Berchtoldstage (January 2), Independence Day (August 1)

Turkey: National Day (April 23), Youth Day (May 19), Constitution Days (May 27 and 28), Victory Day (August 30), Declaration of the Republic Days (October 29 and 30)

A Week or Two before the Trip

With travel arrangements out of the way, use the last 7 to 14 days before the trip to plan coverage for your office and home responsibilities while you are away.

- Arrange an itinerary. List all scheduled meetings and activities, including times, locations (with directions on how to get there if necessary), and agendas.
- Create an information file to leave with your secretary or coworker. Include your itinerary, the numbers where you can be contacted at all times, photocopies of your passport data page and airline tickets, traveler's check numbers, and insurance information. Take a duplicate copy of this file with you; leave another copy at home.
- Make arrangements for pressing work responsibilities to be covered by a coworker or rescheduled. Leave instructions with your secretary or colleagues on handling your work, mail, and calls while you are away.
- Get the necessary guidebooks or phrase books if you are traveling abroad.
- Arrange for traveler's checks and a small amount of local currency from the country you will visit.
- Take care of personal affairs such as having someone water your plants, walk the dog, and pick up your mail. You may want to have your mail held at the post office.

Three Days before Leaving

When your trip is just around the corner, check the arrangements once more. Then you can pack and get ready to enjoy the trip.

- Confirm all reservations, including flights, hotels, and car rentals.
- Check the weather forecast for your destination, and pack accordingly. Clothing that can be layered for unexpected weather changes is best.
- Pack only what you absolutely need and label all luggage. Place a business card inside each piece in case the tags are lost.

WEATHER IN CITIES OF THE WORLD

	Average daily temperature (F)			
	January		July	
	Low	High	Low	High
Amsterdam	34	40	59	69
Athens	42	54	72	90
Atlanta	34	52	73	89
Berlin	26	35	55	74
Boston	21	38	62	83
Budapest	26	35	61	82
Buenos Aires	63	85	42	57
Cairo	47	65	70	96
Chicago	16	31	64	79
Copenhagen	29	36	55	72
Dublin	35	47	51	67
Geneva	29	39	56	74
Istanbul	36	45	65	81
Jerusalem	41	55	63	87
London	35	44	55	73
Los Angeles	47	67	63	83
Madrid	33	47	62	87
Mexico City	42	66	54	74
Montreal	7	22	61	79
Moscow	9	21	55	76
New York	26	39	68	83
Paris	32	42	55	76
Prague	25	34	58	77
Rome	39	54	64	88
San Francisco	41	56	53	70
Sydney	65	78	46	60
Tokyo	29	47	70	83
Toronto	17	31	60	80
Vienna	26	34	59	75
Washington	28	43	70	88

- Take into account the time difference (Figure 11.1) where you are going and begin trying to adjust to reduce the effects of jet lag. (*See also* Minimizing Jet Lag, page 427.)

The Final Countdown

Just before leaving, make sure you have the following:

- your wallet, with credit cards, traveler's checks, cash, and driver's license
- your passport, plane tickets, transportation passes or vouchers, and reservation numbers
- your itinerary, other business papers and materials, contact numbers, personal phone and address book, and travel expense log (*see* Keeping a Record of Travel Expenses, page 311)
- any medications and prescriptions you need (*see* First-Aid Kit for Travelers, page 426)
- your copy of the information file containing photocopies of your passport data page, plane tickets, traveler's check numbers, and insurance information

Things You'll Need: Passports, Visas, and International Driving Permits

Passports

A valid passport is required to enter most foreign countries. If you have never had one or yours has been lost, you must fill out an application (Form DSP-11). This form is available in post offices, courthouses, and at passport agencies (located in many major cities). Proof of U.S. citizenship is required—you can present a certified copy of your birth certificate, a Certificate of Naturalization, or a Certificate of Citizenship. You must also present a picture I.D., such as a current driver's license or a government I.D. card. In addition, you must supply two identical 2″ × 2″ front-view photographs of yourself. The photos should be recent and should feature your face and head only, on a white background. (Most photography studios will take passport photos for a small fee.) After presenting your proof of citizenship and proof of identity, you will turn in your application, with photos, and pay the required fee. The cost of a passport is $55, plus $10 application execution fee.

If you have an expired passport that was issued less than 12 years ago, you may renew it by mail. Fill out Form DSP-82 (also available at post offices, court-houses, and passport agencies). Mail the form, your expired passport, two recent passport photographs as described previously, and $55 to National Passport Center, P. O. Box 371971, Pittsburgh, PA 15250-7971. (An execution fee is not required for renewals.) Report lost or stolen passports immediately by calling or writing

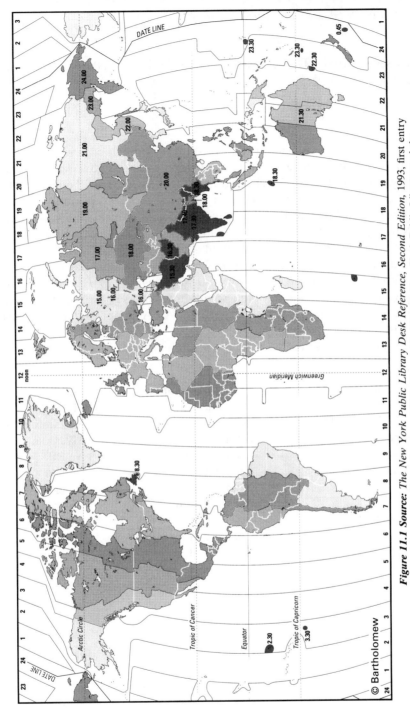

Figure 11.1 Source: *The New York Public Library Desk Reference, Second Edition,* 1993, first entry in the Atlas section that follows page 436. Copyrighted by the New York Public Library and the Stonesong Press, Inc., and published by Prentice-Hall.

Passport Services, Department of State, 1425 K Street NW, Washington, DC 20524, phone 202-647-0518.

Visas

A visa is usually a stamp affixed to your passport. It signifies that your stay in a certain country has been authorized by that country's government. When a visa is required, you will not be allowed to enter the country without one. The consular office of that country will issue your visa by mail or via a personal visit to the office. (Consular offices are located in major U.S. cities, including New York, Chicago, New Orleans, Washington, and San Francisco.) Or you may hire a service to take care of obtaining a visa for you. Find out if you will need a visa as soon as possible to avoid a costly last-minute rush. You may call a consular office to get specific information, or order a copy of *Visa Requirements of Foreign Countries,* a free government brochure. To request the brochure, send a self-addressed, stamped envelope to Bureau of Consular Affairs, CA/PA Room 2807, Department of State, Washington, DC 20520.

Visas are required to enter the following countries:

Afghanistan	El Salvador	Mauritania
Albania	Equatorial Guinea	Moldova
Algeria	Ethiopia	Mongolia
Angola (travel restricted)	Gabon	Mozambique
Armenia	Gambia	Myanmar
Australia	Ghana	Nauru
Azerbaijan	Guatemala	Nepal
Bahrain	Guinea	Niger
Benin	Guinea-Bissau	Nigeria
Bhutan	India	Oman
Brazil	Iran (travel restricted)	Pakistan
Brunei	Iraq (travel restricted)	Panama
Burkina Faso	Jordan	Qatar
Burundi	Kazakhstan	Romania
Byelorus	Kenya	Russia
Cameroon	Kiribati	Rwanda
Cape Verde Islands	Kuwait	São Tomé and Principe
Central African Republic	Kyrgyzstan	Saudi Arabia
Chad	Laos	Sierra Leone
China	Lebanon (travel restricted)	Somalia
Congo	Liberia	South Africa
Cuba (travel restricted)	Libya (travel restricted)	Sudan
Djibouti	Lithuania	Suriname
Dominican Republic	Madagascar	Syria
Egypt	Mali	Taiwan

Tajikistan	Ukraine	Venezuela
Tanzania	United Arab Emirates	Yemen
Turkmenistan	Uzbekistan	Zambia
Uganda		

Countries that do not require visas usually place a limit on how long you are allowed to stay without notifying the government—often 90 days, though it may be as little as two weeks. If you plan to spend an extended period of time in a foreign country, notify the country's consulate before leaving, even if a visa is not required for short visits.

International Driving Permits

Your U.S. driver's license will be accepted in many foreign nations, but some (mainly in Asia, Central America, and Africa) require an International Driver's Permit (IDP) for foreign drivers. In fact, the governments of most countries other than Canada and Mexico, our neighbors, would prefer that you have an IDP, even though they will accept a U.S. driver's license. An IDP should be obtained before leaving the United States. It is available from the American Automobile Association (AAA), the American Automobile Touring Alliance (AATA), and other auto clubs (*see* Foreign Driving, page 453, for addresses/ phone numbers). You must be at least 18 years old and have a valid U.S. driver's license to obtain an International Driving Permit. An application, two recent passport photos, and a fee are required.

Should You Drive in a Foreign Country?

There are some clear advantages to renting a car when traveling abroad. It eliminates waiting for public transportation and figuring out complex schedules. You may also be able to reach some places by auto that are not accessible by public transport. However, there are a number of reasons to think twice before driving abroad.

Traffic in most foreign cities, as in the United States, is terrible; parking is often impossible; and drivers can be very aggressive and reckless. Auto theft—particularly of rental cars—is a big problem in all countries, especially in poorer areas. Gasoline tends to be much more expensive outside the United States and can be extremely difficult to find in less developed countries. Even the price of renting a car can be staggeringly expensive in areas such as South America, Eastern Europe, and Africa. In these regions and in Asia and Central America as well, it is less expensive to hire a car and driver than to rent a car and drive it yourself. In Europe and Japan, road tolls can be prohibitive, and many countries require the purchase of special insurance before allowing foreign citizens to drive.

In less developed nations, country roads are often unpaved, unlighted, and dangerous. Driving can be very hazardous in mountainous or rainy regions of Africa, Asia, Central America, and South America. Animals roam freely on the roads in many countries and can cause serious problems for drivers. In addition, communication difficulties can make getting around—or getting help—very difficult. In developed countries, driving problems and dangers arise from unfamiliar road rules and customs. Europeans, for instance, tend to drive very fast on highways, up to 100 miles per hour. In Japan, the United Kingdom, Ireland, and Cyprus, cars are driven on the left side of the road. Familiarizing yourself with universal road signs in advance will help you drive safely when abroad. A good source is Bill Meier's *Autorental Europe* (*see* Foreign Driving, page 453, for more information).

If you are considering driving a car in a foreign country, make sure that you are properly insured and familiar with the local driving laws and customs. Your auto club, AAA, or AATA can supply more information about the areas you intend to visit.

Immunization Requirements for Foreign Travel

Before traveling abroad, check with your travel agent about necessary immunizations and/or special health warnings for the country of your destination. Then see your physician. You probably received routine vaccinations against a number of diseases during childhood, but periodic boosters are required in many cases:

- tetanus/diphtheria booster (required every 5 to 10 years)
- mumps inoculation, if you have not had the disease
- measles/rubella vaccination, if you have not had the disease
- polio booster
- influenza shot for the elderly and those with chronic disorders such as heart disease, diabetes, or cancer
- pneumococcal vaccine for the elderly and others at special risk

Other vaccinations are also recommended before traveling to areas where certain infectious diseases are a problem. Inoculations against Japanese encephalitis, typhoid, hepatitis, meningitis, plague, rabies, smallpox, influenza, and pneumococcus may be advisable. Gamma globulin injections to boost your immune system may also be needed.

In addition, proof of vaccination against yellow fever is required before entering the following countries if you are coming from an area where yellow fever is prevalent:

Benin	Côte d'Ivoire	Niger
Burkina Faso	French Guiana	Panama
Cameroon	Gabon	Rwanda
Central African Republic	Ghana	Senegal
Chad	Liberia	Togo
Congo	Mali	

Yellow fever inoculation is required before entering these countries if you are coming from an infected area and staying over two weeks:

Afghanistan
Albania
Algeria
Angola
Antigua and Barbuda
Aruba
Australia
Bahamas
Bahrain
Bangladesh
Barbados
Belize
Bhutan
Bolivia
Bonaire
Brazil
Brunei
Burundi
Cambodia
Cape Verde Islands
China
Curacao
Djibouti
Dominica
Ecuador
Egypt
El Salvador
Equatorial Guinea
Ethiopia
Fiji
French Polynesia
Gambia
Greece
Grenada
Guadeloupe
Guatemala

Guinea
Guinea-Bissau
Guyana
Haiti
Honduras
India
Indonesia
Iran
Iraq
Jamaica
Jordan
Kenya
Kiribati
Laos
Lebanon
Lesotho
Libya
Madagascar
Madeira
Malawi
Malaysia
Maldives
Malta
Martinique
Mauritania
Mauritius
Mexico
Montserrat
Mozambique
Myanmar
Namibia
Nauru
Nepal
New Caledonia
Nicaragua
Nigeria
Oman

Pakistan
Papua New Guinea
Paraguay
Peru
Philippines
Qatar
Reunion
St. Eustatius
St. Kitts and Nevis
St. Lucia
St. Martin
St. Vincent and the Grenadines
Samoa
São Tomé and Principe
Saudi Arabia
Sierra Leone
Singapore
Solomon Islands
Somalia
South Africa
Sri Lanka
Sudan
Suriname
Swaziland
Syria
Taiwan
Tanzania
Thailand
Tonga
Trinidad and Tobago
Tunisia
Tuvalu
Uganda
Vietnam
Yemen
Zimbabwe

Cholera immunization is required in a few countries as well, but the U.S. Centers for Disease Control and Prevention (CDC) has issued a statement that the cholera vaccination available in the United States confers only a very brief immunity. Further, CDC literature states that the chances of contracting cholera are very low, and it can usually be avoided by careful attention to the cleanliness of food eaten abroad. Check with your physician or look for details on all immunization recommendations at the CDC's website (*http://www.cdc.gov*).

International Certificate of Vaccination (ICV)

Before traveling to areas requiring immunizations, it is a good idea to get an ICV. This is a small booklet issued by the U.S. Department of Health and Human Services documenting your inoculation history. It should be presented on entering a foreign country. An ICV will also indicate whether you have been tested for the HIV virus, an increasingly pressing requirement for long-term visits to many countries because of growing concern about AIDS. To request an ICV, write the Government Printing Office, Washington, DC 20402, or call the Centers for Disease Control and Prevention at 404-639-2572. Or you may want to request a copy of the government publication *Health Information for International Travel*. It is available by sending $5 to the Government Printing Office. This booklet contains detailed information on required immunizations for foreign travel.

TAKING THE OFFICE WITH YOU VIA PORTABLE COMPUTER

Business travelers with laptop or notebook computers are so common-place that some hotels (the Nob Hill Lambourne in San Francisco, for instance) now provide Internet connections in every room. But most accommodations are not so user-friendly, so be sure to take all necessary equipment with you if on-line access is critical, including an ordinary extension cord and an adapter to connect your portable to any phone.

Also be aware of special safety precautions when traveling with your laptop—portable computers are prime targets for airport thieves. Make sure you have a carrying case with an over-the-shoulder strap and keep the computer with you at all times. Setting it down for even a moment while filling out luggage tags or standing in line is all the opportunity needed for someone to take it and disappear. It is also a good idea to carry your laptop with you on the plane rather than check it with your luggage, as thieves snatch laptops from baggage carousels. Be especially vigilant when going through the security checkpoints, too; make sure the guard is watching your laptop when you put it on the carrier, and do not allow anyone to step ahead of you in line after putting down your computer or other valuables on the moving surface. (*See also* Portable Computers, page 145, and Taking Presentations on the Road, page 162.)

Reservations and Other Logistics

Finding a Good Travel Agency

If you travel frequently, consider using a travel agency to make your arrangements. A good agent can help you save money and get the most out of your trips. Assess your business travel needs before choosing an agent. How much do you plan to use this service? Will your firm choose one agency for all its travel needs? Are there any specific aspects of business travel, such as frequent visits to a particular region or site, that may require an agent with a specialty in that area? Try to have as definite an idea as possible of your travel plans before approaching an agent.

Ask friends and business associates for referrals to travel agencies, but remember that an agency that works well for one type of travel is not always the best choice for other needs. When you find an agency you would like to consider, ask if that firm belongs to trade associations such as the International Air Transport Association and the Airline Reporting Corporation. You may call the American Society of Travel Agents to inquire about their membership.

Next, call the agency to schedule a meeting. When you visit, ask these questions:

1. How well are the agents trained? Are they required to keep up with travel industry changes by attending seminars or reading publications? Are they familiar with the latest techniques used in the business?
2. What kind of equipment do agents use? A good agency will have a computer system to book flights, car rentals, and hotels. Accounts and clients' travel histories should also be computerized.
3. What volume discounts or other incentives does the agency offer? Compare its prices with those of other agencies to find the best prices and service.
4. What is the rate of employee turnover at the agency? Working with the same agent for each trip allows you to develop a relationship in which the agent understands your needs and can be trusted to fill them. Generally, a stable staff also indicates productive workers.
5. What is the agency's reputation? Can it provide good references? Ask for the names of clients you may contact to discuss the firm's strengths and weaknesses.

After retaining a travel agency, observe whether personal attention is given to your firm's travel needs and whether problems are satisfactorily addressed. Do you interact well with the agent assigned to your account? Communicate any questions or requests you have. Continue to monitor service delivery throughout your relationship with the travel agency.

Making Your Own Arrangements: Useful Toll-Free Numbers

If you do not use a travel agent when planning your trip, you will want to compare the prices and packages available from a number of travel services. Many airlines offer discounts to people who travel often; some credit card companies, hotels, and car rental agencies have agreements allowing their clients to earn airline discounts. The following lists of toll-free numbers for airlines, frequent flier programs, hotels, and rental agencies should make your planning a little easier. In addition, the Major Cities Travel Guide, page 429, includes telephone numbers for some of the finest restaurants and hotels in 50 large cities throughout the world as well as data on local transportation and other services. It is also easy now to compare prices, packages, and change-over information and to reserve tickets using the Internet.

U.S. Airline Companies

Alaska Airlines, 800-426-0333
American Airlines, 800-433-7300
America West Airlines, 800-235-9292
Continental Airlines, 800-525-0280
Delta Airlines, 800-221-1212
Hawaiian Airlines, 800-367-7637
Northwest Airlines, 800-225-2525 domestic, 800-447-4747 international
Southwest Airlines, 800-435-9792
Tower Air, 800-221-2500
TWA, 800-221-2000 domestic, 800-892-4141 international
United Airlines, 800-241-6522
USAir, 800-428-4322

AIRPORT SECURITY MEASURES

In the wake of increasing terrorist activities, hijackings, and bombings, airport security measures continue to grow tighter in an effort to protect passengers from harm. Due to the increasing sophistication of weapons that could be smuggled aboard, it is best to check with your airline before making a long trip to see if security measures have changed since your last flight. Most airlines continue to allow passengers to carry laptop computers and other electronic equipment with them onto the plane, but this may change. Also, check to see if your cellular phone can be taken through security, and be sure to follow posted rules about using telephone and computer equipment during flights. Arrive early enough to have time to spare for waiting in line at security checkpoints.

Foreign Airline Companies

Aer Lingus (Ireland), 800-223-6537
Aeroflot Russian International Airlines, 800-995-5555
Aerolineas Argentinas, 800-333-0276
Aeromexico, 800-237-6639
Air Afrique, 800-456-9192
Air Canada, 800-776-3000
Air France, 800-237-2747
Air New Zealand, 800-262-1234
Alitalia (Italy), 800-223-5730
All Nippon Airways (Japan), 800-235-9262
Ansett Australia, 800-366-1300
Asiana Airlines (Korea), 800-227-4262

Austrian Airlines, 800-843-0002
British Airways, 800-247-9297
Canadian Airlines, 800-426-7000
China Airlines, 800-227-5118
Czechoslovak Airlines, 800-223-2365
El Al (Israel), 800-223-6700
Finnair, 800-950-5000
Gulf Air (Persian Gulf), 800-553-2824
Iberia Airlines (Spain), 800-772-4642
Japan Airlines, 800-525-3663
KLM Royal Dutch Airlines, 800-374-7747
Korean Air, 800-438-5000
Kuwait Airways, 800-424-1128
Lan Chile, 800-735-5526
Lufthansa (Germany), 800-645-3880
Mexicana Airlines, 800-531-7901
Olympic Airways (Greece), 800-223-1226
Pakistan International Airlines, 800-221-2552
Qantas (Australia), 800-227-4500
Royal Air Maroc, 800-344-6726
Royal Jordanian, 800-223-0470
Sabena Belgian World Airlines, 800-950-1000
Scandinavian Air, 800-221-2350
South African Airways, 800-722-9675
Swissair, 800-221-4750
TAP Air (Portugal), 800-221-7370
Turkish Airlines, 800-874-8875
Varig Brazilian Airlines, 800-468-2744
Virgin Atlantic (Great Britain), 800-862-8621

Frequent Flier Programs

- American Airlines AAdvantage, 800-882-8880
  AAdvantage Department MD 5400
  P. O. Box 619688
  DFW Airport, TX 75261-9688
    Partners: Airlines—American Eagle, British Airways, Canadian Airlines,
                  Cathay Pacific, Qantas, Singapore Airlines, TWA
              Hotels—Hilton, Inter-Continental, Marriott, Ritz Carlton, Sheraton,
                  Vista, Wyndham
              Car rentals—Alamo, Avis, Hertz
              Other—Citibank AAdvantage VISA/MasterCard, Diners Club, MCI
                  Long Distance
- America West Airlines FlightFund, 800-247-5691
  FlightFund Service Center

P. O. Box 20050
Phoenix, AZ 85036-0050
    Partners: Airlines—Aeromexico, Air France, Northwest Airlines
            Hotels—Colony, Doubletree, Hilton, Radisson, Westin
            Car rentals—Budget, Thrifty
- Continental Airlines OnePass, 800-344-1411
OnePass Service Center
P. O. Box 4365
Houston, TX 77210-4365
    Partners: Airlines—Aer Lingus, Air Canada, Alitalia, Austrian Airlines, Cayman Airways, Continental Express, Iberia Airlines, KLM, Lan Chile, Malaysia Airlines, SAS
            Hotels—Aston, Camino Real, Doubletree, Marriott, Radisson
            Car rentals—Dollar, National, Thrifty
            Other—American Express, Diners Club, OnePass Marine Midland Bank VISA/MasterCard
- Delta Airlines Frequent Flyer, 800-323-2323
Frequent Flyer Service Center
Hartsfield International Airport, Dept. 745
P. O. Box 2532
Atlanta, GA 30320-2532
    Partners: Airlines—Air New Zealand, Atlantic Southwest Airlines, COMAIR, Japan Airlines, KLM, Lufthansa, Singapore Airlines, Sky West, Swissair
            Hotels—Forte, Hilton, Hyatt, Marriott
            Car rentals—Alamo, Avis
            Other—American Express, Diners Club
- Midwest Express Airlines Frequent Flyer, 800-452-2022
Midwest Express Frequent Flyer Service Center
P. O. Box 37136
Milwaukee, WI 53237-0136
    Partners: Airlines—Northwest Airlines, SAS, Skyway Airlines
            Hotels—American Club, Loews, Wyndham
            Car rentals—Avis, National
            Other—Midwest Parcel Express
- Northwest Airlines WorldPerks, 800-435-9696
WorldPerks Service Center
P. O. Box 11001
St. Paul, MN 55111-0001
    Partners: Airlines—Airlink, Alaska Airlines, America West Airlines, Big Sky, Horizon, KLM, USAir (some)
            Hotels—Holiday Inn, Hotel New Otani, Hyatt, Marriott, Radisson, Westin
            Car rentals—Budget, Hertz, National

Other—American Express, Diners Club, Dining for Miles, MCI Long
Distance, WorldPerks VISA
- Southwest Airlines Company Club, 800-445-5764
Company Club Service Center
HQ 1CC
P. O. Box 36657
Dallas, TX 75235-1657
Partners: American Express, Diners Club
- TWA Frequent Flight Bonus, 800-325-4815
Frequent Flight Bonus Service Center
P. O. Box 800
Fairview Village, PA 19409-0800
Partners: Airlines—Air India, Alaska Airlines, American Airlines, Philip-
pine Airlines
Hotels—Adam's Mark, Doubletree, Forte, Marriott
Car rental—Dollar
Other—Diners Club, Getaway Card, Metromedia Long Distance,
NY Helicopter
- United Airlines Mileage Plus, 800-421-4655
Mileage Plus Service Center
P. O. Box 28870
Tucson, AZ 85726-8870
Partners: Airlines—Air Canada, Air France, Alitalia, Aloha Airlines, Ansett
Australia, British Airways, British Midland, Iberia, KLM,
Lufthansa, SAS, Swissair
Hotels—Hilton, Hyatt, Inter-Continental, Sheraton, Westin
Car rentals—Alamo, Dollar, Hertz, National
Other—Diners Club, First Card Classic VISA/MasterCard, Princess
Cruises, Royal Caribbean Cruises
- USAir Frequent Traveler, 800-872-4738
Frequent Traveler Service Center
P. O. Box 5
Winston-Salem, NC 27102-0005
Partners: Airlines—Air France, Air New Zealand, Alitalia, All Nippon Air-
ways, British Airways, Lufthansa, Northwest Airlines, Sa-
bena, Swissair
Hotels—Hilton, Hyatt, Marriott, Omni, Radisson, Stouffer, Westin
Car rentals—Alamo, Hertz, National
Other—American Express, Carnival Cruises, Diners Club, USAir/
NationsBank VISA
- Other airlines with frequent flier programs with U.S. phone numbers:
Aer Lingus Travel Award Bonus, 800-223-6537
Aeromexico Aeromiles, 800-247-3737
Air Canada Aeroplan, 800-361-8253
Air France Fréquence Plus Air France, 800-237-2747

Air New Zealand Air Points, 800-262-1234
Alaska Airlines Mileage Plan, 800-654-5669
All Nippon Airways Goldpass, 800-262-4653
Ansett Australia Airlines Frequent Flyer, 800-366-1300
Asiana Airlines Bonus Club, 800-227-4262
British Airways Executive Club, 800-955-2748
Canadian Airlines Canadian Plus, 800-426-7007
China Airlines Dynasty Flyer Club, 800-227-5118
Finnair Plus North America, 800-950-3387
Hawaiian Airlines Gold Plus, 800-367-7637
Iberia Airlines Plus, 800-772-4642
Japan Airlines Mileage Bank Americas, 800-525-6453
KLM Flying Dutchman, 800-556-1300
Korean Air Mileage Dividend, 800-438-5000
Lan Chile Lan Pass, 800-735-5526
Lufthansa Miles and More, 800-247-8200
MarkAir TravelMark, 800-478-0800
Mexicana Airlines Frequent Flyer, 800-531-7901
Qantas Frequent Flyer, 800-348-5607
Scandinavian Airlines System (SAS) EuroBonus, 800-437-5807
Swissair QualiFlyer, 800-221-4750
Virgin Atlantic Airlines Freeway, 800-365-9500

For additional frequent flier information, call the *USA Today* Frequent Flier Hotline at 900-555-5555, then choose option 1. There is a charge per minute for each call.

SAFE FLYING TIPS

Although many seasoned travelers ignore the safety instructions drill provided by airline staff at the beginning of each flight, safety experts recommend paying close attention no matter how often you fly. In particular, the location of the nearest exit and how to operate that door may be of great importance if you are involved in a crash or need to exit quickly due to fire or other emergency. The nearest exit is different in relation to each seat on the plane, and every type of plane is different, too. Emergencies usually involve split-second decisions by passengers and crew who may be injured or in shock; knowing what to do in advance may save your life and that of others. Even if you are not seated next to an exit, it may be necessary for you to open it or help someone else do so.

It is equally important to ensure that you are familiar with seat belt operation so that yours can be disengaged quickly, even in the dark. Airline statistics indicate that many passengers in disabled craft fail to exit safely because of time spent groping for a seat belt latch by their sides (as in automobile seat belts) rather than correctly reaching for a latch in the center. Also pay attention to the instructions on how to put yourself in the brace position, and be sure to do so immediately if a crash seems imminent. Most accidents occur during takeoffs and landings—be alert for trouble at those times.

Domestic Car Rental Agencies

Agency, 800-321-1972
Alamo, 800-327-0400
Avis, 800-331-1212
Budget, 800-527-0700
Courtesy, 800-252-9756
Dollar, 800-421-6878
Enterprise, 800-325-8007
General, 800-327-7607

Hertz, 800-654-3131
National, 800-CAR-RENT
Payless, 800-PAYLESS
Rent-a-Wreck, 800-421-7253
Sears, 800-527-0770
Thrifty, 800-367-2277
Ugly Duckling, 888-811-8059
Value, 800-327-2501

International Car Rental Agencies

Auto Europe, 800-223-5555
Avis, 800-331-2112
Bon Voyage by Car, 800-272-3299
Budget, 800-472-3325
Carey International Limousine Service, 800-336-4646
National Car Rental Europcar, 800-227-7368

European Car Reservations, 800-535-3303
Hertz, 800-654-3001
Kemwel Holiday Auto, 800-678-0678
Meier's International, 800-937-0700

Hotel Franchises

Best Western, 800-528-1234
Budget Hosts, 800-283-4678
Clarion, 800-252-7466
Colony, 800-777-1700
Comfort Inn, 800-228-5150
Days Inn, 800-325-2525
Doubletree, 800-528-0444
Econo Lodge, 800-553-2666
Embassy Suites, 800-362-2779
Forte, 800-225-5843
Four Seasons, 800-332-3442
Friendship Inns, 800-453-4511
Guest Quarters, 800-424-2900
Hilton, 800-HILTONS
Holiday Inn, 800-HOLIDAY
Hotel Express, 800-866-2015
Howard Johnson, 800-654-HOJO
Hyatt, 800-233-1234

Inter-Continental, 800-327-0200
La Quinta, 800-531-5900
Le Meridien, 800-543-4300
Marriott, 800-228-9290
Motel 6, 800-466-8356
Nikko International, 800-645-5687
Omni, 800-843-6664
Quality Inn, 800-228-5151
Radisson, 800-333-3333
Ramada Inn, 800-2-RAMADA
Red Lion, 800-547-8010
Ritz Carlton, 800-241-3333
Sheraton, 800-325-3535
Sleep Inn, 800-221-2222
Stouffer, 800-468-3571
Super 8, 800-848-8888
Westin, 800-228-3000
Wyndham, 800-822-4200

TELEPHONE DIRECTORY: FOREIGN AIRPORTS

Before or during your trip, you may wish to contact a foreign airport for information about flights, car rentals, airport shuttles, or other details. The main telephone numbers for airports in major world cities are listed below.

Amsterdam: Schiphol Airport, 0635-034050

Athens: Ellinikon Airport, 01-96991

Beijing: Beijing Airport, 1-456-4466

Berlin: Tegel Airport, 030-41011; Schönefeld Airport 030-67870

Bombay: Bombay Airport, 22-8366700

Brussels: Zaventem Airport, 02-7222111

Budapest: Ferihegy Airport, 1-1577-155

Buenos Aires: Ezeiza International Airport (no direct number)

Cairo: Cairo International Airport, 202-244-1050

Copenhagen: Copenhagen Airport, 3-250-9333

Dublin: Collinstown Airport, 1-379900

Geneva: Cointrin Airport, 22-799-3111

Jerusalem: Ben Gurion Airport, 3-971-1071

Lisbon: Portela Airport, 01-802060

London: Heathrow Airport, 0181-7595511; Gatwick Airport, 01293-535353

Madrid: Barajas Airport, 91-205-8343

Montreal: Dorval Airport, 514-633-3105; Mirabel Airport, 514-476-3010

Moscow: Shevemetyevo International Airport, 095-578-9101 or 095-578-7816

Paris: Charles de Gaulle Airport, 48-62-12-12; Orly Airport, 49-75-52-52

Prague: Ruzyně Airport, 02-367814

Rome: Fiumicino (Leonardo da Vinci Airport), 06-65951

Sydney: Kingsford-Smith Airport, 612-667-9111

Tokyo: Narita Airport, 047-632-2800

Toronto: Lester B. Pearson International Airport, 416-676-3506

Vienna: Schwechat Airport, 0222-71110-2231

Warsaw: Okecie Airport, 022-46-96-70

Zurich: Kloten Airport, 01-8121212

Major U.S. Airports

International airports are large, busy, and confusing places. A general idea of the layout may help you find your way to connecting flights, restaurants, and comfort stations. The best way to get an idea of the layout is to consult an airport map ahead of time. These maps are available from a number of places—travel agents, airlines, and airports. You may even obtain one on-line at an airline or airport website.

AIR MILEAGE BETWEEN MAJOR U.S. CITIES

	Atla	Bost	Chic	Clev	Dal	Den	Detr	Hou	L.A.	Mia	Min	N.O.	N.Y.	Phila	Phoe	Pitts	St.L	S.F.	Seatt	Was
Atlanta	—	1037	674	672	795	1398	699	789	2182	655	1068	479	841	741	1793	687	541	2496	2618	608
Boston	1037	—	963	628	1748	1949	695	1804	2979	1504	1368	1507	206	296	2604	561	1141	3095	2976	429
Chicago	674	963	—	335	917	996	266	1067	2054	1329	405	912	802	738	1713	452	289	2142	2013	671
Cleveland	672	628	335	—	1159	1321	170	1273	2367	1264	740	1030	473	413	1992	129	529	2467	2348	346
Dallas	795	1748	917	1159	—	781	1143	243	1387	1300	936	496	1552	1452	998	1204	630	1753	2078	1319
Denver	1398	1949	996	1321	781	—	1253	1019	1059	2037	841	1273	1771	1691	792	1411	857	1235	1307	1616
Detroit	699	695	266	170	1143	1253	—	1265	2311	1352	671	1045	637	573	1957	287	513	2399	2279	506
Houston	789	1804	1067	1273	243	1019	1265	—	1538	1190	1157	356	1608	1508	1149	1313	779	1912	2274	1375
Los Angeles	2182	2979	2054	2367	1387	1059	2311	1538	—	2687	1889	1883	2786	2706	389	2426	1845	379	1131	2631
Miami	655	1504	1329	1264	1300	2037	1352	1190	2687	—	1723	856	1308	1208	2298	1202	1196	3053	3273	1075
Minneapolis	1068	1368	405	740	936	841	671	1157	1889	1723	—	1214	1207	1143	1616	857	552	1940	1608	1076
New Orleans	479	1507	912	1030	496	1273	1045	356	1883	856	1214	—	1311	1211	1494	1070	673	2249	2574	1078
New York	841	206	802	473	1552	1771	637	1608	2786	1308	1207	1311	—	100	2411	368	948	2934	2815	233
Philadelphia	741	296	738	413	1452	1691	573	1508	2706	1208	1143	1211	100	—	2331	288	868	2866	2751	133
Phoenix	1793	2604	1713	1992	998	792	1957	1149	389	2298	1616	1494	2411	2331	—	2051	1470	763	1437	2256
Pittsburgh	687	561	452	129	1204	1411	287	1313	2426	1202	857	1070	368	288	2051	—	588	2578	2465	221
St. Louis	541	1141	289	529	630	857	513	779	1845	1196	552	673	948	868	1470	588	—	2089	2081	793
San Francisco	2496	3095	2142	2467	1753	1235	2399	1912	379	3053	1940	2249	2934	2866	763	2578	2089	—	808	2799
Seattle	2618	2976	2013	2348	2078	1307	2279	2274	1131	3273	1608	2574	2815	2751	1437	2465	2081	808	—	2684
Washington	608	429	671	346	1319	1616	506	1375	2631	1075	1076	1078	233	133	2256	221	793	2799	2684	—

AIR MILEAGE BETWEEN MAJOR CITIES OF THE WORLD

	Beijing	*Cairo*	*London*	*L.A.*	*MexCty*	*Montreal*	*Moscow*	*N.Y.*	*Paris*	*Rome*	*Tokyo*
Beijing	—	4698	5074	6250	7753	6519	3607	6844	5120	5063	1307
Cairo	4698	—	2185	7520	7700	5427	1803	5619	1998	1326	5958
London	5074	2185	—	5439	5558	3254	1564	3456	214	895	5959
Los Angeles	6250	7520	5439	—	1542	2427	6068	2451	5601	6326	5470
Mexico City	7753	7700	5558	1542	—	2317	6676	2086	5725	6737	7035
Montreal	6519	5427	3254	2427	2317	—	4401	331	3432	4104	6471
Moscow	3607	1803	1564	6068	6676	4401	—	4683	1554	1483	4660
New York	6844	5619	3456	2451	2086	331	4683	—	3628	4280	6757
Paris	5120	1998	214	5601	5725	3432	1554	3628	—	690	6053
Rome	5063	1326	895	6326	6377	4104	1483	4280	690	—	6142
Tokyo	1307	5958	5959	5470	7035	6471	4660	6757	6053	6142	—

Making Your Way Through Customs

Customs inspections are often quick and easy. Some customs agents accept travelers' declarations without question, but choose a few people at random for more detailed searches. In any event, it is best to know in advance exactly what items may be brought into a country without paying exorbitant duties for the privilege of doing so. The following general information may give you some idea of what to expect. For more detailed information on customs matters, order the free U.S. government booklet *Know Before You Go* by writing or calling the U.S. Customs Service, P. O. Box 7407, Washington, DC 20044, phone 202-927-6724.

Foreign Customs

Before entering a foreign country, you must pass through customs. The practices of foreign customs agents vary; some are tougher and more restrictive than others. Most countries have reasonable rules that allow travelers to bring in tourist supplies such as cameras. But you may be charged a duty on certain items such as jewelry, perfume, guns, or legal drugs in excess of personal need if an agent suspects you will try to sell them while abroad. If you must pay a fee, try to register the items in order to get refunds on those taken with you when you leave.

Carnets

A carnet is an official document issued by the International Chamber of Commerce based in New York City. It includes vouchers listing the items you are bringing into a foreign country with you and specifies your travel timetable. It guarantees a foreign nation's customs service that all duties and taxes will be paid on articles brought into the country and not taken with you when you leave. If you do not have a carnet, you must leave a deposit or post bond with customs in each country entered to cover any items a customs agent suspects you will try to sell before leaving.

A carnet is valid for up to one year. It can be taken into each country visited unless there is a change in your travel schedule or in the articles you are carrying. If such a change occurs, you will need a new carnet. The minimum price for a carnet is $150, and the price rises according to the value of the items carried. If you suspect that you will be charged duties or taxes on items such as product samples, computer equipment, or business display materials, it would be wise to consider using a carnet.

For carnet information and applications, contact the U.S. Council, International Chamber of Commerce, 1212 Avenue of the Americas, New York, NY 10036, or call 212-354-4480.

U.S. Customs

Upon reentering the United States, you must declare any items acquired while abroad. Declaration forms are usually given to airline passengers a few minutes before landing. You must list each item and the price you paid for it; if an article was a gift, list its market value. The U.S. customs inspector will ask to see this form.

Each person is allowed to bring goods with a total value of $400 into the United States duty-free. Goods valued between $400 and $1,000 will be charged a 10 percent duty (for example, if you have goods worth $500, a $10 duty will be charged). Items totaling more than $1,000 in value are charged varying amounts of duty. (When returning from a trip to any U.S. territory, you are allowed a $1,200 exemption from duty. When coming back from Central America or the Caribbean, a $600 exemption is allowed.)

Restrictions

You must be abroad at least 48 hours to qualify for the standard $400 exemption. In addition, you may receive the exemption only once within a 30-day period. Reentering the United States a second time within 30 days will result in an exemption of only $25 for that trip. Items brought into the country must be for your own use and not for resale. Certain plants, animals, foods, and medicines may not be brought into the United States. No more than one liter of alcoholic beverage, 100 non-Cuban cigars, and 200 cigarettes are allowed. Antiques and art more than 100 years old are duty-free.

If you leave the United States with items made in foreign countries or not marked as made in the United States, you are advised to register them with the customs office before leaving. Or carry receipts or insurance forms as proof that you purchased them in the United States or acquired them before leaving on this trip abroad. This includes jewelry you may be wearing—you could be charged a hefty duty on a $2,500 gold necklace that you have worn for ten years unless you can show proof that you did not purchase it while abroad.

When in Rome . . .

Foreign Business Etiquette

To make a good impression on business associates in foreign countries, remember that everyday etiquette may be quite different abroad. The casual manners typical of U.S. citizens are very different from the formalities observed in other countries. For instance, it is customary to use courtesy titles rather than first names when referring to associates abroad even if you have known these colleagues for a while. Outward signs of gender equality that are important in U.S. business etiquette are much less common overseas. Even in westernized countries, it is often considered inappropriate for a man to shake hands with a woman unless she initiates the handshake. In many countries, women rarely hold business positions, and even businessmen's wives are not included in business-related social gatherings. Research local customs before your trip to reduce the possibility of a disastrous faux pas that could ruin a business deal.

Be sensitive about the religious practices of your foreign contacts. You should know, for example, that observant Moslems do not drink alcohol and that Hindus do not eat beef. And it is best to avoid using gestures unless you are certain you know what they mean to your host. Before confusing or insulting a foreign associate, make sure that what you intend to communicate will be understood. It may also be best to avoid attempts at humor, as you risk alienating foreigners if the punch lines are misunderstood. Many jokes lose something in translation, or depend on subtleties of language to make their point. Even if you do not insult someone by mistake, you may be the only one laughing at your puns. Eliminate any potential awkwardness or offense by staying away from jokes.

Business cards often play a more important role in foreign corporate culture than in the United States. Cards are exchanged often with rather formal procedure. Present your card with both hands (or at least with your right hand). When given a card, read it completely before putting it away. As noted previously, it is best to have cards printed in the local language. Be sure to include your business title on the cards (*see* Business Cards, page 366).

As in the United States, many foreign countries use universal signs to denote restrooms, stairs, areas off limits to unauthorized personnel, taxi stands, and other important information. You may even see a sign in Asia that means remove your shoes. Reviewing these before traveling abroad will increase your confidence and may save you a few blunders. You may find Henry Dreyfuss's *Symbol Sourcebook* helpful (*see* Travel Guides and Literature, page 454, for more information).

DO'S AND DON'TS IN ASIA

Do:
- Greet business associates with a slight bow throughout Asia.
- Use formal titles and family names throughout Asia.
- Remove your shoes when entering a Japanese home.
- Receive gifts with both hands throughout Asia.

Don't:
- Emphasize the colors white and blue; they are colors of mourning in China.
- Give clocks as gifts in China; they symbolize death.
- Discuss business during meals in China.
- Blow your nose in public in Korea.
- Touch another person's head in Thailand.

Guide to Tipping

Even experienced travelers are often confused by the complexities of tipping appropriately at home and abroad. Here are some guidelines to help you find your way through an increasingly complicated gratuity system.

In the United States

Airport:

Flight personnel—none
Skycap—$1 or more for all of your baggage

Barbershop or hairdresser:	Hair stylist—15%
	Manicurist—15%
	Washer—$1 to $2
Hotel:	Bellhop—$1 per bag
	Cleaning person—$1 to $2 per night
	Concierge, lobby attendant, desk clerk—none, except for special services, then $5 to $10
	Room service—15% if a tip is not already included in the bill
	Elevator operator—50¢ to $1 (optional)
Restaurant:	Waiter—15% to 20%
	Busboy—none
	Headwaiter or maitre d'—none, except for special services, then about $5
	Wine steward—15% of wine bill
	Bartender—10% to 15% of bar bill
	Coat check attendant—$1 per coat
	Restroom attendant—50¢
	Valet parking attendant—50¢ or $1
Miscellaneous:	Shoe shiner—$1 to $2
	Taxi driver—15% to 20% of the fare
	Doorman—$1 for hailing cab or carrying bags
	Delivery person—$1
	Limousine driver—$5 per hour (unless already included)

In Other Countries

In Europe, follow U.S. tipping guidelines in most cases, with these exceptions:

- when you see *service compris* or *servizio compresso,* meaning service is included (you may still tip, but only to recognize exceptional service)
- in Iceland and Scandinavia, as tipping may be considered an insult
- in English pubs; also note that just 5% is customary in restaurants
- in taxis, where a gratuity is sometimes included in the fare
- in eastern Europe, where tipping is acceptable but not customary

In Asia and the South Pacific, the general rule is no tipping, as gratuities may be perceived as insults. Hong Kong is an exception, however, as are American-style hotels and restaurants in all Asian countries. Tip according to U.S. custom in Hong Kong and American-style establishments.

Tips are optional for all services in South America and Africa. Some prices include service charges. Tipping is usually reserved for special services not included in a person's regular job description. However, tips are always appreciated. When in North America and the Caribbean, follow U.S. tipping guidelines.

In very poor countries such as Mexico, Egypt, and India, many people make a living by providing small services to tourists and residents. In those countries, it is customary to tip for every little task performed, even opening a door for someone. Carry lots of small change to give whenever necessary. You will often be reminded that U.S. citizens have a relatively affluent lifestyle by the gratitude with which small amounts of money are received by less fortunate individuals.

METRIC CONVERSIONS
(Conversions are approximate.)

Length and Distance

To change:	Into:	Multiply by:
inches	millimeters	2.54
feet	centimeters	30.5
yards	meters	0.9
miles	kilometers	1.6

Length and Distance

To change:	Into:	Multiply by:
millimeters	inches	0.4
centimeters	feet	0.03
meters	yards	1.1
kilometers	miles	0.62

Volume

To change:	Into:	Multiply by:
ounces	milliliters	30
pints	liters	0.47
quarts	liters	0.95
gallons	liters	3.8
milliliters	fluid ounces	0.033
liters	pints	2.1
liters	quarts	1.05
liters	gallons	0.26

Weight

To change:	Into:	Multiply by:
ounces	grams	28
pounds	kilograms	0.45
grams	ounces	0.036
kilograms	pounds	2.2

Area		
To change:	*Into:*	*Multiply by:*
square inches	square centimeters	6.5
square feet	square meters	0.093
square yards	square meters	0.84
acres	hectares	0.4
square miles	square kilometers	2.6
square centimeters	square inches	0.154
square meters	square feet	10.75
square meters	square yards	1.2
hectares	acres	2.5
square kilometers	square miles	0.38

Temperature		
To change:	*Into:*	*Do this:*
C° (degrees Celsius)	F°	Multiply by 1.8, then add 32.
F° (degrees Fahrenheit)	C°	Subtract 32, then multiply by 0.556.

Foreign Currencies

Calculating prices, tips, and other expenditures in a foreign currency can be very confusing. If you travel frequently, you may want to invest in a calculator specifically designed to convert foreign denominations into U.S. equivalents. Visiting several countries in one trip may complicate matters, as similar names for money may not indicate the same units of currency. For instance, the dollars of Canada, Australia, and the United States are not the same, and may represent very different monetary values. The following list of nations and their basic currencies will help to keep it all straight.

Country	*Currency*	*Fractional Unit*
Afghanistan	afghani	100 puls
Algeria	dinar	100 centimes
Argentina	austral	100 centavos
Australia	dollar	100 cents
Austria	schilling	100 groschen
Bahamas	dollar	100 cents
Bahram	dinar	1,000 fils
Barbados	dollar	100 cents
Belgium	franc	100 centimes
Belize	dollar	100 cents
Benin	franc	100 centimes

Country	Currency	Fractional Unit
Bolivia	boliviano	100 centavos
Botswana	pula	100 thebe
Brazil	cruzeiro	100 centavos
Brunei	dollar	100 cents or sen
Bulgaria	lcv	100 stotinki
Cameroon	franc	100 centimes
Canada	dollar	100 cents
Cayman Islands	dollar	100 cents
Central African Republic	franc	100 centimes
Chad	franc	100 centimes
Chile	peso	100 centavos
China	yuan	10 fen
Colombia	peso	100 centavos
Congo	franc	100 centimes
Costa Rica	colon	100 centimos
Cuba	peso	100 centavos
Czechoslovakia	koruna	100 halers
Denmark	krone	100 ore
Djibouti	franc	100 centimes
Dominican Republic	peso	100 centavos
Ecuador	sucre	100 centavos
Egypt	pound	100 piastres
El Salvador	colon	100 centavos
Ethiopia	birr	100 cents
Fiji	dollar	100 cents
Finland	markka	100 pennia
France	franc	100 centimes
Gabon	franc	100 centimes
Gambia	dalasi	100 bututs
Germany	deutsche mark	100 pfennige
Ghana	ccdi	100 pescwas
Greece	drachma	100 lepta
Guatemala	quetzal	100 centavos
Guinea	franc	100 centimes
Guyana	dollar	100 cents
Haiti	gourde	100 centimes
Honduras	lempira	100 centavos
Hong Kong	dollar	100 cents
Hungary	forint	100 liller
Iceland	krona	100 aurar
India	rupee	100 paise
Indonesia	rupiah	100 sen
Iraq	dinat	1,000 fils
Ireland	pound	100 pence
Israel	shekel	100 agorot
Italy	lira	100 centesimi
Ivory Coast	franc	100 centimes
Jamaica	dollar	100 cents
Japan	yen	100 sen
Jordan	dinar	1,000 fils
Kenya	shilling	100 cents
Kuwait	dinar	1,000 fils
Lebanon	pound	100 piastres

Country	Currency	Fractional Unit
Luxembourg	franc	100 centimes
Malawi	kwacha	100 tambala
Malaysia	ringgit	100 sen
Maldives	rufiyaa	100 laari
Malta	lira or pound	100 cents
Mauritania	ouguiya	5 khoums
Mauritius	rupee	100 cents
Mexico	peso	100 centavos
Mongolia	tugrik	100 mongo
Morocco	dirham	100 centimes
Nepal	rupee	100 paisa
Netherlands	guilder	100 cents
New Zealand	dollar	100 cents
Nicaragua	cordoba	100 centavos
Niger	franc	100 centimes
Nigeria	naira	100 kobo
Norway	krone	100 ore
Oman	riyal-omani	1,000 baiza
Pakistan	rupee	100 paisa
Papua New Guinea	kina	100 tpea
Paraguay	guarani	100 centimos
Peru	nuevo sol	100 centimos
Philippines	peso	100 centavos
Poland	zloty	100 groszy
Portugal	escudo	100 centavos
Qatar	riyal	100 dirhams
Romania	leu	100 bam
Saudi Arabia	rival	20 Italali
Senegal	franc	100 centimes
Scychelles	rupcc	100 cents
Sierra Leone	leone	100 cents
Singapore	dollar	100 cents
Solomon Islands	dollar	100 cents
Somalia	shilling	100 cents
South Africa	rand	100 cents
South Korea	won	100 chon
Spain	peseta	100 centimos
Sri Lanka	rupcc	100 cents
Sudan	pound	100 piastres
Suriname	guilder	100 cents
Sweden	krona	100 ore
Switzerland	franc	100 centimes
Syria	pound	100 piastres
Taiwan	dollar	100 cents
Tanzania	shilling	100 cents
Thailand	baht	100 satang
Togo	franc	100 centimes
Trinidad & Tobago	dollar	100 cents
Tunisia	dinar	1,000 millimes
Turkey	lira	100 kurus
Uganda	shilling	100 cents
United Arab Emirates	dirham	1,000 fils

Country	Currency	Fractional Unit
United Kingdom	pound	100 pence
United States	dollar	100 cents
Uruguay	peso	100 centesimos
Venezuela	bolivar	100 centimos
Vietnam	dong	100 xu
Western Samoa	tala	100 sene
Zambia	kwacha	100 ngwee
Zimbabwe	dollar	100 cents

EUROPEAN CLOTHING SIZE CONVERSIONS

Women's coats, dresses, and suits:

United States	2	4	6	8	10	12	14	16	18
United Kingdom	24	26	28	30	32	34	36	38	40
Continental Europe	30	32	34	36	38	40	42	44	46

Women's blouses and sweaters:

United States	30	32	34	36	38	40	42	44
	(10)	(12)	(14)	(16)	(18)	(20)	(22)	(24)
United Kingdom	32	34	36	38	40	42	44	46
Continental Europe	38	40	42	44	46	48	50	52

Women's shoes:

United States	5	5½	6	6½	7	7½	8	8½	9	9½	10
United Kingdom	3½	4	4½	5	5½	6	6½	7	7½	8	8½
Continental Europe	36	36½	37	37½	38	38½	39	39½	40	40½	41

Men's suits and coats:

United States	34	36	38	40	42	44	46	48
United Kingdom	34	36	38	40	42	44	46	48
Continental Europe	44	46	48	50	52	54	56	58

Men's shirts:

United States	14	14½	15	15½	16	16½	17	17½
United Kingdom	14	14½	15	15½	16	16½	17	17½
Continental Europe	36	37	38	39	41	42	43	44

Men's socks:

United States	9	9½	10	10½	11	11½	12	12½
United Kingdom	9	9½	10	10½	11	11½	12	12½
Continental Europe	38	39	40	41	42	43	44	45

Men's shoes:

United States	8	8½	9	9½	10	10½	11	11½	12

United Kingdom	7½	8	8½	9	9½	10	10½	11	11½
Continental Europe	41	42	42	43	44	44	45	46	46

Men's hats:

United States	6¾	6⅞	7	7⅛	7¼	7⅜	7½	7⅝
United Kingdom	6⅝	6¾	6⅞	7	7⅛	7¼	7⅜	7½
Continental Europe	54	55	56	57	58	59	60	61

Health and Safety Issues for Travelers

Eating Right (and Safely)

Food poisoning and parasitic infections can be serious, causing long-term health problems, or even fatal. Many foreign countries do not have the same health standards as those maintained by the United States, and their food and water may not be safe for consumption by visitors. Also, travelers tend to overindulge in spicy, rich, and sweet foods because so many delicious choices are available. Enjoy local foods, but be careful not to overdo it. A weight gain of five or ten pounds need not be one of your souvenirs.

General Tips

To avoid discomfort and illness, use the following tips as a guide to eating sensibly and safely while in a foreign country:

• Peel fruits and vegetables yourself before eating them.
• Avoid eating unpackaged foods bought from street vendors or restaurants that do not seem to be clean.
• Make sure meats, eggs, and poultry are fully cooked and hot before eating.
• Be wary of fish and seafood, as they may contain toxins from polluted waters.
• Limit your intake of very spicy or greasy foods.
• Avoid unpasteurized milk and dairy products.
• Make sure plates and cutlery appear to be clean and sanitary.
• Drink only bottled water.

DRINKING WATER

Only about a quarter of the world's nations have tap water that is considered safe for consumption by U.S. citizens. Consult your travel guide or another reliable source to find out whether the water is safe to drink at your destination. If it is not, limit your liquid intake to bottled water, other bottled beverages, and boiled tap water drinks such as hot tea and coffee. In addition, avoid all drinks and food that may have tap water added after cooking, and do not drink any beverages containing ice. If bottled water is not available, you may boil tap water to sterilize it or use one of the portable water filters available commercially. Water that is very hot to touch is usually safe. When you are not sure if the water is drinkable, assume that it is not, just to be safe.

In many areas, major hotels (especially American chains) have their own water treatment systems to make their water safe for consumption. Check with your travel agent, or ask when making your own reservations. Many travelers find it a nuisance to brush their teeth with bottled water, and it may be difficult to remember to do so. So you may prefer to find accommodations with hygienic tap water, when feasible.

Dealing with Diarrhea

In addition to food and water safety recommendations, ask your physician if you should take an antibiotic or other medication to prevent digestive disorders while traveling. If you develop traveler's diarrhea anyway, speed your recovery by drinking lots of bottled water to avoid dehydration; eating salted crackers and toast; avoiding caffeine and alcohol; and avoiding acidic and dairy foods. Take an over-the-counter medication such as Pepto-Bismol or Immodium A-D to relieve the diarrhea (follow label directions carefully). If your physician prescribed an antibiotic for daily or as-needed use, take it as directed. With proper care, the discomfort should be temporary. However, if diarrhea or other intestinal upset continues for more than a day or two, see a physician as soon as you get home. For information on getting medical assistance when traveling in a foreign country, *see* Medical and Safety Resources, page 453.

First-Aid Kit for Travelers

Seasoned travelers know that basic medical supplies are sometimes hard to procure in foreign countries due to language and labeling differences. Thus, it is wise to have some rudimentary home treatments available at a moment's notice. A well-stocked first-aid kit for traveling should include the following:

- adhesive bandages
- aspirin or other pain reliever
- cough drops or lozenges
- diarrhea medication
- insect repellent
- motion sickness medication
- sunscreen
- thermometer
- vitamins, if you are accustomed to taking them at home
- prescription medications taken regularly—enough to last the duration of your trip plus a few more days in case of delays or schedule changes
- prescription and medical information (for example, on allergies or blood type) and your home physician's phone number, especially if you have a serious medical condition

All prescription medications should be in the original, labeled containers. Over-the-counter medications should also be in the original containers. Sometimes, for customs inspections, it is best for nonprescription drugs to be in sealed packages that have not been opened. (Small, individual packets are best—you can use these as needed, and the unused packets remain unopened.)

You may also want to investigate devices that prevent or ease earaches resulting from pressure changes during flights. (The long, slow ascents and descents of transcontinental and overseas flights cause major discomfort to some passengers.) Prevention devices include ear pads that can be filled with warm water in the cabin's rest room and placed over the ears during takeoff and landing. In the absence of special equipment, ear pain may be lessened by asking a flight attendant for a hot towel to hold over your ears for a few minutes. Remember that any upper respiratory infection can cause an earache when flying, so see your doctor for treatment if you have a cold or sore throat just before a trip.

MINIMIZING JET LAG

- Maintain a proper diet by not overeating and not skipping meals. Eat plenty of proteins for long-term energy during the day and carbohydrates for short-term energy at night.
- Drink plenty of water or juice, and avoid alcohol.
- Get plenty of oxygen. Take deep breaths occasionally, and rest frequently when at high altitudes.
- Schedule your trip according to the jet lag you can expect to experience. When traveling east, schedule meetings later in the day than you would normally so you will be awake and alert. When traveling west, make earlier appointments than usual, as you will probably awaken early and be tired by afternoon or early evening.
- Begin adjusting your schedule before leaving by gradually moving meals and bedtimes closer to the times that would be appropriate if you were already at your destination.
- Make sure you are well rested at the start of your trip. Try not to overwork in the days just before leaving.
- Relax as much as possible during the flight. Get first-class or business-class seats if possible.
- Exercise during the trip to keep your body alert and active, but use common sense. If you have a sedentary lifestyle at home, take some long walks in the weeks before leaving. Traveling abroad almost always involves a good deal of walking, often while carrying heavy luggage.
- Give yourself a while to adjust to the new time schedule. If possible, plan not to work on the first day of your trip.
- Spend time outdoors in the sunlight. Go outside at sunset if you can, especially on the first day of your trip. This will help your body and mind adjust to the new time schedule.

For a program of diet regulation that has proved effective in reducing or eliminating the effects of crossing time zones very quickly, read *Overcoming Jet Lag* by Charles F. Ehret and Lynne Waller Scanlon.

Safety Tips for Business Travel

To be safe when traveling, use the same common sense that you use at home. In general, be aware of the people and environment around you at all times, so that a thief or attacker cannot surprise you. Leave expensive jewelry and most of your cash and valuables in a safe-deposit box at your hotel. Carry credit cards and traveler's checks in a money belt (available in many department stores), and be discreet about displaying large amounts of money. Take special security precautions when traveling in regions where there is political or severe economic unrest. Even countries known for the gentle nonviolence of their people may be unsafe if the basic necessities of life have become scarce and costly, or if the people are anxious and frightened by unstable conditions.

- Know the political situation in countries you will visit. When possible, avoid volatile areas. If you must go into a dangerous region, be careful not to aggravate the situation.
- Register with the local U.S. consulate or embassy when you arrive. Leave your hotel and passport information and the numbers where you can be reached.
- Learn how to contact the local police, the U.S. embassy, or a hospital in case of emergency.
- Keep your passport with you, and put a copy of its data page in your luggage.
- Lock important documents, such as business contracts and airline tickets, as well as jewelry and other valuables, in your hotel's safe-deposit box.
- Avoid attracting attention in countries hostile to the United States, and in any area of political unrest. Try to blend in with the natives so that you do not stand out as an American. Do not carry any sort of U.S. military I.D. unless it is absolutely necessary.
- Be wary of disclosing business or travel plans to others, even guides or cab-drivers.
- Keep a low profile and do not resist your captors if you are involved in a hijacking or hostage situation. Talk as little as possible and avoid making eye contact, but try to stay mentally and physically alert. Be prepared for anything.

ESPECIALLY FOR WOMEN

For the most part, the travel concerns of businesswomen are the same as those of men. Both men and women are at risk in foreign cities just as they are in the United States, and sometimes more. Exercise as much caution as is comfortable for you.

Remember that gender equality is not as prevalent in many countries as it is in the United States. You may experience subtle or overt forms of sexism in business dealings. For example, a foreign businessman may not offer to shake your hand. Though this can be frustrating, such matters are beyond your control. When dealing with business associates, continue to act professionally in spite of others' behavior unless you are treated in a manner that makes you feel endangered.

In more conservative countries, be especially conscious of dressing appropriately. Avoid short skirts and low necklines, loud colors, and tight-fitting clothes. Offending foreign colleagues by inappropriate or too casual attire could affect the outcome of your business there.

Major Cities Travel Guide

The following list of 24 U.S. cities and 26 world cities provides information on transportation, accommodations, sightseeing, restaurants, and other areas of interest to travelers. If local transit data are not listed, have your travel agent arrange for ground transportation from the airport. If you are planning your own trip, call the convention and visitors' center numbers listed—these offices generally offer excellent assistance. To obtain tickets for concerts, games, or other events, try the local Ticketmaster office if no other source is provided.

The hotel and restaurant choices listed are among the finest in these cities, according to several reputable travel publications. To make a good impression on business associates, or if you just like to travel in style, these are the places for you. If you are on a budget, however, be advised that these are among the most expensive places to stay or dine. Most convention and visitors' centers can provide a list of local establishments and their prices relative to others in the area. Your travel agent may also have useful brochures on prices, accommodation, dining, and entertainment. Most of the hotels listed are not part of large hotel chains. Many of the restaurants listed require or suggest reservations. It may be a good idea to call weeks before your trip in some cases, as these are usually popular dining places. Also, ask about their dress code when you call. (For telephone numbers of hotel franchises and car rental agencies, *see* Making Your Own Arrangements: Useful Toll-Free Numbers, page 407.)

Publications in entertainment listings are noted as daily (d), weekly (w), biweekly (bw), monthly (m), or bimonthly (bm). All foreign publications are in English unless otherwise noted. Telephone numbers are local to each city, so be sure to dial the area code or country and city code given after the city's name before dialing a local number. However, numbers under foreign city listings that have the designation "(U.S.)" are American telephone numbers and do not require additional area codes, country, or city codes. (*See also* Domestic Area Codes, page 70, and International Country and City Codes, page 73.)

The United States

Atlanta (area code 404)

- Convention and Visitors Bureau, 521-6600
  235 Peachtree Street NE, Suite 1414
  Atlanta, GA 30303
- Airport shuttle: Atlanta Airport Shuttle, 766-5312
- Taxis/limousines: Executive Limousine, 223-2000; Yellow Cab, 521-0200

- Hotels: Nikko, 800-645-5687; Swissôtel, 800-253-1397
- Restaurants: Bone's (American), 3130 Piedmont Road, 237-2700; Ciboulette (French), 1529 Piedmont Avenue NE, 874-7600
- Sights: CNN Center; Georgia Capitol; Martin Luther King Jr. Center; Underground Atlanta
- Museums: Fernbank Museum of Natural History, 378-0127; Fernbank Science Center, 378-4311; High Museum of Art, 892-4444
- Sports: Baseball—Braves, 577-9100; Basketball—Hawks, 827-DUNK; Football—Falcons, 223-8000
- Entertainment listings: *Creative Loafing* (w); *Journal-Constitution* (d)

Baltimore (area code 410)

- Area Convention and Visitors Association, 837-4636
  300 West Pratt Street
  Baltimore, MD 21202
- Airport shuttle: BWI Ground Transportation, 859-7545
- Taxis/limousines: Diamond, 947-3333; Yellow Cab, 685-1212
- Hotels: Harbor Court, 800-233-1234; Latham, 800-528-4261
- Restaurants: Chiapparelli's (Italian), 237 South High Street, 837-0309; Tio Pepe (Spanish), 10 East Franklin Street, 539-4675
- Sights: Edgar Allan Poe House; Fell's Point; Fort McHenry; Harborplace
- Museums: Baltimore Museum of Art, 396-7100; Maryland Science Center, 685-5225; Walters Art Gallery, 547-9000
- Sports: Baseball—Orioles, 685-9800; Football—Ravens, 554-1010
- Entertainment listings: *Baltimore* (m); *City Pater* (w); *Sun* (d)

Boston (area code 617)

- Boston Convention and Visitors Bureau, 536-4100
  Prudential Tower
  P. O. Box 490
  Boston, MA 02199
- Airport shuttle: Logan Express, 800-235-6426
- Taxis/limousines: Checker, 536-7000; Independent Taxi Operators, 426-8700
- Hotels: Boston Harbor, 800-752-7077; Copley Plaza, 800-223-7434
- Restaurants: Jasper's (American), 240 Commercial Street, 523-5560; L'Espalier (French), 30 Gloucester Street, 262-3023
- Sights: Beacon Hill; Boston Common; Bunker Hill Monument; Copley Square; Faneuil Hall; Freedom Trail; Harvard Yard; Old Ironsides; Old State House
- Museums: Commonwealth Museum, 727-9268; Harvard University Art Museums, 495-9400; Institute of Contemporary Art, 266-5151; Museum of Fine Arts, 267-9300
- Sports: Baseball—Red Sox, 267-1700; Basketball—Celtics, 931-2000; Football—New England Patriots, 508-543-0350 (in Foxboro); Hockey—Bruins
- Entertainment listings: *Boston* (m); *Globe* (d); *Herald* (d); *Phoenix* (w)
- Tickets: Bostix, 723-5181; Out of Town Ticket Agency, 492-1900

Chicago (area code 312)

- Chicago Convention and Visitors Bureau, 567-8500
  North Michigan Avenue
  Chicago, IL 60611
- Airport shuttle: Continental Air Transport, 454-7800
- Taxis/limousines: American United Cab, 248-7600; Yellow and Checker, 829-4222
- Hotels: Drake, 800-533-7256; Fairmont, 800-527-4727
- Restaurants: Ambria (French), 2300 North Lincoln Park West, 472-5959; Charlie Trotter's (American), 816 West Armitage Avenue, 248-6228; Spiaggia (Italian), 980 North Michigan Avenue, 280-2750
- Sights: Grant Park; Halstead Street; John Hancock Center; Lake Shore Drive; Lincoln Park Zoo; Marshall Fields; Miracle Mile; Sears Tower; Water Tower
- Museums: Art Institute of Chicago, 443-3600; Field Museum of Natural History, 922-9410; Museum of Contemporary Art, 280-5161; Museum of Science and Industry, 684-1414
- Sports: Baseball—Cubs, 404-2827, White Sox 924-1000; Basketball—Bulls, 733-5300; Football—Bears, 294-2200; Hockey—Blackhawks, 733-5300
- Entertainment listings: *Chicago* (m); *New City* (w); *Reader* (w); *Sun-Times* (d); *Tribune* (d)
- Tickets: Hot Tix, 977-1755

Cleveland (area code 216)

- Convention and Visitors Bureau of Greater Cleveland, 621-4110
  3100 Tower City Center
  Cleveland, OH 44113
- Taxis/limousines: AmeriCab, 881-1111; Yellow Cab, 623-1500
- Hotels: Omni International; Ritz Carlton
- Restaurants: Jim's Steak House (American), 1800 Scranton Road, 241-6343; Sammy's (eclectic), 1400 West 10th Street, 523-5560
- Sights: The Flats; Old Arcade; Public Square; Rock and Roll Hall of Fame; Rockefeller Park; Terminal Tower
- Museums: Cleveland Center for Contemporary Art, 421-8671; Cleveland Museum of Art, 421-7340; Cleveland Museum of Natural History, 231-4600
- Sports: Baseball—Indians, 420-4200; Basketball—Cavaliers, 420-2000
- Entertainment listings: *Cleveland* (m); *Free Times* (w); *Plain Dealer* (d)

Dallas (area code 214)

- Dallas Convention and Visitors Bureau, 746-6677
  1201 Elm Street, Suite 2000
  Dallas, TX 75270
- Airport shuttles: Shuttlejack 484-7577; Super Shuttle, 817-329-2000
- Taxis/limousines: Lone Star Limousine, 243-8880; Yellow/Checker Cab, 565-9132
- Hotels: Adolphus, 800-221-9083; The Mansion on Turtle Creek, 800-442-3408

- Restaurants: Baby Routh (Southwestern), 2708 Routh Street, 871-2345; French Room (French), 1321 Commerce Street, 742-8200
- Sights: Deep Ellum; JFK Memorial; Texas School Book Depository; Thanksgiving Square; West End Marketplace
- Museums: Dallas Museum of Art, 922-1200; Dallas World Aquarium, 720-2224; Museum of Natural History, 421-DINO
- Sports: Baseball—Texas Rangers, 817-273-5100 (Arlington); Basketball—Mavericks, 939-2712; Football—Cowboys, 579-5000; Hockey—Stars, 467-8277
- Entertainment listings: *Morning News* (d); *Observer* (w); *Texas Monthly* (m)
- Tickets: Rainbow, 787-2000

Denver (area code 303)

- Denver Metro Convention and Visitors Bureau, 892-1112
  225 West Colfax Avenue
  Denver, CO 80202
- Airport shuttle: Airporter, 321-3222
- Taxis/limousines: Metro Taxi, 333-3333; Yellow Cab, 777-7777
- Hotels: Brown Palace, 800-321-2599; Oxford, 800-228-5838
- Restaurants: Buckhorn Exchange (American), 1000 Osage Street, 534-9505; Tante Louise (French), 4900 Colfax Avenue, 355-4488
- Sights: Capitol; Larimer Square; 16th Street Mall; U.S. Mint
- Museums: Denver Art Museum, 640-2295; Denver Museum of Natural History, 322-7009; Museum of Western Art, 296-1880
- Sports: Baseball—Colorado Rockies, 866-0428; Basketball—Nuggets, 893-3865; Football—Broncos, 433-7466; Hockey—Colorado Avalanche, (303) 830-8497
- Entertainment listings: *Colorado Homes and Lifestyles* (m); *Post* (d); *Rocky Mountain News* (d); *Westword* (w)
- Tickets: Ticket Bus (at 16th Street Mall)

Detroit (area code 313)

- The Metropolitan Detroit Convention and Visitors Bureau, 567-1170
  Tower 100 RenCen
  Detroit, MI 48243
- Airport shuttle: Kirby Tours, 800-521-0711
- Taxis/limousines: Checker Cab, 963-7000; Metro Cars, 800-456-1701
- Hotels: Atheneum, 800-772-2323; Hotel St. Regis, 800-333-3333
- Restaurants: Rattlesnake Club (eclectic), 300 River Place, 567-4400; Whitney (eclectic), 4421 Woodward Avenue, 832-5700
- Sights: Belle Isle; the Fist; Ford Plant; Greektown; Greenfield Village; Motown Museum; Philip A. Hart Plaza; Renaissance Center
- Museums: Detroit Historical Museum, 833-1805; Detroit Institute of Arts, 833-7900
- Sports: Baseball—Tigers, 962-4000; Basketball—Pistons, 377-0100; Football—Lions, 335-4151; Hockey—Red Wings, 396-7600
- Entertainment listings: *Detroit Monthly* (m); *Free Press* (d); *Metro Times* (w)

Honolulu (area code 808)

- Hawaii Visitors Bureau, 923-1811
  2270 Kalakaua Avenue, Suite 801
  Honolulu, HI 96815
- Airport shuttle: Terminal Transportation, 836-0317
- Taxis/limousines: Charley's, 531-2333; SIDA, 836-0011
- Hotels: Halekulani, 800-367-2343; Hawaii Prince, 800-321-6284
- Restaurants: La Mer (French/Hawaiian), 2199 Kalia Road, 923-2311; Maile (Hawaiian), 5000 Kahala Avenue, 734-2211
- Sights: Aloha Tower; Chinatown; Diamond Head; International Market Place; Iolani Palace; Kapiolani Park; Pearl Harbor; Tantalus Drive; Waikiki Beach
- Museums: Contemporary Museum, 526-1322; Honolulu Academy of Art, 532-8700; Mission Houses Museum, 531-0481
- Entertainment listings: *Advertiser* (d); *Honolulu* (m); *Honolulu Weekly* (w); *Star Bulletin* (d)

Houston (area code 713)

- Greater Houston Convention and Visitors Bureau, 227-4422
  801 Congress Street
  Houston, TX 77002
- Airport shuttles: Airport Express, 523-8888; Shuttles, 644-8359
- Taxis/limousines: Galveston Limousine, 223-2256; Yellow Cab, 236-1111
- Hotel: La Colombe d'Or, 524-7999
- Restaurants: Café Annie (Southwestern), 1728 Post Oak Boulevard, 840-1111; La Colombe d'Or (French), 3410 Montrose Boulevard, 524-7999
- Sights: Astroworld; International Strip; LBJ Space Center; Sam Houston Park; Tranquility Park
- Museums: Contemporary Art Museum, 526-3129; Museum of Fine Arts, 639-7300; Museum of Natural Science, 639-4600
- Sports: Baseball—Astros, 799-9555; Basketball—Rockets, 627-2115; Football—Oilers, 797-1000
- Entertainment listings: *Chronicle* (d); *Press* (w); *Texas Monthly* (m)
- Tickets: Houston Ticket Company, 877-1555

Las Vegas (area code 702)

- Las Vegas Convention and Visitors Authority, 892-0711
  Convention Center
  3150 Paradise Road
  Las Vegas, NV 89109
- Airport shuttle: Grayline, 739-5700
- Taxis/limousines: Bell Trans Limousine, 736-4428; Yellow and Checker Cab, 837-2000
- Hotels: Caesar's Palace, 800-634-6001; Star's Desert Inn, 800-634-6906
- Restaurants: Chin's (Chinese), 3200 Las Vegas Boulevard South, 733-8899; Palace Court (French), 3570 Las Vegas Boulevard South, 731-7110

- Sights: Caesar's Palace; Circus Circus; Golden Nugget; MGM complex; MGM Grand; Mirage; the Strip
- Museums: Clark County Heritage Museum, 455-7955; Hoover Dam Museum, 294-1988
- Sports: Football—Posse (CFL), 242-4200
- Entertainment listings: *Review Journal* (d); *Showbiz* (w); *Sun* (d)

Los Angeles (area codes 213, 310, 818)

- Los Angeles Visitors and Convention Bureau, 213-624-7300
  633 West Fifth Street, Suite 6000
  Los Angeles, CA 90071
- Airport shuttles: L.A. Top Shuttle, 310-670-6666; SuperShuttle, 310-782-6600
- Taxis/limousines: Bell Cab, 213-221-1112; Showcase Limousine, 800-421-6808, United Independent Taxi, 213-653-5050
- Hotels: Bel Age, 800-424-4443; Biltmore, 800-245-8673
- Restaurants: Chasen's (eclectic), 9039 Beverly Boulevard, West Hollywood 310-271-2168; L'Orangerie (French), 903 North La Ciega Boulevard, 213-652-9770; Spago (eclectic), 1114 Horn Avenue, West Hollywood, 310-652-4025
- Sights: Beverly Hills; Burbank Studios; Disneyland; Griffith Park; Hollywood Studio Museum; Hollywood Walk of Fame; La Brea Tar Pits; Little Tokyo; Mann's Chinese Theatre; Sunset Strip; Universal Studios; Venice Beach
- Museums: J. Paul Getty Museum, 310-458-2003; Los Angeles Museum of Art, 213-857-6000; Museum of Contemporary Art, 213-621-2766; Natural History Museum, 213-744-3466
- Sports: Baseball—Dodgers, 213-224-1500, Angels, 714-937-7200 (Anaheim); Basketball—Clippers, 213-748-6131, Lakers, 310-419-3100; Football—Raiders, 213-747-7111; Hockey—Kings, 310-673-1300, Anaheim Mighty Ducks, 714-704-2400
- Entertainment listings: *Daily News* (d); *LA Weekly* (w); *Los Angeles* (m); *Reader* (w); *Times* (d)
- Tickets: Good Time Tickets, 213-464-7383

Miami (area code 305)

- Greater Miami Convention and Visitors Bureau, 539-3000
  701 Brickle Avenue, Suite 2700
  Miami, FL 33131
- Airport shuttle: SuperShuttle, 871-2000
- Taxis/limousines: Central Cab, 532-5555; Metro Taxi, 888-8888
- Hotels: Colonnade, 800-533-1337; Grand Bay, 800-341-0809
- Restaurants: A Mano (tropical), 1440 Ocean Drive, Miami Beach, 531-6266; Grand Café (eclectic), 2669 South Bay Shore Drive, 858-9600
- Sights: Art Deco District; Bayside Marketplace; Coconut Grove; Freedom Tower; Holocaust Memorial; Little Havana; Metro-Dade Cultural Center; Venetian Pool
- Museums: Bass Museum of Art, 673-7533; Vizcaya Museum, 250-9133; Wolfsonian Museum, 531-1001

- Sports: Baseball—Florida Marlins, 620-6100; Basketball—Heat, 577-HEAT; Football—Dolphins, 620-2578; Hockey—Panthers, 768-1900; Jai-alai—633-6400
- Entertainment listings: *Herald* (d); *New Times* (w); *South Florida* (m)
- Tickets: PACE Free Concert Line, 948-9285

Minneapolis (area code 612)

- Greater Minneapolis Convention and Visitors Association, 661-4700
  1219 Marquette
  Minneapolis, MN 55403
- Airport shuttle: Airport Express, 726-6400
- Taxis/limousines: Airport Taxi, 721-0000; Yellow Taxi, 824-4444
- Hotels: Marquette Inn, 800-328-4782; Whitney, 800-248-1879
- Restaurants: 510 (French), 510 Groveland Avenue, 874-6440; Goodfellow's (American), 800 Nicollet Mall, 332-4800
- Sights: Como Park (St. Paul); Crystal Court; Dinkytown; Falls of St. Anthony; Foshay Tower; Minnehaha Park
- Museums: Frederick R. Weisman Art Museum, 625-9641; Minneapolis Institute of Arts, 870-3131; Minnesota Museum of Art, 292-4355 (St. Paul); Walker Art Center, 375-7600
- Sports: Baseball—Minnesota Twins, 375-1116; Basketball—Minnesota Timberwolves, 337-3865; Football—Minnesota Vikings, 333-8828
- Entertainment listings: *City Pages* (w); *Mpls.-St. Paul* (m); *St. Paul Pioneer Press* (d); *Star Tribune* (d); *Twin Cities Reader* (w)

New Orleans (area code 504)

- Greater New Orleans Tourist and Convention Commission, 566-5011
  1520 Sugar Bowl Drive
  New Orleans, LA 70112
- Airport shuttle: Airport Shuttle, 522-3500
- Taxis/limousines: United Cabs, 522-9771; Yellow/Checker Cabs, 525-3311
- Hotels: Fairmont, 800-527-4727; Windsor Court, 800-262-2662
- Restaurants: Antoine's (Creole), 713 St. Louis Street, 581-4422; Grill Room (American), 300 Gravier Street, 522-1992
- Sights: Audubon Park; Bourbon Street; Canal Street; Custom House; French Quarter; Garden District; Jackson Square; Lafayette Cemetery; Old U.S. Mint; Preservation Hall; St. Louis Cathedral; Woldenberg Park
- Museums: Confederate Museum, 523-4522; Contemporary Art Center, 523-1213; New Orleans Museum of Art, 488-2631
- Sports: Football—Saints, 522-2600
- Entertainment listings: *Gambit* (w); *New Orleans* (m); *Times-Picayune* (d)

New York (area code 212, outer boroughs 718)

- New York Convention and Visitors Bureau, 212-397-8222
  Two Columbus Circle
  New York, NY 10019

- Airport shuttle: Gray Line Air Shuttle, 212-757-6840
- Taxis/limousines: NYC Taxi and Limousine Commisssion, 221-TAXI
- Hotels: Carlyle, 800-227-5737; Pierre, 800-PIERRE-4; Plaza, 800-228-3000
- Restaurants: Four Seasons (eclectic), 99 East 52nd Street, 212-754-9494; Gotham Bar and Grill (eclectic), 12 East 12th Street, 212-620-4020
- Sights: Brooklyn Bridge; Central Park; Chinatown; Chrysler Building; Ellis Island; Empire State Building; Fifth Avenue; Greenwich Village; Lincoln Center; Little Italy; Rockefeller Center; SoHo; South Street Seaport; Statue of Liberty; Times Square; United Nations; Wall Street; World Trade Center
- Museums: American Museum of Natural History, 212-769-5000; Guggenheim Museum, 212-423-3500; Metropolitan Museum of Art, 212-879-5500; Museum of Modern Art, 212-708-9400; Whitney Museum of American Art, 212-570-3600
- Sports: Baseball—Mets, 718-507-8499 (Queens), Yankees 718-293-6000 (Bronx); Basketball—Knicks, 212-465-6741, New Jersey Nets, 201-935-8888; Football— Giants, 201-935-8222 (New Jersey), Jets, 516-538-6600 (Long Island; games in New Jersey); Hockey—Rangers, 212-465-6741, Islanders, 516-794-4100 (Long Island), New Jersey Devils, 201-935-8888; Tennis—U.S. Open, 718-271-5100 (Queens)
- Entertainment listings: *Daily News* (d); *Newsday* (d); *New York* (w); *New Yorker* (w); *New York Times* (d); *NYPress* (w); *Post* (d); *Village Voice* (w)
- Tickets: TKTS, 212-768-1818

Philadelphia (area code 215)

- Convention and Visitors Bureau, 636-1666
  1515 Market Street, Suite 2020
  Philadelphia, PA 19102
- Airport shuttle: Philadelphia Airport Shuttle, 969-1818
- Taxis/limousines: Limelight Limousine, 342-5557; Yellow Cab, 922-8400
- Hotels: Barclay, 800-421-6662; Rittenhouse, 800-635-1042
- Restaurants: Le Bec Fin (French), 1523 Walnut Street, 567-1000; Old Original Bookbinder's (American), 125 Walnut Street, 924-7027
- Sights: Betsy Ross House; Boathouse Row; Christ Church; City Hall; Congress Hall; Headhouse Square; Italian Market; Liberty Bell; Penn's Landing; U.S. Mint
- Museums: Franklin Institute Science Museum, 448-1200; Pennsylvania Academy of the Fine Arts, 972-7600; Philadelphia Museum of Art, 763-8100
- Sports: Baseball—Phillies, 463-1000; Basketball—76ers, 336-3600; Football— Eagles, 463-5500; Hockey—Flyers, 336-3600
- Entertainment listings: *City Paper* (w); *Daily News* (d); *Inquirer* (d); *Philadelphia* (m); *Welcomat* (w)

Phoenix (area code 602)

- Phoenix and Valley of the Sun Convention and Visitors Bureau, 254-6500
  505 North Second Street, Suite 300
  Phoenix, AZ 85004

- Airport shuttle: SuperShuttle, 244-9000
- Taxis/limousines: Yellow Cab, 252-5071
- Hotels: Biltmore, 800-528-3696; Buttes, 800-843-1986
- Restaurant: Christopher's (French), 2398 East Camelback Road, 957-3214
- Sights: Arizona Center; Borgata, Heritage Square; Mercado; Pueblo Grande Indian Ruins; Scottsdale; Taliesin West
- Museums: Heard Museum, 252-8840; Phoenix Art Museum, 257-1222
- Sports: Baseball seven pro teams spend spring training in Phoenix; call 969-1307 for information; Basketball—Suns, 258-6711; Football—Cardinals, 379-0102; Hockey—Coyotes, 379-7800
- Entertainment listings: *Arizona Republic* (d); *New Times* (w); *Phoenix Gazette* (d); *Phoenix Metro* (m)

Pittsburgh (area code 412)

- Greater Pittsburgh Convention and Visitors Bureau, 281-7711
  Four Gateway Center
  Pittsburgh, PA 15222
- Airport shuttle: Airline Transportation Service, 471-7887
- Taxis/limousines: People's Cab, 441-5334; Yellow Cab, 665-8100
- Hotels: Priory, 231-3338; Vista International, 800-367-8478
- Restaurants: Grand Concourse (seafood), One Station Square, 261-1717; Le Mont (French/Italian), 1114 Grandview Avenue, 431-3100
- Sights: Carson Street; Mt. Washington; Oakland; Point State Park; PPG Place; Shadyside; Station Square; Strip District
- Museums: Carnegie, 622-3131; Carnegie Science Center, 237-3400; Cathedral of Learning (University of Pittsburgh), 624-6000; Frick Art Museum, 371-0600; Stephen Foster Memorial, 621-3342; Warhol Museum, 237-8300
- Sports: Baseball—Pirates, 323-5000; Football—Steelers, 323-1200; Hockey—Penguins, 642-1985
- Entertainment listings: *City Paper* (w); *Pittsburgh* (m); *The Pittsburgh Press* (d); *Post-Gazette* (d)

St. Louis (area code 314)

- St. Louis Convention and Visitors Commission, 421-1023
  10 South Broadway, Suite 1000
  St. Louis, MO 63102
- Airport shuttle: Airport Express, 429-4950
- Taxis/limousines: Yellow Cab, 361-2345
- Hotels: Majestic, 800-451-2355; Seven Gables Inn, 800-433-6590
- Restaurants: Cardwell's (eclectic), 8100 Maryland Street, 726-5055; Tony's (Italian) 410 Market Street, 231-7007
- Sights: Anheuser-Busch Brewery; Cherokee Street; Gateway Arch; Laclede's Landing; the Levee; Maryland Plaza; St. Louis Centre; U. City Loop
- Museums: Mercantile Money Museum, 421-1819; St. Louis Art Museum, 721-0067; St. Louis Science Center, 289-4400

- Sports: Baseball—Cardinals, 421-3060; Football—Rams; Hockey—Blues, 644-0900
- Entertainment listings: *Post-Dispatch* (d); *Riverfront Times* (w); *St. Louis* (m)

San Diego (area code 619)

- San Diego Convention and Visitors Bureau, 232-3101
  401 B Street, Suite 1400
  San Diego, CA 92101
- Airport shuttle: SuperShuttle, 278-8877
- Taxis/limousines: SuperShuttle Airport Limousine, 800-948-8853; Yellow Cab, 234-6161
- Hotels: Del Coronado, 800-468-3533; U.S. Grant, 800-237-5029
- Restaurants: Dobson's (eclectic), 956 Broadway Circle, 231-6771; George's at the Cove (eclectic), 1250 Prospect Street, La Jolla, 454-4244
- Sights: Balboa Park; Coronado; Embarcadero; Gas Lamp Quarter; Horton Plaza; La Jolla Tide Pools; Mission Bay Park; Old Town Plaza; San Diego Zoo; Sea Caves; Sea World
- Museums: Junípero Serra Museum, 297-3258; Museum of Contemporary Art, 454-3541; San Diego Museum of Art, 232-7931; San Diego Museum of Man, 239-2001
- Sports: Baseball—Padres, 283-4494; Football—Chargers, 280-2111
- Entertainment listings: *Reader* (w); *San Diego* (m); *Union-Tribune* (d)
- Tickets: ARTSTIX, 238-3810

San Francisco (area code 415)

- San Francisco Convention and Visitors Bureau, 974-6900
  201 Third Street, Suite 900
  San Francisco, CA 94103
- Airport shuttles: SAMTRANS, 800-660-4287; SuperShuttle, 558-8000
- Taxis/limousines: Yellow Cab, 626-2345
- Hotels: Donatello, 800-227-3184; Sherman House, 563-3600
- Restaurants: Ernie's (French), 847 Montgomery Street, 397-5969; Stars (California-style), 150 Redwood Alley, 861-7827
- Sights: Alcatraz Island; the Cannery; Chinatown; Coit Tower; Embarcadero Center; Fisherman's Wharf; Ghirardelli Square; Golden Gate Park and Bridge; Japan Town; Lombard Street; Nob Hill; North Beach; SoMa; Transamerica Pyramid; Union Square
- Museums: Ansel Adams Center, 495-7000; Asian Art Museum, 668-7855; M. H. De Young Memorial Museum, 750-3600; San Francisco Museum of Modern Art, 357-4000; San Francisco Performing Arts Library and Museum, 255-4800
- Sports: Baseball—Giants, 467-8000, Oakland Athletics, 510-638-4900; Basketball—Golden State Warriors, 510-638-6300; Football—49ers, 468-2249; Hockey—San Jose Sharks, 800-BE-SHARK
- Entertainment listings: *Bay Guardian* (w); *Chronicle, Examiner* (d); *SFWeekly* (w)
- Tickets: BASS, 776-1999; TIX, 433-7827

Seattle (area code 206)

- Seattle/King County Convention and Visitors Bureau, 461-5840
  800 Convention Place
  Seattle, WA 98101
- Airport shuttles: Grayline Airport Express, 626-6088; Shuttle Express, 622-1424
- Taxis/limousines: Farwest, 622-1711; Yellow Cab, 622-6500
- Hotels: Alexis, 800-426-7033; Vintage Park 800-624-4433
- Restaurants: Canlis (eclectic), 2576 Aurora Avenue North, 283-3313; Elliott's Oyster House (seafood), 1203 Alaskan Way, Pier 56, 623-4340
- Sights: International District; Pike Place Market; Pioneer Square; Seattle Center; Space Needle; Westlake Center
- Museums: Burke Museum, 543-5590; Pacific Science Center, 443-2001; Seattle Art Museum, 625-8900
- Sports: Baseball—Mariners, 628-3555; Basketball—SuperSonics, 281-5800; Football—Seahawks, 827-9777
- Entertainment listings: *Post-Intelligencer* (d); *Seattle Weekly* (w); *Times* (d)
- Tickets: Ticket/Ticket, 324-2744

Washington, D.C. (area code 202)

- Washington Convention and Visitors Association, 789-7000
  1212 New York Avenue NW, Suite 600
  Washington, DC 20005
- Airport shuttle: Washington Flyer, 703-685-1400
- Taxis/limousines: Diamond, 544-1212; Yellow Cab, 387-6200
- Hotels: Hay-Adams, 800-424-5054; Watergate, 800-424-2736
- Restaurants: Jean-Louis (French), 2650 Virginia Avenue NW, 298-4488; Le Lion d'Or (French), 1150 Connecticut Avenue NW, 296-7972
- Sights: Adams Morgan; Arlington Cemetery; Capitol; Dupont Circle; the Ellipse; Ford's Theatre; Georgetown; Jefferson Memorial; Lafayette Square; Library of Congress; Lincoln Memorial; the Mall; the Pentagon; Supreme Court; Vietnam Veterans Memorial; Washington Monument; the White House
- Museums: Corcoran Gallery, 638-3211; Holocaust Memorial Museum, 488-0400; National Archives, 501-5205; National Gallery of Art, 737-4215; Renwick Gallery, 357-2531; Smithsonian Institution, 357-2700
- Sports: Basketball—Bullets, 301-350-3400; Football—Redskins, 547-9077; Hockey—Capitals, 301-350-3400
- Entertainment listings: *City Paper* (w); *Washington* (m); *Washington Post* (d); *Washington Times* (d)
- Tickets: Ticketplace, TIC-KETS

The World

Amsterdam (country code 31, city code 20)

- Netherlands Board of Tourism, 212-370-7367 (U.S.)
  355 Lexington Avenue, 21st Floor
  New York, NY 10017

- Airport transportation: KLM bus, 649-1393
- Taxis: Taxi Central, 677-7777
- Public transportation: Trams, buses, and one subway line run through the city until midnight, and some buses run through the night. Tickets can be bought at the Central bus station or tobacco shops. Day passes (dagkaart) or multiple-use tickets (strippenkaart) are available.
- Hotels: Americain, 623-4813; Pullman Capitool, 800-21-4542 (U.S.)
- Restaurants: D'Vijff Vlieghen, 624-8369; Excelsior, 623-4836
- Sights: Albert Cuyp Market; Anne Frank House; Dam Square; Flea Market; Heineken Brewery; the Jordaan; Leidesplein; New Church; Rembrandt House; Rembrandtsplein; Royal Palace; Vondelpark; Welletjes; Zeedijk
- Museums: Jewish Historical Museum, 626-9945; Museum of History, 523-1822; Rijksmuseum, 673-2121; Stedelijk Museum, 573-2911; Vincent Van Gogh Museum, 570-5200
- Entertainment listings: *Holland Herald* (m); *What's On in Amsterdam* (bw)
- Tickets: Uitburo, 621-1211

Athens (country code 30, city code 1)

- Greek National Tourist Organization, 212-421-5777 (U.S.)
  645 Fifth Avenue, Fifth Floor
  New York, NY 10022
- Airport transportation: Bus to Syntagma Square
- Taxis: Cosmos Radio Taxi, 493-5811; Proodos Radio Taxi, 643-3400
- Public transportation: One subway line connects downtown with Piraeus Airport and Kifissia, a suburb. Buses and electric trolleys run through the city until around midnight.
- Hotels: Astir Palace, 364-3112; Grande Bretagne, 800-221-2340 (U.S.)
- Restaurants: Bajazzo, 729-1420; Gerofinikas, 362-2719
- Sights: Acropolis; Agora; Areopagus; Greek Orthodox Cathedral; Hadrian's Arch; Keramikos; Monastiraki Square; National Gardens; Omonia Square; Panathenaic Stadium; Plaka; Pnyx; Syntagma Square; Temple of the Olympian Zeus
- Museums: Acropolis Museum, 323-6665; Byzantine Museum, 721-1027; Museum of Cycladic Art, 722-8321; National Archaeological Museum, 821-7717; National Historical Museum, 323-7617
- Entertainment listings: *Athenian* (m); *Athens News* (d); *Greek News* (w)
- Tickets: Athens Festival box office, 322-1459; Hellenic American Union (English language events), 362-9886

Beijing (country code 86, city code 1)

- China National Tourist Office, 212-867-0271 (U.S.)
  60 East 42nd Street, Suite 3226
  New York, NY 10165
- Airport transportation: Car with driver—Beijing Car Company, 594-441; Red Flag Limo, 863-664
- Taxis: Beijing Taxi, 782-561; Shoudou Taxi, 557-461

- Public transportation: Two subway lines run until 11:00 P.M., and four main bus routes run until 5:00 P.M.
- Hotels: Beijing Hotel, 513-7766; China World Hotel, 505-2266
- Restaurants: Fang Shan, 401-1889; Feng Ze Yuan, 721-1331
- Sights: Ancient Observatory; Bei Hai Park; Drum Tower; Forbidden City; Grand View Garden; Great Hall of the People; Great Wall; Imperial Gardens; Jing Shan Park; Mao Zedong Memorial Hall; Marco Polo Bridge; Ming Tombs; Summer Palace; Sun Yat-sen Park; Temple of Heaven; Tiananmen Square; Zhongnanhai
- Museums: Capital Museum; Cultural Palace of the Nationalities; Gugong Museum; Museum of Chinese History; Museum of the Revolution
- Entertainment listings: *China Daily* (d)
- Tickets: CITS, 512-2256

Berlin (country code 49, city code 30)

- German National Tourist Office, 212-661-7200 (U.S.)
  122 East 42nd Street, 52nd Floor
  New York, NY 10168
- Airport transportation: Bus to downtown, or shuttle bus to the S-Bahn
- Taxis: Taxi 69022, 210102
- Public transportation: The U-Bahn (subway) and S-Bahn (elevated train) cover the city, as do buses and streetcars. Most run until about midnight, with some buses running through the night. Day passes and four-packs of tickets are available.
- Hotels: Bristor Kempinski, 884-340; Steigenberger, 21080
- Restaurants: Bamberger Reiter, 218-4282; Frühsammers, 803-8032
- Sights: Brandenburg Gate; Checkpoint Charlie; East Side Gallery; International Congress Center; Kurfurstendamm; Martin Gropius Building; New Synagogue; Nikolai Quarter; Old Palace; Potsdammer Platz; Prinz Albrecht Gelände; Reichstag; Schloss Charlottenburg; Tiergarten; Victory Column
- Museums: Dahlem Museum Center, 83011; Kunstgewerbemuseum, 266-2911; New National Gallery, 266-2666
- Entertainment listings: *Berlin Programm* (m); *Tip* (bw); *Zitty* (bw) (German)
- Tickets: Europa-Center, 261-7051; Theaterkasse, 212-5258

Bombay (country code 91, city code 22)

- India Tourist Office, 212-586-4901 (U.S.)
  30 Rockefeller Plaza
  Room 15, North Mezzanine
  New York, NY 10020
- Airport transportation: Airport City Coach Service available at terminal
- Taxis: Car and driver—Sita World Travel, 240-666; Travel Corporation India, 202-1881
- Public transportation: Trains and buses are available, but hiring your own car and driver is very inexpensive.
- Hotels: Oberoi Towers, 202-4343; Taj Hotel, 495-0808
- Restaurants: Mewar, 202-4343; Tanjore, 202-3366

- Sights: Bassein Fort; Elephanta Caves; Gateway of India; Hanging Gardens; High Court; Jain Temple; Kamala Nehru Park; Rajabhai Tower; Surya Narayan Temple; Victoria Gardens; Victoria Terminal
- Museums: Jahangir Art Gallery; Prince of Wales Museum; Victoria and Albert Museum
- Entertainment listings: *India Magazine* (m); *Imprint* (m)

Brussels (country code 32, city code 2)

- Belgian National Tourist Office, 212-758-8130 (U.S.)
  780 Third Avenue
  New York, NY 10017
- Airport transportation: Autolux airport taxi, 425-6020. Buses and trains are also available.
- Taxis: Taxis Oranges, 513-62-00; Taxis Verts, 349-49-49
- Public transportation: The metro, trams, and buses all use the same ticket system. Tickets can be bought for a single ride, full-day access, or multiple-day access, and are available at metro stations and newsstands.
- Hotels: Amigo, 511-59-10; Conrad, 542-42-42
- Restaurants: Comme Chez Soi, 512-29-21; La Maison du Cygne, 511-82-44
- Sights: Catédrale de St. Michel; Church of Notre Dame du Sablon; Colonnc du Congrès; European Community Headquarters; Galeries St. Hubert; Grand Place; Maison du Roi; Menneken-Pis; Parc de Bruxelles; Place Royale; Tour Noir; Waterloo
- Museums: Musée d'Art Ancien, 513-96-30; Musée d'Art Modern, 513-96-96; Musées Royaux d'Art et Histoire, 741-72-11
- Entertainment listings: *The Bulletin* (w)

Budapest (country code 36, city code 1)

- IBUSZ Hungarian Travel Company, 800-367-7878 (U.S.); 201-592-8585 in New Jersey
  One Parker Plaza, Suite 1104
  Ft. Lee, NJ 07024
- Airport transportation: Airport shuttle, 1578-555
- Taxis: Budataxi, 1294-000; Citytaxi, 1533-633; Fotaxi, 1222-222
- Public transportation: Buses, streetcars, and trolleys run until midnight, and there is also a metro. Tickets are available at tobacco shops and metro stations—yellow tickets for the metro, streetcar, and trolley, blue tickets for the bus. Day passes are available.
- Hotels: Forum, 1178-088; Gellért, 1852-200
- Restaurants: Gundel, 1221-002; Légrádi Testvérek, 1186-804
- Sights: Andrássy Street; City Park; Dohenyi Street Synagogue; Fisherman's Bastion; Heroes' Square; Inner City Parish Church; Main Square (Obuda); Matthias Church; Parliament; Royal Palace; St. Stephen's Basilica; Várhegy (Castle Hill)
- Museums: Fine Arts Museum, 1429-759; Hungarian National Museum, 1382-122; Museum of Contemporary History, 1757-533; National Gallery, 1757-533

- Entertainment listings: *Budapest Panorama* (m); *Budapest Week* (w); *Daily News* (d); *Post* (d); *Programme in Hungary* (m)
- Tickets: Budapest Tourist, 1173-555; Central Booking Agency, 1176-222

Buenos Aires (country code 54, city code 1)

- Argentine Consulate, 212-603-0443 (U.S.)
  12 West 56th Street
  New York, NY 10019
- Airport transportation: Manuel Tienda León, 394-4948
- Taxis: Pídalo Radio Taxis, 903-4991; Teletaxi Pronto, 981-9853
- Public transportation: Buses and five subway lines run until about midnight. Tickets and transfers are available on the bus or at subway stations.
- Hotels: Alvear Palace, 800-44-UTELL (U.S.); Caesar Park, 800-228-3000 (U.S.)
- Restaurants: Au Bec Fin, 801-6894; La Cabaña, 381-2373
- Sights: Avenida Lavalle; Avenida 9 de Julio; Cabildo; Casa Rosada; Catedral; Colón Theater; Costanera Sur; Edifico de Congreso Nacional; France Plaza; Jardín Japonés; La Boca; La Recoleta; Obelisco; Palermo; Plaza de Mayo; Plaza San Martín; San Isidro; San Telmo
- Museums: Boca Museum of Fine Arts, 21-1080; City of Buenos Artes, 331-9855; Museo de Bellas Artes, 803-0714; National Historical Museum, 23-6254
- Entertainment listings: *Herald* (d)

Cairo (country code 20, city code 2)

- Egyptian Government Tourist Office, 212-246-6960 (U.S)
  630 Fifth Avenue
  New York, NY 10111
- Airport transportation: Cars with drivers are available from major car rental companies.
- Taxis: Limo Bank Naser, 915-348
- Public transportation: The Metro is relatively new and extensive. Buses and minibuses are also available, though taxis are very inexpensive.
- Hotels: Mena House Oberoi, 387-7444; Shepheard, 355-3800
- Restaurants: Arabesque, 759-896; Darna, 350-6092
- Sights: Abdin Palace; Blue Mosque; Cairo Tower; Citadel; City of the Dead; Coptic Churches; Garden City; Gates of Cairo; Joseph's Well; Manyal Palace; Memphis; Muhammed Ali Mosque; Pharaonic Village; Pyramids; Qubbah Palace; Roda Island; Sphinx; Tombs of the Caliphs
- Museums: Coptic Museum; Egyptian Antiquities Museum; Egyptian Civilization and Gezira Museum; Modern Art Museum; Moukhtar Museum; Museum of Islamic Art
- Entertainment listings: *Cairo Today* (m); *Egyptian Gazette* (d)

Copenhagen (country code 45, city code 1)

- Scandinavian Tourist Board, 212-949-2333 (U.S.)
  655 Third Avenue
  New York, NY 10017

- Airport transportation: Bus to central station
- Taxis: Taxi, 31-35-35-35
- Public transportation: Buses in the city and S-trains in the suburbs run until about 12:30 A.M. Tickets are for either buses or S-trains, and can be bought at train stations or from bus drivers. Day passes and Copenhagen Cards (multiple-day passes that also provide travel and museum discounts) are available.
- Hotels: D'Angleterre, 800-223-6800 (U.S.); Scandinavia, 800-223-5652 (U.S.)
- Restaurants: Els, 33-12-13-41; Kong Hans, 33-11-68-68
- Sights: Amalienborg Palace; Carlsberg and Tuborg Breweries; Christianborg Castle; City Hall; Gammeltorv; Harbor; Kronborg Castle; Lake Pavilion; Lur Blower's Column; Our Lady's Church; Rosenborg Castle; Runde tårn; Slotsholmen; Strøget; Tivoli; Tycho Brahe Planetarium
- Museums: Liberty Museum, 33-13-77-14; Louisiana Modern Art Museum, 42-19-07-19; National Art Gallery, 33-91-21-26; National Museum, 33-12-12-24; Thorvaldsens Museum, 33-32-15-32
- Entertainment listings: *Copenhagen This Week* (w)
- Tickets: Dansk Musik Information Center, 33-11-20-66

Dublin (country code 353, city code 1)

- Irish Tourist Board, 212-418-0800 (U.S.)
  757 Third Avenue
  New York, NY 10017
- Airport transportation: Bus to central station
- Taxis: Blue Cabs, 676-1111; City Cabs, 286-8888; Co-op Taxi, 676-6666
- Public transportation: Buses run throughout the city, and DART trains go to the suburbs. You may buy tickets on board or get an Explorer Pass for multiple-day travel.
- Hotels: Berkeley Court, 800-44-UTELL (U.S.); Shelbourne, 661-6006
- Restaurants: The Commons, 872-5597; Le Coq Hardi, 668-9070
- Sights: Christ Church Cathedral; Custom House; Dublin Castle; Grafton Street; Guinness Brewery; Leinster House; Merrion Square; Moore Street Market; O'Connell Bridge; Parliament House; Phoenix Park; St. Audoen's Arch; St. Patrick's Cathedral; St. Stephen's Green; Temple Bar; Trinity College
- Museums: Dublin Writers' Museum, 874-7733; Irish Museum of Art, 671-8666; Municipal Gallery of Modern Art, 874-1903; National Gallery, 661-5133; National Museum, 661-8811
- Entertainment listings: *Dublin Event Guide* (bw); *In Dublin* (bw); *Irish Independent* (d); *Irish Press* (d); *Irish Times* (d); *What's On* (w)

Geneva (country code 41, city code 22)

- Swiss National Tourism Office, 212-757-5944 (U.S.)
  608 Fifth Avenue
  New York, NY 10020
- Airport transportation: Train to central train station or bus
- Taxis: Ask at hotel desk.

- Public transportation: Buses and streetcars are available. Tickets (including day passes, multiple-day passes, and tourist Swiss Passes) can be purchased at stations.
- Hotels: Beau-Rivage, 731-0221; Le Richmond, 800-223-6800 (U.S.)
- Restaurants: Le Béarn, 321-0028; Le Gentilhomme, 731-1400
- Sights: Cathédrale St. Pierre; Confédération Centre; Eglise St. Germain; Hôtel de Ville; Ile Rousseau; Jet d'Eau; Lake Geneva; Palais des Nations (UN); the Quays; Reformation Monument; Vieille Ville
- Museums: Musée Barbier-Mueller, 786-4646; Musée d'Art et d'Histoire, 290-011; Musée de l'Histoire des Sciences, 731-6985; Watch Museum, 736-7412
- Entertainment listings: *This Week in Geneva* (w)

Istanbul (country code 90, city code 1)

- Turkish Tourist Office, 212-687-2194 (U.S.)
  821 UN Plaza
  New York, NY 10017
- Airport transportation: Bus to downtown, 245-4208
- Taxis: Dolmus (shared)
- Public transportation: Buses are common, and single tickets or ten-packs can be bought at bus stops. The Tünel, a small train, carries passengers up the steep hill to Istiklal Caddesi.
- Hotels: Çiragan Palace, 258-3377; Pera Palace, 251-4560
- Restaurants: Club, 29-263-5411; Körfez, 332-0108
- Sights: Blue Mosque; Cistern Basilica; Dolmabahçe Palace; Egyptian Bazaar; Flower Market; Galata Tower; Grand Bazaar; Hippodrome; Ibrahim Paşa Palace; Sacred Column; Sancta Sophia; Süleymaniye Mosque; Topkapi Palace
- Museums: Archaeological Museum; Museum of the Ancient Orient; Museum of Turkish and Islamic Arts
- Entertainment listings: *The Guide* (bm); *Turkish Daily News* (d)
- Tickets: Istanbul Foundation for Culture and Arts, 261-3294

Jerusalem and Tel Aviv (country code 972, city codes 2 and 3)

- Israel Government Tourist Office, 212-566-0600 (U.S.)
  350 Fifth Avenue
  New York, NY 10118
- Airport transportation: Bus to the central bus station
- Taxis/limousines: Hapalmach, 02-792333; Nesher, 02-253233; Rehavia, 02-254444
- Public transportation: Buses run until midnight (except from sundown Friday to sundown Saturday). Tickets can be purchased on the bus.
- Hotels: Dan, 03-524-1111 (Tel Aviv); King David, 02-251111
- Restaurants: Casba, 03-602-2617 (Tel Aviv); Cow on the Roof, 02-259111
- Sights:
  Jerusalem—Ben Yehuda Street; Cardo; Church of the Holy Sepulcher; Dome of the Rock; Garden Tomb; Hatachana; Knesset; Old City; Talpiot; Temple Mount; Tower of David; Western Wall; Yad Vashem; Zion Square

Tel Aviv—Allenby Street; Carmel Market; Dizengoff Center; Habimah Square; Jaffa; Nahalat Binyamin; Shalom Tower
- Museums: Diaspora Museum, 03-646-2020 (Tel Aviv); Herzl Museum, 02-511108; Israel Museum, 02-708873; Tel Aviv Museum of Art, 03-696-1297 (Tel Aviv)
- Entertainment listings: *Hello Israel* (m); *Jerusalem Post* (d); *This Week in Jerusalem* (w)
- Tickets: Bimot, 02-240896; Naim, 02-254008

London (country code 44, city code 71)

- British Tourist Authority, 212-986-2200 (U.S.)
  551 Fifth Avenue, Suite 701
  New York, NY 10176
- Airport transportation: Train or bus to Victoria Station, or the Underground
- Taxis: Ask the concierge to call, or hail one on the street.
- Public transportation: The Underground (also called the tube) has 13 lines and runs until around 12:30 A.M., as do both single- and double-decker buses. Day and week passes are available at stations or on buses, and a Visitor's Travel Pass—good for tube, bus, and other discounts—is available through agents in the United States
- Hotels: Claridge's, 800-223-6800 (U.S.); Savoy, 800-63-SAVOY (U.S.)
- Restaurants: La Garroche, 408-0881; Nico at Ninety, 409-1290
- Sights: Bond Street; Buckingham Palace; Chelsea; Covent Garden; Hyde Park; Kew Gardens; Madame Tussaud's; the Mall; Oxford Street; Parliament; Picadilly Circus; Regent's Park; Soho; St. James Palace; St. Paul's Cathedral; Tower of London; Trafalgar Square; Westminster Abbey; Whitehall
- Museums: British Museum, 636-1555; National Gallery, 839-3321; Royal Gallery, 439-7438; Tate Gallery, 821-1313; Victoria and Albert Museum, 938-8441
- Entertainment listings: *City Limits* (w); *Evening Standard* (d); *Guardian* (d); *Independent* (d); *Time Out* (w); *Times* (d)
- Tickets: Society of West End Theatre (half-price tickets) in Leicester Square First Call, 240-7200; London Theatre Bookings, 439-3371

Madrid (country code 34, city code 1)

- National Tourist Office of Spain, 212-759-8822 (U.S.)
  665 Fifth Avenue
  New York, NY 10022
- Airport transportation: Bus to downtown Plaza de Colón
- Taxis: Radio-Taxi, 404-9000; Radio-Teléfono Taxi, 247-8200
- Public transportation: The Metro runs until 1:30 A.M. and buses until midnight. Single or ten-pack tickets can be bought for both, and a Metrotour Card is available for multiple days.
- Hotels: Palace, 800-223-6800 (U.S.); Villamagna, 800-233-1234 (U.S.)
- Restaurants: El Cenador del Prado, 429-1561; Zalacaín, 561-5935
- Sights: Casa de Campo; Convento de las Descalzas Reales; Jardín Botánico; Mercado Puerta de Toledo; Parque del Retiro; Plaza de Cibeles; Plaza de la Villa; Plaza Mayor; Puerta de Alcalá; Puerta del Sol; Royal Palace

- Museums: Museo de la Real Academia de Bellas Artes, 522-1491; Museo Municipal, 522-5732; Museo Nacional de Art Reina Sofía, 467-5062; Prado Museum, 420-2836
- Entertainment listings: *Guia del Ocio* (w) (Spanish)

Mexico City (country code 52, city code 5)

- Mexican Ministry of Tourism, 212-838-2949 (U.S.)
  405 Park Avenue, Suite 1401
  New York, NY 10022
- Airport transportation: Transportación Terrestre stands at airport
- Taxis: Servi-Taxis 516-6020; Super-Taxis, 566-0077
- Public transportation: There are nine Metro lines that cover the city and run until 1:00 A.M. Buses and peseros (minibuses or vans) are also available.
- Hotels: Camino Real, 800-7-CAMINO (U.S.); Marco Polo, 800-223-9868 (U.S.)
- Restaurants: Isadora, 520-7901; Maxim's de Paris, 281-3687
- Sights: Alameda Central; Anahuacalli; Catedral Metropolitana; Chapultepec Park; Ciudad Universitaria; Convento Carmen; Cuicuileo; Palacio de Iturbide; Palacio Nacional; Plaza de las Tres Culturas; Plaza de Santo Domingo; Plaza Garibaldi; Templo Mayor; Xochimilco, Zócalo, Zona Rosa
- Museums: Museo de Bellas Artes, 510-1388; Museo de la Ciudad de México, 542-0671; Museo Nacional de Art, 521-7320; Museo Nacional de Historia, 286-0700
- Entertainment listings: *Daily Bulletin* (d); *Gazer* (w); *News* (d)
- Tickets: Ticketmaster, 325-9000

Montreal (area code 514)

- Greater Montreal Convention and Tourism Bureau, 800-363-7777 (U.S.)
  1555 Rue Peel, Suite 600
  Montreal, Québec
  Canada H3A 1X6
- Airport transportation: Aérocar bus, 397-9999; Aéroplus, 476-1100
- Taxis: Aérocar, 397-9999
- Public transportation: Four Metro lines and the bus system run until about 12:30 A.M. and operate on the same ticket system. Tickets and transfers can be purchased at stations, and multiple-ride tickets are available.
- Hotels: Hôtel de la Montagne, 800-361-6262 (U.S.); Hôtel Vogue, 800-363-0363 (U.S.)
- Restaurants: Café de Paris, 842-4212; Les Halles, 844-2328
- Sights: Carré St. Louis; Complexe Desjardins; Crescent Street; La Ronde; Latin Quarter; Marché Bonsecours; Mount Royal Park; Notre Dame Basilica; Olympic Park; Place Bonaventure; Place d'Armes; Place des Arts; Place Jacques-Cartier; Place Ville Marie; Rue St. Amable; St. Lawrence Boulevard; Underground City; Vieux Montreal
- Museums: McCord Museum of Canadian History, 398-7100; Musée d'Art Contemporain de Montréal, 873-2878; Musée des Artes Décoratifs de Montréal, 259-2577; Musée des Beaux-Arts, 285-1600

- Sports: Baseball—Expos, 800-361-4595 (U.S.); Hockey—Canadiens, 932-2582
- Entertainment listings: *Gazette* (d); *Mirror* (w)
- Tickets: Admission, 522-1245

Moscow (country code 7, city code 095)

- Intourist Travel Information Office, 800-982-8416 (U.S.)
  630 Fifth Avenue, Suite 868
  New York, NY 10111
- Airport transportation: Car with driver—Intourist, 203-1487
- Taxis: Taxi, 927-0000 or 227-0000
- Public transportation: Nine subway lines, buses, trolleys, and trams run throughout the city until 1:00 A.M. Subway tokens are available at stations. Other tickets are available at newsstands and from bus, trolley, and tram drivers.
- Hotels: Metropol, 800-327-0200 (U.S.); Savoy, 929-8500
- Restaurants: Aragui, 229-3762; Kropotkinskaya, 36-201-7500
- Sights: Arbat Street; Bolshoi Theater; Gorky Park; Gum; Ilyinsky Garden; KGB; Kremlin; Lenin Mausoleum; New Maiden Convent; Pushkin Square; Red Square; St. Basil's Cathedral; Tsentr; Tverskaya Street
- Museums: Central V.I. Lenin Museum, 925-4808; Pushkin Museum of Fine Arts, 203-6974; State History Museum, 928-8452; USSR Exhibition of Economic Achievements (VDNKh), 181-9162
- Entertainment listings: *Commersant* (d); *Times* (d)
- Tickets: IPS Theater Box Office, 927-6729

Paris (country code 33, city code 1)

- French Government Tourist Office, 212-757-1125 (U.S.)
  610 Fifth Avenue, Suite 222
  New York, NY 10020
- Airport transportation: Air France buses—42-99-20-18 (De Gaulle), 42-23-97-10 (Orly)
- Taxis: Radio Taxi, 47-39-33-33; Taxi Bleu, 49-36-10-10
- Public transportation: The 13 Metro lines run until 1:00 A.M.; they share tickets with city buses and the suburban RER trains. Buy single tickets, a carnet (ten tickets), weekly or monthly passes, or a Paris-Visite card (unlimited travel for one to five days).
- Hotels: Crillon, 42-65-24-24; George V, 47-23-54-00; Le Bristol, 42-66-91-45
- Restaurants: Chez Benoît, 42-72-25-76; La Tour d'Argent, 43-54-23-31
- Sights: Arc de Triomphe; Champs-Elysées; Eiffel Tower; Ile de la Cité; Ile St. Louis; Jardin des Tuileries; L'Hotel des Invalides; Latin Quarter; Le Centre Georges Pompidou; Montparnasse; Notre Dame; Opéra de la Bastille; Palais Bourbon; Pantheón; Pere-Lachaise Cemetery; Place de la Concorde; Place Vendôme; Rue de Rivoli; Sacré Coeur; Sorbonne
- Museums: Louvre, 42-97-48-16; Musée d'Orsay, 40-49-48-14; Musée Picasso, 42-71-25-21; Musée Rodin, 47-05-01-34; Orangerie, 42-97-48-16

- Entertainment listings: *Paris Selection* (m); *Paris Boulevard* (m)
- Tickets: Madeleine ticket kiosk (reduced price); SOS-Théâtre, 42-25-67-07

Prague (country code 42, city code 2)

- Czechoslovak Travel Bureau, 800-800-8891 (U.S.)
  10 East 40th Street, Suite 3604
  New York, NY 10016
- Airport transportation: Czechoslovak Airlines bus, 800-223-2365 (U.S.)
- Taxis: Radio Taxi, 202951
- Public transportation: Buses, trams, and the three Metro lines run on the same tickets, which can be bought at stations, newsstands, or tobacco shops. Day and multiple-day passes are available as well.
- Hotel: Diplomat, 3314111
- Restaurants: U Malířů, 531833; U Zlaté Hrušky, 531133
- Sights: Charles Bridge; Charles Square; Church of Our Lady of Victory; Clock Tower; Golden Lane; Jewish Quarter; Kafka's birthplace; Old Town Square; Petřín Gardens; Powder Tower; Prague Castle; Royal Summer Palace of Belvedere; St. Vitus Cathedral; Vyšehrad; Welienstein Palace; Wenceslas Square
- Museums: Lobkovic Palace, 537306; Museum of Musical Instruments, 530843; National Gallery, 352441; National Museum, 269451
- Entertainment listings: *Post* (w); *Prognosis* (bw)
- Tickets: Bohemia Ticket International, 228738; Čedok, 2318255

Rome (country code 39, city code 6)

- Italian Government Tourist Office, 212-245-4822 (U.S.)
  630 Fifth Avenue, Suite 1565
  New York, NY 10111
- Airport transportation: Train to central station
- Taxis: Radio Taxi—3570, 3875, 4994, or 8433
- Public transportation: Two Metro lines and buses run until about midnight and some buses continue through the night. Tickets are available as singles, five- or ten-packs, or daily or weekly passes. They can be purchased at stations, tobacco shops, or newsstands.
- Hotels: Hassler, 800-223-6800 (U.S.); Majestic, 650881
- Restaurants: El Toulá, 687-3750; Relais le Jardin, 322-0404
- Sights: Arch of Constantine; Catacombs of St. Calixtus; Circus Maximus; Colosseum; Fontana di Trevi; Jewish Ghetto; Largo Argentina; Palatine Hill; Pantheon; Piazza Barberini, Piazza del Campidoglio; Piazza del Quirinale; Piazza di Spagna; Porta Portese; Roman Forum; Vatican City; Via Appia Antica; Via Condotti; Via Veneto; Village Borghese
- Museums: Galleria Nazional d'Arte Antica, 481-4591; Galleria Nazional d'Arte Moderna, 322-4152; Museo di Roma, 687-5880; Museo Nazional Romano delle Terme, 488-0530; Vatican Museums, 698-3333
- Entertainment listings: *Metropolitan* (bw); *Wanted in Rome* (bw)

Sydney (country code 61, city code 2)

- Australian Tourist Commission, 212-687-6300 (U.S.)
100 Park Avenue, 25th Floor
New York, NY 10017
- Airport transportation: Airport Express bus, 231-4444
- Taxis/limousines: ABC Taxis, 897-4000; Astra Hire Cars, 699-2233
- Public transportation: Buses run throughout the city, and trams cover the suburbs. A monorail and ferries are also available. Tickets can be bought from the bus driver or at tram stations and newsstands. Travelpasses and SydneyPasses offer unlimited use of all public transportation; SydneyPasses include sightseeing cruises.
- Hotels: Regent, 238-0000; Sebel Town House, 358-3244
- Restaurants: Bennelong, 250-7578; Rockpool, 252-1888
- Sights: Admiralty House; Atherden Street; Camp Cove; Fort Denison; Garden Island; King's Cross; Kirribilli House; Macquarie Street; Nielsen Park; Observatory Hill; Point Piper; the Rocks; Royal Botanic Gardens; State Parliament House; Sydney Cove; Sydney Harbour; Victoria Barracks
- Museums: Art Gallery of New South Wales, 225-1700; Australian Museum, 339-8111; Museum of Contemporary Art, 252-4033
- Entertainment listings: *Morning Herald* (d)
- Tickets: Halftix, 1-1681; Ticketek, 266-4800

Tokyo (country code 81, city code 3)

- Japan National Tourist Organization, 212-757-5640 (U.S.)
630 Fifth Avenue, Suite 2101
New York, NY 10111
- Airport transportation: Airport Express Bus; Airport Limousine Bus
- Taxis: Hinomaru, 3505-0707
- Public transportation: Ten subway lines, four trains, and a bus system run throughout the city until midnight. Multiple-ride passes are available—Metrocards for the subway and Orange Cards for the train.
- Hotels: Akasaka Prince, 3234-1111; Asakusa View, 3842-2111; Hotel Okura, 3582-0111
- Restaurants: Edo Gin, 3543-4401; Inakaya, 3408-5040
- Sights: Akasaka; Akihabura; Asakusa; Chinzanso; Edo Mura; Imperial Palace; Jimbocho; Kabuki Za; Kanda; National Diet Building; Onsen; Pagoda of the Kaneii Temple; Ropongi; Shibuya; Shinjuku; temples; Tokyo Station; Ueno; Yasukuni Jinja Shrine
- Museums: National Museum of Modern Art, 3214-2561; Tokyo Metropolitan Art Museum, 3823-6921; Tokyo National Museum, 3822-1111; Ueno no Mori Royal Museum, 3833-4191; Yamatane Museum of Art, 3669-4056
- Entertainment listings: *Mainichi Daily News* (d); *Tokyo Journal* (m)
- Tickets: Ticket Pia, 5237-9999; Ticket Saison, 3286-5482

Toronto (area code 416)

- Metropolitan Toronto Convention and Visitors Association, 800-668-2746 (U.S.)
  207 Queen's Quay West, Suite 509
  Toronto, Ontario
  Canada M5J 1A7
- Airport transportation: Grey Coach, 393-7911
- Taxis: Diamond, 366-4141; Metro, 363-5611
- Public transportation: Buses, streetcars, and trolleys run all night and are on the same system. Single tickets, ten-packs, day passes, or monthly passes are available. A two-line subway runs until 2:00 A.M., with tickets sold at stations and in some stores; transfers to the bus are available.
- Hotels: L'Hôtel, 800-828-747 (U.S.); Park Plaza, 800-268-4927 (U.S.)
- Restaurants: La Bistingo, 598-3490; La Fenice, 585-2377
- Sights: BCE Place; Campbell House; Casa Loma; Chinatown; CN Tower; Dominion Centre; Eaton Centre; Exhibition Place; Fort York; Harbourfront; Hazelton Lanes; Kensington Market; Ontario Place; Queen's Park; Queen Street West; Royal Bank Plaza; Skydome; Toronto Islands; Underground City; Yorkville
- Museums: Art Gallery of Ontario, 977-0414; Ontario Science Center, 696-3127; Royal Ontario Museum, 586-5549
- Sports: Baseball—Blue Jays, 341-1111; Basketball—Raptors; Football—Argonauts (CFL), 595-1131; Hockey—Maple Leafs, 977-1641
- Entertainment listings: *Eye* (w); *Globe and Mail* (d); *Now* (w); *Star* (d); *Sun* (d); *Toronto Life* (m)
- Tickets: Ticketmaster, 872-1111

Vienna (country code 43, city code 1)

- Austrian National Tourist Office, 212-944-6880 (U.S.)
  P. O. Box 1142
  Times Square Station
  New York, NY 10108
- Airport transportation: Mazur Shuttle, 604-9191
- Taxis: Radio Taxi, 31300 or 60160
- Public transportation: The U-Bahn (subway), S-Bahn (suburban train), buses, and trams operate on the same tickets, available at tobacco shops and machines in stations. Buy single tickets, five-packs, or day passes for one, three, or eight days.
- Hotels: Bristol, 800-221-2340 (U.S.); Sacher, 514560
- Restaurants: Korso, 5151-6546; Zu den Drei Husaren, 522-1092
- Sights: Bermuda Triangle; Donner Brunnen; Gloriette; Grinzing; Imperial Palace (Hofburg); Kärntnerstrasse; Palais Ferstl; Prater; St. Stephen's Cathedral; Schloss Belvedere; Schönbrunn Palace; Stattsoper; Vienna Woods
- Museums: Albertina, 534830; Art History Museum, 521770; Mozart Museum, 513-6294; Museum of Fine Arts, 5211770; 20th Century Museum, 782550
- Entertainment listings: *Falter* (w) (German); *Wiener* (m) (German)
- Tickets: Bundestheaterkassen, 514440; Vienna Ticket Service, 587-9843

Sources of Further Information

Credit Cards, Money Wire Services, Traveler's Checks, and ATM Access Information

Credit Cards

Many financial institutions and other organizations issue major credit cards such as VISA or MasterCard. When traveling, take the lost/stolen card reporting numbers for each of those companies with you, and call those numbers first. (If you travel often, you may want to consider joining one of the credit insurance plans that provides one number to report all missing cards.) The emergency numbers listed below may be used if you do not have a credit insurance plan number or your card-issuing company's number.

American Express, 800-327-2177; American Express Global Assistance Hotline, 301-214-8228; card members may call collect from any location outside the United States for assistance with emergency situations, including financial assistance

Diners Club/Carte Blanche, 800-525-9135

Discover, 800-DISCOVER

MasterCard, 800-MASTERCARD

VISA, 800-VISA-911

Money Wire Services

American Express MoneyGram, 800-543-4080

Western Union, 800-325-6000

Traveler's Checks

American Express, 800-221-7282

Bank of America, 800-227-3460

Barclays, 800-221-2426 –

Citicorp, 800-645-6556

Thomas Cook (MasterCard), 800-223-7373

VISA, 800-227-6811

Automatic Teller Machine (ATM) Access

American Express—Express Cash, 800-CASH-NOW (to enroll)

CIRRUS, 800-4-CIRRUS

Plus, 800-THE-PLUS

Customs Inspections and Carnets

Carnet information and applications: Contact the U.S. Council, International Chamber of Commerce, 1212 Avenue of the Americas, New York, NY 10036; or call 212-354-4480.

Know Before You Go. Booklet available from the U.S. Customs Service, P. O. Box 7407, Washington, DC 20044, 202-927-6724.

Foreign Driving

American Automobile Association (AAA), 407-444-7000
1000 AAA Drive
Heathrow, FL 32746

American Automobile Touring Alliance (AATA), 415-777-4000
Bayside Plaza 188
The Embarcadero
San Francisco, CA 94105

Meier, Bill. *Autorental Europe: A Guide to Choosing and Driving a Rental Car in Europe.* Pleasanton, CA: Lansing Publications, 1993

Inoculations, ICVs, and Health Recommendations

To request a copy of *Health Information for International Travel* or to request an International Certificate of Vaccination, contact either of these organizations:

U.S. Government Printing Office
Washington, DC 20402

Centers for Disease Control and Prevention, 404-639-2572

Medical and Safety Resources

American Express Global Assistance Hotline, 301-214-8228; card members may call collect from any location outside the United States for assistance with any number of emergency situations, including legal and financial assistance

Centers for Disease Control Traveler's Health Section, 404-332-4559 (general information on traveling safely); 404-329-2572 (information on drugs and poisons)

Europe Assistance Worldwide Services, 202-347-2025 (medical help and evacuation information in Europe and Asia)

International Association for Medical Assistance to Travelers, 716-754-4883 (medical referrals to physicians around the world)

International SOS Assistance Inc., 800-523-8930 (medical help)

Nationwide/Worldwide Emergency Ambulance Return (NEAR), 800-654-6700

Poison Control Center, 800-282-3171

U.S. State Department Advisories, 202-647-5225 (information on potentially dangerous situations, areas to avoid, and current political climates)

U.S. State Department Overseas Citizen's Emergency Center, 202-647-1512 (information on health conditions and evacuations)

Weather Data

Airdata, 800-247-3282 (75¢ for the first minute, 50¢ for each additional minute)

American Express Weather Information, 800-554-2639 (when calling from within the United States; for card members only); American Express Global Assistance Hotline, 301-214-8228 (when calling from outside the United States; card members only; collect calls accepted)

Weather Channel Connection 900-WEATHER (95¢ per minute)

Travel Guides and Literature

Axtell, Roger, and John Healy. *Do's and Taboos of Preparing for Your Trip Abroad.* New York: John Wiley & Sons, 1994.

Dreyfuss, Henry. *Symbol Sourcebook: An Authoritative Guide to International Graphic Symbols.* New York: Van Nostrand Reinhold, 1984.

Egypt & the Sudan: A Travel Survival Kit. Berkeley, CA: Lonely Planet, 1990.

Insight Guides: East Asia. Boston: Houghton Mifflin/APA Publications, 1994.

Insight Guides: India. London: APA Productions, 1987.

Israel On Your Own. Lincolnwood, IL: Passport Books, 1994.

Uspensky, Gleb. *The Insider's Guide to Russia.* Edison, NJ: Hunter Publishing, 1993.

Updated editions of the following books are published yearly or every two years; get the most recent version when planning a trip:

Birnbaum's Europe. New York: HarperCollins.

Birnbaum's Mexico. New York: HarperCollins.

Birnbaum's South America. New York: HarperCollins.

Birnbaum's United States. New York: HarperCollins.

Fodor's 19___: Australia and New Zealand. New York: Fodor's Travel Publications.

Fodor's 19___: Canada. New York: Fodor's Travel Publications.

Fodor's 19___: Europe. New York: Fodor's Travel Publications.

Fodor's 19___: Japan. New York: Fodor's Travel Publications.

Fodor's 19___: Mexico. New York: Fodor's Travel Publications.

Fodor's 19___: South America. New York: Fodor's Travel Publications.

Fodor's 19___: USA. New York: Fodor's Travel Publications.

Frommer's Canada '92–'93. New York: Prentice-Hall Travel, 1992.

More recent versions of these travel guides may also be available:

Fodor's China. New York: Fodor's Travel Publications, 1992.

Fodor's Egypt. New York: Fodor's Travel Publications, 1992.

Fodor's India. New York: Fodor's Travel Publications, 1993.

Fodor's Israel. New York: Fodor's Travel Publications, 1995.

Fodor's Russia and the Baltic Countries. New York: Fodor's Travel Publications, 1993.

On-Line Resources

All the Hotels on the Web *http://all-hotels.com*

Airlines of the Web: Frequent Flyer Program Web sites *http://www.itn.net/airlines/airff.html*

Inoculations and travelers' health information from the World Health Organization *http://www.who.ch*

Travel Round the World Travel Guide *http://www.digimark.net/rec-travel/rtw/html/faq.html*

Business Resources

Information at Your Fingertips

Because the amount of information is accelerating at such a rapid pace, it is virtually impossible for one person to know every fact necessary to run a business. Instead, it is more important to know where to find the facts when you need them. Research skills and the willingness to use them are invaluable tools in themselves. Finding information is sometimes daunting—logic may suggest that a particular reference book will be most useful, but locating that book may be difficult or impossible. Learning what reference materials are available and where to find them is an important part of the process.

Basics of Research: Getting What You Need Quickly

Comprehensive information resources, some with worldwide scope, can help to scale down a search and locate specific pieces of information. Such references may contain the facts you need or direct you to well-defined areas and specific sources. Common sources of information include the following:

- Almanacs. Many one-volume almanacs are essentially portable reference libraries. They supply a vast amount of facts on countries, people, events, governments, businesses, and a host of other topics, and they are updated annually. *The World Almanac and Book of Facts* and *Irwin Business Investment Almanac* are two of the best known.
- Bibliographies of business information. Gale Research's *Encyclopedia of Business Information Sources* (published yearly) is an excellent resource for those seeking any type of business data; it lists numerous publications in many forms for use in research.
- Encyclopedias. These are excellent resources for quick but thorough exploration of many topics. In-depth articles are concise, easy to comprehend, and frequently illustrated. Encyclopedias usually come with detailed indexes and annual supplements. In addition to traditional printed volumes, electronic encyclopedias are now available via CD-ROMs and on-line technology.
- Handbooks. Business handbooks (such as the one you are now reading) are usually excellent references for introduction to the concepts, procedures, and techniques of specific business functions. Topics may include personnel management, public relations, accounting, finance, marketing, purchasing, and many other aspects of doing business.
- Yearbooks. These differ from almanacs in that they give more information about one particular area, specialty, or field of interest, such as current events, modern nations, or economic trends. An example is *The Statesman's Year-Book World Gazetteer* by John Paxton, which covers world governments, including national history, area, population, economy, industry, trade, communications, and natural resources. A yearbook published for an individual country presents detailed re-

views of various factors influencing the business and economic developments affecting that nation.

Essential Books for the Office

Fundamental reference and research material should be available in every office:

1. a good dictionary
2. a thesaurus
3. local and major metropolitan newspapers
4. a weekly newsmagazine such as *Time* or *U.S. News & World Report*
5. a zip code directory
6. a small selection of trade journals and books about the company's particular field of business

This collection represents a bare minimum of basic resources, and each publication must be up to date or its information will be useless.

Following are some of the better primary business sources available. These will make researching easier and provide a great deal of in-office source material.

Communicating Facts and Ideas in Business by Leland Brown is a broad-based text giving general background on the role of oral and written communications and their business applications. Appendixes provide rules of grammar, letter forms, punctuation, and other information necessary to good communications.

The *Dictionary of Business and Management* by Jerry M. Rosenberg contains concise definitions for over 10,000 business and management terms, including acronyms, associations, and abbreviations.

Directory of Computerized Data Files: A Guide to U.S. Government Information in Machine Readable Format (U.S. National Technical Information Services, updated regularly) is the closest thing to a one-stop shopping guide for government files available to the public.

Editor & Publisher International Year Book (published yearly) has indexes of over 1,600 newspapers from around the world, including dailies, weeklies, and specialty publications.

The *Encyclopedia of Business Information Sources* (published yearly) contains a detailed listing of information sources for businesses.

The Wall Street Journal Index is a monthly publication covering corporate and business news.

CD-ROMs for Reference

For quick access and saving valuable storage space, reference materials on CD-ROM are the answer. One of the best offerings currently available is Compton's Reference Collection 1996, which contains a compact form of the 26-volume print version. An on-line atlas, dictionary, and business section are also included. Another valuable resource is Merriam-Webster's Collegiate Dictionary Deluxe Electronic

Edition, which contains both the Tenth Edition of the dictionary and *Merriam-Webster's Collegiate Thesaurus*. CD-ROM telephone directories, credit rating directories, travel guides, legal guides, Internet connection search engines, and market research databases also provide needed information.

On-Line Database Services

Electronic databases are no longer the wave of the future. They are here now, and here to stay. Businesses of any type without computers will soon be left behind by their computerized competitors. The recent and rapid advances in business computer use have made storing and retrieving information much easier, revolutionizing modern offices.

The term "database" generally refers to a collection of information on a specific subject or interrelated areas. Some resources will help you wade through all of the available material:

1. *CD-Rom Professional* (Online, Inc., updated regularly) is the leading journal for CD-ROM users. It reviews new CD-ROM databases, evaluates hardware, and covers trends affecting business in the electronic industry.
2. *Database* (Online, Inc., updated regularly) examines all aspects of electronic information delivery and presents good coverage of business databases. One of the more important sources for on-line searches.
3. *Directory of Online Databases* (Gale Research, updated regularly) contains pertinent data about on-line collections that are available to businesses. It provides two reference databases (a *bibliographic database* and a *referral* or *directory database*), a dictionary database, and a directory of full or source texts.
4. *Encyclopedia of Information Systems and Services* (Gale Research, published yearly) is one of the more comprehensive guides, describing not just on-line database publishers but also information retrieval software, information networks, video/telex systems, and data collection and research centers.

A number of major information providers have introduced small business on-line database stations. Services such as SBA OnLine make it easy to access the types of information needed by small companies. New services appear regularly, so there are many others in addition to the following major services now in operation:

- America Online—phone 800-827-6364
  This service was initiated by *The New York Times* to list department editors and subjects and to feature current and past coverage in the newspaper as well as many other newspapers, periodicals, and information sources. America Online handles more than 1 million sessions each day. It has so many categories of data access that users are advised to purchase its 500-page reference guidebook, *The Official America Online Tour Guide* by Tom Lichty, already in its third edition. Get the latest version available at bookstores or by computer ordering procedures.

- AT&T Business Network—phone 800-660-2299
  A service created especially for business use, this network offers 2,500 information sources. Such diverse data as credit reports, business case studies, information on starting home-based enterprises, success stories from business schools, and tips on writing business plans are available. The Business Network puts you in touch with professional information from such resources as CNN Business News, Dow Jones, Dun & Bradstreet, the Entrepreneur Magazine Group, the Kiplinger Washington Editors, and TRW Business Information Services.

- CompuServe—phone 800-848-8990
  Billed as "the electronic highways of the world's most diverse information service," CompuServe has more than a million members and an expanding international network of more than 2,000 databases. The basic package provides access to information on news, sports, and weather, electronic mail, research, health counseling, reference libraries, forums on many subjects, financial databanks, consumer reports, hot lines, electronic shopping, entertainment and games, travel advisories, and dozens of support services.

- IBEX—phone 800-537-4239
  IBEX is a service of the International Business Exchange. In addition to information, IBEX has many special aids available to small business users, including matching buyers to sellers (locally, regionally, or internationally); providing forums for negotiations; issuing credit and bank references for its clients; and searching for potential business partners. Members can use IBEX to advertise products and services at a small fee for each on-line posting. Offers to buy can also be posted. For these purposes, IBEX maintains a directory of some 8 million companies worldwide.

- Lexis-Nexis Small-Business Service—phone 800-543-6862
  One of the first firms to enter the on-line commercial information market, Lexis-Nexis has helped to reduce prices among the initial cyberspace providers by introducing low-cost small business services on the Internet and through Prodigy. The firm's E-mail number is *http://www.directory.net/lexis-nexis/sba/.*

- Microsoft Network—phone 800-386-5550 or 206-882-8080
  Microsoft had enrolled 530,000 members by the end of its first three months of service in the fall of 1995, stating that its goal was to provide the suppliers of information and services with better technology and tools. The network is advertised as "a complete multimedia news experience," making extensive use of color photographic images, sound files, and shortcuts to related Internet websites.

- Prodigy—phone 800-776-3449
  In conjunction with Lexis-Nexis, Prodigy provides information compiled from thousands of computers that trade information. The information is organized into hundreds of news groups and special-interest data groups. Like other on-line services, Prodigy maintains a huge electronic library, with more than 700,000 articles and access to hundreds of magazines, newspapers, books, and maps. Resources are divided by category to make it easier for users to select topics of interest.

- Profound—phone 800-435-7560 or 800-270-9896
  Launched by Market Analysis and Information Database, Inc., Profound offers small business members the use of its database of market research at a much

smaller monthly fee than that charged to large corporations. The service features news from more than 4,000 newspapers, periodicals, and wire services such as the Associated Press and Reuters; some 40,000 full-text research reports from publishers; and financial reports on millions of companies.

- PSINet—phone 703-904-4100

  This subsidiary of Performance Systems International offers users a 24-hour interactive presence on the Internet, providing access to a wide and diverse range of information about subject areas such as manufacturers' product data, corporate announcements, news, advertising, foreign trade, and software exhibitions. One of PSINet's facilities is InterRamp, specially targeted to the small business and home office market; it provides affordable, direct, and unrestricted access to a full range of database functions. Available services include E-mail, news services, research services, and World Wide Web, which provides a 24-hour interactive presence on the Internet.

- SBA OnLine—phone 800-697-4636

  SBA OnLine is an electronic bulletin board developed by the Small Business Administration to expedite information and assistance to the small business community. It provides up-to-the-minute, relevant information 24 hours a day, 365 days a year, about such subject areas as SBA publications, information points of contact, access to other government on-line services, special-interest groups, Internet mail and news groups, data compiled by federal agencies, state profiles for small businesses, training-course workbooks, business software, and the many resources available to small and home-based business owners and managers. SBA makes no basic charge for the above access number. There is a charge of 10 cents per minute for an expanded data service, available through 900-463-4636. For access to either number, you need a computer, modem, phone line, and communications software. Call your local SBA office for information about establishing this on-line service.

The Public Library: An Unfailing Resource

Libraries are excellent first choices for business information. Although library staff are present to assist you, it is best to know something about doing research on your own. Some useful resources for business research follow:

- Handbooks. These are good choices for abbreviated introductions to many business functions. They are comprehensive and concise, well indexed and organized, and provide easy access to facts and explanations. They are usually meant to be used as easy reference resources, not to be read cover to cover
- Indexes and abstracts. Sometimes a book is not the best source for a subject. If the information required is based on new developments or is too specific for full-length treatment, abstracts may be most helpful. They provide valuable information on a variety of subjects. Two excellent listings are the *Business Periodicals Index* (H. W. Wilson, published annually) and *Business Publications Index and Abstracts* (Gale Research, published annually).

- Loose-leaf services. These provide businesses with ever changing updates relating to federal and state laws regulating business, keeping subscribers informed on all legal matters that affect daily business operations. Each service contains an introduction with a master index and list of tables.
- Microforms and cassettes. Microfilm and microfiche are used in most libraries because they reduce vast amounts of information to tiny bits of film. Microfilm consists of published works on a film reel, read via a machine that can also make copies. Microfiche are 4-inch by 6-inch sheets of film displaying up to 70 pages or images per sheet. Micropublications have risen dramatically in recent years. Audiocassette tapes are now a popular information resource as well.

Additional library sources can be found at universities, colleges, and business schools. There are also private research and information brokers who will do research for a fee.

Directory of Business Organizations and Associations

The following associations, societies, foundations, institutes, and alliances are among the most significant in existence. They help advance the causes of business and industry in general, and their own fields and professions in particular. For additional information, consult a directory of associations, which can be found in the reference section of your local public library.

Advertising Council
    261 Madison Avenue, New York, NY 10016
    phone 212-922-1500, fax 212-922-1676
Advertising Research Foundation
    641 Lexington Avenue, New York, NY 10022
    phone 212-751-5656, fax 212-319-5265
American Advertising Federation
    1101 Vermont Avenue NW, Washington, DC 20005
    phone 202-898-0089, fax 202-898-0159
American Association of Advertising Agencies
    666 Third Avenue, New York, NY 10017
    phone 212-682-2500, fax 212-953-5665
American Bankers Association
    1120 Connecticut Avenue NW, Washington, DC 20036
    phone 202-663-5000, fax 202-828-4535

American Bar Association
    750 North Lake Shore Drive, Chicago, IL 60611
    phone 312-988-5000, fax 312-988-6281
American Bureau of Shipping
    Two World Trade Center, New York, NY 10048
    phone 212-839-5000, fax 212-839-5130
American Business Association
    292 Madison Avenue, New York, NY 10017
    phone 212-949-5900, fax 212-949-5910
American Business Press
    875 Third Avenue, New York, NY 10017
    phone 212-661-6360, fax 212-370-0736
American Business Women's Association
    9100 Ward Parkway, Kansas City, MO 64114
    phone 816-361-6621, fax 816-361-4991

American Compensation Association
14040 North Northsight Boulevard, Scottsdale, AZ 85260
phone 602-922-2020, fax 602-483-8352

American Economic Development Council
9801 West Higgins Road, Rosemont, IL 60018
phone 708-692-9944, fax 708-696-2990

American Institute of Certified Public Accountants
1211 Avenue of the Americas, New York, NY 10036
phone 212-575-6209, fax 212-596-6213

American Law Institute
402 Chestnut Street, Philadelphia, PA 19104
phone 215-243-1600, fax 215-253-1664

American League of Lobbyists
Post Office Box 30005, Alexandria, VA 22310
phone 703-960-3011, fax 703-960-4070

American Management Association
135 West 50th Street, New York, NY 10020
phone 212-586-8100, fax 212-903-8168

American Marketing Association
250 South Wacker Drive, Chicago, IL 60606
phone 312-648-0536, fax 312-993-7542

American Public Power Association
2301 M Street NW, Washington, DC 20037
phone 202-467-2900, fax 202-467-2910

American Small Business Association
1800 North Kent Street, Arlington, VA 22209
phone 800-235-3298

American Society for Industrial Security
1655 North Fort Meyer Drive, Arlington, VA 22209
phone 703-522-5800, fax 703-243-4954

American Society for Training and Development
1640 King Street, Alexandria, VA 22313
phone 703-683-8100, fax 703-683-8103

American Society of Appraisers
Post Office Box 17265, Washington, DC 20041
phone 703-478-2228, fax 703-742-8471

American Society of Association Executives
1575 I Street NW, Washington, DC 20005
phone 202-626-2723, fax 202-371-8825

American Society of Women Accountants
1255 Lynnfield Road, Memphis, TN 38119
phone 901-680-0470, fax 901-680-0505

American Water Resources Association
950 Herndon Parkway, Herndon, VA 22070
phone 703-904-1225, fax 703-905-1228

Associated Business Writers of America
1450 South Havana Street, Aurora, CO 80012
phone 303-751-7844, fax 303-751-8593

Association of Area Business Publications
5820 Wilshire Boulevard, Los Angeles, CA 90036
phone 213-937-5514, fax 213-937-0959

Association of Small Business Development Centers
1313 Farnam Street, Omaha, NE 68182
phone 402-595-2387

Business Marketing Association
150 North Wacker Drive, Chicago, IL 60606
phone 312-409-4262, fax 312-409-4266

Business Software Alliance
2001 L Street NW, Washington, DC 20036
phone 202-872-5500, fax 202-872-5501

Business Technology Association
12411 Wornall Road, Kansas City, MO 64145
phone 816-941-3100, fax 816-941-2829

Center for Entrepreneurial Management
180 Varick Street, New York, NY 10014
phone 212-633-0060, fax 212-633-0063

Center for Workforce Preparation
1615 H Street NW, Washington, DC 20062
phone 202-463-5525, fax 202-463-5730

Council of Better Business Bureaus
4200 Wilson Boulevard, Arlington, VA 22203
phone 703-276-0100, fax 703-525-8277

Council of Logistics Management
2803 Butterfield Road, Oak Brook, IL 60521
phone 708-574-0985, fax 708-574-0989

Credit Research Foundation
8815 Centre Park Drive, Columbia, MD 21045
phone 410-740-5499, fax 410-740-5574

Direct Marketing Association
1120 Avenue of the Americas, New York, NY 10036
phone 212-768-7277, fax 212-768-4547

Direct Selling Association
1666 K Street NW, Washington, DC 20006
phone 202-293-5760, fax 202-463-4569

Disabled Businesspersons Association
9625 Black Mountain Road, San Diego, CA 92126
phone 619-586-1199, fax 619-578-0637

Employee Benefit Research Institute
2121 K Street NW, Washington, DC 20037
phone 202-659-0670, fax 202-775-6312

Entrepreneurship Institute
3892 Corporate Drive, Columbus, OH 43231
phone 614-895-1153, fax 614-895-1473

Environmental Industry Associations
4301 Connecticut Avenue NW, Washington, DC 20008
phone 202-244-4700, fax 202-966-4818

Equipment Leasing Association
1300 North 17th Street, Arlington, VA 22209
phone 703-527-8655, fax 703-527-2649

Financial Accounting Foundation
401 Merritt Street, Norwalk, CT 06856
phone 203-847-0700, fax 203-849-9714

Financial Executives Institute
10 Madison Avenue, Morristown, NJ 07962
phone 201-898-4600, fax 201-898-4649

Hazardous Materials Advisory Council
1101 Vermont Avenue, Washington, DC 20005
phone 202-289-4550, fax 202-289-4074

Industrial Distribution Association
Three Corporate Square, Atlanta, GA 30329
phone 404-325-2776, fax 404-325-2784

Industrial Research Institute
1550 M Street NW, Washington, DC 20005
phone 202-296-8811, fax 202-776-0756

Industrial Telecommunications Association
1110 North Glebe Road, Arlington, VA 22201
phone 703-528-5115, fax 703-524-1074

Institute of Certified Business Counselors
Post Office Box 70326, Eugene, OR 97401
phone 503-345-8064, fax 503-726-2402

Insurance Information Institute
110 William Street, New York, NY 10038
phone 212-669-9200, fax 212-732-1916

International Association of Business Communicators
One Hallidie Plaza, San Francisco, CA 94102
phone 415-433-3400, fax 415-362-8762

International Council for Small Business
674 Lindell Boulevard, St. Louis, MO 63108
phone 314-977-3628, fax 314-977-3627

International Franchise Association
1350 New York Avenue NW, Washington, DC 20005
phone 202-628-8000, fax 202-628-0812

International Licensing Industry Merchandisers Association
360 Fifth Avenue, New York, NY 10118
phone 212-244-1944, fax 212-563-6552

International Personnel Management Association
1617 Duke Street, Alexandria, VA 22314
phone 703-549-7100, fax 703-684-0948

International Television Association
6311 North O'Connor Road, Irving, TX 75039
phone 214-869-1112, fax 214-869-2980

International Trade Council
3114 Circle Hill Road, Alexandria, VA 22305
phone 703-548-1234, fax 703-548-6126

Magazine Publishers of America
919 Third Avenue, New York, NY 10022
phone 212-872-3700, fax 212-888-4217

Marketing Research Association
2189 Silas Deane Highway, Rocky Hill, CT 06067
phone 203-257-4008, fax 203-257-3990

Multilevel Marketing International Association
119 Stanford Street, Irvine, CA 92715
phone 714-854-0484, fax 714-854-7687

Multimedia Telecommunications Association
2000 M Street NW, Washington, DC 20036
phone 202-296-9800, fax 202-296-4993

National Association for the Self-Employed
1023 15th Street NW, Washington, DC 20005
phone 202-466-2100, fax 800-551-4446

National Association of Broadcasters
1771 N Street NW, Washington, DC 20036
phone 202-429-5300, fax 202-429-5343

National Association of Development Companies
4301 North Fairfax Drive, Arlington, VA 22203
phone 703-812-9000

National Association of Private Enterprise
Post Office Box 612147, Dallas, TX 75261
phone 817-428-4235, fax 817-332-4525

National Association of Purchasing Management
2055 East Centennial Circle, Tempe, AZ 85285
phone 602-752-6276, fax 602-752-7890

National Association of Realtors
430 North Michigan Avenue, Chicago, IL 60611
phone 312-329-8200, fax 312-329-8576

National Association of Small Business Investment Companies
1199 North Fairfax Street, Alexandria, VA 22314
phone 703-683-1601, fax 703-683-1605

National Association of Temporary and Staffing Services
119 South Asaph Street, Alexandria, VA 22314
phone 703-549-6287, fax 703-549-4808

National Business Association
Post Office Box 700728, Dallas, TX 75370
phone 214-458-0900, fax 214-960-9149

National Business Owners Association
1200 18th Street NW, Washington, DC 20036
phone 202-737-6501, fax 202-737-3909

National Executive Service Corps
257 Park Avenue South, New York, NY 10010
phone 212-529-6660, fax 212-228-3958

National Federation of Independent Business
600 Maryland Avenue SW, Washington, DC 20024
phone 202-554-9000, fax 202-554-0496

National Foreign Trade Council
1625 K Street NW, Washington, DC 20006
phone 202-887-0278, fax 202-452-8160

National Newspaper Association
1525 Wilson Boulevard, Arlington, VA 22209
phone 703-907-7900, fax 703-907-7901

National Retail Federation
325 7th Street NW, Washington, DC 20004
phone 202-783-7971, fax 202-737-2849

National Small Business United
1155 15th Street NW, Washington, DC 20005
phone 202-293-8830, fax 202-872-8543

National Vehicle Leasing Association
Post Office Box 281230, San Francisco, CA 94128
phone 415-548-9135, fax 415-548-9155

North American Free Trade Association
1130 Connecticut Avenue, Washington, DC 20036
phone 202-296-3019, fax 202-296-3037

Property Management Association
8811 Colesville Road, Silver Spring, MD 20910
phone 301-587-6543, fax 301-589-2017

Public Relations Society of America
33 Irving Place, New York, NY 10003
phone 212-995-2230, fax 212-995-0757

Radio Advertising Bureau
1320 Greenway Drive, Irving, TX 75038
phone 214-753-6750, fax 214-756-6727

Sales and Marketing Executives International
Statler Office Tower, Suite 977, Cleveland, OH 44115
phone 216-771-6650, fax 216-771-6652

Service Corps of Retired Executives
409 Third Street SW, Washington, DC 20024
phone 202-205-6762, fax 202-205-7636

Small Business Exporters Association
4603 John Tyler Court, Annandale, VA 22003
phone 703-642-2490, fax 703-750-9655

Support Service Alliance
102 Prospect Street, Schoharie, NY 12157
phone 518-295-7966, fax 518-295-8556

Telecommunications Industry Association
2500 Wilson Boulevard, Arlington, VA 22201
phone 703-907-7700, fax 703-907-7727

Television Bureau of Advertising
850 Third Avenue, New York, NY 10022
phone 212-486-1111, fax 212-935-5631

Trademark Research Corporation
300 Park Avenue South, New York, NY 10010
phone 212-228-4084, fax 212-228-6275

Women in Communications
10604 Judicial Drive, Fairfax, VA 22030
phone 703-359-9000, fax 703-359-0603

Young Presidents Organization
451 South Decker Drive, Irving, TX 75062
phone 214-650-4600, fax 214-650-4777

Directory of Government Resources

In addition to the government resources listed, you may call the Federal Information Center, 800-688-9889, or write them at P.O. Box 600, Cumberland, MD 21501-600 to request specific information.

U.S. Department of Commerce

Many owners and managers of small businesses turn to the U.S. Department of Commerce for information, counsel, and help. The following offices within the department may be especially helpful to you. All web addresses begin http://

Bureau of Economic Analysis (BEA)—202-606-9600; www.bea.doc.gov
 The bureau measures and evaluates U.S. economic activity and prepares, develops, and interprets economic reports. These regional, national, and international reports, supplemented by the BEA's own summaries and leading economic indicators, provide businesses with basic information on key issues, such as inflation, business outlook, economic growth, regional development, balance of payments, the world economy, and international investments.

Bureau of Export Administration (BXA)—202-482-1455; www.bxa.doc.gov
 This central agency administers the nation's security, foreign policy, and export controls. It develops and implements programs and policies to ensure a strong American industrial defense base, processes export and import license applications, and enforces export control laws. Business owners and managers can obtain detailed information on export/import matters from this agency, as well as assistance in establishing foreign trade programs or solving existing problems. The central office is in Washington, DC, with field offices in Boston; Chicago; Dallas; Los Angeles; Miami; New York; San Jose, California; and Springfield, Virginia.

Bureau of the Census—301-763-4100; www.census.gov
 The government's principal fact-finding agency collects, processes, analyzes, and disseminates statistics on important aspects of the country's social and economic life. Through the bureau, you can quickly find data, not only on population figures, but on such matters as government, commerce, and industry, retail and wholesale operations, foreign trade, construction, and housing. Regional offices are maintained in a dozen major cities across the United States.

Economics and Statistics Administration (ESA)—202-482-3727; sunny.stat.usa.gov
 This agency collects, analyzes, and publishes most of the economic and social data produced by the federal government, including censuses of businesses, surveys of manufacturers, estimates of foreign domestic investments, merchandise trade balances, and other indicators of business activity. These are available through an on-line Economic Bulletin Board (phone 202-482-1986).

Economic Development Administration (EDA)—202-482-5081; www.doc.gov/eda
   The EDA helps communities that are experiencing, or threatened with, persistent
   and substantial unemployment to take effective steps in planning and financing
   public works and economic development. The agency coordinates these projects
   with local and regional businesses to combat unemployment, find solutions to
   underemployment, and strengthen the affected economy. Regional offices are in
   Atlanta, Austin, Chicago, Denver, Philadelphia, and Seattle.

International Trade Administration (ITA)—202-482-2867; fax 202-482-3508;
   www.ita.doc.gov
   The ITA is responsible for trade operations of the government (except agriculture).
   It supports the trade policies and negotiation efforts of the U.S. Trade Representative and administers import trade laws, including antidumping and countervailing
   duty laws. The ITA is an indispensable contact for export/import firms and all businesses affected by international economic policies, trade development, and global
   commercial services. The agency maintains an Advocacy Center to promote American economic health, assist the private sector, and strengthen export-related employment.

Minority Business Development Agency (MBDA)—202-482-061; chev.eda.dog.
   gov/agency/mbda/index.html
   The MBDA fosters minority entrepreneurship in the United States. It offers an
   array of services to minority-owned businesses in a number of fields, including
   administration, marketing, finance, law, government, training, and technology.
   Regional or district offices are maintained in Atlanta, Boston, Chicago, Dallas,
   Los Angeles, Miami, New York, Philadelphia, and San Francisco. Minority Enterprise Growth Assistance Centers are located across the country.

National Institute of Standards and Technology (NIST)—301-975-2300;
   www.nist.gov
   The NIST is the only federal technological agency with the primary mission
   of helping U.S. industry strengthen its competitiveness. It assists businesses in
   planning, adapting, and commercializing technologies that lead to higher quality,
   greater productivity, and new and improved products and services. Some of
   the NIST's unique research facilities, including laboratories in Maryland and
   Colorado, are open to companies, and qualified recipients are provided with seed
   money to conduct research on high-risk technologies that have broad commercial potential.

National Oceanic and Atmospheric Administration (NOAA)—202-482-3436;
   www.noaa.gov
   This agency promotes global ecological stewardship to conserve and manage the
   country's marine and coastal resources and to describe, monitor, and predict
   changes in Earth's environment. One of its major goals is to ensure and enhance
   sustainable economic opportunities by improving the world's ecological health
   and minimizing pollution and damage to the natural cycle of production. The
   NOAA's five major divisions are concerned with satellite data and information
   services, marine fisheries, ocean services, the weather, and oceanic and atmospheric research.

National Technical Information Service (NTIS)—703-487-4636; www.fedworld.gov/ntis/ntishom.html
The NTIS reports describe scientific research by federal agencies, contractors, and foreign governments. Supplementing the more than 2 million titles in the NTIS collection are data files and software produced by government agencies and *FedWorld* (phone 703-321-8020), an electronic gateway to more than 100 government bulletin boards and on-line databases.

National Telecommunications and Information Administration (NTIA)—202-482-1840; www.ntia.doc.gov
This agency has six basic responsibilities:

- providing advice to White House staff on global telecommunications and information policies
- developing and presenting U.S. administration policies
- managing federal use of radio broadcasting
- serving as the federal transfer center for telecommunications research and engineering, performance standards, and technology
- providing grants to extend public telecommunications services throughout the country
- administering the National Endowment for Children's Educational Television

The value of NTIA to the business community lies in its proficiency in coordinating telecommunications activities and policies for companies of all sizes and kinds.

Office of Business Liaison—202-482-3942, fax 202-482-4054; www.osec.doc.gov/obl
This office serves as the primary point of contact between the government and the business community. Its objectives follow:

- to develop a proactive, responsive, and effective outreach program and relationship with the business community
- to inform the Commerce Department and its officials of critical issues and problems facing American businesses
- to inform the business community of government resources, policies, events, and programs
- to provide outreach to the business community, including the arrangement of regular conferences and briefings with government officials
- to guide businesses, groups, and individuals through government channels by using the Commerce Department's Business Assistance Program, whose specialists field questions on policies, programs, and services and refer inquirers to published materials and other sources of data

Office of Consumer Affairs (OCA)—202-482-5001; www.nt.gov.au/caft/ghindex. html
The OCA advises the Department of Commerce to ensure that consumer needs and interests are given strong priority in the marketplace. The OCA also serves as a resource on consumer issues for other government agencies

and serves as a coordinating force in serving the business community. The OCA encourages business responsiveness to consumer interests; educates consumers with marketplace problems and informs them about the agency's resources and programs; and represents the Commerce Department in matters relating to consumer groups and federal, state, county, and municipal governments.

Office of Small and Disadvantaged Business Utilization (OSDBU)—202-482-3387; www.safsb.hq.af.mil

This office serves as a small business advocacy and advisory center. Its primary mission is to reserve the maximum number of suitable opportunities exclusively for small and minority-owned businesses to ensure that they receive a fair share of government contracts and other benefits. The OSDBU publishes regular forecasts of opportunities for those businesses; sets realistic goals for business contracts and development; screens all procurements so that suitable contracts can be channeled to small and minority businesses; assists small businesses through counseling and seminars; and administers an Innovation Research Program to increase the technological capabilities of small businesses so they can compete for government contracts.

Patent and Trademark Office (PTO)—703-305-8600; www.uspto.gov

The PTO administers the patent and trademark laws of the United States, reviews applications from individuals and firms seeking protection for their inventions and innovations, and reviews and registers qualified trademarks. The office also collects, assembles, publishes, and distributes technological data disclosed in patents. The PTO maintains one or more libraries in each state; these contain trademark collections and CD-ROM and other communications materials that provide businesses with patent and trademark information.

Small Business Administration (SBA)—800-827-5722; www.sba.gov

The SBA offers an extensive selection of information and counsel for owners and managers of small businesses of all kinds and for entrepreneurs intending to start their own firms. It maintains offices throughout the country. (Locations can be found in the "U.S. Government" section of local telephone directories.) The SBA's many programs include financial assistance, training workshops, educational seminars, counseling services, and professional referrals. One of its ongoing missions is to increase the number of government contracts to small businesses, and for this purpose it sponsors programs to develop management skills. Principal units of the agency follow:

- Service Corps of Retired Executives (SCORE); onyx.pucc.cc.va.us/score.html— This national organization has a membership of some 14,000 experienced business executives, volunteers who provide free counseling, workshops, and seminars to small business owners and managers and those seeking help in starting small or home-based businesses. SCORE offices are located throughout the United States, often in space provided at no cost by chambers of commerce.
- Small Business Development Centers (SBDCs)—Sponsored by the SBA in partnership with state and local governments, the educational community, and the

private sector, SBDCs provide assistance, counseling, and training to prospective and active small business entrepreneurs.

- Small Business Institutes (SBIs)—Organized by the SBA to function on more than 500 college campuses nationwide, the institutes provide counseling by qualified students and business faculty members to small business owners and managers.
- Minority Small Business Program—This unit is designed to help improve the standings of minority-owned and managed businesses through a variety of programs that include education, counseling, placement, and financial assistance. A companion program is geared to promote the growth of businesses owned or managed by women.
- SBA loans—These loans are available to small companies that have sought and been refused financing from other lending institutions before applying to the SBA for assistance. Most, however, are made in conjunction with private lenders, in which the lender furnishes the funds and the SBA guarantees up to 90 percent of the amount loaned. Although interest rates are negotiated between the borrower and the lender, they are subject to SBA guidelines and review. The SBA also provides specialized loan guarantee programs that include international trade, lines of credit, contractor financing, community development funds, and pollution control.
- Answer desk—SBA headquarters maintains an answer desk with a toll-free number (800-827-5722). This service provides an automated guide to information on a wide range of subjects of concern to small business, such as starting a business, obtaining loans and grants, and marketing. For those with specific questions, SBA representatives are available to supply answers or make referrals. SBA field offices have similar facilities, using both automated answering machines and live respondents.

For inquiries by mail, write:
Small Business Administration
409 Third Street NW
Washington, DC 20416
You may also obtain specific information on the following subjects by dialing the numbers provided:

disaster assistance 202-205-6734
financial assistance 202-205-6490
international trade 202-205-6720
minority small business development 202-205-6540
research and technology 202-205-6450
small business development 202-205-6766
surety bonds 202-205-6540
women's business ownership 202-205-6673

Technology Administration—202-482-1575; www.ta.docgov
This agency provides businesses with information and assistance in the creation, production, and commercial success of technology-based goods and services. It

also conducts programs and services that help to improve organizations' scientific and technological capabilities and facilities.

United States Travel and Tourism Administration (USTTA)—phone 202-482-0136 This agency formulates and executes national tourism and recreation policies and programs to help achieve economic prosperity and produce a favorable balance of trade in world marketplaces. The USTTA administers a wide range of marketing, technical assistance, and consumer research programs to assist private industry in achieving these objectives.

Internal Revenue Service (IRS)

As a division of the Treasury, the IRS administers all internal revenue laws and regulations except those relating to alcohol, tobacco, firearms, and explosives. Most familiar to citizens and businesses as the collector of individual and business taxes, the IRS consists of seven regions and sixty-four districts. It maintains dozens of free tax-assistance programs. Here are a few of the most-used services, publications, and programs. Telephone listings are for IRS headquarters offices, but you may also obtain source information by calling the nearest IRS office, as listed in your local phone directory. www.irs.ustreus.gov

- *Federal Income Tax Guide for Older Americans,* a publication available through the Committee on Aging of the U.S. House of Representatives, covers tax provisions that especially benefit senior citizens with moderate incomes. It also lists numerous Internal Revenue Service publications and recorded telephone messages that provide pertinent details. Call 202-226-3375 to request a copy.
- Volunteer Income Tax Assistance (VITA) is an IRS program that schedules courses to assist people who may have particular difficulty with filing tax forms, whether because of age, disability, language, or any other reason. The volunteers hold sessions in convenient community locations, such as libraries, schools, churches, and shopping malls. VITA also welcomes professionals and other experienced volunteers who will commit themselves to four to five days of training and provide this kind of instruction to those who need help. Call 202-622-7827 to schedule training.
- Legal assistance, if you are audited or have deduction claims rejected, is available through the Volunteer and Education branch of the IRS. Your local taxpayer education coordinator can inform you about this kind of assistance and/or tax clinics being held in your locale. Call 202-622-7827 for more information.
- The International Office of the Internal Revenue Service offers assistance to Americans living abroad, to those who receive foreign incomes, and to organizations that have business dealings outside the United States. The IRS maintains overseas offices in key locations in Europe, South America, Canada, Australia, Japan, and Saudi Arabia. This branch of the IRS also becomes involved in negotiations in cases where U.S. taxpayers require relief from the threat of double taxation by foreign governments. Call 202-287-4311.

- A community outreach program of the IRS was established to help civic organizations, associations of private citizens, small businesses, and other groups in joint efforts to provide better understanding of and relief from taxation. The assistance is provided in the form of seminars, question-and-answer sessions, videotapes, films, and other media. Small-business owners or managers who need help can form groups and request special programs for orientation purposes. Call 202-622-7827 for assistance.
- The IRS provides experienced speakers for civic, municipal, professional, and other interested groups who would like to know more about taxation, particularly ways to reduce individual and company taxes. This branch also arranges tax clinics and has even, on occasion, sponsored call-in radio and TV programs for listeners who want answers to specific questions about their filing methods or financial assessments. Call 800-829-1040.
- If you are planning to establish a small business, are experiencing financial problems because of the growth of your company, or have other problems that involve the nature and extent of your taxes, you may want to attend an IRS Tax Workshop for Small Business. These free workshops explain many pertinent business-related matters, such as withholding tax, employment tax returns, and tax forms. For information about workshops, contact the Taxpayer Education Coordinator in your tax district, or call 202-622-7827. You may also obtain the following useful publications by phoning 800-TAX-FORM. Request Publication 334, *Tax Guide for Small Business,* and Publication 583, *Taxpayers Starting a Business.*
- The IRS has videocassettes and audiocassettes available for loan to the public. Some provide step-by-step instructions for filing forms. Other topics on tape or film include tax audits, electronic filing, reporting requirements for small businesses, updates regarding changes in tax laws, and even a history of taxation. Call 202-622-7541 for more information. (Foreign language editions are also available.)
- The Taxpayer Ombudsman Service was established by the Problem Resolution Staff of the IRS Commissioner as a means of solving tax problems that were not resolved through normal procedures. The program is geared to the interests of the taxpayer, whether an individual or organization, and to preventing future problems by identifying root causes and seeking solutions. Each IRS district, service center, and regional office has a Problem Resolution Officer (an ombudsman serving the public) who can be contacted for assistance with previously unresolved tax problems. Call 202-622-4300 to learn more about this service.

There are other programs and services offered, free of charge, by the IRS. These include publications covering corporation tax statistics, procedures and instructions for electronic tax filing, foreign language assistance, forecasts of future tax legislation and major revisions, hot lines, strategies for the collection of delinquent child support payments, walk-in service centers, tax information in Braille, and even a service through which you can voice your opinions on existing laws and make recommendations or proposals for changes in the tax system.

Government Printing Office (GPO)

The GPO was established by Congress to print and distribute federal publications that now include the *Congressional Record* and some 30,000 others. Along with the National Technical Information Service, the GPO is Uncle Sam's most prolific publisher. Through its Superintendent of Documents, it offers a wealth of titles for businesses of all sizes, individuals, families, and every conceivable kind of organization in America. Topics range from how-to guides and professional manuals to in-depth studies on thousands of subjects. An encyclopedic *Publications Reference File* lists all of the GPO titles, most of which can be accessed by mail, fax, or computer modem, as well as through a nationwide system of almost 1,500 libraries and many bookstores across the country. The latter will order publications that are not in stock and will accept major credit cards.

Consult one or more of the GPO's 320 *Subject Bibliographies,* described in the *Subject Bibliography Index,* free upon request. Or contact the GPO by phone, fax, or mail to request lists of publications on specific topics. www.acess.gpo.gov

Major publication groups that have been assembled over the years follow:

- *Congressional Record* and calendars—The GPO publishes all major congressional publications, including House and Senate calendars, bills, laws, and related information, and the *Congressional Record.* All are available to companies and individuals by subscription.
- *Bestsellers from Uncle Sam*—This is a free catalog listing the most popular books sold by the government on subjects such as boating, crafts and hobbies, dieting, exercise, fishing, health, history, recreation, schooling, and much more.
- Graphic arts—The GPO makes available illustrations, maps, charts, posters, decals, and other visual matter for both educational and decorative use. Among the most popular items are depictions of nature, sketches of national monuments and historic places, sports posters, and reproductions of such documents as the *Constitution* and the *Declaration of Independence.*
- *Catalog of Federal Domestic Assistance*—This exhaustive volume contains a goverment-wide summary of federal financial (and many nonfinancial) assistance programs and services for the American public. The catalog describes the types of assistance available, eligibility requirements, and guidelines for applicants. It may be of critical importance to entrepreneurs and small business owners who are seeking assistance in starting, improving, or reorganizing their ventures. For information, contact the Superintendent of Documents, Government Printing Office, Washington, DC 20402, phone 202-783-3238, fax 202-512-2233.

Consumer Information Center of the U.S. General Services Administration

Of particular interest to individuals, families, and professionals are publications offered by the Consumer Information Center (CIC). It maintains a list of more than 200 useful government publications, ranging from leaflets to full-length books, many of which are free or priced under $1. Subjects include cars, children, employment, federal programs, food and nutrition, health, hobbies, housing, money, small business, and travel. Offerings in the small business section include data on patents, trademarks, commercial credits for women and minority business owners, and guidelines on the administration of pension and welfare plans. www.pueblo.gsc.gov

Write the Consumer Information Center, P.O. Box 100, Pueblo, CO 81002. Orders can be placed and charged on major credit cards by fax, if desired, at fax number 719-948-9724. Publications listed in the catalog, consumer news, updates, and information for individuals or firms are also available on-line. The electronic bulletin board service number is 202-208-7679, or use the Internet World Wide Web number: *http://www.gsa.gov/staff/pa/cic/cic/htm.*

Equal Employment Opportunity Commission (EEOC)

For a copy of the EEOC Compliance Manual, posters, and fact sheets on discrimination, as well as information on any issue concerning employment discrimination, call or write:

Equal Opportunity Employment Commission
1800 L Street NW
Washington, DC 20507
Phone 800-USA-EEOC or 202-663-4900; www.eeoc.gov

Glossary of Business, Legal, and Financial Terms

acceptance   an agreement by a buyer to the terms and offer of a seller

account payable   a liability to a creditor, usually for goods and services

account receivable   a claim against a debtor, usually for products delivered or services rendered

accrual method (accrual basis)   the accounting method that states that a transaction is recorded when it is actually made, regardless of whether the product or service purchased has been paid for

acquisition   usually a company or other substantial entity acquired by a business

additional named insured   a person or business named as a beneficiary on an insurance policy in addition to the primary beneficiary

advertising   the action of attracting public attention and potential customers through various paid media

affidavit   a sworn written statement signed and witnessed by a notary or other authority

agency   the legal relationship wherein one party has given to another (its agent) the right to act on its behalf and in its interest in business dealings

amortization   depreciation on intangible assets

antitrust laws   federal regulations designed to prevent the development of monopolies that limit free trade

arbitrage   the purchase of shares, commodities, and currencies with the objective of reselling them quickly for a higher price

arbitration   submission to the authority of a predetermined nonjudicial party for settlement of a dispute

articles of incorporation   a document filed by the original owners (creators) of a corporation specifying the objectives, policies, place of business, and capitalization of the corporation, plus the names of its creators and appointed directors

as is   a term indicating that goods are being sold without warranty

asset   anything with monetary value owned by a business or individual; an entry on a balance sheet showing a financial/tangible property that is owned by the business or that can be readily converted to ownership by the business

assignment   the legal contractual transfer of property or obligation from one party to another

audit   a formal examination of the financial statements of a business or individual, usually performed by a certified public accountant

balance sheet   the financial statement showing total assets, liabilities, and capital of a business

bankruptcy   a situation in which liabilities exceed assets, resulting in assets being surrendered voluntarily or involuntarily to creditors

bear   an investor who speculates that stock market prices will fall and sells certain securities with the hope of rebuying them more cheaply at a later date

blue chip   stocks and other securities with a long record of stability and reliability, considered safe purchases and likely to be profitable in the long run

boilerplate   standard, repeatable language that appears in common contracts

bona fide   actual; in good faith

bond   an officially registered certificate of indebtedness

break even   the point at which profits and losses are in balance

bull   an investor who speculates that stock market prices will rise and buys securities with the expectation of selling them later at a higher price

business climate   the attitudes, outlook, and economic conditions that prevail in a given locale

buy-sell agreement   an agreement among shareholders to buy and sell shares only to each other (in case of a shareholder's death or decision to sell stock) in order to keep control of the company

bylaws   rules concerning the management of a business, adopted by its original owners

capital   any form of material wealth, such as money or property, that is used or accumulated by an individual or corporation

capitalization   the sum of the par value of a company's stock and bonds outstanding

cash flow   the movement of money into and out of a business

cash method (cash basis)   an accounting method that records transactions only when they are completed; that is, when payment is made or received

certified public accountant (CPA)   an accountant who meets certain state requirements, including the passing of a uniform examination prepared by the American Institute of Certified Public Accountants

Chapter 7   a provision of bankruptcy laws wherein a company is required to liquidate its assets to pay off its creditors

Chapter 11   a provision of bankruptcy laws allowing a bankrupt company to remain in business while its owners attempt to pay its debts

chart of accounts   a list of account numbers used to identify the bookkeeping accounts of a company

coborrower   a person who is a joint borrower for a loan, bearing equal responsibility with the borrower for repayment of the loan

collateral   property or assets pledged as security for repayment of a loan, which can be seized by the lender if the borrower defaults on the loan

consideration   something of value given by one party to a contract to another party to the contract as an inducement for the second party to enter the contract

consignment   delivery of goods to a buyer with payment to be made only after the buyer has resold those goods

contingency   a contract provision requiring the satisfaction of or existence of one or more conditions before the provision is considered binding

corporation   a business that has been granted the right to operate as a separate entity legally distinct from its owner or owners

cosigner   a person who promises to accept responsibility for paying a loan in the event that the primary borrower does not pay

CPA   see *certified public accountant*

d.b.a.   abbreviation for *doing business as;* used to indicate any name used by a company other than its original or incorporated name

debenture   a fixed-interest bond with a long-term outlook and guarantee issued by a government body or private organization

debt ratio   a calculation used in evaluating loads; it is obtained by dividing the applicant's total gross monthly income by total monthly expenses: the result is the percentage of the applicant's income that is owed to creditors

deductible   the amount of loss an insured party is required to pay (absorb) before an insurance policy takes effect and begins to pay

delivery   the act of transferring a completed contract back to the original party, which is necessary for it to take effect

demographics   data researched and computed statistically to present specific information about the characteristics of groups of people or population segments

depreciation   a universal accounting principle assuming that all fixed assets wear out in time, so that the cost of a fixed asset is spread out over the period of its useful life

direct mail   mail addressed directly to prospective customers or clients during an advertising, promotion, or merchandising campaign

discount rate   the rate of interest that is deducted in advance, as in the case of purchasing Treasury bills

discretionary dollars   funds used for variable monthly expenses—a term used in loan evaluations that indicates how much money an applicant will have remaining after all necessary bills are paid

distribution   the process of moving goods from a manufacturer to consumers or points of sale

diversification   extending a business into other fields to increase profits or otherwise improve the value of the organization

Dow Jones Index   the listing of prices on the New York Stock Exchange, based on the average price of shares

equity   the basic value of a business or property, beyond any liabilities connected with it

estimated taxes   see *self-employment taxes*

excise   an indirect tax levied on the production, sale, or consumption of certain commodities (such as tobacco or alcohol) within a country

exclusions   those items in an insurance policy that are specifically listed as not being covered by the policy

execute   make a contract legally valid by signing it

fiscal year   an accounting period of 12 months for financial and investment purposes, which is instituted arbitrarily and may differ from the calendar year

fixed assets   the resources of a business that are not intended for resale, such as furniture or company office buildings

floating   a term describing any currency with an exchange rate determined by supply and demand, without government mediation or intervention

FOB   abbreviation meaning *free on board;* used in contracts to indicate property that is transferred from seller to buyer upon shipment (the buyer handles the transportation of goods and assumes liability)

franchise   authorization (from a manufacturer or business proprietor) granted to a dealer, distributor, or independent operator to sell the manufacturer's/proprietor's products or services subject to certain terms and conditions

fringe benefits   benefits, other than wages or salaries, or other things of value given to employees by an employer

futures   securities, especially commodities, that are purchased or sold at an agreed-upon price on one date for future delivery on another date

garnishment   money withheld from an employee's wages by an employer and paid to a creditor of that employee based on a court order

Generally Accepted Accounting Principles (GAAP)   the universal rules used for determining the information to be included in financial statements and the ways in which the information will be presented

general partner   a partner (owner) who is liable for the total debts of a business and must use personal assets to pay those debts if necessary; also, a partner who bears responsibility for day-to-day operations and management of the business (in general partnerships, all owners are general partners; in limited partnerships, there are one or more general partners in addition to a limited partner or partners)

general partnership   an unincorporated business in which all partners (owners) equally share management responsibilities for business operations, ownership of business assets, and the obligation to pay the partnership's debts or liabilities, with no limit to the amount of risk borne by each general partner

gilt-edged securities (gilts)   fixed-interest securities, generally having a low price, that are issued by the government

gross income   the overall income received by a company prior to deductions such as expenses, taxes, and interest

guarantor   a person or party who promises to uphold a guarantee made by another person or party

implied contract   a contract created neither in writing nor orally, but rather inferred from the actions of the parties involved

income statement (profit and loss statement)   the financial statement of a business that provides information about business revenue, expenses, and profit or loss over a given period

incorporation   the act of legally establishing a business as a corporation

independent contractor   a person or company contracted by another to do a limited and specific job

injunction   a court order obtained to prohibit another party from performing a specific act

intellectual property   trade secrets, proprietary information, or information protected by a company or individual through trademarks, copyrights, or patents

inventory   the total quantity of goods and materials held by a business

joint venture   a partnership agreement between two or more businesses or people to work together on a project that is limited in scope

journal   a record of the daily transactions of a business, showing the date, a brief description, the amount of money, and the asset, liability, capital, or type of income or expense involved in each transaction

ledger   the book or file in which transactions for several accounts are recorded

letter of credit   authorization (in letter form) permitting the person(s) named to draw a stated sum of money from a financial institution or another specified party

liabilities   monetary obligations of a business or individual, including claims of creditors against business/individual assets

license   a legal certificate authorizing a person or company to perform a specific service

lien   a creditor's right to claim property given by a debtor as collateral to secure a loan

limited partner   a partner whose liability for the financial obligations of a business is limited to the amount of money he or she invested in the company; usually a partner whose responsibility for day-to-day operations of the business is also limited

limited partnership   an unincorporated business in which the liability and responsibility of all partners (owners) are not equal; a partnership in which there are both limited and general partners

liquidate   convert assets to cash, often in order to repay a debt

logo (logotype)   a symbol used to identify a company

market   the area in which a company can realistically (and logically) conduct its business, which can be described in terms of size, location, and nature

markup   the amount added to the cost of materials or products to determine the final price paid by consumers, usually calculated to cover overhead expenses and the desired amount of profit

mechanical warranty   a guarantee that property or merchandise will perform as promised for a specified period or be repaired at no cost to the buyer

media   commonly used to refer to all means of mass communication (for example, newspapers, radio, television, and magazines) used as vehicles for conveying information to consumers

merchandising   promoting goods and services via advertising, publicity, sales campaigns, etc.

merger   the joining of two or more businesses into one legal entity

mutual fund   a securities portfolio containing selections made and sold, as a package, by a mutual fund brokerage firm

named perils   the types of losses for which an insurance policy provides coverage

noncompete agreement   a contract or contract provision that prohibits a person or company from operating a similar business, often limited to a certain geographic area

offer   a provision put forward to indicate willingness to enter into an agreement, which would constitute a contract if accepted

option   reservation of the right, usually through payment, to buy something at a specified price during a specified period of time

organizational chart   a graphic chart, table, or diagram depicting the positions and relationships of people in an organization, or the layout of its different departments

partnership   an unincorporated business owned by two or more persons or business entities

par value (nominal value)   the face value of a stock or other security

point of sale (point of purchase)   the location at which customers select goods to buy in a retail establishment

policy   a plan or course of action established by business owners/managers that is designed to guide managers and employees in their actions and decisions to promote the good of the business

portfolio   the combined lists of securities held by an investor

power of attorney   the legal authority of one person to act for another in legal matters; or the signed document authorizing such a relationship

preferred stock   a fixed-interest security issued with a guarantee that dividends will be paid to the holder before any dividends are assigned to ordinary shares (that is, before ordinary stockholders are paid dividends)

profit and loss statement   see *income statement*

promissory note   a written document promising to pay a specified sum of money to a specified person

proposal   a formal presentation of data designed to encourage its recipient or audience to view its creator's suggestions favorably

proprietary   something owned or held privately by a person or company, such as information or material

public relations   actions and methods used to promote public goodwill toward an organization or person

quality control   systems and procedures designed to maintain quality in manufacturing, production, or processing

real property   tangible but unmovable property such as land or buildings

receipt   an acknowledgment of payment given to a buyer by a seller

retail the sale of products, goods, and related services directly to consumers, in limited quantities

retainer a fee paid to a company or individual to secure services for future use

risk management the administration of loss reduction and prevention arrangements, such as security measures to prevent losses from theft, insurance to reduce liability for costs of accidents or illnesses, and personnel training to reduce or prevent on-the-job injuries

S corporation a company incorporated specifically as a small business, with a limited number of stockholders, limited liability, and a lower tax burden than many regular corporations

secured loan a loan in which the borrower provides collateral to guarantee payment of the loan

securities stocks, bonds, shares, certificates, or other evidence of ownership or entitlement of worth, whether fixed or fluctuating in market value and price

self-employment earning an income by the provision of services or products directly to others, rather than as an employee of a business owned by someone else

self-employment taxes Medicare and Social Security taxes that must be paid by self-employed individuals

settlement the completion of a transaction through the satisfaction of all necessary conditions

sole proprietorship a business owned by one person only in which there is no legal distinction between the owner and the business

stock split the issuance of one or more extra shares of stock to stockholders for each share they already own

subcontractor a business or person hired by a general contractor to complete a specialized part of a job

subsidiary a business in which a majority interest is owned by another company, known as the parent company

taxpayer identification number a number used by the Internal Revenue Service to identify a business

terms and conditions the provisions of a contract describing the actions and agreements being made

trademark a distinguishing symbol legally registered for exclusive use by an organization

Treasury bill an obligation of the U.S. Treasury, bearing no interest, but sold at a discount and maturing within one year

trial balance an accounting process in which all debit account balances are totaled, all credit account balances are totaled, and the two are compared to see whether the company's accounts are in balance

umbrella coverage insurance coverage that provides limits in addition to what is provided on the standard policy

underwriter an individual or firm that guarantees the value of an issue of a security by endeavoring to purchase any shares that are not bought by others

unfair competition business advantages gained through illegal or deceptive practices

unsecured loan a loan that is granted solely on the basis of the creditworthiness of the borrower, with no collateral

vendor   a seller of goods and supplies

venture capital (risk capital)   funds made available for investment in an unproven enterprise

void   cancel or annul and make unenforceable

voucher   a written document attesting that a transaction has been made

warranty   a promise attesting to the truth of claims

wholesale   the sale of goods in large quantities at a lower price than retail, usually to retailers but sometimes directly to consumers

zoning   the designation by government authorities of certain geographical areas to be used for specific purposes only, such as for commercial, industrial, or residential uses

Index

References to figures and tables are in *italics*.